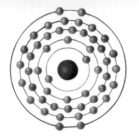

CONTENTS

WEATHER AND CLIMATE

THE WORLD AROUND US

SPACE

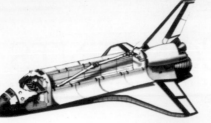

LIFE ON EARTH

SCIENCE

HOW THINGS WORK

WEATHER AND CLIMATE

HOW DOES THE SUN CREATE WEATHER?

There would be no weather at all without the Sun. Heat and light energy from the Sun keep the air in the Earth's atmosphere moving, which directly and indirectly causes everything from wind and rain to fog, snow and thunderstorms. The changing position of the Earth in relation to the Sun is responsible for much of the variation in climate on our planet.

WHY IS THE SKY BLUE ON A SUNNY DAY?

LIGHT FROM the Sun is made up of several different colours, each of which has its own wavelength. The wavelength of the blue part of the Sun's light is shorter than the size of an oxygen atom. When the blue light waves hit the oxygen atoms in the Earth's atmosphere, they are scattered, making the sky appear blue. The light waves of other colours (with greater wavelengths than blue) are also affected, but blue waves are scattered more than most.

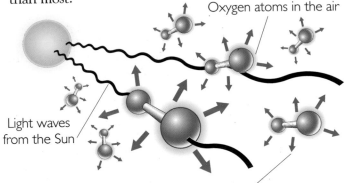

Oxygen atoms in the air

Light waves from the Sun

Blue light waves scattered by oxygen atoms

Heat generates air movement, producing wind and other weather.

The Sun heats the sea.

People enjoy the sunshine.

The Sun heats the land.

HOW IS THE SUN HARMFUL TO US?

MOST PEOPLE enjoy the sunshine, and the ultraviolet (UV) rays produced by the Sun help us to produce certain vitamins in our bodies. However, too much exposure is very harmful and can lead to serious diseases such as skin cancer. Always protect yourself with sunscreen and try to keep covered up for most of the time that you spend in the sunshine.

DO SUNSPOTS AFFECT THE EARTH'S WEATHER?

SOME SCIENTISTS believe that sunspot activity may have an effect on the Earth's weather. Sunspots seem to occur in cycles of 11 years. Research has shown that major periods of drought have occurred roughly every 22 years, or two sunspot cycles. We have yet to discover the exact relationship between the two.

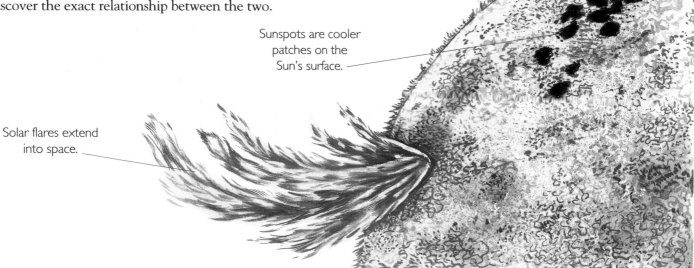

Sunspots are cooler patches on the Sun's surface.

Solar flares extend into space.

WHAT IS SOLAR WIND?

SOMETIMES, INTENSE amounts of electromagnetic energy are released from the Sun in the form of solar wind, or flares. The Earth is protected from solar wind – essentially an extremely hot gas – by its magnetic field, which stretches out into space. The particles of solar winds are known to affect satellites and even cause power blackouts on Earth. Scientists are still investigating the possible long-term effects of this activity on the Earth's climate.

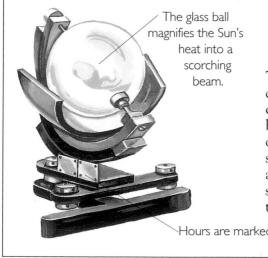

The glass ball magnifies the Sun's heat into a scorching beam.

Hours are marked on a cardboard scale.

HOW IS THE AMOUNT OF SUNSHINE IN A DAY RECORDED?

THE NUMBER of hours of sunshine in a day is recorded on an instrument called a parheliometer. A solid glass ball focuses the Sun's rays on to a strip of card. The intensified rays leave scorch marks on the card, moving along as the Sun moves through the sky. The longer the marks, the longer the period of sunshine.

HOW DOES A SUNDIAL WORK?

A SUNDIAL SHOWS the time of day by casting a shadow across its face. With the needle – the *gnomon* – of the sundial pointing north–south, the shadow indicates the time as the Sun passes through the sky from sunrise to sunset.

The shadow moves around the dial.

The time of day is indicated by the shadow.

WHY IS IT HOT AT THE EQUATOR?

HOW DOES THE SUN HEAT THE EARTH?

ENERGY FROM the Sun arrives on the Earth in the form of radiation. Some of the radiation is absorbed or reflected back into space by the Earth's atmosphere and clouds, but most of it reaches the surface, where it heats up the land and sea. As the Earth heats up, some of this heat is also reflected back into space.

The temperature of an area is largely determined by the way that the Sun's rays strike that part of the Earth. The way the Earth is tilted and curved means that the Sun's rays strike different places at different angles. Generally, temperatures are highest close to the Equator, where the Sun's rays hit the Earth straight on. At the poles, the rays hit the Earth at an angle, and the area tends to be much cooler.

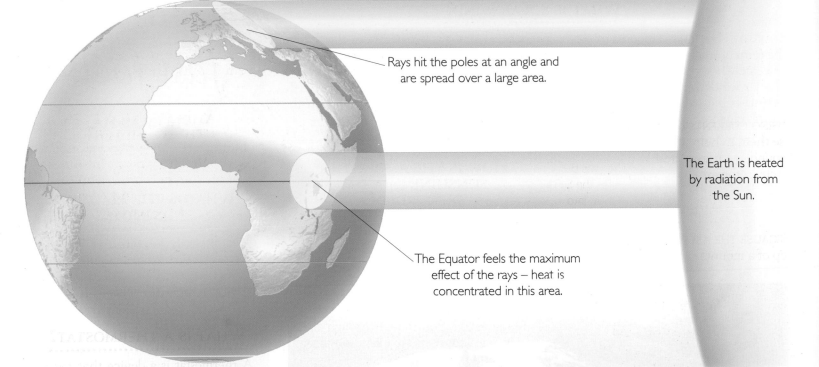

The Sun's rays hit the Earth in parallel.

Rays hit the poles at an angle and are spread over a large area.

The Earth is heated by radiation from the Sun.

The Equator feels the maximum effect of the rays – heat is concentrated in this area.

WHAT IS ALBEDO?

THE RELATIVE "shininess" of the Earth's surface in a certain area will affect the local temperature – this is called *albedo*. Icy, snowy areas reflect most of the radiation of the Sun and remain cold. Forests and areas of bare soil absorb the radiation and tend to stay warm.

In areas where the land is covered in ice and snow, most of the solar radiation is reflected back into the atmosphere. This helps to explain how it can be cold and sunny at the same time.

Forested regions have a low albedo – they tend to absorb the Sun's radiation. This helps to keep the surface temperature relatively high.

WHAT ARE CONVECTION CURRENTS?

WHERE COOL AIR lies above a warm area of land, the air will be heated. As the air warms up, it expands, becomes less dense (its molecules become less tightly packed) and it begins to rise. The surrounding cooler air replaces the rising warm air. As the warm air rises, it cools down and its density increases. These currents of warm and cold air are called convection currents.

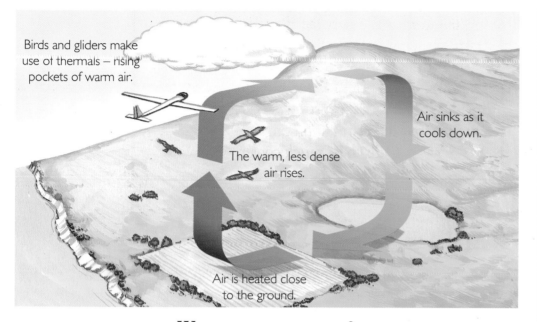

Birds and gliders make use of thermals – rising pockets of warm air.

Air sinks as it cools down.

The warm, less dense air rises.

Air is heated close to the ground.

WHAT ARE THERMALS?

RISING CURRENTS of warm air are called thermals. They are useful to glider pilots, who use them to help lift their craft into the air. Thermals can form over "hot spots" on the ground, such as a freshly ploughed field. Some large birds make use of thermals to circle in the air.

WHY IS IT COLD AT THE TOP OF A MOUNTAIN?

BECAUSE THE AIR is warmed by heat rising from the ground, the air temperature at the top of a mountain will always be lower than it is at the bottom.

Air temperatures at the top of this mountain are generally very low, as illustrated by its snow-capped peaks. The warmer temperatures found at the foot of the mountain result in a lush, green landscape.

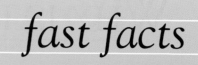

fast facts

WHAT WAS THE HIGHEST RECORDED TEMPERATURE?

A temperature of 58°C (136°F) was recorded near the Sahara Desert in Libya in 1922.

WHAT WAS THE LOWEST RECORDED TEMPERATURE?

In July 1983, a temperature of −89°C (−129°F) was recorded at a meteorological research station in Antarctica.

DO HIGH TEMPERATURES AFFECT PEOPLE?

Studies in the USA have shown that incidences of murder and violent crime increase when the temperature rises above 32°C (90°F).

WHAT IS THE LIQUID IN A THERMOMETER?

Thermometers contain either mercury or coloured alcohol – liquids that expand easily in response to air temperature.

WHO INVENTED THE THERMOMETER?

An early thermometer was made by Galileo in the 16th century.

WHAT IS A THERMOSTAT?

A thermostat is a device that regulates heating systems in buildings.

WHY IS TEMPERATURE MEASURED IN THE SHADE?

If the temperature was measured in direct sunlight, it would give a false reading because the thermometer would be heated by both the air and the direct heat of the Sun.

WHAT CAUSES THE SEASONS?

As the Earth orbits the Sun, different parts of the planet face towards or away from it, receiving varying amounts of heat. The Earth is tilted at an angle and always tilts the same way. This means that when the Earth is on one side of the Sun, the Northern Hemisphere leans towards the Sun and experiences summer. At the same time, the Southern Hemisphere is leaning away from the Sun and is having winter weather. Six months later, the Earth is on the other side of the Sun and the situation is reversed. Spring begins in a hemisphere at the moment at which it starts to lean towards the Sun; Autumn starts when it begins to lean away from it.

DECEMBER

When a hemisphere is tilting towards the Sun, it experiences long, hot days with the Sun high in the sky – this is summer.

The hemisphere leaning away from the Sun will be having shorter, darker days and colder temperatures – this is winter.

JUNE

WHAT ARE THE SEASONS IN TEMPERATE ZONES?

In winter, the days are short and the skies may be filled with dark, grey cloud. Many trees are bare, and the ground is often covered with frost, snow or ice.

Spring brings warmer weather. Flowers come into bloom, trees regain their leaves and blossom. Some sunshine will be accompanied by cool breezes and light showers of rain.

In summer, the days are long and the land receives a lot of sunshine. Temperatures are high and trees and plants are green and leafy. Thunderstorms will bring rain.

Temperatures drop during autumn, as the days begin to get shorter. Some places may experience violent storms at this time of year. Leaves go brown and fall from the trees.

WHERE CAN YOU SEE THE SUN AT MIDNIGHT?

IN THE PARTS of the world that are close to the poles, the way the Earth tilts means that the summer months in those regions are marked by constant daylight. Parts of Scandinavia, for instance, are known as the "land of the midnight Sun". In mid-winter, these areas experience the opposite – total darkness for 24 hours a day.

In places where the Sun does not set during the summer, the midnight sky will have a dusk-like appearance. It will quickly turn from dusk to dawn, with no real "night-time".

WHAT IS SEASONAL AFFECTIVE DISORDER?

MANY PEOPLE suffer from the "winter blues". Feeling tired, run down and a bit sad is a natural response to the long, dark days, cold weather and the effects of colds and flu. A few people experience exaggerated symptoms, which doctors have recognized as a medical condition known as Seasonal Affective Disorder, or SAD. A lack of daylight can cause sufferers of SAD to become very depressed and have problems sleeping and eating.

Some sufferers of Seasonal Affective Disorder (SAD) use a light box to simulate daylight during the dark winter months. The additional daylight fools the patient's brain into thinking that the day is longer. The treatment has proved very successful and is especially helpful for those sufferers who live in places that experience many hours of winter darkness.

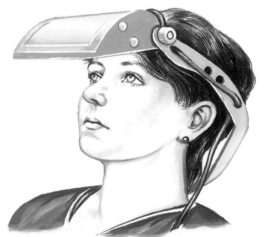

WHAT IS A SOLSTICE?

WHEN THE SUN is directly overhead at its most northern or southern position, it is called the solstice. The Northern Hemisphere's summer solstice occurs when the Sun is above the Tropic of Cancer – on 20, 21 or 22 June – and marks the beginning of summer. Its winter solstice (the Southern Hemisphere's summer solstice) is on 21 or 22 December. The summer solstice is the longest day of the year; the winter equivalent is the shortest.

It is thought that ancient peoples understood the significance of the solstices. Many ancient monuments, such as Stonehenge, England (above), are built in such a way that when the Sun rises on a solstice, it is aligned with a particular part of the structure.

fast facts

WHERE ARE THE SEASONS HOT AND COLD?

Areas between the poles and the tropics have hot and cold seasons.

WHERE ARE THE SEASONS WET AND DRY?

Places close to the Equator have two seasons – one dry and one wet.

WHY IS "FALL" SO CALLED?

Fall (also called autumn) takes its name because it is the season when leaves fall from the trees.

WHAT IS AN EQUINOX?

An equinox is one of the two days of the year when the Sun lies directly above the Equator.

WHEN ARE THE EQUINOXES?

The equinoxes occur on 20 or 21 March and 22 or 23 September.

WHAT HAPPENS ON AN EQUINOX?

On an equinox, the days and nights are about the same length everywhere on Earth.

WHAT DOES EQUINOX MEAN?

Equinox means "equal night".

WHY ARE THERE DIFFERENT CLIMATES?

A region's climate is the general pattern of weather that it experiences over a long period of time. Climate depends on a number of factors. The position of the area on the Earth's surface, and its height above sea level are two factors. Warmth carried around the world by ocean currents affects the climate on land, and those areas far from the sea will have a different climate from those on the coast. There are eight main types of climate, but there are variations to be found within them.

WHAT IS A TEMPERATE CLIMATE?

THERE ARE two types of temperate climate – cool and warm. Cool temperate areas have rainfall throughout the year, warm summers, and winters with temperatures often below freezing. The warm temperate climate features mild, wet winters where the temperature rarely gets below 4°C (39°F). The summers are hot and dry, with temperatures averaging 20°C to 27°C (68°F to 81°F).

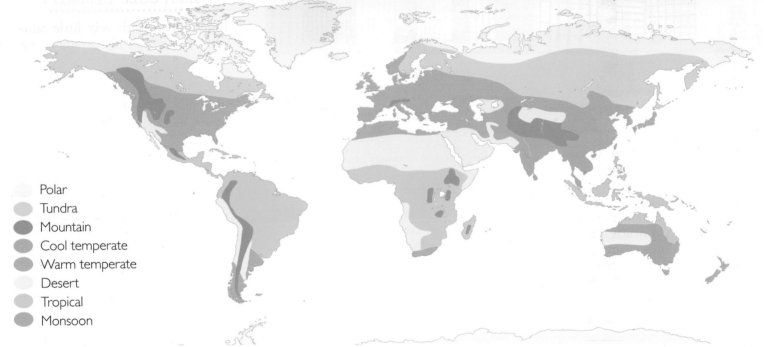

- Polar
- Tundra
- Mountain
- Cool temperate
- Warm temperate
- Desert
- Tropical
- Monsoon

WHAT IS A TROPICAL CLIMATE?

AREAS WITH A TROPICAL climate have high temperatures (24°C to 27°C (75°F to 81°F)) throughout the year. The atmosphere is very humid (full of moisture) and the levels of rainfall are very high – at least 150cm (59in) – particularly in those regions close to the Equator.

WHAT IS A MOUNTAIN CLIMATE?

IN THE MOST mountainous regions of the world, the climate will often be very different from that of the land that surrounds them. The freezing climate of the Himalayas, for example, is surrounded by desert, warm temperate, and monsoon climates.

WHAT IS A MICROCLIMATE?

SOME RELATIVELY small areas have their own climate, which differs slightly from the climate surrounding it – a microclimate. Cities often have a microclimate, due to the concentration of buildings, people and vehicles generating heat. This creates a "heat island" – a warm mass of air that sits over the city, making it up to 6°C (11°F) warmer than the surrounding area.

Rising warm air may give rise to clouds and rain.

Buildings absorb and generate a lot of heat.

Tall buildings affect wind direction.

DOES IT EVER GET WARM AT THE POLES?

THE POLAR CLIMATE is very dry and windy, as well as being exceptionally cold. Inland, it is nearly always below freezing, and temperatures often reach –40°C (–40°F). Only near the coasts do temperatures reach about 10°C (50°F) in the summer.

Penguins are found on the coastal areas of Antarctica – the warmest part of that region.

WHAT IS IT LIKE TO LIVE IN A MONSOON REGION?

PARTS OF INDIA and Southeast Asia have a monsoon climate. In these areas, it changes very suddenly from a wet to a dry season, according to the direction of the prevailing wind. The dry period is extremely hot, and the powerful monsoon winds that blow in from the sea bring torrential rain, often without warning. Such violent extremes of weather can make daily life very difficult, with heavy flooding, damage to property and loss of life commonplace.

In monsoon regions, houses are sometimes built on stilts to avoid being flooded. They also have steep-sided roofs to allow the water to run off easily.

CAN CLIMATES BE SIMULATED?

IT IS POSSIBLE to simulate the conditions of certain climates inside a greenhouse. Glass and other materials can be used to create a space within which the heat and light from the Sun is intensified, making it much warmer than it is outside. The temperature, humidity and air movement can be controlled, recreating the atmosphere of a particular climate.

The Eden Project in Cornwall, England – the largest botanical garden of its kind – uses the latest technology to recreate different climates from around the world.

DO CLIMATES CHANGE?

The world's climates have been through many changes since the planet was formed over 4000 million years ago. The Earth has been both hotter and colder than it is now. In the age of the dinosaurs, there were no polar ice caps, and tropical and desert climates were predominant. Since that time, there have been several Ice Ages, when the polar ice sheets expanded to cover up to one-third of the planet. The planet will continue to experience such dramatic changes, as well as minor fluctuations in the weather. Many people are concerned that the activities of mankind will have a catastrophic effect on our planet's weather patterns.

During the 150 million years that dinosaurs walked the Earth, the climate was warmer than it is today. They probably walked through tropical landscapes, covered with lush vegetation and, later, huge forests. Some scientists believe that a dramatic change in the climate, possibly caused by the impact of an asteroid, led to the extinction of the dinosaurs.

In the last Ice Age, the world was much colder than it is now. Mammoths roamed the Earth towards the end of this time. Their woolly coats protected them from the extreme cold.

WHAT CAUSES AN ICE AGE?

THE CAUSES of an Ice Age are not clear. One theory is that the Earth's tilt and its orbit of the Sun have changed. An orbit that took our planet further from the Sun would result in a cooler climate.

WHAT IS AN INTERGLACIAL PERIOD?

IT IS THOUGHT that Ice Ages occur roughly every 100,000 years. The last one ended around 10,000 years ago, so we may experience another in 90,000 years time. Scientists call the time between Ice Ages an interglacial period.

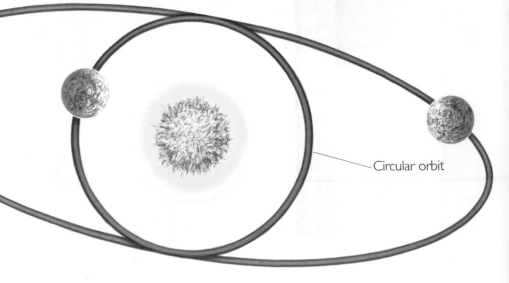

Elliptical orbit

Circular orbit

It is thought that the Earth's orbit has shifted between an elliptical (oval) shape and one that is closer to a circle. In an elliptical orbit, the Earth will have travelled further from the Sun, resulting in less solar energy reaching the planet's surface. Ice Ages possibly occur at these times.

HOW CAN TREES TELL US ABOUT PAST CLIMATES?

BY STUDYING the growth rings in ancient trees, scientists can gather information about climates of the past. This science is called dendroclimatology. In each year of a tree's growth, new layers are added to the centre of its trunk, producing a growth ring. Warm, wet growing seasons produce several layers, creating a wide growth ring. In a cold, dry period, fewer layers are produced, and the ring will be narrower.

Wide rings suggest a period of warm, wet weather.

Narrow rings indicate a year of cold, dry weather.

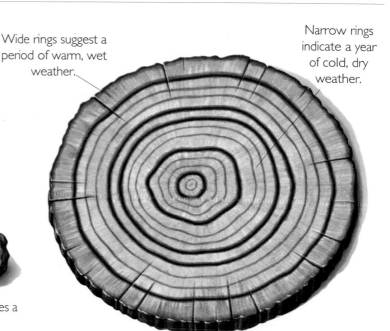

HOW CAN ROCKS TELL US ABOUT CLIMATE CHANGE?

FOSSILS CONTAINED in layers of rock can reveal details about the climate millions of years ago. Rock that contains a large variety of fossils was formed during a time when the climate was warm; fewer fossils indicate a cooler climate. Rocks that show signs of glacial erosion were part of the Earth's surface during an Ice Age. Geologists can work out the age of the layers, which tells us when the changes took place.

Fossil-rich rock indicates a warm climate.

Ice Age rock shows signs of glacial movement.

DO VOLCANOES AFFECT CLIMATES?

LARGE VOLCANIC ERUPTIONS can have an almost immediate effect on the world's weather. The dust that is thrown into the atmosphere creates a kind of screen, which reflects more of the Sun's energy back into space. As a result, temperatures around the world can drop slightly and weather patterns may be affected for several years.

WHAT MAKES SEA LEVELS RISE?

RISING TEMPERATURES cause sea levels to rise in two ways. A warmer sea is less dense, so its volume increases and the level rises as it expands. A warmer climate can also cause glaciers to melt into the sea, raising its level.

fast facts

WHO WAS JAMES CROLL?

James Croll was a British scientist who, in the 19th century, proposed that ice ages were caused by the changing tilt of the Earth.

HOW WILL GLOBAL WARMING AFFECT THE WEATHER?

A hotter Earth will have a dramatic effect on weather in the future. Tropical areas will receive more rain than they do at present, which could lead to severe flooding. Places that have little rainfall will have even less, creating more deserts.

WHEN DID HUMANS START TO AFFECT THE CLIMATE?

Pollution of the atmosphere on a large scale began in the 19th century, as many places in the world became industrialized.

HOW MUCH WARMER WILL EARTH BE IN THE FUTURE?

Estimates of exactly how much warmer the Earth will be in the future vary. Most scientists suggest that unless emissions of greenhouse gases are reduced dramatically, the world's average temperature will rise by 2–4°C (1.8–3.6°F) by 2030.

WHAT IS THE ATMOSPHERE?

The Earth's atmosphere is a covering of gases that surrounds the planet to a depth of 1000km (600 miles). Without it, no life would exist, and there would be no weather. Scientists divide the atmosphere into five separate layers: the exosphere, thermosphere, mesosphere, stratosphere and troposphere. The troposphere is the layer nearest the surface and is the only part of the atmosphere where weather happens.

In a view of the Earth from space, weather systems can clearly be seen moving around the atmosphere.

WHAT HAPPENS IN THE TROPOSPHERE?

THE TROPOSPHERE is sometimes called the weather layer. Here, the air is constantly moving as it is heated and cooled in a process known as convection. Clouds form as water in the atmosphere evaporates and then condenses. This movement of air, heat and water creates the world's weather systems.

HOW FAR UP DOES THE TROPOSPHERE REACH?

THE HEIGHT of the troposphere varies between different areas of the Earth. At the Equator, for example, it stretches to about 20km (12 miles) above the surface. At the poles, the layer reaches a height of about 10km (6 miles).

Mountain ranges can have a significant effect on local weather.

Convection – the movement of air that causes the weather – only happens in the troposphere.

Water circulates throughout the atmosphere.

Different types of clouds form at different levels.

WHAT IS ABOVE THE TROPOSPHERE?

THE LAYER directly above the troposphere is called the stratosphere. The stratosphere is warmer than the upper part of the troposphere and this warm, relatively heavy air acts like a lid, trapping clouds in the troposphere. Going up through the layers, the air gets thinner and thinner – only in the lower parts of the troposphere is there enough air to breathe normally.

EXOSPHERE
The exosphere is the very outer limit of the atmosphere, where space begins. At a height of about 900km (500 miles) above the surface, the air is very thin. Some satellites orbit just above the exosphere.

THERMOSPHERE
The thermosphere is the hottest part of the atmosphere, because the few air molecules there directly absorb radiation from the Sun. Here, radio waves bounce off layers of electrically-charged particles called the ionosphere.

MESOSPHERE
The mesosphere starts at about 50km (30 miles) above the surface and stretches for about the same distance again. It is very cold here, often less than −100°C (−148°F).

STRATOSPHERE
The temperatures in the stratosphere range from about −60°C (−75°F) at the bottom to around freezing at the top. Jet aircraft fly through the stratosphere because the air is much calmer than it is in the troposphere below.

The ozone layer lies between the stratosphere and the troposphere.

fast facts

WHAT DID JAMES GLAISHER DISCOVER?

James Glaisher was a 19th-century scientist who, after travelling in a hot-air balloon, discovered that the temperature dropped the higher he went.

WHO WAS JOSEPH PRIESTLEY?

English chemist Joseph Priestley discovered that the air is made up of several gases in 1774.

WHO WAS ANTOINE LAVOISIER?

French chemist Antoine Lavoisier identified and named oxygen a year after Priestley's discovery.

HOW MUCH OF THE AIR IS OXYGEN?

Oxygen makes up 21% of the air.

WHERE DO METEORS APPEAR?

Fragments of "space rock" called meteoroids enter the Earth's atmosphere and burn up as meteors in the mesosphere.

DO OTHER PLANETS HAVE ATMOSPHERES?

All of the planets have atmospheres, but none of them have the same properties as the Earth's.

WHAT IS THE TROPOPAUSE?

The tropopause is the very upper part of the troposphere, where it meets the stratosphere.

HOW HIGH CAN AIRCRAFT FLY?

Some military jets can fly into the exosphere. They are described as flying on the "edge of space".

WHAT CAUSES AIR PRESSURE?

Air pressure is created by the effect of gravity pulling the atmosphere towards the Earth. It can vary according to temperature, causing different amounts of pressure in different parts of the world. It also changes according to altitude – pressure is greater at sea level because there is more air pushing down than there is at higher altitudes.

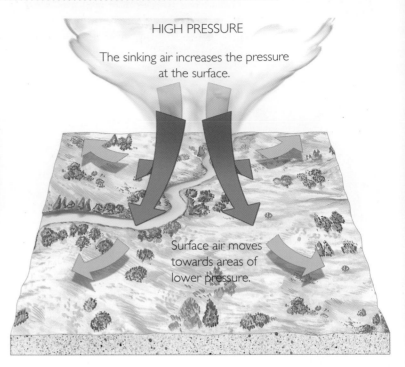

HIGH PRESSURE

The sinking air increases the pressure at the surface.

Surface air moves towards areas of lower pressure.

HOW DOES A LOW-PRESSURE AREA FORM?

AN AREA of warm air can create low pressure because warm air rises, reducing the level of air pressure. If the warm air evaporates water on the surface, clouds may form, producing the rain and bad weather associated with low pressure.

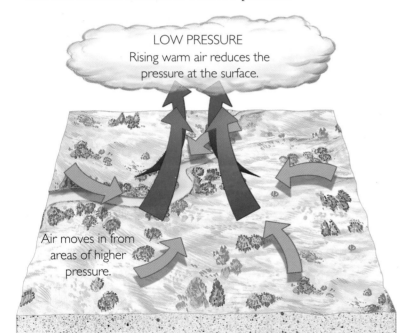

LOW PRESSURE

Rising warm air reduces the pressure at the surface.

Air moves in from areas of higher pressure.

HOW DOES A HIGH-PRESSURE AREA FORM?

AN AREA of high pressure is created where the air is cold. The cold air sinks, pushing down and creating high pressure. This causes the air molecules to be squashed together, creating heat. As the air warms up, it tends to bring warm and pleasant weather.

HOW IS AIR PRESSURE MEASURED?

AN INSTRUMENT called a barometer is used to measure air pressure. A mercury barometer consists of a glass tube standing in an open dish of mercury. The air pressure pushes against the mercury and forces it up the tube. The level of the mercury is recorded against a scale. Mercury barometers are clumsy, and mercury is poisonous, so aneroid barometers are more commonly used. A sealed metal box inside the barometer is connected to the pointer on the clock-like face. The vacuum inside the metal box means that an increase in pressure will squash it; a drop in pressure will make it expand. These changes make the pointer move around the dial.

Aneroid barometer

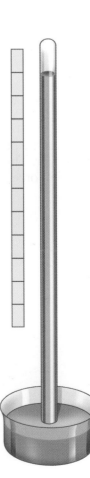

Mercury barometer

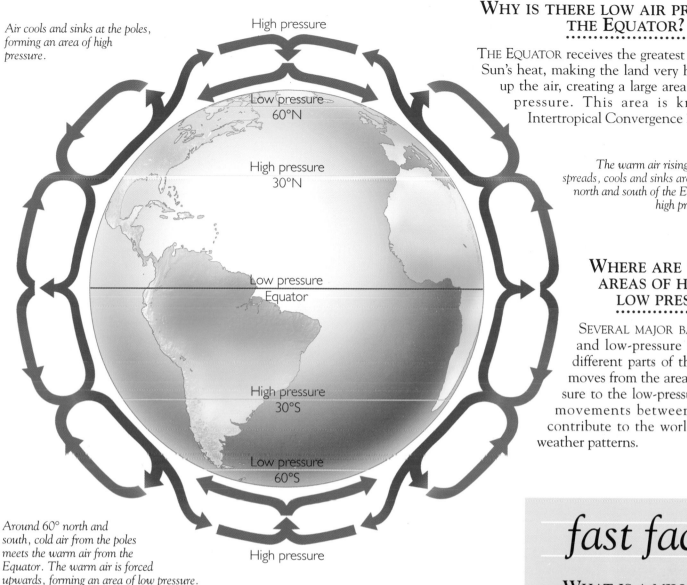

Air cools and sinks at the poles, forming an area of high pressure.

High pressure

Low pressure
60°N

High pressure
30°N

Low pressure
Equator

High pressure
30°S

Low pressure
60°S

High pressure

Around 60° north and south, cold air from the poles meets the warm air from the Equator. The warm air is forced upwards, forming an area of low pressure.

WHY IS THERE LOW AIR PRESSURE AT THE EQUATOR?

THE EQUATOR receives the greatest amount of the Sun's heat, making the land very hot. This heats up the air, creating a large area of mainly low pressure. This area is known as the Intertropical Convergence Zone (ITCZ).

The warm air rising from the Equator spreads, cools and sinks around latitudes 30° north and south of the Equator. A band of high pressure forms here.

WHERE ARE THE MAIN AREAS OF HIGH AND LOW PRESSURE?

SEVERAL MAJOR BANDS of high- and low-pressure areas exist in different parts of the world. Air moves from the areas of high pressure to the low-pressure areas. The movements between these areas contribute to the world's winds and weather patterns.

WHY DO SOME AIRCRAFT HAVE PRESSURIZED CABINS?

AT THE ALTITUDE at which many jet aircraft fly, the air pressure is extremely low – less than the pressure inside the human body. This makes it impossible for the body to take in air. There is also very little oxygen, so the air inside the plane has to be pressurized in order to simulate the level of air pressure on the surface.

fast facts

WHAT IS A MILLIBAR?

A millibar is the standard unit that meteorologists use to measure atmospheric pressure.

WHAT IS THE AVERAGE ATMOSPHERIC PRESSURE?

The average pressure of the atmosphere has been set as 1013mb (29.91psi – pounds per square inch).

WHAT IS AN ISOBAR?

An isobar is the curving line on a weather map that links together all the areas of equal pressure.

WHO WAS EVANGELISTA TORRICELLI?

Evangelista Torricelli was an Italian scientist who invented the mercury barometer in 1643.

WHAT IS A WEATHER FRONT?

Swirling masses of high- and low-pressure air are constantly moving around the Earth. When two masses of air with different characteristics meet, they do not mix, and a boundary develops between them. This boundary is called a front. On the ground, the arrival and departure of a front is felt by sharp changes in the weather.

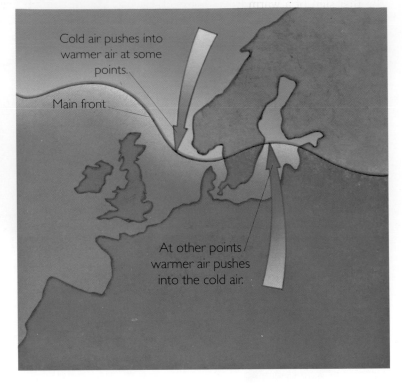

Cold air pushes into warmer air at some points.

Main front

At other points warmer air pushes into the cold air.

WHAT HAPPENS WHEN AIR MASSES MEET?

WHEN DIFFERENT air masses meet, varying pressure differences cause two things to happen. Warm air either bulges into the cold air, or the cold air pushes into the warm air. The collision causes the warm air to rise rapidly over the cold air, creating an area of low pressure called a frontal depression. The weather in this area becomes very unsettled and is worse when the differences in pressure and temperature are greatest. Depressions cover huge areas but tend to pass over in less than a day.

WHICH ARE THE MAIN AIR MASSES?

FOUR MAJOR masses of air lie over different parts of the world. The tropical maritime mass is warm and moist; the tropical continental mass is hot and dry. The polar continental mass is cold and dry, and the polar maritime mass is cold and wet. These air masses are blown around by high-level winds, and their interactions have a major influence on the world's weather. The kind of weather experienced depends on the nature of the air mass – tropical masses bring warm, humid weather, and the polar masses tend to bring snow. In places where these masses meet, the weather can be very changeable indeed.

TROPICAL CONTINENTAL

TROPICAL MARITIME

POLAR CONTINENTAL

POLAR MARITIME

WHAT HAPPENS UNDER A WARM FRONT?

AS ITS NAME suggests, a warm front has an area of warm, moist air behind it. The warm air rises above the cold air, and clouds are formed along the front. From the ground, the first sign of a warm front approaching is the sight of high, wispy cirrus clouds and maybe some light rain. When the warm front has passed, there is usually a short period of dry weather.

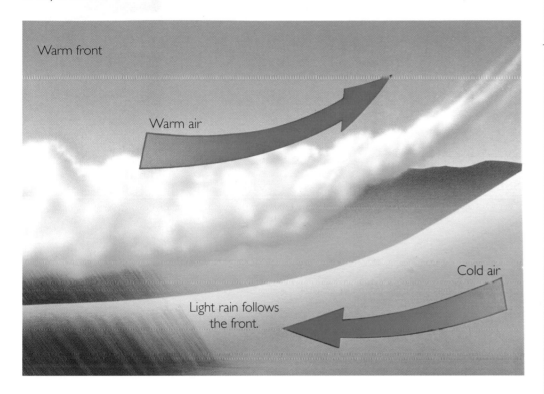

Warm front

Warm air

Cold air

Light rain follows the front.

WHAT HAPPENS UNDER A COLD FRONT?

A COLD FRONT is followed by an area of cold air. Thick, dark clouds, heavy rain and sometimes violent storms arrive immediately. If seen from the side, a cold front looks much steeper than a warm front. Cold air pushes beneath the warm air and rising water vapour condenses into clouds and then rain. Showers of rain will often follow as the front passes over.

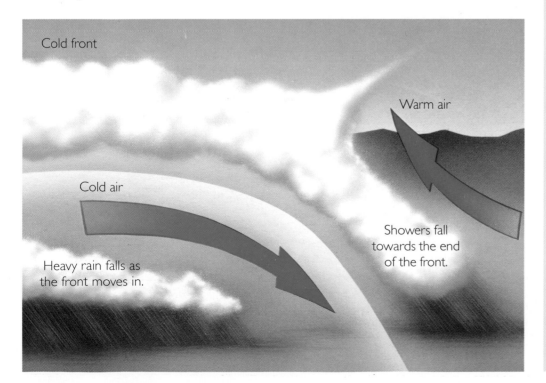

Cold front

Cold air

Warm air

Showers fall towards the end of the front.

Heavy rain falls as the front moves in.

fast facts

WHAT IS AN OCCLUDED FRONT?

When a cold front catches up with a warm front, the cold front moves underneath the warm air and lifts it up. This produces an occluded front, which can bring massive clouds and very heavy rain.

WHAT IS A SQUALL?

The sudden, often violent gusts of wind that accompany a cold front are known as squalls. The clear edge seen along a front is sometimes called a squall line.

WHAT IS AN ANTICYCLONE?

Meteorologists refer to an area of circulating high pressure as an anticyclone. An anticyclone often has descending air, light winds and bright, clear skies.

WHAT IS A DEPRESSION?

A depression is a circulating area of low pressure. It often has rising air and strong winds, and may bring clouds, rain or snow.

DO DEPRESSIONS AND ANTICYCLONES ROTATE IN THE SAME DIRECTION?

In the Northern Hemisphere, air travels clockwise around an anticyclone and anticlockwise around a depression. In the Southern Hemisphere, the directions are reversed.

WHAT IS THE BUYS-BALLOT LAW?

According to the Buys-Ballot Law, if you stand with your back to the wind in the Northern Hemisphere, the pressure will be lower on the left. In the Southern Hemisphere, the pressure will be lower on the right. It was devised by the Dutch meteorologist Christian Buys-Ballot.

WHAT MAKES THE WIND BLOW?

The wind is created by differences in air pressure and temperature – winds blow from areas of high pressure to those of low pressure. Rising warm air creates a low-pressure area, and the gap created is filled by high pressure produced by cooler air. The greater the difference in pressure, the stronger the wind.

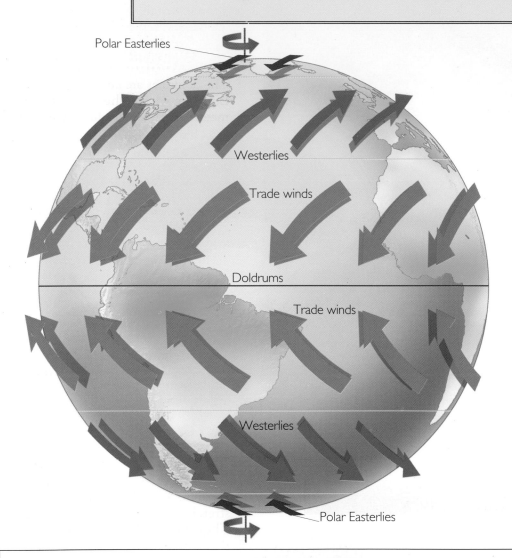

Polar Easterlies

Westerlies

Trade winds

Doldrums

Trade winds

Westerlies

Polar Easterlies

WHAT IS THE CORIOLIS EFFECT?

THE MOVING AIR that produces the winds tries to take the most direct route possible between the different areas of pressure. However, it is deflected by the rotating movement of the Earth. This is known as the Coriolis effect. In the Northern Hemisphere, the winds are deflected to the right of the direction in which they are headed; in the Southern Hemisphere, they are deflected to the left.

WHAT ARE PREVAILING WINDS?

PREVAILING WINDS are those that blow constantly in certain parts of the world. They are produced by hot air moving north and south from the Equator and by cold air moving away from the poles. The prevailing winds are the Polar Easterlies, found in the extreme north and south; the Westerlies, blowing between 30° and 60° north and south of the Equator; and the Trade winds, which blow north-east and south-east, either side of the Equator.

WHAT IS THE WIND-CHILL FACTOR?

THE WIND CAN make the air temperature feel colder than it actually is. A thin layer of warm air normally surrounds your body, creating an insulating "blanket" of air. If the wind is strong, this warm air gets blown away, making you feel a lot colder. This is known as the wind-chill factor. In a breeze blowing at 9km/h (5.6mph), an air temperature of 0°C (32°F) will feel like –3°C (27°F). If the breeze increases to around 15km/h (9.3mph), the wind-chill factor will make it feel like –10°C (14°F).

People who live in freezing conditions wrap themselves in several layers of clothing to insulate themselves from the cold and the wind.

WHAT CREATES A SEA BREEZE?

ON A HOT and sunny day, coastal areas will experience sea breezes. The land and the sea heat up and cool down at different rates, producing moving currents of air. The land heats more quickly than the sea, producing an area of low pressure, into which the cooler sea air moves. This breeze may move in a completely different direction from the prevailing wind and can blow up to 30km (18 miles) inland.

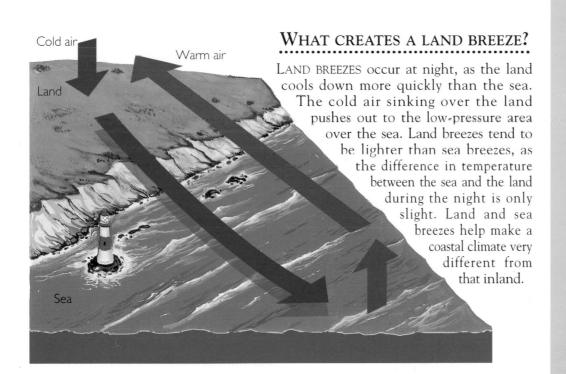

Warm air

Land

Sea

Cold air

WHAT CREATES A LAND BREEZE?

LAND BREEZES occur at night, as the land cools down more quickly than the sea. The cold air sinking over the land pushes out to the low-pressure area over the sea. Land breezes tend to be lighter than sea breezes, as the difference in temperature between the sea and the land during the night is only slight. Land and sea breezes help make a coastal climate very different from that inland.

Cold air

Warm air

Land

Sea

HOW DO WINDMILLS WORK?

WINDMILLS USUALLY face into the prevailing wind, but they can also be adjusted should the wind direction change. Some types of windmills can be completely rotated according to the wind direction; in others, the angle of the sails can be adjusted to receive the maximum amount of wind power. Some wooden sails have spring shutters that open and close according to the wind strength. If the wind gusts, the shutters open up, if it drops, they close. In this way, a constant wind force is maintained on the windmill sails.

fast facts

HOW DID THE TRADE WINDS GET THEIR NAME?

The trade winds are so called because they were the winds that powered sailing ships on their journeys between Europe and the Americas.

WHAT ARE THE DOLDRUMS?

The doldrums are an area along the Equator where the trade winds meet. There is very little wind in the doldrums, and sailing ships were often stuck there for long periods of time while they drifted towards the trade winds.

WHAT ARE LOCAL WINDS?

Local winds are those that blow in a relatively small area. Land and sea breezes are local winds, but there are some with specific names. The Mistral is a cold, northerly wind, which sometimes blows along France's Mediterranean coast. The Chinook is a southerly wind that follows the Rockies in North America.

WHAT IS A JET STREAM?

Jet streams are powerful winds that blow at about 10km (6 miles) above the Earth's surface. Blowing at about 200km/h (125mph), they can stretch halfway around the world. They move major air masses and therefore have a considerable effect on the weather.

WHAT IS A WINDSOCK?

Small airports use windsocks – hollow tubes of material – to show pilots the strength and direction of the wind. In a strong wind, a windsock fills with moving air and billows in the direction the wind is blowing towards. A limp windsock indicates that the wind is very light.

HOW IS WIND STRENGTH MEASURED?

The strength of the wind varies between gentle breezes and destructive storms. Knowing the strength of the wind and its effect is important for the safety of people and property, particularly for those at sea. In 1805, Sir Francis Beaufort devised a scale by which the strength of the wind could be determined by observing its effect on the environment. This is known as the Beaufort scale.

WHY WAS THE BEAUFORT SCALE DEVISED?

THE BEAUFORT SCALE was devised for use by sailors. By observing the wind's effect on the ship's rigging and the waves, sailors would know how much sail should be carried or stowed in order for the ship to sail efficiently and safely. The 12 levels of wind strength have since been adapted for use on land.

FORCE 1
Light air. Smoke seen to drift gently in an average wind speed of 3km/h (1.8mph).

FORCE 2
Light breeze. Some leaves will rustle. Wind speed: 9km/h (5.6mph).

FORCE 3
Gentle breeze. Flags begin to flutter in a wind speed of 15km/h (9.3mph).

WHY ARE SOME BRIDGES CLOSED WHEN IT IS WINDY?

DURING HIGH WINDS, some bridges may be closed for safety reasons. The structure of the bridges is rarely in doubt, although there have been cases of bridges collapsing in strong winds. The chief concern is for the safety of the vehicles that cross the bridge, particularly high-sided lorries and trucks. Those bridges in especially high positions are most prone to closure.

FORCE 7
Near gale. Whole trees will sway; litter bins are blown over in a wind speed of 56km/h (35mph).

FORCE 8
Gale. Twigs broken off trees and walking is difficult. Wind speed: 68km/h (42mph).

The Severn Bridge, which links England and Wales, is often closed to traffic when the wind gets above Forces 7 to 8. This is a good example of how the strength of the wind can disrupt everyday life.

WHEN DOES THE WIND START TO DAMAGE BUILDINGS?

DAMAGE TO BUILDINGS during a storm obviously varies according to the construction and location of the building, but damage generally occurs above Force 9 or 10. Chimney pots, roofing tiles and slates are the parts of buildings most at risk from storm damage.

HOW DOES A KITE WORK?

KITES USE the strength of the wind to keep them in the air. Held by one or more strings, the kite deflects the force of the wind downwards. The wind produces a reaction force that acts in the opposite direction of the pull to the string, supporting the kite in the air. Different designs of kites are suitable for use in different wind strengths.

Flying a kite is a fun way of using the force of a powerful wind.

FORCE 4
Moderate wind. Litter blows around and small branches move in a wind speed of 25km/h (16mph).

FORCE 5
Fresh wind. Small trees start to sway in a wind speed of 35km/h (22mph).

FORCE 6
Strong wind. Large tree branches move; umbrellas difficult to hold. Wind speed: 45km/h (28mph).

FORCE 10
Storm. Buildings damaged and trees blown down. Wind speed: 94km/h (58mph).

FORCE 9
Severe gale. Branches blown off trees; chimney pots blown off buildings. Wind speed: 81km/h (50mph).

FORCE 11
Severe storm. Serious damage caused to buildings. Wind speed: 110km/h (68mph).

FORCE 12
Hurricane. Damage inflicted on whole area with wind speeds of at least 118km/h (73mph).

WHAT IS AN ANEMOMETER?

ANEMOMETERS ARE instruments that measure the speed of the wind. Some early versions had a ball attached to a swinging arm that travelled up a curved scale according to the strength of the wind. Most anemometers consist of three or more cups mounted on arms that spin around a pole. Inside the pole, a mechanism records the number of rotations in a certain period of time. The speed is usually given in kilometres or miles per hour, although marine anemometers may give the speed in knots.

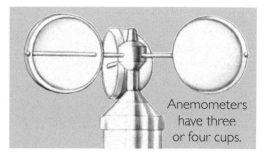

Anemometers have three or four cups.

fast facts

WHO INVENTED KITES?

The Chinese are thought to have invented kites around 500BC.

WHEN WERE ANEMOMETERS INVENTED?

The modern type of anemometer was invented in 1846.

WHY IS IT SO WINDY AT SEA?

Winds tend to be strongest at sea because there is nothing to break them up.

WHAT IS DEAD CALM?

No wind at all is dead calm – Force 0 on the Beaufort scale.

WHAT WAS THE STRONGEST RECORDED WIND?

The record wind speed is 371km/h (231mph), recorded in New Hampshire, USA, in April 1934.

WHAT IS A HURRICANE?

Hurricanes are very powerful, spiralling storms that produce winds of up to 300km/h (185mph). A combination of wind and torrential rain causes widespread flooding of the land and damage to buildings. Meteorologists call hurricanes tropical cyclones, due to the nature of their movement and the areas in which they form. They are also known variously as typhoons and willy-willies.

Hurricanes are powerful enough to uproot trees, overturn cars and destroy buildings.

HOW DOES A HURRICANE FORM?

HURRICANES FORM when moist air is stirred up by heat over warm oceans. It is thought that areas of very low pressure suck air into the centre of the low, producing strong surface winds. The air speeds up and spirals upwards, with water vapour condensing to form massive cumulonimbus clouds. Heat is generated, which makes air rise faster and faster and causes the wind speed to increase even more.

WHERE DO HURRICANES OCCUR?

HURRICANES OCCUR only in tropical areas – between latitudes of 5° and 20° north and south of the Equator. Extreme temperatures and humidity provide the right conditions for a hurricane to develop. They occur when the sea temperature rises above 27°C (80°F). The south-east coast of the USA and south-east Asia see many hurricanes.

Huge rings of cumulonimbus clouds form around a hurricane's centre.

Air rises rapidly at the centre, forming a spiralling column.

When a hurricane hits the land, the population will be evacuated, leaving the streets deserted. Those who live in hurricane hotspots have much to fear.

WHAT HAPPENS IN THE EYE OF A HURRICANE?

IN THE CENTRE of a hurricane there is a column of air 30–50km (20–30 miles) wide. This is known as the "eye" of the hurricane. In the eye, the air is sinking slowly, and the wind is relatively light. As the eye passes over an area, the sky will clear, the rain will stop, and there will be a moment of calm. In the area immediately surrounding the eye – the eye wall – winds can reach up to 240km/h (150mph). Winds increase as the eye becomes narrower.

HOW ARE HURRICANES TRACKED?

METEOROLOGISTS USE satellite images to determine where and when hurricanes may develop. The movement of a hurricane is determined by a combination of high-level winds and the direction of warm ocean currents. By analyzing data and predicting the potential path of the storm, meteorologists can give people living in danger areas an early warning.

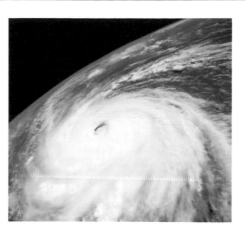

fast facts

HOW ARE HURRICANES NAMED?

A list of alternating male and female names is produced each year. A new hurricane is simply given the next name on the list.

DO ALL HURRICANES SPIN THE SAME WAY?

Hurricanes spin anticlockwise in the Northern Hemisphere and clockwise in the Southern Hemisphere.

WHAT WAS HURRICANE FLOYD?

In October 1987 Hurricane Floyd caused severe damage in Britain.

WHEN DOES A STORM BECOME A HURRICANE?

A storm becomes a hurricane at a speed of 199km/h (74mph).

HOW ARE HURRICANES CATEGORIZED?

Hurricanes are categorized on a scale of 1 to 5 (5 is the strongest).

WHO WAS CLEMENT WRAGGE?

Clement Wragge was the first person to name hurricanes.

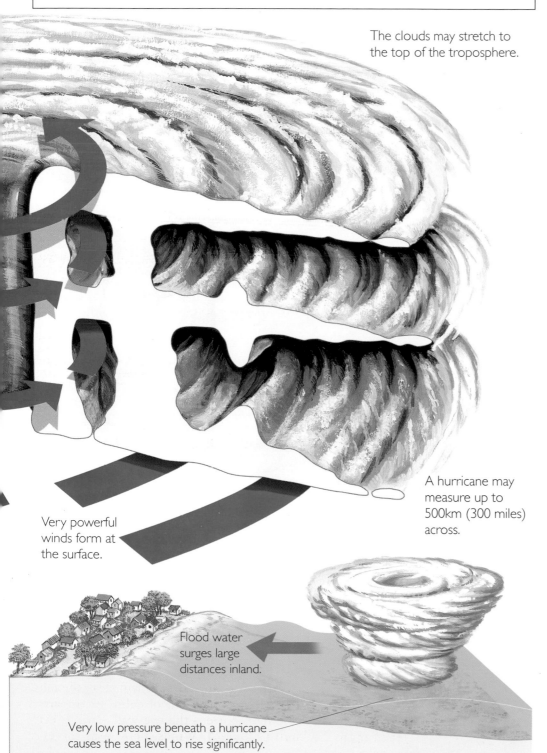

The clouds may stretch to the top of the troposphere.

A hurricane may measure up to 500km (300 miles) across.

Very powerful winds form at the surface.

Flood water surges large distances inland.

Very low pressure beneath a hurricane causes the sea level to rise significantly.

WHAT IS A STORM SURGE?

MUCH OF THE destruction caused by a hurricane comes from the sea. The low pressure in the eye sucks up the sea beneath, raising it by as much as 6m (20ft). At the same time, violent winds whip up waves as tall as houses. The high water level and the freak waves combine to make "storm surges" – towering walls of seawater that surge inland for many kilometres, sweeping away buildings, trees and anything in their path.

WHAT IS A TORNADO?

Violent thunderstorms can often give birth to powerful funnels of wind called tornadoes. The wind in these funnels can reach speeds of over 500km/h (300mph). When they come into contact with the ground, tornadoes can pick up vast amounts of dust and debris. Rising air within the funnel sucks objects upwards, uprooting trees and destroying houses.

HOW MUCH DAMAGE CAN A TORNADO CAUSE?

SEVEN-TENTHS OF TORNADOES are labelled as "weak" tornadoes because they do not cause much damage. The remaining three-tenths are devastating. At its strongest, a tornado can level a well-built house and suck a fully laden juggernaut into the air.

WHEN WAS THE MOST DEVASTATING TORNADO?

IN 1925 A TORNADO carved a path of destruction through the states of Indiana, Missouri and Illinois, USA, killing 689 people.

WHERE ARE TORNADOES MOST COMMON?

TORNADOES are most common in the USA. Although every state has been hit by a tornado at some time, they occur most frequently in the large, central plains of Missouri, Kansas and Texas. As a result, this part of the continent has been nicknamed "tornado alley".

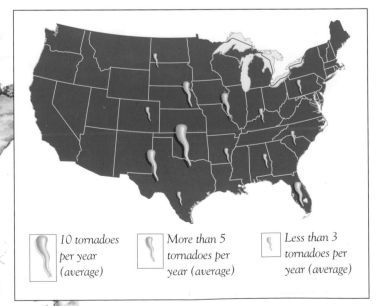

| | 10 tornadoes per year (average) | | More than 5 tornadoes per year (average) | | Less than 3 tornadoes per year (average) |

The map above shows the frequency of tornadoes in affected areas of the United States of America.

HOW ARE TORNADOES GRADED?

THE FUJITA TORNADO INTENSITY SCALE is used to grade how powerful a tornado is, based on the amount of damage it does. The F (for Fujita) scale uses numbers from 0 to 5. An F0 tornado has winds of less than 115km/h (72mph) and does little damage. An F5 tornado has wind speeds greater than 418km/h (261mph) and can be devastating to anything nearby.

F1: Minor damage to homes; vehicles overturned.

F2: Large trees are uprooted by the storm.

F3: Major structural damage to buildings.

F5: Total destruction of nearby buildings.

Cold, dry air

A twisting column of air stretches from the ground to the storm clouds above.

Warm, moist air

HOW DOES A TORNADO FORM?

A TORNADO FORMS in the same way as the funnel created when water drains out of a sink or bath. A whirlpool, or vortex, forms when water drains from a sink because of the downdraft created by the hole. Water is pulled downwards and begins to rotate. The faster the water rotates, the more powerful the vortex becomes. In a tornado, the same process happens with air. Large thunderstorms are formed by hot air rising from the ground, called an updraft. If an updraft is strong enough, a vortex of air forms beneath the cloud, gradually stretching downwards until it touches the ground.

DO TORNADOES JUST OCCUR OVER LAND?

A WATERSPOUT is literally a tornado over water. It may look like a waterfall rising from the water surface as condensed water vapour is pulled into the updraft. Waterspouts are very rarely as powerful as tornadoes, but wind speeds of over 400km/h (250mph) can make them a severe hazard to nearby boats.

WHAT CAUSES A THUNDERSTORM?

Thunderstorms develop when the weather is very hot and humid. Warm, wet air rises and then cools very quickly to produce thunder-clouds. Inside the clouds, the violent movement of air causes the water droplets and ice to bump against one another, knocking charged electrons from the ice, producing a build-up of static electrical charge. The huge amount of energy is released in the form of thunder and lightning.

Lighter, positively charged particles in the upper part of the cloud

WHAT IS THUNDER?

THE SOUND OF thunder is produced when a strike of lightning produces a huge amount of heat. Heated to a temperature of around 30,000°C (54,000°F), the air around the lightning expands very quickly – faster than the speed of sound. This rapid expansion of air causes the crashing thunder sound.

HOW DOES LIGHTNING STRIKE?

LIGHTNING STRIKES the ground due to opposite charges of static building up within the cloud. Positive charge builds up at the top of the cloud, while negative charge builds up at the bottom. The ground becomes positively charged, and lightning flashes between the cloud and the ground to discharge its electrical charge.

Negatively charged particles at the bottom of the cloud

WHAT DOES A LIGHTNING CONDUCTOR DO?

THE POWER contained within a stroke of lightning can easily damage buildings and start fires. To avoid this, many tall buildings are fitted with a lightning conductor. When lightning strikes the conductor, the electricity travels along the metal strip, which extends from a point above the building all the way to the ground.

The ground is positively charged by the negative charge on the underside of the cloud.

WHAT IS THE DIFFERENCE BETWEEN FORKED AND SHEET LIGHTNING?

ALL FORMS OF LIGHTNING are produced when electrical charge passes between positively and negatively charged areas. In forked lightning, an initial stroke (known as a leader) travels to the ground at a speed of around 100km per second (62 miles per second), creating a path of electrically charged air. A return stroke that travels immediately back along the path is what we see. Lightning also flashes between points within the cloud itself and between the cloud and the air, lighting up the sky. If the flash of lightning is hidden by cloud cover, it appears to make the cloud glow. This is called sheet lightning.

Forked lightning takes the quickest path from the underside of the cloud to a point on the ground.

Lightning that discharges within the air and does not reach the ground is sometimes called sheet lightning.

WHERE IS THE SAFEST PLACE TO BE IN A THUNDERSTORM?

BECAUSE A LIGHTNING strike seeks out the quickest route to the ground, it is unwise to shelter close to an isolated tall point, such as a tree, should you find yourself out in the open during a thunderstorm. The inside of a car is one of the safest places to shelter because if the car is struck, the electricity is conducted to the ground over the surface of the car. Of course, a secure building is the safest place to be during a storm.

Zeus was the most powerful of the Greek gods. He is often shown hurling thunderbolts on the world below.

HOW DID EARLY PEOPLE EXPLAIN THE POWER OF THUNDERSTORMS?

LIKE MANY THINGS in the natural world, thunder had a mythological and spiritual significance for some early peoples, who endowed their gods with the power of many natural forces. The Greeks attributed the might of storms to Zeus, the king of the gods. When angry, he would smite the world below with his thunderbolts. In early Scandinavian mythology, the god Thor had some of the same attributes, being the god of the sky and controller of storms, lightning, rain and thunder. Farmers prayed to Thor for good harvests and fine weather.

WHAT DO DIFFERENT TYPES OF CLOUDS INDICATE?

Clouds are named according to their shape, height and size. They are normally associated with rain, snow, sleet or hail, but not all clouds mean that bad weather is on the way. Dark, angry-looking clouds normally bring wet and windy weather, but a sky full of fluffy white clouds on a warm and sunny day usually means that the weather will stay that way.

Cirrus clouds

Cirrus clouds that form into an almost transparent layer high in the sky are called cirrostratus clouds. Wet weather often follows.

A combination of cirrus and cumulus are called cirrocumulus clouds. They are rows of icy particles and indicate a period of unsettled weather.

WHAT ARE CIRRUS CLOUDS?

CIRRUS CLOUDS form at heights above 6000m (20,000ft). At this altitude, it is so cold that the water inside the clouds is frozen into crystals of ice. They have a feathery, wispy appearance and are sometimes called "mares' tails". A large number of cirrus clouds will occasionally form a complete layer of white cloud.

A thin, watery sheet of grey cloud is called altostratus cloud. Rain often follows its appearance.

Cumulonimbus clouds are huge, flat-topped clouds that often bring heavy storms, rain and thunder. Because of their shape, they are sometimes called anvil clouds and may stretch to great heights.

Altocumulus clouds are small, flattened cumulus clouds, grey or white in colour. They may appear after a long period of hot weather, before a thunderstorm.

Cumulus clouds

Stratocumulus clouds are formed from a sheet of cumulus clouds that almost join together. They are probably the most common type of cloud.

WHAT ARE STRATUS CLOUDS?

STRATUS CLOUDS form at the lowest levels of the cloud layer – around 500m (1600ft). They form in layers that can build up across the whole sky. Stratus clouds produce light rain and drizzle and, in hilly areas, will often produce wet fog and mist over the ground.

Nimbostratus clouds are very thick and grey. They bring rain or snow and block out the Sun completely.

WHAT ARE CUMULUS CLOUDS?

CUMULUS CLOUDS form at different heights, although they are most often seen in the middle of the cloud layer. Fluffy in appearance, cumulus clouds are often grey on the bottom and a very bright white at the top. Sometimes known as cauliflower clouds, they are usually seen on dry, sunny days.

Stratus clouds

HOW DO CLOUDS FORM?

THE AIR CONTAINS millions of microscopic dust particles, which absorb water from rivers, lakes and seas. This happens when the water is heated. The heat turns the water into an invisible gas called vapour – a process called evaporation. When the warm, moist air cools down, it condenses (turns back into a liquid) on the surface of the dust particles. When the tiny droplets of water group together, a cloud forms. Clouds can be formed in several different ways, such as by warm air rising up through thermals, or when warm air is forced over hills and mountains. They can also be formed when two air masses meet and the cold air pushes under the warm air, forcing it up.

Warm air cools and water vapour condenses to form convective clouds.

As air at the surface is heated, it expands and rises.

Clouds form when warm air rises above a heated part of the Earth's surface.

Warm air cools down as it is forced over hills and mountains.

Clouds will form over the hills.

Warm air

Cold air

Frontal clouds form as the warm air rises over the cooler air.

Clouds form when warm air is forced over high areas.

Clouds form when two air masses meet.

HOW IS CLOUD COVER MEASURED?

METEOROLOGISTS MEASURE cloud cover in oktas – the number of oktas indicates how much of the sky is covered with cloud. On a scale of 0 to 8, 0 oktas means that there are no clouds; 8 oktas means the sky is completely covered.

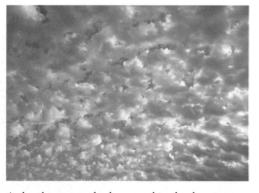

This scene shows a cloud cover of about 4 oktas, meaning that four-eighths (half) of the sky is covered.

A sky almost completely covered in cloud measures at about 7 on the okta scale.

WHAT ARE CONTRAILS?

AIRCRAFT FLYING at high altitudes will leave a white trail behind them when the air is very cold. This is caused by the exhaust gases expelled by the aircraft's engines. The gases contain a large amount of water vapour, which condenses and freezes in the cold, high-altitude air, leaving behind cloud-like trails called contrails.

fast facts

WHO CLASSIFIED CLOUDS?

Amateur meteorologist Luke Howard classified clouds in 1803.

HOW MANY TYPES OF CLOUD ARE THERE?

There are many different clouds, but only ten are officially classified.

WHAT DO THE NAMES MEAN?

Cumulus means "heaped"; cirrus means "feathered", and stratus means "layered". Nimbus is Latin for rain.

HOW IS A CLOUD'S HEIGHT MEASURED?

By reflecting a laser beam off the underside of the cloud to a receiver on the ground, it is possible to calculate the cloud's height.

HOW DOES RAIN FORM?

Rain can form in two ways. In tropical areas, where temperatures are warm, tiny water droplets in the clouds join together to form raindrops that are heavy enough to fall from the clouds. Elsewhere, rain starts life as snow in the freezing temperatures of the high clouds. As the snow falls nearer the ground, it will turn to rain if the temperature is above freezing.

Melting snowflakes will form rain.

Raindrops are made up of millions of tiny particles of water vapour.

Tiny water droplets join together or coalesce to form raindrops.

WHEN WAS THE UMBRELLA INVENTED?

UMBRELLAS HAVE been used for over 1000 years, and it is thought that they probably originated in China. Early umbrellas were made of paper and bamboo and waterproofed with varnish.

WHEN DOES "LIGHT" RAIN BECOME "HEAVY" RAIN?

IF LESS THAN 0.5mm (1/48in) of rain falls in an hour, it is described by meteorologists as light. When more than 4mm (1/6in) falls, the rain is described as heavy. The heaviest rainfall is experienced in the tropical and monsoon regions of the world. In other areas, periods of heavy rain rarely last longer than an hour.

HOW DOES RAINFALL VARY AROUND THE WORLD?

TROPICAL AREAS experience a lot of rain because high temperatures cause a large amount of water to evaporate from the sea to make clouds. Coastal areas of the world tend to experience more rainfall than those inland. One side of a mountain range may be drier than the other, because the mountains block the winds that bring the rain. These and other factors account for the varying amounts of rainfall around the world.

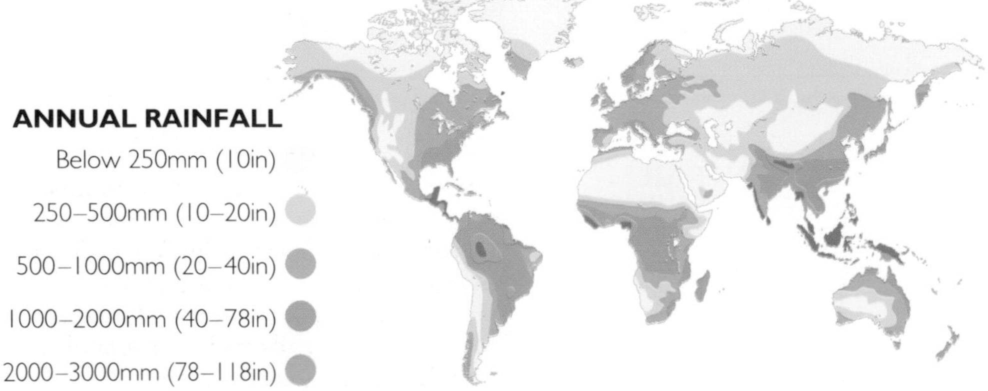

ANNUAL RAINFALL
Below 250mm (10in)
250–500mm (10–20in)
500–1000mm (20–40in)
1000–2000mm (40–78in)
2000–3000mm (78–118in)
Over 3000mm (118in)

WHAT CAUSES A DROUGHT?

A DROUGHT occurs when there is less than 0.2mm (1/100in) of rainfall in an area over a period of about two weeks. Droughts are usually caused by an area of high pressure that remains in one place for a long period of time. This is called a blocking high. The blocking high will prevent the movement of low-pressure systems into an area, meaning that hot, dry weather will dominate that area, leading to a drought. Parts of Africa, Asia and Central America often experience periods of drought.

This pink flower is growing in Death Valley, California, USA – one of the hottest and driest areas of the world.

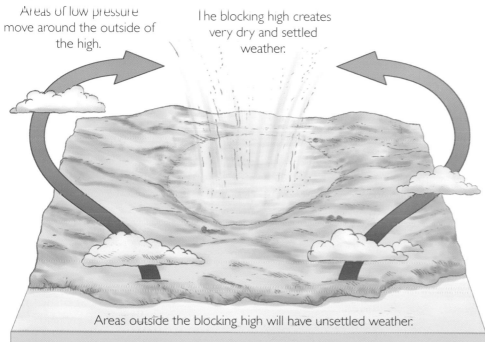

Areas of low pressure move around the outside of the high.

The blocking high creates very dry and settled weather.

Areas outside the blocking high will have unsettled weather.

HOW DO FLOWERS GROW IN A DESERT?

DESERT REGIONS experience very little rainfall, but flowers may still bloom after the rains come. Some flower seeds will survive in the desert soil for years, suddenly coming into bloom at the first sign of rain. These flowers will grow long enough to produce seeds, so that the cycle may continue.

WHY DO FLOODS OFTEN FOLLOW A DROUGHT?

AN AREA that has experienced a very long period of hot, dry weather or drought may suffer a flood should heavy rain follow. This is because the soil will have become baked so hard and dry that the water produced by very heavy rainfall will not be able to drain away. This is sometimes called a flash flood.

Flash floods can occur when heavy rainfall immediately follows a prolonged dry period.

HOW IS RAINFALL MEASURED?

RAINFALL IS usually measured in millimetres or inches. Rain water is collected in a metal drum about 50cm (20in) tall called a rain gauge. The rain gauge is placed on the ground, just high enough to avoid splashes. The rainwater is collected in a funnel at the top and passes into the drum.

Rain gauges are used by weather stations to measure rainfall. They are placed in clear, open spaces.

fast facts

WHY IS IT SAID TO RAIN "CATS AND DOGS"?

The old English saying "raining cats and dogs" may be based on the ancient Chinese spirits of wind and rain – a cat and a dog.

WHAT WAS THE DUST BOWL?

The Dust Bowl was a large area of farmland in North America that suffered drought in the 1930s.

WHAT SHAPE ARE RAINDROPS?

Raindrops are shaped like a flattened ball, rather than a teardrop.

CAN YOU "SMELL" RAIN?

After a dry period, moisture in the air can release oils trapped in the soil. These give off smells that are associated with rain.

HOW DOES SNOW FORM?

Snow forms in clouds when the temperature is within the range −20°C to −40°C (−4°F to −40°F). Ice crystals in the clouds begin to melt and join together with super-cooled water droplets. They then freeze together and form into snowflakes which, provided the air temperature is low enough, fall from the clouds. The process of forming snowflakes is called accretion.

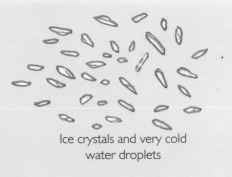

Ice crystals and very cold water droplets

WHAT IS SLEET?

SLEET IS usually snow that has half-melted, or it can be formed from raindrops that have partly evaporated and then cooled down as they fall to the ground. It often feels like very cold, wet rain when it falls on you.

Ice crystals crash together to form snowflakes.

All snowflakes have a six-sided pattern.

ARE ALL SNOWFLAKES THE SAME SHAPE?

THERE ARE thought to be about 80 different varieties of snowflakes, which form into shapes ranging from needles and columns to stars, prisms, plates and hexagons. All snowflakes have a symmetrical, six-sided pattern, but no two snowflakes have been found with exactly the same shape. Scientists think the shape of a snowflake depends on the height and temperature at which it was formed.

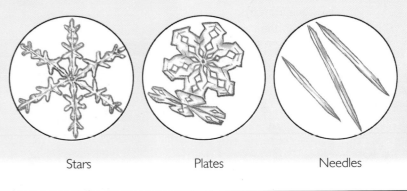

Stars   Plates   Needles

IS ALL SNOW THE SAME?

SNOW IS OFTEN described as being "dry" or "wet". The snowflakes that make wet snow are relatively large and form when the temperature is at freezing point or thereabouts. Wet snow packs together easily when it falls and is the best snow for making snowmen and snowballs. Dry snow is formed at lower temperatures, and the snowflakes are smaller than those that make wet snow. It is referred to as "powder" by skiers and snowboarders and is the best form of snow for such winter sports enthusiasts. It is lighter and much easier to clear away.

Wet snow is the easiest type to form into shapes and is ideal for making snowmen.

Dry snow is much better for skiing.

HOW DOES HAIL FORM?

HAILSTONES ARE essentially frozen raindrops. They are made inside very tall cumulonimbus clouds that have great differences in temperature between the top and bottom. Freezing temperatures at the top and warmer temperatures at the bottom of the cloud create very strong upward and downward currents of air. Ice crystals and super-cooled water droplets are thrown around by these currents and collide with each other. As they do so, they are coated with more and more layers of ice. The layers of ice build up until the hailstones are heavy enough to fall to the ground.

Ice crystals and droplets collide and freeze.

Hailstones are carried around the cloud and covered with more layers of ice.

A new layer of ice freezes around the hailstone.

Very strong air currents take the hailstone from the bottom to the top of the cloud.

Hailstones fall when they are too heavy to be held in the cloud.

Large hailstones can damage crops and break windows.

WHAT DOES THE INSIDE OF A HAILSTONE LOOK LIKE?

IF YOU were to cut through a hailstone, you would see that it is made up of several layers of ice and frost. Each layer is produced by one journey up and down the height of the cloud. The greater the amount of turbulence inside the cloud, the greater the number of layers and the bigger the hailstones.

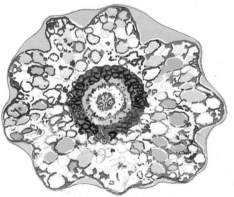

A cross-section of a hailstone shows it to be made up of layers, much like an onion.

WHEN DOES FROST FORM?

Frost most often forms over the land when the air remains clear after a cold winter's day. The ground loses its heat quicker than the air above it, and if the temperature falls below freezing, any moisture in the air will freeze, covering almost any surface with frost. Different conditions can produce different types of frost.

WHAT IS HOAR FROST?

HOAR FROST is the most common type of frost. It covers every exposed surface with layers of crunchy ice crystals. In certain conditions, the ground may be covered with a very thick layer of white hoar frost, which looks like snow.

Frost will cover any freezing-cold surface.

If there is not enough moisture in the air, the ground may freeze without a white covering.

WHY IS IT DANGEROUS TO WALK OR SKATE ON FROZEN WATER?

RIVERS AND LAKES can become frozen over if the temperatures get very low. This will usually depend on the depth of the water – the shallower it is, the more likely it is to freeze over. A layer of ice forms on the surface that is strongest and thickest nearest to the banks. Weaker spots will exist further out, making it very dangerous to walk or skate on the ice – anyone falling in could easily become trapped in the freezing water.

Skating or walking on a frozen lake or river is very dangerous.

HOW DO ICICLES FORM?

ICICLES USUALLY form when the water from thawed ice and snow freezes again. This happens during a bright winter's day when sunny areas are warm, but shaded areas remain below freezing, or when a cold night follows a warmer day. When the melt-water drips over the edge of a surface, the drops will freeze to form an icicle.

Icicles grow in length as more water runs over them and turns to ice.

WHAT IS RIME?

RIME FROST forms on leaves, branches and other solid objects when an icy wind freezes water droplets over them. It forms a solid white crust on the windward side of objects and can cause damage to buildings and other structures if it is allowed to build up. Rime is usually found in very cold, exposed areas.

CAN ICICLES FORM UPSIDE DOWN?

IT IS POSSIBLE for a type of icicle to form upside down. This happens in small, shallow pools of water – ornamental bird baths, for example. When the water freezes, it expands and forms a dome of ice in the centre. A crack in the dome will allow water out, which then freezes. As this happens over time, an "ice spike" will form.

Water freezes and forms into a dome shape.

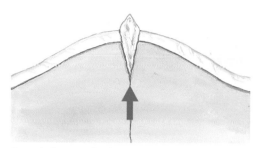

A crack forms in the dome and water expands through it.

As water continues to flow through the gap, it freezes and forms "upside-down" icicles.

WHAT IS FERN FROST?

FROST CAN sometimes create beautiful patterns on the inside of windows. The delicate shapes, called fern frost because of their resemblance to fern plant, form when water vapour condenses into tiny droplets on the window pane. Ice crystals form, making water freeze on to the sharp points of the ice crystals, creating a chain reaction that creates the patterns.

WHAT IS DEW?

DEW IS condensed water vapour, which forms when air comes into contact with a cold surface. It will form on a clear, still night, but it is especially noticeable after a night of fog, when there is a lot of water vapour in the air close to the ground. Dew will appear as water droplets on any cold surface.

Dew drops will form on the petals and leaves of outdoor plants and flowers.

Tiny droplets of morning dew clinging to spiders' webs are a common sight.

fast facts

WHAT IS BLACK ICE?

Black ice is formed when rain falls through very cold air on to ground that is below freezing. The freezing rain forms a transparent layer of ice, making the surface very slippery and hazardous to road-users.

WHY IS ICE SLIPPERY?

When water freezes, the molecules bond together very tightly, making any large surface smooth and slippery. As a sheet of ice melts, the water lubricates the surface, making it even more slippery.

WHY DO PIPES BURST WHEN IT FREEZES?

Water expands as it freezes, creating pressure against any enclosed space that it occupies. This is why cold water pipes may burst in freezing temperatures. Insulating the pipes can help prevent this happening.

WHAT IS THE DEW POINT?

The dew point is the temperature at which dew starts to form.

WHAT IS ANTIFREEZE?

Antifreeze is a chemical used to stop water-cooling systems in engines from freezing up. The most common antifreezes contain a type of alcohol called ethylene glycol. Depending on its concentration, antifreeze can prevent freezing down to temperatures of –35°C (–25°F). Many cars need to have antifreeze added to the water in their radiators in cold weather to make sure that they are able to start on cold mornings.

WHO IS JACK FROST?

Jack Frost is a mythical, devilish character mentioned in folk stories in some parts of the world. In the stories, the frosty patterns left on windows are said to be Jack Frost's fingerprints.

WHAT IS HUMIDITY?

The air absorbs water from oceans, rivers, lakes and also from trees and plants. Humidity describes the amount of water vapour that the air contains. The warmer the weather, the more moisture the air can hold. The air can reach a point of saturation, where it is no longer able to absorb any more water – this is 100% humidity. In such conditions, water vapour condenses to form mist, clouds and rain.

In very high humidity, there is a lot of water in the atmosphere.

Rainforests are very high in humidity – this is why so many plants and animals thrive in them.

WHICH PARTS OF THE WORLD HAVE HIGH HUMIDITY?

HUMIDITY IS highest in tropical areas, where the climate is warm. A continuous cycle of water movement exists, where water evaporates from the sea into the air and falls again in heavy rainfall. The conditions are ideal for plants and other forms of life – the plants themselves add more moisture to the atmosphere.

WHY IS EXERCISE SO DIFFICULT IN HIGH HUMIDITY?

PHYSICAL EXERCISE is difficult in a humid atmosphere if you are not used to it. This is because sweat cannot evaporate into the air properly, making it very difficult for the body to cool down. Athletes and other sports players will train in humid conditions in order to prepare themselves for competition in such an environment.

Strenuous exercise is very difficult in humid conditions.

WHICH PARTS OF THE WORLD HAVE LOW HUMIDITY?

DESERT REGIONS have very low levels of humidity – often less than 10%. The low levels of water vapour in the air and, indeed, the general scarcity of water makes conditions for life very difficult. Agriculture is practically impossible in such areas and is only really successful in places where levels of humidity tend to be moderate.

Levels of humidity are very low in desert regions, making conditions for life very harsh.

WHAT IS RELATIVE HUMIDITY?

TO MEASURE HUMIDITY accurately, meteorologists look at relative humidity. This is the amount of water in the air, relative to the maximum amount of water that it can hold at that temperature. To measure relative humidity, a wet and a dry thermometer are used. The wet bulb is covered with wet muslin. The water in the muslin evaporates, making the temperature around the wet bulb cooler than that around the dry bulb. The amount of water that evaporates increases along with the dryness of the air – the greater the difference in temperature, the lower the humidity. A smaller difference means higher humidity. The thermometers are housed in a Stevenson screen, to shade them from the Sun.

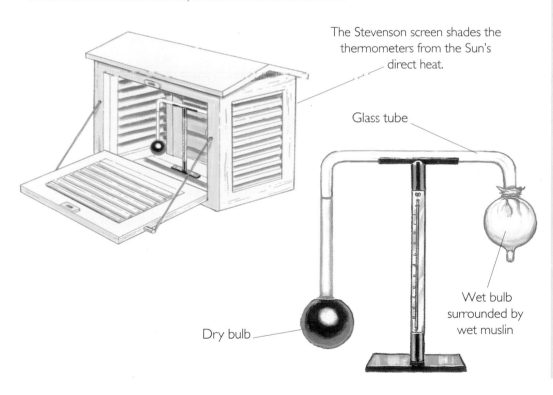

The Stevenson screen shades the thermometers from the Sun's direct heat.

Glass tube

Dry bulb

Wet bulb surrounded by wet muslin

HOW DO GREENHOUSES CREATE HUMIDITY?

Commercial greenhouses create humid conditions by spraying a fine mist into the air and keeping the temperature artificially high.

HOW DOES HUMIDITY AFFECT SILK-MAKING?

The caterpillars that produce silk thread prefer humid conditions and are therefore more productive in these conditions.

WHAT DID FERDINANDO DE MEDICI INVENT?

Ferdinando de Medici was an Italian duke who invented a hygrometer that measured humidity according to the amount of dew collected on a cool surface. The first hygrometer was a sponge.

WHY IS HUMID WEATHER DESCRIBED AS "STICKY"?

Humid weather is often described by people as "sticky" because that is how the air feels to us when it is full of moisture.

HOW IS HUMIDITY HARMFUL?

High levels of humidity in homes can lead to breathing and other health problems due to the high level of moisture in the air.

WHAT IS A HAIR HYGROMETER?

ONE OF THE simplest ways to measure humidity is to use a hair hygrometer. This uses a piece of human hair, which stretches or contracts according to the amount of water in the air. In a weather house – a type of hair hygrometer – a hair attached to a turntable stretches and contracts, making the man appear in humid conditions and the woman appear when it is drier.

The man is outside the house when humidity is high.

The woman is outside the house when humidity is low.

HOW DOES FOG FORM?

Fog is cloud that forms close to the ground. It appears when the wind is light, the air is damp and the sky is relatively clear. It often forms when moisture in the air close to the ground condenses and spreads upwards – this is called radiation fog. It is most common at the beginning or end of the day, when the ground cools down quickly.

Water vapour condenses to form fog

Cooler surfaces

Warmer air

WHAT IS THE DIFFERENCE BETWEEN FOG AND MIST?

THE DIFFERENCE between fog and mist is defined according to the density of the cloud. If the visibility through the cloud is less than 1km (0.6 miles), it is described as fog. If it is between 1km and 2km (0.6 and 1.25 miles), it is called mist.

Cooler surfaces

The city of San Francisco, USA, regularly experiences summer fog, as shown in this picture of its most famous landmark, the Golden Gate Bridge. The fog is created when a cold-water current in the Pacific meets the warm air of the land. It often takes a long time to clear.

WHAT IS ADVECTION FOG?

ADVECTION FOG forms when a warm, moist air blows over a cold expanse of water, such as a river or sea. The fog forms into a layer just above the water and is held in place by warm air above the fog. The fog will only blow inland if the land is low-lying and, when it does, it usually evaporates quickly.

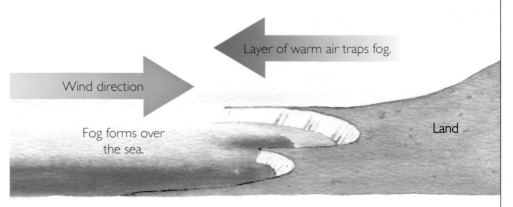

Layer of warm air traps fog.

Wind direction

Fog forms over the sea.

Land

WHY IS DRIVING IN FOG SO DANGEROUS?

THE LOW VISIBILITY that dense fog brings makes driving very hazardous. Low speeds and greater distances between vehicles need to be maintained, while headlights should be dipped at all times. Using them at full beam makes the light reflect off the fog, dazzling both the driver and other road-users.

Headlights must be dipped in fog.

Rear fog lamps shine through the fog.

WHAT IS SPECIAL ABOUT FOG LAMPS?

REAR FOG lamps use high-intensity bulbs filled with a special gas such as halogen. The light they produce is more intense than that of ordinary headlights.

HOW DO SHIPS NAVIGATE IN FOG?

LIGHTHOUSES AND LIGHTSHIPS are used to warn sailors of hazards at sea, but their effectiveness is reduced during dense fog. The beams will be less visible, and it is difficult to judge the actual position of the hazard. In fog, audible warnings – foghorns – are sounded, and most modern ships use sophisticated radar systems to detect hazards and other shipping in the area nearby.

WHAT IS ICEBERG FOG?

FOG OFTEN forms around icebergs when the air surrounding them is very cold but the water is quite warm. As the water evaporates, it condenses when it meets the cold air. It is thought that the ocean liner *Titanic*, which sank on its maiden voyage when it struck an iceberg in 1912, may have been in an area where icebergs were hidden from view by the dense fog surrounding them.

fast facts

WHAT IS A "PEA-SOUPER"?

During the late 19th and early 20th centuries, London, England, used to experience lots of heavy smogs caused by the burning of coal in homes and industries. The yellow-coloured smog caused respiratory problems, cut down visibility and was often described as being as "thick as pea-soup", hence the nickname "pea-souper".

WHAT IS FOG STRATUS?

Sometimes, a layer of fog can be seen with clear air above and below it. This occurs when the Sun's rays pass through the fog, heat the ground and make the bottom of the fog evaporate. The layer that remains is called fog stratus.

HOW DOES A FOG MACHINE WORK?

Fog is produced artificially for special effects in theatres and sometimes in nightclubs. It is made using machines that heat a mixture of an oil-based substance and water, which is then blown into the air. A similar effect is achieved using "dry ice" – made by dissolving frozen carbon dioxide in hot water.

WHY DOES MIST OFTEN FORM IN VALLEYS?

Mist often forms early in the morning in wooded valley areas. Higher up the valley slopes, the temperatures tend to be higher, making moisture on the trees condense to form low-lying mist. The mist gradually evaporates as the Sun warms the ground.

WHAT IS FREEZING FOG?

When fog forms and the temperature drops dramatically soon afterwards, the droplets of water vapour become larger, producing "freezing fog". Visibility is very much reduced in freezing fog.

WHEN DOES A RAINBOW APPEAR?

A rainbow appears when sunlight shines through raindrops. When the light passes through the raindrops at certain angles, the "white" light is split, or refracted into the seven colours of the light spectrum. The best time to see a rainbow is early morning or late evening, when the Sun is low in the sky. You will see a rainbow only when the Sun is shining behind you and it is raining in front of you.

The colours are always seen in the same order.

The colours red, orange, yellow, green, blue, indigo and violet are seen in a rainbow.

From an aircraft, you may see a rainbow as a full circle.

HOW DOES A RAINDROP SPLIT LIGHT?

RAINDROPS ACT like tiny prisms – splitting white light into all the colours of the spectrum. As light rays pass through the raindrop, they are refracted, causing them to split into different colours. The rays bounce off the back of the raindrop and pass out, divided into all the colours seen in the rainbow.

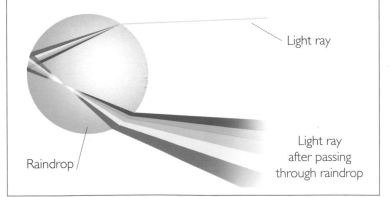

Light ray

Raindrop

Light ray after passing through raindrop

WHAT MAKES A SECOND RAINBOW APPEAR?

A SECOND, fainter rainbow can sometimes be seen a little higher than the main rainbow. It is made by light being reflected twice on the surface of each raindrop. The colours are seen in reverse order, with red at the bottom of the bow. A slight loss of sunlight with each reflection makes the second bow appear fainter.

CAN AURORAS BE SEEN FROM SPACE?

THE SPECTACULAR LIGHT shows known as auroras are seen in the skies above Arctic and Antarctic regions. They are caused by electrically charged particles from the Sun colliding with the Earth's magnetic field and atmosphere. The green, pink and blue lights produce a dazzling display when seen from space. From such a view, the aurora is seen from the beginning of its formation – from the point the particles first make contact with the atmosphere.

Seen from the window of a Space Shuttle, an aurora seems to radiate from the Earth. Of course, the opposite is true – the source of the aurora is the Sun.

HOW DO HALOES FORM AROUND THE MOON?

IN CERTAIN conditions, a bright Moon may appear to be surrounded by glowing "haloes" of light. This happens when moonlight (sunlight reflected by the Moon) passes through ice crystals high in the atmosphere. The light is reflected at certain angles to produce one or two haloes. They are usually incomplete, and they are most often seen when the Moon is at its fullest.

IS THERE EVER A BLUE MOON?

"ONCE IN A BLUE MOON" is a phrase that suggests a rare or unlikely occurrence. However, certain atmospheric conditions can cause the Moon to appear to change colour. A blue Moon has been reported in periods following massive volcanic eruptions. The dust in the atmosphere makes the Moon look blue.

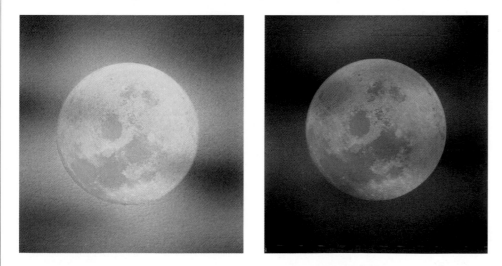

During a lunar eclipse, when the Earth casts a shadow on the Moon, it may appear red, as the Sun's rays are bent around the Earth.

WHAT IS EL NIÑO?

El Niño is a Pacific Ocean current that causes freak weather occurrences around the world. Scientists have noticed that every five to seven years, prevailing winds in the Pacific occasionally change direction, driving warm water east towards South America. This tends to start in January – during the Southern Hemisphere's summer. The effect has been known to occur for centuries, but it is only since the 1970s that scientists have understood El Niño and the way that it upsets the world's climate.

WHAT DOES EL NIÑO MEAN?

EL NIÑO is Spanish for "Boy Child" – a reference to Jesus. It was named in the 17th century by Spanish-speaking fishermen who lived in Peru, South America. It was given this name because the unusual weather associated with El Niño began around Christmas.

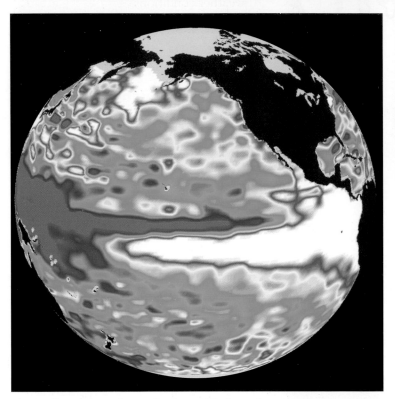

This satellite picture, taken in October 1997, shows the warm El Niño current as a white/red gash extending across the Pacific to the coast of South America.

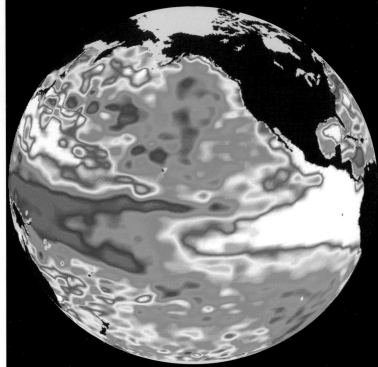

By January of the following year, this picture shows that El Niño had retreated slightly. However, the Pacific waters remained unusually warm.

WHAT ARE THE EFFECTS OF EL NIÑO?

IN AN EL NIÑO year, weather systems around the world become very unpredictable. This is most noticeable in the Pacific region. In the El Niño of 1997–98, massive floods caused widespread devastation in many parts of South America, making many thousands of people homeless. It also triggered a hurricane, bringing torrential rain to the deserts of California and Nevada. In the west of the region, El Niño brings hot, dry weather in what ought to be a rainy season. In the past, this has caused forest fires in Australia and Indonesia.

During an El Niño year, the waters off the coast of California, USA, are much warmer than usual, causing massive storms. Some have produced giant waves that have washed away entire beaches.

The El Niño of 1982 caused some of the most widespread and devastating drought conditions for hundreds of years. In South Africa, the drought virtually wiped out that year's corn crop.

HOW CAN IT RAIN FROGS AND FISH?

THERE HAVE been numerous reports of frogs, fish and other animals falling from the sky during heavy thunderstorms. One possible explanation for this unusual phenomenon is that the unfortunate creatures are sucked into the air by tornadoes, carried a great distance by the moving weather system, and then dropped to the ground along with the rain.

Few weather forecasts predict a heavy shower of fish and frogs!

ARE CROP CIRCLES CAUSED BY WEIRD WEATHER?

THERE ARE MANY theories about the origin of mysterious patterns that appear in fields of corn around the world – commonly known as crop circles. While some people believe they are the work of alien spacecraft, many of them are known to be man-made. Unusual weather, such as small tornadoes or electrical storms, is thought to be the cause of some of the patterns.

Some experts believe that many crop circles are formed by tornadoes.

WHO FORECASTS THE WEATHER?

Meteorologists and weather forecasters are employed by national and regional weather centres, as well as by organizations such as the military and by airports. They make forecasts based on their knowledge of weather patterns and information received from local, national and global sources. The forecasts are delivered to the public through television, radio, newspapers and the Internet.

HOW ARE WEATHER FORECASTS SHOWN ON TELEVISION?

TELEVISION WEATHER forecasts are the most easily understood and widely seen source of weather information for the general public. The weather forecasters may be trained meteorologists who work at a weather centre, or television presenters may read out forecasts provided for them. A detailed forecast is presented as a sequence of weather maps generated on a computer. They usually show temperatures and wind speed and direction, and give some indication of the expected weather conditions for different parts of the country. Local television stations will present a more detailed forecast for their region.

The computer weather maps appear in the blue area.

The weather forecaster stands in front of a blank blue screen.

A monitor helps tells the forecaster where to point on the screen.

The forecaster changes the weather maps by remote control.

HOW FAR AHEAD CAN THE WEATHER BE FORECAST?

DETAILED, SHORT-RANGE weather forecasts can usually be made for the next 24 hours. However, meteorologists today have access to information that enables them to make a fairly accurate, long-range forecast for up to a week ahead.

WHAT DOES A SATELLITE IMAGE SHOW?

WEATHER SATELLITES produce images by interpreting different levels of heat and light. When an area is lit by sunlight, different features – clouds, land, sea, ice, and so on – reflect different amounts of light, which are recorded by the satellite as varying shades of grey. When an area is in darkness, heat emissions are recorded by infrared equipment to produce a similar picture. The information is transmitted to a base station, where it is converted into images. Television forecasts often put a series of satellite images together to produce a "movie" of a moving weather system.

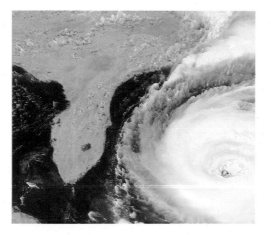

This computer-enhanced satellite picture shows Hurricane Fran approaching the coast of Florida, USA, in September 1996.

WHAT IS A SYNOPTIC CHART?

METEOROLOGISTS DRAW up special weather maps called synoptic charts to show a forecast. The long curved lines – isobars – show areas of equal pressure. Black circles mark the centre of low- and high-pressure areas. Lines of red semicircles indicate a warm front, and a cold front is shown by a line of blue triangles. A combination of triangles and semicircles indicates an occluded front. Ideally, all the observations shown on a synoptic chart should be made at the same time ("synoptic" means "seen together"), but this is rarely possible, so slight variations must be taken into account when interpreting a chart.

The synoptic chart illustrated below shows a weather system over north-west Europe.

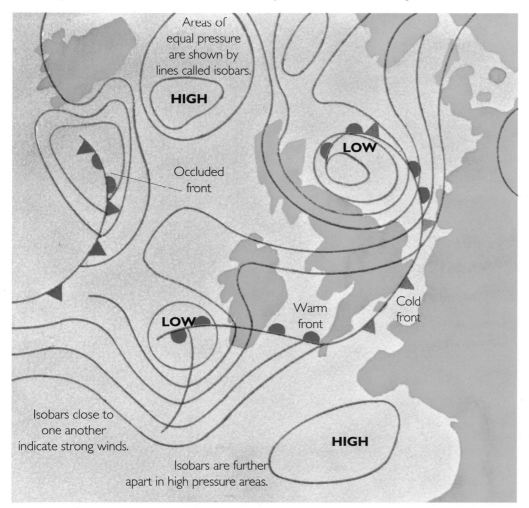

Areas of equal pressure are shown by lines called isobars.

HIGH

LOW

Occluded front

Warm front

Cold front

LOW

Isobars close to one another indicate strong winds.

Isobars are further apart in high pressure areas.

HIGH

HOW IS WEATHER INFORMATION GATHERED?

Meteorologists forecast the weather based on information gathered from a huge variety of sources. To get the clearest picture about the weather, both people and technology are employed around the world to continuously take weather measurements. Instruments on land, at sea, in the air and in space feed the information into a global network, where it is accessed and analyzed by the world's weather experts.

The helium-filled balloons burst when they reach a certain altitude.

Instruments in the long nose of this aircraft record temperature and humidity.

WHAT IS A WEATHER BALLOON?

WEATHER BALLOONS are used to take measurements of humidity, pressure and temperature at altitudes of up to 20km (12 miles). The readings are taken by instruments called radiosondes carried beneath the balloon. These transmit the information to processing stations on the ground. Wind strength and direction is monitored by tracking the movement of the balloon.

The radiosondes return to Earth on a small parachute – they are not always retrieved.

HOW ARE AIRCRAFT USED TO COLLECT WEATHER DATA?

RESEARCH AIRCRAFT are used to obtain detailed information about the atmosphere. They carry very sophisticated radar and laser equipment that records a three-dimensional picture of clouds at various levels in the atmosphere. Some planes are dedicated to monitoring hurricanes, often flying into the centre of the storm itself. The information collected by aircraft is much more detailed than that collected by weather balloons.

HOW IS THE WEATHER MONITORED ON LAND?

WEATHER DATA in remote areas is collected by automated weather stations. Equipped with a wide range of instruments and computers, the stations record and transmit information via satellite every hour. Individual observers with a small number of simple instruments also play an important part in all levels of weather forecasting.

Automated weather stations are located in places such as Antarctica.

HOW ARE COMPUTERS USED TO PREDICT THE WEATHER?

COMPUTERS ARE used to collect weather information and also to help meteorologists predict the weather. Special software uses the data to develop a "model" of the expected weather.

HOW DO SATELLITES HELP FORECAST THE WEATHER?

SATELLITES SERVE two purposes in weather forecasting. Communications satellites are used to send weather data around the world, while dedicated weather satellites monitor the movement of weather systems and the patterns of cloud cover. There are two types of weather satellite. Geostationary satellites are fixed in one position, observing a certain area from their orbit high above the Equator. Polar-orbiting satellites circle the Earth from pole to pole. The planet's rotation means that each orbit takes in a different part of the Earth.

There are around five geostationary weather satellites in orbit around the Earth.

The information from weather satellites is beamed back to weather stations on Earth.

Meteorologists may carry out long-term research on board ships.

A transmitter on the buoy notifies satellites of its position.

HOW IS THE WEATHER MONITORED AT SEA?

AT SEA, weather conditions are monitored by ships, which take measurements of pressure and sea and air temperatures. Ships may be used to launch weather balloons. Free-floating buoys are also used to collect weather data. They drift with ocean currents, transmitting sea-level weather details to satellites. They are much less expensive to maintain than specialist weather ships.

fast facts

WHEN ARE WEATHER BALLOONS RELEASED?

Weather balloons are released around the world twice daily – at midday and midnight, Greenwich Mean Time.

WHICH WAS THE FIRST WEATHER SATELLITE?

The first weather satellite, TIROS, was launched by the United States in 1960. It beamed back the first images from space of clouds moving around the Earth.

WHAT DID LEWIS FRY RICHARDSON DEVISE?

In the 1920s, British mathematician Lewis Fry Richardson devised a way of using mathematics to predict the weather. The calculations involved were so enormous that the system only became practical with the invention of the electronic computer around twenty years after his work was published.

WHAT DOES A WEATHER RADAR SHOW?

Weather radars show where rain, hail or snow is falling and how heavy it is. They work by sending out radiation waves, which bounce off the raindrops or snowflakes and are reflected back to a receiver. The intensity and location of the precipitation is shown in colour on the radar screen.

WHAT IS THE WORLD METEOROLOGICAL ORGANIZATION?

The World Meteorological Organization analyzes the data collected from weather satellites, balloons, ships and land stations operated in 150 countries around the world. The information is shared to produce accurate, up-to-date forecasts.

HOW CAN NATURE TELL US ABOUT THE WEATHER?

People have been forecasting the weather for thousands of years, based on changes seen in the world around them. Many such observations are little more than folklore and superstition, but it is true that certain plants and animals can detect variations in the air that people cannot, providing us with a natural sign of a change in the weather.

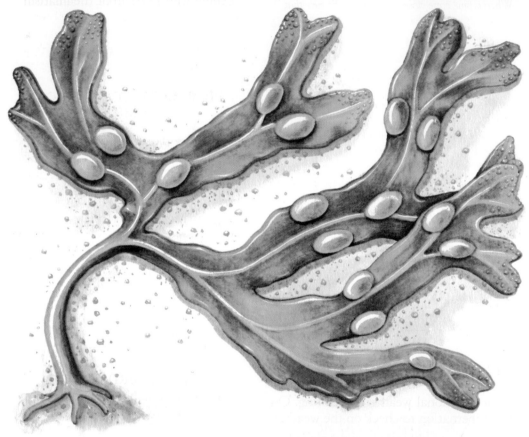

Seaweed is a good indicator of whether it will rain or stay dry.

WHAT DO RED SKIES AT DAWN AND DUSK MEAN?

THE SAYING "red sky at night, shepherd's delight; red sky in morning, shepherd's warning" probably originated in Europe. There, prevailing winds bring weather systems from the west, so a clear red sky at sunset is thought to indicate the arrival of good weather. A similar sight in the eastern skies at dawn could suggest that the fine weather is passing away.

HOW DOES A PIECE OF SEAWEED WARN OF RAIN?

A PIECE OF SEAWEED is an excellent indicator of humidity. Any moisture in the seaweed evaporates when the air is dry, making it brittle and hard to the touch. When humidity levels increase, the seaweed absorbs moisture again, making it expand and become soft. A high level of moisture in the air is a sure sign that rain will follow soon after. Pieces of seaweed are often seen hanging outside the houses in seaside towns.

WILL IT RAIN WHEN COWS LIE DOWN?

IT IS OFTEN said that when cows lie down in a field, rain is on the way. This piece of folklore is based on the idea that the cows can sense dampness in the air, so they lie down to make sure they have a dry space to stay. As much as this saying is well known, it is also rarely accurate. Cows will lie down when they are tired, not just when they think it might rain, so they are probably not the best weather forecasters!

If you see a field full of cows lying down, you do not necessarily need to run for shelter or get your umbrella out. They are probably just having a rest!

WHAT CAN PINE CONES TELL US ABOUT THE WEATHER?

PINE CONES make one of the best natural weather indicators. The scales of a pine cone open out when the weather is dry and close up when the air is humid – a good sign that rain is coming. The natural state of the cone is closed – the scales are shrivelling up when it is dry. When the air is moist, the cone becomes flexible again and returns to its regular shape.

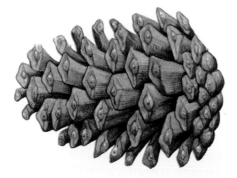 

The opened-out scales of the pine cone above indicate dry air and pleasant weather.

When a pine cone closes up, you can be sure that colder, wetter weather is on the way.

HOW DOES BLOSSOM TELL US ABOUT THE WEATHER?

THE APPEARANCE of blossom on trees is traditionally said to mark the beginning of spring and the end of winter. Trees do only come into bloom in mild weather, but as anyone who lives in a temperate part of the world knows, cold weather will often return after the blossom appears! The dates on which blossom appears have been recorded in some weather records for many years, which helps to show what the weather was like in the past.

The Japanese tradition of noting the date on which cherry blossom (left) appears has been carried out for hundreds of years.

WHAT IS THE ORIGIN OF GROUNDHOG DAY?

IN THE USA, 2 February is an important date for traditional weather forecasting. On this day, it is said that a groundhog emerges from hibernation to check on the weather. If it is sunny on that day, the groundhog will see its shadow and return to its burrow in the belief that the weather will be cold for the following six weeks. A cloudy day (and

no shadow) will keep the groundhog above ground in anticipation of fine weather. The tradition originates in Europe, where 2 February, known as Candlemas, marks the point halfway between the winter solstice and the spring equinox.

Weather records show that the groundhog is not an especially accurate weather forecaster. In fact, a sunny 2 February is more likely to herald six weeks of better weather!

fast facts

WHO WAS ST SWITHIN?

In the United Kingdom, it is said that if it rains on St Swithin's day (15 July), it will rain for forty days and forty nights. St Swithin was a 9th-century bishop of Winchester, England. It is said that it rained heavily on the day that he was buried in the city's cathedral.

CAN PEOPLE FEEL THE WEATHER IN THEIR BONES?

People who suffer from rheumatism (a disease that affects the joints) tend to feel greater pain when the weather is cold and damp because it makes their joints less flexible.

HOW DOES WOOL REACT TO HUMIDITY?

A piece of wool will shrink and become curly when the air is dry. When there is a lot of moisture in the air, the wool expands and straightens.

WHY DO SOME FLOWERS CLOSE THEIR PETALS BEFORE IT RAINS?

Many flowers whose petals are wide open during sunny weather will close up when rain is approaching. It is thought that this response is designed to stop rain washing pollen away.

WHY DO BIRDS GO TO ROOST WHEN A STORM IS APPROACHING?

Birds going to roost during the day is often taken as a sign of an approaching storm. This may be because they find it harder to fly in the low-pressure air that brings the stormy weather. There are also likely to be fewer thermals, which many birds rely upon to gain height.

HOW DO FROGS ACT AS BAROMETERS?

It is thought that frogs croak when the air pressure drops – a natural barometer?

HOW CAN I INVESTIGATE THE WEATHER?

The experiments on these pages will help you to make your own weather record and understand how some weather conditions occur. These experiments are perfect for school projects or just for fun! You may need help with some of them. Remember to record your results.

CAN I MAKE A CLOUD?

YOU CAN create your very own cloud in a bottle with this simple experiment. Be very careful when handling the hot water – ask an adult to help you.

YOU WILL NEED:

Ice cube

Glass bottle   Hot water   Black paper

WHAT TO DO:

1 Fill the bottle with hot water and leave it to stand for about five minutes.

2 Pour about three-quarters of the water away and then place the ice cube on top of the bottle.

3 Put the black paper behind the bottle and watch what happens.

WHAT IS HAPPENING?

The warm air makes some of the water turn into water vapour. When the water vapour rises and meets the cold air beneath the ice cube, it condenses, forming a cloud at the top of the bottle.

HOW DO I MAKE A RAIN GAUGE?

THIS RAIN GAUGE is similar to those used in real weather stations. Record the depth (in millimetres) every morning. An amount too small to register is called a "trace" measurement.

YOU WILL NEED:

Waterproof tape   4 bricks   Waterproof pen

Scissors   Ruler   Plastic bottle

WHAT TO DO:

1 Ask an adult to cut the top off the bottle.

2 Mark a scale on a piece of waterproof tape as shown and stick it to the bottle's base.

3 Fit the upturned top of the bottle into the base as shown – this acts as a funnel.

4 Place the gauge in an open space, supported by the four bricks.

IS IT POSSIBLE TO MAKE RAIN?

THIS EXPERIMENT shows you how rain is created inside a cloud. First, place a large metal spoon in a freezer for about half an hour. Boil a kettle and place a saucer beneath its spout. Using an oven glove, hold the cold spoon in the steam coming from the boiling kettle. "Rain" forms when the steam (water vapour) from the kettle hits the cold spoon. The vapour condenses and forms water droplets, which drop from the spoon.

HOW DO I MAKE A RAINBOW?

THE TWO EXPERIMENTS below show you how to create your own rainbow – outdoors and indoors! Choose a sunny day. All you need to do is to provide a source of water through which the Sun's light can be split into the spectrum. The second experiment works well with a small plant-sprayer if you do not have a garden hose – always ask before you borrow them!

This works best when the Sun is low in the sky – early morning or evening. Stand with your back to the Sun and spray the water into a fine mist. Face a dark background to see the colours clearly.

Place a glass of water on a windowsill in the Sun. Take a piece of white paper and put it on a table just beneath the windowsill. Adjust the position of the paper until you can see rainbow colours.

HOW DO I MAKE AN ANEMOMETER?

REAL ANEMOMETERS are very expensive. Follow the steps below to make your own version of this essential weather instrument. All the things needed to make it are easily available in hardware or craft shops.

YOU WILL NEED:

wooden post

1 red plastic cup

2 x 30cm (12in) pieces of balsa wood

3 large beads

nail

3 white plastic cups

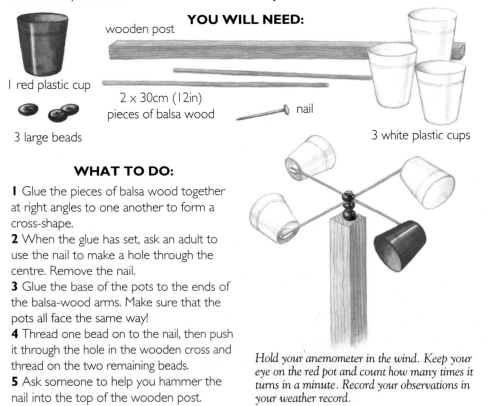

WHAT TO DO:

1 Glue the pieces of balsa wood together at right angles to one another to form a cross-shape.
2 When the glue has set, ask an adult to use the nail to make a hole through the centre. Remove the nail.
3 Glue the base of the pots to the ends of the balsa-wood arms. Make sure that the pots all face the same way!
4 Thread one bead on to the nail, then push it through the hole in the wooden cross and thread on the two remaining beads.
5 Ask someone to help you hammer the nail into the top of the wooden post.

Hold your anemometer in the wind. Keep your eye on the red pot and count how many times it turns in a minute. Record your observations in your weather record.

fast facts

HOW OFTEN SHOULD I MAKE OBSERVATIONS?

To make your weather record accurate, measurements should be taken as often as possible and at the same times each day.

WHAT IS A WEATHER SCRAPBOOK?

You could keep a record of significant weather events in your area in a scrapbook. Fill it with articles and photographs from newspapers, along with that day's weather map.

WHERE CAN I FIND OUT MORE?

Your school will be able to help you discover more about investigating the weather. A trip to the library or a search of the Internet will lead you to sources of relevant information, groups and organizations.

WHAT IS CLOUD SEEDING?

Cloud seeding is a scientific process that makes clouds produce rain and snow. It works by sending tiny particles of silver iodide, or other substances such as dry ice or liquid propane, into rain-bearing clouds, usually by aircraft. These substances stimulate the production of rain by providing something for water droplets to freeze on to – scientists call them ice nuclei. Once enough of the droplets take hold, they become heavy enough to fall to the ground. Cloud seeding cannot produce clouds – it can only make existing clouds produce rain.

Cloud seeding is used in some parts of the world to assist farmers in areas of low rainfall. In the future, it may be possible actually to create rain-bearing clouds and help solve the problems of drought.

The crystals stimulate the production of ice, bringing about rain or snow.

IS IT POSSIBLE TO REDUCE A HURRICANE'S POWER?

HURRICANES ARE probably the most destructive of all extreme weather events – a category 5 hurricane is thought to contain the same amount of energy as all the world's power plants combined. The ability to reduce this power would be a huge benefit. American scientists are looking at ways of cutting off a hurricane's energy source by using cooking oil. The theory is that aircraft would be used to spray a thin layer of oil over the surface of the ocean. This would help prevent water evaporating into the atmosphere – the process that provides a hurricane with its heat and energy. This would work with any kind of oil, but vegetable oil is considered to be the most environmentally friendly substance. It is thought that using a process similar to cloud seeding could also be used to tame a hurricane by "cooling it down".

Being able to control the power of a hurricane would help to reduce the loss of life and damage to property that the most powerful hurricanes bring. The technology involved in controlling hurricanes is only at an experimental stage.

HOW DO SCIENTISTS PLAN TO TAME TORNADOES?

SCIENTISTS BELIEVE that it may be possible to "kill" a tornado. Space satellites could be used to fire beams of microwave energy towards the base of a thunderstorm. The theory is that this would heat up the cool downdraft of air that helps create the tornado, effectively knocking it out. This sounds very much like science fiction, and many scientists claim that it could never work.

The beam heats the downdraft of the tornado, weakening it.

The satellite sends a beam of microwave energy towards the tornado.

IS IT POSSIBLE TO CONTROL LIGHTNING?

THE NEXT generation of lightning conductor could be a type of laser gun. A laser beam fired from the ground into a storm cloud could charge the air molecules along the way, creating a path for the lightning bolt to follow. Once the lightning is set on a direct path, its charge can be neutralized. It is thought that such a device could be used to steer lightning away from exposed structures such as power lines.

HAS ANYONE ATTEMPTED TO STOP HAILSTONES?

THE DAMAGE caused to crops by large hailstones has prompted many attempts to prevent hail forming. Techniques similar to those used in cloud seeding have been tried, aiming to turn hailstones into rain, but this does not seem to work. In the early 20th century, people tried using "anti-hail guns". These would fire huge amounts of debris into the clouds in an attempt to break up the hailstones. They were tried many times, unsuccessfully, in the vineyards of France.

The use of anti-hail guns was largely unsuccessful. More often than not, they caused injury to people on the ground – and the hailstones still fell.

fast facts

DOES WEATHER CONTROL HAVE MILITARY USES?

The use of weather control is a very controversial issue. It is claimed that the United States used cloud seeding during the war in Vietnam to flood areas and make them impassable. The use of weather modification for military purposes is now banned by the United Nations.

WHEN WAS CLOUD SEEDING INVENTED?

The General Electric Company discovered the principle of cloud seeding in its research laboratory in 1947.

HOW DID ANCIENT PEOPLE ATTEMPT TO INFLUENCE THE WEATHER?

In many ancient cultures, rituals would be performed, which asked the gods to bring certain weather conditions, usually rain or sunshine.

HOW HAS THE WEATHER AFFECTED HISTORY?

Throughout history, the weather has had a major influence on the outcome of certain events. Adverse weather conditions have helped decide the outcome of battles and military campaigns, while over longer periods of time, climate change is thought to have brought about the end of some civilizations and the beginning of others.

HOW DID THE WEATHER DEFEAT NAPOLEON IN RUSSIA?

NAPOLEON BONAPARTE was one of the finest military leaders in history. His clever tactics brought a series of victories that allowed him to rule over large parts of Europe over 200 years ago. However, it was the weather that was to prove instrumental in his downfall. He invaded Russia in the summer of 1812 and captured Moscow, following the Russians deeper into the country. By November, a lack of supplies forced Napoleon and his army to retreat, and the extremely harsh winter killed many thousands of troops as they returned to France.

WHAT HAPPENED AT THE BATTLE OF WATERLOO?

THREE YEARS after his retreat from Russia, Napoleon faced the allied forces of Britain and Prussia at Waterloo. Again, the weather was to play its part. Very heavy rain in the region made the ground muddy, which delayed Napoleon's attack. The delay meant that the allies, under the leadership of the Duke of Wellington, were able to send in additional troops and supplies, which ultimately helped them to victory.

Thousands of French troops died as they returned from Russia. They had been made cold, hungry and demoralized by the severe cold of the winter. The retreat from Moscow proved to be the beginning of the end of Napoleon's domination of Europe.

DID DROUGHT BRING ABOUT THE END OF THE MAYAN CIVILIZATION?

1200 YEARS AGO, the Mayan civilization thrived in what are now southern Mexico, Belize and Guatemala. The Mayans were brilliant astronomers and mathematicians, and their society was very stable and established. However, at some point during the 9th century, their civilization suffered a sudden and devastating collapse. Archaeologists have struggled to find an explanation for the Mayans' fate, but recent studies suggest that a massive drought was responsible. Analysis of mud samples from the bottom of Lake Chichancanab in the Yucatan area of Mexico has found that the region's climate in the 9th century was the driest that it had been for 7000 years.

The ruins of spectacular Mayan temples can be found scattered throughout the rainforests of southern Mexico and northern South America. It is difficult to imagine how a drought could affect such a lush, tropical region, but it is thought that a sudden change in climate – possibly caused by El Niño – was responsible for the collapse of one of history's great civilizations.

WHY WERE FLOODS IMPORTANT TO THE STABILITY OF ANCIENT EGYPT?

THE RIVER NILE was the source of life and prosperity in Egypt. The Ancient Egyptians relied on the annual floods of the Nile to irrigate their crops, but studies have shown that the way in which the river floods varies considerably. Working together, historians and climatologists have found links between years of low flooding and periods of instability in Egyptian society. Records show that the famines that followed low floods led to disease and civil unrest – possibly causing the collapse of the Old Kingdom.

The Nile remains an important part of life in Egypt to this day. Did its failure to flood in the past lead to the collapse of the Old Kingdom of Egypt?

DID THE GREAT FLOOD DESCRIBED IN THE OLD TESTAMENT ACTUALLY HAPPEN?

SOME EXPERTS believe that when glaciers melted 7000 years ago, this caused the Mediterranean to overflow into the Black Sea, then a small freshwater lake. This may form the basis of Middle Eastern tales, such as the one recorded in the Old Testament, of a hugely destructive flood.

fast facts

HOW DID EL NIÑO AFFECT THE INCAS?

The Incas of Peru offered up human sacrifices to persuade their gods to send fair weather. The bad weather was probably caused by El Niño.

DID THE RUSSIAN WINTER AFFECT WORLD WAR II?

In 1942, heavy cloud cover prevented German air forces from bombing Russian positions, allowing the Russians to fight back.

DID EL NIÑO HELP PEOPLE REACH EASTER ISLAND?

The reverse currents caused by El Niño probably helped the Polynesians sail 1000 miles south to Easter Island.

WHY WAS CHRISTOPHER COLUMBUS LUCKY?

Christopher Columbus was lucky to avoid disaster as he was in the Caribbean in the hurricane season.

WHEN WAS THE "YEAR WITHOUT SUMMER"?

In the USA, the very cold 1817 was known as "the year without a summer".

WHO USES WEATHER FORECASTS?

Weather forecasts are used by everybody, but some people pay closer attention to them than others. Severe weather conditions can endanger lives on the roads, at sea and in the air, so transport and safety organizations are regularly updated on the weather situation. Many businesses, from farming and fishing to hotels and restaurants can be affected by the weather, so a forecast can help with business planning.

It is useful to know in advance if it is going to rain – we can prepare ourselves by wearing waterproof clothes or taking an umbrella. Weather forecasts have greater importance for people whose lives or livelihood depends on the weather conditions.

WHY ARE WEATHER FORECASTS IMPORTANT FOR PEOPLE AT SEA?

PEOPLE WHO work at sea depend heavily on detailed, specialized weather forecasts because their lives can be at risk when stormy conditions bring high winds and steep seas. Fishermen may decide where to fish according to weather conditions, while sport sailors pay close attention to wind details to plan their racing tactics. All mariners listen to radio stations and coastguard broadcasts for advance warnings of weather conditions, which focus on the speed and direction of the wind, visibility and barometer readings.

Oil rig workers and sailors listen out for gale warnings because their lives may depend on knowing where and when gales will occur.

The nature of farming means that accurate weather forecasts are essential for business.

HOW DO FARMERS MAKE USE OF WEATHER FORECASTS?

FARMERS NEED to pay special attention to the weather in order to tend their crops or feed their animals. Knowledge of a severe frost or rain will influence the time that they sow seeds or harvest crops. Accurate weather forecasts also help farmers to decide when to treat crops with chemicals. For example, should it rain shortly after pesticides are applied, they will be washed away and have little effect – a waste of time and money for the farmer. Forecasts for farmers provide as much information as possible about the weather for the next week or so.

HOW IS SPORT AFFECTED BY THE WEATHER?

MOST OUTDOOR SPORTS events can be affected by adverse weather conditions in one way or another. "Rain stopped play" is a phrase familiar to followers of cricket in England, where the often unpredictable summer weather regularly interrupts a game. Tennis is similarly affected when heavy rain makes play impossible on open-air grass courts. Some sports can be played in almost all weathers (only severe snow and freezing temperatures will stop a soccer or rugby match), but the conditions can influence tactics and the outcome of the game.

Cricket demands excellent light, so an overcast, gloomy day will often cause the game to be stopped because the players are unable to see the ball clearly. Some special evening games are played under flood-lights, using a fluorescent ball and with the players in coloured kits.

Golfers pay particular attention to the strength and direction of the wind, selecting their clubs and playing their shots accordingly.

Humidity can influence a game of tennis. A tennis ball will move faster and further in dry air than it will in air that is full of moisture.

Rain is an important factor in horse-racing. Some horses run better on firm ground and some on softer ground, so gamblers often consider this before placing a bet.

fast facts

HOW DO AIRPORTS USE WEATHER FORECASTS?

Airports use special equipment to clear snow and ice away from their runways. Predictions about the weather help them to prepare the equipment ready for use. Fog and strong winds can present serious safety problems at airports. In extreme cases, flights can be cancelled and incoming aircraft may be directed to other airports.

HOW ARE ROADS PREPARED FOR ICE?

When freezing conditions are expected, the relevant authorities send out trucks to treat roads with grit and salt. This helps prevent the roads from freezing over.

DO PEOPLE BET ON THE WEATHER?

Some bookmakers will take bets on almost anything, including the weather. In the United Kingdom, a popular bet made is whether there will be a white Christmas. Odds are given for snow falling on the roof of the London Weather Centre on Christmas Day.

HOW DOES RAIN AFFECT MOTOR RACING?

Formula 1 racing cars use different types of tyres in different types of weather. When it is wet, tyres with better grip are used to cope with the slippery surface. Average speeds in the wet are slower.

HOW DO LEAVES STOP TRAINS?

In some countries, leaves cause disruption to train services. The problem is that autumn leaves fall on to the tracks, making them very slippery. It is difficult for the trains to stop safely. Special "leaf-clearing" trains are used to tackle the problem.

GLOSSARY

Atmosphere The mixture of gases that surrounds the Earth. They are held in place by the pull of gravity.

Atom The smallest amount of a particle of matter that cannot be split up.

Climate The general pattern of weather conditions that occur in a place over a long period of time.

Climatology The science of climates and climate change.

Condensation A process in which vapour cools and turns back into liquid.

Convection The transfer of heat through the movement of gas or liquid. This is how heat moves through the atmosphere.

Drought An unusually long period of time without rainfall.

Equator An imaginary line that stretches around the Earth, exactly halfway between the two poles.

Evaporation A process in which liquids turn into gases.

Forecast A prediction of weather conditions for a period of up to a week in advance.

Hemisphere One half of the Earth. This usually refers to the Northern and Southern Hemispheres, which are divided by the Equator.

Hurricane This is a violent tropical storm with winds that spiral inwards towards a centre of low pressure called the eye.

Ice Ages These occur when the Earth's climate becomes much cooler, and the amount of ice increases.

Meteorology Science that studies the atmosphere, enabling the weather to be forecast accurately. Weather forecasters are also called meteorologists.

Molecule The smallest amount of a non-elementary substance that can exist whilst still having the basic chemical structure of that substance.

Monsoon These are seasonal winds that affect large areas of the tropics and sub-tropics.

Precipitation Water that falls to the ground in the form of rain, sleet, snow or hail.

Radiation The transmission of heat in waves of energy. The Sun's heat reaches the Earth by radiation.

Refraction The bending of light when it passes through an object or matter. Rainbows are seen when the viewer sees the Sun's light refracted through raindrops.

Seasons These are caused by different regions of the Earth being tilted towards the Sun at different times of the year. For example, spring begins at a particular place on Earth at the moment when it begins to lean towards the Sun.

Synoptic chart Type of chart that shows the weather expected in a certain area for a particular time.

Temperate climate This is a climate that does not generally have extreme weather conditions.

Thermometer Instrument used to measure temperature.

Tropical climate This is a hot climate in the areas roughly between 23° north and south of the Equator.

Vapour A gas that would normally be found in a liquid or solid form, such as water vapour.

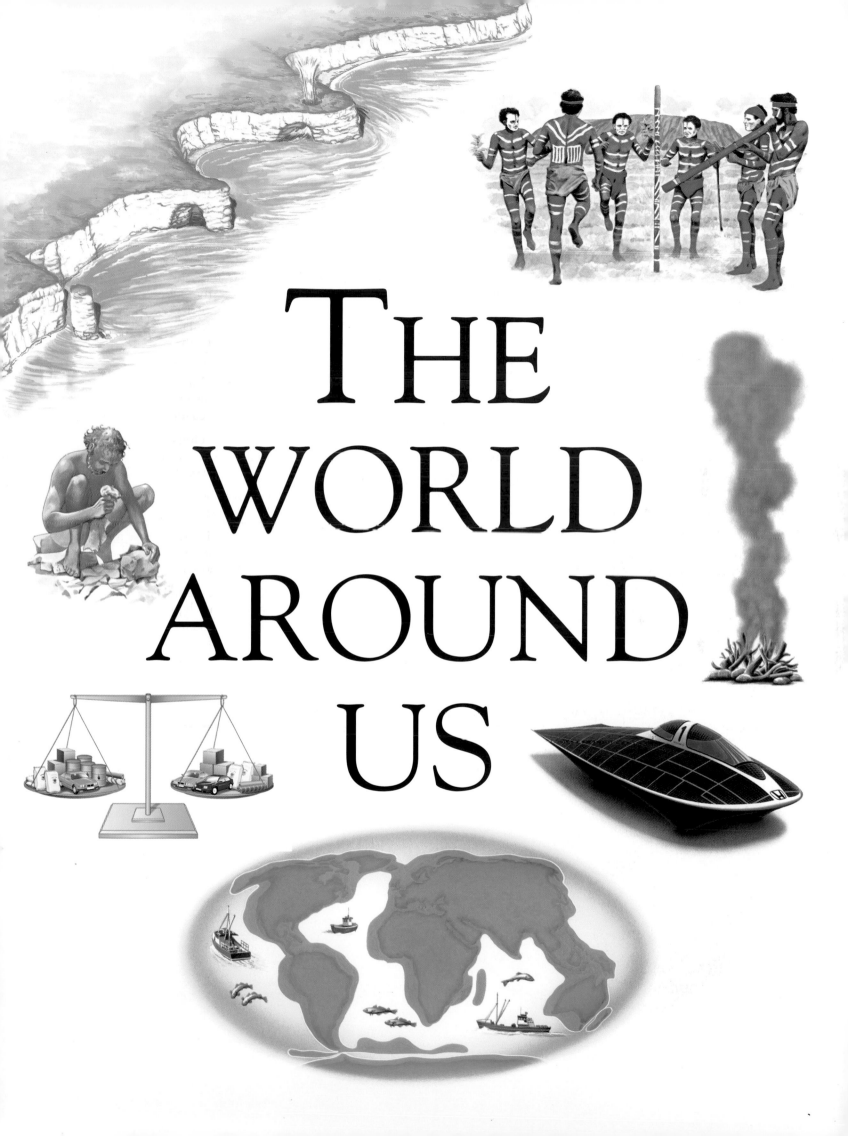

THE WORLD AROUND US

HOW OLD IS THE EARTH?

The amount of time that the Earth has been in existence is immense, and it is impossible to give it an exact age. However, around 5000 million years ago our planet was nothing more than part of a cloud of dust and gas, spinning around in space. Around this time, something caused the material in this enormous cloud to contract, forming the Sun, the Earth and the other planets in our Solar System.

HOW WAS THE EARTH FORMED?

1 The Earth and the other planets in the Solar System formed from solid lumps of ice and rock in a massive cloud.

2 The newly formed Earth became a sphere of molten rock as iron and nickel sank to create the Earth's core.

3 The Earth's crust began to form around 4000 million years ago. Small plates of crust floated on oceans of molten rock.

4 As the crust developed, volcanoes erupted, water vapour condensed to form t oceans, and the continents began to form.

WHAT IS THE EARTH'S TILT?

THE AXIS of the Earth (the imaginary line along which it spins) is set at a slight angle. This tilt affects the Earth's climate because it causes the poles to point towards and away from the Sun at different times of the year. We divide these times into the seasons.

The Earth bulges at the Equator.

The Earth rotates on its axis, tilted at about 23°.

HOW LONG DOES THE EARTH TAKE TO ORBIT THE SUN?

IT TAKES the Earth one whole year to make one full orbit of the Sun.

HOW BIG IS THE EARTH?

THE SIZE of the Earth depends upon how you measure it. If you were to circumnavigate the world (on land and sea) following the Equator, you would travel 40,075km (24,902 miles). Starting at one pole and visiting the other, you would travel 67km (42 miles) less. The Earth's diameter, pole to pole, is 12,714km (7900 miles), while the distance through the Earth at the Equator is a further 43km (27 miles).

WHAT MAKES THE EARTH SPIN?

THE EARTH spins as a result of things colliding with each other when the Solar System was formed. Some scientists believe that the Earth started spinning after a direct collision with the Moon. Kept moving by the force of momentum, the Earth takes one day to make one full rotation.

IS THE EARTH A PERFECT SPHERE?

THE ROTATION of the Earth causes it to bulge slightly in the middle. Centrifugal force makes the Earth's material move away from the centre – the faster the spin, the greater the force. As places at the Equator are moving faster than places at the poles, the centre of the Earth pushes out slightly more than the rest.

Like all the planets in our Solar System, the Earth is a sphere that orbits the Sun. The atmosphere and the oceans give our planet its distinctive blue colour.

fast facts

IS EARTH SLOWING DOWN?

Scientists think that days were shorter 400 million years ago. Maybe the Earth was spinning more slowly.

WHAT MAKES THE EARTH SLOW DOWN?

It is thought that the friction created by the movement of tides has slowed down the Earth's spin.

IF THE EARTH IS SPINNING, WHY DO WE NOT GET THROWN OFF?

All objects in the Universe produce the force of gravity – the larger the object, the stronger the force. It is gravity that keeps us on our planet.

HOW FAST DOES THE EARTH SPIN?

The Earth rotates at a speed of 1609km/h (1000mph).

DOES THE EARTH WOBBLE ON ITS AXIS?

Research has shown that as the Earth spins, it wobbles slightly on its axis. This very slight movement (a few feet) has been named the Chandler Wobble.

WHAT IS THE EARTH MADE OF?

The surface of the Earth, the crust, makes up a very small part of the whole planet. While it is relatively straightforward to find out about the Earth's surface, investigating deep within the Earth is part science, part guesswork. What is known is that there are three main layers: the crust, the mantle and the core, and that these consist of rocks and metals in various states and forms.

WHAT IS THE EARTH'S CRUST?

THE CRUST is the hard, outer layer of the Earth that forms the land and the ocean floor. The continental crust (the land masses) is the oldest and thickest part and made up mostly of silica and aluminium. The oceanic crust, made up mostly of silica and magnesium, is around 200 million years old.

HOW FAR IS IT TO THE EARTH'S CORE?

THE OUTER CORE begins at a depth of 2935km (1822 miles) below the Earth's surface. It is a further 3432km (2134 miles) to the very centre of the Earth.

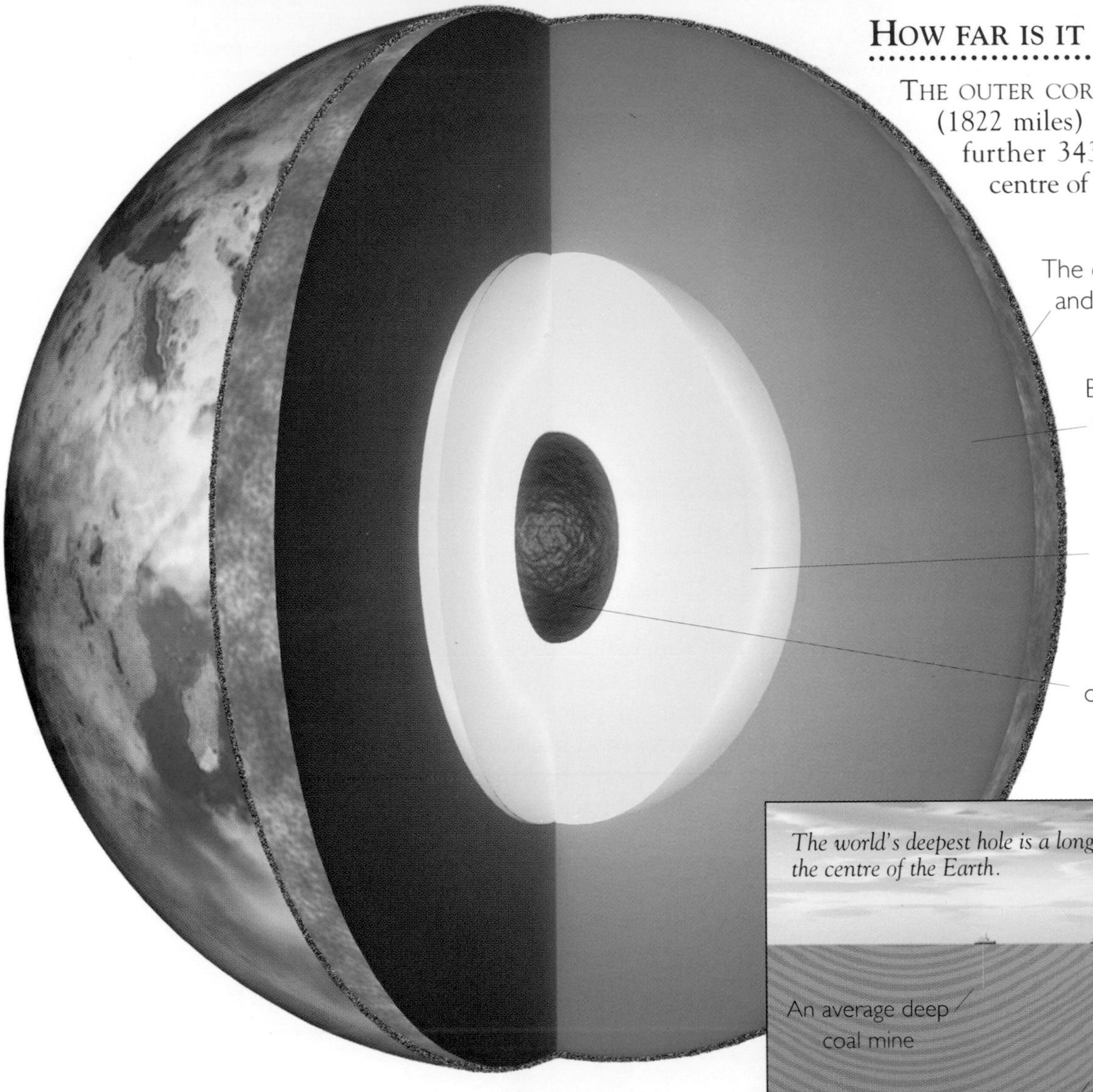

The crust is made of rocks familiar to us and other substances.

Both solid and partly melted rock make up the mantle.

The outer core is probably made up of liquid iron, nickel and oxygen.

The inner core is thought to consist of solid iron and nickel.

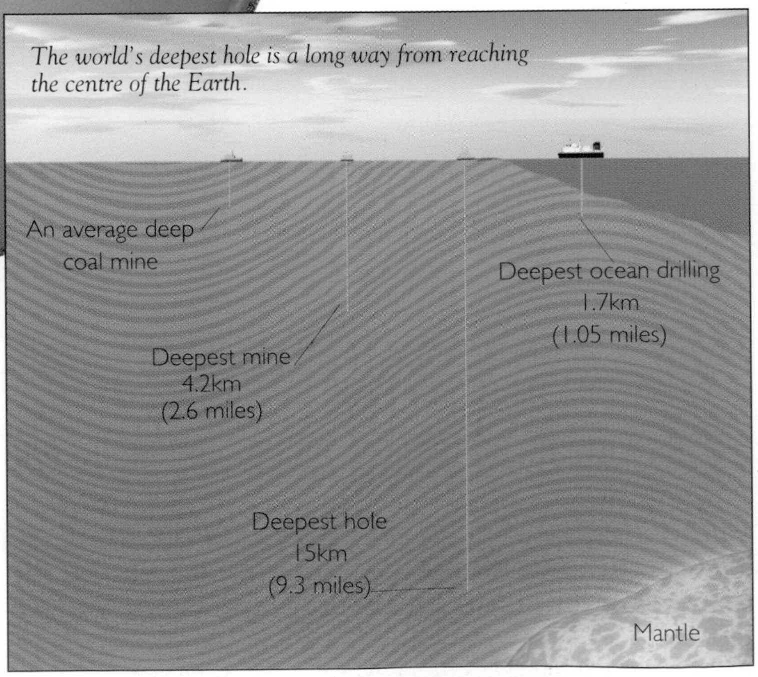

The world's deepest hole is a long way from reaching the centre of the Earth.

An average deep coal mine

Deepest ocean drilling
1.7km
(1.05 miles)

Deepest mine
4.2km
(2.6 miles)

Deepest hole
15km
(9.3 miles)

Mantle

HAS ANYONE BEEN TO THE CENTRE OF THE EARTH?

IN 1990, A GEOLOGICAL exploration began to find out more about the Earth's crust. A hole drilled into the ground in the Kola peninsula, Russia, has reached a depth of around 15km (9.3 miles). Nobody has been down it, and it is still well short of the Earth's centre.

WHAT MAKES THE EARTH MAGNETIC?

THE MOLTEN IRON that partly makes up the Earth's core continually flows around. As this happens, it generates powerful electric currents that create the Earth's magnetic field. This is similar to the way magnetic currents are generated by an electric motor.

The Earth's magnetic field reaches out to some 60,000km (37,000 miles).

WHAT IS THE MAGNETIC FIELD?

THE EARTH is rather like an enormous magnet. Otherwise known as the magnetosphere, the Earth's magnetic field stretches out into space, helping to protect the Earth from the Sun's radiation. The magnetic poles are close to the geographic North and South Poles.

The alignment of the Earth's magnetic field is shown on a compass.

WHAT MAKES SOME ROCKS MAGNETIC?

THE MAGNETIC FIELD of the Earth at any given time is preserved in the magnetic minerals within rocks that solidified during that period. Geologists are thus able to study the magnetic field of rocks thousands of years old, such as those used to build the pyramids at Giza, Egypt.

In industry, iron and steel need to be heated to around 1900°C (3500°F) for them to melt. These are the kinds of temperatures that are found at the Earth's core.

fast facts

HOW DO WE KNOW WHAT THE EARTH IS MADE OF?

Drilling beneath the Earth's surface is very difficult and expensive, so most of what we know about the Earth's structure comes from a science called seismology. Vibrations caused by earthquakes, called seismic waves, tell scientists about the Earth's interior by the way they behave as they pass through the Earth.

WHAT IS THE MOHO?

A Croatian scientist called Andrija Mohorovicic was one of the first people to observe the behaviour of seismic waves. The area between the mantle and the crust is named the Mohorovicic discontinuity or Moho.

HOW DOES A COMPASS SHOW DIRECTION?

A compass is a magnet carefully balanced on a pivot or in a fluid. The Earth's magnetic field will align the magnet in a north–south direction.

DOES THE EARTH'S MAGNETIC FIELD EVER CHANGE?

The Earth's magnetic field is always changing. Sometimes, the change is so powerful that the magnetic poles switch positions; this is known as polar reversal. Nobody knows why this occurs, but it last happened around 30,000 years ago.

IS THE EARTH COMPLETELY SOLID?

MOST OF THE EARTH is made of various solid rocks. The 2000km- (1240-mile-) thick outer core is the only part of the Earth that exists in an entirely liquid form. Iron, nickel and other materials are liquified by the extremely high temperatures. Molten rock is found in parts of the mantle, some of which comes to the surface as lava.

WHAT IS CONTINENTAL DRIFT?

It may not be apparent to us, but the major land masses of the Earth, the seven continents, are not in fixed positions. They are constantly shifted around by forces deep within the Earth. Around 250 million years ago, the land on Earth was made up of one huge continent known today as Pangaea. Over time, this broke up into the continents we know today. This continual movement of the land is known as continental drift.

WHAT ARE TECTONIC PLATES?

THE EARTH'S CRUST is divided into enormous slabs of rock called tectonic plates. There are about 15 major plates, covering both the land masses and the ocean floor. They fit together like a huge jigsaw puzzle and, due to continental drift, their boundaries are either colliding with or pulling away from each other.

This map shows (in red) the boundaries of the world's tectonic plates.

WHAT MAKES THE LAND MOVE?

THERE ARE A NUMBER of theories about the causes of continental drift. One puts forward the idea that hot rocks rise through ocean ridges, cool down and then drag the plates downwards. Another theory suggests that the heat from inside the Earth creates movement in the mantle. The resulting currents then shift the plates around. The third idea is the simplest. At the ocean ridges, the plates are higher than elsewhere, resulting in the force of gravity pulling the plates downwards.

Mountain ranges are formed where continental plates collide. This is called convergence.

The subduction zone is where two plates collide and one is forced over the other.

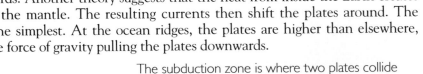

Mid-ocean ridges occur where two plates are pulling apart. Where this occurs on land, they produce steep-sided valleys.

WHAT GIVES THE CONTINENTS THEIR SHAPE?

A GLANCE AT a modern map of the world makes it easy to see that all the continents were once joined together. Perhaps the clearest example is the east coast of South America and the west coast of Africa. Their shapes suggest that they would fit closely if brought together.

Present day map: the shapes of the continents suggest that they were once joined together.

Future map: this map shows Europe and Africa joined together, Australia attached to Antarctica, and Asia and the Americas divided.

WILL THE CONTINENTS EVER BE PUSHED TOGETHER AGAIN?

CONTINENTAL DRIFT is still happening, and the continents will continue to move in the future. They are unlikely to return to the shape of Pangaea, but a map of the world 150 million years from now could look significantly different from today's.

IS THERE EVIDENCE THAT THE LAND HAS MOVED?

FOSSILIZED REMAINS found in different parts of the world are good evidence that the continents were once joined together. Remains of the same animal have been found in both South America and Africa, which means it must have lived at a time when the continents were part of the same land mass. Plant fossils of the same type and age have been found all over the world, and geologists have identified parts of the same mountain range in different continents.

IS THE BOTTOM OF THE SEA MOVING?

THE WHOLE of the Earth's crust is subject to continental drift, including the ocean floor. Most of the tectonic plates are both continental (part of the land) and oceanic (part of the ocean floor). Evidence of movement on the sea bed is found in different magnetic alignments in the rock and volcanic activity on the ocean floor.

Volcanic activity on the ocean floor is evidence of continental drift beneath the oceans.

fast facts

WHICH IS THE LARGEST CONTINENT?

Asia is the world's largest continent. It covers an area of 44,485,900 sq km (17,176,090 sq miles) and accounts for 30% of the world's total land area.

WHICH IS THE SMALLEST CONTINENT?

Australasia is the smallest continent. It covers an area of 8,924,100 sq km (3,445,610 sq miles).

WHAT IS THE ASTHENOSPHERE?

The asthenosphere is a fairly soft layer of the Earth's mantle. It helps to lubricate the movement of the plates above it.

HOW QUICKLY IS THE LAND MOVING?

The land is moving extremely slowly. Although some of the plates move faster than others, the average rate of movement is no more than 2.5cm (1 inch) a year.

WHAT IS THE LITHOSPHERE?

The crust and top part of the mantle are known as the lithosphere.

WHY ARE EARTHQUAKES SO DESTRUCTIVE?

Earthquakes are one of the most destructive forces on Earth. They happen quite frequently, though most of them are relatively minor. Powerful quakes, depending on where they happen, cause severe damage, toppling buildings and sometimes killing many thousands of people. They happen when tension created by the movement of the Earth's tectonic plates is released, causing the rocks to shift and break suddenly. The incredible amount of force required to break the rocks is what makes earthquakes so devastating.

The side-effects of an earthquake can be almost as destructive as the quake itself. Here, a bridge has been demolished by a landslide triggered by a powerful earthquake.

WHERE ARE EARTHQUAKES MOST LIKELY TO HAPPEN?

EARTHQUAKES CAN HAPPEN anywhere, but they occur most frequently above the boundaries of the Earth's tectonic plates. The most powerful earthquakes occur where the plates are moving deep below the surface. These boundaries are known as transform faults or fault lines.

This map shows the world's earthquake zones (in red).

HOW ARE EARTHQUAKES RECORDED?

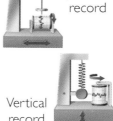

Horizontal record

Vertical record

THE SIZE, or the magnitude, of an earthquake is recorded using an instrument called a seismometer. Using very heavy weights that remain still while the room it is in is shaking, the machine records the amount of movement on a rotating drum of paper. This type of record is measured on the Richter scale. The physical and visible effects of a quake are measured using the Modified Mercalli scale (see below).

The Modified Mercalli scale:
1 Only detected by instruments. Doors begin to swing.
2 Some people inside high buildings may feel a tremor.
3 Rapid vibrations possibly felt indoors.
4 Stationary cars rock; windows shake; people indoors feel something.
5 Effects felt outdoors; small objects fall over; some buildings shake.
6 Trees begin to shake; crockery broken; everyone in the area feels it.
7 People alarmed; chimneys begin to crack; windows break.
8 Cars crash; buildings and trees damaged.
9 Many people panic; cracks in the ground; buildings fall down.
10 Buildings destroyed; underground services disrupted; rivers affected.
11 Bridges collapse; landslides happen; railways affected.
12 Widespread devastation; landscape changed.

WHAT HAPPENS AT THE FOCUS OF AN EARTHQUAKE?

DEEP BENEATH the Earth's surface, the place where the earthquake actually occurs is called the focus. This is where the greatest amount of rock movement is to be found. The ground directly above the focus is known as the epicentre. This is where the most damage occurs.

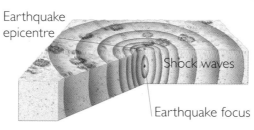

Earthquake epicentre

Shock waves

Earthquake focus

DO EARTHQUAKES HAVE ANY SIDE-EFFECTS?

THE SHOCK WAVE of a powerful earthquake can easily destroy buildings and other structures, but there are some side-effects of the quake itself. Underground gas pipes may rupture, leading to serious fires and explosions. The health of survivors is put at risk by damaged sewerage systems allowing disease to spread. In mountainous areas, landslides or avalanches can be triggered, and an undersea earthquake can generate a huge wave called a tsunami.

WHAT IS THE SAN ANDREAS FAULT?

PERHAPS THE WORLD'S best known fault line is the San Andreas Fault. Situated in California, USA, it is an area of the world where earthquakes and tremors occur frequently. The citizens of San Francisco know that a very powerful quake (often referred to as "The Big One") could occur at any time.

IS IT POSSIBLE TO BUILD EARTHQUAKE-PROOF BUILDINGS?

MODERN BUILDING technologies mean that homes, offices and other buildings can be designed to withstand the effect of an earthquake. Tall buildings are built with a strong central column from which the structure "hangs". Conical or triangular designs are able to absorb shocks more easily, while the use of new materials allows buildings to be constructed in earthquake zones at a relatively low cost.

The TransAmerica building is one of San Francisco's landmarks. Known as "the Pyramid", its distinctive shape comes from being designed to resist the effects of an earthquake.

fast facts

HOW LONG DOES AN EARTHQUAKE LAST?

Earthquakes generally last for less than a minute. However, some of the most destructive have lasted for up to four minutes.

CAN ANIMALS DETECT EARTHQUAKES?

It is thought that some animals can sense that an earthquake is about to happen. Dogs are known to become uneasy and start to howl in the moments before a quake.

WHICH IS THE STRONGEST RECORDED EARTHQUAKE?

An earthquake in Chile in May 1960 measured 9.5 on the Richter scale.

WHICH WAS THE MOST DESTRUCTIVE EARTHQUAKE?

An earthquake in China in 1566 killed almost one million people, while a 1923 earthquake in Japan destroyed around 575,000 homes.

WHO DEVISED THE RICHTER SCALE?

American seismologist Charles Richter devised the method of measuring earthquakes in 1935.

WHAT HAPPENS WHEN A VOLCANO ERUPTS?

Volcanoes erupt when molten rock, known as magma, is forced to the Earth's surface by the movement of the Earth's tectonic plates. Sometimes a volcano explodes, sending thick clouds of ash high into the atmosphere. Other volcanic eruptions produce rivers of red-hot lava that flow over the landscape covering everything in their path. Whichever way a volcano erupts, it is one of the natural world's most powerful and destructive forces.

ARE THERE DIFFERENT TYPES OF VOLCANO?

STEEP-SIDED, cone-shaped andesitic volcanoes are formed by melted plates exploding to the surface. These types of volcano are extremely violent, and their eruptions are very destructive. Basaltic volcanoes form where molten rock rises slowly to the surface from the mantle. They are broad and low and when they break the surface they can spray their lava into the air, producing blobs of lava known as volcanic bombs.

Andesitic volcano

Volcanic bomb

Magma chamber

Sometimes, the lava from an andesitic volcano produces a cloud of gas, rock and ash called a nuée ardente. This cloud crashes down the hillside at high speed.

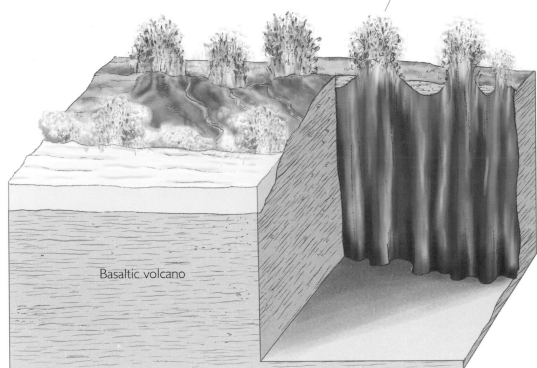

Basaltic volcano

WHAT IS A VOLCANIC HOT SPOT?

AREAS OF VOLCANIC activity in the Earth's mantle are known as hot spots. As plates move over these areas, basaltic volcanoes are formed above, often resulting in a chain of several volcanoes.

CAN VOLCANOES ERUPT UNDERWATER?

BASALTIC VOLCANOES are found mainly beneath the ocean. The lava that erupts cools very quickly, forming round lumps of rock called pillow lava.

Is all lava the same?

LAVA DIFFERS between volcanoes according to the type of rock it is made from, the gases it contains, and where it erupts. Pahoehoe lava moves quickly and looks rather like coils of rope when it cools. The thicker, lumpier aa lava cools into chunky rocks.

Pahoehoe lava moving across a road.

Hot lava flowing from a volcano.

How does volcanic activity affect the landscape?

WHEN WATER is heated by volcanic activity, strange and spectacular landscapes are created. Known as hydrothermal areas, they can feature steaming hot springs, gurgling pools of mud and jets of water spouting hundreds of feet into the air.

Water heated underground by hot volcanic rock rises to the surface to form a hot spring.

Foul-smelling jets of volcanic gas and steam are released from vents in the ground known as fumaroles.

Where corrosive volcanic gases dissolve mineral particles around pools of hot water, pools of hot mud are formed.

Ancient volcanic activity can leave unusual rock formations, such as this "Fairy Chimney" in Turkey.

fast facts

CAN VOLCANIC ERUPTIONS BE PREDICTED?

Volcanic eruptions are very difficult to predict. They do not occur at regular intervals, and dormant volcanoes (those that have been "sleeping" for years) can erupt without warning.

WHICH WAS THE BIGGEST VOLCANIC ERUPTION?

The biggest volcanic eruption on record occurred in Indonesia in 1815. One on the island of Sumbawa sent over 100 cubic km (24 cubic miles) of ash into the air. Around 100,000 people were killed, and the island sank by 1250m (4100ft).

WHICH IS THE LARGEST ACTIVE VOLCANO?

With a diameter of 100km (62 miles), Mauna Loa in Hawaii is the world's largest active volcano.

WHAT ARE PYROCLASTS?

All volcanic eruptions produce solid products known as pyroclasts, consisting of dust, ash, lapilli (stone fragments) and bombs or blocks.

ARE THERE VOLCANOES ON OTHER PLANETS?

Scientists have found evidence of volcanoes elsewhere in the Solar System. It is thought that Venus has many active volcanoes, while huge volcanic eruptions have been recorded on Io, one of Jupiter's moons.

WHAT HAPPENED AT POMPEII?

The Roman city of Pompeii was completely buried under hot ash when Vesuvius erupted in AD79.

Geysers burst out from underground chambers of heated water. The now-extinct Waimangu Geyser in New Zealand reached 445m (1500ft).

WHAT ARE ROCKS MADE OF?

All rocks are made of various natural substances called minerals. Each mineral has its own chemical make-up, and the different minerals combine together in various ways. Most rocks contain around six different minerals that grow together in a crystal structure.

Scientists called petrologists study rocks in close-up. A very thin slice of rock is examined under a microscope that uses polarized light. Each mineral produces its own colour and texture, and this helps to identify the type of rock. This picture shows a sample of marble under a petrologist's microscope.

ARE THERE DIFFERENT TYPES OF ROCK?

THE EARTH'S ROCKS are divided into three main types. Igneous rock is the original material that makes up the Earth, formed when magma rises to the surface and cools. The planet's oldest rocks are all of the igneous type. Sedimentary rock is made up of particles of other rock that has been affected by contact with the atmosphere. Erosion caused by water, wind and ice breaks the rock down into tiny particles that are carried away and settle in rivers, lakes and other areas. Over time, the particles compress to form sedimentary rock. Metamorphic rock is formed by the natural effects of heat and pressure changing igneous and sedimentary rock.

Igneous rock tends to be very hard. When broken up, it makes good material for road-building. Granite is one of the most common types of igneous rock.

Sandstone and limestone are good examples of sedimentary rock. Though relatively hard, they are easy to cut and are often used in construction.

Marble is found in layers of metamorphic rock. It can be used to create attractive and impressive surfaces in important buildings.

WHAT IS THE ROCK CYCLE?

THE ROCK CYCLE is the process through which all the Earth's rock is continually changing.

Particles of eroded rock are washed away to the sea and river beds where they form sedimentary rock.

Igneous rocks are worn down by atmospheric conditions.

Where molten rock rises to the surface, it cools to form various types of igneous rock.

Pressure from mountain-building and heat from under the Earth transform igneous and sedimentary rock into metamorphic rock.

WHAT SHAPES DO CRYSTALS FORM?

CRYSTALS are formed from minerals that melt or are dissolved in liquids. Crystals in different types of rocks and minerals form one of six different geometric shapes. These shapes were discovered in the 18th century by Abbé René Haüy.

CRYSTAL SHAPES

CUBIC — Diamond is an example of a mineral with a cubic structure.
HEXAGONAL — Beryl has a hexagonal crystal shape.
TETRAGONAL — Zircon has a tetragonal crystal structure.
MONOCLINIC — Gypsum has a monoclinic design.
ORTHOHOMBIC — Sulphur has an orthohombic crystal structure.
TRICLINIC — Turquoise has crystals in a triclinic shape.

Cubic   *Hexagonal*   *Tetragonal*

Monoclinic   *Orthohombic*   *Triclinic*

WHY ARE GEMSTONES VALUABLE?

SOME MINERALS are very precious. Diamonds, rubies, emeralds and sapphires are examples of gemstones that are valued for their rarity and beauty. They are difficult to find and expensive to extract from the Earth. Some of them also have particular uses in science and industry that can increase their value.

fast facts

WHAT IS GEOLOGY?

Geology is the science of studying rocks.

WHAT DOES A GEOLOGIST DO?

Geologists are scientists who take specimens of rocks and study them in the laboratory.

WHAT ARE ORGANIC GEMSTONES?

Organic gemstones are those that are formed from plant or animal materials. Pearls and amber are examples of these.

WHICH IS THE WORLD'S LARGEST PEARL?

The Pearl of Lao-tze was found inside a giant clam. Weighing 6.37kg (14lb 1oz), it was found in the Phillipines in 1934.

HOW ARE DIAMONDS CUT?

The only way to cut the hardest mineral is by using tools tipped with diamond. Diamond-tipped tools are also used extensively in industry to cut materials finely.

HOW IS A PEARL FORMED?

PEARLS ARE PRECIOUS STONES formed inside shellfish such as oysters, mussels and clams. They form when a piece of grit enters the creature's shell. The most valuable pearls are those from oysters.

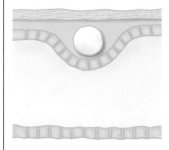

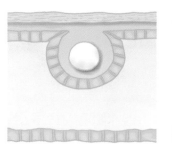

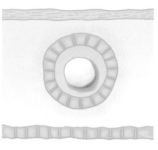

A small piece of grit enters the shell and begins to irritate the creature.

Mother-of-pearl is secreted from within the creature around the grit.

As the grit becomes surrounded by mother-of-pearl, it separates, forming the precious stone.

WHY ARE SOME MINERALS HARDER THAN OTHERS?

THE HARDNESS OF MINERALS varies according to the structure of their atoms. A mineral's hardness is measured using the Mohs scale. Diamond is the hardest mineral and thus has a rating of 10 Mohs.

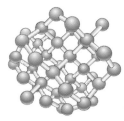

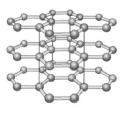

Diamond atoms are strongly bonded to each other, making them very hard.

The atoms of graphite are layered apart, giving it a fairly soft structure.

WHAT IS GLACIATION?

Glaciation occurs when layers of snow build up in areas over a long period of time. The layers become compressed and form a mass of ice. Where this happens in the valley areas of mountain ranges, the layers form into glaciers that, over time, move slowly down the mountainside. In the polar regions, vast frozen areas known as ice caps are formed.

Glaciers begin high in a mountain range.

HOW QUICKLY DO GLACIERS MOVE?

THE SPEED AT WHICH glaciers move depends on the steepness of the slope, though they average a speed of around 2m (7ft) a day. It generally takes ice several thousand years to move from one end of a glacier to the other.

The front of the glacier is called the snout.

The glacier scours out rocks as it slowly tumbles down the valley.

Cracks in the glacier are called crevasses.

Meltwater forms at the lower areas of the glacier.

WHAT HAPPENS WHEN GLACIERS MELT AWAY?

AFTER THOUSANDS of years, the climate may warm and the glacier melts away. During glaciation, the valley's shape will have changed from a V-shape to a U-shape. Water can fill the area to form fjords and lakes.

Before glaciation

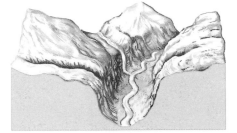

After glaciation

HOW DOES AN ICE CAP FORM?

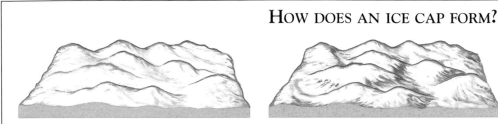

In the far north and south, glaciation causes vast sheets of ice to form over the land. The temperature never rises enough for the ice to melt completely.

Ice caps move outward towards the sea. Snow in the centre of the cap becomes ice at the edges.

The two largest ice caps are in Greenland and Antarctica. With the global climate warming up, the Antarctic ice cap is beginning to melt.

HOW ARE ICEBERGS FORMED?

ICEBERGS ARE FORMED from freshwater ice brought to the sea by glaciers, or when chunks are broken off an ice cap due to the effect of the tide and waves. This effect is known as calving. Icebergs contain large amounts of rock fragments that make them heavy, and they sit low in the sea. Once an iceberg has broken off, its movement depends upon the wind and sea currents.

Around 88% of an iceberg lies below the surface of the water. It is estimated that around 10,000 icebergs break off the ice caps of Greenland each year.

DOES THE SEA EVER FREEZE?

WHEN THE TEMPERATURE of the sea dips below –1.9°C (28°F), it can freeze. This happens off the Antarctic coast and other glaciated regions. The whole of the North Pole is in fact frozen sea that is never more than a few metres thick. Sea ice is often referred to as pack ice.

Specially designed ships known as icebreakers can penetrate areas of sea ice in the polar regions. Their hulls are strengthened to enable them to batter their way through the ice and also to withstand the force of the ice when the sea freezes around the ship.

WHAT CAN SCIENTISTS DISCOVER IN THE POLAR REGIONS?

SCIENTISTS WHO STUDY glaciers and polar ice are called glaciologists. There are permanent research stations based in polar regions, manned by glaciologists who can discover a great deal about the Earth. Working in laboratories dug out of the ice, they investigate layers of ice that contain gases and substances from climatic conditions of the past. Ice cores are also drilled from the ice and taken back to laboratories for detailed testing.

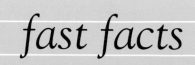

fast facts

WILL THERE BE ANOTHER ICE AGE?

There are times when the Earth's climate grows so cold that the ice caps become huge. These periods are called Ice Ages. Scientists think that there have been around five Ice Ages in the last million years, the last one ending around 10,000 years ago. If Ice Ages happen in cycles, then another one could be a distinct possibility.

HOW BIG WAS THE LARGEST ICEBERG?

One iceberg was measured at 335km (208 miles) long and 97km (60 miles) wide.

WHERE IS THE THICKEST ICE IN THE WORLD?

Ice in Antarctica has been measured at 5km (3 miles) deep.

HOW OLD ARE ICEBERGS?

It is thought that the ice in icebergs is about 5000 years old.

WHAT CAUSES AN AVALANCHE?

AVALANCHES are huge masses of snow that suddenly crash down a mountainside. They are caused by a combination of heavy snow and a sudden rise in temperature. Avalanches can be up to 1km (0.6 miles) across and generate winds of up to 300km/h (185mph). Their effects on towns and local populations can be devastating.

Sometimes, a skier can accidentally trigger an avalanche.

HOW ARE MOUNTAINS FORMED?

Mountain ranges make up some of the world's most impressive landscapes. Like earthquakes and volcanoes, they are formed as a consequence of the activity of the Earth's tectonic plates. Where the plates push up against one another, the Earth's crust buckles and folds, resulting in ranges of rocky mountains. Volcanoes also make up some of the world's greatest mountains.

WHAT ARE THE DIFFERENT TYPES OF MOUNTAIN?

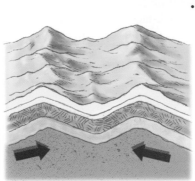

Fold mountains
Fold mountains form where tectonic plates collide, and the crust bends and buckles.

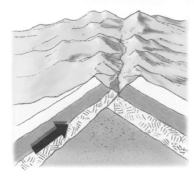

Fault-block mountains
When layers of rock crack or snap to form faults, slabs of rock may be forced upwards to form block mountains. Some of these are flat-topped.

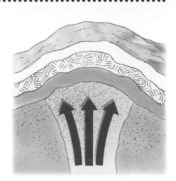

Dome mountains
Dome mountains form above a rising layer of molten rock. Where the rock moves outwards, a dome shape is formed.

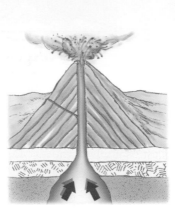

Volcanoes
Volcanoes form mountains as layers of solidified lava pile up into a cone shape.

WHERE ARE THE WORLD'S HIGHEST MOUNTAINS?

NO FEWER THAN ten of the highest mountains in the world are in the Himalayas. Highest of all is Everest, which lies on the border of Nepal and China. At a height of 8848m (29,028ft), it is almost 2000m (6562ft) higher than the highest mountain outside the Himalayas – Aconcagua in Argentina, South America.

The highest peak in the Himalayas, Everest, has long represented a challenge to adventurous mountaineers. It was first climbed in 1953.

Ancient mountain ranges such as the Scottish Highlands are evidence of continents colliding millions of years ago. Once massive, they have eroded over time.

ARE SOME MOUNTAINS OLDER THAN OTHERS?

MOUNTAINS FORM OVER many millions of years, and due to the continual movement of the Earth's plates, they are still being formed. Young mountain ranges are those that have formed in the last 50 million years or so, such as the Himalayas in Asia. Older mountain ranges, such as the Urals in Russia or the Scottish Highlands, were formed many more millions of years ago and have eroded significantly.

HOW IS A RIVER VALLEY FORMED?

OVER TIME, rainfall has the effect of eroding the land to form valleys and other features. At mountain peaks, the rainwater flows quickly to form narrow gullies. Slowing down as it moves further downhill, the water forms a wide valley.

Narrow valley in higher area

Valley widens in the lower reaches.

WHAT ARE RIFTS AND CANYONS?

RIVER WATER does not always carve out wide valleys. In some areas, where there are fairly soft rocks, for instance, very deep, narrow valleys with vertical sides called canyons are formed. In places where continents are drifting apart, very wide rift valleys and flat areas known as plateaux can appear. The Great Rift Valley in Africa is the biggest example of these.

The Grand Canyon in Arizona, USA, was formed by the Colorado River that runs along its base. Reaching depths of over 1.5km (1 mile) and running for 350km (217 miles), the surrounding cliffs are made of a striking, multi-coloured rock.

HOW DO CAVES FORM?

CAVES can form in different ways, depending on the type of landscape in which they are situated. Limestone is a very soft rock, and caves are quite common in limestone areas as it dissolves in rainwater. Caves can be formed out of coastal cliff faces by waves crashing against them, and ice caves may appear where streams of meltwater run beneath a glacier. The hardened lava of a volcanic eruption may also leave a hollow beneath, producing a lava cave.

fast facts

WHICH IS THE WORLD'S LONGEST MOUNTAIN RANGE?

The Andes in South America is the world's longest mountain range, stretching for 7200km (4500 miles).

WHICH IS THE HARDEST MOUNTAIN TO CLIMB?

K2, the second highest mountain in the Himalayas, is notoriously difficult to climb because of its acutely-angled rock-faces. Many have died trying to reach its summit.

WHICH IS THE WORLD'S DEEPEST CANYON?

Contenders for the world's deepest canyon include Hell's Canyon in the USA, the Colco Canyon in Peru and the Yalung Zambo in the Himalayas.

WHO CLIMBED MOUNT EVEREST FIRST?

Sir Edmund Hillary and Sherpa Norgay Tenzing climbed Mount Everest in 1953.

WHY DO SOME CAVES HAVE STALACTITES AND STALAGMITES?

STALACTITES AND STALAGMITES can be found in limestone caves. As water drips down through limestone, it dissolves it and leaves behind deposits of a mineral called calcite. This produces distinctive stalactites that hang from the roof of the cave. When the calcite forms in pools of water on the cave floor, deposits grow upwards, forming stalagmites. Where the two features meet, they form columns.

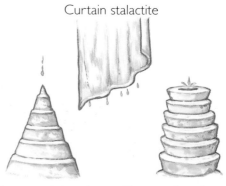

Curtain stalactite

Fir-cone stalagmite   Plate-stack stalagmite

HOW MUCH OF THE EARTH IS COVERED BY WATER?

Though the bulk of our planet is made of rock, around 70% of its surface is covered with water. The Earth's seas and oceans account for most of this coverage – the Pacific Ocean alone covers more than a third of the Earth.

HOW ARE WAVES MADE?

WIND BLOWING ACROSS the surface of the sea creates ripples of energy in the water. Although it appears that the water is moving along, it is actually moving in a circle. At the shore, the circular movement is broken, and the crest of a wave topples over as it meets the land. Powerful waves create a tremendous force when they crash against the shore – in storms they can cause severe damage. The height and power of a wave depends on the power of the wind.

WHAT CAUSES OCEAN CURRENTS?

CURRENTS OF WATER in the world's oceans and seas are generated by wind and the movement of warm and cold water. Warm currents created by wind flow near the surface of the water and move away from the Equator. Cold water from the poles sinks below the warm water and moves into its place. Warm and cold currents often flow in the same area in different directions. The rotation of the Earth affects some currents by turning them into twisting movements called gyres.

Surf is produced where large waves pass over a beach that becomes shallow slowly. The wave breaks over a relatively long period, creating large crests. A surfer uses a surfboard to travel along the "tube" that the circular motion of the wave creates.

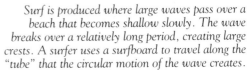
Cold current →

Warm current →

Arctic Ocean: 3.65% of total sea area

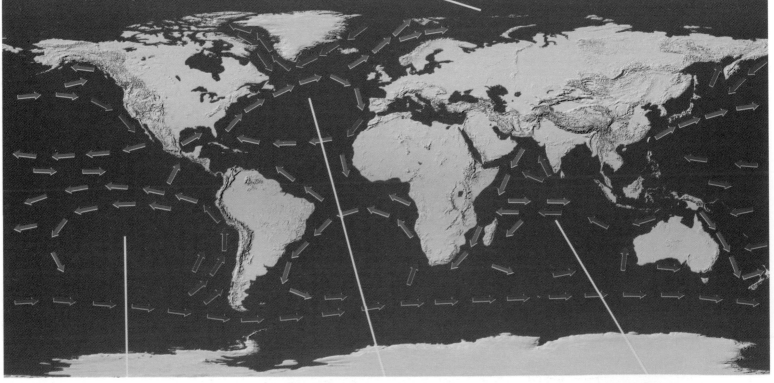

Pacific Ocean: 45.7% of total sea area   Atlantic Ocean: 22.7% of total sea area   Indian Ocean: 20.3% of total sea area

WHAT CAUSES A WHIRLPOOL?

WHIRLPOOLS ARE CAUSED where ocean currents, tidal flows, winds and irregularities in the coastline and ocean floor combine to form a swirling mass of water. Whirlpools powerful enough to produce a twisting vortex capable of sucking boats down beneath the surface are rare and only found near coasts, not in open seas. The Charybdis whirlpool, which is found between Sicily and mainland Italy, is a well known example.

HOW WERE THE OCEANS FORMED?

THE OCEANS were formed many millions of years ago. Water vapour thrown into the atmosphere by volcanoes condensed, resulting in rainfall. Hollow areas of the crust filled with water to form the oceans.

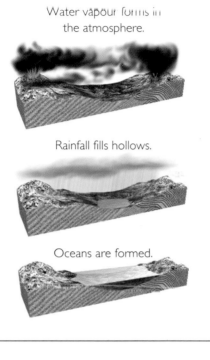

Water vapour forms in the atmosphere.

Rainfall fills hollows.

Oceans are formed.

HOW ARE ISLANDS FORMED?

ISLANDS VARY in size and type. They can be formed by volcanoes erupting beneath the ocean, depositing lava that eventually builds up to the surface. Some volcanic islands form long chains, known as arcs. Islands in tropical areas may form when tiny marine organisms called coral build up in shallow water. Sometimes, the sea may rise to such an extent that it cuts off an area of land to form an island.

The Whitsunday Islands on the coast of Queensland, Australia, form part of the Great Barrier Reef – the world's largest group of coral islands.

fast facts

IS THE OCEAN FLOOR FLAT?

The ocean floor is far from flat. It is almost as varied as the continental landscape, with mountainous areas, plains and ridges.

WHICH IS THE BIGGEST OCEAN?

The Pacific is the world's biggest ocean with a total surface area of 165,384,000sq km (63,855,000sq miles).

ARE THE WORLD'S OCEANS CONNECTED?

None of the world's five oceans is completely surrounded by land; they flow into one another through open water.

WHAT IS AN ATOLL?

A ring of coral around a sunken island is called an atoll.

HOW DO SCIENTISTS STUDY THE OCEAN?

OCEANOGRAPHY IS THE SCIENCE concerned with the study of oceans and seas. Because of the vastness and great depths of the oceans, there is a great deal to study, and many things are not yet understood. Modern technology has helped oceanographers immensely. Computer analysis of water and sediment samples can give an accurate picture of the content of oceans, and currents can be electronically monitored and predicted. Robotic submersibles and sonar imaging help in the study of the sea floor.

Mother ship

Submersible carrying sonar equipment

Towing cable

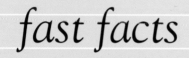

Sonar imaging helps oceanographers build up a picture of the ocean floor. Sound waves are beamed on to the seabed, from which they bounce back to a receiver. A computer then translates the information into a sonic "image" called a sonograph.

WHERE DOES A RIVER BEGIN AND END?

Rivers begin in places where water collects and eventually trickles over the land. The water in all rivers comes from rain or snow. Sometimes rain falls on to a mountainside and flows directly into gullies that flow into small streams and eventually into a river. Mountain springs form when rainwater soaks into the ground through permeable rocks and then bubbles up again, usually at the foot of a mountain. The water from the spring then forms a river flow. Other rivers begin where glaciers melt, and some rivers, such as the Nile, have a lake as their source. All rivers flow into the sea through an estuary.

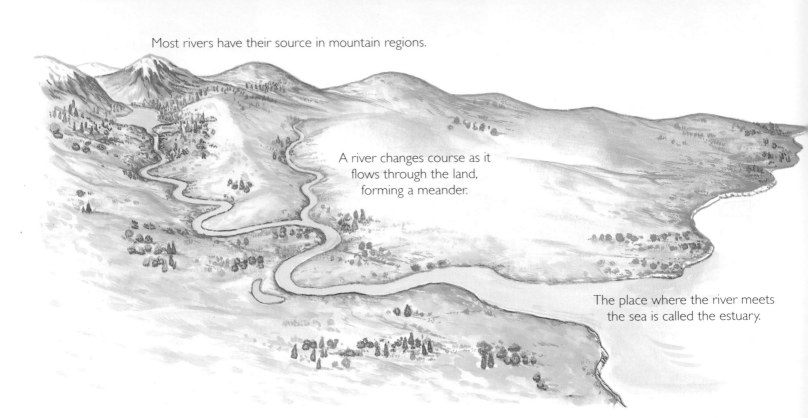

Most rivers have their source in mountain regions.

A river changes course as it flows through the land, forming a meander.

The place where the river meets the sea is called the estuary.

HOW ARE WATERFALLS FORMED?

WATERFALLS ARE GENERALLY found near the source of a river, where it is flowing fastest. They form where a layer of soft rock lies below a layer of hard rock. Because the soft rock wears away faster than the hard rock above it, a ledge forms, and the water crashes over it. The water will continue to erode the soft rock, moving the waterfall's position gradually backwards.

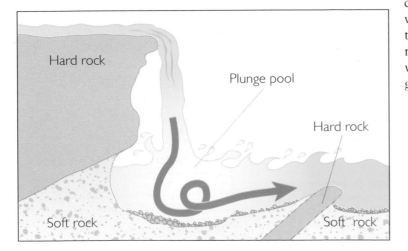

Hard rock

Plunge pool

Hard rock

Soft rock

Soft rock

This waterfall is in Yellowstone National Park in the USA.

WHAT MAKES A RIVER FLOOD?

THERE ARE A NUMBER of reasons for rivers flooding. Heavy rainfall, such as that in tropical regions during the monsoon season, will produce more water than a river is able to hold, making it burst its banks. A flood can also happen if a river is blocked by something, such as a landslide. Tidal rivers can flood when very high tides and strong winds combine to force more water upstream. In cold countries, melting snow has the same effect as heavy rainfall, while ice melting upstream before it does further downstream can cause ice blockages in the channel, resulting in a flood.

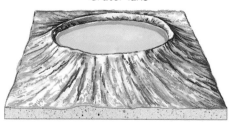

Some kinds of flooding can be prevented by building dams or water barrages. The Thames Barrier in London, England, is one such example. If a flood is expected, the Barrier's gates can be raised to help prevent serious flooding in the city.

ARE THERE DIFFERENT TYPES OF LAKES?

LAKES ARE AREAS of water surrounded by land. They occur where water collects in hollows in the Earth's surface. The type of lake depends on how the hollow was formed.

Artificial lake

Lakes can form in disused gravel pits, quarries or open-cast mines. Dammed rivers may also flood areas to make artificial lakes.

Glacial lake

Lakes can form in areas where ice sheets and glaciers have carved out hollows in hard rock. Finland has many lakes formed in this way.

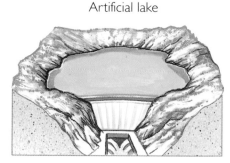

Rift-valley lake

Where the Earth's crust slips down to form a rift valley, water may collect to form a lake. Lake Nyasa in East Africa is an example of a rift-valley lake.

Crater lake

Water may collect in the hollow of a long-extinct volcano, such as that at Crater Lake in Oregon, USA. Some meteorite craters may also form lakes.

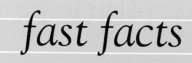
fast facts

ARE THERE ANY RIVERS WITHOUT WATER?

Ephemeral rivers are found in many desert areas. They are completely dry, except during periods of freak rainfall.

WHICH IS THE WORLD'S LONGEST RIVER?

The River Nile, which stretches for 6,695km (4,160 miles) through Africa, is the world's longest river.

WHERE IS THE WORLD'S DEEPEST LAKE?

Lake Baikal, in Siberia, Russia, is the world's deepest lake at 1620m (5315ft).

WHICH IS THE HIGHEST WATERFALL IN THE WORLD?

The Angel Falls in Venezuela drop 979m (3212ft), making them the highest in the world.

WHAT IS IRRIGATION?

When water is diverted from a river or lake to farmland, it is known as irrigation.

WHICH IS THE BIGGEST LAKE?

The Caspian Sea is, despite its name, the world's largest lake.

DO LAKES LAST FOR EVER?

LAKES may eventually disappear. This happens as they drain away through man-made barriers, fill up with sediment from rivers, or evaporate as the climate changes.

WHY ARE COASTLINES SO VARIED?

The world's coastlines show more varied features than any other kind of landscape. The type and appearance of a coastline depends on the kind of rock present where the land meets the sea, as well as the strength and direction of the prevailing winds, tides and currents.

HOW ARE COASTLINES ERODED?

THE STRENGTH of the sea is such that many coastlines are easily eroded. Caves and arches are created as the waves attack a headland from all sides. These features then continue to be eroded in two ways. Stones thrown up by the sea scrape away at the rocks, wearing the cliffs into the sea. Cracks in the rock are then made bigger as air forced into them by the water expands when the waves retreat.

The distinctive white cliffs found along the south coast of England are this colour because the rocks in the area are made mainly of chalk.

Headlands are made of hard rocks, which resist the force of the sea.

The air in a sea cave may be forced through the roof, creating a blowhole.

Cracks in the head-land erode to make sea caves.

Arch

Stack

This natural arch has formed in the coastline at Durdle Door, Dorset, England.

WHAT ARE ARCHES AND STACKS?

PERHAPS THE MOST DRAMATIC coastlines are seen where rocky headlands have been eroded into arches and stacks. As the sea erodes the rocky coastline, only the toughest rocks remain, sometimes forming arch-shaped head-lands. Eventually, the roofs of these arches may fall, leaving tall, rocky columns known as sea stacks.

These stacks are found in the Magdalen Islands, Canada.

HOW ARE BEACHES FORMED?

BEACHES ARE MADE as rocks, worn away from headlands, are ground down into shingle and sand. The sea then deposits these particles in a sheltered place, forming a beach.

Some beaches have special walls called groynes to help prevent the effect of longshore drift.

Sand may be carried away from the beach to form a spit.

You can see how the sand and shingle is moved about by the way it piles up against groynes and sea walls.

DO BEACHES ALWAYS REMAIN THE SAME?

BEACHES ARE changing all the time. Shingle and sand on beaches is constantly shifted around by the action of the wind and waves – a process known as longshore drift. The same beach may be made of pebbles at one time of the year, yet be sandy a few months later.

CAN COASTLINES BE PROTECTED FROM THE SEA?

IT IS POSSIBLE to prevent or, at least, slow down the erosion of some coastlines. Groynes help to prevent longshore drift, while trees and grasses can be specially planted to stop sand dunes being blown away. Sea walls help to prevent coastal erosion and protect low-lying areas from flooding.

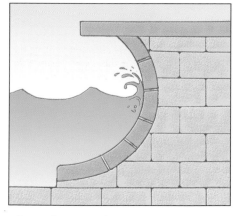

Sea walls can be designed to repel waves, protecting the coast.

Concrete barriers, or breakwaters, extend into the sea to break up waves.

WHAT IS SPECIAL ABOUT CORAL REEFS?

CORAL REEFS are special areas of coastline made from living things. They grow in areas where the water is particularly warm, clear and shallow. Tiny sea animals cling to the coastline. When they die, they create limestone skeletons to which more creatures attach themselves. As these die, more creatures cling on, and the process continues. Coral reefs are among the strongest structures on Earth, as well as making up some of the world's most beautiful coastlines.

Coral reefs are most commonly found near the shoreline. The reef above is known as a fringing reef – it is connected directly to the land. Barrier reefs create a lagoon of calm water between the reef and the land.

fast facts

WHICH IS THE WORLD'S LONGEST BEACH?

The longest beach, Cox's Bazar, Bangladesh, is 121km (75 miles) long.

WHAT IS A RIA?

A ria is an inlet on a coastline that appears when the land sinks or the sea level rises.

WHY DOES THE SEA CHANGE COLOUR?

The colour of the sea depends on two things: what the weather is like and what the sea bed is made up of. For example, stormy weather stirs up sediment from the sea bed, making it a brown colour. The sea also reflects the colour of the sky, so a sunny day will mean blue seas; cloudy skies make the sea appear murky.

DO INLAND LAKES HAVE BEACHES?

Some inland lakes have beaches, although they do not change as dramatically as those on the coast.

WHAT IS A SAND SPIT?

Longshore drift can carry sand away out to sea to form a sand spit.

WHERE DO FORESTS GROW?

Forests will grow in areas where the temperature rises above 10°C (50°F) in the summer and the annual rainfall is more than 200mm (8in). The type of forest depends upon the local climate, the soil and the altitude. Forests that grow in the extreme north of the Northern Hemisphere are called boreal forests; temperate forests grow in areas of moderate climate in both the Northern and Southern Hemispheres. Tropical regions are best known for their vast, dense areas of rainforest.

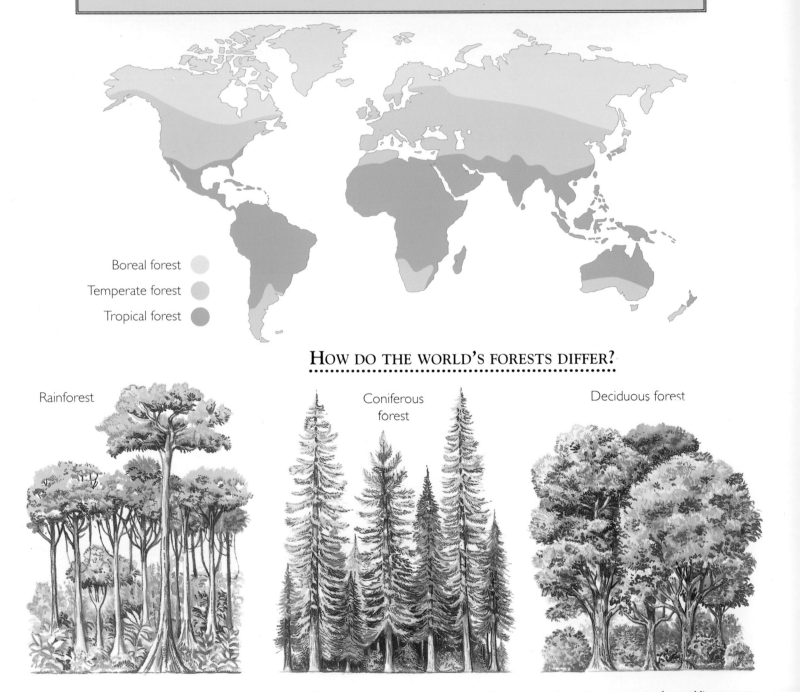

Boreal forest

Temperate forest

Tropical forest

HOW DO THE WORLD'S FORESTS DIFFER?

Rainforest

Coniferous forest

Deciduous forest

Rainforests feature an extremely wide variety of broadleaved trees, characterized by long, slim trunks. Most of the greenery is at the top of the tree and is known as the canopy. Temperate rainforests grow in parts of North America. They are home to some of the oldest and largest trees on Earth.

All boreal forests are of the coniferous type. The harsh climate (very cold winters, hot summers and little rainfall) means that only hardy conifers, such as spruce, fir and pine trees, can grow in these areas. These "evergreen" trees usually have needle-shaped leaves.

Deciduous forests grow in the world's temperate regions. The trees in these areas shed their leaves during winter or the dry season. High rainfall and a relatively mild climate mean that broadleaved trees such as oak and beech thrive in these areas.

WHAT IS IT LIKE ON THE FOREST FLOOR?

THE FLOOR of a forest is teeming with wildlife. Decaying vegetation provides food for insects and allows many kinds of fungi to grow. The warm, humid atmosphere of a tropical rainforest is the perfect environment for plants and mosses that thrive in shady areas. Palm trees will grow here amongst other young trees growing towards the forest canopy. Climbing plants such as liana twist and curl around the trunks of the trees.

WHY ARE FORESTS DESTROYED?

THE WORLD'S FORESTS provide many resources for human beings. Trees are cut down for timber, which is used for many different purposes, from building materials and fuel to making paper and chemicals. Forest areas are also cleared to create land for farming and other uses. There is a great deal of concern about the rate at which rainforests in particular are being destroyed. It is thought that an area of rainforest the size of a soccer pitch disappears every second. Such devastation has a dramatic effect on plant and animal species, as well as on the land itself.

Deforestation – the destruction of forests is happening at an alarming rate. Some forests are carefully managed, and trees are replanted to create sustainable forests for the future. However, many tropical rainforests are destroyed for economic reasons, without any replanting. Half of the world's rainforests were cut down during the twentieth century.

WHICH ANIMALS LIVE IN RAINFORESTS?

TROPICAL RAINFORESTS ARE home to an incredible range of animal life. Over half of the world's known species exist in the Amazon rainforest alone. Colourful birds, such as toucans, parrots and macaws, live alongside gorillas or other primates, while tigers, pumas and wolves may roam among countless poisonous snakes and insects.

fast facts

HOW MUCH OF THE WORLD IS COVERED BY FOREST?

Around one-third of the Earth's surface is covered by forest, although the number of trees is decreasing steadily.

WHICH IS THE WORLD'S LARGEST FOREST?

The world's largest forest is in Siberia. It covers around 11 million sq km (4.2 million sq miles).

WHICH IS THE WORLD'S LARGEST RAINFOREST?

Covering an area of 7 million sq km (2.7 million sq miles), the Amazon rainforest is the largest of its kind.

WHAT IS COPPICING?

Cutting down areas of woodland to promote the growth of new wood is known as coppicing.

WHAT IS THE UNDERSTOREY?

The layer just above the floor of a rainforest is called the understorey.

HOW CAN RAINFORESTS BE REGENERATED?

WITH CAREFUL PLANNING, areas of rainforest can be re-established, although it takes over a hundred years for the forest to return to its original state. However, if the land is damaged, only scrubby vegetation will grow again.

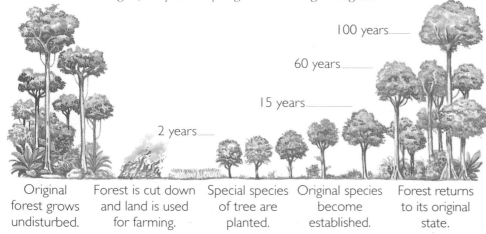

100 years

60 years

15 years

2 years

| Original forest grows undisturbed. | Forest is cut down and land is used for farming. | Special species of tree are planted. | Original species become established. | Forest returns to its original state. |

WHAT ARE THE MAIN FEATURES OF A DESERT?

Deserts are hot, dry areas formed by the constant weathering and erosion of the land by fierce winds, extreme temperatures and occasional flows of water. They can contain barren mountain ranges, vast canyons cut into the Earth and huge plains covered with rocks or sand dunes. Many deserts have unusual rock formations, produced by certain kinds of erosion caused by wind and sand.

Strange rock formations are a common sight in many of the world's deserts. Winds stir up sand that wears away softer rocks, leaving only the hard layers visible. These red rocks in the Painted Desert, Arizona, USA, are one such example.

Sand dunes form in flat areas.

Isolated areas of eroded rock are called buttes.

A river may flow through a deep canyon. The water comes from outside the desert.

Water oases appear in some hollows. Vegetation will grow here.

Steep-sided, flat-topped hills called *mesas* form where soft rock is eroded.

HOW ARE SAND DUNES FORMED?

SAND DUNES FORM when sand is heaped up by the desert winds. They do not remain still but are being constantly shifted around by the wind. Dunes form in several different ways, producing various shapes.

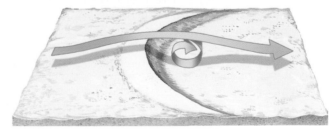

Barkhan sand dune
The most familiar types of sand dunes are the crescent-shaped barkhan dunes. The sand at either end of the crescent is being blown faster than that in the middle.

Seif sand dunes
In areas where there is little sand and a powerful wind, seif sand dunes can form. Long ridges of sand are heaped up in lines, parallel to the wind's direction. The wind slows down at the edges of the ridges, producing eddies of sand.

ARE THERE DIFFERENT TYPES OF DESERT?

ALL DESERTS FORM in areas where there is very little rainfall – less than 250mm (10in) a year. While they share many features, deserts around the world form because of varying climatic conditions. Tropical deserts form when dry air drops all its rain at the Equator. Continental deserts are found in areas so far inland that there is no moisture in the air – the Gobi Desert in central Asia is one example. Rain-shadow deserts exist near mountain ranges where all the rain in the region falls, while cold ocean currents can force dry air downwards, creating coastal deserts.

The Sahara is a continental desert. Too far inland to receive any moisture, vast, shifting sand seas known as ergs make up a typical Saharan landscape.

Monument Valley in Arizona, USA, is a typical rain-shadow desert. These types of desert often have a mainly rocky landscape.

CAN PEOPLE LIVE IN DESERTS?

DESPITE THE HARSH CONDITIONS of deserts, people have lived in these areas for thousands of years. The nomadic people of the Middle East and Africa – the Bedouin – move herds of camels through the desert, settling near oases and river valleys.

The Bushmen of the Kalahari in Africa live off the native wildlife and have developed special skills for finding water.

The Bedouin have travelled through the desert for centuries. In the modern age, there are more people than ever living in deserts. The desert locations of valuable mineral resources such as oil have led to the growth of permanent settlements in areas that were previously seen as uninhabitable. Modern engineering means that water can now easily be supplied to these areas.

WHAT IS A MIRAGE?

HOT DESERT AIR can distort light in a way that makes objects in the distance appear in the wrong place. Light travels more quickly through warm air close to the ground than it does through the cooler air above it. This causes light from an object to bend, making it appear upside-down and nearer to the viewer. The shimmering effect can look a bit like a lake – an effect often seen on hot roads as well as in deserts.

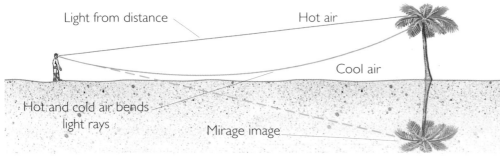

Light from distance   Hot air

Cool air

Hot and cold air bends light rays

Mirage image

fast facts

HOW DOES A SANDSTORM HAPPEN?

Strong desert winds whip up the sand and transport it many miles to produce a sandstorm.

WHERE IS THE HOTTEST PLACE IN THE WORLD?

The hottest place in the world is Death Valley, California, USA, where temperatures can reach 57°C (134°F).

HOW LONG CAN A HUMAN BEING SURVIVE IN THE DESERT?

With adequate water, shade, food and clothing, people could survive happily in the desert. Without these, at temperatures in excess of 46°C (115°F), the average person would be dead within a day.

WHY ARE SOME DESERTS COLD AT NIGHT?

Clear skies in desert areas mean that the heat escapes during the night, often making them very cold.

WHICH IS THE LARGEST DESERT?

The Sahara is by far the world's largest desert. Covering an area of 8,600,000 sq km (3,320,000 sq miles), it is almost four times bigger than the next largest, the Arabian Desert.

WHAT IS DESERTIFICATION?

Intensive farming methods and the destruction of forests are two ways in which humans have increased the size of deserts. Such activity damages soil. When deserts grow because of this, it is known as desertification.

WHAT IS A DREIKANTER?

A pebble that has been eroded flat by desert wind and sand is called a dreikanter.

WHERE DOES COAL COME FROM?

Coal is the fossilized remains of plants that have been put under high pressure beneath the ground for millions of years. Ancient trees and plants became buried in swampy areas, where the process of decay was very slow. The first level of decay produced a soft, earthy material called peat. As the material became covered with more and more sediment, the pressure gradually transformed it into coal. The type of coal varies according to the amount of water and carbon that it contains. The more deeply coal is buried, the more carbon and the less water it contains, forming a drier, better-quality coal. Coal is found in layers called seams. The lower a seam is found, the narrower it tends to be.

Trees and plants become buried in swamps.

First layer of decay produces peat.

Brown coal, or lignite, is quite soft, as it still contains a lot of water. It is about 70% carbon.

Bituminous coal is slightly harder, with an 85% carbon content.

The hardest type of coal, with a carbon content of 90%, is called anthracite.

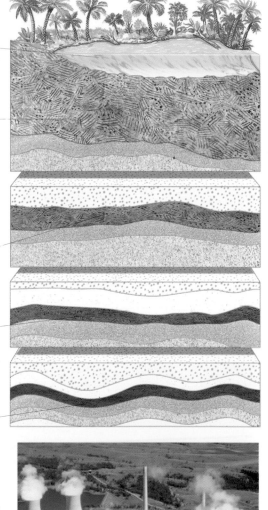

ARE THERE DIFFERENT WAYS OF MINING COAL?

A DIFFERENT MINING technique will need to be used according to the depth at which the coal is found. Where coal is found deep underground, a mine shaft is drilled to reach it. Shaft-mining is the most expensive and potentially dangerous form of mining. Drift mines can be used in hilly areas, where a coal seam can be accessed through a horizontal tunnel. Open-cast or strip mining is the simplest method; layers of ground are stripped away to access the coal found close to the surface.

Strip or open-cast mining has dramatically altered landscapes in the past. Modern methods involve refilling areas that have been dug out. The reclaimed land can then be put to other uses. Around two-thirds of modern coal extraction is carried out in this way.

Coal is an efficient source of energy and is widely used in power stations. Burning coal releases carbon dioxide into the atmosphere, which is harmful to the environment. The cooling towers of this power station (right) are actually releasing steam, not smoke.

WHAT IS COAL USED FOR?

THE PRIMARY USE of coal is as fuel. Although it is now used less as a domestic heating fuel, many power stations around the world use coal to drive their generators. Coal is also used to produce other products. Coke is a form of processed coal used in blast furnaces to make metals. It is made by heating coal without air, a process that removes ammonia and coal tar. These two products can then be processed into other chemicals to make products such as pesticides, paints and medicines.

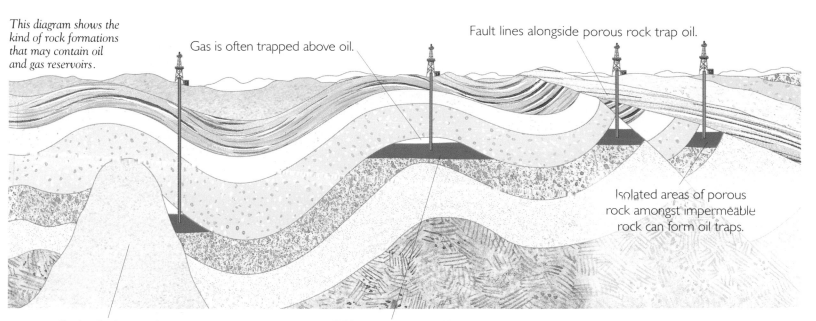

This diagram shows the kind of rock formations that may contain oil and gas reservoirs.

Gas is often trapped above oil.

Fault lines alongside porous rock trap oil.

Isolated areas of porous rock amongst impermeable rock can form oil traps.

Beds of salt may rise beneath rock to form a dome, trapping oil.

Oil becomes trapped in porous rock between layers of impermeable rock.

HOW DOES OIL AND GAS FORM?

OIL AND NATURAL gas are the remains of living organisms that inhabited the sea millions of years ago. They sank to the sea bed and became buried by layers of mud and sand, in a similar way to the plants that formed coal. As the remains became more deeply buried, they were broken down by bacteria, heat and pressure and gradually turned into oil and gas. These fuels are trapped in layers of porous rock, either beneath the sea bed or deep below land that was once covered by sea. Geologists call oil and natural gas "petroleum".

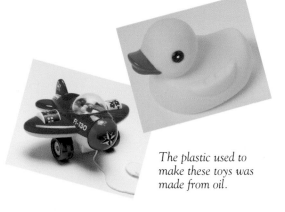

The plastic used to make these toys was made from oil.

WHAT IS OIL USED FOR?

OIL IS SUCH a valuable resource because it has many uses. Crude oil (its natural state) is refined into different types of oil. Fuel oil comes in many forms: gasoline (petrol) for motor vehicles; gas oil for diesel and central heating fuel; kerosene for aircraft jet engines. These and other oil products can be processed to make chemicals used in plastics, lubricants, drugs and solvents.

HOW IS OIL AND GAS TRANSPORTED?

OIL AND GAS are carried around the world in two ways – by ship and through miles and miles of pipelines. Oil tankers are usually very large, capable of carrying over 100 million litres (22 million gallons) of oil. Pipelines carry oil and gas from fields and platforms directly to refineries to be processed or transferred to oil tankers.

Pipelines carry oil and gas across great distances. One of the largest is the Trans-Alaska pipeline, which stretches for over 1290km (800 miles) between the north and south coasts of Alaska, USA.

fast facts

WHAT IS GAS USED FOR?

Gas is used as a domestic heating fuel, but it is also refined in a similar way to oil to produce useful chemicals.

WILL WE EVER RUN OUT OF OIL?

Oil will not last for ever. It is thought that current oil supplies will begin to run out by around 2040.

WHY DOES GAS SMELL?

Gas in its natural form – methane – has its own smell, but when it is refined for use in the home, the smell disappears. A scent is then added to make gas leaks easy to detect.

WHEN WAS PLASTIC INVENTED?

The first usable plastic was "Bakelite", developed in 1909 by Henrik Baekeland.

HOW IS OIL FOUND?

Oil and gas are found by surveying and analyzing the shock waves of test explosions. Exploratory drilling will then be carried out. On land, oil sometimes rises to the surface, giving a clue to its location under the ground.

WHAT IS RENEWABLE ENERGY?

Hydroelectric power is produced by turbines and generators when water is held behind huge dams.

Reservoirs or lakes may supply water for the turbine.

Renewable energy systems use resources that are constantly being replaced. Unlike fossil fuels, they are usually cleaner and less harmful to the environment. Examples of renewable energy sources include the Sun, wind, and geothermal energy (energy derived from heat within the Earth). We can also get renewable energy from trees, plants, water, and even waste products.

The flow of water spins the generator.

HOW IS WATER USED FOR POWER?

WATER IS used to generate electricity in three ways. Hydroelectric power is one of the most commonly used forms of renewable energy, accounting for around 7% of the world's electricity production. Specially-built dams feed falling water into turbines that drive electricity generators. A similar system controls the flow of water in tidal areas, with a barrier built across an estuary or river. Wave power can also be harnessed by using floating generators that transform wave movement into electricity.

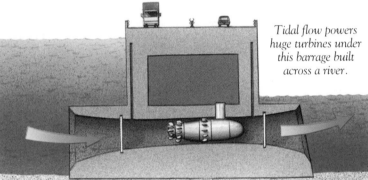

Tidal flow powers huge turbines under this barrage built across a river.

WHAT IS GEOTHERMAL ENERGY?

IN VOLCANICALLY ACTIVE areas of the world, heat energy inside the Earth is used for power. Geothermal powerplants use the heat produced by molten rocks to create hot water and steam. The steam powers turbines, while the hot water is piped to homes. Iceland and New Zealand are two countries where geothermal energy is used.

Geothermal power plants use very deep wells to reach volcanically-heated water.

HOW IS THE WIND USED TO GENERATE ELECTRICITY?

THE POWER of the wind can be used to generate electricity using huge wind turbines. The blades of a wind turbine drive a generator that produces electricity. Large groups of wind turbines, called wind farms, are built in areas where the wind blows fairly constantly. Flat, open areas of land and coastal areas are popular locations for wind farms. The electricity produced by these farms is fed into the electricity grid along with that coming from other sources.

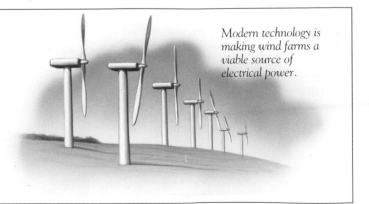

Modern technology is making wind farms a viable source of electrical power.

WHAT IS SOLAR POWER?

SOLAR-POWER SYSTEMS convert light energy from the Sun into electricity using photo-voltaic cells. These cells are similar to those used to power pocket calculators, but used on a larger scale they can provide electricity for homes and businesses in areas away from a regular power supply. Most solar-power systems work by charging batteries that store the electricity for later use, or act as a back-up system for a conventional power supply. Solar power is also used to heat water.

This experimental car uses solar power. The entire surface of the vehicle is covered in photovoltaic cells that create enough electricity to power the wheels. It is highly energy-efficient but not very practical.

CAN WASTE PRODUCTS BE USED FOR ENERGY?

SOME POWER STATIONS are able to burn waste products that would otherwise be buried in the ground. Even waste that is already buried can be put to use by harnessing the methane gas that decaying matter gives off. Once purified, the gas can be piped to homes, or used in power stations. However, while it solves the problem of what to do with rubbish, burning waste releases gases into the atmosphere, creating a pollution problem of its own.

WHERE DOES NUCLEAR ENERGY COME FROM?

NUCLEAR POWER PLANTS use radioactive materials such as uranium or plutonium to power their steam turbines. The atoms of these materials decay, producing heat energy inside a nuclear reactor. Nuclear energy is a "clean" fuel, in that it does not produce the polluting gases that burning fossil fuels do. However, the disposal of used nuclear fuel is hazardous, expensive and poses serious environmental risks.

The two dome structures in this nuclear power station hold the reactors in which the energy to drive its generators is produced.

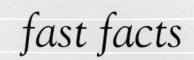

fast facts

WHAT IS BIOMASS ENERGY?

Biomass energy is derived from burning natural materials such as wood. Woodchips can also be processed to produce a gas to be burnt.

WHAT IS LPG?

LPG stands for Low Pressure Gas – an alternative to petrol.

WHAT IS ETHANOL?

Ethanol is a type of alcohol derived from grain, which may prove to be a useful fuel.

WHY IS NUCLEAR ENERGY DANGEROUS?

Nuclear fuels emit radiation, which can cause cancer in people and animals. If it enters the atmosphere, it can damage plants and trees and make large areas of land uninhabitable.

WHAT IS A SALTER DUCK?

In the 1970s, engineer Stephen Salter developed a method of harnessing power with his "ducks" – paddles that float on the water surface and transform wave energy into electricity.

HOW DOES INDUSTRY USE RAW MATERIALS?

Trees are cut into logs, which are then broken into woodchips.

Most of the world's industry involves working with raw materials extracted from the Earth. As well as fossil fuels, minerals such as salt, clay and sulphur, and metals including copper and iron ore are all extracted for industrial purposes. The extraction of such materials is described as primary industry; activities that convert them into other products are known as secondary industries.

Chemicals and dyes are added, depending on the type of paper being produced.

HOW ARE TREES USED TO MAKE PAPER?

TREES ARE MADE up of thousands of tiny fibres. The paper-making process extracts these fibres and arranges them in a criss-cross pattern. Wood is broken up into small pieces and then chemically treated to break it down into fibres. Most paper is produced from softwood trees such as spruce and pine.

The pulp is poured out on to a mesh.

The paper is compressed, smoothed out and placed on a roll.

The woodchips are pulped in water and treated with alkalis or acids to release the fibres. Used paper may be added at this point.

Liquid is removed from the pulp by squeezing it through rollers.

WHAT ARE CERAMICS?

CERAMICS ARE materials made from stony or earthy material taken from the ground. Some ceramics, such as pottery and bricks, are moulded into shape and then baked (fired) to make them set. Glass is a type of ceramic that is heated first and then moulded into shape. Some ceramic materials are able to withstand very high temperatures and are used for specialist applications in industry and engineering.

HOW DOES MINING FOR MINERALS AFFECT THE ENVIRONMENT?

MINING CAN CREATE a number of environmental problems. In the search for useful minerals, other substances are often discarded in the landscape. If these substances are toxic and they enter the water supply, wildlife and people may be affected. Mining can also cause serious physical damage to a landscape.

Clay pots are made from a mixture of kaolin (china clay), which has a smooth texture, and ball clay, which gives strength. Once shaped, the pottery is baked in a kiln.

This iron-ore mine in Brazil has made a huge impact on the landscape.

HOW IS IRON TURNED INTO STEEL?

IRON HAS BEEN extracted from iron ore since around 1500BC. Most iron is now turned into steel because this is a much more flexible metal. Steel is made by removing more carbon from the iron and adding other metals, depending on the type of steel that is being produced. Steel is made in an oxygen furnace. Molten iron mixed with scrap steel is poured into a furnace and oxygen is blown over it. The oxygen mixes with the carbon and removes it in the form of carbon monoxide.

Molten iron

Scrap

1 Molten iron and scrap steel is poured into the furnace.

Oxygen

Lime

2 Oxygen is added to produce carbon dioxide. Lime added to the mix helps to remove impurities.

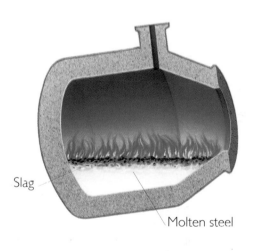

Slag

Molten steel

3 Impurities float on the surface of the molten steel as "slag".

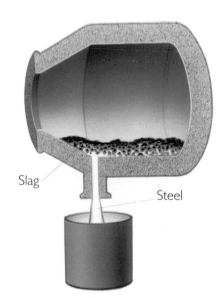

Slag

Steel

4 The slag is separated from the steel when it is poured out of the furnace.

WHY IS GLASS SO USEFUL?

GLASS IS ONE of the world's oldest man-made materials. It is made from sand that is heated, mixed with other materials, and then shaped as it cools. Glass is easily shaped, cheap to make and easy to recycle over and over again. It has a huge range of uses, from buildings and optical instruments to bottles and glasses. Modern communication systems rely heavily on fibre-optic cables, which are made from very fine glass fibres.

Glass is used to make fibre-optic cables, which allow information to be sent around the world at the speed of light.

fast facts

WHERE DOES MOST OF THE WORLD'S GOLD COME FROM?

Much of the world's supply of precious metals comes from the countries of southern Africa. Gold exports account for around 30% of South Africa's earnings.

DO ANY COUNTRIES NOT HAVE ANY RAW MATERIALS?

Japan is one of the world's leading producers of electronics, cars and ships, yet it has to import almost all of its raw materials.

WHERE DOES SILICON COME FROM?

Silicon is the most common solid element on Earth, although it is quite difficult to extract from the rocks and clays in which it is found. It is a semi-metal, or semiconductor, which means that it conducts electricity in certain conditions. Silicon is used to make electronic components such as microchips.

WHERE DOES MOST OF THE WORLD'S TIMBER COME FROM?

The USA is the world's largest producer of timber, providing around 14% of the global supply of wood.

WHERE DOES ALUMINIUM COME FROM?

Aluminium is the most common metal on Earth, but it is difficult to extract in a pure form. Most aluminium comes from bauxite – an ore found in rocks that contain aluminium, oxygen and silicon. Aluminium is useful because it is both lightweight and strong.

WHY IS WATER SO IMPORTANT?

All living things depend upon water for their survival; life on Earth would not exist without it. A clean supply of water is essential for people, not only to drink but for sanitation and health reasons. There is plenty of water on Earth, but not everyone has access to the same amount. Demand for water is always increasing, and supplies in many parts of the world are overstretched. In such areas, supplying fresh water can be a time-consuming and expensive business. For many people, a safe, regular supply of water is taken for granted, but without it life, and indeed industry, would come to a halt.

HOW DOES WATER GET INTO OUR HOMES?

WATER IS SUPPLIED into most homes by underground pipes. It starts its journey in a lake or man-made reservoir and passes through a process of purification before coming out of the tap in your home.

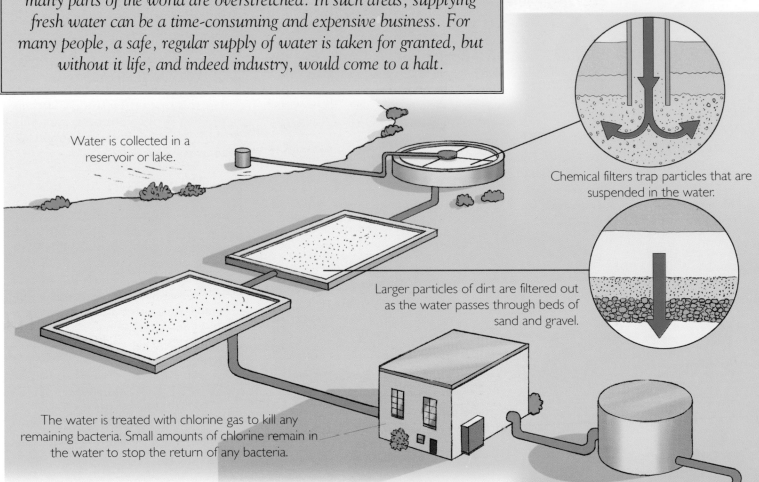

Water is collected in a reservoir or lake.

Chemical filters trap particles that are suspended in the water.

Larger particles of dirt are filtered out as the water passes through beds of sand and gravel.

The water is treated with chlorine gas to kill any remaining bacteria. Small amounts of chlorine remain in the water to stop the return of any bacteria.

Water is held in storage towers, ready to be supplied to people's homes through the water mains.

WHAT DOES INDUSTRY USE WATER FOR?

WATER HAS an enormous range of industrial uses, which means that industry needs a huge amount of water. Companies that produce chemicals use water as a solvent to dissolve other substances and also as a coolant. Power stations use water to generate steam for their turbines, and, of course, water is used in all industries for cleaning.

The electricity-generating industry is one of the biggest users of water. Most power stations use water to produce steam to drive their turbines; nuclear power stations also use it to cool their reactors. This hydroelectric power station uses water directly to power huge turbines.

WHY IS WATER PURIFIED?

HARMFUL BACTERIA that may cause serious diseases and death need to be removed from water before it can be used for domestic purposes. Dirt particles are removed because they can wear away pipes or damage industrial equipment.

HOW DO COUNTRIES WITH LITTLE RAINFALL GET WATER?

IN PARTS of the world that receive little rainfall, access to water can be difficult. In such areas, wells may be dug deep underground, or water can be piped from natural springs. Some countries even process seawater at a desalination plant. The seawater is heated, and only pure water evaporates. When it condenses, it is collected, leaving behind the salt in a concentrated form.

WHERE DOES MINERAL WATER COME FROM?

MINERAL WATER comes from natural sources of water beneath the ground. The types of minerals in the water will depend on the type of rock over which the water has been running – different areas produce mineral water containing different types of minerals. Calcium, sodium and sulphur are examples of minerals commonly found in mineral water. Sources of mineral water are most often in mountainous and hilly regions.

WHICH DISEASES CAN UNCLEAN WATER CAUSE?

MANY MILLIONS of people in developing countries do not have access to clean drinking water and sanitation. In the countryside, people may be forced to use the same ponds, streams, rivers and lakes for drinking and for sewage. In cities, water supply and sewage systems are often inadequate and, in both cases, people may be exposed to serious illnesses such as malaria, cholera and yellow fever.

Many people in the western world drink bottled mineral water in the belief that it is healthy.

fast facts

HOW IS WATER QUALITY MEASURED?

Water quality is measured by what is in the water. Bacteria, phosphates and metals may all be present, and the amount of such substances in the water will determine its quality. Water used for drinking needs to be of better quality than that used to water land.

WHAT IS LIMESCALE?

The green-coloured deposit that is sometimes found in kettles is known as limescale. It comes from minerals that are in the water. Water that leaves a lot of limescale is sometimes described as "hard" water.

WHICH COUNTRIES USE THE MOST WATER?

Unsurprisingly, countries with large populations use most of the world's water. Between them, the USA, the Commonwealth of Independent States (formerly USSR), India and China use 45% of the world's water supply.

WHAT IS ALUMINIUM HYDROXIDE?

This is a chemical used in water treatment to remove impurities.

WHAT IS THE WATER CYCLE?

MOST OF THE Earth's water (around 97%), is contained in the oceans. The polar ice caps hold a further 2%. The remainder (just 1%) is continually recycled through a natural process called the water cycle. The heat of the Sun evaporates water from the sea, lakes and rivers. This produces water vapour, which is held in warm air in the atmosphere. When the vapour moves to a cool area it condenses, forming clouds, and eventually falls to the surface as rain, hail or snow. This waters the land and feeds the world's water supplies. Most of the water then returns to the oceans, and the cycle continues.

Clouds

Rain and snow

Ground water

Lakes and rivers

Evaporating water

Sea

HOW LONG HAVE HUMAN BEINGS BEEN FARMING?

The first farmers grew and cultivated crops in the Middle East around 12,000 years ago. Different varieties of wheat and barley were the main crops. They were grown, as they are today, to produce grain to make bread. Knowledge of farming spread from the region into Europe and Asia, while the native peoples of North and South America began farming around 7000BC.

Springtime is when the fields are ploughed, ready for the crops to be planted.

WHAT IS INTENSIVE FARMING?

DEMAND FOR FOOD in the modern world means that the production of crops and livestock needs to be maximized. Many farms use a range of machinery and chemicals to practice what is known as intensive farming. Tractors plough fields and plant seed, while combine harvesters cut the crops at harvest time. Animal pests are controlled with pesticides, and weeds are destroyed with herbicides. Intensive farming methods often raise concerns about animal welfare, as livestock may be kept indoors in cramped conditions for long periods of time.

Combine harvesters are used to harvest grain.

Seeds are sown by machinery that automatically covers them with soil.

Pesticides and herbicides are applied with a sprayer.

WHAT IS SUBSISTENCE FARMING?

IN MANY DEVELOPING countries, subsistence farming is a common way of life. Farmers will normally grow just enough to food to feed themselves and their families, occasionally selling or trading surplus produce at local markets. They will keep small numbers of animals, sometimes for their meat, but more often to work the land.

In some countries, farming methods are employed that have remained unchanged for thousands of years. In such circumstances, the way of life is hard and is very much dependent on the weather and the quality of the harvest.

WHICH IS THE MOST WIDELY-GROWN CROP?

GRAIN IN the form of wheat, corn (maize) or rice is the most important food crop in the world. As the basic ingredient of bread, wheat is grown throughout the world, often in very large quantities. Rice is grown in paddy fields throughout Asia, forming the basic foodstuff in that part of the world. Intensive farming methods mean that the amount of grain grown per hectare (the yield) in the USA is four times that produced from the same area in Africa.

WHAT IS SELECTIVE BREEDING?

ONLY VARIETIES of crops that grow and taste the best have been cultivated over time, resulting in improved size, flavour and appearance of crops. Certain breeds of animals have been bred to produce livestock that gives more meat. This is known as selective breeding.

Modern breeds of cattle have been developed through years of selective breeding.

HOW DOES A COMBINE HARVESTER WORK?

A COMBINE HARVESTER is an important machine on a modern grain farm. It allows a very large amount of grain to be harvested very quickly. A combine harvester is so called because it does both of the processes involved in harvesting the grain – cutting the crop and separating the grain from the plant. Before the combine harvester, one or both of these jobs was done by hand or by two separate machines.

The thresher separates the grain from the stalks.

Two more augers are used to unload the grain.

An auger works like a screw to send stalks to the conveyor.

The rotating reel sends the stalks to the cutting bar.

The conveyor takes the stalks to the thresher.

The cutter at the front slices the wheat stalks.

WHAT IS GENETIC MODIFICATION OF FOOD?

The genetic modification of food sets out to improve crops and livestock by altering their genetic make-up. Crops can be bred that are resistant to pesticides or extreme weather conditions, allowing them to be grown more efficiently, or in places that they could not grow before. Many people are concerned about the effects this may have on the environment and public health.

WHAT IS ORGANIC FARMING?

Organic farming is very different from intensive farming. It uses natural fertilizers and pesticides rather than artifical ones. Animals are often allowed to enjoy a more natural life than in "factory" farming.

WHAT IS A FOOD MOUNTAIN?

Sometimes, the amount of a crop grown for a market exceeds the demand. Large quantities of the foodstuff may be stockpiled, hence the term "food mountain".

WHAT ARE CASH CROPS?

Cash crops are those grown specifically for trade and economic reasons. Coffee and rubber grown in developing countries may be described as "cash crops".

HOW DOES A FAMINE HAPPEN?

Famines normally occur in areas that rely heavily for food on crops grown locally. Should weather conditions result in a poor harvest, there may be a severe shortage of food in the whole area.

WHAT IS AGROFORESTRY?

Agroforestry is a system of growing trees and crops together.

WILL THE WORLD EVER RUN OUT OF FISH?

Fishing is a very important global industry, but it can only exist as long as there are fish to catch. In some parts of the world, stocks of fish have decreased dramatically, due in part to modern fishing methods. As demand for fish has increased, so greater numbers of boats have fished the same areas. Technology has also made locating fish easier. Using nets too fine to allow small fish to escape has decreased the numbers of younger fish, which affects breeding and future stocks. While it is unlikely that stocks of fish will run out completely, many countries place strict controls on fishing, in an attempt to limit the damage.

Trawling: nets are trawled at various depths, depending on the type of fish being caught.

Purse-seining: the nets are towed in a large circle to catch the fish.

WHAT ARE THE DIFFERENT WAYS OF CATCHING FISH?

THE FISHING INDUSTRY uses several different methods to catch large numbers of fish. They mostly involve the use of nets. Trawling uses a cone-shaped net towed behind the fishing boat (known as a trawler). Purse-seining involves surrounding a school (group) of fish with a net and drawing the net lines together. Drift nets may be as long as 95km (60 miles). Left to drift in the water, they can catch many millions of fish at once.

Drift nets are very effective but can harm other marine life.

WHERE ARE THE BEST PLACES TO CATCH FISH?

THE AREAS OF SEAS and oceans where most fish are caught are called fishing grounds. Most of the world's fishing grounds are found above the continental shelf – relatively shallow areas around the coastlines of the world. Fish are attracted to these areas because ocean currents create feeding grounds there.

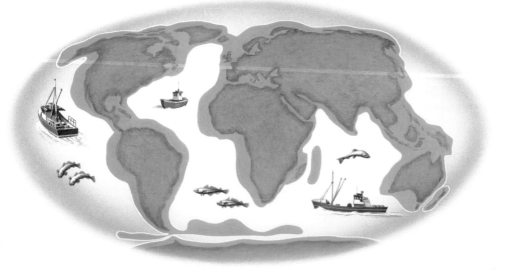

The blue areas of this map show where most of the world's fish are caught.

HOW ARE SHELLFISH CAUGHT?

SHELLFISH SUCH as crabs and lobsters are caught using baskets or netting pots. These baskets or pots sit on the seabed, with their position marked on the surface by a floating buoy. The opening of the basket or pot is designed so that the fish can get inside easily but cannot get out.

Shellfish are caught in fairly shallow waters close to the coastline. The fishermen lay the pots or baskets and return later to retrieve the catch.

WHAT ARE FISH FARMS?

SOME FISH are bred in controlled conditions called fish farms. Fish farmers build special pens in lakes, ponds or estuaries. Here, they hatch fish from eggs and keep them until they are big enough to sell. Also known as "aquaculture", fish-farming is becoming increasingly common. Freshwater fish farms breed salmon, carp and trout. Oysters and other shellfish are popular in coastal fish farms.

Fish farms are an efficient way of supplying stocks of fish. This farm in Iceland is used to produce salmon, one of the most commonly farmed fish.

IS EARTH THE ONLY PLANET TO SUPPORT LIFE?

As far as we know, the Earth is the only planet in our Solar System capable of supporting life. It has all the things necessary to support life as we know it – water, carbon, oxygen, nitrogen and an abundant supply of food. Life on Earth is incredibly diverse, and the systems that support it are very complex.

Despite the efforts of astronomers and other space scientists, we have yet to find evidence of life on a planet other than our own.

HOW DO SCIENTISTS STUDY THE BIOSPHERE?

SCIENTISTS WHO study the relationships between different forms of life on Earth are called ecologists. They divide up the biosphere into different, related sections, which makes the relationships easier to understand. These sections are the *niche*, the *habitat*, and the *ecosystem*.

WHAT IS THE BIOSPHERE?

THE BIOSPHERE is the part of the Earth in which life exists. It covers an area that stretches from the very bottom of the oceans to some way above the surface of the Earth.

An ecosystem is a particular part of the biosphere that contains living things.

A habitat is an area in which communities of different species live together.

A niche is where a plant or animal exists within its habitat, and includes its relationship to other plants and animals.

HOW BIG IS AN ECOSYSTEM?

AN ECOSYSTEM is any area that can support different living things, and as such can be almost any size. A droplet of rain may contain bacteria and other microscopic living things that live off one another, and could therefore be described as an ecosystem.

An ecosystem may be as small as a droplet of water or as large as a forest.

DOES THE EARTH RECYCLE ITS RESOURCES?

THE EARTH is continually recycling the essential ingredients for life – carbon, oxygen, nitrogen and water. All plants and animals play their part in this recycling process.

All living things need the oxygen in the atmosphere.

Plants and trees take in carbon dioxide and give out oxygen during the day.

Carbon is the basis for all living things and is found in carbon dioxide gas.

At night, plants and trees take in oxygen and give out carbon dioxide.

Living things use the nitrogen in the atmosphere to create proteins.

Animals breathe in oxygen and give out carbon dioxide.

Bacteria in the soil help release nitrogen and carbon dioxide back into the environment.

Decaying plant matter and animal wastes release nitrogen into the soil.

WHAT DOES THE OZONE LAYER DO?

OZONE IS a very important gas in the Earth's atmosphere. It screens out some of the harmful ultraviolet rays that come from the Sun. The ozone layer is a very fine layer of the gas that surrounds the Earth at a height varying between 15 and 50km (between 9 and 30 miles).

Ozone makes up a very small part of the Earth's atmosphere.

fast facts

WHAT IS BIODIVERSITY?

If a habitat or ecosystem has a large number of different species living within it, it is said to have a high degree of biodiversity. Ecologists use biodiversity as a measure of the relative ecological "health" of an area.

WHAT WOULD EARTH BE LIKE WITHOUT LIFE?

If there were no longer any life on Earth, the atmosphere would probably be very similar to that of the planet Mars – dry and low in oxygen. All the nitrogen in the atmosphere would move to the oceans.

WHAT IS THE GAIA THEORY?

The idea that the Earth is a single living organism that looks after itself is known as the Gaia theory. Named after a Greek term meaning "Mother Earth", it was developed by the scientist James Lovelock in the 1970s.

HOW LONG HAVE HUMANS BEEN ON EARTH?

Humans have lived on Earth for around 35,000–40,000 years. In the context of the history of the Earth, which is around 4.6 billion years old, it is a very short period of time.

WILL LIFE ON EARTH EVER END?

This is a question that is often asked. Dinosaurs lived for around 10 million years, until they were wiped out by a major catastrophe, generally thought to have been an asteroid colliding with our planet. Such an event, or the long-term ecological destruction of the Earth, could see the elimination of certain species, but some kind of life would probably replace them.

WHO WAS ERNST HAECKEL?

The German biologist Ernst Haeckel coined the word "ecology" in 1869.

HOW HAS HUMANKIND ENDANGERED THE EARTH?

Human beings have affected the Earth's environment like no other species on the planet. The destruction of rainforests, pollution from industry and transport, and wasteful use of resources are just some of the ways in which people have put the Earth in danger.

Oil spillages at sea can cause serious damage to coastlines and marine wildlife. Cleaning up afterwards is costly and time-consuming.

WHAT IS GLOBAL WARMING?

THE "GREENHOUSE EFFECT" is a natural process through which gases in the atmosphere trap the Sun's heat and warm the Earth. Industrial activities such as burning fossil fuels have added to the levels of carbon dioxide and other "greenhouse gases" in the atmosphere. This has increased the greenhouse effect, causing the Earth to get hotter than it would have done naturally.

Heat from the Sun

Some heat radiates back into space.

Some heat is reflected back by Earth, clouds and the atmosphere.

Heat is trapped in the atmosphere.

The Earth is warmed by heat trapped in the atmosphere.

The atmosphere warms up.

The Earth is warmed by the Sun.

Water in the air mixes with gases.

Poisonous gases are released from factories and power stations.

Polluted water falls as acid rain, snow or sleet.

The environment is damaged.

WHAT IS ACID RAIN?

WASTE GASES from factories, such as sulphur dioxide and nitrogen dioxide, combine with water in the air to produce sulphuric and nitric acid. This falls as acid rain, sleet or snow. It pollutes rivers and lakes, kills trees and even eats away at buildings.

WHAT ARE CFCs?

CFCs (CHLOROFLUOROCARBONS) are another example of greenhouse gases. They are found in aerosol sprays, refrigeration and air-conditioning systems, and certain types of foam packaging. Awareness of the damage caused by CFCs has meant that some products are labelled as "CFC Free".

Some aerosol sprays contain CFCs, but awareness of the damage that they cause has led to safer alternatives being used.

IS THERE A HOLE IN THE OZONE LAYER?

GIVEN THE RIGHT CONDITIONS, CFCs can also damage the ozone layer. The CFCs combine with very cool air, producing chlorine – a substance that eats away at ozone. Ozone loss is worst at the area above the South Pole, where a complete "hole" was confirmed in 1985. Reduced ozone levels mean that a greater amount of the Sun's harmful ultraviolet rays will reach the Earth's surface, affecting human and animal health, as well as damaging food crops.

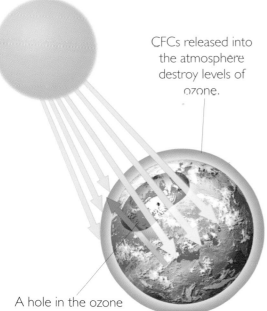

CFCs released into the atmosphere destroy levels of ozone.

A hole in the ozone layer allows ultraviolet (UV) radiation through.

You need to protect yourself from exposure to UV radiation when in the sunshine. It is UV rays that cause sunburn and can cause skin cancer in the long term.

WHAT CAN I DO TO HELP PROTECT THE ENVIRONMENT?

EVERYONE CAN do things to help save the environment – here are a few things you could do. Using recycled paper and card is a good way to start, as is making sure that all the glass, cans, and paper that your family uses is sent for recycling. Try to use public transport instead of travelling by car and encourage others to do the same. Switch off lights and other electrical appliances when they are not in use. Make sure that all aerosol products you use do not contain any CFCs.

High levels of traffic in cities are the main cause of smog. Some countries have attempted to deal with the problem by restricting traffic and encouraging the use of cleaner fuels. Smog, and air pollution in general, continues to be a major problem and is the cause of some respiratory diseases, such as asthma.

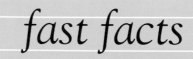
fast facts

WHERE DOES MOST ACID RAIN FALL?

Acid rain tends not to fall in the regions in which it is created as it is carried away by weather systems. Scandinavian counties are affected by pollution created by the heavily-industrialized areas of Britain, Eastern Europe and Germany. It is thought that half of the acid rain that falls in Canada comes from its neighbour, the USA.

ARE GOVERNMENTS DOING ANYTHING TO HELP SAVE THE EARTH?

In the last 50 years, people have become aware of environmental problems and some countries have entered agreements to reduce the use of CFCs, cut levels of vehicle emissions and control industrial pollution. The problem is that many governments and companies will avoid employing environmentally-friendly systems if they are costly.

WHAT IS A CATALYTIC CONVERTER?

Emissions from petrol engines contain harmful chemicals, such as carbon monoxide and nitrogen oxide, that produce smog and affect people's health. A catalytic converter attached to a vehicle's exhaust converts these chemicals into less harmful carbon dioxide, nitrogen and water.

WHAT IS A LANDFILL SITE?

Most household rubbish is buried in a hole in the ground called a landfill site.

WHAT IS SMOG?

Many of the world's large cities suffer from smog (literally smoke + fog). Exhaust emissions from motor vehicles are the main source of smog. The situation is made worse in strong sunlight, when warm air above the level of smog traps it at ground level.

WILL THE WORLD'S POPULATION CONTINUE TO GROW?

Around a thousand years ago, the world's population began to increase dramatically, with the sharpest increase occurring during the 20th century. In the year 2000, the world's population reached six billion, and its growth shows no sign of stopping. Many people fear that an ever-increasing population will lead to serious problems with food supply and overcrowding.

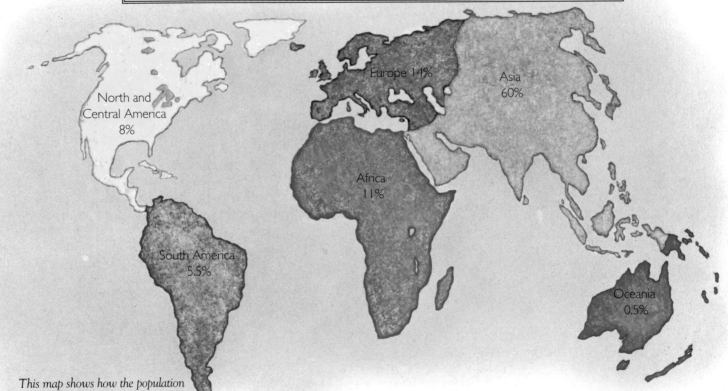

Europe 14%

Asia 60%

North and Central America 8%

Africa 11%

South America 5.5%

Oceania 0.5%

This map shows how the population is distributed throughout the world.

WHICH IS THE WORLD'S MOST POPULATED COUNTRY?

CHINA HAS been the world's most populated country for some time. This vast country is home to over one billion people – around one sixth of the world's total. In an effort to control the growth in numbers of people there, the government has encouraged families to have only one child.

IS THE WORLD'S POPULATION GETTING OLDER OR YOUNGER?

THE AVERAGE age of a population varies from country to country. In the more developed parts of the world, the population is generally older. High standards of healthcare allow people to live longer, and families tend to have fewer children. In poorer countries, life expectancy is shorter and many babies die at birth. As a result, families have more children, which means that the population is generally younger.

WHAT IS URBANIZATION?

IN THE MODERN WORLD, more and more people live in towns and cities. This is mainly because of employment opportunities – there are generally more jobs to be found in urban areas – but also because modern building methods allow more people to live in a smaller area. Roughly half of the world's population lives in cities, and this proportion is expected to increase.

More and more people are moving to the world's cities in search of jobs. This is especially true in developing countries, where cities are becoming very overcrowded.

WHY DO SOME PEOPLE MIGRATE TO OTHER COUNTRIES?

THE MOST common reason that people move to other countries is to seek work. Modern North America was founded through mass immigration – its population grew from 31 to 92 million between 1860 and 1910. Some people may leave their home country because of war, or for political or religious reasons. These people are known as refugees.

The first European immigrants arrived in America in 1620. They sailed in a small ship called the Mayflower. *The Pilgrim Fathers, as they are known, named their settlement Plymouth, after the town in England from which they set sail.*

During the 19th and 20th centuries, millions of immigrants arrived in the United States from Europe. The first thing many saw on their way into New York was the Statue of Liberty. Nearby Ellis Island was the site of the USA's main immigration station for many years.

WHAT ARE INDIGENOUS PEOPLES?

The human race is made up of many different nationalities and groups of people. Indigenous people are those who are native to a certain area. The term is often used to describe the original inhabitants of areas that are now populated by people from other parts of the world.

WHO ARE THE NATIVE AMERICANS?

AROUND 20,000 YEARS AGO, the first settlers of North America arrived from Asia. They were able to travel over land, because at the time, the two continents were joined together. These early settlers gradually formed different tribes and spread themselves throughout the whole country. When the first Europeans arrived during the 15th century, they thought they had landed in Asia, and called the Native Americans "Indians". The relationship between the Indians and the new settlers was difficult, and many battles were fought.

Some Native American peoples were nomadic, travelling the Great Plains in pursuit of buffalo. They erected temporary shelters made from buffalo hides when they made camp.

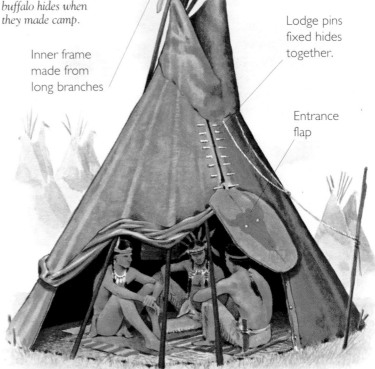

Lodge pins fixed hides together.

Inner frame made from long branches

Entrance flap

Many Native Americans live on reservations – areas of land specially set aside for them by the US government during the 19th century.

The Inuit traditionally build temporary hunting lodges, called igloos, from blocks of ice.

WHO ARE THE INUIT?

THE INCREDIBLY HARSH environment of the Arctic is home to a group of people who settled there around 4000 years ago. They inhabit parts of Siberia, Alaska, Canada and Greenland. Those who live in North America are known as Inuit, which literally means "real men". Many Inuit continue their traditional lifestyle – hunting for food and furs to sell – but being part of both modern and traditional worlds can be hard, especially for young people.

WHO ORIGINALLY LIVED IN AUSTRALIA?

THE FIRST PEOPLE to live in Australia arrived there about 40,000 years ago from Southeast Asia. These people were named "Aborigines" (people who have lived there since early times) by the European settlers who arrived in Australia during the 18th century. Life has been difficult for many Aboriginal Australians, forced to adapt to the settlers' ways of life. Today, youngsters are being taught about their own rich heritage.

WHAT IS THE DREAMTIME?

THE NATURAL environment is very important to Australian Aborigines. This is because they traditionally believe that the world was created by human, animal and plant ancestors in something called the Dreamtime. The Dreamtime is celebrated and communicated through art, songs, dancing and story-telling.

WHO LIVED ON EASTER ISLAND?

ONE OF THE great mysteries of the world is the identity of the people who inhabited Easter Island in the South Pacific. The island is famous for the mysterious stone statues found there. It is believed that they were carved by tribes of people who lived there during neolithic times (more than 1000 years ago). Very little is known about these people, but they are thought to be the ancestors of the people of the islands of Polynesia.

There are more than 600 ancient statues on Easter Island. Some of them are over 20m (65ft) tall.

The fortress city of Machu Picchu was an Inca stronghold. Built over a series of terraces in the spectacular setting of a remote Peruvian mountain, it remained undiscovered by the Spanish conquistadors.

HOW ARE CIVILIZATIONS WIPED OUT?

GROUPS OF PEOPLE can be wiped out when their way of life is threatened by a sudden change of circumstances. One of the best known examples of this happened in the early 16th century, when Spanish conquistadors conquered the Incas and Aztecs of South America. More than 70 million indigenous people were wiped out by diseases such as smallpox and measles, which were brought from Europe by the Spanish. With no history of these diseases, the Incas and Aztecs had few natural defences against these illnesses.

fast facts

WHAT IS COLONIALISM?

During the 19th century, many European countries set about gaining influence in countries around the world. This "colonialism" was usually done for economic or military reasons, and often resulted in the exploitation of the native peoples.

WHO WERE THE LAST PEOPLE TO BE "DISCOVERED"?

Tribes of people living in the forests of Papua New Guinea were unknown to the West until the 1930s.

WHERE DID THE MAORIS COME FROM?

The Maoris arrived in New Zealand around 1000 years ago from the islands of Polynesia, thousands of miles away in the Pacific Ocean. According to Maori legend, they arrived in just seven small canoes.

WHERE DO PYGMIES LIVE?

There are many groups of Pygmies – "small people" – many of whom live in the rainforests of Central Africa.

WHO ARE THE MASAI?

The Masai are a nomadic tribe of cattle-herders who roam around the borders of Kenya and Tanzania in Africa.

WHAT IS RELIGION?

A religion is a set of beliefs that attempts to make sense of the things in life that are difficult to understand, such as why we are here. Human beings have always sought explanations about the world, and various religions have developed in order to provide some answers. Most religions are based around the teachings of one God or several gods – supreme beings who created the world and determine what happens in it. Religions have been an extremely powerful force in human history, inspiring art and culture and shaping countries and empires.

The story of Jesus was passed on through the gospels in the New Testament part of the Bible. These seem to have been written by the Apostles – men who knew Jesus.

WHAT DO CHRISTIANS BELIEVE?

CHRISTIANITY is a religion that has one God. Its followers – Christians – believe that Jesus Christ was the Son of God and that he lived to show people the way to eternal life with God through the forgiveness of sins (wrongdoing). A key Christian belief is that Jesus was killed by his enemies and then rose from the dead to join God in heaven. Christianity is the world's largest religion, with more followers than any other.

WHO WAS MOHAMMED?

MOHAMMED WAS a 7th-century prophet who founded the religion of Islam. Islam's followers – Moslems (or Muslims) – believe that many prophets, including Jesus Christ and Moses, have carried the word of one God, named Allah. For Moslems, Mohammed was the greatest prophet of them all. His word is revealed in the Koran – the sacred book of Islam.

WHICH WAS THE FIRST RELIGION TO HAVE ONE GOD?

JUDAISM, the religion of the Jewish people, was the first to have only one God. Jews believe that Judaism began in the Middle East 4000 years ago when God's word was revealed to Abraham, the father of the Jewish people. God told Abraham that the Jews would be his chosen people in return for obeying his laws and spreading his message. Throughout their history, Jewish people have suffered persecution in many parts of the world.

The city of Jerusalem is a holy city for Christians, Moslems and Jews. Partly for this reason, it has become a place of tension and conflict instead of peace and understanding.

WHAT IS BUDDHISM?

BUDDHISM BEGAN in Northern India about 2500 years ago. It was founded by an Indian prince called Siddhartha Gautama, who had become upset by the suffering of the world. After travelling and meditating for three years, he adopted the name Buddha, which means "Enlightened One". Buddhists, like Hindus, believe in reincarnation and karma. The ultimate aim of all Buddhists is to achieve Nirvana – a state of absolute peace.

Images of the Buddha represent him sitting on a lotus flower. The image reminds Buddhists of his goodness.

WHERE DID HINDUISM ORIGINATE?

HINDUISM IS one of the world's oldest religions. It began in India some 5000 years ago and developed gradually from various early beliefs in the region. Those who follow the Hindu religion worship many different gods, and there are lots of different Hindu sects. Most Hindus believe in reincarnation – that a person's soul moves to another body after death. Those who lead good lives are reborn in a higher state; those who do not may return as an animal or insect.

Shiva rules over life and death.

Brahma is the creator.

Vishnu brings peace and order.

Vishnu, Brahma and Shiva are the three most important Hindu gods.

fast facts

WHAT IS ANIMISM?

Early religions were based around the belief that a spirit or god existed in everything. This is called animism.

WHAT IS A MISSIONARY?

Missionaries are people who travel to spread the word of their own religion to those who have not adopted its beliefs.

WHAT IS SECULARISM?

Secularism is the belief that people should be taught things without a religious emphasis.

WHAT IS A SECT?

A sect is a group of people with particular views within a religion. They sometimes demand strict conformity and may be shunned by the mainstream leaders of their religion.

WHAT IS SHINTOISM?

This is a Japanese religion based on the worship of the gods of nature.

WHEN DID SIKHISM BEGIN?

THE SIKH FAITH is a relatively new religion, which began in about 1500. Its founder, Guru Nanak, came from the Punjab region of Northern India. He and nine other "gurus" set out the basic beliefs of Sikhism in the Guru Granth Sahib – the religion's sacred book. Sikhs believe that God is found in all things.

WHAT IS MEDICINE?

All human beings are likely to suffer from disease or illness at some point in their lives. Medicine is a science that attempts to identify, prevent and treat diseases that affect humans. Diseases are usually treated with drugs or surgery, although preventative treatments, such as vaccinating against diseases before they occur, are an important part of medical science today.

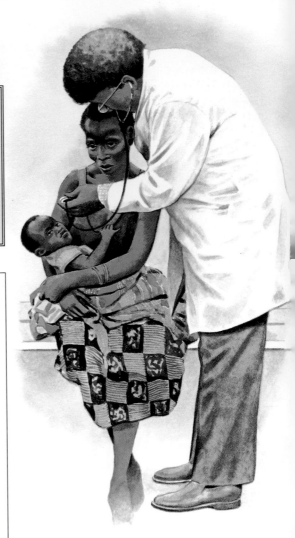

Visiting a doctor is taken for granted by most people in the western world. In some countries, however, there may on be one doctor for many thousands of people.

HOW HAS TECHNOLOGY CHANGED MEDICINE?

MODERN TECHNOLOGY allows doctors and other medical specialists to make a more accurate diagnosis of a problem and to treat patients more effectively. Scanners can produce an x-ray or ultrasound image of the whole body, making it possible to identify problems and begin treatment at an early stage. This helps to increase the chance of the patient making a good recovery.

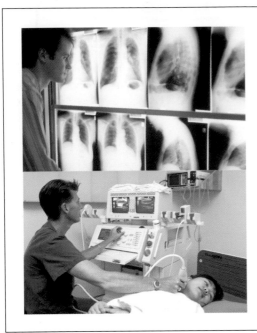

Ultrasound and x-ray machines are just two examples of the way in which technology has revolutionized modern medicine.

HOW ARE DRUGS PRODUCED?

MODERN MEDICINE uses thousands of different types of drugs, which come from a variety of sources. They can be broadly divided into those that are derived from natural sources such as plants and herbs, and those that are produced artificially from chemicals. A recent development involves genetically engineering certain bacteria to produce a drug for a specific purpose.

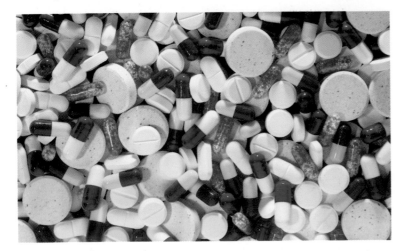

The production of pharmaceuticals is one of the world's biggest industries.

WHAT CAUSES DISEASE?

DISEASES ARE CAUSED in many different ways. Infectious diseases are those that can be passed from person to person. They are usually caused by tiny organisms called viruses and bacteria. Influenza (flu) is a disease caused by a virus; typhoid and cholera are caused by bacterial infections. Certain diseases are passed on to children by their parents at conception. These are called hereditary diseases.

The flu virus is spread amongst people by coughing and sneezing.

WHICH PEOPLE ARE MOST AT RISK FROM DISEASE?

SOME PEOPLE MAY be more at risk from disease than others. In many developing countries, people may be short of food or may not have access to clean water. In such circumstances, they are at risk from nutritional diseases such as scurvy and rickets, as well as those that thrive in areas with poor sanitation, such as cholera and hepatitis. In industrialized nations, the population may have an increased risk of cancer and heart disease, brought about by high-fat diets and unhealthy lifestyles.

Despite having good medical services, people in the West risk their health through an unbalanced diet.

WHAT IS IMMUNIZATION?

PEOPLE CAN be protected from certain diseases by being given a weakened version of the germ that causes a disease. This is called immunization. A successful immunization programme has completely eliminated the disease of smallpox. Immunization programmes are especially important for developing countries.

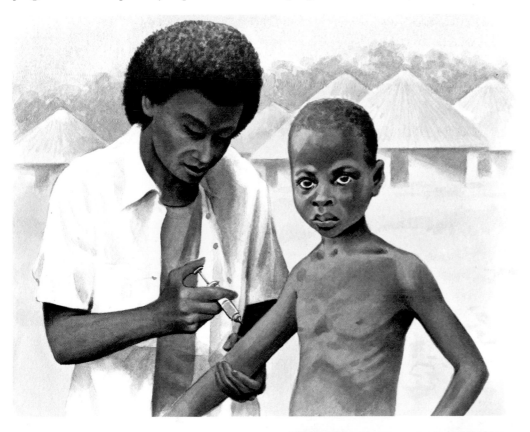

WHAT ARE ANTIBIOTICS?

SPECIAL DRUGS called antibiotics are used to treat diseases caused by bacteria. Early antibiotics were made from moulds and fungi, but today they are produced artificially from chemicals. Antibiotics work by breaking down the cells of the bacteria. There is some concern that the continued use of antibiotics could create problems for the future because the bacteria are becoming resistant to the drugs.

WHO DISCOVERED PENICILLIN?

Penicillin was the first antibiotic drug. It was discovered by chance by Alexander Fleming in 1928. It was not suitable for use in its natural state and 11 years of development were needed before it was of practical use.

WHAT IS COMPLEMENTARY MEDICINE?

Mainstream medicine is not the only way that illness and disease are treated. There are a number of treatments that are used as an alternative to, or alongside, regular medical treatment. Therapies such as acupuncture or homeopathy often take a "holistic" approach – treating the whole person, not just the illness.

WHAT IS A MEDICINE MAN?

In some cultures, illness is believed to be caused by the presence of evil spirits in the body. The community will look to a Shaman, also known as a witch-doctor or medicine man, to provide a cure. The medicine man will perform a ritual that involves communicating with the spirit world and using herbal preparations.

WHAT IS AN EPIDEMIC?

An epidemic describes a situation where a disease affects a large number of people at the same time. Malaria, a disease carried by mosquitoes in tropical countries, has killed more people than any other disease. It infects around 10 million people every year, most of them in Africa.

WHAT IS ACUPUNCTURE?

Acupuncture is a form of alternative medicine that involves puncturing the skin with needles at certain specific points.

Antibiotics, created in laboratories, have been very effective in controlling bacteria-based diseases.

WHEN DID PEOPLE FIRST BUILD HOUSES?

In very early times, people probably lived in caves, moving from one cave to another as they roamed around, hunting for food. It is thought that some of the first people to settle down in one place did so in what is now Palestine, around 13,000 years ago. The Natufians, as they are known, built circular huts made from mud, reeds and wood. They lived in these and used them to store grain.

Wooden chalets in Alpine regions have steep-sloped roofs to prevent snow collecting on them.

Wood is a plentiful material in cold, forested areas and makes an ideal building material.

WHY DO BUILDINGS VARY BETWEEN COUNTRIES?

THE CONSTRUCTION and style of houses vary greatly from country to country. This is due mainly to a combination of the materials available locally and the type of weather that the region experiences.

Mud houses often have small windows and thick walls, which help to keep out the fierce heat of the day.

In very hot countries, houses are often made of mud. Low levels of rainfall mean that the mud stays hard.

Space is limited in large towns and cities, so the best option is to build upwards. Flats can house large numbers of people in a small area.

DOES ANYONE STILL LIVE IN CAVES?

THERE ARE some parts of the world where people still live in caves. However, they are often far removed from the prehistoric dwellings of our ancestors. Indeed, many of them are in spectacular locations and have all the facilities of any other modern home.

This is a modern cave dwelling in Matmata, Tunisia, Africa.

These skyscrapers dominate the skyline in an area of Paris, France. Very tall buildings offer architects the chance to use interesting shapes and surfaces.

Reinforced concrete is made by combining liquid concrete with steel rods.

A crane is used to lift building materials into position.

The strength of the frame allows lightweight materials such as glass and aluminium to be used on the outside of a skyscraper.

HOW DOES A SKYSCRAPER STAY UP?

SKYSCRAPERS – very tall buildings – are a familiar sight in many of the world's large cities. Ordinary buildings are constructed in such a way that the walls provide support for the whole structure. A skyscraper is so tall, and the weight of the building is so great, that a frame of steel or concrete is needed to support it. The foundations of the skyscraper are also important. Beams (piles), also made of steel or concrete, are driven into the ground with a powerful machine called a pile-driver.

HOW ARE TUNNELS BUILT?

TUNNELS ARE built for many different reasons, such as carrying water and sewage beneath cities and providing access for people, trains and motor vehicles. "Cut-and-cover" is a common method of building tunnels in urban areas – a deep trench will be dug and then covered over. Long transport tunnels, which may go through mountain-sides or underwater, are usually made with enormous boring machines. As a rotating cutting head cuts out rock at the front of the machine, sections of tunnel-lining are fitted in behind. Two machines will often be used, one starting at each end.

Subways keep pedestrians safe.

Transport tunnels carry cars and trains.

Service tunnels carry water or sewage.

fast facts

WHICH WAS THE WORLD'S FIRST SKYSCRAPER?

The first building to be called a skyscraper was the 10-storey Home Insurance Building in Chicago, USA. It was completed in 1885.

HOW DO WE FIND OUT ABOUT RUINED BUILDINGS?

Archaeologists can tell us a lot about buildings from the past. The foundations, walls and other parts of a building's structure can be uncovered by digging through layers of earth. Using knowledge of other buildings, archaeologists can build up a picture of what the building looked like.

WHAT WILL HOUSES BE LIKE IN THE FUTURE?

A big feature of houses in the future will be energy conservation. They will probably be better insulated and use alternative fuel sources.

WHAT IS ARCHITECTURE?

Architecture refers to the style and design of a building. Architects aim to design buildings that are visually attractive and comfortable to inhabit.

WHAT IS A SHANTY TOWN?

Cities in developing countries are often surrounded by "shanty towns" – groups of makeshift houses built by those who have nowhere else to live.

WHAT IS ADOBE?

Bricks of sun-baked mud used to build houses are called adobe.

WHAT IS A YURT?

A yurt is a type of tent used by nomads in Mongolia, Asia.

HOW IS INFORMATION SENT AROUND THE WORLD?

Satellites receive signals from transmitters on Earth and send them back to various receivers.

In the modern world, we can access information in ways that could only be dreamt about just 50 years ago. Information can travel around the world via television, radio, telephone and computer networks, all of them connected by satellite or cable links. Modern communication systems, or media, allow almost anyone to transmit and receive verbal, visual and written information wherever they are in the world.

Signals are used for communication and provide navigation assistance for ships and planes.

WHAT WERE THE EARLIEST FORMS OF COMMUNICATION?

Early people probably communicated through a combination of primitive sounds and basic sign language. Languages may have evolved through a need for survival – warning others of danger, for instance. They developed gradually as people used the spoken word for instruction and entertainment. Oral communication, particularly through story-telling, was and still is an important part of a society's culture.

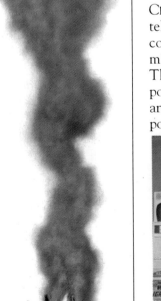

WHAT IS MASS MEDIA?

CERTAIN FORMS of media, particularly television and newspapers, are able to communicate to thousands, or even millions of people at the same time. These mass media can have a very powerful influence on their audience, and often reflect the particular viewpoint of the media-owner.

In early times, news could only travel as fast as a messenger could travel. Smoke signals were one of the first attempts at long-distance communication.

WHY DO COMPANIES ADVERTISE?

COMPANIES USE all forms of media to advertise their products and services. Advertising began simply as a way of telling people about a product, but it is now much more sophisticated. It is used to present the image of a company in a certain way and also to target a particular audience that the company feels it can attract. In this way, the company associates itself with a certain lifestyle. Advertising is a huge business, with large companies investing huge sums of money in anything from sports sponsorship to putting their logo on the side of a milk carton.

We are exposed to advertising almost everywhere. These electronic hoardings are advertising products in Tokyo, Japan.

HOW DOES THE INTERNET WORK?

THE INTERNET is a global network of millions of computers that can communicate with one another. Information can be sent and received across the network in the form of text, pictures, video and sound. Home computers often connect to the Internet using a normal phone line and a modem – a device that connects the computer to an Internet Service Provider (ISP). Businesses and other large organizations may have their own network, known as a Local Area Network (LAN), which connects to an ISP with a high-speed link.

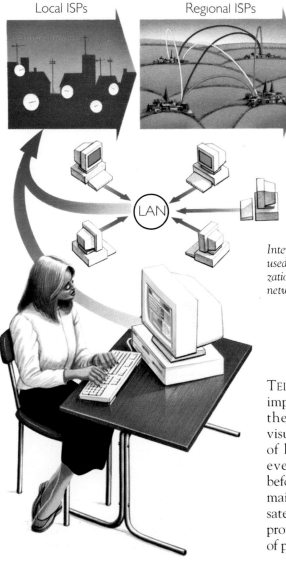

Local ISPs   Regional ISPs   Global ISPs

LAN

Internet Service Providers (ISPs) connect computers used in homes, businesses, schools and other organizations to the Internet. The Internet is all of these networks of computers connected together.

HOW HAS TELEVISION CHANGED OUR LIVES?

TELEVISION WAS undoubtedly the most important communications invention of the 20th century. Its ability to bring visual information directly into millions of homes made people aware of world events in a way that they never were before. It quickly overtook cinema as the main form of entertainment, and modern satellite, cable and digital television now provides people with an incredible choice of programmes, 24 hours a day.

fast facts

WHEN WAS THE FIRST TELEVISION BROADCAST?

Scottish engineer John Logie Baird demonstrated a mechanical "visual wireless" in 1926, but the first television service began in Britain in 1936.

WHAT IS PROPAGANDA?

Propaganda is the spreading of information, usually used to promote a certain kind of religious or political thinking. The use of mass media to spread propaganda has had a very powerful and influential effect.

CAN YOU WATCH TELEVISION IN SPACE?

When television signals are transmitted, they pass through the atmosphere and into space. This means that even astronauts can tune in to their favourite TV shows!

WHAT WAS TELSTAR?

Telstar was the name of the first satellite to send television pictures. It was used to transmit live images from the USA to Europe in 1962.

WHAT WAS CUNEIFORM?

Cuneiform was an early form of writing that used symbols to represent the sounds of words.

The Apollo Moon landing of July 1969 was a global television event when over 700 million people tuned in to watch live pictures of the landing.

WHAT IS A SOCIETY?

A society is a community of people. All societies around the world are based on families, but the way societies are organized and governed varies from country to country. Religion, politics, economics and climate all influence the way that a society develops and organizes itself.

HOW DO FAMILIES DIFFER?

THE WAY that families live together can vary hugely from country to country and even within the same country. The term "nuclear family" describes an arrangement where two parents bring up their children in the same home. Extended families are those where several generations live together. In some societies, men and women may live separately most of the time, each with defined social roles.

The nuclear family is a common living arrangement in some parts of the world.

In extended families, many relatives live, and very often work, together.

HOW ARE COUNTRIES GOVERNED?

IN THE MODERN WORLD, most countries are led by governments. A government makes decisions on behalf of the population to organize public services, maintain law and order and manage the economy. It is also responsible for the defence of the country. A government raises taxes from its people to finance its activities. In a democracy, the people choose the government by voting for candidates in an election. An autocratic government is not elected by its people and is normally ruled by one person.

WHAT IS A PARLIAMENT?

IN MANY DEMOCRATIC countries, such as the United Kingdom, political matters are debated in an elected assembly. The political party with the most elected members forms the government, headed by the Prime Minister. Laws and decisions are passed (or rejected) on the basis of votes cast by the members of parliament (MPs). Many parliamentary systems have two assemblies. The United Kingdom has the House of Commons and the House of Lords. The House of Commons has the most power and makes most of the decisions.

The speaker chairs debates.

Members of the government, including the Prime Minister, sit together.

Representatives of the opposition parties sit opposite the government.

In the United Kingdom, debate between MPs takes place in a formal room called the "Chamber".

WHAT IS A REPUBLIC?

A REPUBLIC is a country where the head of state (the leader) is a president elected by the people. The president appoints heads of administrative departments to help make decisions. Their decisions are discussed by an assembly of elected representatives, who can pass or block the laws. In the USA, the assembly is called Congress. Congress may suggest its own laws, which the president has the power to overrule. Most republics have a third level of government, a judiciary, which reviews the laws. The highest judiciary in the USA is the Supreme Court.

The Capitol Building in Washington DC houses the US Congress, the elected representatives of the United States government.

Karl Marx was a German philosopher.

WHAT IS COMMUNISM?

COMMUNISM is a type of political and economic system devised by the German thinker Karl Marx in the 19th century. The idea of the communist system was that property and wealth should be shared by the people and that everyone should be treated equally. Unfortunately, many countries that adopted Communism found it difficult to put these high ideals into practice. Many people lost their freedom, and the governments struggled to control the economy.

Defence lawyer   Judge   Prosecution lawyer

Witness

Defendant on trial

Jury

In some countries, ceremonial dress, such as gowns and wigs, is still worn by officers of courts of law.

HOW ARE PEOPLE TRIED FOR CRIMES?

IN MANY COUNTRIES, someone accused of a serious crime will be tried in a court of law in front of a judge and jury. The jury is chosen at random from the general public and is usually made up of 12 people. The accused person – the defendant – will be represented by a lawyer, who will try to convince the jury that his or her client is not guilty. The prosecution lawyer will try to establish guilt. Judges are usually appointed by the state. They advise the jury and decide on any punishment necessary.

fast facts

WHAT DOES "GOVERNMENT" MEAN?

The word government is taken from a latin word – *gubernare* – meaning "to steer".

WHY DOES A COUNTRY NEED LAWS?

The laws of a country are usually decided upon by the government and enforced by the police and a legal system. Laws are designed to protect society from crime and also to settle disagreements over such things as money and property.

WHO INVENTED POLITICS?

Politics has its origins in Ancient Greece. The philosopher Plato was the first to discuss government and politics in *The Republic*, over 2000 years ago. Democratic traditions and the discussion of ideas became central to the way Greece was governed.

WHO MADE THE FIRST LAWS?

The first laws were probably made by the Babylonians, whose civilization flourished in the Middle East around 4000 years ago. The laws covered things like property, slaves and wages. Penalties were enforced for those who broke the laws.

WHAT IS CAPITAL PUNISHMENT?

In some countries, people may be sentenced to death if they have committed a very serious crime. This is called capital punishment. Many countries have abolished the death penalty, and in places where it still exists, it is often never applied. In the USA, prisoners facing the death penalty can spend many years in prison on "Death Row" while their sentence is subject to appeal.

WHAT IS INDUSTRY?

Industry organizes the provision of things that people need to live their lives, from essential items such as food and water, to luxury goods like toys and chocolate. Without industry, we would have to produce everything we need ourselves. Not all industries produce goods. Service industries offer a service – washing clothes, for example – in return for money.

WHAT IS MANUFACTURING?

MANUFACTURING FORMS the basis of what most people think of as "industry". It means using materials to make a product. There are often many stages of manufacturing between the raw material and the finished product. Many industries involve the assembly of component parts, which will have been made by any number of separate companies.

WHAT IS A PRODUCTION LINE?

IT IS RARE in modern manufacturing that something will be made from start to finish by one person. Most factories use a production line to manufacture their products. Each worker has a specific task in the production process – adding a particular component or operating a certain machine, for example. As each task is completed, the product passes along the line for the next stage of production. Some production lines, particularly in the motor industry, are entirely or partly automated. Robots play a large part in the assembly of many products.

The car body is assembled from component parts.

The body is sprayed in the paint plant.

The assembled body is treated and prepared for painting.

The body is attached to the chassis, and the engine is fitted.

The interior and other components are added, and the car is ready to be driven away.

WHAT IS MASS PRODUCTION?

MASS PRODUCTION is the manufacture of goods on a large scale. It aims to produce the maximum number of goods for the lowest possible cost. The use of production lines and automation allows the manufacture of near-identical, interchangeable parts. Modern techniques of mass production were pioneered by the American motor-car manufacturer Henry Ford. Production of the Ford Model T revolutionized the way that all manufacturing industries carried out their business.

Over 15 million Ford Model Ts were made between 1908 and 1927. It was the first car to be made using methods of mass production. The car was inexpensive, reliable and cheap to run. It brought motoring to those who could not previously afford it.

WHAT WAS THE INDUSTRIAL REVOLUTION?

AROUND THE middle of the 18th century, changes took place that greatly affected the way that people lived and worked. The Industrial Revolution, as it is known, began in Britain and spread to Europe and then to the United States. New machines and inventions allowed goods to be produced more quickly, and huge factories were built, leading to the rapid growth of industrial towns. People began to move from the countryside to the towns in search of work, but they often ended up living in miserable conditions.

Steamships travelled the world.

Bridges and other structures were built from iron and steel.

Railways and canals revolutionized passenger travel and the transportation of goods.

Towns grew rapidly as factories were built, along with houses for the workers.

WHEN WERE TOOLS FIRST USED?

THE EARLIEST human beings began to make use of tools around 35,000–40,000 years ago. Sharpened flints were used to skin animals and fashion implements from wood and bone.

HOW ARE GOODS MOVED AROUND THE WORLD?

ALL FORMS of transport are used to move goods around the world. Cargo planes are by far the quickest method, but are very expensive. Where large amounts of goods need to be transported over great distances, ships are the cheapest method. Container ships carry metal containers of a standard size, which can hold almost anything. Once in port, the containers are easily transferred to trains or lorries. For shorter sea journeys, lorries and their cargoes are driven on to Ro-Ro (roll on, roll off) ferries in one port and driven off at another.

Container ships are the main way of transporting goods across the world. The largest ships can carry several thousand containers.

WHAT IS THE WORLD ECONOMY?

Most of the world's countries trade goods and services between themselves. The transactions that take place make up the world economy. The global marketplace exists partly because countries need things that they cannot produce themselves. Also, richer countries will buy goods from places where the costs of production are low and the goods are cheap. Modern transport and communications have allowed the world economy to develop.

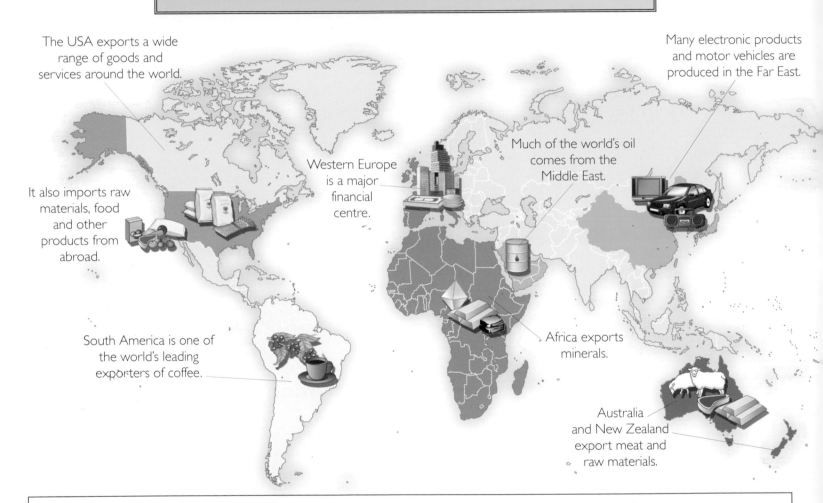

The USA exports a wide range of goods and services around the world.

It also imports raw materials, food and other products from abroad.

South America is one of the world's leading exporters of coffee.

Western Europe is a major financial centre.

Much of the world's oil comes from the Middle East.

Many electronic products and motor vehicles are produced in the Far East.

Africa exports minerals.

Australia and New Zealand export meat and raw materials.

WHAT IS A BALANCE OF PAYMENTS?

THE GOODS OR SERVICES that one country sells to another are called exports; the things that it buys from abroad are called imports. Imports need to be paid for with the money made from exports – the balance between the two is called the balance of payments. Not all countries can afford to pay for everything that they need, so they borrow money from wealthier countries and large banks. This has led in part to the large gap between the world's richest and poorest countries. Many so-called "developing countries" need to use all the money they make from trade simply to repay the interest on loans.

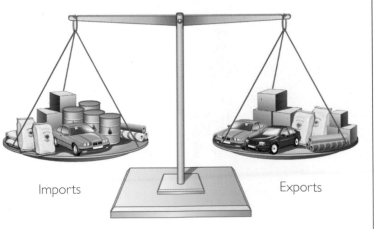

Imports   Exports

HOW ARE BANKNOTES PRINTED?

PAPER MONEY needs to be designed and made in such a way that it is very difficult to forge. Banknotes have extremely complicated designs, with pictures and backgrounds made up of very fine lines and patterns. These are printed from hand-engraved steel plates. The notes are also printed on a special type of paper, which is hardwearing and has a strip of plastic or metal embedded in it.

HOW HAS SHOPPING CHANGED IN THE PAST CENTURY?

SHOPPING HABITS have changed enormously in the past 100 years. At one time, goods were mainly purchased from various specialist shops – meat from a butcher and vegetables from a greengrocer, for example. In many countries, it is now more common for households to buy everything from one store and to visit shopping centres, where individual shops are housed under one roof. Also, since the late 1990s, the Internet has allowed more and more people to do their shopping without leaving home.

HOW DID MARKETS BEGIN?

MARKETS HAVE been around for thousands of years – long before the first shops. They were set up in towns where trading routes crossed. Salesmen, known as pedlars, travelled between markets, buying and selling goods. People also sold surplus goods or things that they had made. Goods were often exchanged for other goods, a practice known as bartering, and people always argued, or haggled, over a price.

Markets are still common all over the world. They are often good places to find a bargain, if you know what to look for. In some countries, it is still common to negotiate a price with the stallholder.

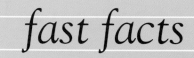

fast facts

WHAT IS A STOCK MARKET?

Companies may allow people to invest in them by offering "shares". These are known as stocks and are bought and sold on a stock market.

WHAT IS A TRADE AGREEMENT?

Countries often sign trade agreements between themselves to try to ensure economic stability. They may fix a price for a certain product and restrict or exclude other countries. Breaking trade agreements can lead to fierce disputes and, sometimes, war.

WHAT IS A MINT?

A mint is a factory where both coins and paper currency are produced. Coins are usually made of copper, nickel, brass or a combination of all three metals. They are stamped with a design, the coin's value and its year of manufacture – a process known as minting.

WHAT IS THE "BLACK ECONOMY"?

The "black economy" involves the trade of illegal goods, such as drugs, and transactions that avoid taxation and other official controls.

WHEN WAS MONEY INVENTED?

It is thought that "money" in the form of various weights of silver was used in Mesopotamia over 4000 years ago. The first coins were probably used in what is now Turkey around 2700 years ago.

WHAT IS A "CRASH"?

A very large and rapid drop in the price of shares is called a crash.

WHAT IS A "TAKE-OVER"?

When one company buys another, the event is called a take-over.

GLOSSARY

Architecture The style and design of buildings.

Biosphere The parts of the Earth's atmosphere, land and water where living things can exist.

CFCs (Chlorofluorocarbons) Chemicals used in aerosols, refrigerators and air conditioning systems that are partly responsible for damaging the ozone layer.

Civilization A group of people or a nation that, through its organization, customs and culture, has become historically important.

Coke Fuel produced by refining certain types of coal to remove impurities. Used as an industrial and domestic fuel.

Community A group of people identified by belonging to a certain group, organization or place.

Coral A marine organism, which has a skeleton made from calcium carbonate (lime) extracted from the sea in which it lives. Large numbers of coral skeletons build up to form coral reefs.

Crust The rocky outer layer of the Earth.

Deforestation The destruction and clearing of forests for agricultural and other uses without replanting.

Democracy A system in which a country's government is chosen by the people.

Desertification A process in which areas of land turn to desert. It is caused by climate change, some intensive farming methods and deforestation

Ecology The science of the relationship between living things and the environment in which they live.

Ecosystem A community of living organisms and the particular area in which they exist.

Erosion The process by which rocks and soils are broken up, worn down and taken away. It can be caused by the action of wind, water, glaciers or a change in the rock itself.

Geology The science of the Earth, its history and structure.

Glacier A huge mass of ice, which forms in areas where layers of snow and ice build up over long periods.

Igneous A type of rock formed from solidified lava.

Immigration The movement of people into a country for the purpose of settling there.

Irrigation Diverting water supplies to land or crops by digging channels or building pipelines.

Magma Molten rock that lies beneath the Earth's surface. Lava is magma that emerges through a volcano.

Media Means by which information is communicated, often to large numbers of people at the same time.

Metamorphic A type of rock formed by the effects of heat and pressure over time.

Mineral A naturally occurring, non-living substance with a certain chemical make-up. Rocks are made from one or more minerals.

Oceanography The study of the oceans and the living things that inhabit them.

Ozone A highly reactive gas that forms a layer in the atmosphere. It protects life on Earth from the Sun's damaging ultraviolet rays.

Pangaea A name for the Earth's original "supercontinent" that existed around 220 million years ago.

Petroleum The term scientists give to naturally occurring oil and gas.

Plateau An area of very level ground. Plateaux may be found at the bottom of rift valleys.

Sedimentary rock A type of rock formed when layers of material are compressed over long periods.

SPACE

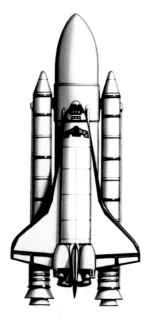

WHAT DOES THE UNIVERSE CONTAIN?

The Universe contains quite literally everything – from you and me to the most distant stars. It is everything and anything that exists, occupying an unimaginably vast area. Distances in space are so immense that light from the furthest galaxies takes over 10 billion light years to reach Earth, even though light travels fast enough to go round the Earth several times every second. Everything that you can see in the night sky lies in our Universe, from the Sun to far-off gas clouds like the Eagle Nebula (right).

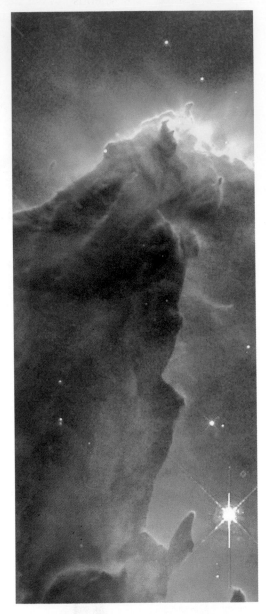

HOW DID THE UNIVERSE BEGIN?

ALTHOUGH NOBODY can be sure how the Universe began, most scientists believe that it was born from an enormous explosion 13 billion years ago. This explosion, called the "Big Bang", was the point where space and time came into existence and all of the matter in the cosmos started to expand. Before the Big Bang, everything in the Universe was compressed into a minuscule area no bigger than the nucleus of an atom. The Big Bang was an unimaginably violent explosion that sent particles flying in every direction. A process called cosmic inflation caused the Universe to expand into an area bigger than the entire Milky Way in less than a second. Moments later, the temperature began to decrease, and the Universe began to settle down. Stars and galaxies began to form roughly one billion years after the Big Bang.

The temperature of the Universe during the first second of its existence was over 100 million trillion trillion degrees. During this second, the building blocks of the Universe formed.

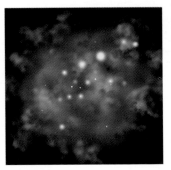

After three minutes the Universe cooled to one billion degrees. Protons and neutrons began to combine, forming heavier elements such as helium.

300,000 years after the Big Bang, the temperature dropped to 3000 degrees. Electrons began to join with atomic nuclei to form neutral atoms.

These incredible cloud patterns are actually stellar nurseries, where stars are being born all the time. Everything that can be seen in the night sky is part of the known Universe.

CAN WE PROVE THERE WAS A BIG BANG?

THE IDEA OF THE "Big Bang" was first suggested in the 1920s by an astronomer named Edwin Hubble. He discovered that the Universe was expanding and suggested that it must have been much smaller in the past. The most convincing argument for the Big Bang lies in the presence of cosmic background radiation. This is an echo of the energy released by the Big Bang, and was detected in 1965 by two astronomers. Scientists believe that the only possible source of this radiation is the dying heat of the Big Bang.

In 1992 the COBE satellite took this microwave image of the Universe. The ripples are the afterglow of the Big Bang.

DOES THE UNIVERSE HAVE AN EDGE?

ALTHOUGH WE KNOW THE UNIVERSE is expanding, nobody knows for sure what it is expanding into. Some scientists claim that it is not expanding into anything because nothing exists outside the Universe. Instead, space itself is stretching to accommodate the expanding matter. The Universe has no outside edge, and no centre because the force of gravity distorts everything within it.

Gravity affects everything in the Universe, even space itself. If the Universe contained enough matter, then space could bend so much that it doubled back on itself. A spaceship leaving Earth and travelling in a straight line would never find the edge of the Universe…

…but would arrive back at Earth trillions of years later. This concept is called a closed universe. Although it extends forever, it has no edges.

HOW DO WE KNOW IF THE UNIVERSE IS CHANGING SIZE?

ASTRONOMERS CAN GAUGE the movement of a star using a technique called the Doppler effect. All stars and galaxies emit electromagnetic radiation. The wavelengths of any form of electromagnetic energy are affected by movement – the radiation emitted by an object moving towards an observer is squeezed, moving towards the blue end of the spectrum where wavelengths are shorter (blueshift). The wavelengths of an object moving away are stretched, and move towards the red end of the spectrum (redshift). Most of the stars and galaxies in the Universe have redshifted, meaning that everything is drifting apart.

The electromagnetic energy from a star moving away from Earth is stretched, making it appear red.

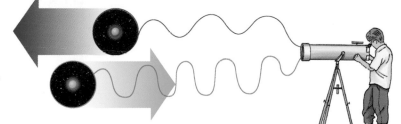

fast facts

IS THE BIG BANG THE ONLY THEORY ABOUT HOW THE UNIVERSE BEGAN?

There have only been a handful of alternative theories to the Big Bang. The Steady State Theory suggested that the Universe had no beginning, and that although it is expanding, it stays in perfect balance all the time.

WHAT IS A CELESTIAL OBJECT?

Any object seen in the sky, such as a planet, moon, star or galaxy, is called a celestial object.

HOW BIG IS THE UNIVERSE?

In 1995 the Hubble Space Telescope took a photograph of a speck of the sky no bigger than a grain of sand. In this small space alone were thousands of galaxies. If the entire sky is as densely populated as this, then the Universe must be large enough to contain over fifty billion galaxies.

WHAT IS THE MOST DISTANT THING IN THE UNIVERSE?

Quasars – the powerful cores of remote galaxies – are the most distant things in the Universe. Some were formed over twelve billion years ago.

WHERE IS EARTH IN THE UNIVERSE?

It is impossible to pinpoint exactly where the Earth lies in the Universe because of the distortion of space. However, astronomers are able to tell where Earth lies in relation to its surroundings.

Our planet orbits one of 200 billion stars in the galaxy called the Milky Way. The Milky Way stretches over 100,000 light years.

The Milky Way itself is part of a collection of galaxies called the Local Group, the diameter of which is over 5 million light years.

The Local Group is part of one of millions of Local Superclusters that stretch across hundreds of millions of light years.

WHAT IS THE SOLAR SYSTEM?

The Solar System is everything that orbits our star – the Sun. Caught in the Sun's immense gravitational pull are nine planets, over 60 moons and millions of asteroids, meteoroids and comets. Pluto is the furthest planet from the Sun, but the Solar System does not end there. Surrounding the planets is a vast sphere of comets – the Oort Cloud. Objects beyond this are pulled away from the Solar System because the Sun's gravity is not strong enough to hold them.

WHAT IS AN ORBIT?

AN OBJECT'S ORBIT is the path it takes around another, more massive object in space. Each of the nine planets in the Solar System is held in orbit by the Sun's gravitational pull. However, the planets do not orbit the Sun in circular paths but in elliptical (oval) ones. Orbit lengths, and the orbital period (the time it takes a planet to complete one orbit) increase with successively distant planets.

Inner planets: Mercury, Venus, Earth and Mars

Outer planets: Jupiter, Saturn, Uranus, Neptune and Pluto

Mercury, 57.9 million km (36 million miles) from the Sun

Venus, 108.2 million km (67 million miles) from the Sun

Earth, 150 million km (93 million miles) from the Sun

Mars, 228 million km (142 million miles) from the Sun

Jupiter, 779 million km (484 million miles) from the Sun

Saturn, 1.4 billion km (886 million miles) from the Sun

Uranus, 2.9 billion km (1.8 billion miles) from the Sun

Neptune, 4.5 billion km (2.8 billion miles) from the Sun

Pluto, 5.9 billion km (3.7 billion miles) from the Sun

WHAT IS THE DIFFERENCE BETWEEN THE INNER AND THE OUTER PLANETS?

THE PLANETS in the Solar System form two very different groups – inner and outer. The inner planets, often called terrestrial planets, are composed mainly of rock and metal, with solid surfaces, no rings and few satellites. The outer planets, called Jovian or Gas Giants, are much larger than their inner neighbours. They are composed primarily of hydrogen and helium, have very deep atmospheres, rings and lots of satellites.

ARE PLANETS AND MOONS THE ONLY THINGS IN THE SOLAR SYSTEM?

PLANETS AND MOONS are just a few of the objects orbiting the Sun. Astronomers already know of thousands of large rocky bodies called asteroids (shown right), and icy objects called comets. Millions of smaller rocks, called meteoroids, also orbit the Sun.

HOW DID THE SOLAR SYSTEM FORM?

OUR SOLAR SYSTEM formed from the force of an exploding star. When some stars reach the end of their lives, they can explode into a supernova, sending shockwaves of energy deep into space. Roughly 4.6 billion years ago, a shockwave from a supernova, travelling at 30 million kilometres (19 million miles) per hour, hit a cloud of ice, dust and gas. The force of the impact caused the cloud to flatten and rotate. From this spinning disc, our Solar System began to form.

1 A dying star exploded, shedding energy and material into space. When the shockwave hit a nearby cloud of debris and gas, it enriched it with elements such as carbon.

2 The cloud began to rotate and shrink, causing many of the particles within it to group at its centre. As they impacted against each other, they heated up, becoming a protosun.

3 Throughout the cloud, pieces of debris collided against each other and joined together. These rocky lumps grew larger and larger, and gradually formed into planets.

4 When the centre of the cloud reached 10 million °C (50 million °F), nuclear reactions began, and the Sun was born. The force of the explosion blew away the loose dust and gas.

WHAT ARE PLANETS MADE OF?

ALL OF THE planets in the Solar System formed from the same cloud of debris. The inner planets have solid cores of iron, surrounded by rocky mantles, topped with a very thin silicate crust. The Gas Giants have solid cores of rock and ice, but these are much smaller in proportion to those of the inner planets. Jupiter and Saturn are made of hydrogen and helium, which becomes denser towards their centres. Uranus and Neptune both have mantles of icy water, methane and ammonia.

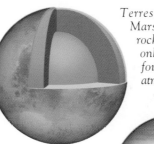

Terrestrial planets like Mars are made up of rock and metal. The only gases are those found in their small atmospheres.

Jupiter and Saturn are roughly 90% hydrogen and 10% helium. This is very close to the make-up of the original gas cloud from which the Solar System formed.

WHY ARE PLANETS SPHERICAL?

WHEN THE PLANETS were forming, they were in a molten state. In any object, gravity pulls from the centre, and parts of the object at the same distance from the centre are pulled inward with equal force, creating a sphere. This will only happen to objects with sufficient mass, such as planets and stars. Smaller objects, such as asteroids, have a weaker gravitational force, so they cannot pull themselves into a spherical shape. Gravity is also responsible for denser materials being pulled to the centre of a star or planet.

fast facts

HOW BIG IS THE SOLAR SYSTEM?

Measured from opposite ends of the Oort Cloud, the Solar System is roughly 1.6 light years in diameter. It fills a volume of 15 trillion kilometres.

WHICH PLANET HAS THE LONGEST ORBIT?

The orbits of the planets increase the further they are from the Sun. This makes Pluto the planet with the longest orbit. It takes 247.68 Earth years to complete one circuit of the Sun. This is so long that it has not even travelled half its orbit since its discovery in 1930.

WHY IS PLUTO THE ODD PLANET OUT?

Pluto is a mystery to astronomers because it is so different from both the inner and the outer planets. It is much smaller than any other planet in the Solar System and made of rock, metal and snow.

WHICH PLANET HAS THE HIGHEST VOLCANOES?

Venus, Earth and Mars all have enormous volcanoes, but those on Mars are the most impressive. Because of its smaller size, Mars has weaker gravity than Earth or Venus, allowing the lava from volcanic eruptions to build up higher. Also, Mars' crust is in a fixed position, meaning that volcanoes happen in the same place many times, each lava flow adding to the height of the last.

WHERE DO ASTEROIDS AND COMETS COME FROM?

After the planets formed, a great deal of loose material remained, but it was no longer being thrown together with the force needed to create planets. This debris became asteroids and comets.

WHY IS THERE LIFE ON EARTH?

Earth is the only place in the Solar System on which scientists have encountered life. Conditions on our planet are perfect for sustaining life – the surface temperature averages around 15°C (59°F), allowing water to exist in liquid form. Water is a vital ingredient for life, and its presence on Earth has enabled an incredible variety of creatures to live on every part of the planet. Also, Earth is large enough to contain a protective atmosphere, but not big enough to become a suffocating gas planet like Jupiter or Saturn.

The Earth began to form around 4.6 billion years ago. It started life as a huge ball of liquid rock. Gradually, the surface began to cool and harden.

HOW DID LIFE DEVELOP ON EARTH?

FOR MUCH OF ITS EARLY HISTORY, Earth was a bubbling, volcanic ball – far too hot to sustain life. Over millions of years, the surface of the planet began to cool and harden, releasing enormous clouds of steam and gas. The moisture in these clouds eventually became rain, forming the seas. Scientists believe that the first life-forms originated in shallow pools of water, where different chemicals were concentrated to form single-celled organisms. These gradually evolved into more complex life-forms. All living creatures on Earth are still evolving.

Simple organisms began to form in shallow pools around four billion years ago.

These organisms gradually evolved into fish. Some of these fish made their way on to land, where they became amphibians.

As the Earth became drier, some amphibians evolved into reptiles that could survive better on dry land. Around 220 million years ago the first dinosaurs appeared. They are believed to have been wiped out by a huge meteorite around 65 million years ago.

The first mammals evolved around 200 million years ago. Early ancestors of humans only appeared less than two million years ago. Today, millions of different species cohabit our planet.

WILL THERE ALWAYS BE LIFE ON EARTH?

LIKE ALL STARS, our Sun will eventually die. In around five billion years its supply of hydrogen will run out, and it will become a red giant, expanding to well over thirty times its current size. As it grows, the Sun will engulf all the inner planets, making them far too hot for life to survive.

WHAT IS THE ECOSPHERE?

THE ECOSPHERE is a narrow band around the Sun where the temperature is neither too hot nor too cold for life to exist. Earth is the only planet in this zone, and is therefore the only planet in the Solar System able to support life. Mercury and Venus are too close to the Sun for water to exist in liquid form. The remaining planets lie well beyond the ecosphere, where it is too cold for life. The temperature on Pluto can reach as low as –223°C (–370°F)!

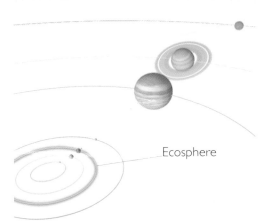

Ecosphere

HOW DID LIFE BEGIN ON EARTH?

NOBODY KNOWS WHAT conditions are needed for life to begin. Some scientists have suggested that living cells may have been brought to Earth by a comet. When the Giotto probe investigated Halley's comet in 1986, it found molecules that were similar to living cells. If a comet like this collided with Earth at the right time, then life may have taken hold. Another theory is that powerful lightning bolts flashing through Earth's early atmosphere may have caused chemical reactions, which created living cells.

HOW LONG HAVE HUMANS LIVED ON EARTH?

HUMAN BEINGS are late arrivals on planet Earth. Humankind's earliest ancestor – *Australopithecus afarensis* – appeared over two million years ago. Neanderthals had evolved by 400,000 years ago, and *Homo sapiens*, modern humans, only existed around 100,000 years ago. Just how short a time this is can be seen when we look at the history of the Earth as a clock, with 12 o'clock midnight being the time that Earth was formed 4.6 billion years ago. Each hour on the clock represents 383 million years.

For the first two hours the planet was forming. Primitive life evolved over billions of years (blue). Dinosaurs appeared at 11.30, lasting less than 30 minutes (purple). Mammals (green) have been around for a very short time, and humans (yellow) for less than a minute.

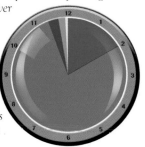

WHAT IS EVOLUTION?

All living creatures exist as they do now because of evolution. This is a process of natural change in a species over many generations. This change enables it to adapt to its surroundings, and therefore to increase its chances of survival. Over many years, the changes that are most successful survive.

CAN WE SEE EVOLUTION AT WORK?

Evolution occurs very gradually and over many generations, so it is very difficult to see. However, scientists experimenting with mice have found that, in cold conditions, some evolve with thicker coats and are therefore more likely to survive.

WHAT IS THE OXYGEN CYCLE?

All plants and animals on Earth depend on each other because of something called the oxygen cycle. Animals breathe oxygen because it is needed to release energy from food. When the oxygen is used up, it is breathed out as carbon dioxide. All plants on Earth need carbon dioxide in order to survive, and they, in turn, change it back into oxygen.

HAS THE EARTH ALWAYS LOOKED THE WAY IT DOES TODAY?

EARTH IS THE ONLY planet in the Solar System that has a surface split into geological plates. These plates are constantly moving, carried on oceans of rocky mantle no faster than two centimetres each year. 250 million years ago all of the plates on Earth were compressed together in a giant super-continent called Pangaea. Over millions of **years** this land mass was pulled apart as forces caused the plates to **move away** from each other.

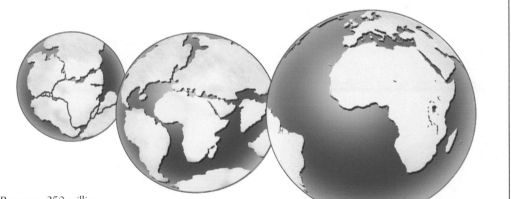

Pangaea, 250 million years ago. Heat from inside the planet caused the individual plates to move slowly apart.

Carried on the partly molten rock of the mantle, the plates move no faster than human hair grows.

The continents will continue to move. If we were able to look at earth in another 250 million years, it would look totally different.

IS THERE ICE ON MERCURY?

Mercury is the closest planet to the Sun, and as a result is a dry, barren planet scorched by solar heat. Parts of Mercury's surface often exceed 450°C (840°F) when the planet is closest to the Sun. However, at night, temperatures can drop by over 600°C (1,100°F), and some scientists believe that there is actually ice in deep craters that never see the Sun. Radar imaging of the planet has revealed areas of high reflectivity near the planet's poles. This may be frozen water carried to Mercury by meteorites.

IS MERCURY A DEAD PLANET?

PLANETS ARE BORN from the countless collisions of rocks and space debris that were part of the early Solar System. The heat from these impacts remains deep within the core of the planet, released through volcanic eruption. Mercury's cratered appearance shows that there has been no volcanic activity on the planet for billions of years. This makes Mercury a dead planet.

WHY DOES MERCURY GET SO COLD?

DESPITE BEING the closest planet to the Sun, often orbiting less than 60 million kilometres away from the star, temperatures on Mercury can drop below –180°C (–290°F). This is because Mercury is too hot and too small to be able to hold on to much gas. With no clouds to stop heat from escaping into space at night, temperatures on Mercury plummet.

WHY IS MERCURY HEAVY?

ALTHOUGH MERCURY is the second smallest planet in the Solar System, it is heavier than Mars, and almost as heavy as Earth. The reason for this is that Mercury has an enormous core of iron – almost 3600km (2237 miles) in diameter.

Craters on Mercury are not as deep as those on the Moon. This is because material ejected by meteorite impacts does not travel so far, due to Mercury's stronger gravity.

There is no wind or water on Mercury, as on Earth's Moon, meaning that its scarred landscape has remained unchanged since the early days of the Solar System.

WHY IS MERCURY DIFFICULT TO SEE?

BECAUSE OF ITS proximity to the Sun, Mercury is a very difficult planet to explore. It is normally obscured by the Sun's glare, which prevents even observatories such as the Hubble Space Telescope from peering at it because of the risk to light-sensitive equipment. Mariner 10 is the only probe to have visited Mercury, but it too could only photograph half the planet.

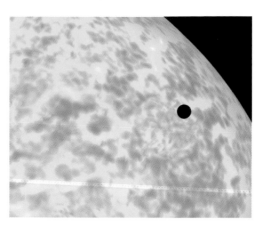

WHAT IS UNUSUAL ABOUT MERCURY'S ORBIT?

MERCURY ORBITS THE SUN more quickly than any other planet, but turns slowly on its axis, completing one rotation in 59 Earth days. The planet spins three times for every two complete orbits of the Sun, meaning that anybody born on Mercury would technically be two years older each day!

WHY IS MERCURY SCARRED?

MERCURY IS ONE of the most heavily scarred objects in the Solar System. Thousands of meteor craters cover the planet, including the largest – the Caloris Basin. This was formed when a piece of rock 100km (60 miles) wide collided with Mercury 3.6 billion years ago. Mercury is also shaped by wrinkles and cracks that formed when the surface of the planet cooled and shrank (right).

fast facts

HOW ARE MERCURY'S SURFACE FEATURES NAMED?

Mercury's surface features are all named after men and women famous for their contributions to the arts. The Beethoven crater is the second largest on the planet, and there are smaller landmarks named after writers, such as Milton, philosophers, such as Sophocles, and musicians, including Mozart and Vivaldi.

DOES MERCURY HAVE ANY ATMOSPHERE AT ALL?

Mercury has a very slight atmosphere consisting of atoms blown from its surface by the power of the solar wind – charged particles released from the Sun.

WHO DISCOVERED MERCURY?

Mercury was known about in ancient times, but the eighteenth-century astronomer Johan Hieronymous Schroeter was the first to make detailed illustrations of Mercury's surface.

HOW DO CRATERS FORM?

Craters form when smaller objects from space collide with a planet or moon. These objects, called meteorites, travel at very fast speeds and are often pulled towards larger objects by their gravitational pull.

When a meteorite collides with a planet or moon, it does so with tremendous force. The impact creates an enormous dent in the ground. Vast quantities of dirt and debris are blasted upwards, making the hole much bigger than the meteorite.

The dirt and debris form rings of mountains around the crater. Chunks of rock make smaller crater holes. Some impacts can be so powerful that they send shockwaves through the planet, creating mountain ranges on the other side.

WHY IS VENUS A KILLER PLANET?

Early astronomers claimed that Venus was Earth's sister planet. They believed that the light and dark areas they saw on the planet through their telescopes were oceans and continents. Modern astronomy has proved that nothing could be further from the truth! The light and dark areas are Venus' suffocating atmosphere – a layer of clouds containing sulphuric acid released by volcanic eruptions. The temperature on Venus can rise to 464°C (867°F), and the heavy layers of cloud make the air pressure on the surface over 100 times that of Earth.

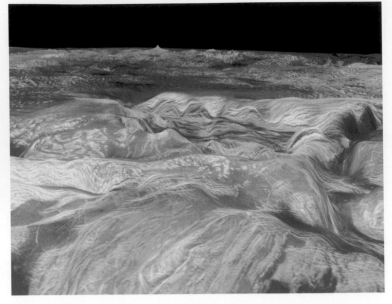

HOW CAN WE SEE PAST VENUS' CLOUDS?

VENUS' ATMOSPHERE is formed from clouds of carbon dioxide, nitrogen and sulphuric acid. This heavy layer of clouds is over 30km (18 miles) deep in some places, meaning that no part of the planet's surface can be seen with the naked eye. Only since the 1970s have scientists been able to "look" past these clouds to see the solid ground beneath. This has mainly been done with equipment mounted on space probes. Radar technology allows probes to record the geography of the planet, and to produce a map of surface features.

WHAT WAS THE MAGELLAN MISSION?

THE MOST DETAILED information about Venus was acquired by a space probe called Magellan. Launched in 1989, Magellan travelled to Earth's neighbour and spent three years building a complete map of the planet. Flying as low as 294km (183 miles) above the surface, Magellan bounced radar pulses off the solid ground beneath and sent the data back to Earth to be analyzed. It measured strips of land 24km (14 miles) wide and 10,000km (6000 miles) long each time it circled the planet, while its altimeter measured its height above the surface.

To the naked eye, Venus appears as a mass of cloud, like the left-hand side of the image above. With the data from Magellan, scientists can see what Venus looks like beneath the clouds (right-hand side above).

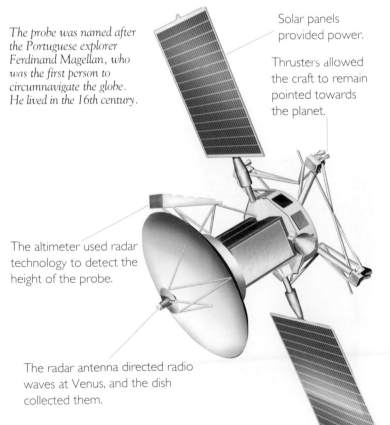

The probe was named after the Portuguese explorer Ferdinand Magellan, who was the first person to circumnavigate the globe. He lived in the 16th century.

Solar panels provided power.

Thrusters allowed the craft to remain pointed towards the planet.

The altimeter used radar technology to detect the height of the probe.

The radar antenna directed radio waves at Venus, and the dish collected them.

HOW DOES RADAR TECHNOLOGY WORK?

RADAR WORKS IN THE same way as an echo. When you shout loudly at a distant wall, you will hear the echo of your voice a few seconds later. This is because the sound waves hit the solid wall and bounce back towards you. Radar uses high-frequency waves that travel much faster and much further. The radar sends out a short burst of radio waves and then listens for an echo, which tells it how far away the target is, and what it is made of.

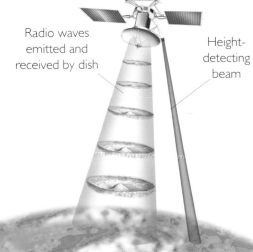

Radio waves emitted and received by dish

Height-detecting beam

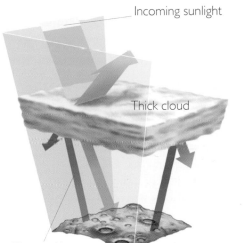

Incoming sunlight

Thick cloud

Trapped heat

WHY IS VENUS LIKE A GREENHOUSE?

LESS THAN 20% of sunlight falling on Venus breaks through the clouds. Despite this, Venus has the hottest surface temperature of any planet in the Solar System. This is because infrared radiation (heat) released from the planet cannot escape back into space. The atmosphere traps heat inside, like the glass in a greenhouse, meaning that the temperature is over 400°C (750°F), greater than it would be if Venus had no atmosphere.

WHY ARE THERE SO MANY VOLCANOES ON VENUS?

VENUS IS covered by hundreds of thousands of volcanoes. This is because the surface of the planet is a thin skin floating on hot molten rock. This lava is vented wherever possible, meaning that, unlike Earth, Venus has volcanoes everywhere. Most of these volcanoes are around 3km (2 miles) wide and 90m (395ft) high, but there are over 160 much larger than this. Some volcanoes on Venus are over 100km (60 miles) in diameter! The volcanic activity on Venus means that the surface of the planet is always changing.

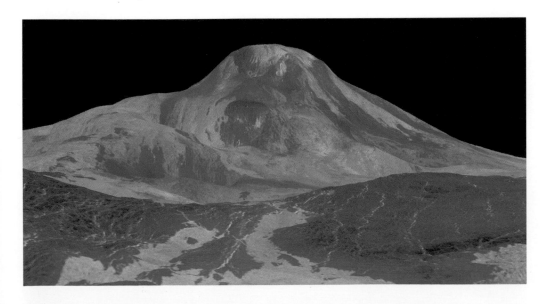

fast facts

WHERE DOES THE TERM RADAR COME FROM?

The word radar is made up of the initial letters of the phrase "RAdio Detecting And Ranging".

HOW BIG ARE VENUSIAN VOLCANOES?

One of the largest volcanoes on Venus is Maat Mons, which rises over 9km (5.5 miles) above the surrounding terrain. Its diameter measures over 200km (120 miles). It lies in a region called Aphrodite Terra, which contains several enormous volcanoes.

WHICH PLANET HAS THE LONGEST DAY?

It takes Venus 243 Earth days to spin once, giving the planet a longer day than any other in the Solar System.

CAN VENUS BE SEEN FROM EARTH?

Venus' clouds reflect a great deal of the Sun's light, which means that the planet can usually be seen clearly from Earth. In fact, Venus is often called a star because it is the brightest object in the sky in the early morning or late evening (depending on the season).

HOW LONG CAN PROBES SURVIVE ON VENUS?

Over twenty spacecraft have landed on Venus since 1970, sending back information about the planet's composition, pressure and weather. Once they have landed, however, the probes do not have long to complete their tasks. The Russian lander Venera 13, which sent back the picture on the left, lasted just over two hours on the surface before it was destroyed by the planet's immense pressure.

HOW FAR AWAY IS THE MOON?

The Moon is Earth's closest neighbour in space. Its orbit around Earth is elliptical, rather than circular, which means that its distance from us varies. At its closest point to Earth (its perigee), the Moon is 363,300km (225,600 miles) away. However, at its furthest distance from the planet (its apogee) it is 405,500km (252,000 miles) away. Incredibly, the Moon's orbit is slowly carrying it away from Earth at a rate of around 5cm (2in) a year.

WHAT IS THE MOON MADE OF?

ALTHOUGH THE MOON'S interior structure is difficult to study, scientists believe that it has a small iron core. Surrounding this is a partially molten zone called the lower mantle. Above this lies the mantle, which is made up of dense rock, and the crust, which is also made of rock. Together, the mantle and the crust form the lithosphere, which can be up to 800km (500 miles) thick. There are only two basic regions on the Moon's surface – dark plains called *maria* and lighter highlands. These heavily cratered highlands are the oldest parts of the Moon's crust, dating back over four billion years. The darker plains are craters that were filled with lava.

IS THE MOON HOT OR COLD?

THE MOON EXPERIENCES temperatures both hotter and colder than those on Earth. When the Sun is directly overhead, the temperature on the Moon's surface is higher than the boiling point of water – 100°C (212°F). However, at night, the Moon becomes very cold, with temperatures dropping to –173°C (–280°F). Earth and the Moon are approximately the same distance from the Sun, and therefore receive the same amount of heat. But the lack of an atmosphere on the Moon means that its temperature range is much more extreme. The Sun's radiation is not filtered out by gases in the atmosphere, and there are no clouds to stop heat escaping at night.

HOW DID THE MOON FORM?

NOBODY KNOWS EXACTLY HOW the Moon formed. The most common theory is that shortly after Earth formed, it was hit by an object the size of Mars. The impact was so powerful that it sent billions of tonnes of molten material into space. This debris was held in orbit around Earth, and eventually solidified to form the Moon.

A large object strikes the young Earth, ejecting material into space.

Caught by Earth's gravity, this material clumps together to form a solid sphere. Over millions of years, it cools and hardens.

Waxing crescent   *First quarter*   *Waxing gibbous*   *Full Moon*   *Waning gibbous*   *Last quarter*   *Waning crescent*

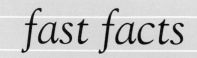

fast facts

WHY DOES THE MOON HAVE PHASES?

LIKE THE EARTH, half of the Moon is always lit by the Sun, while half remains in darkness. Its orbit around the Earth, and Earth's orbit around the Sun, mean that we see the Moon with different amounts of sunlight on its surface. Although it appears to be altering its shape, only the position of the Sun's light on the Moon's surface is changing. These phases follow a cycle from a new Moon, where the dark side is facing us and the Moon appears invisible, to a full Moon, where the entire sunlit part is visible.

WHY IS THE SKY ALWAYS BLACK ON THE MOON?

IF YOU ARE STANDING ON THE MOON, the sky would always appear black, whether it was night or day. This is because there is no atmosphere to scatter sunlight. On Earth, atoms of oxygen and nitrogen in the atmosphere have an effect on sunlight passing through them. Light scatters when it passes through particles that are one tenth as large as the light's wavelength. The atoms of oxygen and nitrogen are one tenth the size of the blue wavelength, so blue light is scattered more effectively than other colours.

WHY DO WE ALWAYS SEE THE SAME SIDE OF THE MOON?

The Moon takes the same time to rotate on its axis as it does to orbit the Earth. Because of this, we always see the same side of the Moon. The far side remained a mystery to astronomers until 1959, when the Russian Luna 3 space probe travelled behind the Moon and sent back photographs.

DOES THE MOON PRODUCE LIGHT?

The Moon has no light of its own. It shines because it is reflecting light from the Sun.

HOW POWERFUL IS THE MOON'S GRAVITY?

The gravitational pull of the Moon is so strong that it is actually slowing the Earth's rotation. This is only happening at a rate of less than two seconds a year, but over thousands of years it can have a serious effect. Scientists studying the growth lines of coral fossils have discovered that a day on Earth was around three hours shorter 350 million years ago.

WHAT HAPPENS DURING A LUNAR ECLIPSE?

A LUNAR ECLIPSE OCCURS when the Earth comes directly between the Sun and the Moon. As the Moon moves through Earth's shadow, the planet prevents direct sunlight from reaching the surface of the Moon. The Moon does not disappear but turns red because Earth's atmosphere bends the Sun's rays.

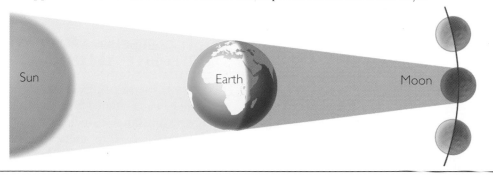

Sun   Earth   Moon

HOW DOES THE MOON AFFECT EARTH?

DESPITE BEING much smaller than the Earth, the Moon still has a great deal of influence on its parent planet. Its gravity is constantly pulling on Earth's surface. This is not noticeable in relation to solid ground, but can clearly be seen in the movement of Earth's tides. Twice a day, the oceans on Earth rise and fall. This is because the Moon's gravitational pull is strongest on the side of Earth that is facing the Moon. Oceans on this side will be pulled into a bulge – high tide. Water on the opposite side is least affected by the Moon's gravity, so it flows away from Earth in another bulge, resulting in another high tide. Areas of Earth at right angles to the Moon, will have low tide.

The Moon's gravity pulls the oceans into a tidal bulge. When the Sun and the Moon are in line, their combined gravitational pull creates larger bulges and a greater tidal rise and fall – called spring tides.

When the Sun and Moon are at right angles to one another, their gravitational pulls tend to cancel one another. This produces smaller tidal pulls that are known as neap tides.

HAS THERE EVER BEEN LIFE ON MARS?

Of all the planets in the Solar System, Mars most resembles Earth. Its day is only slightly over 24 hours, and it is tilted at the same angle as our planet, meaning that seasons are very similar to ours. Early on in its history, Mars had water on its surface. Oceans formed, kept warm by volcanic activity, and primitive life may have started here. Today, freezing conditions on Mars, and the planet's thin atmosphere, mean that life can no longer exist on the planet's surface.

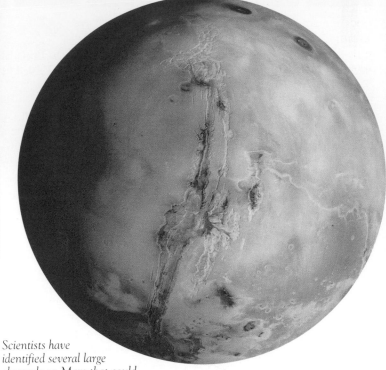

Scientists have identified several large channels on Mars that could only have been formed by running water.

ARE THERE CANALS ON MARS?

IN THE 19TH CENTURY, the astronomer Giovanni Schiaparelli claimed that Mars was covered by a network of channels. Many people believed that these were canals created by an intelligent civilization to help carry water from the polar regions to drier areas around the Equator. Recent photographs of Mars have shown that there are many channels on the planet, but scientists believe these were created naturally by running water billions of years ago.

DOES MARS HAVE AN ATMOSPHERE?

WHEN MARS FIRST FORMED it had a very thick atmosphere. However, the gases have long since disappeared into space due to the planet's weak gravity. Mars' atmosphere is now very thin, and made mainly of carbon dioxide.

WHY IS MARS KNOWN AS THE RED PLANET?

MARS HAS been known as the red planet for thousands of years. The Ancient Romans named the planet Mars because it reminded them of their God of anger and war. Mars gets its striking colour from large amounts of iron oxide (rust) in its soil.

WHAT IS SPECIAL ABOUT THE METEORITE ALH84001?

THE MOST CONVINCING evidence for life on the red planet comes from a Martian meteorite that landed on Earth around 13,000 years ago. This meteorite contained microscopic structures that could have been formed by living organisms.

WHAT IS TERRAFORMING?

TERRAFORMING IS THE process of changing the environment of a planet to make it more like Earth. Many scientists have proposed terraforming Mars as a way of dealing with overcrowding on Earth. Nobody knows exactly how terraforming would work, and whether it would have a damaging effect on Mars' natural environment, but in theory, Mars could be transformed into a second Earth, where many forms of life could live naturally. The diagrams to the right show how it could be done.

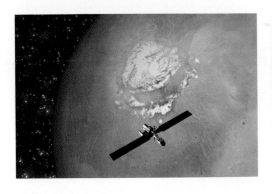

Before beginning, scientists would need to know more about Mars. Probes would visit the planet to find out how much water it contains, and whether there is enough carbon dioxide in its atmosphere to support plant life.

Once these factors are ascertained, the first major step would be to warm the planet by creating a greenhouse effect. This could be done by unfreezing the carbon dioxide locked in the planet's polar caps, either by giant mirrors, or with nuclear waste.

IS THERE STILL WATER ON MARS?

WHEN MARS FIRST formed it had a much thicker atmosphere than it does today. Because the planet's gravity is not very strong, this atmosphere gradually escaped into space. The climate became increasingly cold, and all the water on Mars froze. Today, the water on Mars exists only as an icy, permafrost layer deep in the soil. Temperatures in Mars' polar regions are so low that carbon dioxide in the atmosphere freezes, covering sheets of water ice with a layer of frosty crystals of dry ice.

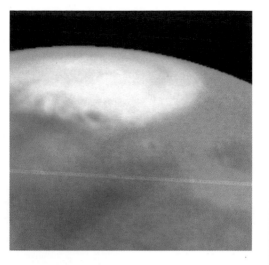

CAN ANYBODY LIVE ON MARS?

AS IT EXISTS TODAY, Mars is a planet hostile to life. Unlike Earth, Mars has no ozone layer to protect life from the Sun's lethal ultraviolet radiation. There is no breathable oxygen in the air, and giant dust storms are common around the planet. The first astronauts to live on Mars will probably do so in large domes that can contain an artificial, Earth-like atmosphere.

WHAT IS THE SURFACE OF MARS LIKE?

MARS HAS ONE of the most dramatic surfaces of any planet in the Solar System. Enormous volcanoes dominate the landscape, the largest of which – Olympus Mons – is over 25 kilometres (15.5 miles) tall. This is three times larger than Mount Everest on Earth! The giant canyon Valles Marineris is long enough to stretch across the entire United States of America.

fast facts

DOES MARS HAVE MOONS?

Mars is orbited by two tiny moons called Phobos and Deimos (which mean "fear" and "panic"). They are so different to Mars that scientists believe they were asteroids captured by the planet's gravitational pull.

WHAT WERE THE VIKING LANDERS?

In 1976, two Viking spacecraft landed on Mars. They were designed to carry out numerous experiments on the planet to determine if there was any sign of life. The landers tested the soil, looking for gases that could have been produced by living organisms. The Viking landers found no conclusive evidence of life on Mars, but some scientists still believe that microscopic organisms may exist there.

This photograph was taken by the spacecraft Pathfinder, which landed on Mars in 1997.

After many centuries, Mars would have a suitable atmosphere. Tiny, car-sized factories on the surface would pump certain chemicals and gases such as nitrogen into the air, allowing plants to grow. Eventually, an ozone layer would develop.

Although the temperature and air pressure would be bearable to humans, they would initially have to carry oxygen tanks because of the lack of breathable air. Eventually, oxygen produced by plants would allow humans to exist naturally.

Gravity on Mars is only one-third that of Earth, which means that people born on Mars might not be able to visit Earth because their bodies would not be able to cope with the pressure. The first Martians to visit Earth could be humans!

WHAT ARE ASTEROIDS?

Planets and their moons are not the only objects in our Solar System. Billions of small rocky bodies, called asteroids, also orbit the Sun. An asteroid, often called a minor planet, is a small body made up of rock and metal left over from the formation of the Solar System. Asteroids can range in size from almost 1000km (610 miles) in diameter, to the size of a small car.

WHAT IS THE ASTEROID BELT?

MOST OF THE ASTEROIDS in the Solar System orbit the Sun in a band between Mars and Jupiter. This band is nearly 550 million km (340 million miles) wide and is called the asteroid belt. There are billions of asteroids in this zone, each moving independently around the Sun and spaced many thousands of kilometres from each other.

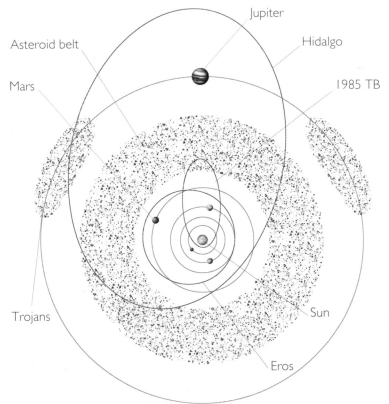

WHAT IS BODE'S LAW?

BODE'S LAW states that there is a pattern in the way the planets are spaced from the Sun. Bode started with the number 0, then took 3, and began doubling: 0, 3, 6, 12, 24, 48, 96, 192, 384, 768. He then divided each number by 10 and added 4. The numbers that he discovered were similar to planetary distances from the Sun in astronomical units. According to Bode's theory, there should be a planet between Mars and Jupiter.

HOW DID THE ASTEROID BELT FORM?

THERE ARE MANY THEORIES about how the asteroid belt developed. Some astronomers believe that it is the remains of a planet that was torn apart billions of years ago. Conversely, others argue that the asteroids in the belt are pieces of a planet that never formed. According to this theory, the immense gravitational pull of the young planet Jupiter prevented the rocks from forming one large body.

HOW CLOSE DO ASTEROIDS FLY TO EARTH?

ALTHOUGH MOST ASTEROIDS DRIFT harmlessly around the Sun for billions of years, some are occasionally knocked out of their orbits. Some of these asteroids pass very close to Earth. In 1994, an asteroid measuring 10m (32ft) in diameter passed within 105,000km (65,000 miles) of our planet – around one third of the distance to the Moon. If a large asteroid were to collide with Earth, the impact could be powerful enough to annihilate all life on the planet. Vast waves of water, dust and fire would flatten cities in seconds, and billions of tonnes of dust entering the atmosphere would block out the Sun's light for hundreds of years.

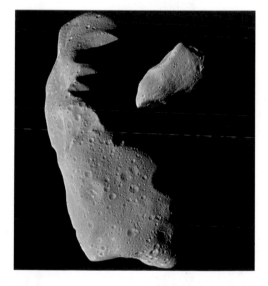

CAN ASTEROIDS HAVE MOONS?

ALTHOUGH ASTEROIDS ARE very small compared to planets, some have a powerful enough gravitational pull to attract natural satellites. As the space-craft Galileo travelled towards Jupiter in 1993, it flew by an unusual pair of asteroids called Ida and Dactyl. Ida is 56km (35 miles) long, and was found to have a moon, Dactyl, that is smaller than 1.6km (1 mile) across (above).

HOW CAN WE FIND OUT MORE ABOUT ASTEROIDS?

SCIENTISTS ARE INTERESTED in finding out more about asteroids. Many are thought to contain minerals and metals that could benefit industries on Earth. The Near Earth Asteroid Rendezvous (NEAR) space probe (below) visited two asteroids, Mathilde and Eros, in 1997 and 1998. It took photographs that showed Mathilde to be entirely covered by craters. Soon, expeditions may be launched from Earth to mine asteroids in space.

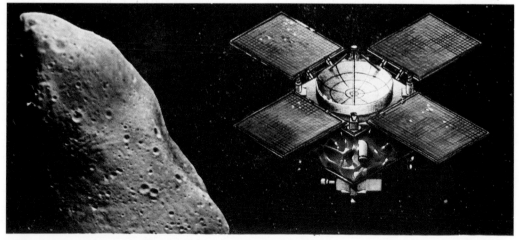

fast facts

WHAT IS THE LARGEST KNOWN ASTEROID?

Ceres is the largest known asteroid. It is almost 1000km (610 miles) in diameter, and contains one-third of the total mass of all the asteroids.

HAVE THERE ALWAYS BEEN SO MANY ASTEROIDS?

When the Solar System was first forming, the asteroid belt consisted of fewer than 700 rocky lumps. Each of these asteroids was larger than Ceres. In the turbulent conditions of the early Solar System, these asteroids collided and began to break up, eventually forming thousands of smaller bodies.

IF THE ASTEROIDS IN THE BELT FORMED A PLANET, HOW BIG WOULD IT BE?

If the asteroids in the main belt could overcome the gravitational battle between the Sun and Jupiter, they might form a planet the size of our Moon.

WHAT IS THE DIFFERENCE BETWEEN ASTEROIDS AND COMETS?

Asteroids are solid lumps of rock and metal, varying in size from 900km (560 miles) to a few metres across. Comets are usually a similar size, but are made up of ice and dust.

COULD JUPITER BECOME A STAR?

Jupiter formed from the same cloud of gases as the Sun. If this giant planet had continued to grow, its core would have ignited into a nuclear furnace, and Jupiter would have become a star. Theoretically, Jupiter could still become a star. If it expands to forty times its present mass, then self-sustaining nuclear reactions will begin within its core – the defining factor of a star.

WHY DOES JUPITER HAVE BANDS OF CLOUDS?

THERE ARE THREE LAYERS of clouds on Jupiter, each made of different molecules. The outer cloud deck is made from ammonia, the middle deck from a combination of ammonia and sulphur, and the inner deck from ordinary water clouds. Heat from Jupiter's interior, and the planet's rapid rotation, cause ferocious winds that create the cloud patterns. The white bands are areas of rising gas, called zones. The dark bands are called belts, and are areas of falling gas. In these belts we are seeing much further into Jupiter, so they appear darker.

WHAT IS JUPITER'S RED SPOT?

THE GREAT RED SPOT is Jupiter's fiercest storm. It is a hurricane over three times as large as Earth that has been raging continuously for over 300 years. Made from gases such as ammonia and clouds of ice, it towers 8km (5 miles) over surrounding clouds. Damp air rising inside the Great Red Spot causes the clouds to rotate, coming full circle every six Earth days.

Jupiter's cloud tops consist of ammonia ice.

Ammonium sulphide clouds lie around 20km (12 miles) below the cloud tops.

Around 30km (18 miles) below the cloud tops lies a layer of water ice.

The deeper the gases in Jupiter's atmosphere, the more pressure they are under. Gases here react to form complex, coloured molecules.

Voyager 1

WHAT WERE THE VOYAGER MISSIONS?

SEVERAL PROBES have flown as far as Jupiter. In 1973, the Pioneer 10 probe flew by the giant planet taking close-up photographs. The Voyager 1 and 2 probes, launched in 1977, flew by the four gas planets – Jupiter, Saturn, Uranus and Neptune – taking pictures and measurements. The primary Voyager missions were completed in 1989, but both craft are now continuing into the depths of the outer Solar System at a speed of over 56,300km/h (35,000mph). Even at this speed it could take the probes over 30,000 years to reach the outer edges of the Solar System!

WHY ARE JUPITER'S MOONS SO VARIED?

Jupiter has at least 16 moons. Twelve of these are smaller than 200km (125 miles) in diameter, but the four enormous Galilean moons are of great interest to astronomers.

Callisto has more scars than almost any other body in the Solar System. These craters were caused by meteorite impacts billions of years ago. Callisto may have a salty ocean beneath its crust of ice.

Ganymede is Jupiter's largest satellite – bigger even than the planets Mercury and Pluto. Its surface is dark and covered with craters.

Io is the most volcanic world in the Solar System. It is caught in a gravitational tug-of-war between Jupiter, Ganymede and Europa. The conflicting pressures mean that heat is generated as molecules on the planet collide with each other, creating numerous violent volcanoes, molten sulphur lakes and enormous lava flows.

Europa is completely covered with a sheet of ice.

HOW DID JUPITER GET ITS RINGS?

JUPITER HAS A VERY FAINT system of rings that was discovered by the Voyager space probes in the 1970s. There are three distinct rings, all formed by material knocked off the planet's four inner moons. Adrastea, Metis, Amalthea and Thebe all orbit very close to the planet, and are constantly bombarded by meteorites. The dust blasted from these tiny moons is added to the planet's rings.

DOES JUPITER HAVE A SURFACE?

NONE OF THE GAS GIANTS has a surface like the terrestrial planets. Instead, the gases that make up Jupiter are put under more and more pressure the deeper they are, so that they gradually change from a gas into a liquid. Further in, the pressure is so great that the gases are squeezed into solid form.

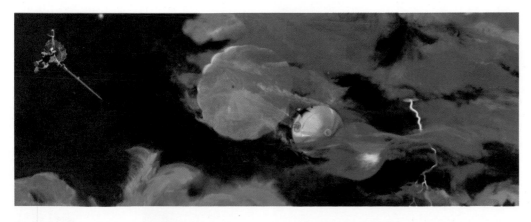

Jupiter has no surface on which to land a space probe, so any craft investigating the giant planet's atmosphere must take a suicidal journey deep into its interior. In 1995, NASA's Galileo Orbiter dropped a small probe into Jupiter's atmosphere. It took readings and measurements for almost an hour before being crushed by the intense pressure.

fast facts

HOW FAST DOES JUPITER SPIN?

Considering its size, Jupiter spins incredibly quickly, rotating fully in 9 hours and 55 minutes. The speed of its rotation makes Jupiter bulge at its Equator.

WHAT IS A PLANET'S MAGNETOSPHERE?

A magnetosphere is the bubble around a planet where the magnetic field is strong enough to block the solar wind. Jupiter's magnetosphere is over 20,000 times stronger than Earth's, and stretches past Saturn.

IS THERE LIFE ON EUROPA?

Scientists believe that beneath Europa's icy crust there may be a liquid ocean. Volcanic activity may have allowed this ocean to form under the crust, with heat from the moon's core rising up through thermal vents in the ocean bed. It is possible that primitive aquatic life may have developed here.

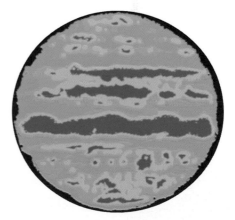

WHY DOES JUPITER GIVE OUT SO MUCH HEAT?

Jupiter has been contracting and cooling down since its birth 4.6 billion years ago. It was once an incredible 700,000km (435,000 miles) in diameter – over five times its present size. Jupiter shrinks by around 2.5cm (1in) each year, and as it does so, it generates an enormous amount of heat. Scientists now know that Jupiter gives out more heat than it receives from the Sun.

WHAT ARE SATURN'S EARS?

In 1610, when Galileo Galilei first began to look at Saturn through his homemade telescope, he thought that Saturn's rings were actually two moons. He called these moons "Saturn's ears". Forty-five years later, the astronomer Christiaan Huygens realized that these moons were actually a series of beautiful rings surrounding the planet. With the photographs provided by the Pioneer and Voyager probes, scientists now know more about these rings than ever before.

WHAT ARE SATURN'S RINGS MADE FROM?

SATURN'S RINGS are made from millions of tiny individual satellites, or moonlets. Each of these particles is like a dirty snowball of ice, dust and rock. These range in size from less than a centimetre to over a kilometre in diameter.

Each tiny particle in Saturn's rings is a natural satellite of the planet. Some scientists believe that Saturn's gravity may eventually cause the rings to group together and form a moon.

HOW MANY RINGS DOES SATURN HAVE?

THE VOYAGER SPACE PROBES took many pictures of Saturn's rings, showing them to be made up of countless hundreds of ringlets. These have been separated into different divisions. Three of these divisions can be seen from Earth: the outer A ring, the bright B ring and the inner C ring. The E ring is the furthest from Saturn, stretching nearly 500,000km (310,000 miles) from the planet. None of the rings is ever more than 1.5km (0.9 miles) thick.

Saturn   D ring   C ring   Bright B ring   A ring   F ring

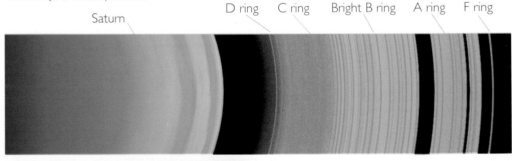

DO OTHER PLANETS HAVE RINGS?

FOR A LONG TIME astronomers believed that Saturn was the only planet with rings. However, in 1977, astronomers studying Uranus noticed that as it moved through the sky, the light from stars behind it twinkled, suggesting the presence of rings. In 1986, the Voyager 2 space probe flew past the planet and photographed 11 very faint, black rings. Both Jupiter and Neptune have ring systems that are very difficult to spot from Earth.

This false-colour image of Uranus' rings was taken by Voyager 2 as it flew by the planet. The ring systems of the planets appear beautifully coloured because the ice refracts sunlight in the same way as a garden sprinkler.

ARE THERE STORMS ON SATURN?

ALTHOUGH SATURN IS considered a more beautiful planet than its neighbour Jupiter, its weather is no less violent. It spins so quickly that it bulges at its centre, creating 1600k/ph (1,000mph) winds. Every 30 Earth years, a giant raging storm breaks out on Saturn, spreading across the entire planet. Such storms start when bubbles of hot gas rise up in the atmosphere.

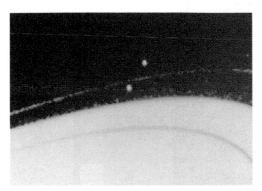

WHAT ARE SHEPHERD MOONS?

TWO OF SATURN'S MOONS – Pandora and Prometheus – are known as shepherd moons. They orbit either side of the narrow F rings, and have earned their name because their gravitational pull prevents the particles in this ring from straying out into space.

Pandora and Prometheus, shown left, were discovered in 1980 by Voyager 1.

HOW DO RINGS FORM?

NOBODY KNOWS FOR sure how planets get their rings. In the 19th century, the French mathematician Edouard Roche suggested that if any large object, such as a moon or comet, got too close to a planet, it could be torn apart by the planet's tidal force. The object would be pulled one way by its orbit and another by the planet's gravity. Once it reached the "Roche limit", it would break apart into tiny fragments.

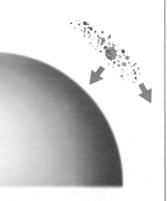

WHY ARE SCIENTISTS INTERESTED IN TITAN?

ONE OF SATURN'S satellites, Titan, is the only moon in the Solar System to have a substantial atmosphere. It is covered in thick clouds, and scientists believe conditions beneath these clouds may be similar to those on Earth billions of years ago. Although temperatures on the planet are believed to be well below freezing level, some scientists believe that internal heating may allow areas of liquid water to exist on the moon's surface. Some believe that primitive life may even exist on the moon. The European Space Agency's Huygens probe has been designed to parachute down through Titan's atmosphere in order to investigate the moon at first hand (right).

fast facts

HOW MANY MOONS DOES SATURN HAVE?

Saturn has the largest family of moons in the Solar System. Astronomers know of over 20 already, but there may be more. These range from Titan, which is the second largest moon in the Solar System after Jupiter's Ganymede, to tiny Pan, which is less than 20km (12 miles) in diameter.

WHAT IS THE CASSINI MISSION?

The Cassini probe was launched in 1997 on a seven-year journey to Saturn. Once there, it will spend four years in orbit, taking photographs and measurements of the planet, its rings and its moons.

WHY WOULD SATURN "FLOAT"?

Although Saturn is the second largest planet in the Solar System, it is the least dense – with an average density of less than three-quarters that of water. The particles that make up Saturn are spread so thinly that if the planet was placed in a large enough ocean, it would float!

WHY IS URANUS LIKE A BARREL?

Uranus is the third largest planet in our Solar System. It is unusual because it appears to lie on its side. Because the planet's axis is tilted, Uranus "rolls" around the Sun like a barrel, rather than spinning like a top. Its 11 faint rings and 17 moons spin around it like cars on a ferris wheel. Nobody knows exactly why Uranus behaves this way. Many believe the planet was struck by an enormous object billions of years ago, the impact knocking the planet on its side.

IS THERE ANY ACTIVITY ON URANUS?

THE SURFACE OF URANUS may look as motionless as that of a snooker ball, but in reality the planet is no less turbulent than Jupiter and Saturn. Like its larger neighbours, Uranus does have bands of clouds that blow around the planet at incredible speeds, but because of an overlying layer of methane in the upper atmosphere, they are very faint. Only enhanced infrared pictures, like those taken by the Voyager space probe (right), show the weather on Uranus.

HOW ARE URANUS' MOONS UNUSUAL?

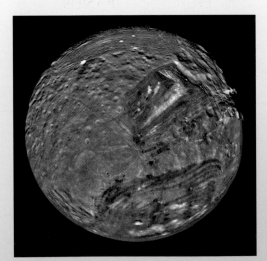

ALTHOUGH URANUS IS DEVOID OF SURFACE FEATURES, its many moons display a fascinating portrait of a violent history. The cracked and distorted surfaces of Uranus' moons are believed to have been caused by water. As liquid water rose from the interior of the moons, it froze and expanded, causing the crust to buckle outward. Miranda, one of Uranus' larger outer moons, has one of the most chaotic surface patterns of any body in the Solar System. The moon, shown left, resembles a patchwork, with parts of its core now on the surface, and parts of the crust buried deep underground. Scientists believe that this is because the moon was at one time pulled apart, and has gradually reformed.

WHY ARE URANUS AND NEPTUNE BLUE?

URANUS' COLOUR COMES FROM the presence of methane clouds in the planet's atmosphere. Methane absorbs red light, reflecting only blue and green. Neptune's upper atmosphere contains more methane than Uranus', which gives the planet's clouds their striking blue colour.

HOW WAS NEPTUNE DISCOVERED?

NEPTUNE'S DISCOVERY WAS UNUSUAL in that it was found with calculations rather than with a telescope. Astronomers observing Uranus noticed that it was drifting off the expected path of its orbit. Two mathematicians, working independently of each other, thought that this was because the gravitational pull of an unknown planet was disturbing Uranus' orbit. The calculations of both men led to the planet being discovered in 1845.

Voyager 2 found a raging storm on Neptune that was named the Great Dark Spot (below). It was as large as Earth, but had disappeared by the time the Hubble telescope took pictures of the planet in 1994.

WHAT IS THE WEATHER LIKE ON NEPTUNE?

NEPTUNE BOASTS one of the most violent weather systems known. When the Voyager 2 spacecraft flew by in 1989, it discovered that winds around the planet's equator reached speeds of 2000km/h (1240mph) – faster than anywhere else in the Solar System. Heat from inside the planet means that Neptune's atmosphere is turbulent and constantly changing.

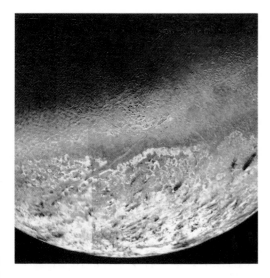

WHICH IS THE COLDEST BODY IN THE SOLAR SYSTEM?

TRITON, ONE OF NEPTUNE'S MOONS, has been found to be the coldest world in the Solar System. Parts of its surface reach temperatures as low as –235°C (–391°F), which is only 38°C (100°F) above the coldest temperature possible – absolute zero. Voyager 2 discovered that the moon is also geologically active. In several places, pockets of nitrogen gas explode from vents, sending plumes of gas, dust and ice up to 8km (5 miles) into the air. Wind blows the plumes into long streaks that can stretch for 150km (90 miles).

WHY ARE URANUS AND NEPTUNE ICE GIANTS?

SCIENTISTS STUDYING URANUS and Neptune discovered that these planets were very different from Jupiter and Saturn. They are much younger than their bigger neighbours, and therefore unable to feed on the enormous clouds of hydrogen and helium that made Jupiter and Saturn so large. Uranus and Neptune have been called ice giants as opposed to gas giants because beneath their cloud tops they may have oceans of water, heated by the energy from their cores.

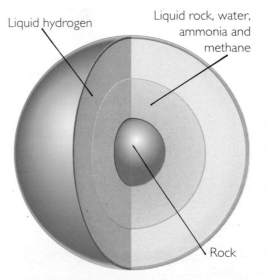

Liquid hydrogen

Liquid rock, water, ammonia and methane

Rock

fast facts

HOW WAS URANUS DISCOVERED?

Uranus was discovered by accident by the astronomer William Herschel. He was studying the night sky with his homemade telescope in 1781, when he spotted the planet. Uranus was the first planet to be discovered that could not be seen with the naked eye.

HOW MANY MOONS DOES URANUS HAVE?

Uranus has a family of 17 moons. Ten of these were discovered by the Voyager 2 space probe when it flew by the planet in 1986. They are named after characters from the writings of William Shakespeare and Alexander Pope.

DOES URANUS HAVE RINGS?

Uranus has a series of very faint rings made from particles of rock and ice about 1m (3ft) wide.

IS PLUTO REALLY A PLANET?

Pluto is the most mysterious planet in the Solar System because it is the one that astronomers know least about. Many have questioned Pluto's status as a planet, arguing that it is too small, and its orbit too elliptical, to be classified as such. Pluto may be the largest of the asteroids in the Kuiper Belt. Or it may once have been one of Neptune's moons that broke free of its parent's gravity. However, there are no plans to demote Pluto yet.

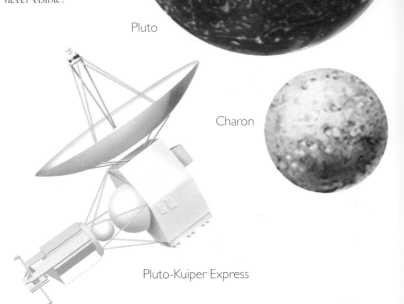

Pluto and Charon are in synchronized orbits. This means that they keep the same side, facing each other as they turn. From one side of Pluto, Charon always appears at the same point in the sky. On the other side of the planet, the moon is never visible.

Pluto

Charon

Pluto-Kuiper Express

HOW MUCH DO WE KNOW ABOUT PLUTO?

BECAUSE PLUTO is so far away from Earth, it is very difficult to explore the planet using telescopes. Even the Hubble Space Telescope cannot make out the planet in very much detail. So far, no probes have visited the ninth planet. However, NASA's Pluto-Kuiper Express is due to fly by the planet between 2006 and 2008.

WHAT ARE CONDITIONS LIKE ON PLUTO?

AT NEARLY 5900 million km (3670 million miles) from the Sun, Pluto is a cold, dark world, even in the middle of the day. The Sun appears over 1000 times fainter from the surface of Pluto that it does from Earth – little more than a bright star. Because of this, surface temperatures average around –230°C (–382°F). In summer, Pluto has a slight atmosphere because the surface warms up enough to turn some of the ice to gas. As Pluto moves away from the Sun, the gas freezes and becomes ice again.

WHAT IS A DUAL PLANET SYSTEM?

PLUTO'S ONLY MOON, Charon, is over half the diameter of Pluto, making it the biggest moon in relation to its parent planet in the Solar System. They are only 20,000km (12,430 miles) apart, and are caught in a gravitational headlock that scientists call a dual-planet system. They are so similar in size that they can be thought of as a double planet, as shown below.

WHAT LIES BEYOND PLUTO?

THE SOLAR SYSTEM does not end at Pluto but stretches outwards in all directions for billions of kilometres. Many scientists believe that the boundary of the Solar System could be an immense cloud of comets, called the Oort Cloud, which surrounds the planets like a spherical cage. Scientists believe that there are over ten trillion comets in this spherical halo, stretching nearly 8 million million kilometres (5 million million miles) from end to end.

The Oort Cloud, named after the Dutch astronomer Jan Oort, is made up of trillions of comets. Objects outside the Oort Cloud are pulled away from the Solar System because the Sun's gravity is not strong enough to hold them.

IS THERE A TENTH PLANET?

SOME SCIENTISTS ARE CONVINCED that the orbits of Uranus and Neptune are being distorted by the gravitational pull of a planet beyond Pluto. The recent discovery of minor members beyond Pluto which could be responsible for this distortion makes the existence of a tenth planet unlikely. New planets are being discovered continually, however, not in our Solar System, but orbiting other stars.

A comet orbiting the Sun from the outer edge of the Oort Cloud would take millions of years to complete one orbit.

WHAT IS THE KUIPER BELT?

BEYOND THE ORBIT OF NEPTUNE, stretching deep into the outer Solar System, lies a belt of celestial bodies made of rock and ice. The astronomer Gerard Kuiper first suggested the existence of this zone of comet-like objects, and so it was named the Kuiper Belt. There are at least 70,000 minor members in the Kuiper Belt with a diameter of over 100km (62 miles). The largest of these is 1992QBI, otherwise known as Smiley, which is 220km (137 miles) across.

IS PLUTO ALWAYS THE MOST DISTANT PLANET?

Pluto's highly elliptical orbit means that it is not always the most distant planet from the Sun. For a 20-year span in each 248-year orbit, Pluto comes closer to the Sun than Neptune. It was like this between 1979 and 1999.

WHAT IS PLUTO MADE OF?

Pluto is a tiny ball of ice and rock, a great deal smaller than Earth. It has a large rocky core and a small mantle of water ice below the surface. Pluto's thin crust is made up of rock and frozen methane. Pluto is only 2274km (1413 miles) in diameter – only one-fifth the size of Earth.

HOW DID PLUTO GET ITS MOON?

Nobody really knows how Pluto came to have so large a moon. Some believe that both Pluto and Charon are former moons of Neptune that escaped and found their own orbit around the Sun. The most common theory, however, is that Charon is made from ice that was knocked off Pluto during a collision.

WHO DISCOVERED PLUTO?

Pluto was discovered in 1930 by the astronomer Clyde Tombaugh.

If all the planets in the Kuiper Belt joined together, they would form an object roughly the size of Earth. The mass of all the objects in the Oort Cloud is roughly the same as three Earths.

HOW DO COMETS GET THEIR TAILS?

Although all comets seen from Earth have tails, they do not always look like this. When a comet is a long distance from the Sun, it exists purely as a lump of ice, frozen gas and rocky dust. However, as the comet's orbit takes it closer to the Sun, the temperature rises, and the ice begins to melt. Gas and dust are released, forming a huge cloud around the comet. This cloud is blown by the solar wind to form a tail.

A comet usually has two tails: a blue-coloured gas tail and a yellow or white dust tail. A comet's tails can stretch for hundreds of millions of kilometres into space.

WHAT ARE COMETS MADE FROM?

ALL COMETS BEGIN their lives as dirty snowballs. They are relics from the birth of the Solar System around 4.6 billion years ago, and are made up mainly of ice, gas and rock. As the comet approaches the inner Solar System, the Sun's heat causes the ice to evaporate. It turns into gas and forms a glowing head around the nucleus.

The nucleus is the only solid part of a comet. It is made up of ice, dust and rock.

HOW MANY TAILS DOES A COMET HAVE?

COMETS USUALLY HAVE two tails – one of gas and one of dust. The gas tail is normally blue, and is pushed away from the Sun by particles in the solar wind. The dust tail is yellow or white, and although it too is pushed away from the Sun, the star's gravity causes the tail to curve.

DOES A COMET'S TAIL ALWAYS FOLLOW THE NUCLEUS?

BECAUSE OF THE SOLAR WIND, a comet's tail always points away from the Sun. If a comet is travelling away from the Sun, its tail will be in front of the nucleus, as shown below.

The coma is formed of gas released by melting ice in the nucleus. It can measure 100,000km (62,000 miles) across.

HOW CLOSE HAS A PROBE FLOWN TO A COMET?

THE SPACE PROBE GIOTTO was the first to visit a comet up close. In 1986, it flew into Halley's comet and photographed the nucleus in incredible detail. It was able to gather data for almost 10 hours before dust and gas hitting the probe put the cameras out of action. From just 600km (373 miles) away, Giotto determined that Halley's nucleus measures 15km by 8km (9 miles by 5 miles), and is made up of ice and dust.

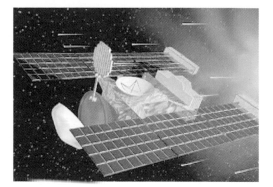

Giotto was named after a 14th-century Italian artist, who painted a comet on the wall of a chapel in Padua, Italy, in 1303. The probe was equipped with 10 instruments that photographed and analyzed Halley's comet.

HOW WILL SCIENTISTS FIND OUT MORE ABOUT COMETS?

SEVERAL MORE PROBES have been designed and built to visit comets in the near future. Stardust, above, will investigate and photograph comet Wild 2 in early 2004. It will bring a sample of dust and gas back to Earth for scientists to study.

WHEN WAS THE FIRST RECORDED SIGHTING OF A COMET?

UNLIKE MANY OTHER minor bodies in the Solar System, comets have been known about for thousands of years. The Chinese recorded Halley's comet as far back as 240BC. The famous Bayeux Tapestry, which was made to commemorate the Norman conquest of England in 1066, shows Halley's comet (right).

Comet

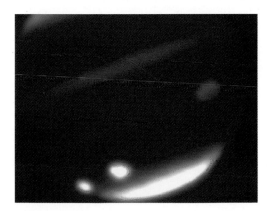

WHAT HAPPENS WHEN A COMET HITS A PLANET?

IF A COMET collided with Earth, the results could be disastrous – possibly meaning the end of all life on our planet. Comets can often be caught by the strong gravitational pulls of planets. In 1994, the Shoemaker-Levy 9 comet crashed into Jupiter's atmosphere. It impacted at more than 200,000km/h (124,000mph), creating balls of fire larger than Earth.

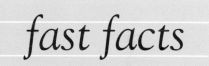

HOW LONG DO COMETS HAVE THEIR TAILS?

Comets develop new tails each time their orbit takes them close to the Sun. Their tails only last for a short time, often less than two months.

WHICH IS THE MOST FREQUENT COMET?

The most frequent cometary visitor is comet Encke, which passes by the Sun every 3.5 years. Halley's comet orbits every 76 years. In contrast, the Great Comet of 1864 will pass by Earth only once every 2,800,000 years.

WHAT KIND OF ORBITS DO COMETS HAVE?

MOST COMETS HAVE very long orbits that cover millions of kilometres. They travel into the Solar System from about one light year away, before swinging round the Sun and heading back out into space for thousands of years. These are called long-period comets. Some comets, particularly those that are trapped by the gravity of large planets, orbit the Sun in less than 200 years. These are called short-period comets.

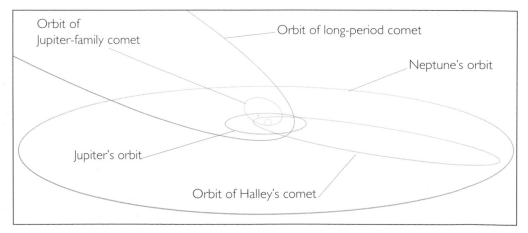

Orbit of Jupiter-family comet

Orbit of long-period comet

Neptune's orbit

Jupiter's orbit

Orbit of Halley's comet

HOW MANY METEORITES LAND ON EARTH?

Amazingly, thousands of rocks from space hit the surface of Earth each day. Every year our planet puts on nearly 10,000 tonnes in weight due to meteoroids entering the atmosphere. Many of these are minuscule grains of dust, but some can be many metres in length. The world's largest known meteorite was discovered in Namibia, Africa, in 1920 (right). It weighs an incredible 55,000kg (120,000lbs).

WHAT IS THE DIFFERENCE BETWEEN A METEOROID, A METEOR, AND A METEORITE?

SPACE IS TEEMING with millions of tiny pieces of rock and dust left over from the formation of the Solar System 4.6 billion years ago. These fragments are called meteoroids. They range in size from minuscule dust particles no larger than one-millionth of a gram to large rocks weighing many tonnes. Meteoroids travel through space and are often caught by Earth's gravitational pull. When a meteoroid enters Earth's atmosphere, it begins to heat up because of friction. As it heats up, it starts to glow, becoming a meteor – better known as a shooting star. Most meteors burn up in the atmosphere before they reach the ground. Those that hit the Earth's surface are called meteorites.

WHAT ARE METEORITES MADE FROM?

THERE ARE THREE MAIN types of meteorite. More than 90% of meteorites found on Earth are made of stone. Stony meteorites are divided into chrondites, which contain particles of solidified rock, and achrondites, which do not. Iron meteorites are composed of iron and nickel. Less than 1% of all meteorites are a mixture of rock and iron, and are called stony-iron meteorites.

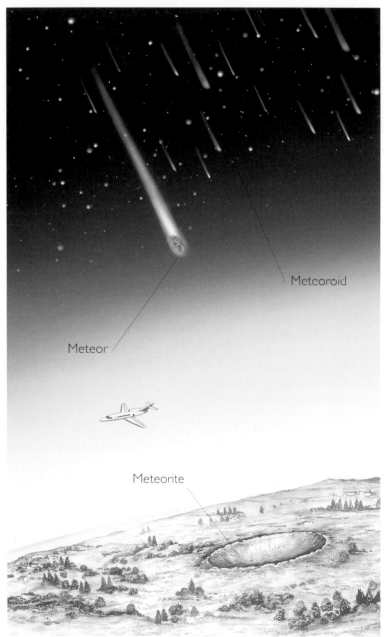

Meteoroid

Meteor

Meteorite

Iron meteorite

Stony-iron meteorite

Stony meteorite

WHY DO METEOR SHOWERS OCCUR?

A GREAT DEAL OF the material that makes up meteorites comes from short-period comets. As comets travel close to the Sun, they lose material, creating a trail of debris behind them. These trails, called meteoroid streams, can take many hundreds of years to form, but gradually build up to contain a large amount of loose dust and rock fragments. If Earth's orbit carries it through one of these streams, then hundreds of meteoroids will enter the atmosphere in a very short time, creating a meteor shower.

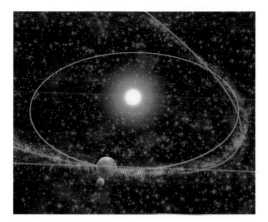

WHY ARE THERE SO FEW CRATERS ON EARTH?

UNLIKE MANY of the planets, moons and smaller bodies in the Solar System, Earth appears to be covered by very few craters. In the early days of the Solar System, Earth was as much a target for meteorites as any other planet, and suffered intensive cratering in the first one billion years of its existence. However, unlike bodies such as Mercury and the Moon, Earth has many geological processes that "hide" craters. Constant weathering and erosion from winds and water wear away or cover up craters. Some may also be hidden by vegetation or lie under the sea, although in the last hundred years, aerial photography and other forms of imaging have given us a clearer view of many remaining craters.

CAN SCIENTISTS PREDICT METEOR SHOWERS?

BECAUSE EARTH PASSES THROUGH meteor streams at roughly the same time each year, meteor showers can be predicted highly accurately. Astronomers have now even worked out which comets are responsible for each annual shower. Two meteor showers come from the trail left by Halley's comet: the Orionids in October, and the Eta Aquarids in May. Although meteors in a shower fall to Earth over a large distance, perspective makes them seem to be falling from the same point in the sky, called the radiant.

HOW FAST DO METEORITES IMPACT WITH THE EARTH?

THE AVERAGE METEORITE enters the Earth's atmosphere at around 50km/s (31mi/s), but particles in the atmosphere cause the speeding rocks to slow down. All but the largest meteorites are decelerated to around 150km/h (93mph) by the time they impact. Larger meteorites will not be slowed by atmospheric friction and hit the ground travelling at deadly speed.

fast facts

HOW ARE METEOR SHOWERS NAMED?

Meteor showers are named after the constellation in which their radiant is located. For example, the Orionids appear to fall from the Orion constellation (the hunter).

HAS ANYBODY EVER BEEN HIT BY A METEORITE?

Although ancient Chinese records describe deaths by meteorite impacts, no human in the last 1000 years has been killed by one. However, some have been known to crash into houses and gardens, and in 1992 an empty car was flattened by a falling meteorite.

WHICH IS THE WORLD'S LARGEST CRATER?

The largest crater on Earth lies near the city of Progreso, in Mexico. It is almost 300km (180 miles) in diameter, and was created when a 10km (6 miles) wide meteorite impacted with the Earth around 65 million years ago. Many think that this impact was responsible for the death of the dinosaurs, and 70 per cent of all life on Earth.

HOW MUCH DAMAGE COULD A METEORITE IMPACT DO?

WE KNOW THAT EARTH is bombarded by thousands of meteorites every day, none of which does our planet much damage. Any meteorite up to 10m (33ft) in diameter will normally burn up in the atmosphere before it reaches Earth, separating into tiny fragments. If a meteorite larger than this falls to Earth, it can cause considerable damage – impacting with the energy of five nuclear warheads. Approximately once every 1000 years, a larger meteorite does fall to Earth, and several large craters caused by such impacts can still be seen. One such was the nickel–iron meteorite that created the Barringer Crater in Arizona, USA (shown on the left from the air). The meteorite was an incredible 45m (148ft) wide, creating a crater nearly 1.5km (1 mile) in width. However, it would take an impact by an object roughly 5km (3 miles) wide to cause mass extinctions and threaten life on Earth.

How hot is the Sun?

Temperatures in and around the Sun vary considerably. On the Sun's surface, called its photosphere, the temperature is around 5500°C (10,000°F). Above this lies a hotter section of the atmosphere called the chromosphere, where temperatures can reach 15,000°C (27,000°F). Temperatures in the core of the Sun can exceed an incredible 15 million°C (27 million°F).

How does the Sun generate energy?

LIKE ALL STARS, the Sun generates nuclear energy. In the Sun's core, the temperature is so high that particles of gas cannot form completely. Instead, atomic nuclei and electrons travel around at very high speeds, moving so fast that if they collide, they join to form new particles. This process is called nuclear fusion, and it converts hydrogen into helium whilst also releasing vast amounts of energy. The Sun converts over four million tonnes of matter into energy every second.

Why does the Sun have spots?

THE SURFACE OF THE SUN often appears to be dotted with small dark patches. These are called sunspots. They form when the Sun's magnetic field blocks the heat rising from inside the Sun. Sunspots are actually very bright but appear dark because of their surroundings.

Once the energy has been released in the core, it travels outwards in the form of radiation such as gamma rays.

Energy travels through the radiative zone and the convective zone. As it moves, each photon of radiation collides with gas particles, losing energy with each impact. Because of this, radiation from the core can often take thousands, even millions of years to reach the surface of the Sun. The radiation has lost so much energy by this time that it leaves as visible light and infrared radiation.

Radiative zone

Convective zone

Core

Sunspots are around 1500°C (2730°F) cooler than the rest of the photosphere.

Earth

What are sunquakes?

SUNQUAKES ARE violent eruptions on the Sun around areas of hot gas. These explosions send out shockwaves more powerful than the detonation of a billion tonnes of high explosives.

At least 109 Earth-sized planets would fit side-by-side across the diameter of the Sun.

How big is the Sun?

THE SUN is a large ball of gas 1.4 million km (900,000 miles) in diameter. It is so large that, if it was hollow, one million Earth-sized planets could fit inside it!

WHAT IS AN ECLIPSE?

A SOLAR ECLIPSE occurs when the Moon comes directly between the Earth and the Sun. When this happens, the Sun's light is blocked, and the Moon's shadow falls on Earth. During an eclipse, the Moon and the Sun appear to be exactly the same size in the sky, because although the Moon is much smaller, it is also much closer. Total eclipses occur once every 18 months around our planet. However, it is estimated that any one place on Earth only sees a total eclipse every 360 years.

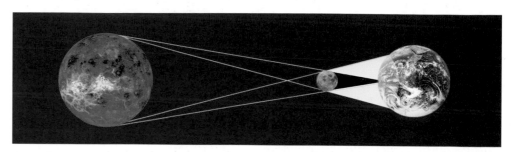

As a solar eclipse occurs, people in different locations on Earth will see different things. Anybody inside the complete shadow of the Moon, called the umbra, will see a total eclipse. Anybody in the outer shadow, called the penumbra, will witness a partial eclipse. A solar eclipse will reach a point of totality, where the Sun is completely covered by the Moon. This lasts for up to seven minutes.

During a total eclipse, the Moon covers up the Sun completely. All that can be seen of the star is its faint outer atmosphere, the corona, like a cloud of gas around a dark centre. As the Moon appears to devour the Sun, a brilliant bright spot can be seen on the edge of the Moon. This is caused by the last fingers of sunlight filtering through mountain ranges on the Moon.

HOW DOES SOLAR WIND AFFECT EARTH?

THE SUN is constantly sending out a stream of charged particles into space, called the solar wind. The strength of the solar wind varies. It is usually at its strongest when the number of sunspots is highest. As these particles pass by Earth, some are trapped by the planet's magnetic field, interacting with gases in the atmosphere. The reaction between particles and gases creates a multicoloured lightshow that can be seen from Earth.

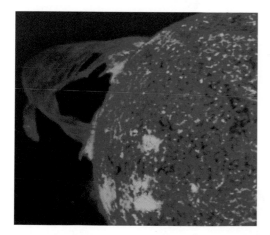

WHAT IS AN ANNULAR ECLIPSE?

THE MOON'S ORBIT around Earth is elliptical rather than circular, which means that sometimes the Moon appears slightly smaller in the sky than the Sun. If this happens during an eclipse, then a ring of brilliant sunlight remains visible, like a circle of fire around the Moon. This is called an annular eclipse (the word *annular* means "ring-shaped").

HOW HIGH CAN SOLAR PROMINENCES SHOOT?

GIANT JETS OF flaming hydrogen can often be seen erupting from the chromosphere. These are called solar prominences. They shoot from the Sun at incredible speeds. The average length of a prominence is 100,000km (60,000 miles), but many can reach distances of over 500,000km (310,000 miles). Some prominences, like the one on the left, make giant loops, following the magnetic field of the Sun.

HOW CAN WE OBSERVE THE SUN?

BECAUSE OF ITS extreme brightness, it is very dangerous to look at the Sun directly or through a telescope. Professional astronomers use tower telescopes to record the Sun's activity. These are large telescopes with moving mirrors (heliostats) that reflect light down a long shaft to data-recording instruments on the ground.

fast facts

IS THE SUN ON FIRE?

Scientists in the early 19th century believed that the Sun was an enormous lump of burning coal. However, scientists today know that the Sun is not actually on fire but is powered by nuclear reactions.

HOW FAST DOES THE SUN ROTATE?

Because the Sun is a giant ball of gas, all parts do not rotate at the same speed or in the same way as a planet or a moon. The inner part of the Sun rotates every 27 days, whereas the Sun's Equator rotates roughly every 25 days. Areas near the Sun's poles take around 35 days to make one complete rotation.

WHAT IS A SOLAR FLARE?

Solar flares are powerful explosions from the Sun, caused by sudden releases of energy heating up matter in the Sun's atmosphere. Flares eject charged particles into space. These particles carry so much radiation that when they reach Earth they can cause magnetic storms and interfere with radio communications. If a particularly powerful flare hit Earth, it could strip the planet of its protective ozone layer.

WHERE ARE STARS BORN?

Stars are born in giant stellar nurseries of gas and dust called molecular clouds. The gas that forms these vast clouds is much thinner than the atmosphere on Earth, yet there is just enough gravity to force clumps of gas and dust to contract into a ball. This is the beginning of a star. It will continue to grow until it is large enough for nuclear reactions to begin in its core. A molecular cloud remains dark until the light from new stars illuminates the surrounding gas, turning it into a nebula.

DO STARS COME IN DIFFERENT SIZES?

ALTHOUGH THE STARS in the night sky may appear to be similar in size, they can vary greatly. Red supergiants are the largest stars, growing up to 500 times the size of the Sun. Stars like the Sun are the most common in the night sky. When these stars die, they become white dwarfs, shrinking to the size of Earth. Neutron stars are even smaller than this, their gravitational pull so strong that they have shrunk to a few kilometres in diameter.

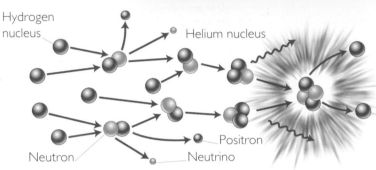

Hydrogen nucleus
Helium nucleus
Neutron
Positron
Neutrino

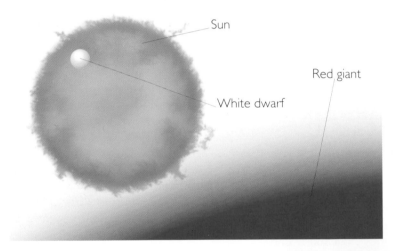

Sun

White dwarf

Red giant

WHAT IS CORE FUSION?

A STAR PRODUCES ENERGY by nuclear fusion. Inside the core of the star, the temperature is so hot that particles cannot form properly, leaving a soup of atomic nuclei and electrons. These nuclei travel at incredibly fast speeds and often collide. If two hydrogen nuclei (protons) collide, they will join together in a process called nuclear fusion, creating heavy hydrogen (deuterium). If another hydrogen nucleus collides with the deuterium, then a light variety of helium is formed, called helium-3. If two helium-3 nuclei collide, an ordinary helium nucleus (helium-4) is formed. At each stage of the process, vast amounts of energy are released in the form of particles called positrons and neutrinos, and in packets of radiation called gamma-ray photons.

HOW LONG IS A STAR'S LIFESPAN?

A STAR'S LIFE CYCLE can last millions, if not billions, of years. All stars begin in the same way – from material in a giant cloud of gas and dust called a molecular cloud. Stars remain alive as long as there is enough hydrogen to make helium, so a star's lifespan depends on its mass. Stars like the Sun will burn steadily for around 10 billion years before running out of hydrogen. Larger stars convert hydrogen much more quickly and therefore have much shorter lives.

A giant cloud of gas and dust begins to contract under its own gravitational pull.

The cloud separates into clumps. As each clump shrinks, its core begins to heat up.

When the core reaches critical density, nuclear reactions begin with a violent release of energy.

The new star shines steadily, converting hydrogen into helium by nuclear fusion.

HOW DO LARGE STARS DIE?

LARGE STARS, with a mass much greater than our Sun's, die a very violent death. As the hydrogen in a large star is used up, nuclear reactions produce heavier and heavier elements until a large iron core develops. This core eventually collapses under its own immense gravity, and the force of this collapse creates a tremendous explosion called a supernova. Most of the star's matter is blown into space by this explosion, leaving a tiny, dense remainder – either a neutron star or a black hole.

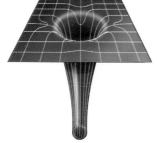

The matter inside a neutron star is so densely packed that a single thimbleful would weigh more than the Eiffel Tower in Paris, France.

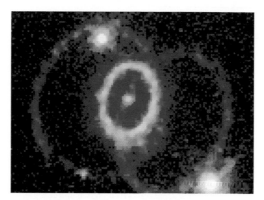

Supernova explosions can be brighter than a billion Suns, and are so violent that they send shockwaves of energy into space at millions of kilometres per hour.

WHAT ARE NEUTRON STARS?

WHEN A STAR explodes into a supernova, all that remains is a very small, extremely dense ball. This star is not made of gas, but rather of a liquid centre of subatomic particles called neutrons, surrounded by a solid iron crust. The matter in a neutron star is packed so tightly that the star is often no bigger than a few kilometres in diameter.

fast facts

WHAT IS A PULSAR?

After the power of a supernova, some neutron stars spin very quickly. They send beams of radio energy out into space in much the same way as a lighthouse beam. From Earth, these beams appear to flash on and off very quickly as the star spins. These neutron stars are called pulsars.

DO STARS COME IN PAIRS?

Our Sun is unusual because it is alone in space. Over half the stars in space are actually double stars, so close together that they appear to be only one. Double stars orbit around each other, held together by the pull of each other's gravity.

WHY ARE BLACK HOLES SO POWERFUL?

IF A STAR'S CORE after a supernova is more than three times the mass of the Sun, it will collapse in on itself even further than a neutron star, shrinking into an unimaginably small space called a singularity. Its gravity becomes immensely strong, creating a gravi-

tational well in space. If space was a stretched out sheet, such as in the diagram on the left, a black hole would create such a steep well in the sheet that any object passing too close would be sucked inside for ever. The force is so strong that nothing can escape, not even light.

A black hole is so massive that it will create a very deep well in the fabric of space. Objects travelling too close to this well will be drawn towards it and swallowed. Everything that enters a black hole is compressed into the singularity, which is no bigger than an atom.

HOW CAN BLACK HOLES BE DETECTED?

BLACK HOLES emit no light. However, scientists can find them if they are located close to another star. The enormous gravitational pull of the black hole will tear gas from the star, pulling in streams of material. This gas will circle the black hole with such force that its temperature can exceed 100 million°C. This is so hot that x-rays will be released. Satellites such as the RXTE are used by astronomers to detect these x-rays.

The dust cloud around the star becomes a disc. Particles join together and may form planets.

The star will spend most of its life on its main sequence, turning hydrogen into helium.

As its hydrogen fuel runs out, the star expands, becoming a red giant.

The star burns helium, turning it into carbon. Its core heats up, and its surface cools.

When the helium runs out, the star blows off its outer layers to form a planetary nebula.

Once the planetary nebula has blown away, all that remains is a white dwarf.

HOW FAST DOES LIGHT TRAVEL?

Light is the fastest thing in the Universe. It travels almost 300,000km (186,000 miles) in one second. In a single year, light travels 9,500,000,000,000km (5,900,000,000,000 miles) – or 9.5 trillion km (5.9 trillion miles). This distance is called a light year. It is used by astronomers to describe the enormous distances between stars and galaxies in space.

HOW ARE STARS CLASSIFIED?

THERE ARE COUNTLESS billions of stars in the Universe, each at different stages of development. Astronomers use a special chart called the Hertzsprung–Russell (H–R) diagram to help understand the different types of stars better. By plotting stars on the H–R diagram based on their temperature and absolute magnitude, astronomers can sort the stars into groups and learn more about them.

CAN WE LOOK BACK IN TIME?

BECAUSE STARS ARE so far apart from each other, even light can take billions of years to travel between them. The further away a star is from Earth, the longer it takes its light to reach us. This means that when we look up at the stars at night, we are gazing back in time. Even the Sun's closest neighbour, Proxima Centauri, is more than four light years away, which means that we are seeing it as it was over four years ago.

WHAT ARE LUMINOSITY AND MAGNITUDE?

THE ACTUAL BRIGHTNESS of a star compared to the Sun is called its visual luminosity, which ranges from 100,000 times to 1/100,000 of the Sun's brightness. A star's apparent magnitude is how bright it appears from Earth. Brighter stars have low, or negative, magnitudes.

Stars are measured by their luminosity down the side of the chart, and their temperature along the top.

Surface temperature

Luminosity

White dwarfs lie along the bottom of the chart because they are hot but not very bright.

Red giants lie along the top of the chart because, although they are much cooler than newer stars, they are much larger and brighter.

Most stars lie in a band stretching from left to right. This is the main sequence.

WHAT IS LIGHT?

LIGHT IS A FORM OF ENERGY that can travel on its own even through a vacuum. Humans can see visible light, from red to violet, but there are also many other forms of light that cannot be seen with the naked eye. Light consists of energy in the form of electric and magnetic fields, and is therefore referred to as electromagnetic radiation. Light travels like a wave, and light waves come in many sizes. The size of a wave is measured by the distance from one peak to the next, which is called the wavelength. Light waves also come in many frequencies – the number of waves that pass a certain point every second. Gamma rays have the highest frequencies and the shortest wavelengths, and therefore the most energy.

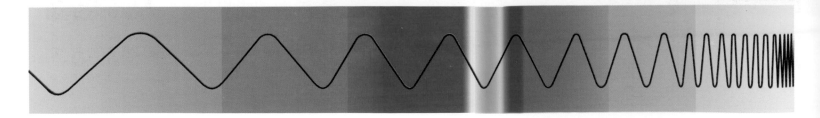

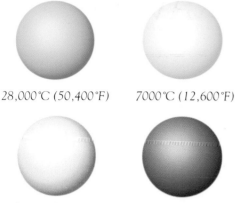

28,000°C (50,400°F)   7000°C (12,600°F)

5500°C (9900°F)   3000°C (5400°F)

WHY ARE STARS DIFFERENT COLOURS?

STARS IN THE NIGHT SKY appear to glow in a variety of different colours. This is because they have different temperatures and emit light with different wavelengths. Hot stars, with temperatures greater than 28,000°C (50,400°F), glow blue. Stars like our Sun, which have a surface temperature of around 5500°C (9900°F), appear yellow, whereas cooler stars glow red. Astronomers divide stars into seven spectral types: O (hottest), B, A, F, G, K and M (coolest).

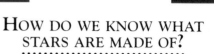

A spectograph of the Sun (right) shows that it is made up of many elements, including sodium, hydrogen and helium. In contrast, a spectograph of pure white light (left) will reveal no absorption lines because it contains no elements. Joseph von Fraunhofer invented the spectograph in the early 1800s.

HOW CAN WE TELL HOW FAR AWAY STARS ARE?

SCIENTISTS HAVE TO KNOW how far away a star is before they can begin to analyze details such as its age, size, temperature and mass. The most effective way of measuring a star's distance from Earth is called the parallax method. If you are travelling in a car and looking out of the window, nearer objects seem to pass by much more quickly than distant ones. In the same way, as Earth orbits the Sun, nearer stars appear to move more quickly through the sky than those further away. The angle through which a certain star moves over a period of six months is called its parallax. This angle is used by astronomers to work out how far away the star is.

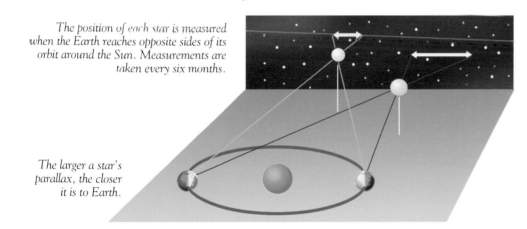

The position of each star is measured when the Earth reaches opposite sides of its orbit around the Sun. Measurements are taken every six months.

The larger a star's parallax, the closer it is to Earth.

HOW DO WE KNOW WHAT STARS ARE MADE OF?

EACH STAR PRODUCES its own individual light. By splitting the light into a spectrum, astronomers can discover the chemical elements that make up the star. This is because different elements in the star's atmosphere absorb light of different wavelengths. Sodium atoms, for example, only absorb light from the yellow part of the spectrum. A dark line across this part of the spectrum, called an absorption line, tells scientists that there is sodium in the star. By studying the various lines made on the spectrum, scientists can determine what the star is made up of.

WHAT LIES IN BETWEEN THE STARS?

MUCH OF THE SPACE BETWEEN the stars may be black, but it certainly isn't empty. Tiny amounts of dust and gas, called interstellar medium, occupy the space between stars. Interstellar medium has an average density of less than one atom per cubic centimetre, but in some places it is concentrated into vast clouds called nebulae. Nebulae come in many different shapes, sizes and colours. Emission nebulae (left) are the most beautiful. Their striking colours come from the presence of hydrogen atoms that release red light. Reflection nebulae (centre) are illuminated by light reflected from nearby stars. They appear blue because the light is scattered by dust grains. Absorption nebulae (right) are dark because there are no nearby stars to light them. They can be spotted because they block out the light from more distant stars.

fast facts

HOW DOES GRAVITY AFFECT LIGHT?

Gravity affects everything, including light. The Einstein cross appears in the sky as five points of light. However, it is really only one. The light comes from a distant quasar and is bent on its way to Earth by the gravitational pull of a galaxy.

WHAT ARE VARIABLE STARS?

Variable stars seem to get much brighter, then much dimmer over a regular period of time. Cepheid variables are stars that expand and shrink as they become hotter and cooler.

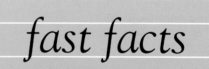

WHAT ARE ISLAND UNIVERSES?

In 1755, the philosopher Immanuel Kant claimed that some bright objects in space were giant collections of stars, and he named them island universes. The work of Edwin Hubble in the 1920s proved that these island universes were galaxies that lay beyond our own. A galaxy is an enormous collection of stars, dust and gas, held together by its own gravity. Even the smallest galaxies contain hundreds of thousands of stars, and it takes light many thousands of years to travel from one side to the other.

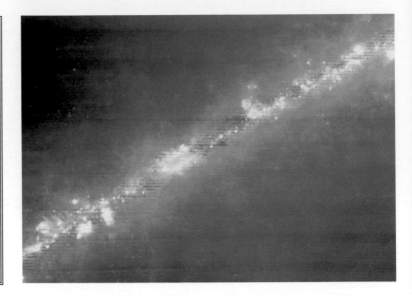

WHAT IS THE MILKY WAY?

THE MILKY WAY IS OUR home in the Universe. It is made up of over 200 billion stars, including the Sun, as well as large amounts of gas and dust. It looks like a giant spiral from above, but if it was viewed from the side it would appear as a flat band of stars. This is because the Milky Way is over 100,000 light years long, but only 2000 light years thick. The centre of the Milky Way is made up of a bright nucleus of old, cool stars. Emerging from the central galactic bulge are several spiral arms made up of gas, dust and young stars.

WHERE IS THE SUN IN THE MILKY WAY?

OUR SOLAR SYSTEM LIES ROUGHLY two thirds of the way from the centre of the galaxy, on the inner edge of a spiral arm called the Orion Arm, or the Local Arm. From Earth, the Milky Way appears as a river of milk stretching across the night sky. This is because we are viewing it from inside. The infrared image above gives a clearer view of the Milky Way as it stretches across space.

The Sun lies on the inner edge of one of the spiral arms.

The central galactic bulge is full of old, red stars.

WHAT ARE SATELLITE GALAXIES?

JUST AS THE SUN'S GRAVITY holds the objects of the Solar System in their orbits, the gravitational pull of the Milky Way keeps two smaller galaxies in tow. The two Magellanic Clouds consist of thousands of star clusters that orbit the Milky Way every 1.5 billion years. The Large Magellanic Cloud (right) is made of the same mix of gas and stars as the Milky Way, but is less than one-twentieth as large. The Small Magellanic Cloud is slowly being pulled apart by the gravity of our galaxy.

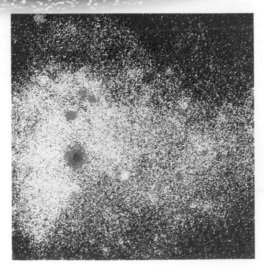

WHAT IS AT THE CENTRE OF THE MILKY WAY?

ASTRONOMERS CANNOT SEE what lies at the centre of the Milky Way because of the large amounts of dust in the way. Radio waves are not affected by dust, however, so scientists have been able to make detailed maps of the galaxy. They have found that at the centre of the Milky Way lies an enormous black hole – as large as Jupiter's orbit around the Sun – which is sucking in matter and pouring out energy with the strength of almost 100 million Suns.

ARE THERE DIFFERENT KINDS OF GALAXIES?

GALAXIES COME IN ALL SHAPES AND SIZES, but astronomers divide them into just a few main types. More than half of all galaxies are elliptical, named because of their egg-like shape. They are made up of large numbers of old, red stars and have very little gas and dust with which to make new ones. Around a third of all galaxies are spiral in shape, like the Milky Way. Old stars are packed tightly in their centres, while new stars are continually being born from the large amounts of gas and dust in their spiral arms. Some spiral galaxies are classed separately because their nucleus is elongated into a bar. This bar is made up of stars in motion, and the spiral arms extend from the ends of the bar. Some galaxies cannot be classed as either spirals or ellipticals because they have no recognizable shape. These galaxies are called irregulars, and are full of gas in which new stars are forming.

Elliptical galaxy (E)   *Spiral galaxy (S)*

Barred spiral galaxy (BS)   *Irregular galaxy (Irr)*

WHAT HAPPENS WHEN GALAXIES COLLIDE?

GALAXIES ARE NORMALLY SEPARATED by vast, empty gulfs. Occasionally, however, two galaxies can pass close enough to one another to collide. They are travelling at millions of kilometres per hour, and the resulting impact can be incredible. The individual stars in a galaxy do not collide, but the vast clouds of interstellar gas and dust smash into one another, triggering a ferocious birth of new stars. Only gravity holds

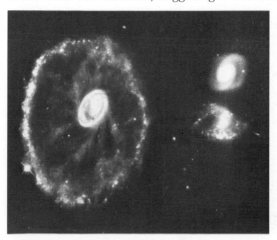

these galaxies together, so an amazing battle of strength follows an impact. Sometimes galaxies merge to form even larger galaxies. At other times, galaxies can be distorted, or even ripped apart, by the impact. The Cartwheel galaxy (left) was hit by another galaxy 300 million years ago.

The Cartwheel galaxy used to be a spiral galaxy, but a smaller galaxy, travelling very fast, smashed through its centre. The blue ring around the central region is made up of millions of new stars triggered by the impact.

HOW ARE GALAXIES CLASSIFIED?

GALAXIES ARE CLASSIFIED using a very simple code that describes their basic shape. "E" is used to describe an elliptical galaxy, and a number from 0 to 7 is added to further define its form. An E0 galaxy looks like a ball, whereas an E7 galaxy resembles a short, fat sausage. Spiral galaxies are defined by the letter "S", and barred spiral galaxies by the letters "BS". Both these forms of galaxy are given further definition by the addition of a letter a, b, c or d. Galaxies with tightly wound arms are labelled Sa, and galaxies with looser arms are labelled Sd.

DO GALAXIES COME IN GROUPS?

GALAXIES THEMSELVES MAY APPEAR to be enormous, but even they do not exist independently in space. They gather together in groups – from pairs to clusters that can contain thousands of galaxies. The Milky Way is only one of a cluster of around 30 galaxies that make up the Local Group, an enormous collection of galaxies that stretches over millions of light years. The largest known cluster is the Virgo cluster, which contains over 2000 galaxies. Just as gravity causes galaxies to form clusters, it also brings clusters together to form superclusters. These are the largest structures in the Universe, stretching hundreds of millions of light years across space.

WHEN DID ASTRONOMY BEGIN?

Astronomy has been around ever since humankind first looked up at the stars and wondered about the sparkling lights above. There is evidence to suggest that people have been charting the skies for over 15,000 years. Cave paintings in France and Spain include maps of star clusters, such as the Pleiades. The Akkadians, who lived in Babylonia 4500 years ago, kept many astronomical records, including the path of the Sun, the Moon and the planets. Stonehenge, in England, was built in around 3000BC. It is a giant astronomical calendar with stones aligned to the Sun.

WHO WAS PTOLEMY?

THE ANCIENT GREEKS turned astronomy into a science. Ptolemy (above right), who was born around AD100, published his *Almaghest* in AD140. This was an encyclopedia of the patterns of the stars and planets, and he used it to support his argument that the Earth was at the centre of the Universe. His "system of the world" claimed that surrounding Earth were seven transparent spheres, each containing a moving object such as the Sun, the Moon, or a planet. An eighth sphere, which surrounded everything, held the stars. His theory, which we now know to be incorrect, was a very accurate way of predicting the motions of the planets, and was the dominant theory in astronomy for over 1000 years.

Ptolemy's celestial sphere placed the Earth at the centre of the Universe, orbited by the Sun, Moon and planets.

WHO FIRST SUGGESTED A HELIOCENTRIC UNIVERSE?

NOT EVERYBODY BELIEVED that the Earth was at the centre of the Universe. Aristarchus, another Greek who lived in the same age as Ptolemy, claimed that the Sun was at the centre of everything, orbited by the Earth and the planets. This is known as a heliocentric theory. Nobody took him seriously because he could not explain why, if the Earth moved through space, the stars did not change their positions in relation to each other.

WHO WAS COPERNICUS?

IT WAS NOT UNTIL the 16th century that Ptolemy's system was challenged seriously. A Polish churchman named Nicolaus Copernicus claimed that the Earth and the planets orbited the Sun. His ideas were backed up in 1610 when Galileo Galilei used a telescope to view the moons of Jupiter, proving that not everything orbited the Earth.

Copernicus' Universe (left), with the Sun at its centre, is very similar to the Solar System that we know today.

HOW DID THE PLANETS GET THEIR NAMES?

THE NAMES OF THE PLANETS in our Solar System originate from characters they resembled in ancient Greek and Roman legends. Mercury was named after the nimble messenger of the gods because of its fast orbit. Venus was named after the goddess of beauty and love because of its brightness in the night sky. Mars was named after the god of war because of its colour. Jupiter was given the name of the king of the gods because of its size, and Saturn was named after the god of the harvest. Planets discovered later were named in the same way – Uranus after the father of the gods, Neptune after the god of the sea, and Pluto after the god of the underworld.

WHAT IS THE ECLIPTIC?

WHEN PEOPLE FIRST BEGAN to study the movement of the Sun, they believed that it orbited the Earth. It seemed to move along the same path through the skies every day, and the path was named the ecliptic. We now know that the Earth orbits the Sun, and that this line is actually a projection of Earth's orbit around the Sun on to the stars beyond (left).

There are so many stars in the night sky that it is possible to find almost any image you like. The brightest stars have been grouped together into similar patterns by people all over the world.

WHAT ARE CONSTELLATIONS?

FOR THOUSANDS OF YEARS, societies all over the world have grouped together the brightest stars in the sky to form patterns and pictures called constellations. People have projected characters, natural images and human beings on these groupings – from animals such as the Great Bear to mythological heroes such as Hercules. There are 88 officially recognized constellations in the night sky.

WHAT IS THE ZODIAC?

THE ZODIAC IS A GROUP of twelve constellations that lie along the ecliptic. Of the 88 constellations that are officially recognized today, the twelve of the ecliptic are the most ancient. They are regarded as special because the Sun appears to pass through them as it moves through the sky. Even today they act as markers in astrology – the belief that human life is affected by the position of the stars and planets.

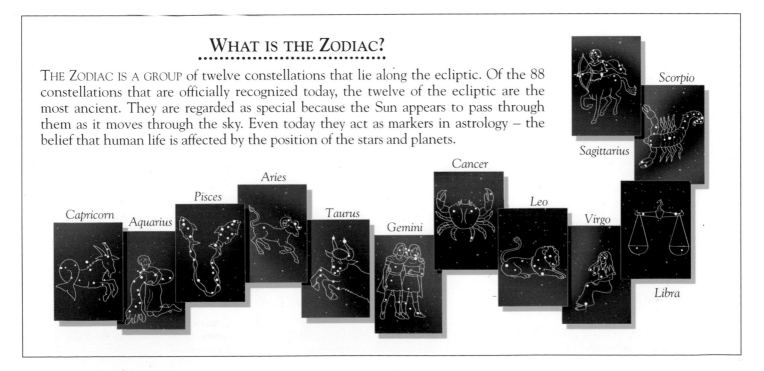

WHO INVENTED THE TELESCOPE?

The first telescope was created by the Dutch spectacle-maker Hans Lippershey in 1608. It was a simple design that could only magnify objects a small number of times, but the idea spread like wildfire through Europe. The Italian inventor Galileo Galilei was the first person to use the telescope to study the movement of the stars and planets, one year later.

HOW DO OPTICAL TELESCOPES WORK?

ASTRONOMERS USE TWO different types of visual telescope: reflectors and refractors. The idea behind both is to capture as much light as possible from distant objects, and direct that light to the human eye, or to data-recording equipment. Refractor telescopes, which are used by most amateur astronomers, work by capturing light through a main lens. This light is then magnified by a second lens, which focuses it into an image. Most professional astronomers prefer to use reflector telescopes (right), which use mirrors to capture light.

Light from objects in space enters here and is collected by the main mirror.

The image is formed in the main mirror. Because it is curved, the mirror focuses the image, directing it towards a second mirror.

The secondary mirror reflects the light of the main image to an eyepiece, or to data-recording equipment.

Data-recording equipment

Unlike the lenses in a refracting telescope, which are limited in size, mirrors in a reflecting telescope can be any size.

DO TELESCOPES ONLY STUDY VISIBLE LIGHT?

VISIBLE LIGHT ONLY MAKES UP a tiny fraction of the electromagnetic spectrum – less than 0.00001 per cent. Objects in space emit radiation in many different forms, from radio waves to gamma rays. By studying these forms of radiation, astronomers can learn more about space. Astronomers use different kinds of telescope to study different types of radiation.

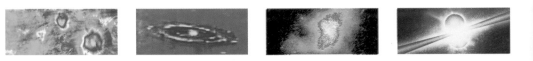

WHAT OTHER TYPES OF ASTRONOMY ARE THERE?

RADIO ASTRONOMY COLLECTS the radio signals given out by objects in space, which can be used to put together a picture of something that cannot be seen with the naked eye, such as volcanoes on Venus (above left). Many objects in space emit energy in the form of infrared waves, such as the Andromeda galaxy (second left). Ultraviolet astronomy is used to track down the hottest stars in space, such as the Crab supernova (second right). Radiation with the highest energy levels is called gamma ray (right).

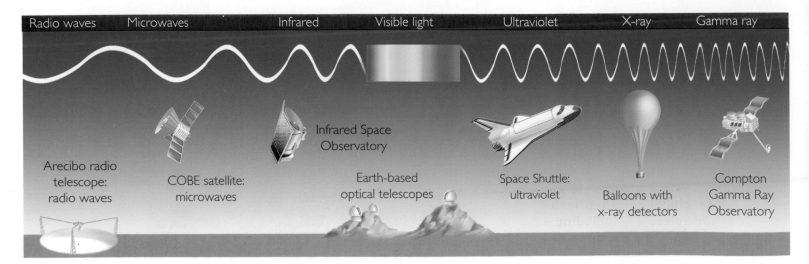

| Radio waves | Microwaves | Infrared | Visible light | Ultraviolet | X-ray | Gamma ray |

Arecibo radio telescope: radio waves

COBE satellite: microwaves

Infrared Space Observatory

Earth-based optical telescopes

Space Shuttle: ultraviolet

Balloons with x-ray detectors

Compton Gamma Ray Observatory

HOW HAVE MODERN TELESCOPES BEEN IMPROVED?

MODERN ASTRONOMY RELIES AS MUCH upon computers as upon telescopes. Data collected by telescopes and satellites is processed by computers to produce images that can be stored and studied at leisure. Telescopes are becoming bigger and more powerful. The twin Keck telescopes, built on the 4200m (13,780ft) summit of an extinct Hawaiian volcano, are eight storeys tall, with mirrors 10m (33ft) wide.

WHICH IS THE LARGEST TELESCOPE?

THE BIGGEST TELESCOPE in the world is aptly named the Very Large Telescope, and is located in Chile. It is made up of four separate 8.2m (27ft) mirrors, each one more than a billion times more powerful than the naked eye. It is so powerful that it is even able to spot an astronaut on the Moon. The Arecibo telescope in Puerto Rico is the world's largest curved focusing antenna. Its dish is 305m (1000ft) in diameter, and made up of almost 40,000 aluminium panels.

Satellites such as the Compton Gamma Ray Observatory are carried into space by the Space Shuttle.

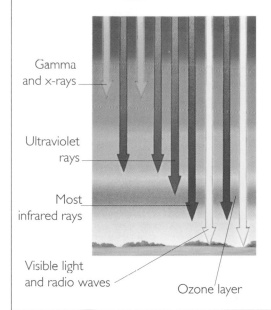

Gamma and x-rays

Ultraviolet rays

Most infrared rays

Visible light and radio waves

Ozone layer

WHY DO WE NEED TELESCOPES IN SPACE?

EARTH'S ATMOSPHERE SHIELDS the planet against radiation from space. Gamma rays, x-rays and most ultraviolet rays are absorbed by the atmosphere, preventing them from reaching the surface. Because of this, these types of radiation are best studied from space. There are many different satellites in orbit around the Earth, such as the Compton Gamma Ray Observatory (above), that allow these forms of radiation to be studied.

Only visible light, some infrared, ultraviolet and radio waves reach Earth's surface.

WHAT IS THE HUBBLE SPACE TELESCOPE?

LAUNCHED IN 1990 AFTER nearly half a century of planning, the Hubble Space Telescope was a dream come true for astronomers. It orbits 610km (380 miles) above the Earth's surface, meaning that its view is not blocked by the planet's turbulent atmosphere. Hubble's main telescope is a reflector telescope, like those used on Earth. This can take crystal clear pictures of the most distant parts of the Universe. Hubble also has many other kinds of telescope, including a faint-object camera, infrared cameras and a wide-field telescope.

Faint-object camera

Wide-field and planetary camera

Near-infrared camera

Main mirror

Light enters here.

Solar panels power Hubble.

HOW DO SATELLITES GET INTO SPACE?

Everything that enters space, from satellites to astronauts, does so through the incredible power of rocket propulsion. In order to escape Earth's strong gravitational pull, a space launcher has to reach a speed of over 27,000 kilometres (17,500 miles) per hour. Once the rocket is in orbit, its power is shut off. Although it is still being affected by Earth's gravity, it does not fall back down to the ground because its speed cancels out the gravitational pull.

WHAT IS PROPULSION?

PROPULSION IS THE act of driving something forwards. Rockets, cars, boats, planes and all other vehicles use some form of propulsion in order to move.

HOW DO ROCKETS WORK?

A ROCKET NEEDS to produce enough thrust to overcome gravity and lift its own weight. Rockets burn liquid hydrogen and oxygen in a specially built combustion chamber. For every pound of rocket fuel burned, a pound of exhaust gas is allowed to escape from a nozzle at the base of the rocket. As the high-temperature, high-velocity gases are fired downwards, they exert an equal, opposite force that fires the rocket upwards.

WHAT ARE NEWTON'S LAWS OF MOTION?

SIR ISAAC NEWTON, a scientist who lived between 1642 and 1727, completely changed our understanding of the Universe when he proposed his three laws of motion:

  1 *An object remains motionless or travelling in a straight line until a force acts upon it.*
  2 *The acceleration of an object is equal to the overall force acting on it divided by its mass.*
  3 *Every action has an equal and opposite reaction.*

This last law is most important in relation to rocket propulsion. When firemen spray water from a hose, they have to struggle to hold it still. This is because the hose is firing water forwards, and the firemen are struggling against the opposite reaction.

The nose cone, also called the fairing, reduces air resistance during take-off.

Typical rocket payloads include satellites and space-station components. Small engines on the satellite will boost it into orbit at exactly the right time.

Second-stage tanks and combustion chamber

Liquid oxygen tank. Oxygen is needed for combustion. Without it, the fuel would not burn.

Liquid hydrogen tank

Pipes carry the liquid oxygen and liquid hydrogen to the main combustion chamber.

The liquid helium container pressurizes the fuel tanks, preventing leakage.

Main engine combustion chamber. This is where fuel is mixed and ignited.

Exhaust gases are ejected from the exhaust nozzle, giving the rocket lift.

WHY DOES A ROCKET HAVE DIFFERENT STAGES?

ROCKETS HAVE TO carry an enormous amount of fuel in order to make the journey into orbit. So much fuel is needed that most rockets are made up of enormous chambers in which to store the liquid hydrogen and oxygen. Rockets such as the Ariane need maximum thrust for the first few seconds of take-off, so the main engine and two extra boosters fire at full power. After about two minutes, all the fuel in the two boosters has been used up, so they are jettisoned in order to lighten the payload. The less a rocket weighs, the less fuel it has to use.

WHEN WERE ROCKETS INVENTED?

SOLID-FUEL ROCKETS were first used by the Chinese over 1000 years ago. They were powered by gunpowder made from sulphur, saltpetre and charcoal, and used as weapons. In 1926, the American scientist Robert Goddard launched the first liquid-fuelled rocket. Long-range rockets were perfected in 1942 when Wernher von Braun developed the powerful V-2 for the German army.

WHAT IS A ROCKET'S PAYLOAD?

The payload is the cargo that a rocket carries into space. This is usually an artificial satellite or parts for a space station.

WHAT IS AN AIR LAUNCH ROCKET?

Air-launch rockets are small rockets launched from aircraft. The aircraft carries the rocket to a certain altitude, usually around 12km (8 miles) before releasing it. After around five seconds, the rocket's boosters ignite, carrying it into space.

WHY DO ROCKETS CARRY OXYGEN?

Oxygen is needed for all combustion. Because space contains no oxygen, a rocket must carry its own.

WHAT IS A SPACE LAUNCHER?

SPACE LAUNCHERS ARE rockets that carry payloads into space. Just as there are many sizes of truck to carry different goods from place to place, there are many different space launchers, each suited to different purposes. Rockets such as the Mercury-Atlas (left) were designed to be small and light, as they only had to carry one man. Russia's Soyuz series (middle) are incredibly powerful, able to carry 20 tonnes into a low-Earth orbit. NASA's Saturn V (right) was designed to be powerful enough to carry three men to the Moon.

WHAT HAPPENS AT MISSION CONTROL?

MISSION CONTROL IS a rocket's contact back on Earth. All missions into space require constant technical support from scientists and engineers on the ground. The staff at Mission Control have many important jobs, such as ensuring the craft is on the right course, maintaining vital communication links, and making sure there is enough oxygen and fuel to complete the mission safely.

WHEN DID THE SPACE AGE BEGIN?

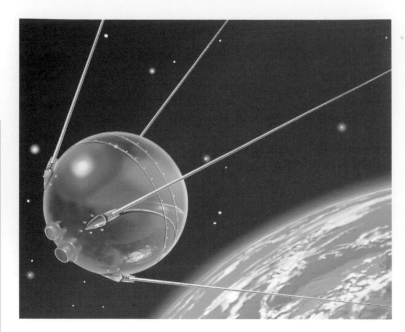

From the early 1950s, the USSR and the USA were engaged in a ferociously competitive war of supremacy against one another, each trying to be the country to begin the space age. Vast amounts of money were invested in space exploration, and in October 1957, the Union of Soviet Socialist Republics (USSR) launched the world's first ever artificial satellite, Sputnik 1. It did very little other than transmit a simple radio signal, but it marked a new stage in the history of humankind.

Many frightened people believed that Sputnik 1 (above) was spying on their activities from space. In reality, all the probe did was emit a simple tracking signal for the 21 days that it was in orbit.

WHO WAS THE FIRST PERSON IN SPACE?

THE SOVIET Yuri Alekseyevich Gagarin was the first person to be launched into space. He travelled aboard Vostok 1, and blasted off from Earth in April 1961. After completing one orbit, he returned safely to Earth. John Glenn was the first American to be sent into space in 1962.

Russian cosmonaut Yuri Gagarin was the first man in space.

WHAT WAS THE FIRST LIVING THING IN SPACE?

LESS THAN ONE MONTH after Sputnik 1 had been launched, the Soviets claimed a second amazing achievement by sending the first living creature into orbit. Sputnik 2, which blasted off from Earth in November 1957, contained a small dog called Laika. The spacecraft was specially designed for the dog, with life-support facilities and a cradle. Laika survived the launch and the journey into space, but died when her supply of oxygen ran out in orbit. Three years later, in August 1960, two more dogs, named Belka and Strelka, became the first creatures to survive the journey into space and return, travelling aboard Sputnik 5.

WHICH COUNTRY WAS FIRST TO EXPLORE THE MOON?

LUNA 2 (left) was launched from the USSR in 1959, and was the first probe to visit the Moon's surface, although it did not so much land as crash. Ranger 7, an American probe, also crashed on the Moon's surface in 1964. It managed to take over 4000 close-up pictures. Luna 9 was the first probe to land successfully on the Moon in 1966. It sent back television pictures of the barren surface.

WHAT WERE THE APOLLO MISSIONS?

THE APOLLO LUNAR PROGRAMME was launched in 1961 by the President of the USA, John F Kennedy. He ambitiously claimed that human beings would set foot on the Moon by the end of the decade. It was one of the most complicated and technically challenging projects of the twentieth century, but resulted in a manned mission being sent to the Moon in 1969. A very powerful rocket, called the Saturn V, was built especially for the journey. It was able to carry the 52 tonnes of equipment needed for a successful visit to the lunar surface. Apollo 8 carried the first men around the Moon in 1968, but it was not until one year later, in July 1969, that humankind first set foot on the surface of the Moon.

WHAT ARE CONDITIONS LIKE ON THE MOON?

GRAVITY ON THE MOON is only one-sixth of that on Earth, which means that astronauts can jump several metres effortlessly. There is no atmosphere on the Moon, so sound cannot be carried even over a small distance. Radios have to be used to communicate over a few centimetres. Because there is no weather, the astronauts' footprints will last for thousands of years (below).

HOW DID THE APOLLO ASTRONAUTS GET TO THE MOON?

SATURN V held the Apollo spacecraft, which was made up of three parts – the Command, Service and Lunar Modules. Neil Armstrong and Buzz Aldrin touched down on the Moon's surface in the Lunar Module. As well as providing their transport, the Lunar Module was the astronauts' home for the three days they spent on the Moon. Michael Collins remained in orbit aboard the Command and Service Module. When it was time to leave the Moon, Aldrin and Armstrong blasted back into orbit in the top half of the Lunar Module, before docking with the Command and Service Module and beginning the journey back to Earth.

1 Saturn V blasts off from Florida and begins its journey to the Moon.

2 Saturn V's boosters are jettisoned, leaving the modules to continue to the Moon.

4 The astronauts head back to Earth in the Command Module.

3 The Lunar Module descends to the surface as the Command and Service Modules orbit.

WHAT KIND OF EXPERIMENTS WERE DONE ON THE MOON?

THERE HAVE BEEN SIX APOLLO missions to the Moon, during which 12 astronauts have explored its composition and conditions. Thousands of photographs have been taken, and 176kg (388lbs) of Moon-rock were brought back to Earth to be studied. Scientists are interested in finding out what the Moon is made of because this may determine its origin and history. Astronauts also measured the amount of solar particles reaching the lunar surface, the amount of dust in the air, and the power of moonquakes, which are slight movements in the Moon's crust.

WHAT WAS THE MOON BUGGY?

ON APOLLO 17, the last manned mission to the Moon, the astronauts took with them a small buggy called the Lunar Rover. It was battery powered and could travel at just under 20km/h (12mph), enabling astronauts to explore much more of the Moon than their predecessors had been able to do on foot. It had a small television camera and a satellite dish that sent the footage back to Earth. The Moon Buggy, as it is often called, had rubber tyres that could not be punctured, and was steered by a small hand control. It could be folded up and stored away when it was not needed.

fast facts

DID THE USSR AND THE USA WORK TOGETHER?

Despite their battle for political supremacy, the USA and the Soviet Union co-operated on one space mission. During the Apollo–Soyuz rendezvous, the crews docked their craft with one another. Over a period of a few days, they worked together on various experiments.

WILL ASTRONAUTS EVER RETURN TO THE MOON?

Scientists are already considering sending astronauts back to the Moon in order to build lunar bases. Astronauts will investigate the Moon's surface in order to find suitable locations in which to construct laboratories and telescopes.

WERE OTHER ANIMALS SENT INTO SPACE?

The Russians sent at least ten dogs into space after Laika, Belka and Strelka in order to test equipment prior to manned missions. The Americans sent several chimpanzees and monkeys into orbit, the first of which was named Gordo. Turtles, flies and worms have also been on trips into space.

WHAT IS THE SPACE TRANSPORTATION SYSTEM?

Sending a rocket into space is a very expensive procedure, especially considering that each launcher can be used only once. The Space Transportation System (STS), better known as the Space Shuttle, was designed to be the world's first reusable space vehicle.

WHY IS THE SHUTTLE ECONOMIC TO RUN?

MOST ROCKETS either burn up in Earth's atmosphere or are decommissioned after they have completed their mission. A new rocket has to be built from scratch for the next launch. All but one part of NASA's Space Shuttle returns to Earth intact. After these parts have been checked for damage, they are ready to be used again, therefore saving the cost of rebuilding.

WHAT ARE THE DIFFERENT COMPONENTS OF THE SHUTTLE?

THE STS IS COMPRISED of four main parts: the orbiter is the main section of the Shuttle, housing the crew, the control centre and the payload. The orbiter is the only part of the Shuttle to reach orbit, after which it returns to Earth, landing like a plane. An external fuel tank contains the liquid hydrogen and liquid oxygen needed for propulsion. Two solid rocket boosters propel the orbiter to a height of 45km (28 miles) before they are jettisoned.

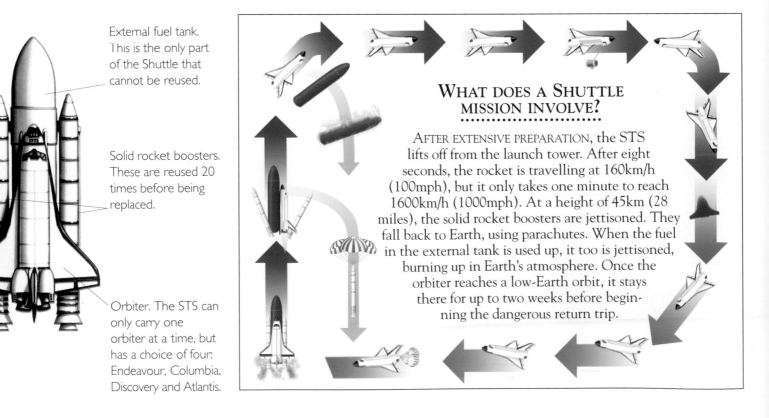

External fuel tank. This is the only part of the Shuttle that cannot be reused.

Solid rocket boosters. These are reused 20 times before being replaced.

Orbiter. The STS can only carry one orbiter at a time, but has a choice of four: Endeavour, Columbia, Discovery and Atlantis.

WHAT DOES A SHUTTLE MISSION INVOLVE?

AFTER EXTENSIVE PREPARATION, the STS lifts off from the launch tower. After eight seconds, the rocket is travelling at 160km/h (100mph), but it only takes one minute to reach 1600km/h (1000mph). At a height of 45km (28 miles), the solid rocket boosters are jettisoned. They fall back to Earth, using parachutes. When the fuel in the external tank is used up, it too is jettisoned, burning up in Earth's atmosphere. Once the orbiter reaches a low-Earth orbit, it stays there for up to two weeks before beginning the dangerous return trip.

WHAT DOES THE ORBITER CONTAIN?

THE ORBITER is the most important section of the Space Shuttle. Although it looks a great deal like a small plane, it is actually a high-tech laboratory and storage area, with facilities to hold up to seven crew members for over two weeks. The front end of the orbiter is comprised of three levels: the flight deck, the mid-deck, where the crew live whilst in space, and the lower deck, which contains vital life-support equipment. Most of the orbiter is taken up by a vast payload bay.

The flight deck is the equivalent of a cockpit in a normal aircraft. This is the control centre for the entire Shuttle, with power, communications, lighting and life support being overseen from here.

A remote-controlled manipulator arm is used to move cargo.

The orbiter has several different types of engine. The three main engines are used to help the Shuttle into orbit. Orbital-manoeuvring engines help the craft to move in space. Smaller thrusters allow the orbiter to change its position more accurately.

The orbiter's wings are designed to help the craft land back on Earth.

The mid-deck can be accessed from the flight deck by a ladder. It contains almost everything that the astronauts use during the mission, such as the galley (kitchen), bathroom and sleeping stations.

The lower deck houses life-support equipment designed to keep the Shuttle's environment cool and comfortable.

The payload bay holds the Shuttle's cargo, which varies from satellites to equipment such as the Hubble Space Telescope.

ARE ALL SHUTTLE MISSIONS SUCCESSFUL?

UNFORTUNATELY THERE ARE MANY risks relating to space travel. With the tremendous forces involved, accidents inevitably occur. In 1986, the Challenger orbiter exploded when a joint between two segments of one of the boosters came loose. Tragically, everybody on board died.

WHAT IS THE PAYLOAD BAY?

THE PAYLOAD BAY is where the Shuttle's cargo is kept during flight. It measures 18.3m by 4.6m (60ft by 15ft), which is large enough to hold two small buses end to end. The two large bay doors can be opened when the Shuttle reaches low-Earth orbit, allowing the cargo to be lifted into space.

fast facts

WHEN WAS THE FIRST SHUTTLE FLIGHT?

The orbiter Columbia was the first Shuttle to enter orbit. It was launched on 12 April 1981.

HOW DOES THE SHUTTLE LAND?

The Shuttle begins to slow down half a world away from the landing site in Florida, USA. It is travelling so quickly that it does not need its engines to power it. Instead, it acts in the same way as a glider, using the air to slow it down as it approaches the 4.5km-long (2.8-mile-long) runway.

WHY DOES THE SHUTTLE HEAT UP ON RE-ENTRY?

EARTH'S ATMOSPHERE IS MADE UP of minuscule particles of rock and gas. When an orbiter re-enters the atmosphere, it impacts with these particles, heating up because of friction. Parts of the Shuttle can reach up to 1500°C (2732°F), which is hot enough to cause them to melt. Because of this, the nose tip and wing edges are protected by heat-absorbing tiles that prevent the orbiter from getting too hot.

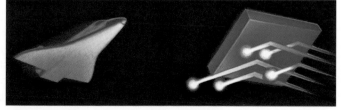

The orbiter is travelling so quickly as it re-enters the atmosphere that tiny particles hit it with great force. In the same way that your hands heat up when you rub them together, the rapid movement of particles against the craft causes it to heat up.

WHAT ARE ION DRIVES?

Ion technology is the future of space travel. It is a cheap, efficient form of propulsion that enables crafts to travel at incredible speeds. Ion drives are one of many technologies that are set to change the way we think about space travel, allowing us to travel further from Earth than ever before.

HOW DOES ION PROPULSION WORK?

ION PROPULSION ENGINES WORK using the same principles as conventional rockets – they expel a force in one direction that propels the craft in the opposite direction. However, instead of using liquid propellant, an ion drive works by accelerating and expelling positively charged atoms (ions). These ions are fired at more than 31km/s (24mps), which is much faster than the exhaust gases of liquid-fuelled rockets. However, their accumulative mass is so small that it would take a spacecraft with an ion drive many months to reach its maximum speed.

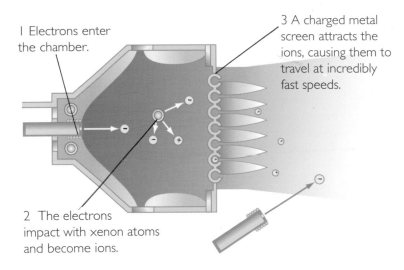

1 Electrons enter the chamber.

3 A charged metal screen attracts the ions, causing them to travel at incredibly fast speeds.

2 The electrons impact with xenon atoms and become ions.

WHICH FORM OF PROPULSION IS MOST EFFECTIVE?

WHILE THE PARTICLES expelled from an ion drive travel much faster than the gases from a conventional rocket, they are not massive enough to provide sufficient thrust. Rockets such as the Space Shuttle can produce millions of pounds of thrust at lift-off, whereas, to begin with, an ion drive can only produce around 20-thousandths of a pound of thrust. This is not enough force to escape Earth's gravitational pull. Crafts with ion drives have to be carried into space by a conventional rocket, but once they have left Earth's orbit, their velocity continues to increase, until they reach much faster speeds than rockets. Ion drives are also much more efficient, using only 80kg (176lbs) of xenon in a two-year mission.

ARE ION DRIVES ALREADY IN USE?

NASA'S DEEP SPACE 1 probe (above), launched in 1998, was the first craft to use ion technology in space. It flew close to the near-Earth asteroid Braille (also known as 1992 KD), guided by an automated navigation system. Afterwards, it investigated the comet Borrelly, completing its mission in late 2001. Deep Space 1 is an experimental craft that is also testing several other new technologies, including more efficient solar panels, and an autonomous operations system, which allows the craft to think and act on its own. Its success has made scientists optimistic about the use of ion technology.

WILL CHEAPER ROCKETS LEAD TO HOLIDAYS IN SPACE?

SOME COMPANIES ARE already taking bookings for leisure trips into space. In 2001, the American millionaire Dennis Tito was the first "tourist" in space, flying into orbit in a Russian Soyuz rocket. Other firms have already spent millions on designing hotels and condominiums on the Moon! As the price of travelling into space lessens, more and more people will make plans to go on the ultimate holiday in orbit.

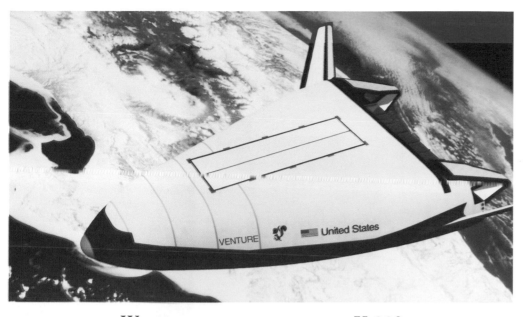

WHAT IS SPECIAL ABOUT THE X-33?

THE X-33 is a single-stage-to-orbit reusable launch vehicle designed by NASA. It is currently a sized-down prototype of a new rocket design called the Venturestar, which will be built if the X-33 is successful. The Venturestar will be able to travel into space and back in one piece, without jettisoning any boosters or fuel tanks, and will lower the cost of putting one pound of payload into orbit by more than 90%.

IS FASTER-THAN-LIGHT TRAVEL POSSIBLE?

IN 1905, ALBERT EINSTEIN published his theory of special relativity. This stated that travel at the speed of light is impossible. He argued that the faster an object moves, the heavier it becomes, so that an object travelling at the speed of light would have infinite mass, which is impossible. Spacecraft are getting faster and faster but may never be able to reach the speeds needed to travel between stars.

Spacecraft like the proposed warp-drive ship above may be able to fly faster than light by creating bubbles of space through which the ship travels.

ARE THERE OTHER ALTERNATIVES TO CONVENTIONAL ROCKETS?

SCIENTISTS AND ENGINEERS are continually working on new ways to carry expensive payloads into space. The X-34 (below left) is a small rocket designed to be launched by an aeroplane. It is hoped that the X-34 will be able to minimise the cost of carrying satellites into orbit. The DC-XA (below right) was a new design for a single-stage-to-orbit vehicle. It made four successful flights before crashing. The Roton is designed to work without the heavy technology needed to pump rocket fuel. Its rotor blades spin, literally throwing propellant into the combustion chamber.

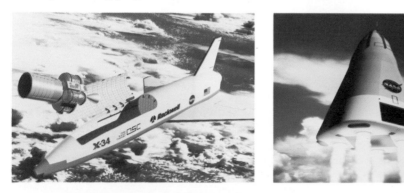

fast facts

HOW DOES AN AEROSPIKE ENGINE WORK?

The Venturestar rocket will be powered by an engine called a linear aerospike. The shape of the engine nozzle, through which gases are released, is designed to allow it to change shape as the rocket changes altitude. This allows the craft to work at maximum efficiency all the way to orbit.

HOW WILL FUTURE SPACECRAFT BE POWERED?

Scientists have suggested giving starships giant sails. Powerful lasers beamed from Earth would propel these craft forwards at incredible speeds. Theoretical warp drives are another possible solution. These would work by contracting space in front of a starship and expanding space behind it. Although the ship itself would not be travelling at the speed of light, the "bubble of space" carrying the ship would be.

WHAT ARE INTERSTELLAR CITIES?

One way of being able to travel beyond the Solar System without having to exceed the speed of light is to build enormous space cities. These would be spaceships capable of sustaining thousands of people, animals and crops for hundreds of years. The journey to other stars would still take thousands of years, but descendants of the original crew would eventually be able to explore distant planets.

WHAT IS HOPE?

The H-II Orbiting Plane, or HOPE, has been designed by the Japanese to carry supplies to and from the International Space Station. It is unique in that it has been developed to fly without a crew. Instead, fully automated systems control the craft on its journey into orbit.

HOW ARE SPACE STATIONS BUILT?

Because space stations are so large, it is impossible to build them on Earth and then carry them into space. Instead, space stations must be built in orbit. This can be a long, difficult and dangerous process. The International Space Station (ISS) is currently in orbit around Earth. It began construction in 1998, but installation of all 100 components will not be finished until 2006. Over forty space flights will be needed to bring parts and equipment to the ISS, and around 160 space walks, totalling nearly 1300 hours, will be required to put it all together.

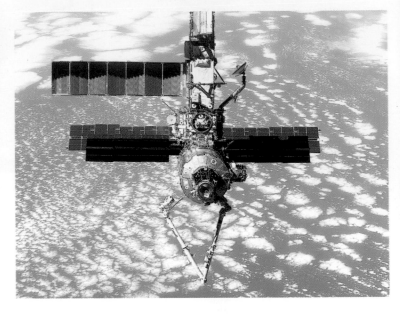

HOW DO SPACE STATIONS KEEP PEOPLE ALIVE?

A SPACE STATION MUST MAINTAIN an atmosphere similar to that on Earth in order for it to be habitable. In the ISS, oxygen is made by electrolysis. A generator splits water into oxygen and hydrogen. Carbon dioxide is collected by special materials and released into outer space. Water is recycled for maximum efficiency. It is collected from various sources including urine, sinks and showers, and cleaned for reuse. The ISS is heated by all the electronic equipment on board.

HOW IS THE ISS POWERED?

LIKE MANY OF THE SATELLITES in orbit around Earth, electricity on the ISS will be generated by solar power. Eight giant solar arrays collect energy from the Sun and transform it into electricity. When the ISS passes through the Earth's shadow it is powered by three rechargeable battery stations. The ISS needs to be boosted periodically in order to prevent it losing speed and altitude. This is done by small rocket engines mounted on the command modules.

Many different countries have contributed materials to the ISS. NASA is responsible for most of the station, but Russia is providing many vital elements.

Thermal panels to control temperature

In case of an emergency, on board the ISS there is a specially designed escape vehicle called the X-38. The X-38 is like a giant glider. It can carry seven people safely down to the surface.

The Japanese external experiment platform, Kibo (Hope)

There will be several laboratories on board the ISS, including the European Space Agency's Columbus Orbital Facility.

HOW DOES SOLAR POWER WORK?

SOLAR TECHNOLOGY CONVERTS sunlight into electricity. Solar cells are made of special materials called semiconductors, mainly silicon. When light strikes, the cell part of it is absorbed into the silicon, and knocks electrons loose. The cell's natural electrical field forces the loose electrons to form a flow, which is an electric current.

The solar panels are provided by NASA. Each solar array is 33m (109ft) long and covers an area of 2508 sq m (27,000 sq ft).

The Space Shuttle can easily dock with the ISS for repairs and supply trips.

WHAT IS IT LIKE INSIDE A SPACE STATION?

CONDITIONS ON BOARD A SPACE STATION can be very strange. There is no gravity, which means that astronauts can float in mid-air and lift heavy objects with ease. In a space station, there is no up or down, which can be very confusing, so the walls, floor and ceiling are painted different colours to help the crew orientate themselves. The lack of gravity means that astronauts can eat or sleep on the walls, or even the ceiling, but it can also prove troublesome. Scientists have to strap themselves to the walls when they are working to stop themselves floating away. The planned ISS habitation module is equipped with everything astronauts need to live normally for long periods in space, including a gym, a galley, medical facilities and a meeting area.

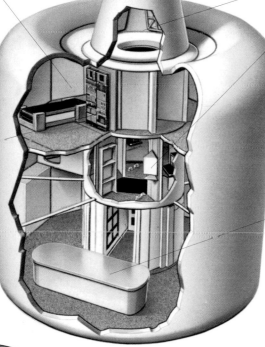

The station gym will be where astronauts work out every day to prevent muscle and bone wastage. It will contain a treadmill and an ergometer (shown below).

The exercise area also contains vital medical equipment.

Although there is no "up" or "down", the ISS will be arranged with carpets, and lights in the ceiling to help astronauts feel at home.

Pressurized tunnel leading to the ISS

The habitation module will sleep four astronauts. The sleeping bags are fixed upright to the wall and are mainly used to keep the astronauts securely in place while they sleep.

The wardroom will be where the astronauts eat and relax. It will contain a large table, a galley area and storage space for their belongings.

Treadmill

Ergometer

WHY IS EXERCISE ESSENTIAL IN SPACE?

BECAUSE THE BODY does not have to fight against gravity in space, there is a serious danger of it losing bone and muscle mass. Astronauts must exercise every day to prevent their muscles wasting away. In the ISS there is a treadmill and a stationary exercise bike, but astronauts must remember to strap themselves on or they will float away.

HOW DO ASTRONAUTS GO TO THE TOILET IN SPACE?

BECAUSE OF THE LACK OF gravity, going to the toilet in space can be a tricky operation. Toilets on board space stations are equipped with restraints to hold an astronaut in place. A powerful vacuum pump is used to create a seal between the body and the seat. Waste products are collected. Some are recycled, while solid waste is disposed of safely.

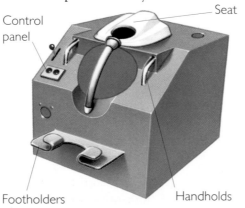

Control panel

Seat

Footholders

Handholds

fast facts

WHAT IS SPACE DEBRIS?

In the same way that humans have discarded many unwanted materials into the ground and oceans, there is now a great deal of pollution in space. Millions of pieces of space debris orbit the Earth, mainly the remains of spacecraft or satellites that have been discarded.

HOW CAN SPACE DEBRIS AFFECT SPACE TRAVEL?

It is estimated that there are over 10,000 items of space debris larger than 10cm (4in) orbiting the Earth. Because craft such as the Space Shuttle move at incredibly high speeds, this orbiting junk can prove very dangerous. A fleck of paint travelling in the opposite direction to a Space Shuttle could impact at speeds of 40,000km/h (25,000mph). Such an impact could easily smash the orbiter window, depressurizing the cabin and killing everybody on board the Shuttle.

WHAT HAPPENS WHEN A SPACE STATION IS NO LONGER NEEDED?

When a space station is no longer needed, or it is too old to be of any use, it is abandoned and destroyed. In early 2001 the Russian Mir space station, which had orbited Earth for fifteen years, was abandoned. Its rocket engines were fired to slow it down, and it lost altitude. As it entered the Earth's atmosphere, it burned up.

WHAT DO ASTRONAUTS DO FOR FUN?

Early space missions on the Space Shuttle and Mir involved astronauts doing a great deal of work and having no leisure time. This proved unhealthy. All astronauts aboard the ISS will have time to themselves, so that they can e-mail friends, play games, read or just watch Earth from the window.

WHAT IS SPACE SCIENCE?

Space stations have given scientists a unique laboratory that can be found nowhere on Earth – one that is unaffected by gravity. Gravity influences everything on Earth, from the way that the human body works to the growth of crystals used in semiconductors for computers. In orbit, however, a space station's speed cancels out the Earth's gravitational pull, so scientists can carry out experiments in weightless conditions.

In a space station, such as Skylab (above), experiments can be carried out in microgravitational conditions. Although there are gravitational pulls present, none are strong enough to affect the scientific tests.

WHAT IS GRAVITY?

EVERY OBJECT WITH MASS has a gravitational pull, even you and I. The more material that an object contains, the stronger its gravitational pull. Objects such as a football have tiny gravitational pulls that are barely noticeable, whereas much larger things, such as planets and stars, have very strong forces of gravity. Imagine that space is a thin rubber sheet. If you placed a large object such as a bowling ball on the sheet, it would create a dent. Other objects would roll into this dent, towards the bowling ball, if they passed by too closely. In a similar way, stars and planets create deep gravitational wells in space. The more massive the object, the deeper the gravitational well.

Earth creates a moderate gravitational well towards which all nearby objects are attracted. A ball thrown upwards will always be pulled back down because the force of gravity pulls it towards Earth's core.

ARE SPACE STATIONS AFFECTED BY GRAVITY?

SPACE STATIONS TYPICALLY ORBIT BETWEEN 192 and 576km (120 and 360 miles) above the Earth's surface. The Earth's gravitational pull is still quite strong, even at this altitude. If you were standing on Earth and dropped a ball, it would fall to the ground. If an astronaut on a space station dropped a ball, it would fall, too. However, the ball would appear to float in mid-air because it, the astronaut and the space station are all falling at the same speed. They are not falling *towards* the Earth, but *around* it. This condition is called microgravity.

WHAT KIND OF EXPERIMENTS ARE DONE IN SPACE?

WORKING IN SPACE ALLOWS scientists to explore how different things are affected by gravity. The European Space Agency's Spacelab was designed with two pressurized laboratories where microgravity experiments could be carried out. Special racks held hundreds of different kinds of cells and organisms including bacteria, lentil seedlings and shrimp eggs. Tests were run on these organisms, and on human beings, to determine whether they behaved differently in space.

DO HEAVY AND LIGHT OBJECTS FALL AT THE SAME RATE?

IT WAS ISAAC NEWTON who discovered that all falling bodies accelerate at the same rate. His second law of motion states that the greater an object's mass, the greater the force required to accelerate it. A bowling ball weighing 7kg is pulled to Earth by a gravitational force 100 times as strong as a 70g tennis ball. However, because the bowling ball's mass is 100 times greater to start with, the acceleration of the two balls will be exactly the same.

WHAT TECHNOLOGIES HAVE BEEN DEVELOPED IN SPACE?

SPACE SCIENCE HAS LED TO many amazing developments in technology. Scientists have studied combustion in microgravity in order to design more efficient jet engines. We have all benefited from technology that was designed for use in space. Microchips found in digital watches, computers and mobile phones were first developed so that lots of equipment could fit into a small spacecraft. Many household items have come about because of space technology, including air-tight cans and tin foil. Technologies such as solar power and keyhole surgery have also advanced largely due to the space programme.

WHAT OTHER FORCES ARE THERE IN THE UNIVERSE?

GRAVITY IS ONE OF ONLY FOUR FORCES that govern every event in the entire Universe. Gravity binds together the Universe, while electromagnetic force is responsible for light and electricity. A strong nuclear force holds together basic particles, and a weak nuclear force causes the decay of unstable atoms. These four forces may have been united during the Big Bang, emitted as one superforce bound by extremely high temperatures. As temperatures began to cool, the superforce was gradually broken down into four separate forces. All four forces are linked with special particles that act in the same way as couriers, transferring the force from one place to another. Electromagnetism and gravitation can work over large distances, but the two nuclear forces only operate on an atomic level.

IS THERE A THEORY OF EVERYTHING?

TOGETHER, THE FOUR FORCES can explain everything that happens in the Universe. Many scientists are now working to prove that they are all separate parts of the same universal force that once existed at the birth of the Universe (see above).

WHAT HAPPENS DURING A NUCLEAR EXPLOSION?

NUCLEAR REACTIONS are the result of the strong nuclear force, which binds together the particles that form atoms. During a nuclear explosion, this powerful force is released, expelling vast amounts of energy.

Gravity broke away first as temperatures began to cool. Gravity is responsible for the attraction between matter in the Universe.

The electromagnetic force, which binds atoms together into molecules, and the weak nuclear force were the last to separate.

In the extreme conditions of the Big Bang, there may have been only one force.

The strong nuclear force, responsible for atomic fission and fusion, separated next.

WHY IS SPACE DANGEROUS?

From Earth, space can seem calm and quiet, but in actual fact it is deadly. If humans ventured into space without the protection of a spacesuit they would die almost instantly. The lack of oxygen would mean suffocation. But before this, the lack of pressure would cause gases in the blood to separate as if it were boiling. With no protection from the Sun's harmful ultraviolet radiation, the astronaut would be burned to death.

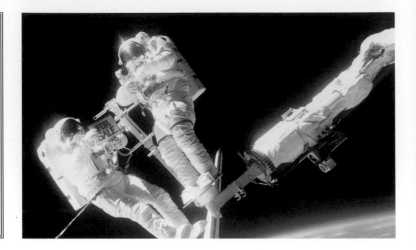

HOW ARE ASTRONAUTS PROTECTED IN SPACE?

EVERY ASTRONAUT who leaves a spacecraft has to wear a specially designed spacesuit. It is called an Extra-Vehicular Activity (EVA) suit and acts like a miniature spaceship. Layers of material protect the astronaut from the Sun's rays, as well as tiny particles of space dust that travel at hundreds of thousands of kilometres per hour. The suit provides everything that an astronaut needs to survive in space for short periods of time, including oxygen to breathe and water to drink. It also provides heating and cooling, communication devices and toilet facilities.

WHAT KINDS OF JOBS DO ASTRONAUTS DO?

ASTRONAUTS HAVE TO PERFORM many different duties that involve leaving their spacecraft. The International Space Station, which is currently under construction, requires many adjustments that can only be done by trained personnel. Robotic equipment is used to put the components of the space station together, but much of the construction can only be done by hand. Astronauts also have to make repairs to complicated items such as the Hubble Space Telescope and damaged satellites.

A camera on board the Manned Manoeuvring Unit allows scientists and mission controllers to see what the astronaut is doing.

Spacesuits have shiny, gold-plated visors that protect the astronaut's eyes from harmful solar radiation.

Spacesuits are heavily insulated with 13 different layers to cope with the extremes of temperature. They are white to reflect the Sun's light.

Small thrusters built into the Manned Manoeuvring Unit allow astronauts to adjust their position very slightly, or to move rapidly through space.

Astronauts wear a large, specially designed nappy, called a Maximum Absorption Garment, to absorb waste products.

Specially designed life-support systems in the astronaut's backpack supply a pure oxygen atmosphere and remove the dangerous carbon dioxide that the astronaut exhales.

Spacesuits maintain a constant pressure around the body by surrounding it with a giant balloon. Neoprene-coated fibres restrict the outer side of the balloon, keeping the air pressure inside at a constant level.

WHAT IS THE MANNED MANOEUVRING UNIT?

MOVING AROUND IN SPACE is much like trying to move underwater. Wearing a large suit makes movement even more difficult, and when time is short, an astronaut must be able to move quickly. The Manned Manoeuvring Unit was specially designed to allow astronauts to move swiftly and safely through space. The MMU is like an armchair with small thrusters attached. It is operated by a hand control similar to those used in computer games.

HOW DO ASTRONAUTS STOP THEMSELVES FLOATING AWAY?

MOVEMENT IN SPACE is very difficult because if you push on something, you will move in the opposite direction. Astronauts on the Gemini missions complained that when they tried to use a spanner in space they spun in the opposite direction. Microgravity means that an astronaut is in danger of floating away mid-job, or losing a vital tool into outer space. To aid astronauts to move around outside, spacecraft are equipped with handles and special footholders into which feet can be locked.

CAN ASTRONAUTS EAT OR DRINK IN SPACE?

BECAUSE ASTRONAUTS CAN BE in their spacesuits for up to seven hours, they need water to avoid dehydration. Spacesuits are equipped with the In-suit Drink Bag (IDB), a plastic pouch connected to the inside of the suit's torso. It can hold nearly 2 litres (32oz) of water that can be accessed via a straw. The helmet also has a slot for rice-paper-covered fruit and a cereal bar, should the astronaut get hungry.

WHO FIRST WALKED IN SPACE?

THE FIRST HUMAN BEING to leave the confines of a spacecraft and take a "walk" in space was the Soviet cosmonaut Alexei Leonov. He crawled through the airlock of Voskhod 2 in 1965 and was so overwhelmed by the view that he shouted out the first words he could think of: "The Earth is round!" During his twenty minutes in space, Leonov's spacesuit expanded, due to the lack of pressure, and he was barely able to fit back in the airlock.

fast facts

HOW MUCH DO SPACE-SUITS COST TO MAKE?

Because each EVA suit acts like a miniature spacecraft that can act independently of the space station, each one costs around 12 million US dollars to construct.

HOW DO ASTRONAUTS TRAIN TO SPACE WALK?

Astronauts train to move around in space in enormous water tanks on Earth. They wear a spacesuit similar to the one used in orbit, and practice space walking and using tools. Water tanks are used because the buoyancy of an inflated suit in water is a very accurate simulation of microgravity.

WHAT WILL FUTURE SPACESUITS BE LIKE?

Scientists are constantly working on new ways to make suits less expensive and easier to move around in. For the planned missions to send astronauts to Mars, NASA are working on suits that are much more lightweight than those used by Apollo astronauts on the Moon, which were clumsy and heavy. The new suits should allow the astronauts to explore the planet much more freely.

WHY DO SPACECRAFT NEED AIRLOCKS?

AIRLOCKS ARE VITAL FOR PROTECTING the crew of a spacecraft. In a submerged submarine, if there was no airlock, the vessel would instantly be flooded with water as soon as the hatch was opened. In the same way, a space station with no airlock would depressurize the instant the door was opened, killing anybody on board who was not wearing a spacesuit. This is because air always tries to remain at a level pressure. If the pressure inside a spacecraft is greater than the pressure outside, as soon as the hull is breached, air will rush out into outer space.

Astronauts entering a space station will open an outer door to the airlock. Once inside, the airlock will be pressurized to a level safe for humans.

Only when the pressure in the airlock is the same as the pressure inside the rest of the space station will the inner airlock door be released.

HOW DOES A SPACE PROBE NAVIGATE?

Space probes are highly advanced robotic craft, often the size of a large car, launched into space to investigate celestial objects. They use radio transmitters to communicate with mission specialists on Earth. All probes have highly sensitive electronic equipment on board.

1 The first probe to visit Neptune was Voyager 2 in 1989. It sent pictures back to Earth that took over four hours to reach us.

2 The Mariner 10 probe passed within 327km (203 miles) of Mercury's surface when it flew by three times in 1974.

3 The Viking probes that visited Mars in 1976 landed on the surface and took samples of Martian soil for analysis.

ARE THERE DIFFERENT KINDS OF SPACE PROBE?

SPACE PROBES are designed to do different jobs. Some fly by their target at a distance of several thousand kilometres, taking pictures of the planet's surface and surveying its atmosphere. Other probes are designed to enter a planet's orbit, which allows them to survey the planet in more detail.
The probes that provide the most information about planets are called landers because they touch down on the planet's surface.

WHEN WAS THE FIRST SUCCESSFUL SPACE PROBE LAUNCHED?

THE FIRST SPACE PROBE to complete its mission was Luna 2. It was launched by the USSR in 1959 and successfully landed on its destination – the Moon. Its predecessor, Luna 1, was launched towards the same target several months earlier but missed by 6000km (3730 miles).

Independent rovers such as the one shown here can travel short distances across a planet, analyzing the terrain.

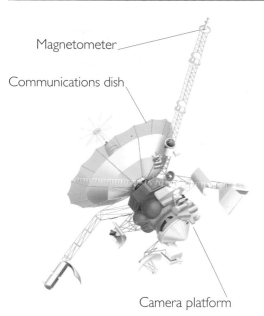

Magnetometer

Communications dish

Camera platform

The Galileo probe used the Sun's gravity to catapult it across the immense distance to Jupiter.

HAVE PROBES VISITED EVERY PLANET IN THE SOLAR SYSTEM?

SO FAR SPACE PROBES have visited every planet in the Solar System except Pluto. Venus was the first planet to be investigated as Mariner 2 flew by in 1962. Mariner 10 orbited Mercury in 1975. Mars is the most visited planet in the Solar System, with over five probes landing on its surface. The Pioneer and Voyager probes, launched between 1979 and 1989, investigated the outer planets Jupiter, Saturn, Uranus and Neptune. The Pluto-Kuiper Express aims to visit Pluto between 2006 and 2008.

DO PROBES ONLY INVESTIGATE PLANETS?

SCIENTISTS have sent probes to investigate many kinds of celestial objects. In 1995, the Ulysses probe was launched towards the Sun and took readings of the solar wind and the star's magnetism. The Giotto probe, launched in 1986, battled its way past flying debris and gas into the heart of Halley's comet, taking incredible pictures of its nucleus. Asteroids have also been visited by space probes. The Near Earth Asteroid Rendezvous probe landed on the asteroid Eros in 2001.

WHAT SORT OF EXPERIMENTS DO PROBES CONDUCT?

PROBES investigate as much of their target as they can. Cameras take an assortment of photographs from different angles and distances, while antennae detect magnetism and radio waves. Lander probes, such as the Vikings that touched down on Mars, can take soil samples and analyze the atmosphere.

fast facts

DO PROBES TRAVEL IN A STRAIGHT LINE?

The Ulysses probe was actually launched towards the planet Jupiter although its destination was the Sun. This was so that the giant planet's gravitational pull could be used as a free source of energy to catapult the probe millions of miles across the Solar System.

CAN PROBES FULLY INVESTIGATE THE SUN?

The Sun's intense heat means that it is impossible for probes to fly too close to it. However, NASA's Solar Probe is set to fly within several million kilometres of the surface, taking measurements from within the Sun's corona.

WHAT IS THE FARTHEST DISTANCE A PROBE HAS TRAVELLED?

The Pioneer and Voyager probes did not stop when they flew by their target planets but continued deep into the dark outer regions of the Solar System. They will continue travelling for millions of kilometres before their power source runs out.

HOW ARE IMAGES SENT FROM PROBES TO EARTH?

Images are transmitted as radio signals that are received by radio telescopes on Earth. There are receiving stations placed around the world so that it does not matter where the Earth is in its rotation when the signals arrive.

HOW ARE PROBES POWERED?

Most probes are powered by electricity generated by solar panels attached to the probe's casing. Others use a nuclear generator. One modern method of propelling a space probe is the ion drive, which uses reactions in a chemical gas instead of combustion.

HOW DOES A PROBE LAND?

A PROBE'S LANDING PROCEDURE is a complicated and dangerous one. Because scientists do not know everything about a target planet, they can never be sure what the conditions will be like when a probe lands. Mars, for example, suffers from enormous dust storms that could seriously damage a probe descending to the surface. The diagram below shows a procedure for a landing.

1 In orbit, the lander separates from the main body of the probe. Once it is deep inside the planet's atmosphere, it releases a parachute.

2 Despite its parachute, the probe is still travelling at speed when it hits the surface. Probes like Pathfinder have inflatable cushions that ease the landing.

3 Once landed, a probe begins its experiments. Pathfinder released a robotic rover called Sojourner to investigate beyond the landing site.

WHAT IS A SATELLITE?

Any object in orbit around a celestial body is called a satellite. Earth has had its own natural satellite – the Moon – for billions of years. Since 1957, however, hundreds of artificial satellites have been launched into orbit around Earth, each transmitting a cacophony of radio signals to locations across the planet. Satellites are now vital to modern life and are used in many areas of technology, including communications, entertainment and espionage.

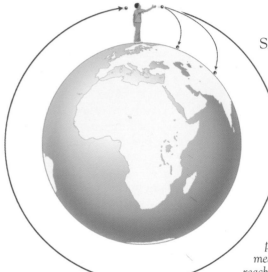

Although the ball is in freefall towards Earth, the planet's curve means that it never reaches it.

HOW DO SATELLITES STAY IN ORBIT?

SATELLITES MUST BE LAUNCHED into orbit with enough speed to prevent Earth's gravity from pulling them back down to the ground. Imagine throwing a ball horizontally. Gravity pulls the ball back to Earth very quickly. If the ball could be thrown hard enough, however, then it would have enough force to keep on travelling horizontally for ever. It would be in orbit. A satellite at an altitude of 200km (120 miles) must be travelling at 7.8km/s (4.8mp/s) to prevent it being pulled back down to Earth.

HOW ARE MILITARY SATELLITES USED?

A GREAT MANY of the satellites sent into space by the USA and Russia are used for military activities. These range from eavesdropping on important telephone calls to detecting the x-rays and electromagnetic pulses given off by nuclear explosions. Early military satellites were used to take close-up pictures of enemy territory but had to return home to have their film developed. Modern satellites use digital technology to take photographs, so they never run out of film. Amazingly, they can photograph things as small as the headlines on a newspaper.

HOW DO COMMUNICATIONS SATELLITES RELAY INFORMATION?

COMMUNICATIONS SATELLITES are used for many different tasks, including television broadcasts and telephone calls. A telephone call made from England to the USA would be sent to the nearest Earth station, which would use its giant antenna to beam the call into space in the form of radio waves. The satellite would receive these radio waves and beam them back down to an antenna on the other side of the planet.

The American Defense Support Programme (DSP) satellites, shown right, are used to detect the launch of enemy missiles. Infrared sensors detect the heat released when a ballistic missile is launched, and a warning message is instantly transmitted to Earth.

Communications satellites such as the Intelsat V send and receive signals via antenna dishes. They can send messages to boats and planes as well as to receiving stations on the ground.

WHAT KIND OF ORBITS DO SATELLITES HAVE?

SATELLITES ARE PROGRAMMED to follow one of four different orbits. A satellite in geostationary orbit takes the same time to orbit the Earth as the Earth does to spin, therefore always remaining over the same point on the planet. This orbit is mainly used for communications satellites. Low-Earth orbits, often used by spy satellites, can be lower than 250km (155 miles) above the planet. Polar-orbit satellites orbit at around 800km (590 miles), while highly-elliptical-orbit satellites have very low altitudes when they are closest to Earth, but pass far beyond the planet when they are at their most distant.

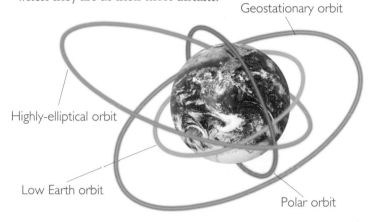

Geostationary orbit

Highly-elliptical orbit

Low Earth orbit

Polar orbit

HOW DO SATELLITES PREDICT THE WEATHER?

METEOROLOGY SATELLITES, which orbit in geostationary and polar orbits, can keep a constant watch over the weather systems at work around the planet. They record data, such as cloud formation and movement, pressures, wind speeds and humidities, and send them to Earth, where scientists can use them to predict weather in preparation for weather forecasts. Satellites are also used to detect hurricanes – fierce tropical storms with wind speeds of over 130km/h (80mph). These storms can strike with very little warning, but satellites can detect them before they hit land, warning people of danger in time for them to take cover.

WHAT ARE EARTH-RESOURCES SATELLITES?

SATELLITES CAN HELP SCIENTISTS learn a great deal more about the planet than instruments on aircraft and ships can. They use Earth-resources satellites to monitor every part of the world in order to find out information about the planet's condition. Satellites can detect things such as the amount of water in a field of crops, which will give early warning of a harvest failure. They can also detect large areas of deforestation, showing changes over large periods of time.

HOW DO SATELLITES REMAIN STABLE IN SPACE?

A SATELLITE CANNOT do its job properly if it is not stable. A satellite dish must always point towards its location, or signals will be lost in space. In order to keep satellites from flying out of control, some are deliberately designed to spin. In the same way that a spinning top remains stable if it is spinning quickly, a satellite that is spinning will not deviate from its course. Some satellites have small, spinning wheels at various points on their frame. These wheels can be used to realign the satellite if it moves off course.

WHAT IS GPS?

GPS, or the Global Positioning System, is designed to aid navigation around the planet. It consists of 24 satellites in six different orbits around Earth. Their position in these orbits means that any receiver, anywhere on Earth, can always receive a signal from four satellites or more. Using data from these signals, a GPS receiver can work out its position, including altitude, to within a few metres.

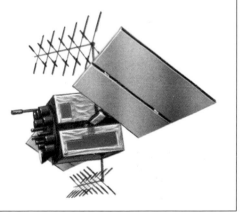

HOW DO GPS RECEIVERS WORK?

GLOBAL POSITIONING SATELLITES beam signals to special receivers on Earth. These receivers, which are not much larger than mobile phones, know the difference between when the satellite signal was sent and when it was received. This allows the receiver to work out the distance between each of the satellites and itself, and therefore calculate its position.

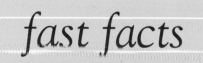

fast facts

WHEN WERE SATELLITES FIRST USED?

The idea of transmitting radio signals across the world by beaming them through space was first put to use in 1954. The US Navy sent a message from Washington DC to Hawaii by bouncing a signal off the Moon.

WHAT WAS ECHO?

Echo was an aluminized balloon launched by NASA in 1960. It was used to reflect radio signals across North America.

HOW DO SATELLITES AID MINING?

Industry depends on a continuous supply of non-renewable resources such as oil, gas and coal. Because most of the easily obtained supplies of these resources have already been depleted, satellites are used to scan the surface for harder-to-spot supplies. Oil can be spotted from space as it seeps into the sea from deposits beneath the seabed.

ARE THERE OTHER SOLAR SYSTEMS?

Four hundred years ago, an astronomer named Giordano Bruno was burned at the stake for suggesting the existence of other Earth-like worlds. Today we know that there are potentially billions of extrasolar planets in the Milky Way. None found so far resemble Earth. Indeed, many are shockingly different from our world. Although none of the planets investigated so far have shown any signs of life, many astronomers believe that it is only a matter of time before Earth's twin planet is discovered.

HOW CAN WE DETECT OTHER SOLAR SYSTEMS?

EXTRASOLAR PLANETS ARE very difficult to see because they are outshone by the light from their parent stars. It can be determined whether or not a star has a planetary system by observing whether or not the star's light "wobbles". As a planet orbits a star, its gravitational pull will cause the star's light to bend slightly, and thus to change colour. This technique only works for giant planets, however, because an Earth-sized world would have little effect on its parent.

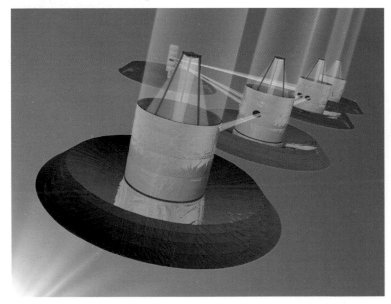

WHAT IS THE PLANET FINDER?

NASA's Terrestrial Planet Finder (above), due to be launched in 2010, will be powerful enough to search the brightest 1000 stars in the galaxy. It will be able to spot Earth-like planets, and will even be able to detect what their atmospheres are like.

HOW LIKELY IS ALIEN LIFE?

THE ASTRONOMER FRANK DRAKE pioneered the search for intelligent life elsewhere in the Universe. He claimed that for intelligent life, capable of communicating over interstellar distances, to arise on a planet, conditions must be perfect. He came up with an equation to estimate the number of civilizations in the galaxy with the means of communicating with Earth:

$$N = R^* fp\ ne\ fl\ fi\ fc\ L$$

N = the number of civilizations with the ability to communicate over long distances.

R = the rate of formation of suitable stars.

fp = the fraction of those stars with planets.

ne = the number of Earth-like worlds in a planetary system.

fl = the fraction of Earth-like worlds on which life develops.

fi = the fraction of life-forms that develop intelligence.

fc = the fraction of intelligent life-forms that develop electromagnetic communication technology.

L = the lifetime of these communicating civilizations.

How can we search for aliens?

RADIO ASTRONOMY IS THE MOST effective way to search for alien life. Radio telescopes can be positioned all over the world – as radio waves are not affected by the Earth's atmosphere, and can pick up signals from across the Universe. Radio telescopes such as Arecibo (below) in Puerto Rico, and the Very Large Array, enable astronomers to view space in all directions for signs of alien intelligence.

fast facts

What are UFOs?

UFO stands for Unidentified Flying Object. Thousands of reports of mysterious objects in the skies are made every year. Over 95% of these can be explained in terms of everyday things such as weather balloons.

What happened in Roswell?

One of the most famous UFO encounters was in Roswell, USA, in 1948. A craft was seen by several witnesses crashing next to a military base. A strange metallic material was found next to the crash site. The metal was thin, but was resistant to extreme heat and very strong.

Can we communicate with aliens?

AS WELL AS RECEIVING SIGNALS from outer space, radio telescopes such as Arecibo can also broadcast signals to the entire galaxy and beyond. In 1974, radio waves beamed from the Arecibo telescope carried a message deep into space. The message consisted of 1679 pulses that, when arranged into a grid 23 columns wide and 73 rows tall, creates an image (below). The message was aimed at a dense ball of stars called M13, which is so far away from Earth that it could take up to 50,000 years for a possible reply.

The message contained information about life on planet Earth, including:

The numbers 1–10 in binary code

The most important elements of life

A strand of DNA, which carries the blueprint of life

The image of a human, the world's population and the average height of a human

Earth's position in the Solar System

An image of the Arecibo telescope

Lights from big cities, burning oil wells and large fleets of boats are visible from space at night (above). The Pioneer probes each had plates showing a man and woman giving a greeting, and Earth's position in the Solar System.

How could aliens find out about Earth?

IN 1990, THE GALILEO SPACE PROBE began to investigate Earth. It was determining whether it is possible to detect signs of life on a planet when viewed from space. The probe detected that Earth had water on its surface and oxygen in its atmosphere, which told scientists that the planet contained life. As well as this, Earth at night is like a glowing neon signpost, alerting aliens to our whereabouts. The Pioneer space probes (above) had special plates engraved with symbols in case the probes ever encountered intelligent life on their journeys into space.

GLOSSARY

Absolute zero The coldest temperature possible, or –273°C (–459°F).

Asteroid A small rocky body orbiting the Sun. Asteroids can range in size from smaller than a few metres in diameter to larger than a thousand kilometres across.

Big Bang A theory of the beginning of the Universe which states that it started from a violent explosion around 13 billion years ago.

Black hole The core of a collapsed star with a gravitational pull so strong that nothing can escape from it, not even light.

Celestial body Any object in the sky such as a moon, planet or star.

Comet An object composed of dust and ice that orbits the Sun. When a comet travels too close to the Sun, the solar wind melts ice from the comet, thereby forming its tail.

Elliptical This term is used to describe an elongated circle.

Galaxy An enormous body of stars, gas and dust that is held together by gravity. Galaxies are separated from one another by voids of empty space.

Gravitational pull The mutual force of attraction between masses. The gravitational pull of a planet or star is very strong because of its large mass.

Halley's comet One of the most famous comets to be seen from Earth. It orbits the Earth once every 76 years.

Light year A unit of measurement based on the distance that light travels in an Earth year.

Meteor These are streaks of light that appear briefly in the night sky. They occur when particles of rock or dust left by comets burn up in the Earth's atmosphere. They are also known as shooting stars

Microgravity This is extremely low gravity. Astronauts experience this when floating in orbit, as there are no objects with large enough mass to pull them to any surface.

Orbit This is the path of one celestial object around another celestial object with a greater mass. For example, the Earth orbits the Sun.

Planet A planet is a spherical celestial body that orbits the Sun, or any star. There are nine known planets in our Solar System.

Quasars These are exploding centres of remote, aged galaxies.

Radar Short for RAdio Detecting And Ranging. It works by sending out a short burst of radio waves and then listening for the echo. In this way operators can determine how far away an object is and what it is made of.

Solar flare These are enormous and unpredictable explosions that occur in the Earth's atmosphere.

Solar System This is everything that orbits our star, the Sun. It includes 60 moons, millions of asteroids, meteoroids and comets. It also includes the Oort Cloud, which is a vast sphere of comets.

Supernova A star that suddenly increases greatly in brightness due to an internal explosion ejecting most of its mass.

Terraforming The process by which a planet's atmosphere can be changed, thereby making it able to support human life.

Total eclipse During a total eclipse, the Moon appears (from Earth) to cover the Sun completely. Total eclipses occur once every 18 months.

Universe The Universe is everything that exists, including humankind, planets, stars, moons and galaxies.

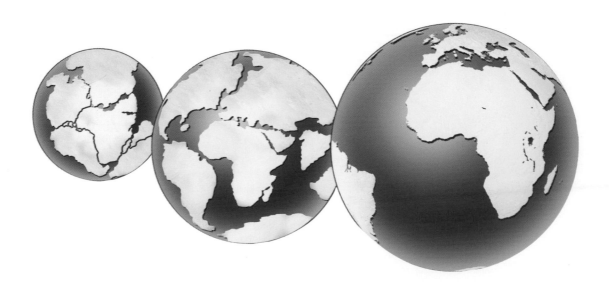

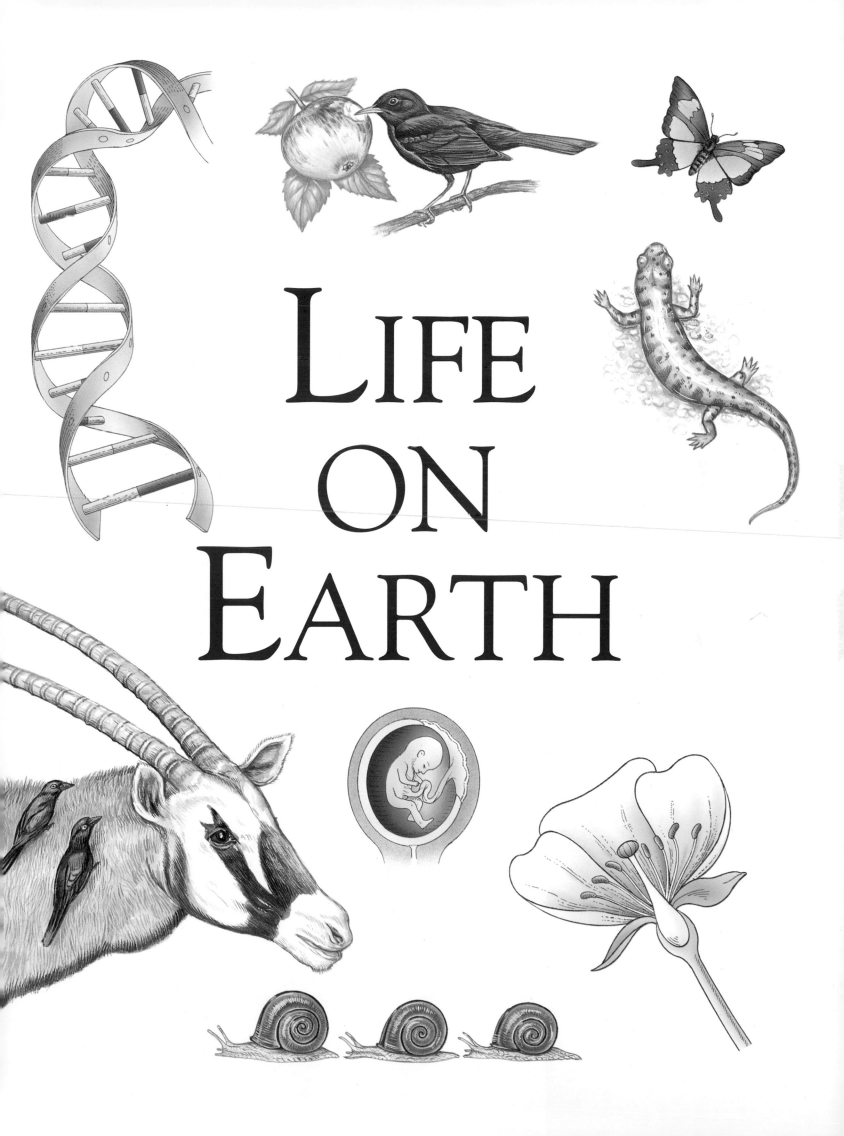

LIFE ON EARTH

WHERE IN THE UNIVERSE ARE WE?

The universe is the name we give to all of space. Astronomers use huge telescopes, both on Earth and in space, to measure light, x-rays and radio waves from objects that are billions of light years away. Earth is one of the nine planets that orbit our Sun. It is part of the Milky Way Galaxy, one of billions of galaxies in the universe.

Sun Venus Mars Saturn Neptune

Mercury Earth Jupiter Uranus Pluto

WHICH IS THE NEAREST STAR?

THE SUN is our nearest star. It is 149.6 million km (92.9 million miles) away from Earth. Stars are massive nuclear reactors, generating energy in their cores. It is the heat and light from the Sun that makes life on Earth possible. The huge gravity pull of the Sun keeps the planets of our Solar System orbiting around it.

WHAT ARE THE PLANETS OF THE SOLAR SYSTEM?

THE FIRST FOUR planets are known as the Inner Planets. The remaining five are the Outer Planets.

Planet	Diameter	Length of year	No. of moons
Mercury	4878km	88 Earth days	0
Venus	12,103km	225 Earth days	0
Earth	12,756km	365 Earth days	1
Mars	6794km	687 Earth days	2
Jupiter	142,800km	11.9 Earth years	16
Saturn	120,000km	29.5 Earth years	18
Uranus	52,400km	84.0 Earth years	15
Neptune	49,400km	164.8 Earth years	8
Pluto	1100km	248.5 Earth years	1

WHAT IS A GALAXY?

A GALAXY is an enormous group of stars held together by gravity. Our galaxy, the Milky Way, is in the shape of a spiral. Other galaxies are elliptical or irregular. There may be 100 billion galaxies in the universe. Many of them are grouped together in clusters, with huge areas of space in between.

spiral galaxy   elliptical galaxy   irregular galaxy

WHY DO CONSTELLATIONS HAVE SUCH STRANGE NAMES?

HUMAN BEINGS have always tried to see pictures in the patterns the stars make. The names given to those pictures by European scholars in medieval times and earlier are often used by astronomers today. Most of them are in Latin as that was the language of scholarship in Europe for hundreds of years.

Aquila (the eagle)   *Scorpius* (the scorpion)

fast facts

IS THERE LIFE ELSEWHERE IN THE UNIVERSE?

As there are so many billions of planets in the universe, it may be that life exists on some of them. In 1996 scientists believed they had discovered signs of fossilized life in a meteorite that landed on Earth from Mars.

WHAT ARE SHOOTING STARS?

Shooting stars are meteors, made of particles of rock and dust, that shine brightly as they burn up in the Earth's upper atmosphere.

WHY IS IT SOMETIMES HARD TO SEE THE STARS?

The stars are still there! It may be that cloud is covering the night sky. Also, there is so much artificial light at night now, from homes and street lighting, that it is often not dark enough to see the stars.

WHAT IS AN ECLIPSE?

Eclipses happen for a brief period when the Moon, Earth and Sun are in line. A lunar eclipse happens when the Earth lies between the Moon and the Sun, blocking off the light to the Moon, so that the Moon seems to vanish. A solar eclipse is when the Moon blocks the Sun's light from the Earth, so that the Sun seems to disappear.

Space travel gave human beings their first opportunity to see the Earth from outside the Earth's atmosphere.

WHEN DID SPACE EXPLORATION BEGIN?

THE FIRST ARTIFICIAL SATELLITE, *Sputnik 1*, was launched by the USSR in October 1957. The same year, a dog called Laika was the first living creature to travel in space in *Sputnik 2*. It was the USSR again that put the first human in space in 1961, when Yuri Gagarin travelled in *Vostok 1*. In 1969, US astronauts were the first to land on the Moon in *Apollo 11*.

As there is no wind or weather on the Moon to erase them, the footprints left by astronauts are still there!

WHY DOES THE MOON CHANGE SHAPE EACH MONTH?

OF COURSE, the Moon does not really change shape – it just seems as though it does. The Moon orbits the Earth once every 27.3 days. It has no light of its own, but as it moves around, it is lit by the Sun. Only the part of the Moon that is both turned towards the Earth and lit by the Sun is visible on Earth. The amount of the Moon's surface that can be seen changes as the Moon's position changes.

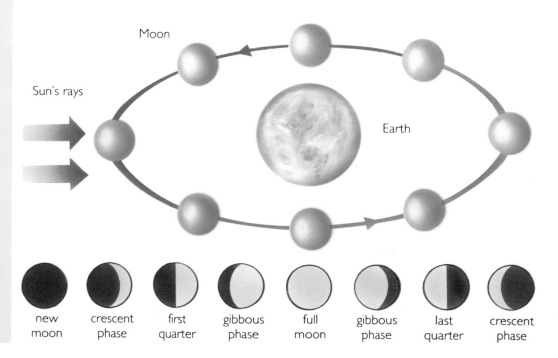

Moon

Sun's rays

Earth

new moon   crescent phase   first quarter   gibbous phase   full moon   gibbous phase   last quarter   crescent phase

WHAT IS INSIDE THE EARTH?

Beneath the land and water that cover the Earth's surface lie layers of rock and metal at very high temperatures. The deepest mines ever dug have not reached the bottom of the outer layer, called the crust. Under the crust, a layer called the mantle is thought to be made partly of solid and partly of molten rock. At the centre of the Earth, there is an outer core of molten metal and an inner core of solid metal, probably largely iron.

crust
between 5 and 80km
(3 and 50 miles) thick

mantle
2900km (1800 miles)
thick

HOW ARE EARTHQUAKES MEASURED?

THE SIZE of the shock waves from an earthquake is measured on the Richter scale. No earthquake has ever measured more than 9 on this scale. However, the size of the shock waves cannot tell us how much damage the earthquake has done. That depends on many factors, such as the kind of soil on which buildings are constructed, how they are built and so on. The effects of earthquakes are measured on the Modified Mercalli scale. The highest point on this scale is 12, which describes the total destruction of all buildings but has luckily rarely been used.

outer core
2255km (1400 miles) thick

inner core
1200km (745 miles) thick

WHAT CAUSES EARTHQUAKES?

THE EARTH'S CRUST is made up of 15 pieces or "plates", which float on the molten rock below. The places where these plates meet are called faults. Along the lines of faults, the plates move and push against each other. Sometimes this causes a violent shock, with waves of tremors moving out and shaking the Earth's surface.

The San Andreas fault runs along the west coast of the United States of America. Most older houses in San Francisco, which lies near the fault, are built of wood. They do not collapse as easily as brick buildings if the ground shakes.

CAN ANY BUILDING WITHSTAND AN EARTHQUAKE?

NO STRUCTURE can withstand very large earthquakes, but by using reinforced materials and foundations that allow for movement, architects have been able to design buildings able to survive even quite strong shocks.

In Tokyo new buildings are designed to withstand most earth tremors.

WHAT IS A GEYSER?

IN SOME AREAS, underground lakes, rivers and springs are heated by molten rocks below. The hot water bubbles to the surface in springs and forms pools, or it may shoot upwards under great pressure, forming a geyser.

This famous geyser in Yellowstone National Park, USA, is known as "Old Faithful".

fast facts

CAN EARTHQUAKES BE PREDICTED?

Not very well. Scientific instruments attempt to detect early signs, and the behaviour of birds and animals may give warning of a shock, but none of these methods is currently foolproof.

WHAT IS THE EPICENTRE OF AN EARTHQUAKE?

The epicentre is the point on the Earth's surface directly above where the earthquake occurs. Shock waves move out from the epicentre to surrounding areas.

WHAT IS A TSUNAMI?

A tsunami is a huge tidal wave, caused by an undersea earthquake. It is dangerous to shipping and can also cause damage on land when it breaks over the coast.

ARE THERE VOLCANOES UNDER THE SEA?

Most active volcanoes *are* under the sea! Their effects are usually not noticed on land.

WHAT IS A DORMANT VOLCANO?

Dormant means "sleeping". A dormant volcano might erupt in the future. An *extinct* volcano, on the other hand, will not become active again.

WHY DO VOLCANOES ERUPT?

LIKE EARTHQUAKES, volcanoes mainly occur along fault lines. Molten rock, gases and ash are forced out through a gap in the Earth's crust to release the pressure beneath. Over thousands of years, cooled rock sometimes builds up around the fissure in the ground to form the familiar conical shape of a volcano.

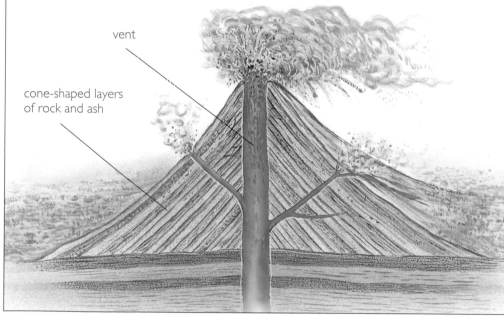

vent

cone-shaped layers of rock and ash

WHAT CAN VOLCANOES TELL US?

ONE interesting aspect of volcanic eruptions is that surrounding areas are covered rapidly in molten rock or ash, sometimes preserving the animals, plants and structures underneath. Archaeologists have been able to study life in Roman times, for example, by examining the remains of Pompeii, in Italy, buried when Vesuvius erupted in AD 79.

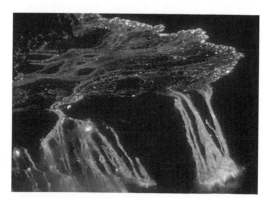

The lava flow from a volcano can be spectacular, as this photograph of Kilauea Volcano, Hawaii, shows.

WHEN DID LIFE BEGIN ON EARTH?

The Earth began to be formed over 4.5 billion years ago, but for millions of years nothing could live here. Gradually, the Earth's crust and the atmosphere formed. The simplest forms of life, bacteria and algae, probably began to grow less than four billion years ago. Human beings did not appear until about two million years ago.

On the coast of Western Australia, strange formations called stromatolites have been found. They are formed of layers of fossils of blue-green algae and may be over three billion years old.

WHAT WERE THE FIRST LIVING THINGS ON EARTH?

ALTHOUGH VIRUSES are the simplest living things, they need to live and reproduce themselves inside a larger organism, so they are unlikely to have been the first living things on Earth. The earliest evidence of life that has been found is tiny fossils of primitive bacteria in rocks about 3800 million years old. Later, blue-green algae evolved. They could use energy from the Sun and in so doing gave off oxygen. Modern plants and animals share these simple organisms as ancestors.

HOW DO WE KNOW ABOUT PREHISTORY?

ALMOST EVERYTHING that we know about the living things on Earth before humans evolved has been learnt from fossils. Fossils are the remains of dead animals and plants that have been turned to stone over millions of years.

An animal dies and is covered by sediment washed on top of it.

Under great pressure, the sediment slowly solidifies into rock.

Minerals fill the space left by the body or bones and also become rock.

Over thousands of years, weather and the Earth's movement may bring the fossil to the surface.

HOW ARE PREHISTORIC TIMES DESCRIBED?

THE PERIODS when the Earth was forming and early kinds of life were developing have been given names. There is also a short way of saying "55 million years ago": 55mya.

WHEN DID THE EARTH BEGIN TO LOOK AS IT DOES TODAY?

THE SURFACE of the Earth is changing all the time. When living things first began to evolve on Earth, there was just one huge continent. Over millions of years, this continent broke up and moved to become the land masses we recognize today. This is why similar dinosaur fossils have been found in very different parts of the world, although dinosaurs were land creatures and could not cross the oceans.

PRECAMBRIAN 4600–590mya	PALEOZOIC 590–248mya						MESOZOIC 248–65mya		
	Cambrian	Ordovician	Silurian	Devonian	Carboniferous	Permian	Triassic	Jurassic	Cretaceous

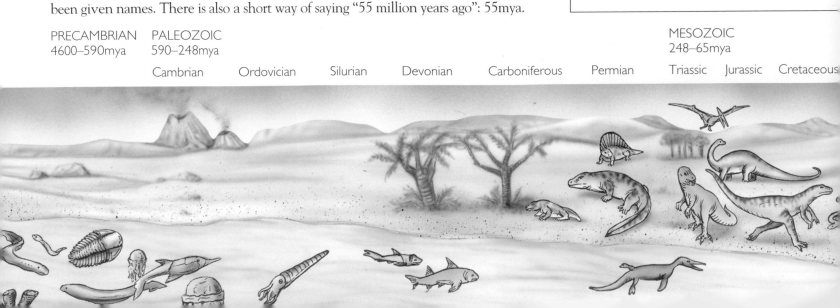

fast facts

WHAT IS PREHISTORY?

Prehistory is what we call the time before written records.

CAN WE SEE EVOLUTION HAPPENING?

It takes many, many generations for evolutionary changes to take place, so we cannot usually see them happening. But as some insects live for a day or less, scientists can trace changes in them in only a few years.

WHAT IS PALAEONTOLOGY?

Palaeontology is simply the scientific name for the study of fossils.

ARE NEW FOSSILS STILL BEING FOUND?

Every year fossils are found that add to our knowledge of prehistoric life. Very often they are discovered by ordinary people walking in the countryside. Places where soil is frequently being washed away from rocks, such as at the bottom of cliffs, are good places to look.

WHAT IS EVOLUTION?

LIVING THINGS inherit characteristics from the generations that have gone before, but each individual is slightly different. Over many generations, the differences that are more successful survive, so that the species gradually adapts. In time, these changes, called evolution, can lead to major adaptations and even new species. All living things have evolved from the simple organisms that began to grow in the Earth's waters. Many of these, such as the dinosaurs, have since become extinct, although they may have lived successfully on Earth for millions of years.

WHEN WERE FOSSILS DISCOVERED?

EVER SINCE HUMAN BEINGS first lived on Earth they have been finding fossilized remains. But it was really only in the nineteenth century that scientific study of the fossils took place. Until then, people believed that the fossils came from dragons, giants or even unicorns!

There are large gaps in the fossil record that have puzzled scientists. That is why there was once talk of "missing links" – living things that had evolved to a point between early fossil forms and modern creatures and plants. Although some modern reptiles look as ancient as dinosaurs, they are not directly descended from them, but they may share a common ancestor.

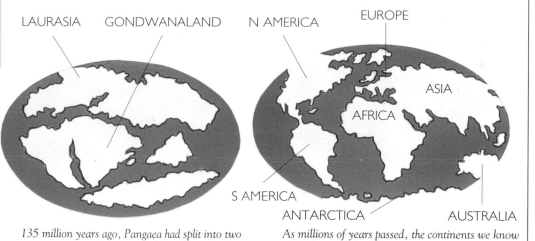

LAURASIA GONDWANALAND   N AMERICA   EUROPE   ASIA   AFRICA   PANGAEA   S AMERICA   ANTARCTICA   AUSTRALIA

250 million years ago, there was one giant continent, now named Pangaea.

135 million years ago, Pangaea had split into two main continents: Laurasia and Gondwanaland.

As millions of years passed, the continents we know today began to form.

CENOZOIC
65mya–today

Tertiary   Quaternary

DID DINOSAURS RULE THE EARTH?

During the 150 million years that they lived on Earth, dinosaurs certainly included the largest creatures to live on land and the fiercest hunters. But they were not the only animals to live successfully on Earth by any means. There were many species of insect and the earliest winged animals could be seen in the skies. The seas were teeming with fish and other sea-life. The first mammals were also thriving, ready to become the dominant creatures when the dinosaurs became extinct.

WHAT COLOUR WERE DINOSAURS?

DINOSAUR FOSSILS, even when they show the skin of the animal, cannot show us what colour it was. Dinosaurs may have been green and brown in colour, camouflaging them amongst the leaves and rocks. It is also possible that some of them were very brightly coloured, just as some tropical lizards are today.

This scene shows what the landscape may have looked like during the Cretaceous period. In many parts of the world there were plentiful streams and rivers, with marshy plains in between. Lush vegetation allowed the plant-eating dinosaurs to grow even larger.

Iguanodon was a plant-eater, tearing leaves from high branches.

Baryonyx had sharp claws and teeth. It is likely that it ate fish from streams and lakes.

Polacanthus was a plant-eating dinosaur, browsing near the ground. Its spines helped to protect it from attack.

Fossil footprints show that some dinosaurs, such as *Hypsilophodon*, seem to have moved in groups. As with herds of browsing animals today, this meant that they were safer from predators.

ARE FOSSILS THE ONLY EVIDENCE OF LIFE IN PREHISTORIC TIMES?

OVER TIME, the remains of plants and animals decay. Fossilization is one way in which their forms have survived to give us information about prehistoric times. Since the time of the dinosaurs, however, the climate of parts of the Earth has cooled. In recent years, frozen remains of mammoths and even humans have been found, preserved in the ice of polar or mountainous regions.

Another source of information about prehistoric life is cave painting. In several parts of the world, early paintings have been found on rocks, often hidden from view for thousands of years. Viewed by the flickering light of torches, as they would have been when first painted, the animals almost seem to move.

WHAT HAPPENED TO THE DINOSAURS?

ONE THEORY is that climate changes gradually led to a drop in dinosaur numbers. Another is that a huge meteorite hit the Earth, throwing up a massive dust cloud. Mammals managed to survive the climate change, but dinosaurs did not.

WHO WERE THE FIRST HUMANS?

SCIENTISTS believe that humans and apes had a common ancestor. About five million years ago in Africa, some hominids (early humans) began to walk on two legs. Over millions of years, they developed bigger brains and began to spread out to other parts of the world. Later hominids began to make tools, develop language, use fire and wear clothes. The scientific name for modern people is *Homo sapiens sapiens*. They invented farming about 9000 years ago. Their early settlements led to the first civilizations.

Homo habilis made stone tools.

Homo erectus used fire and could live in cooler climates.

Homo sapiens neanderthalensis lived in Europe and had burial ceremonies.

Homo sapiens sapiens, modern man, does not seem to have evolved from Homo sapiens neanderthalensis.

fast facts

DID DINOSAURS HAVE COLD BLOOD?

Like modern reptiles, dinosaurs were probably cold-blooded creatures, although this is difficult to prove. Some dinosaurs may have had "sails" on their backs to help them to regulate their body heat.

HOW MANY KINDS OF DINOSAUR WERE THERE?

Fossils of over 350 different species of dinosaur have been discovered, but it is likely that there were many more than this. There are certainly many more fossils of all kinds waiting to be found.

DID DINOSAURS ATTACK HUMANS?

Dinosaurs became extinct about 65 million years ago, over 60 million years before humans lived on Earth.

WHICH WERE THE LARGEST DINOSAURS?

The plant-eating *sauropods* were the largest dinosaurs. They are the biggest land animals ever to have lived on Earth. Some were over 30m (100ft) long.

WERE DINOSAURS CLEVER?

Dinosaurs were very successful – they lived on Earth for over 150 million years – but as far as we know they all had quite small brains. *Stegosaurus'* brain was only 5cm (2 inches) long.

DID DINOSAURS CARE FOR THEIR YOUNG?

It used to be thought that dinosaurs laid their eggs and left them to hatch, as turtles do. Discoveries of the fossils of young dinosaurs with adult members nearby now suggest that some dinosaurs did care for their young, perhaps even sitting on the eggs to hatch them.

HOW ARE LIVING THINGS CLASSIFIED?

Living things are classified in groups that have certain characteristics in common. The largest groups are called kingdoms. All living things can be classified as belonging to one of the five kingdoms: animals, plants, fungi, protists and monerans. Kingdoms can be divided into phyla (singular: phylum) or divisions and subphyla, which in turn can be separated into classes. Classes are divided into orders and suborders. These are separated into families and then into genera (singular: genus). Finally, each genus contains a number of species.

WHICH ARE THE SIMPLEST LIVING THINGS?

MEMBERS of the moneran and protist families are the simplest organisms. Individuals are much too small to be seen without a microscope.

HOW IS A LION CLASSIFIED?

LIONS belong to the:

Animal (*Animalia*) kingdom
Chordate (*Chordata*) phylum
Mammal (*Mammalia*) class
Carnivore (*Carnivora*) order
Cat (*Felidae*) family
Big cat (*Panthera*) genus
Lion (*leo*) species

The scientific name for lions is *Panthera leo*, the last two divisions.

WHICH IS THE LARGEST GROUP OF LIVING THINGS?

THE CLASS of insects is the largest class of living things, containing over one million different species.

WHY DO LIVING THINGS HAVE LATIN NAMES?

THE SYSTEM of classifying living things was invented by a Swedish botanist called Carolus Linnaeus (1707–78). Latin was traditionally the language used by scholars, so the classifications have Latin names. This also means that living things can be identified by scientists in every country, no matter what the local name for a species might be.

Classifying millions of living things is very complicated. This chart has been simplified to include the main groups of plants and animals.

KEY

KINGDOM

phylum

class

MONERANS

single-celled organisms without a cell nucleus, such as bacteria

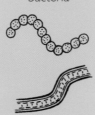

PROTISTS

single-celled organisms with a cell nucleus, such as amoebas and diatoms

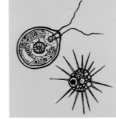

FUNGI

organisms with bodies made of a mass of threads, feeding on plants and animals, such as moulds, mildews and mushrooms

PLANTS

have cell walls of cellulose, and most make their food from sunlight by photosynthesis

mosses

ferns

ANIMALS

can move for at least part of their lives, feeding on plant or animal matter

sponges

molluscs

sea anemones, jellyfish, corals

flatworms, tapeworms

star fish, sea urchins

roundworms

leeches, worms

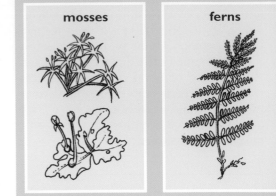
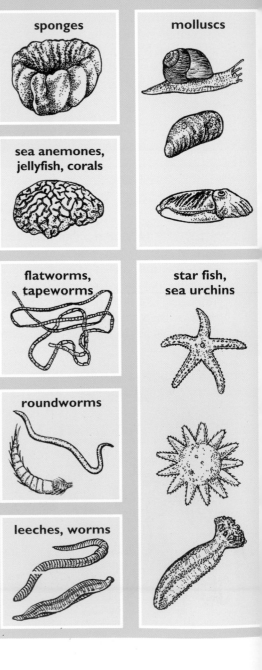

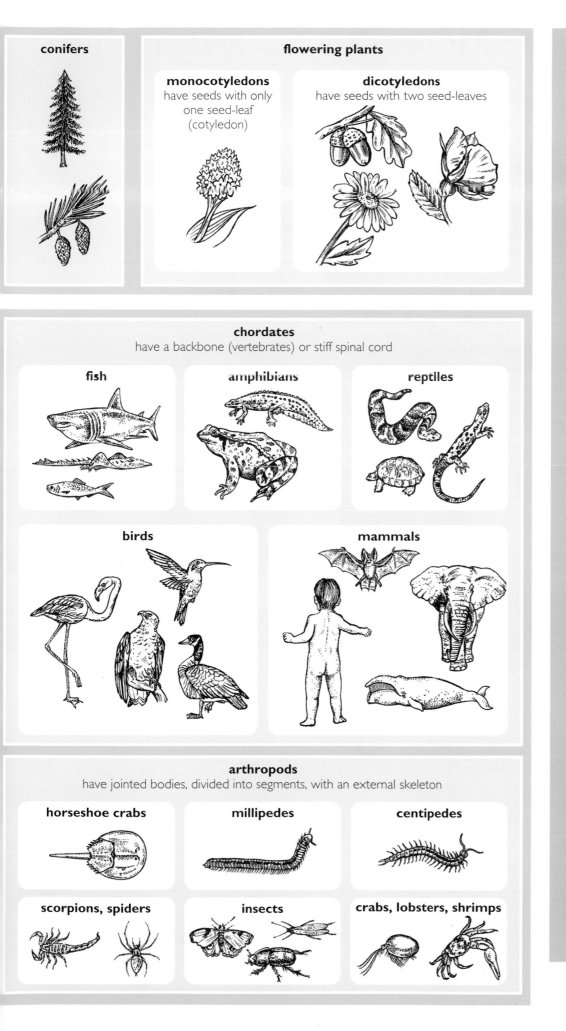

conifers

flowering plants

monocotyledons
have seeds with only
one seed-leaf
(cotyledon)

dicotyledons
have seeds with two seed-leaves

chordates
have a backbone (vertebrates) or stiff spinal cord

fish

amphibians

reptiles

birds

mammals

arthropods
have jointed bodies, divided into segments, with an external skeleton

horseshoe crabs

millipedes

centipedes

scorpions, spiders

insects

crabs, lobsters, shrimps

fast facts

ARE NEW SPECIES STILL BEING DISCOVERED?

There are many parts of the Earth where new species are still being discovered, including the rainforests, which are teeming with living things, and the oceans, still the least explored part of our planet.

HOW ARE NEW SPECIES NAMED?

Usually new species can be fitted into an existing genus. The species name may describe a characteristic of the new discovery or show where it was found, or it may be named after the person who found it.

WHAT IS AN EXTINCT SPECIES?

An extinct species is one where there are no more living examples on Earth.

HOW MANY SPECIES HAVE BECOME EXTINCT?

Species are evolving all the time. The climate, new predators, or the success of other species may cause them to become extinct. It is thought that as many as 95% of the species that have ever lived on Earth are now extinct.

DOES THE CLASSIFICATION OF LIVING THINGS EVER CHANGE?

When Linnaeus first proposed his system of classification, he based his decisions mainly on the appearance of the living things. Since then, scientists have been able to study the physical and chemical structures of organisms and form views on how they evolved historically. This has meant that some living things have been reclassified as more is known about them.

HOW DO PLANTS LIVE?

flower

leaf

stem

root

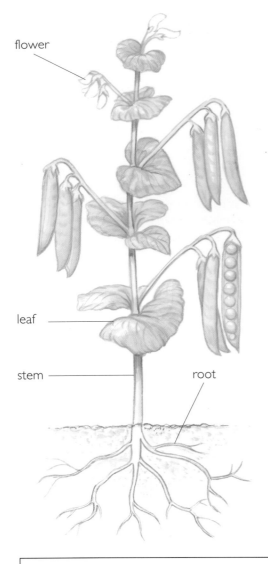

Like animals, plants need food for energy to survive and grow, but while animals can move about to catch their food or find new areas of vegetation, plants are usually rooted to one spot. But plants can do something that no animal can do. They can make energy from sunlight. This process is called photosynthesis. As well as light, plants also need water and nutrients.

HOW DOES PHOTOSYNTHESIS WORK?

A PLANT'S LEAVES contain a green substance called chlorophyll. The chlorophyll enables chemical reactions to take place. These use energy from the Sun and carbon dioxide gas from the air to make food for the plant to live and grow. As photosynthesis happens, oxygen is given off into the air.

carbon dioxide from the air

light energy from the Sun

oxygen given off

water and nutrients taken in from the soil

WHAT ARE PLANTS USED FOR APART FROM FOOD?

OVER THOUSANDS OF YEARS, human beings have found many uses for plants. Some of the most common ones are shown here.

Both linen and cotton threads, used to make fabric, come from plants.

Most paper is made from the cellulose fibres found in wood pulp.

Rubber comes from the sap of a tropical tree.

Sisal and hemp are tough plant fibres used for ropes and matting.

Many objects, including buildings, are made from wood.

Plant extracts are used in perfumes and many cosmetic and cleaning preparations.

WHY ARE PLANTS IMPORTANT?

IF THERE WERE NO PLANTS, there could not be animal life on Earth. All animals either eat plants or eat other animals that in turn eat plants themselves. In this way, every living thing on Earth indirectly gets its energy from the Sun, although only plants can convert the Sun's light into a usable form.

Humans use milk and meat from cows for energy. Cows take in energy from plants. Plants convert energy from the Sun. This is called a food chain.

HOW DO PLANTS REPRODUCE?

THERE ARE TWO MAIN WAYS in which plants reproduce. In sexual reproduction, pollen is transferred by insects or the wind from one part of a flower to another, in such a way that fertilization can take place. Seeds are then formed. These seeds in turn are distributed in different ways to a spot where they can germinate and grow.

Seeds may be surrounded by fleshy fruit. Some fruits, such as cherries, contain just one seed. Others, like this papaya, have many seeds inside.

This popular houseplant produces small plants at the end of stems. If put in soil, these will grow and can be separated from the parent plant.

In asexual reproduction, a plant can reproduce without fertilization taking place. It may, for example, reproduce by sending out runners from its roots or by growing new plants on the tips of its leaves or branches.

DO PLANTS REALLY EAT INSECTS?

SOME PLANTS do gain extra minerals and other nutrients by trapping and "eating" insects. They are usually found in areas where there are not enough nutrients in the soil for healthy growth.

When an insect lands on tiny hairs on the Venus' flytrap's sensitive leaf tips, the pairs of leaves snap shut, trapping the insect inside.

HOW HAVE HUMANS CHANGED PLANTS?

ABOUT 9000 years ago, human beings invented farming. Since then, they have carefully selected the crops that give the best harvests under different conditions. Particularly in the last two hundred years, selective plant breeding has developed the characteristics that farmers and consumers require. Now that machines are used to pick most crops, and large stores prefer to package fruits and vegetables in regular sizes, many commercial varieties have been bred to produce even fruits that ripen together.

In the wild, flowers appear over a period of weeks. Commercial growers have bred varieties that will flower and can be picked all at one time.

fast facts

WHAT IS A WEED?

A weed is simply a plant that is growing somewhere inconvenient for a gardener or farmer.

WHAT IS A PARASITIC PLANT?

A parasitic plant does not grow in the soil but on another plant. It does not photosynthesize but takes the food it needs through its roots or stem from its host plant.

CAN PLANTS FEEL?

Although plants do not have feelings in the way that we do, they can certainly respond to different stimuli. They are able to grow towards a light source, even if turned upside down. Some plants have very sensitive leaves, which will fold up if touched.

ARE ALL PLANTS GREEN?

Most plants are green, but a few also have other pigments that mask the green colour. Red seaweed is an example of this kind of plant.

WHICH ARE THE SMALLEST PLANTS?

Green algae are single-celled plants. They form, for example, the greenish film often found on the bark of trees. Millions of cells of the algae are needed to cover the tree trunk.

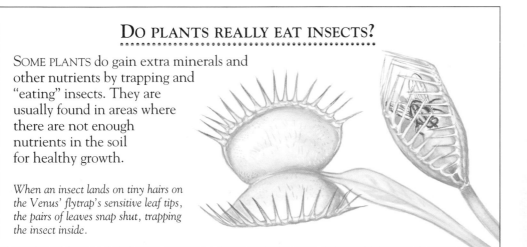

DO ALL PLANTS HAVE FLOWERS?

Flowering plants are known as angiosperms. Although there are plenty of plants that do not have flowers, such as mosses, ferns, algae and conifers, the majority of plants on Earth are flowering ones. That does not mean that they are what we generally think of as flowers – colourful blooms that can be presented in bouquets. Most trees and grasses, for example, are flowering plants, but their flowers may be so small that they usually go unnoticed.

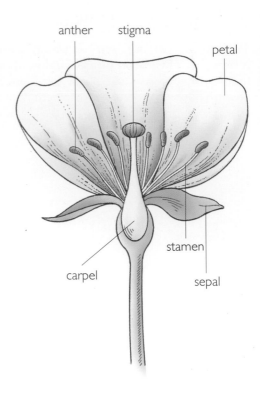

Although many plants have flowers with both male and female parts, as in this cross-section, some have male and female flowers on the same plant, and some have only male or only female flowers. Holly trees are an example of this. In order for a female holly to produce berries, it must be fertilized by a nearby male holly, which will never produce berries.

WHAT ARE FLOWERS FOR?

FLOWERS are the reproductive parts of a plant. Usually, one flower has both male and female parts. The male parts are the stamens, which consist of filaments and anthers. Filaments are like little stalks that support the anthers. Anthers produce tiny dust-like grains called pollen. The female part of a flower is called the carpel. This consists of an ovary, ovules, a style and a stigma. The ovary is hidden in a bulb-shaped receptacle at the base of the flower. Inside the ovary are one or more ovules, which become seeds if the flower is fertilized. Rising from the ovary is a small, sticky stem called the style, the tip of which is the stigma. In order for a flower to be fertilized, pollen must be transferred from the male stamen to the female stigma.

WHY ARE THERE SO MANY FLOWER SHAPES?

THE DIFFERENT SHAPES of flowers help to ensure that they are fertilized. Flowers that rely on insects for pollination must make sure that the insect is carrying pollen from the same kind of plant. The shape of the flower ensures that only certain kinds of insect can pollinate it. Flat flowers, such as daisies and sunflowers, can be visited by hoverflies and some bees. Flowers that are formed into tubes only attract insects that have long tongues. As flowers bloom at different times of the year, there are usually only a few different species available to each insect at any one time, so the chances of pollination are increased.

The ancestors of these garden flowers developed different formations of petals, stamens and carpels. Over the centuries, horticulturists have developed these shapes further by selective breeding.

fast facts

WHICH IS THE LARGEST FLOWER?

The largest flower in the world is *Rafflesia arnoldii*, from Asia. Its flowers can measure over 1m (3ft) across.

WHAT ARE PERENNIALS, BIENNIALS AND ANNUALS?

Some plants grow from a seed, flower, produce their own seeds and die all in one year. They are called annuals. Those taking two years to complete their life cycle are called biennials. Plants that live for several years, even if they die down in the winter, are called perennials.

WHAT IS POT-POURRI?

This fragrant mixture is usually made from dried flower petals, spices and sweet-smelling oils. It was very useful in the days when rooms – and people – were dirtier and smellier than we would like today, but pot-pourri is still popular for its sweet scent.

WHAT IS THE LANGUAGE OF FLOWERS?

From early times, flowers have been thought to have a special meaning when presented to a loved one. The Victorians developed this to a fine art. An admirer sending a red rose to signify "pure love" might receive the reply of a Michaelmas daisy, meaning "farewell"!

HOW HAVE FLOWERS HELPED HISTORIANS?

Flowers seem very delicate, but parts of them last almost indefinitely in the right conditions. This is particularly true of pollen, which can still be recognized long after it was part of a growing plant. Historians have been able to tell which plants grew in ancient times by examining the pollen found in tombs and graves thousands of years old.

HOW ARE FLOWERING PLANTS FERTILIZED?

THE POLLEN that fertilizes the stigma may come from the same flower or from a nearby flower. Many flowers are fertilized (or pollinated) by insects. The flowers produce drops of a sweet liquid called nectar at the base of their petals. When insects visit the flower to drink the nectar, pollen from the anthers rubs off onto their wings, bodies and legs. When the insect visits another flower, the pollen is deposited on its sticky stigma.

Some plants, such as willows and hazels, have long dangling flowers called catkins. The wind is their pollinator, as great clouds of pollen blow off in the breeze and find their way to neighbouring catkins.

HOW ARE SEEDS DISPERSED?

WHEN THE FLOWER has been fertilized, the ovary swells to form a fruit, inside which one or more seeds will grow. These seeds may simply fall to the ground below, or the plant may have methods of ensuring that its offspring grow much further away.

Some seeds in fruits and berries have tough outer cases with fleshy fruits around them. The seeds can pass through the digestive system of birds and grow wherever the birds' droppings fall.

Dandelion seeds are dispersed by the wind. Each seed has a hairy parachute that can carry it for many metres.

Some trees rely on animals to carry their seeds far away. Squirrels, for example, collect acorns and nuts and may bury them to eat later. Often these stores are forgotten, and the seeds grow where they were buried.

HOW ARE NEW FLOWERS BRED?

FLOWERS that are closely related often cross-pollinate in the wild, creating a variety of flower shades and shapes. Under controlled conditions, plant breeders ensure that their parent plants are not pollinated naturally. They then transfer pollen from a selected "father" plant to the stigma of the "mother" plant and wait for seeds to form. These are sown to see what kind of flowers result. It may be years before the results are known and even then only a few of the plants will prove to be different and attractive enough to be launched as new varieties.

WHICH ARE THE BIGGEST PLANTS?

*Trees are the largest plants on Earth and play a
very important part on the planet. They cover
almost a quarter of the Earth, helping to stabilize
the atmosphere by taking in huge amounts of
carbon dioxide from the air and giving off oxygen.
In addition, tree roots help to retain fertile soil and
stop the rain from washing it down hillsides, while
the huge amount of water vapour given off by
trees has an important effect on the weather.*

WHY ARE TREES IMPORTANT?

AS WELL AS directly affecting the environment, trees supply
homes and food for millions of other living creatures, including
people. They are also the source of wood, which is used in buildings and for making such essential items as furniture and paper.

DO TREES HAVE FLOWERS?

TREES can be divided into two groups. Broad-leaved trees, which may also be
deciduous, meaning that they drop their leaves in winter, are flowering plants.
Sometimes their flowers are very small and difficult to spot. Conifers, most of
which are evergreen, retaining their leaves all year round, are cone-bearers. They
have small male cones and larger female cones instead of flowers.

apple-tree flowers   cone

*The trunk, branches,
leaves and roots of this
tree provide food and
shelter for many insects,
birds and animals. Some
plants, too, grow on these
much larger plants.*

HOW ARE YOUNG TREES PRODUCED?

TREES PRODUCE SEEDS just as smaller plants do. Their flowers or cones are fertilized by the wind, or insects or birds. But a parent tree takes up large amounts of water from the area around it, and its leaves prevent sunlight from reaching the ground beneath, so it is important that all the seeds do not fall directly beneath the tree. Some trees produce fruits that are eaten by birds or animals and carried far away in their digestive systems. Others bear seeds that have "wings" and can be blown far away by the wind.

HOW CAN YOU TELL HOW OLD A TREE IS?

IN TEMPERATE CLIMATES, a tree makes rapid growth in the warm spring and summer months and much slower growth in the autumn and winter. This growth shows in the trunk as a light ring during times of fast growth and a darker ring for slower growth. It is therefore possible to count the pairs of light and dark rings to see how many years the tree has been growing.

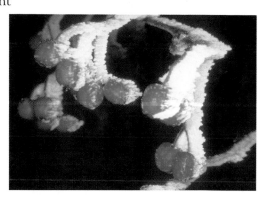

Hawthorn berries pass through the digestive system of birds before the seeds germinate. In winter, birds are glad of fruits to eat, as insects are hard to find.

Counting the rings of some ancient trees shows that they were growing when the pharaohs ruled Egypt.

HOW CAN YOU IDENTIFY A TREE?

OFTEN the easiest way to identify a deciduous tree is to look at the shape of its leaves. The general shape of the tree, the way in which the branches join and the pattern of the bark also give clues, especially in winter when the leaves have fallen.

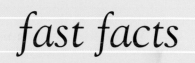

fast facts

WHAT IS THE TALLEST TREE IN THE WORLD?

The giant sequoia is not only the tallest tree in the world but the tallest living thing of any kind. It can reach over 90m (270ft).

WHICH TREES LIVE THE LONGEST?

Yew trees can live to a very great age, but the oldest living tree is probably a bristlecone pine, in the western United States, which is over 4300 years old.

HOW MANY SPECIES OF TREE ARE THERE?

There are thought to be about 40,000 species of tree, of which about 700 are conifers.

WHAT WERE THE FIRST TREES LIKE?

Trees have been on Earth longer than many animals. The first trees were cone-bearing.

DO ALL TREES GROW TALL?

The dwarf willow, which grows in the Scottish highlands, reaches only 2.5cm (1 inch) in height.

WHAT IS AN INVERTEBRATE?

The leech has 33 segments in its body.

> *An invertebrate is an animal without a backbone. More than 90% of all animals are invertebrates. Insects form the largest group of invertebrates. Like millipedes and centipedes, crustaceans and spiders, they are arthropods, with jointed bodies and an outer protective casing. There are also many soft-bodied creatures, such as worms and jellyfish, often living in water or damp areas where sun and air will not dry out their bodies. Molluscs are also soft-bodied, but many of them are protected by an outer shell.*

WHICH INVERTEBRATES CAN BE MISTAKEN FOR PLANTS?

CNIDARIANS are invertebrates, mainly living in the sea, that have a single space inside them where food is digested. A mouth leads from the outside to the space, which is called the coelenteron. Often the mouth is surrounded by tentacles, which help to catch food and pass it into the coelenteron. Corals, sea anemones and jellyfish are all cnidarians. Both corals and sea anemones can look like plants at first sight.

Brightly coloured sea anemones look like exotic flowers but are in fact made of jelly. Their waving tentacles have stinging cells to attack any small fish that swims through them. The tentacles then shorten to draw the fish into the body of the anemone, where it is slowly digested.

HOW MANY DIFFERENT KINDS OF WORM ARE THERE?

THERE ARE well over fifty thousand different kinds of worm, divided into three main groups. The annelids have bodies that are divided into segments. They include earthworms and leeches. Roundworms, also known as nematodes, do not have segments. Many of these are crop pests, eating plants and making crops prone to diseases. Others are parasites, living on or in other animals, some causing serious diseases in humans. Finally, flatworms also include several parasites, including some with a complicated life cycle that involves them living in two different animal hosts one after the other.

Tapeworms are flatworms that live and lay eggs inside an animal. The eggs are passed out in the animal's waste matter and can then infect another host.

Tiny bristles enable the earthworm to move through the soil.

Earthworms improve the quality of the soil by mixing up different layers as they burrow and allowing water to drain freely through the soil.

Earthworms "eat" soil and digest small pieces of plant material in it as it passes through their bodies. Undigested soil is passed out of the other end of the worm to form wormcasts on the surface.

The coral reefs to be found in tropical waters are made from millions of little creatures, rather like sea anemones, called polyps. They live in colonies begun by just one polyp that "buds" and produces new polyps. Each polyp builds a hard skeleton around itself. When the polyps die, their skeletons remain.

HOW DOES A MAN O' WAR CATCH ITS FOOD?

ALTHOUGH at first sight the man o' war appears to be a jellyfish, in fact it is made up of a whole colony of polyps, each of which has a particular job to do. Some form stinging tentacles; others digest food; and one large polyp is filled with gas to form the "sail" that allows the man o' war to float, powered by the wind.

WHICH ANIMALS HAVE THEIR SKELETONS ON THE OUTSIDE?

ARTHROPODS have skeletons on the outside, which give them several advantages over soft-bodied animals. The skeleton forms a waterproof casing, preventing the body from drying out and allowing the animal to live outside water or damp places. In addition, skeletons on the outside, just like those on the inside, give muscles a firm anchoring point, so that the animal is often stronger than soft-bodied creatures of a similar size.

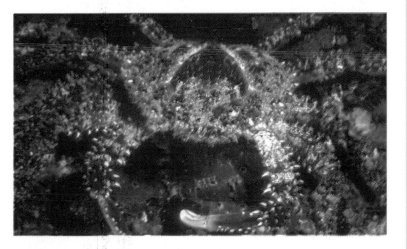

Centipedes, millipedes, spiders, insects and crustaceans are all arthropods. Some crustaceans, such as many crabs and lobsters, have particularly hard outer casings. Shrimps and barnacles are also crustaceans.

WHAT IS A MOLLUSC?

AFTER INSECTS, molluscs form the largest group of animals. Molluscs have soft, muscular bodies, often covered by a protective shell. Some, such as snails, move on a muscular foot, which can be withdrawn into the shell for protection. Other, sea-dwelling molluscs, such as squid and scallops, take in water and squirt it out to jet-propel themselves along.

CAN ALL INSECTS FLY?

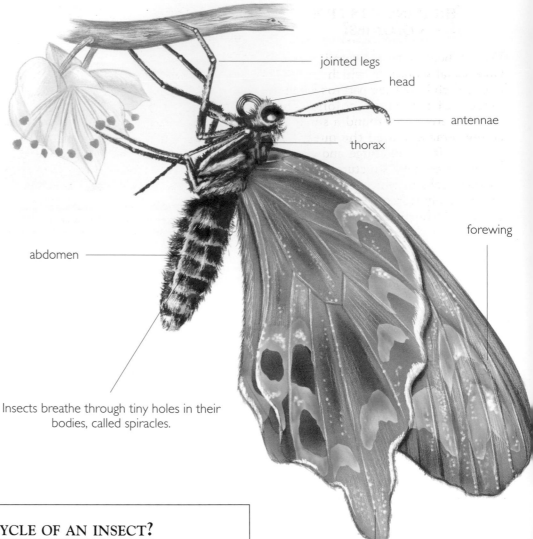

jointed legs

head

antennae

thorax

forewing

abdomen

Insects breathe through tiny holes in their bodies, called spiracles.

hindwing

Most insects have wings at one time or another in their lives, although a very few species, such as fleas, silver-fish, firebrats and springtails, do not. Flying insects have two pairs of wings – forewings and hindwings – although not all of them use both pairs for flying. All insects have a tough outer skeleton, six legs and bodies divided into three distinct parts, but there is enormous variation between insect species.

WHAT IS THE LIFE CYCLE OF AN INSECT?

YOUNG INSECTS develop in two main ways. In some species, such as grasshoppers and locusts, the young that hatch from eggs look rather like small adults, and are called nymphs. As they grow, the nymphs shed their skins, looking more and more like adults each time.

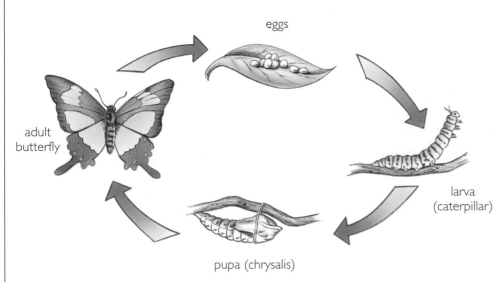

eggs

adult butterfly

larva (caterpillar)

pupa (chrysalis)

Other insects, such as butterflies, bees and beetles, go through a process called metamorphosis. Their eggs hatch into larvae or caterpillars. Later these become a pupa or chrysalis, within which an imago, or adult insect, develops. The larvae may live in a different habitat from the adult and require different foods.

ARE SPIDERS INSECTS?

SPIDERS belong to the class of arachnids, which also includes scorpions, ticks and mites. None of these are insects. They have eight legs, and their bodies are divided into two parts, not three.

Although they are not insects themselves, spiders are meat-eaters, feeding on insects – and other spiders.

WHICH INSECTS LIVE IN COLONIES?

WASPS, bees, ants and termites live in large social groups, in which individual insects each have their part to play in the success of the whole colony. These colonies are built around a single egg-laying female, called the queen. The colonies often build large and elaborate homes. Bees make structures containing six-sided cells in which eggs and honey can be safely stored. Ants and termites often build huge mounds, with tunnels and galleries inside, to house the colony.

Honey bees are able to tell other colony members where good sources of food can be found by performing a special dance on their return to the hive.

DO INSECTS HAVE EYES?

INSECTS' extraordinary compound eyes are made up of hundreds of tiny lenses. The images from all the lenses are made sense of by the insect's brain. Like us, insects can see colour, although in a different way. Flowers that seem dull to us may seem very bright to an insect. As well as having good vision, many insects have sensitive hearing and an acute sense of smell. A female moth, for example, gives off a smell that can be detected by male moths several kilometres away.

HOW DO INSECTS PROTECT THEMSELVES?

THERE ARE almost as many different ways in which insects protect themselves from enemies as there are different insects. Some insects, such as wasps and ants, have powerful stings or are able to shower their attackers with poisonous fluid. The hoverfly does not sting, but its colouring is so like that of a wasp or bee that enemies are very wary of it! Other insects, such as stick insects and praying mantises use camouflage. They look like the leaves and twigs among which they feed.

fast facts

WHICH IS THE BIGGEST INSECT?

The goliath beetle (*Goliathus*) can weigh well over 100g (3.5oz).

ARE THERE STILL INSECTS TO BE DISCOVERED?

Well over a million species of insect are known, yet many hundreds of previously unknown insects are discovered each year.

DO INSECTS HAVE BLOOD?

Insects do have blood, but it may be blue, yellow or green!

HOW CAN TINY INSECTS BE DANGEROUS TO HUMANS?

Insects are very helpful to humans. While searching for food, they help to pollinate crops. By eating dead plant and animal material, they help to clean up the environment. But insects are also pests, sometimes devouring whole fields of crops in a matter of hours. They also carry diseases to plants, animals and humans. Finally, some insects have painful or deadly bites and stings.

HOW DO INSECTS HELP TO CATCH MURDERERS?

Very soon after death, bodies begin to break down. This process is helped by a number of insects that feed or lay their eggs on the body. Scientists have found that these insects appear in a particular order. Examining the insects found in a body can help to pinpoint the time of death, and in many cases this has helped the police to find a killer.

The leaf katydid of Borneo is wonderfully camouflaged amongst leaves and branches. It is only when it begins to move that predators take a closer look. The burying beetle, found in the deserts of Arizona, has colouring that warns enemies that it may be poisonous.

HOW DO FISH BREATHE?

Fish are the oldest vertebrates on Earth. They are cold blooded and spend all their lives in water. They breathe by taking in oxygen dissolved in the water. Most fish breathe by using gills. They gulp in water through their mouths and pass it out through the gills, which are rich in blood and extract oxygen from the water as it passes through them.

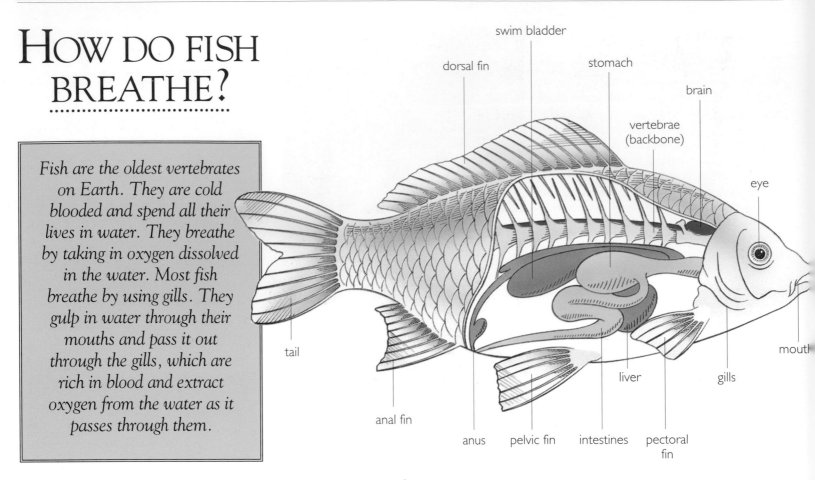

The illustration of the fish above shows features shared by all teleosts. Fish scales may be silvery or, in the tropics, glowing in bright rainbow colours.

HOW DO BONY FISH AND CARTILAGINOUS FISH DIFFER?

THE LARGEST GROUP of fish are bony fish. Most of these, making up 95% of fish species, are known as *teleosts*. They have skeletons made of bone and are usually covered with small overlapping bony plates called scales. They also have swim bladders, filled with gas, to help them remain buoyant. Cartilaginous fish include sharks, skates and rays. Their skeletons are made of flexible cartilage but, as they do not have swim bladders, they must keep moving all the time to keep their position in the water. They usually have tough, leathery skins and fleshy fins.

WHICH FISH TRAVEL THE LONGEST DISTANCES?

THE SALMON hatches in freshwater streams and rivers but then begins an incredible journey of up to 5000km (3000 miles), first to the open sea and then to return to the same river in which it was spawned in order to breed. The salmon only makes the journey once – after spawning, it dies. The European eel makes the reverse journey. It spawns in the Sargasso Sea, in the western Atlantic, and its tiny larvae swim to the shores of Europe and North America, becoming elvers (small eels) on the journey. They then spend several years in freshwater rivers and lakes before returning to the Sargasso Sea to breed. Whales also travel huge distances, this time in search of food. The tiny plankton that they eat are found more abundantly in certain areas during the year.

During its journey upstream to breed, the salmon may leap over rocks and up small waterfalls. In North America, bears wade into the river to catch some of the fish making their annual migration.

IS IT TRUE THAT MALE SEAHORSES BECOME MOTHERS?

OF COURSE, it is the female seahorse that is the real mother, producing and laying eggs. The difference is that she lays the eggs in a special pouch on the male seahorse's body. The babies develop inside the pouch and emerge when they are fully developed. As they emerge, it looks as though they are being born from the male seahorse.

It is easy to see that the seahorse was so named because of the shape of its head. In order not to be swept along by the current, the seahorse can grasp the fronds of seaweeds with its tail.

ARE ALL SHARKS DANGEROUS TO HUMANS?

ALL SHARKS are carnivorous (meat-eaters), and a few species, such as the white shark, which can grow to 9m (30ft), have been known to attack humans or even boats. But 90% of all shark species are not dangerous to humans at all.

The shark's streamlined shape and muscular body enables it to move at great speed through the water. Its keen sense of smell means that it can locate and devour living or dead animals with ease. The shark's teeth are serrated, so that it can saw at the flesh of its victims.

WHAT IS A "MERMAID'S PURSE"?

A VERY FEW FISH give birth to live young, but most lay their eggs in the earth, which is called spawning. A fish may lay millions of eggs, only a small proportion of which will grow into adults. A few fish, such as salmon and sticklebacks, build nests underwater to protect their eggs. They lay fewer eggs because more young survive. Dogfish and skates protect their eggs in black capsules. The empty capsules are often washed up on the beach, and it is these that are known as "mermaid's purses".

fast facts

WHICH FISH HAVE NO JAWS?

Lampreys and hagfish do not have jaws, but they do have teeth. Some of them are parasites, attaching themselves to other fish and feeding on their blood and flesh.

HOW DO SOME FISH USE ELECTRICITY?

Some fish, such as the Atlantic torpedo, the African electric catfish and the electric eel, can store electrical charges in their muscles – sometimes up to 500 volts. They may ward off attackers with electric shocks or use this extraordinary ability when catching food or attracting a mate.

WHAT IS A COELACANTH?

The coelacanth is often called a living fossil. It was known only from fossil examples until a live fish was caught off the coast of Madagascar. Coelacanths have hardly changed in the last 90 million years. They use their fins alternately, like legs, instead of together.

ARE THERE REALLY FLYING FISH?

The flying fish (*Cypselurus heterurus*) has large fins that it can spread out. When escaping its enemies, it can launch itself from the water and glide up to 100m (330ft) through the air.

HOW FAST CAN FISH SWIM?

The marlin can reach speeds of 80km/h (50mph).

WHICH IS THE SMALLEST FISH?

The dwarf goby (*Pandaka pygmaea*), which is also the smallest vertebrate, is a freshwater fish that never reaches more than 1.25cm (0.5 inches) in length.

CAN ALL AMPHIBIANS LIVE BOTH ON LAND AND IN WATER?

Amphibians have different life cycles. Many live mainly on land, but most of them spend at least some of their lives in water. Frogs, toads, newts and salamanders are all amphibians. Frogs and salamanders are able to breathe through their damp skins to a certain extent, both in the water and on land, but toads must rely largely on their lungs and cannot remain in water for long.

WHAT IS THE LIFE CYCLE OF AN AMPHIBIAN?

MOST AMPHIBIANS lay their eggs in water. Frogs' eggs are called spawn. They are protected from predators by a thick layer of jelly. Inside this a tadpole develops. When it hatches out, it is able to swim, using its long tail, and breathes through gills. As the tadpole grows, first hind legs and then fore legs begin to grow. Lungs develop, and the young frog is able to begin to breathe with its head above water. Gradually, the tail shortens until the young frog resembles its adult parents.

HOW DO FROGS AND TOADS DIFFER?

TOADS AND FROGS are similar in many ways, although toads usually have rougher, drier skins and may waddle rather than hopping as frogs do. Some toad spawn is produced in strings, like necklaces, rather than the mass of eggs laid by a frog.

Toads are often well camouflaged, easily blending into a stony or leafy background.

Adult frogs often return to the pond in which they hatched to breed.

Frog spawn hatches into larvae called tadpoles after about a week.

By 16 weeks, the froglet has four legs and almost no tail. Lungs have taken over from the gills.

By about ten weeks, the tadpole has hind legs, internal gills, and can eat small insects, worms and its smaller brothers and sisters.

At first tadpoles feed on algae and breathe through feathery gills.

HOW CAN A TREE FROG CLIMB TREES?

THE RED-EYED TREE FROG lives in the rain-forests of South America. Although it can swim, it spends much of its life out of water, among the leaves of trees where there are plentiful insects for food. The tree frog's toes have sticky pads that enable it to grip branches as it climbs.

Some tree frogs, living high in the Amazon rainforest, use the pools of water in the centre of certain tropical plants. They lay their eggs among the leaves and carry their tadpoles to water on their backs.

fast facts

WHICH IS THE LARGEST AMPHIBIAN?

The Chinese giant salamander grows up to 1.8m (6ft) long.

DO ALL AMPHIBIANS HAVE LEGS?

Caecilians are amphibians that look rather like worms. They are adapted for a life burrowing in soil or underwater. They have no legs and are practically blind, but they feel by means of tiny tentacles on their cheeks.

WHAT IS AN AXOLOTL?

Axolotls are a kind of salamander found in Mexico. Like other amphibians, they begin life as tadpoles, breathing through gills, but they never develop further and breed in the water without ever changing into an adult form.

HOW DO SOME FROGS USE A KIND OF ANTIFREEZE?

In North America, some frogs build up chemicals in their blood at the onset of cold weather. These act as a kind of antifreeze, allowing the frog to survive temperatures as low as –8°C (18°F) without freezing.

WHAT IS SPECIAL ABOUT THE MIDWIFE TOAD?

The midwife toad has a special way of hatching its eggs. The male wraps the string of eggs around its body and back legs, where they remain until they hatch.

WHAT IS THE LEGEND OF THE SALAMANDER?

IN ANCIENT TIMES, it was believed that salamanders could live in the middle of fires, as the cold of their bodies extinguished the flames around them. Of course, this is quite untrue, but the story may have come about because salamanders were often seen to run out of logs thrown onto the fire.

Salamanders and newts, unlike frogs and toads, have distinct necks and long tails in adulthood. Their bright colours warn of their poisonous skin.

HOW DO AMPHIBIANS DEFEND THEMSELVES?

AMPHIBIANS have a wide range of ways of protecting themselves. Some brightly coloured amphibians produce poisons in glands on their skins. The bright colours warn birds and animals not to attempt to eat them. Others use camouflage, blending with their surroundings, to prevent enemies from spotting them. Some frogs and toads puff themselves up or stand on tiptoes to look larger than they really are!

These frogs have skins that are coloured and speckled to blend perfectly with the background of their habitats. Camouflage is their best protection from predators.

HOW MANY DIFFERENT KINDS OF REPTILE ARE THERE?

There are four orders of reptile, by far the largest of which is the order of lizards and snakes. There are nearly 6000 different species of these. The other orders are much smaller. There are about 200 species of turtles, tortoises and terrapins, and only just over 20 species of crocodiles and alligators. Rarest of all is the tuatara, which forms an order all by itself.

WHAT ARE THE SPECIAL CHARACTERISTICS OF REPTILES?

REPTILES are cold blooded, so must gain warmth from their surroundings. This means that they can be found anywhere except in the very coldest regions of the Earth. Those that live in cooler areas usually spend the winter hibernating. Most reptiles lay eggs with hard or leathery shells. Their young hatch into miniature versions of their parents, but as reptiles can continue to grow after they are mature, some reach an enormous size.

The giant dome-shaped tortoise of the Galapagos Islands can live to a great age and considerable size.

Alligators (and crocodiles) are more closely related to dinosaurs than to other living reptiles.

Crocodiles can reach up to 7m (22ft) in length.

HOW CAN YOU TELL A CROCODILE FROM AN ALLIGATOR?

BOTH CROCODILES AND ALLIGATORS spend most of their lives in swamps and rivers in warm climates, although they breathe air through nostrils on the top of their snouts, closing these off when they dive. Caymans and gavials are relatives of crocodiles and alligators. The simple way of telling them apart is that crocodiles show the fourth tooth in their lower jaw when their mouths are closed, while alligators do not. It is probably not wise to go near enough to a live crocodilian to find out, however, as they have been known to attack humans!

The sharp teeth of crocodiles and alligators enable them to grip larger prey and drag them down under the water, where they drown. They have been known to kill farm animals in this way.

HOW DOES A CHAMELEON CHANGE COLOUR?

THE CHAMELEON is able to change colour to match its surroundings by releasing or tightening special cells on its skin. As well as this remarkable ability, chameleons are amazing in other ways. They are able to grip very strongly with their toes and tails to balance on precarious branches. Their extraordinary tongues, which are able to shoot out as far as the chameleon's body length, are sticky and able to scoop back prey like a piece of elastic. Finally, the chameleon's eyes are bulging and can move in any direction, protected by an eyelid that is fused all round the eye, leaving only a tiny hole in the middle. Even stranger, the chameleon can move each of its eyes in a different direction at the same time!

Some snakes kill or immobilize their prey by injecting it with poison from their fangs. Some cobras are particularly dangerous, as they can spit their venom several feet. Other snakes squeeze their prey to death in their muscular coils.

Snakes that eat fairly large prey have flexible joints in their jaws, enabling them to open their mouths incredibly wide to swallow the prey whole.

HOW DO SNAKES MOVE?

MANY SNAKES throw themselves along the ground in waves that pass from head to tail. They have hundreds of pairs of ribs and strong muscles to enable them to do this, while their scales grip the ground. North American sidewinders, however, move as their name suggests, by throwing their coils sideways along the ground.

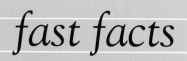

fast facts

WHICH IS THE LONGEST LIVING REPTILE?

The giant tortoise can live for up to 150 years.

ARE THERE ANY VEGETARIAN SNAKES?

All snakes are carnivores, eating anything from insects to small mammals.

CAN LIZARDS REALLY GROW A NEW TAIL?

If they are in serious danger from a predator, some lizards are able to discard part of their tails. The tail continues to wriggle while the lizard escapes. Within a few months, the soft part of the tail will be regrown, although it will not have bones inside it as the original tail had.

WHICH IS THE WORLD'S LARGEST SNAKE?

The anaconda and the reticulated python can both grow to over 9m (30ft) in length.

WHICH SNAKE IS THE DEADLIEST?

Up to a hundred thousand people die each year from snake bites. The snake responsible for more human deaths than any other is the Asian cobra, which is very common on the Indian subcontinent.

DO SNAKES HAVE A SENSE OF SMELL?

Strangely enough, snakes smell by using their tongues! By flicking their tongues in and out, snakes carry air to a special "smelling" gland in their mouths.

HOW DO BIRDS AND MAMMALS DIFFER?

It is likely that birds evolved from reptiles. Like reptiles but unlike most mammals, they lay eggs that hatch outside the mother. All adult birds have feathers, rather than fur or scales, and most can fly. However, birds are similar to mammals in being warm blooded.

IS IT EASY TO TELL MALE AND FEMALE BIRDS APART?

SOME MALE AND FEMALE BIRDS of the same species have very different plumage, with the male usually being more brightly coloured to attract females. Other species show little or no difference between the sexes. As well as having different plumage, birds may make displays to each other during the breeding season. Some dance in elaborate curving patterns, spread their feathers and strut, or sing. Male birds may fight to defend their territories during nesting.

The peacock displays its magnificent tail to attract the much less showy peahen. Remarkably, despite the weight of its tail feathers, a peacock can still fly.

Both male and female flamingos have pink plumage in their native habitats in Africa. They live in colonies and have long legs for wading in shallow waters.

WHAT DO BIRDS EAT?

DIFFERENT SPECIES of birds have different diets, just as mammals do. Some are vegetarian, eating fruits and seeds. Others feed on insects and other invertebrates, such as worms. Birds' beaks are adapted to the kind of food they need. The beaks of meat-eaters are often hooked and sharp, ideal for tearing flesh from carcases. Birds that search for food along the seashore or on mud banks often have long pointed beaks for burrowing into the soft ground.

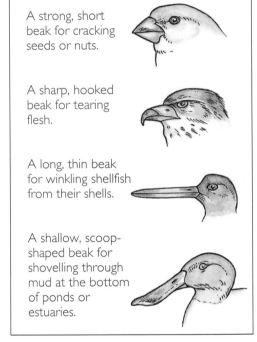

A strong, short beak for cracking seeds or nuts.

A sharp, hooked beak for tearing flesh.

A long, thin beak for winkling shellfish from their shells.

A shallow, scoop-shaped beak for shovelling through mud at the bottom of ponds or estuaries.

HOW DO BIRDS FLY?

BIRDS are specially adapted for flight, whether skimming short distances between branches or flying for weeks at a time above the oceans. The shape of their wings gives a clue to the kinds of flight they make. Birds' bodies need to be light enough for flight. The large surface area of their wings pushes air downwards as they flap to lift the bird. At the same time, birds need immensely powerful chest muscles to move their wings. Feathers are the ideal covering – they are light but strong and flexible. In flight, they can lie flat against the bird's body to reduce wind resistance.

The structure of a bird's legs and wings has much in common with that of the legs and arms of humans, but they are specially adapted for flight and the bird's habitat. Swimming birds, for example, have webbed feet to help propel them through the water.

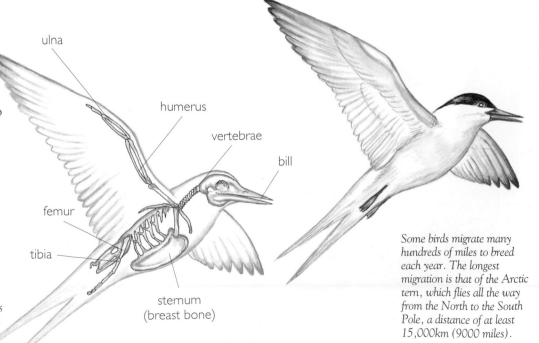

ulna

humerus

vertebrae

bill

femur

tibia

sternum (breast bone)

Some birds migrate many hundreds of miles to breed each year. The longest migration is that of the Arctic tern, which flies all the way from the North to the South Pole, a distance of at least 15,000km (9000 miles).

WHAT ARE FLEDGLINGS?

WHEN THEY FIRST HATCH from the egg, baby birds are called nestlings. At this stage, many of them have no feathers. Blind and helpless, they are completely dependent on their parents for food and protection. As their feathers grow, they become fledglings, with open eyes and hearty appetites. When the fledglings have all their feathers and are strong enough, they are ready to learn to fly and begin to be independent.

WHAT KINDS OF HOMES DO BIRDS MAKE?

BIRDS show extraordinary variety and ingenuity in the nests they build. An untidy mound of sticks, simply dropped on top of one another, is all that a mute swan requires. House martins, on the other hand, literally build their homes. They skim over puddles and ponds, picking up little pieces of mud, which are built up into round-walled structures on the sides of buildings. Cuckoos, of course, are renowned for the fact that they use other birds' nests in which to lay their eggs. They are able to mimic the size, shape and colour of the host-bird's eggs to some extent, so that the additional egg is not immediately obvious.

Skilfully built, this mud nest becomes a strong structure in which several nestlings can be raised.

Dried grass, twigs, moss and feathers are easy to find for nest-building and also help to camouflage the nest.

WHICH IS THE LARGEST BIRD?

THE OSTRICH, running in herds in southern Africa, is the largest bird in the world. It can stand more than 2m (7ft) high. As well as being able to run at enormous speed from danger, the ostrich has powerful legs and sharp claws, which can deliver a kick hard enough to kill many predators.

CAN ALL BIRDS FLY?

MOST BIRDS can fly, but there are also some flightless species. These all have other ways of escaping from predators. The larger flightless birds, such as ostriches and emus, can run very fast. Penguins cannot fly but can swim and dive at great speed, using their wings as flippers to power them through the water.

fast facts

WHAT ARE FEATHERS MADE OF?

Feathers are made of keratin, which is a protein. Hair, hoofs and fingernails also contain keratin.

WHY ARE SOME BIRDS' BONES HOLLOW?

Hollow bones are strong but also help birds to be light enough to fly.

WHICH IS THE SMALLEST BIRD?

The bee hummingbird (*Mellisuga helenae*) is just 5.7cm (2.24 inches) long and weighs only about 1.6g (0.056oz).

HOW FAST CAN BIRDS FLY?

The white-throated spine-tail swift (*Hirundapus caudacutus*) can fly at over 170km/h (105mph).

HOW MANY FEATHERS DO BIRDS HAVE?

It varies, but some birds have more than 25,000 feathers.

WHAT IS SPECIAL ABOUT MAMMALS?

There are around 4000 species of mammal. Some spend their whole lives swimming in the ocean, while others never venture into the water. Most have fur or hair on their bodies at some time in their lives. Some walk on two legs and some on four. What all mammals have in common, however, is that they are warm blooded and breathe air. Mammal mothers feed their young on milk from their mammary glands. Mammals also have lungs, a heart with four chambers and well-developed brains.

WHY IS IT AN ADVANTAGE TO HAVE WARM BLOOD?

WARM-BLOODED ANIMALS are able to control their internal temperature to a greater degree than cold-blooded animals, so that they are less dependent on the temperature of their surroundings. While reptiles slow down when the weather is cold, mammals are able to lead an active life. Mammals have adapted to life in all parts of the world where there is food for them to eat.

WHY ARE SOME MAMMALS' BABIES ABLE TO RUN ALMOST AS SOON AS THEY ARE BORN?

ALMOST ALL MAMMAL BABIES grow inside their mother until they are able to breathe and feed outside, but mammal babies differ very much in the kind of help they need after birth. Human babies, for example, need the attention of their parents for many years before they are able to fend for themselves completely. Most grazing animals, on the other hand, have adapted to life on wide, open grasslands, where they are constantly at risk from attack by predators. It is important that these animals give birth to young that can stand on their own feet and run from danger almost immediately.

Mammal mothers produce milk for their offspring from mammary glands. The babies are able to suck the milk from nipples on their mother's stomach or chest. Usually, animals that have many babies at one time have several nipples. The mother's milk is a complete food for the babies, until they are weaned. This means introducing them to the foods they will eat as adults.

Many mammals sweat or pant to lose heat if they become warm. Dogs, for example, are able to lose heat through their tongues. If the temperature becomes too cold, blood vessels contract, causing goosebumps, and muscles cause shivering in order to warm up the body with movement. Human beings, of course, can also regulate their heat by changing their clothing so that it is suitable for the conditions they meet.

DO ALL MAMMALS GIVE BIRTH TO LIVE YOUNG?

MOST MAMMAL BABIES develop inside their mothers until they are ready to be born. The exceptions are the monotremes, a small group of mammals found in Australia. Like most reptiles, they lay eggs rather than giving birth to live young. Perhaps the best known of these is the duck-billed platypus.

Although the young of the duck-billed platypus hatch from eggs, they are mammals, so they still receive nourishment from their mother's milk. The eggs are laid underground in burrows, where the mother cares for her young until they are able to swim and forage for themselves.

WHICH MAMMAL IS THE FASTEST?

THE CHEETAH (*Acinonyx jubatus*) can reach 105km/h (65mph) when sprinting over a short distance.

WHAT IS A MARSUPIAL?

A marsupial is a very special kind of mammal. Although it does give birth to live young, they are very immature when born. Their mothers have a pouch on their abdomens, where the babies are protected and can drink milk until they are ready to survive in the open.

Female kangaroos have the extraordinary ability to keep an embryo in the womb in a state of suspended animation for several years until conditions are right for a baby (called a joey) to be born.

fast facts

WHICH IS THE LARGEST LAND MAMMAL?

The largest mammal on Earth is not a land mammal at all, but the blue whale (*Balaenoptera musculus*). The largest land mammal is the African elephant (*Loxodonta africana*), which can weigh up to 7 tonnes (6.9 tons).

CAN MAMMALS FLY?

Nowadays human beings can fly, of course, but only with the help of machines. the only mammals that can really fly are bats, which have flaps of skin between their front and hind legs, acting as wings. Other mammals, such as some possums and squirrels, can spread out their bodies and glide tthrough the air but they do not truly fly.

WHICH IS THE LARGEST ORDER OF MAMMALS?

There are over 1600 species of rodent, making them the largest order of mammals. Rodents have chisel-shaped front teeth, called incisors, that can be used for gnawing food. Most rodents, such as rats and mice, are quite small, but the capybara of South America can grow over a metre (3ft) long.

WHAT IS A PANGOLIN?

The pangolin is an extraordinary mammal that is covered with scales rather than fur. The pangolin eats ants, and tthe scales protect its body from the bites of these insects.

WHICH IS THE SMALLEST MAMMAL?

Savi's pygmy shrew (*Suncus etruscus*) weighs less than 3g (0.1oz).

WHICH MAMMALS ARE VENOMOUS?

Male duck-billed platypus, several species of shrews and the solenodon.

WHICH ARE THE MOST NUMEROUS PRIMATES?

There are about 180 different species of primate, most of them living in the tropical regions of the world. The exception, and also the most numerous primate, is Homo sapiens – human beings. All primates have fairly large brains and forward-facing eyes that enable them to judge distances accurately. Instead of claws or hoofs, like other mammals, they have fingers and toes with soft, sensitive tips. They also have the ability to grasp with their fingers, thumbs and toes. The order of primates can be divided into prosimians, also known as primitive primates, and anthropoids, the higher primates, which include marmosets, monkeys, apes and, of course, human beings.

The ring-tailed lemur has a very long tail, like many of its relatives.

WHAT ARE PROSIMIANS?

THE PROSIMIANS include lemurs, the aye-aye, lorises and tarsiers. Lemurs live in the forests of Madagascar and nearby islands, where they eat insects, small vertebrates, shoots and leaves. They spend their time mainly in the trees, coming to the ground occasionally to feed. Most of them have long tails and many are nocturnal. Lorises come from Africa and southern Asia. They have huge, round eyes and eat insects. Tarsiers, living in the forests of Indonesia and the Philippines, also have huge eyes. Although they do not grow to more than 16cm (6.5 inches), they can leap over 1.8m (6ft) from tree to tree.

HOW DO OLD WORLD AND NEW WORLD MONKEYS DIFFER?

The mandrill is one of the largest of the Old World monkeys. It can weigh as much as 20kg (44lb).

THE MONKEYS of the American continent, the "New" World, differ in several ways from those of Africa and Asia. New World monkeys, such as capuchins, spider monkeys, howler monkeys and woolly monkeys, have flat noses and widely spaced eyes. They live in family groups and spend much of their time in the trees, feeding mainly on fruit and leaves. Most of them have long tails, which they can use like an extra arm or leg to cling to branches. Old World monkeys live in a wide variety of habitats. They walk on all fours and, although they may sleep in trees, some species live mainly on the ground. They have narrow noses, and their nostrils face forward. Old World monkeys include macaques, mandrills and mangabeys.

The cotton-top tamarin is a New World monkey, living in the forests of South America.

HOW DO PRIMATES COMMUNICATE?

PRIMATES other than humans communicate with each other in a number of ways. Many primates use touch to establish relationships, grooming each other to show friendship and to remove insects. Howler monkeys, living in the tropical forests of South America, make very loud calls. The male calls to mark his territory and can often be heard over 3km (almost 2 miles) away. Male gibbons, too, have loud calls, used for communicating with family members and to warn off other males. Some Old World monkeys have brightly coloured faces and bottoms, which the males use in courting displays and to frighten off enemies and rivals. Gorillas thump on the ground to warn off rival males, or beat their chests and roar to demonstrate their strength and power. Chimpanzees communicate with each other by using sounds and gestures.

WHICH ANIMALS ARE HUMAN BEINGS' NEAREST LIVING RELATIVES?

THE GREAT APES are the nearest living relatives to *Homo sapiens*. There are four species of great ape: the orang-utan, chimpanzee, gorilla and gibbon. Both orang-utans and gibbons spend most of their time in the trees, where they are very agile, swinging from branch to branch. Gorillas live in family groups, led by a large male, and feed mainly on the ground. The dominant male is often called a "silverback" – like humans, their hair becomes grey with age. Chimpanzees are very intelligent. They can use tools and solve puzzles. Their gestures and expressions often make them seem uncannily like humans.

All primates, including humans, take care of their young for a long time before they become adults. Apes look after their young for up to five years. Usually only one baby is born at a time.

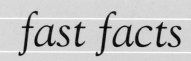

fast facts

DO ALL PRIMATES LIVE IN GROUPS?

Most primates do live in family groups, but the orang-utan often lives alone, joining other orang-utans only to mate.

HOW DO HUMAN FEET DIFFER FROM THOSE OF OTHER PRIMATES?

All primates have opposable thumbs – their thumbs can swivel to be used with the fingers to grip and grasp objects. Most primates have this ability with their feet as well – humans are the only primates that do not have opposable big toes.

WHICH IS THE LARGEST PRIMATE?

The gorilla (*Gorilla gorilla*) is the largest primate. A male can weigh up to 275kg (605lb) – as much as three heavyweight boxers!

WHICH IS THE SMALLEST PRIMATE?

The mouse lemur (*Cheirogaleidae*) has a head and body length of 12.5cm (6 inches).

WHAT IS BIG FOOT?

There is a legend that an apelike animal, behaving like a human being, lives in the forests of North America. No such creature has ever been captured, although many hunters and hikers claim to have seen it or its tracks, which is why it is called Big Foot. Similar tales are told of the yeti of the Himalayas.

ARE ALL PRIMATES VEGETARIANS?

Many humans, of course, eat foods from both animals and plants. Most other primates are mainly vegetarian, but some, like chimpanzees, also eat insects, birds' eggs and small vertebrates at times.

HOW HAVE HUMAN BEINGS CHANGED THE EARTH?

There have been living things on the Earth for thousands of millions of years. It is only during the last million years that one animal has become dominant. In that time, human beings have brought huge changes to the planet, so that today there are very few places untouched by human activity. In fact, many scientists would say that our actions have had such an enormous effect that the climate of the globe has been altered, with serious consequences for every living thing that shares our Earth.

WHAT ARE THE EFFECTS OF FARMING ON THE WORLD'S WILDLIFE?

ONCE HUMAN BEINGS lived a nomadic life, hunting and gathering food as they travelled. Their lives had little effect on the ecosystems of the planet. Gradually, some nomadic peoples began to domesticate animals such as goats and sheep. By taking animals with them on their travels, they ensured a constant supply of milk, meat, skins and wool. But it was when they began to grow crops and settle in one place that humans really began to change the face of the Earth.

In huge areas of the world, natural vegetation has been ploughed up so that crops can be grown. Vast European forests were cleared for farming hundreds of years ago. Large areas of the prairies of America have been cultivated within the last two hundred years. Today the clearance still goes on as rainforests are felled. Even where land has not been ploughed, overgrazing by cattle can destroy grasslands.

Large fields without hedges can suffer from soil erosion as winds sweep across them, blowing away the topsoil.

Pesticides enter the food chain when affected insects or small animals are eaten by birds and other creatures. These in turn feed larger birds and mammals, which may be taking in harmful or even fatal amounts of chemicals.

Large fields are easier for machinery but mean that hedgerows and the habitats they provide are destroyed.

Modern intensive farming relies on chemicals to put nutrients back into the soil and kill pests. These chemicals can seep into river systems, polluting the water and damaging the habitats of many living things.

fast facts

WHY DO LIVING THINGS BECOME EXTINCT?

Living things usually become extinct because of a change in their environment. Attack by a predator, destruction of habitats or food sources and climate change can all be fatal. Humans are only a recent cause of some extinctions.

WHY IS IT IMPORTANT TO SAVE ENDANGERED SPECIES?

Living things depend on each other in complicated ways. The loss of one species may change the balance of a habitat, leading to the loss of other living things. And once a plant, for example, is extinct, it is too late to find out that it might have supplied a life-saving drug or helped to feed people or animals.

CAN THE EARTH FEED EVERYONE?

The Earth is able to produce enough food for everyone on it, but billions of people go hungry each year because they do not have access to the planet's produce.

ARE HUMANS THE BIGGEST THREAT TO LIVING THINGS?

All living things may be attacked by predators or disease, but usually a whole species is not wiped out in this way. Natural disasters, such as volcanic eruptions, fires and floods also have a local effect on wildlife. But humans can affect habitats for a long time and over a huge area.

HOW FAST IS THE WORLD'S HUMAN POPULATION GROWING?

Two hundred years ago the population of the world was around one billion (1,000,000,000). Today it is about six billion. The growth may slow in the twenty-first century, but the population is still likely to reach 10 billion before the year 2100.

WHAT IS ACID RAIN?

WHEN FOSSIL FUELS are burnt, nitrogen oxide and sulphur dioxide are given off. These substances dissolve into the moisture in the air and rise into clouds. These are blown along by the wind and fall as rain, sometimes hundreds of kilometres away. This "acid rain" kills vegetation and the living things that feed on it. It can be difficult to find the source of the problem because of its distance from the damage being done.

WHAT IS GLOBAL WARMING?

BURNING COAL AND OIL gives off carbon dioxide and other gases. At the same time, cutting down forests means that less carbon dioxide is used by plants for photosynthesis. In the modern industrial world, more and more carbon dioxide is being produced. This and other gases are known as greenhouse gases. They are held in the atmosphere of the planet and prevent heat from escaping, so warming the Earth by means of the "greenhouse effect".

CAN CITIES PROVIDE HABITATS FOR LIVING THINGS?

WHEN TOWNS AND CITIES are built, the habitats of the living things in the area are destroyed. Gradually, however, other plants and animals find a foothold in the urban environment, while a few of the original species adapt to the new conditions. Even in the largest cities there are parks, gardens and tree-lined roads. Human beings throw away an enormous amount of food, which can provide nourishment for insects, birds and animals.

At first sight a city such as New York does not appear to be an ideal habitat for wildlife, but even the largest city can provide food and homes for a wide variety of living things. Not all of these are welcomed by the city's human residents, however.

ARE WEATHER AND CLIMATE THE SAME THING?

The lower levels of the Earth's atmosphere are in constant motion. As the atmosphere heats and cools, it expands and contracts, causing changes in pressure and air movement. These changes cause the weather that we experience on Earth. The daily occurrence of sunshine, rain, hail, snow, fog or wind is what we call weather. Climate is the overall weather in a particular area over a longer period of time.

HOW DO WE DESCRIBE THE WIND?

KNOWING THE DIRECTION of the wind is not always enough. People on land and sea also need a way of describing the strength of the wind. In 1805, a British admiral called Beaufort devised the scale that still bears his name.

- **0 Calm** Smoke rises straight upwards
- **1 Light air** Smoke slowly drifts
- **2 Light breeze** Tree leaves rustle
- **3 Gentle breeze** Flags flutter
- **4 Moderate wind** Branches wave
- **5 Fresh wind** Small trees sway
- **6 Strong wind** Umbrellas misbehave!
- **7 Near gale** Large trees bend
- **8 Gale** Small branches break
- **9 Severe gale** Roof tiles dislodge
- **10 Storm** Trees blown over
- **11 Severe storm** Buildings damaged
- **12 Hurricane** Major structural damage

WHAT CAUSES LIGHTNING?

THE WATER DROPLETS in clouds have a positive electrical charge at the top of the cloud and a negative charge at the bottom. When the negative charge comes near enough to an attracting positive charge on the Earth below or on another cloud, the electrical energy is released in a flash of light. There may also be a loud bang, called thunder, at the same time. However, as light travels faster through the air than sound, we see the lightning flash before hearing the thunder.

WHAT IS THE WATER CYCLE?

WATER ON EARTH is constantly recycled. Water evaporates into the air from rivers, lakes and oceans. As it rises into the air, the vapour is cooled and condenses into clouds. The wind blows the clouds along until eventually precipitation – rain, snow or hail – results. The precipitation falls to Earth, where it runs through the soil to join rivers, lakes, oceans and underground reservoirs. Without water, there could be no life on Earth.

Water falls back to the ground as rain, snow or hail.

Water vapour forms clouds.

Water rises by evaporation from rivers, lakes and oceans.

Water runs from rivers into the sea.

Water vapour rises.

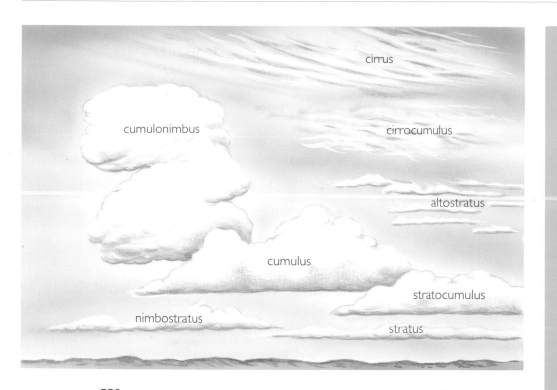

cirrus

cumulonimbus

cirrocumulus

altostratus

cumulus

stratocumulus

nimbostratus

stratus

WHAT ARE THE DIFFERENT KINDS OF CLOUD?

MOST OF THE NAMES given to different kinds of cloud simply describe their shapes and positions or give a clue about what we can expect from them. *Cirro* means "curled"; *cumulo* means "piled up"; *nimbo* means "rain"; *strato* means "in layers or sheets" and *alto* means "high". Higher levels of cloud are made of ice crystals. As you might expect, it is the clouds with the word *nimbus* or *nimbo* in their names that bring rain, hail or snow. The very lowest clouds drift over high ground as fog.

An anemometer measures wind speed.

A simple weather vane is effective for measuring wind direction.

A barograph charts air pressure.

A thermometer measures air temperature.

HOW DO METEOROLOGISTS FORECAST THE WEATHER?

AS EVERYONE KNOWS, predicting the weather can often be difficult. Professional weather forecasters, called meteorologists, use information collected by weather stations on land, at sea and on satellites in space. Rainfall, sunshine and wind speed can all be measured fairly easily, but they only tell us what the weather is like *now*. A better gauge of future weather is to study air pressure and cloud formation. Today's meteorologists use computers to help make sense of all the information received and to predict, based on past events, the weather of the future.

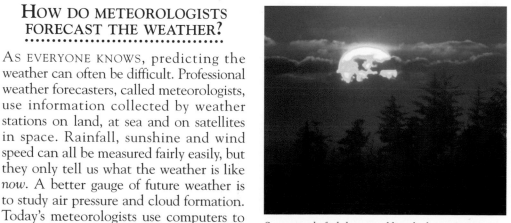

Some people feel that age-old methods are just as effective as computers in predicting the weather. "Red sky at night, shepherd's delight, red sky in the morning, shepherd's warning" is a traditional saying.

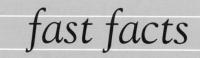

fast facts

WHICH IS THE WINDIEST PLACE IN THE WORLD?

Antarctica holds the record for being the windiest place on Earth. Although higher wind speeds have been recorded for short periods elsewhere, Port Martin regularly has winds of over 100km/h (65mph).

WHICH IS THE DRIEST PLACE IN THE WORLD?

The Atacama Desert, in Chile, is the driest place in the world. Parts of it have never had rain since records have been kept.

WHAT CAUSES THE SEASONS?

As it moves around the Sun on its yearly orbit, the Earth is slightly tilted, so that at different times of the year the northern and southern hemispheres may be slightly nearer or slightly further from the Sun. This is what causes the differences in temperature and weather that we call seasons. The equator is always about the same distance from the Sun, so its climate is the same all the year round.

WHAT IS A TORNADO?

A tornado is a wind that twists violently to form a funnel. Rising air within the funnel can literally suck objects, including buildings and people, into the air. Tornadoes are particularly dangerous because they move at high speed and can change direction very rapidly.

ARE SNOWFLAKES REALLY ALL DIFFERENT?

Examined under a microscope, all snowflakes are made up of six-sided shapes that appear to be different from each other. The problem is that no one can look at all the millions of snow crystals that form to check that there really are not two the same!

WHAT IS AN ECOSYSTEM?

Different parts of the world vary enormously in the kinds of plant and animal life they can support. This is mainly caused by the climate in each place, which allows different kinds of living things to thrive. The climate itself is influenced by the physical characteristics of a region – whether it is mountainous or near the sea, for example – and its position on the Earth – how near to the equator it is. Different parts of the world can share similar conditions, even if they are thousands of miles apart. Each area contains communities of millions of living things that rely on each other for survival. These communities are called ecosystems.

DO ECOSYSTEMS CHANGE?

OVER TIME, ecosystems can alter a great deal. The climate of the Earth has gradually changed many times even within the time when records have been kept. Before that we know that parts of the world experienced Ice Ages, which had huge effects on the environments of living things. Human beings also alter ecosystems, often without realizing the possible results of their actions. Once large areas of North America and Europe were covered with deciduous woodland. Over hundreds of years, trees have been cut down for building, to supply fuel and to clear land for farming, so that remaining areas of woodland are comparatively small.

Human beings have also altered ecosystems by introducing plants and animals from other parts of the world. European settlers in Australia, for example, took rabbits with them, which have bred in the wild and become serious pests, ousting native species.

WHERE ARE THE MAIN ECOSYSTEMS OF THE WORLD?

THE MAP BELOW shows the main ways in which the Earth can be divided into different ecosystems. These are based mainly on the kind of plants that grow in an area, as all other living things rely directly or indirectly on plants for their food. Of course, there are many smaller ecosystems within these broad divisions.

KEY

ice and tundra

coniferous forest

deciduous woodland

Mediterranean

grassland

savannah

tropical rainforest

desert

HOW DO THE MAIN ECOSYSTEMS DIFFER?

Ice and tundra
In the cold conditions of the Poles, very few species can survive, but during the summer the ice around the Arctic and Antarctic Circles melts to reveal tundra, on which sparse vegetation can live.

Coniferous forest
The coniferous forests that stretch across northern Europe, Asia and America are called the taiga. Most of the trees are evergreen, offering food and shelter to animals all the year round.

Deciduous woodland
Deciduous woodlands occur in temperate parts of the world, where the climate is fairly mild for part of the year and there is plenty of rainfall.

Mediterranean
The area around the Mediterranean Sea is known for its long, hot summers and cooler winters. Parts of Australia and North America also have this ecosystem.

Grassland
These areas are too dry to support large plants such as trees but have a variety of grasses and smaller plants on which grazing animals can feed.

Savannah
This is also grassland but it is found in tropical regions. Rainfall usually happens once a year, when grasses can grow up to 3m (10ft) tall.

Tropical rainforest
Rainforests, with their warm, moist climate, support an extraordinary variety of living things.

Desert
Desert areas have little or no rainfall. Plants and animals here have adapted to conserve every drop of available water.

fast facts

WHAT IS A HABITAT?
Within each ecosystem there are many different places for animals to live. In the rainforest, for example, they may live high up in the tree canopy or in the rich soil below. Each place is a habitat.

HOW LARGE IS AN ECOSYSTEM?
An ecosystem can vary from an area of hundreds of square miles to a tiny pool or a single plant. A very small area may support a unique community of living things.

WHAT IS ECOLOGY?
Ecology is really the study of ecosystems – the ways in which living things live together within their surroundings.

WHY ARE THERE BATS ALL OVER THE WORLD BUT NOT ELEPHANTS?
The simple reason is that bats can fly! When the continents split from each other, different species developed on each continent, although sometimes in very similar ways.

WHAT IS THE BIOSPHERE?
The biosphere is the name given to the area on and around our planet in which life can exist.

WHICH ECOSYSTEM HAS THE GREATEST VARIETY OF LIVING THINGS?
It is likely that over half of the Earth's different kinds of living things live in the warm, moist conditions of the tropical rainforest.

DO OCEANS AND RIVERS HAVE ECOSYSTEMS TOO?
There may well be as many different ecosystems underwater as there are on land!

HOW DO LIVING THINGS SURVIVE TOGETHER?

All living things are linked in complicated food webs, relying on each other for nourishment, but some animals and plants have very special relationships, where a partnership may benefit one partner or both.

HOW DO CLOWNFISH AND SEA ANEMONES LIVE TOGETHER?

IN TROPICAL WATERS, clownfish have a symbiotic relationship with sea anemones. They live among the anemone's tentacles, unharmed by its stings but enjoying protection from predators. In turn, the clownfish seem to protect the anemone from some predators too. They may even lure fish into the anemone's tentacles, where they can be caught and digested.

WHAT IS SYMBIOSIS?

WHEN BOTH PARTNERS benefit equally from a partnership, they are said to be in a symbiotic relationship. There are many such relationships in the natural world. For example, when a bee goes to a flower to collect nectar, it also brings about pollination by carrying pollen on its furry body from one flower to the next. Both the bee and the flower benefit.

Symbiosis can sometimes help to kill parasites. Small birds called oxpeckers peck parasites from the skins of antelopes on the African savannah.

HOW DO CUCKOOS FOOL OTHER BIRDS INTO BECOMING BABYSITTERS?

CUCKOOS do not raise their own young. They are said to be brood parasites. They lay a single egg in a nest that already contains several eggs while the parent bird is away. Although cuckoo eggs are often slightly bigger than the other eggs, the female cuckoo has the extraordinary ability partially to match the colour of her egg to the others. The eggs are hatched by the host bird. The young cuckoo is bigger and stronger than the other nestlings and demands more food. To ensure that it receives all the food brought to the nest by the foster parents, it pushes the other young birds out of the nest.

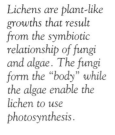

Lichens are plant-like growths that result from the symbiotic relationship of fungi and algae. The fungi form the "body" while the algae enable the lichen to use photosynthesis.

WHY DO SOME DISEASES NEED ANIMAL AND HUMAN HOSTS?

EVEN THE TINIEST living things may be parasites. The micro organisms that cause malaria and sleeping sickness, for example, are parasites that need more than one host to complete their life cycles. The diseases are spread by infected insects, which bite human beings to feed on their blood and in so doing pass on the infection. The organisms multiply in the person's body, causing illness. The cycle is completed when an infection-free insect bites the person and in its turn becomes a carrier of the disease.

A parasite is a living thing that benefits from a relationship with another species but actually causes harm to that species. Some fungi are found on dying birch trees and can also live for a while on the wood after the tree has died.

HOW HAS DOMESTICATING ANIMALS HELPED HUMANS?

BY DOMESTICATING goats, cattle, sheep, pigs and poultry, humans have been able to ensure that food is always available. Horses, mules and camels have been used to carry people and goods over long distances. Pets provide companionship but can also be very useful. Sheepdogs help farmers to round up their flocks. Guide dogs for the blind and hearing dogs for the deaf help their owners to lead full lives. Animals are also used to guard property, perform rescues and carry messages.

Until the introduction of machinery, many tasks on the farm were done using the strength of horses.

Camels are used as beasts of burden in parts of the world where there are often dry conditions.

Near the Arctic Circle, dogs have traditionally been used to pull sleds. They are able to withstand the very cold conditions and move quickly over the snow.

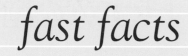
fast facts

WHAT IS COMMENSALISM?

Commensalism is a relationship where one partner gains a benefit but the other is not affected at all.

WHICH WERE THE FIRST PETS?

Dogs were probably the first animals to be domesticated, perhaps to help with hunting. All modern dogs are related to wolves (*Canis lupus*).

WHY CAN IT BE A MISTAKE TO KILL PESTS?

A pest, such as an aphid attacking plants in the garden, may be food to an insect such as a ladybird. If all the aphids are destroyed, the ladybirds will die out too. They will then not be available to go into action if another colony of aphids arrives. Links like this between living things are happening all the time, in complicated relationships. Killing pests can affect the whole balance of an ecosystem.

ARE BACTERIA ALWAYS HARMFUL?

The human body is host to millions of bacteria. Many of these are useful, helping us to digest our food. In fact, some of the foods we eat, such as yoghurt and blue cheese, are made by allowing certain kinds of bacteria to breed in them.

WHY DO SOME ANIMALS HAVE HUNDREDS OF YOUNG AND SOME ONLY ONE?

All animals want to make sure that at least some of their young reach adulthood and reproduce themselves. Some animals do this by looking after a few babies until they can fend for themselves. Other animals produce hundreds of eggs, which they leave to develop by themselves. Most of them will die, but a few will survive, just as in smaller families.

HOW CAN GRASSLANDS SUPPORT SO MANY ANIMALS?

When not shaded by larger plants, grasses grow very quickly, especially if frequently nibbled or cut, as anyone who has to help mow a lawn knows. Up to 30% (almost a third) of the Earth's land is covered by grassland. Grass plants can survive fire, which spreads rapidly across the land but burns for only a short time, as there is little to fuel it. Flash floods are also not a problem, as the shallow, dense roots of the grasses prevent the soil from being washed away.

DO GRASSLANDS ALL OVER THE WORLD HAVE SIMILAR CLIMATES?

THE CLIMATES of the world's grasslands vary a great deal. In Africa there are huge areas of grassland called savannah. These are warm all year round with summer rains. They support large populations of seed-eating birds and grazing animals, which in turn provide food for large meat-eating animals, such as lions, leopards, cheetahs, hyenas and jackals. The North American prairies and Russian steppes are similar in having hot summers but very cold winters. Great herds of bison once roamed the North American "sea of grass", but early settlers killed enormous numbers of them for food and sport. Now the bison is a protected species. South American grasslands, called pampas, and the South African veld have sparser tussocks of grass.

Before hunting severely reduced the numbers of bison on the American prairie, it was said that a herd could take many days to pass.

WHY ARE THERE VERY FEW TREES ON VAST STRETCHES OF GRASSLAND?

IT WAS ONCE THOUGHT that large areas of grassland did not have enough rainfall or had soil that was too poor for trees to grow. Now it is also thought that they may have lost trees through fire. When grazing animals pass frequently over newly growing forest, young trees are soon killed by nibbling and trampling, so that the trees would never have a chance to become established again.

giraffe

Grant's gazelle

hyena

vulture

HOW DO GRASSES KEEP GROWING IF THEY ARE CONSTANTLY EATEN?

GRASSES are well suited to being grazed. Although many will grow to more than two metres (over six feet) if left undisturbed, they do not need to reach this height to reproduce. Even if a flower and seed head are never allowed to form, the plant can reproduce by sending out runners underground, from which new daughter plants can grow. As well as being able to grow upwards from their central stem, grasses also have lower growing points from which new stalks can grow if the central one is cut. In fact, by this means grasses grow more thickly than ever, giving more food for grazing animals to eat.

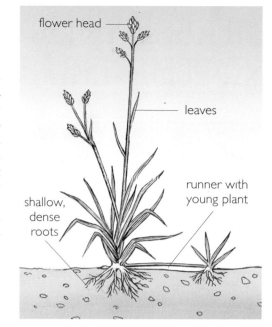

flower head

leaves

runner with young plant

shallow, dense roots

WHAT DEFENCES DO GRAZING ANIMALS HAVE AGAINST PREDATORS?

FOR MOST GRAZING ANIMALS, being part of a herd is their best defence against attack. Although individual animals, especially young, old or sick ones, may be picked off by predators, most animals will be safe. There are also more animals to watch out for danger while the rest graze. When attacked, the best defence of an antelope or zebra is its speed. At least over short distances, it can usually outrun its attackers. Wildebeest and some other heavier animals also have a powerful kick, which can break the bones of a lion or hyena if well aimed.

zebra

lion

WHAT IS A HERBIVOROUS ANIMAL?

Herbivorous animals are plant-eaters, unlike carnivorous animals, which eat meat. Omnivorous animals, like most human beings, eat almost anything!

HOW MANY VERTEBRAE DOES A GIRAFFE HAVE?

Despite its extraordinarily long neck, a giraffe has exactly the same number of vertebrae as a human being – just 24.

DO MALE OR FEMALE LIONS HUNT FOR FOOD?

It is usually the females in a pride, or group of lions, that hunt for food.

WHAT ARE SCAVENGERS?

Scavengers are carnivores that feed on meat that is already dead. They steal meat from the kills of other animals or "clean up" when a larger animal has eaten its fill.

HOW HAVE HUMAN BEINGS CHANGED GRASSLAND WILDLIFE?

Big-game hunters have almost wiped out some kinds of grassland wildlife. Now most larger game is protected by law, but illegal poaching still goes on. In temperate areas, such as Russia and North America, large areas of natural grassland have been ploughed and used for growing crops. Although the soil is very fertile, crops often need more water and protection from the wind than grasses, which can cause problems for farmers.

ARE THERE ALSO ANIMALS LIVING UNDER GRASSLANDS?

AS GRASSLANDS usually have few trees or rocks to offer cover to smaller animals, many of them live in burrows underground. In North America, prairie dogs (*Cynomys ludovicianus*) live in huge numbers in connected burrows, sometimes causing the ground to cave in. The South American pampas also has many burrowing animals, including viscachas (*Lagostomus maximus*) and cavies (*Cavia aperea*), related to guinea pigs.

WHY ARE RAINFORESTS SO RICH IN LIVING THINGS?

Rainforests are tropical evergreen forests. They have at least 4000mm (156 inches) of rain each year. The climate is warm and moist all year round, giving conditions in which green plants can produce huge amounts of vegetation, flowers and fruit. There is always plenty to eat for insects and the animals that, in turn, feed on them. The rainforest also offers an extraordinarily wide range of habitats for living things.

WHERE ARE THE WORLD'S RAINFORESTS?

STRICTLY SPEAKING, tropical rainforests should fall within the *tropics* – between the Tropic of Capricorn and the Tropic of Cancer. In fact, most are found even nearer to the equator. South America, Africa and Asia have large areas of rainforest.

WHAT IS THE DIFFERENCE BETWEEN A LEOPARD AND A JAGUAR?

RAINFORESTS in different parts of the world often have similar species, but because they have developed separately for thousands of years, they each have their own characteristics. Both South American jaguars and African leopards have spotted skins that camouflage them in the dappled light of the forest floor. Like leopards, jaguars have rings of black spots on their coats, but they also have smaller spots within those rings.

Leopards are often nocturnal, hunting by night when lions and other predators are not active. They are also excellent climbers.

Jaguars, the largest wild cats on the American continent, prowl the forest floors of South America in search of prey.

WHY ARE RAINFORESTS IN DANGER?

RAINFORESTS are being cut down at an alarming rate for two main reasons. Both large commercial farming companies and individual families clear the forest to gain land to cultivate and graze animals, although the rainforest soil is not suitable for this use. Secondly, forests have been felled to supply tropical hardwoods for furniture-making and building. Woods such as mahogany have been highly prized in wealthy countries for hundreds of years.

ARE ALL RAINFOREST ANIMALS BRIGHTLY COLOURED?

As in most other habitats, the colouring of animals in the rainforest is very varied. Some are brilliantly coloured, to attract mates or to warn predators that they are poisonous. Other creatures have green or dark colouring to camouflage them amongst the vegetation. This hides them from their enemies and enables them to creep up on their prey unseen.

The scarlet macaw is the largest parrot in South America. Its powerful beak can crack open seeds and nuts – even Brazil nuts.

WHAT DIFFERENT HABITAT LAYERS ARE FOUND IN A RAINFOREST?

THE MANY HABITATS to be found in rainforests can be thought of as layers. In real forests, of course, these layers overlap each other a good deal.

The *emergent layer* consists of the tallest trees, with umbrella-like branches poking through the mass of leaves below. In this layer live free-flying birds and bats, including birds of prey.

The *tree canopy* consists of the leaves of mature trees. Their tops spread out to reach as much of the light as possible. As well as birds and fruit bats, monkeys and squirrels live in this layer, feeding on the fruits, nuts and leaves of the trees in the canopy.

Very little light filters through the leaves of the canopy. In the *mid-zone*, creepers called lianas hang in great ropes among the trees. Here there are monkeys, squirrels, birds and bats again, but also some snakes and tree frogs.

The *forest floor* is very dark. Larger mammals, such as deer, tapirs, elephants, jaguars and bush pigs, forage among the fallen leaves or prey on each other or smaller animals.

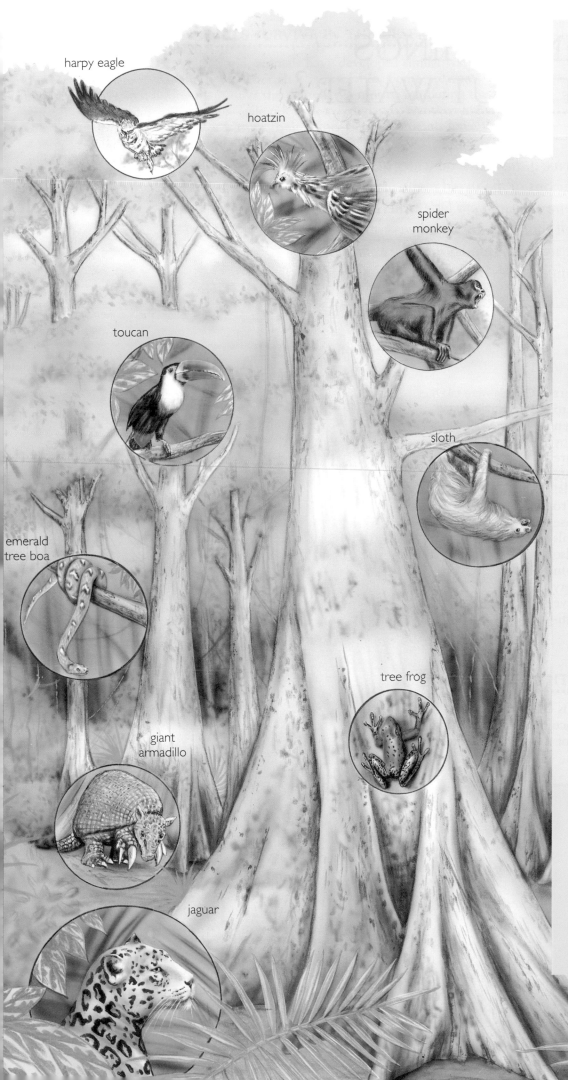

harpy eagle

hoatzin

spider monkey

toucan

sloth

emerald tree boa

tree frog

giant armadillo

jaguar

fast facts

HOW DO PLANTS HIGH IN THE TREES GET WATER?

Some plants, called bromeliads, collect water in their cup-shaped leaves. Insects and even frogs may be found living in the tiny pool.

IS THE SOIL OF RAINFORESTS PARTICULARLY FERTILE?

The hot, moist climate of rainforests means that fallen leaves decay extremely quickly and their nutrients are taken up by the roots of plants almost at once. Nutrients are not held in the soil as happens in other environments. If the rainforest is cut down, the soil is not fertile enough for farming.

ARE SLOTHS SLOTHFUL?

Sloths are tree-dwelling mammals from South America. They hang from branches and eat leaves. It would not be fair to say that sloths are slothful, or lazy, but they do move very slowly. In fact, tiny plants called algae grow on their coats, giving them green fur!

HOW MANY SPECIES LIVE IN RAINFORESTS?

It is estimated that over two million different species of plant and animal thrive in rainforests. So far, only a small proportion of these have been discovered by humans.

WHICH RAINFOREST BIRD HAS CLAWS ON ITS WINGS?

Like many birds that live among the rainforest trees, the South American hoatzin can only fly for short distances – after all, there are too many branches in the way for long flights. Instead it climbs through the branches. Young hoatzins are helped to clamber around by tiny claws on their wings.

WHAT CAN LIVE IN THE COLDEST PLACES ON EARTH?

As in other extreme climates, only specially adapted plants and animals can live in the coldest parts of the world. In fact, at the North and South Poles, almost nothing can survive, but around the edges of the Arctic and Antarctic there are seas rich in plant and animal life. This means that larger animals, living on the edge of the ice, can find food in the teeming waters.

HOW DO THE ARCTIC AND ANTARCTIC DIFFER?

AT THE North and South Poles there are areas that are covered by thick layers of snow and ice all year round, but the two areas are very different. The Antarctic region, around the South Pole, has land far under the ice. The Arctic region, around the North Pole, is actually frozen sea. It is possible for a submarine to travel right under the North Pole. Because in polar regions the sea is warmer than the land or ice, the Arctic, with more sea, is not as cold as the Antarctic.

DO THE POLAR REGIONS HAVE SEASONS?

THERE ARE SEASONAL VARIATIONS at the Poles, but these are much more noticeable in the Arctic than in the Antarctic. During the Arctic summer the sea ice begins to melt and break away in large icebergs. Although the area around the North Pole is always covered by ice, the snow melts around the edges of the Arctic Circle so that Arctic animals can browse on the sparse vegetation. One result of this is that some Arctic mammals, who need camouflage to keep them safe from predators, change the colour of their coats from white in the winter to brown in the summer months.

Arctic hares turn white in the winter. In summer they moult to reveal brown coats that camouflage them against the tundra.

THE ARCTIC

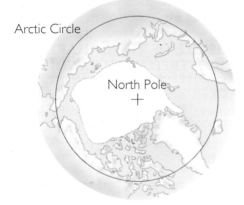

Arctic Circle

North Pole
+

ANTARCTICA

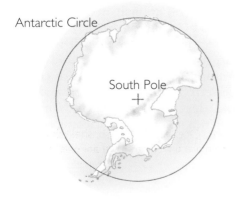

Antarctic Circle

South Pole
+

HOW DO POLAR ANIMALS KEEP WARM?

IN VERY COLD CLIMATES, animals need excellent insulation to stop their body heat from escaping. This may be on the outside, in the form of dense hair, fur or feathers, or on the inside, in the form of a thick layer of fat or blubber.

Many kinds of seal live in the Arctic Ocean, feeding on fish and shellfish. They come out of the water to give birth to their pups.

HOW DO PENGUINS KEEP THEIR EGGS WARM?

PENGUINS are only found in the southern hemisphere, not in the Arctic. Many penguins lay only one egg during the dark days of winter. One penguin "sits" on the egg, holding it off the ice with its feet, until it hatches two months later.

The macaroni penguin huddles over its egg, keeping it warm and protecting it from predators.

HOW DOES THE WALRUS USE ITS TUSKS?

DURING THE BREEDING SEASON, walruses gather on the Arctic ice. The males fight each other for the females, often causing serious wounds with their long tusks. But the main reason for these impressive extended teeth is for digging up shellfish from the ocean floor.

Polar bears are fierce predators. They wait by holes in the ice to catch seals that come up for air. Although they are large, polar bears are very fast and excellent swimmers.

No one is quite sure why the narwhal has such a long tusk. It is a mammal, giving birth to live young underwater.

fast facts

WHERE IS THE COLDEST PLACE ON EARTH?

The average temperature at the South Pole is around –50°C (–58°F), although temperatures 40°C (104°F) lower have been recorded.

WHAT IS THE ARCTIC UNICORN?

Some people believe that stories of unicorns came about because sailors found the horns of narwhals and did not know that they came from a sea mammal.

WHICH IS THE LARGEST POLAR MAMMAL?

Although polar bears in the Arctic are very large, the biggest polar mammal does not live on land at all. It is the blue whale, which swims around the Antarctic Circle and is the largest mammal ever to have lived on Earth. Despite its huge size, the blue whale survives by eating tiny shrimp-like creatures called krill (*Euphausia superba*).

HOW DO POLAR BEARS AVOID SLIPPING ON THE ICE?

Polar bears have very hairy feet! These help them to grip the ice, and their sharp claws enable them to take a firmer grip still.

WHAT IS TUNDRA?

Tundra is the name given to the bleak land of the Arctic that is only covered by ice and snow in the winter. During the summer, many species of plant grow there, but the earth is too cold for their roots to reach down far. Grazing animals, such as reindeer and the musk ox, feed on the low-growing plants.

The Arctic Ocean is rich in fish, shellfish and krill, which are tiny shrimp-like animals. These in turn feed on microscopic plant life.

IS THERE LIFE IN THE DEEPEST OCEANS?

It is likely that life on our planet began in the oceans. As much more of the Earth is covered with water than with land, and the sea can be thousands of metres deep, there is simply more space for living things in the oceans. However, the conditions that they experience there are not so varied, so there are fewer different species than there are on land. Well over 90% of the living things that thrive in the oceans are found in the fairly shallow waters around the continents. However, scientists have found that there is life even in the deepest oceans, although it is not easy to study wildlife in such remote areas.

WHAT IS A CONTINENTAL SHELF?

AROUND THE CONTINENTS of the world there are areas of fairly shallow sea called continental shelves. Here the sea bed is quite flat and only about 130m (430ft) below the surface. There is usually plenty of marine life in these areas. Beyond the shelf, the sea floor drops, so that the sea is much deeper further from shore. In the middle of the oceans, however, the sea bed rises into a ridge, where the plates of the Earth's crust meet.

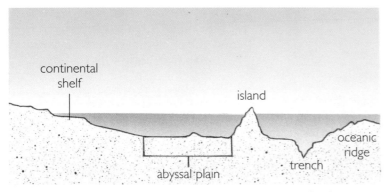

Most commercial fishing takes place in the waters above continental shelves. The deepest ocean is found in trenches where the sea floor plunges hundreds of metres.

HOW DO OYSTERS MAKE PEARLS?

PEARL OYSTERS are molluscs. Their soft bodies are protected by a tough outer shell, hinged at one side. When a piece of grit becomes embedded in the soft body of the oyster, it protects itself by building up layers of a shiny, shell-like material around the foreign body. This happens naturally, but today many pearls are cultivated in oyster farms, where "seeds" are injected into the oysters so that they will form pearls.

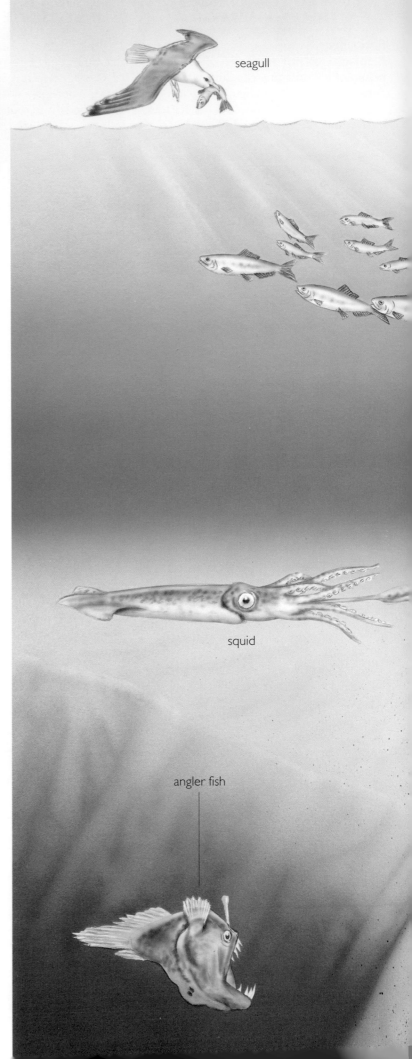

shoal of mackerel

ray

plaice

HOW DO SCIENTISTS INVESTIGATE OCEAN LIFE?

BY CARRYING OXYGEN TANKS, divers can examine the wildlife of the top few metres of the oceans, but for deeper investigations, where the water pressure is higher, they need diving suits or specially adapted submersibles. Mechanical arms can be operated from within the sub to retrieve samples of plants, animals and minerals.

Fortunately, most ocean life is within reach of divers carrying oxygen. Coral reefs are particularly rich in living things.

WHY DO SOME FISH HAVE BOTH EYES ON THE SAME SIDE?

WHILE MANY FISH swim in shoals, eating plankton as they flash through the water, others spend most of their time on the ocean bed. As the fish evolved, their eyes developed on the same side, so that both can see into the water above.

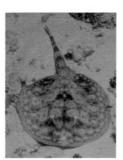

Some fish use camouflage just as land animals do. While they are not moving, it can be very difficult to see them among the sand and stones of the sea bed.

fast facts

HOW MUCH OF THE EARTH'S SURFACE IS COVERED BY SEA?

Over two-thirds (71%) of the Earth's surface is covered by the oceans.

WHAT IS PLANKTON?

Plankton is the millions of tiny plants and animals, too small to see without a microscope, that live in huge numbers in the oceans. They are food for many species, including some of the largest ones – whales.

WHY IS THE SEA SALTY?

The sea is salty because chemicals from rocks and soil have been dissolved in it. These include sodium, chlorine (which together make the salt we put on our food), magnesium, calcium and potassium.

HOW DEEP IS THE DEEPEST OCEAN?

The deepest ocean known is in the western Pacific. It is called the Marianas Trench and is about 11,000m (36,000ft) deep. Mount Everest could be placed in it and there would still be thousands of metres of water above it.

WHICH IS THE FURTHEST MAMMAL MIGRATION?

The longest mammal migration takes place in the oceans. The blue whale travels up to 20,000km (12,500 miles) each year.

CAN DEEP-SEA CREATURES SEE IN THE DARK?

OCEANS offer various habitats at different depths below the surface. These are called zones. The euphotic zone is at the top, ending at a depth of about 200m (660ft). Below this, very little light from the Sun can reach. The bathypelagic zone below is totally dark, so no plants can live there, but a number of fish, squid and crustaceans do make this zone their home, feeding on waste material that sinks down from above and on each other. Deep-sea creatures cannot see in total darkness, but their other senses help them to find food. Some, such as angler fish, carry their own lights. They are not bright enough to search for food by, but they may lure other fish towards them and help fish of the same species to recognize each other.

HOW DO FRESHWATER ECOSYSTEMS OPERATE?

Freshwater habitats include both still and moving water. Living things within rivers and streams can travel through the water to different areas. Many underwater inhabitants of ponds and lakes, however, cannot escape from what may be quite a small area of water. However, even a tiny pool may have a complete, self-contained ecosystem. As well as plants and fish, freshwater ecosystems support living things that visit the water but spend part of their lives on land, such as amphibians, birds and insects. Many mammals also spend time in and around the water. Finally, the kinds of wildlife found in freshwater ecosystems will be affected by the climate and landscape around it. For example, the crocodile may be the fiercest predator in an African river, but its place may be taken by an otter in a European stream.

The wildlife to be found in fresh water varies a great deal, depending on whether the water is still or moving and on the climate of the surrounding countryside. In the Brazilian rainforest, the Amazon is as teeming with life as the forest itself. The giant water lily is the largest in the world. The leaves are strong enough to support a small child!

WHERE DOES THE WATER IN PONDS AND RIVERS COME FROM?

PONDS AND RIVERS are part of the water cycle – the water that is constantly evaporating from the Earth, forming clouds and coming back to Earth as rain or snow. Some of this water seeps into underground streams and pools, which in turn may feed a spring that is the source of a river. Other rivers are fed by melting glaciers or very large lakes.

Although many parts of the world appear to have plenty of surface fresh water, in fact most of the world's fresh water is held underground or as ice. Less than 0.5% is to be found in rivers, lakes and the atmosphere.

DO FISH BUILD HOMES?

ALTHOUGH they often lay hundreds or even thousands of eggs, some fish do build nests to protect their young. The stickleback, found in European ponds and rivers, builds a nest of plant fibres in which the male guards the eggs until they have hatched, chasing away even the female that laid them.

dragonfly

newt

HOW IS AN OXBOW LAKE FORMED?

AS A RIVER FLOWS through countryside, it rarely follows a straight line, but bends and twists following the natural contours of the ground and washing away the softest soil. Water flows fastest on the outer side of the bends, causing that bank to wash away further. In the meantime, soil being carried along in the river water, called silt, is deposited on the opposite bank. Over time, especially if there is flooding, the river may cut across the neck of the bend, creating an oxbow lake beside the river.

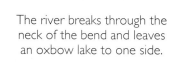

The river meanders as it crosses flat ground.

The river's current causes the bend to become greater and silt to be deposited on the bank opposite.

The river breaks through the neck of the bend and leaves an oxbow lake to one side.

WHY DO BEAVERS BUILD DAMS?

BEAVERS are rodents with very long, sharp front teeth. They use their teeth to gnaw down small trees for use in dam building or for food. Beavers build dams of sticks and mud across a river. This makes a calm pool the other side of the dam in which the beaver can build its home, or lodge. The inside of the lodge is reached by means of underwater tunnels. This keeps the beaver safe from predators such as wolves, even when the surface of the water is frozen in winter.

The beaver's thick fur keeps it warm in wet and icy conditions. In the past it also attracted fur trappers.

WHICH IS THE LARGEST FRESHWATER LAKE?

Lake Superior, one of the Great Lakes on the border between the United States and Canada, is 82,409sq km (31,820sq miles) in area. It is the largest freshwater lake in the world.

WHICH IS THE WORLD'S LONGEST RIVER?

The River Nile in Africa and the River Amazon in South America are similar lengths. The Nile is 6670km (4145 miles) long, while the Amazon stretches to 6437km (4000 miles).

WHICH IS THE HIGHEST WATERFALL?

The Angel Falls in Venezuela is the highest waterfall in the world at 979m (3212ft).

WHY ARE SOME LAKES SALTY ALTHOUGH CUT OFF FROM THE SEA?

Some lakes are salty because minerals from the surrounding soil are dissolved in their water.

WHAT IS AN ESTUARY?

An estuary is the mouth of a large river, where it flows into the sea. The river is often wide and shallow at this point and its mixture of salt and fresh water provides a habitat with its own distinct range of wildlife.

HOW DOES WATER FLOW EFFECT FRESHWATER WILDLIFE?

A FAST-FLOWING RIVER sweeps soil from the riverbed so that plants cannot grow there. On the other hand, there is more oxygen dissolved in the water, so that fish such as salmon thrive. Rivers in areas where the soil is peaty often have very little wildlife, because acid from the soil washes into the water.

moorhen

stickleback

great diving beetle

WHAT ARE LIVING THINGS MADE OF?

Everything in the universe is made of atoms, arranged in different ways. But living things, unlike rocks or metal, have larger building blocks called cells. Some living things have only one cell, while others contain millions. Each cell has a job to do, but they all work together to make a living organism.

WHAT IS A CELL?

CELLS certainly are the building blocks of life, but they are very busy building blocks! Inside each cell thousands of chemical reactions are going on, so that the cell can carry out its tasks. A typical cell has a cell wall or membrane surrounding a kind of watery jelly called cytoplasm. Within the cell there are a number of parts called organelles. These do all the work that the cell is designed to do. The nucleus is a particularly important organelle. It controls all the activities of the cell.

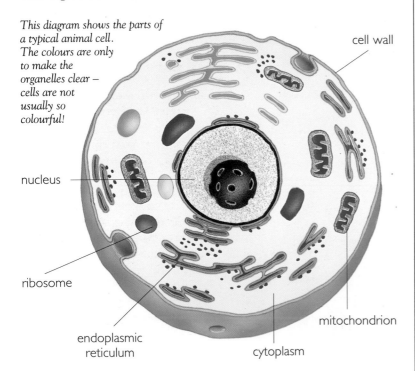

This diagram shows the parts of a typical animal cell. The colours are only to make the organelles clear – cells are not usually so colourful!

cell wall

nucleus

ribosome

endoplasmic reticulum

cytoplasm

mitochondrion

WHAT ARE MITOCHONDRIA?

MITOCHONDRIA are organelles that break up food materials to make energy. Other important organelles are ribosomes, which make proteins, and endoplasmic reticulum. This is a structure, made of double membranes, that is linked to the nucleus and to the cell wall, so that chemicals can be carried around the cell. The cell wall itself is said to be semi-permeable. That means that some chemicals can pass through it into the cell but none can pass out.

WHAT DO ALL LIVING THINGS HAVE IN COMMON?

LIVING THINGS are said to be animate. Inanimate things are not living. Metal, plastic and glass, for example, are inanimate. All animate things are able to do six things that inanimate things cannot.

1. They can feed, taking in nutrients that can be used for energy or to build or renew body parts.

The bodies of living things are adapted to help them find and eat food.

2. They can grow. They may stay the same shape and simply become larger, or they may take on various forms during their life cycle.

Living things may grow to enormous size over hundreds of years.

3. They can respire, taking in gases from the air and using them as part of the process of converting food into energy.

Fish respire by taking in oxygen dissolved in the water through their gills.

HOW DO PLANT CELLS DIFFER FROM ANIMAL CELLS?

ALL CELLS have a cell wall, but in plant cells this is made of a stiff, tough layer of cellulose. Cellulose is made of tiny fibres, layered together to form a strong sheet. Most plant cells also contain organelles called chloroplasts. It is in these that photosynthesis takes place.

Plants do not have skeletons to form a rigid framework for their bodies. Instead, stiff cell walls hold them up.

WHAT IS DNA?

DNA IS AN ABBREVIATION of the name of a chemical: deoxyribonucleic acid. It is DNA that contains the instructions for making and controlling every living thing. Inside the nucleus of a cell, the DNA forms chromosomes. Living things have different numbers of chromosomes. Human beings have 46, arranged in 23 pairs. Each of us has inherited one half of each chromosome pair from our father and the other half from our mother. A gene is a small part of the DNA molecule that can make one of the proteins that the living organism needs.

4. They can excrete, getting rid of waste material through their surfaces or by means of special parts of the organism.

Some animals, such as rhinos, use excretions to mark their territory.

5. They are sensitive, reacting to stimuli from outside.

Horses can be trained to respond to the most delicate touch of a rider.

6. They can reproduce, creating new versions of themselves in order that the species will not die out.

Most larger mammals produce only one or two offspring at a time.

All animals and many plants are also able to move. Plants cannot move their whole bodies in search of food, shelter or a mate, as most animals can, but many can move in a very small way, bending towards light, for example.

The molecules of DNA are in the form of a spiral, making a shape called a double helix.

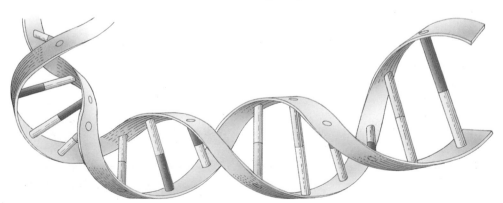

HOW DO LIVING THINGS GROW AND AGE?

Two things affect the way in which living things grow and age. The first is their genetic make-up – the genes that they have inherited from their parents. The DNA in their chromosomes controls the way that cells divide to cause the growth of the young organism, its coming to maturity and its aging. The other important factor is the environment and conditions that the organism experiences – how much of the right kind of food it eats, where it lives, the climate and the kinds of events and accidents that happen to it.

WHAT ARE THE LONGEST ANIMAL LIFE SPANS?

HUMAN BEINGS are far from being the longest-living animals. The giant tortoise can reach 150 years, while several aquatic creatures, such as the killer whale and some species of sea anemone, can survive for well over 80 years. At the other end of the scale, the adult mayfly lives for less than two days. The plant kingdom has far longer-living species. Several trees, such as the yew and giant sequoia, live for thousands of years.

WHAT IS GESTATION?

GESTATION is the length of time between conception – the fertilization of an egg by a sperm – and the birth of the baby that grows from the fertilized egg. The length of gestation varies according to the species.

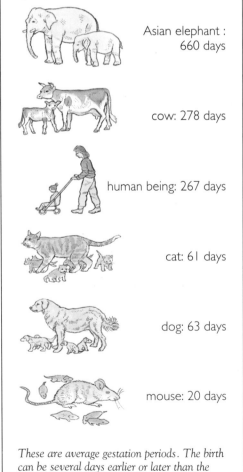

Asian elephant : 660 days

cow: 278 days

human being: 267 days

cat: 61 days

dog: 63 days

mouse: 20 days

These are average gestation periods. The birth can be several days earlier or later than the average.

HOW ARE CHARACTERISTICS PASSED FROM ONE GENERATION TO THE NEXT?

THE CHARACTERISTICS of individual human beings are passed from one generation to the next in their chromosomes. Each of our parents gives us 23 chromosomes, making 46 in all. That means that we have two versions of each of our genes, but one is often dominant. We see the effect of the dominant gene, but the other (recessive) gene is still there and can be passed to our children.

Bb   Bb

BB   Bb   Bb   bb

*In this diagram, **B** stands for brown eyes and **b** stands for blue eyes. If a child inherits one brown-eyes gene and one blue-eyes gene, she will have brown eyes, but she still has a blue-eyes gene to pass on to half of her own children. If her children's father also has brown eyes but a recessive blue-eyes gene, on average one in four of her children will inherit two blue-eyes genes and therefore have blue eyes.*

Our genes are inherited from our parents, which is why resemblances between family members can often be seen.

How do human babies develop?

Human beings are mammals, which means that their young develop inside the mother until they are ready to be born. This development takes place inside the womb or uterus, where the baby gains the nutrients and oxygen it needs for growth from its mother's own blood, supplied through the umbilical cord.

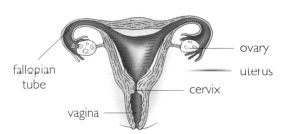

A woman's ovaries usually release one egg each month. As it travels through the fallopian tube towards the uterus, it may be fertilized by a sperm that has entered her body during sexual intercourse.

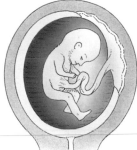

As soon as it is fertilized, the egg cell begins to divide, until it becomes a ball of cells called a blastocyst. This ball then implants itself in the wall of the uterus.

After four weeks, the blastocyst has become an embryo. Its brain, spine and limbs are already forming and its heart will soon begin to beat.

At 12 weeks, the embryo is now called a foetus. All its organs are formed. For the rest of the time before it is born, it simply has to grow.

From 38 weeks onwards, the baby is ready to be born. It moves down into the pelvis. At birth, the cervix gradually opens and the baby is born through the vagina.

Although human babies are quite helpless at birth, by nine months most are on the move by crawling or sliding along, and within a year they will be able to eat solid food, walk and begin to understand language.

How much longer are people living now than in the past?

In many parts of the world, life expectancy – the number of years that a person can expect to live – is increasing. A thousand years ago, 40 might have seemed a good age for an adult to reach. Now we expect to live twice as long. Of course, these are just averages. Since records began there have been exceptional people who lived to 80 and beyond, but for most people, the dangers of dying of disease, accident, war or starvation were very high. Childhood in particular was a dangerous time. A woman might give birth to more than 10 children, none of them living to adulthood. We must not forget that there are parts of the world where this is still true, and billions of people still die each year from lack of food or medical care.

fast facts

Have all human populations increasing numbers of older people?

In the developed world, populations are aging, as better health care means that more people are living longer, while younger people are having fewer children. But in developing countries, where recent improvements in medical attention mean that fewer babies die in their early years, there are far more young people, under the age of 20, in the population than any other group.

Why does skin wrinkle with age?

As we get older, our skin becomes less elastic. We also tend to become thinner, so there is less fat beneath the skin to plump it out.

Why can't people live for ever?

Every living thing has a natural lifespan. Gradually, the parts of the body do not repair and maintain themselves so effectively and most processes become weaker, until one breaks down and the organism dies. However, as scientists learn more about aging, it may be that the human lifespan can be lengthened.

Do human beings shed their skin?

Human beings shed tiny particles of skin all the time. In fact, a large proportion of house dust is made up of human skin!

Do people really become shorter as they age?

In old age, our muscles weaken and there is a tendency to stoop, making us look shorter. In addition, the cartilage between the bones of our spine becomes thinner, reducing our height.

WILL LIFE ON EARTH GO ON FOR EVER?

Life on Earth cannot go on for ever because it depends on the Sun and, like all stars, our Sun will eventually die. However, that will happen billions of years in the future. In the meantime, we need to be concerned about the way in which we are using our planet now, so that it will continue to provide a home for all the living things that share it with us in the next century and beyond.

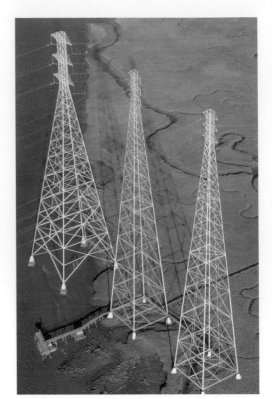

Pylons carrying electricity cables are such a familiar sight that it is hard to remember that two hundred years ago no one had any electrical appliances, lighting or heating.

WHAT ARE NON-RENEWABLE RESOURCES?

LIVING THINGS can grow and reproduce themselves. Given the right conditions, they can continue to do this for millions of years. But some of the Earth's resources cannot renew themselves. When they have been used up, there will be no more. Perhaps the most important of these non-renewable resources are what are known as fossil fuels. Both oil and coal were made millions of years ago when the bodies of prehistoric plants and animals were crushed under enormous pressure beneath moving rock. There is a limited supply of these fuels, making it necessary for us to develop energy sources that cannot run out.

WHICH KINDS OF ENERGY WILL NOT RUN OUT?

WIND, moving water and sunshine are always to be found somewhere on the Earth. All of these can be harnessed to provide energy. Wind farms, consisting of fields of enormous windmills, have been set up in many parts of the world to capture the wind's energy. Hydroelectric power uses the force of water hurtling over dams. Solar panels are warmed by the Sun and can be used to heat water and homes. At the moment, these methods are not able to produce all the energy that the world needs, but they hold out hope for the future.

wind farm

hydroelectric power station

Wood is a renewable resource as new trees can be planted, but it is not suitable for use as fuel on a large scale. After all, it takes only a few hours to burn a tree trunk but thirty years to grow another one.

solar panels

DOES THE PLANET HAVE ITS OWN RECYCLING SYSTEMS?

THE SAYING that there is nothing new under the Sun is strangely true. The stuff that makes up everything on Earth – animals, plants, rocks, water – cannot be destroyed, although it can be changed from one form to another. Living things are almost entirely made up of six elements: carbon, oxygen, hydrogen, nitrogen, phosphorous and sulphur. When a plant or animal dies, it decomposes. Gradually, its body breaks down, and the elements it was made of go back into the soil or water. These elements in time are taken up by new plants, which in turn are eaten by animals. This cycle of elements being released and re-used can take millions of years, but it is quite likely that within your body there are chemicals that were once part of a prehistoric plant – or even a dinosaur!

WHAT ARE THE MAIN PROBLEMS OF SPACE TRAVEL?

THE BIGGEST PROBLEMS of space travel all have to do with the enormous distances that are involved. Using today's technology, it would take years to reach even the nearest planets, and generations of space travellers would live and die on a journey to more distant ones. For this to happen, spacecraft will need to be self-supporting or able to travel faster than the speed of light.

COULD HUMANS FIND HOMES ELSEWHERE IN THE UNIVERSE?

AS THERE ARE BILLIONS of planets in our universe, it is likely that some of them could support life, but the vast distances that would have to be travelled to reach them are at present an immense problem. More possible is the idea that humans could build self-supporting communities on nearby planets. Ideally, these would need to be enclosed, containing their own atmosphere and able to support a variety of plant and animal life just as our planet does. Experiments are being made to see if it is possible to build artificial ecosystems like this here on Earth.

The Moon is so near that it would be possible to take day trips there! But it has no oxygen, so no living thing could survive there except inside a specially constructed building or suit.

COULD SCIENCE FICTION STORIES EVER COME TRUE?

SCIENCE FICTION STORIES do come true all the time. Less than a hundred years ago, space travel was a fantasy invented by storytellers such as H G Wells and Jules Verne. When we consider the extraordinary advances made in the fields of travel and communications in the past century, it is tempting to believe that *Star Trek* may in the future be nearer to reality than at present seems possible!

By studying the way in which the Earth's natural systems renew themselves, scientists hope to learn how to create successful ecosystems on other planets.

HOW CAN HUMANS HELP WITH RECYCLING?

The first step is not to use too many of the Earth's resources in the first place. For example, we can try to use less fuel and buy fewer products that have a great deal of packaging. Many items that we need to use, however, can be recycled. Glass, paper, metals, plastics and even textiles can be recycled. Centres have been set up in many areas where household waste of this kind can be taken for recycling.

CAN OUR PLANET KEEP ITSELF IN BALANCE?

Some people believe that our planet is wiser than the people that live on it. They reason that life has continued on Earth for billions of years, despite natural "disasters" such as Ice Ages. The whole Earth (and the living things on it) is itself like a living organism, constantly adapting to the conditions in which it finds itself. This is a comforting thought, but it is wise to remember that we need the Earth much more than the Earth needs us. After all, life on Earth developed for millions of years before humans evolved.

HOW CAN POLLUTION BE REDUCED?

Pollution is the name we give to waste products that enter the air and soil and water but cannot be quickly broken down by natural processes. Instead, they affect the health of plants and animals, including humans, and the environments they live in. Controlling the emissions of factories and vehicles can help. It is also important, as far as possible, to use materials that can break down in the soil when they are thrown away. Such materials are said to be biodegradable.

GLOSSARY

Antifreeze A substance added to a liquid to raise the temperature at which it will freeze. Antifreeze added to the water in a car's radiator will prevent it from freezing except at very low temperatures.

Atmosphere The gases that form a layer around a planet.

Botanist A scientist who studies plants.

Camouflage The way in which the shape, colour or markings of a living thing can help it to blend into its surroundings and protect it from notice by its enemies.

Carnivorous Meat-eating. An animal that eats both plants and animals is said to be omnivorous.

Classification Organizing items into different classes or divisions. This helps scientists to describe them properly and to observe similarities and differences between them.

Condensation The changing of a gas or vapour into a liquid, often the result of cooling the gas or vapour.

Constellation Stars that appear to form a group or pattern when viewed from Earth.

Continent A very large body of land, surrounded by sea.

Environment The surroundings of a living thing.

Evaporation Molecules of a liquid escaping into the atmosphere to form vapour.

Hibernation Sleeping or greatly slowing down the body's functions during the winter.

Hominid A member of the primate family that walks on two legs, as people do.

Horticulturist A person concerned with growing and breeding plants, especially for gardens.

Life cycle The stages that a living thing normally goes through during its lifetime.

Metamorphosis Literally, changing form. The word is often used of the changing of a larva to a pupa in the insect world.

Nomad A person with no settled home, who moves about in search of food and shelter, often following the migrations of animals throughout the year.

Nutrient Something that gives nourishment. Part of the food of a living organism.

Orbit The path that a body takes as it circles another body, especially a planet or moon circling a star.

Organism A living thing, such as a plant or animal. Living things are made up of one or more cells.

Planet A large heavenly body that is in orbit around a star. A smaller body that is in orbit around a planet is called a moon.

Plankton Microscopic plants and animals that live near the surface of the sea and provide food for many sea creatures.

Predator An animal that hunts other animals for food.

Reproduction The creation of a new living thing similar to its parents. Sexual reproduction requires a male and female parent, while asexual reproduction can be achieved by a single organism.

Satellite Something that orbits a planet. This may be an artificial satellite, put into orbit by scientists, or a natural satellite, such as a moon.

Segment A section of the body of a plant or animal marked off by a clear line or division. Often such an organism has several similar segments making up its body.

Serrated With a saw-like edge.

Stimulus Something that prompts an organism or part of an organism into action or response.

Vegetation Plants of all kinds, especially those with abundant or large leaves.

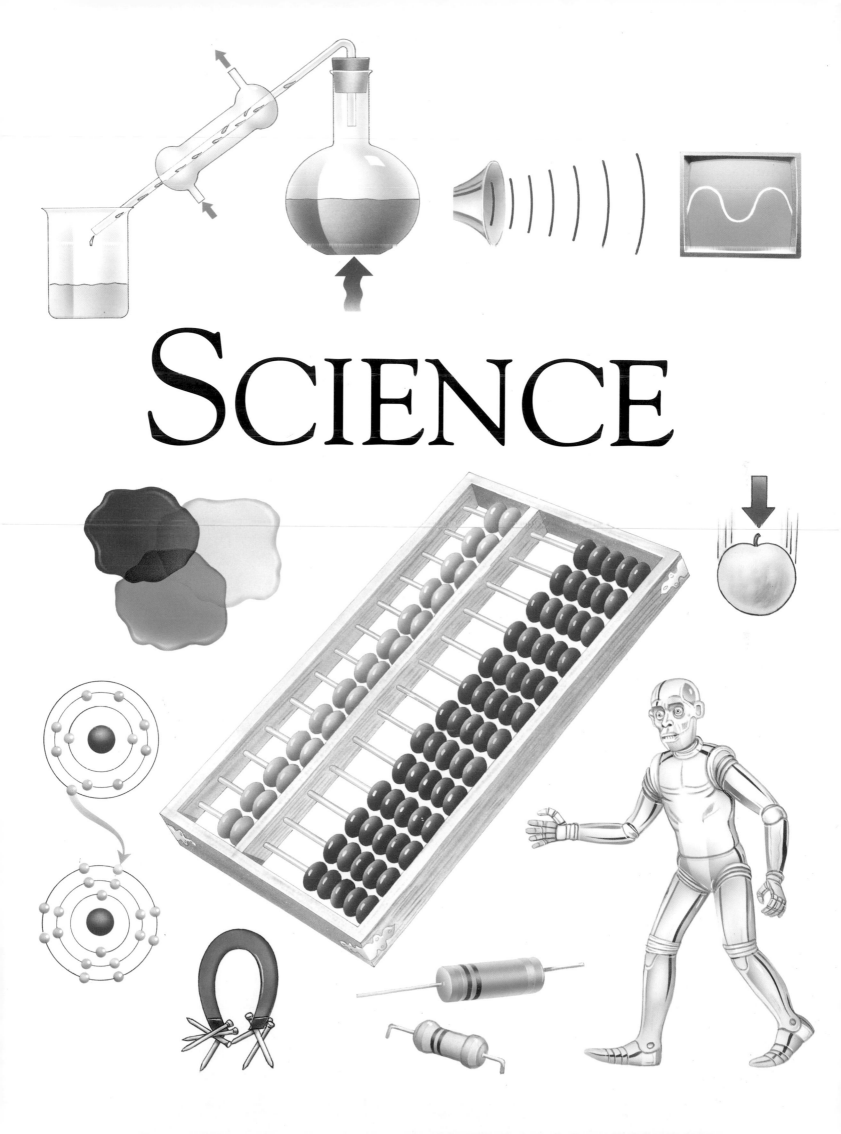

SCIENCE

WHO WAS THE FIRST SCIENTIST?

Scientists study how and why things happen, or why they are as they are. They can use this knowledge in many different ways: to predict what will happen in certain circumstances, to understand why bodies and machines sometimes go wrong and to try to prevent this or put it right, and to develop inventions that will make a difference to the world. The first scientist was probably a very early human, or even human ancestor, who noticed something about the world, began to think about why this might be so and tried to test these ideas.

WHAT ARE THE MAIN FIELDS OF SCIENCE?

TRADITIONALLY, science has been divided into natural science, which deals with living things, and physical science, which is concerned with the matter that makes up the universe and how it behaves. Of course, these two fields overlap a great deal. There are also more detailed labels for different areas of scientific study.

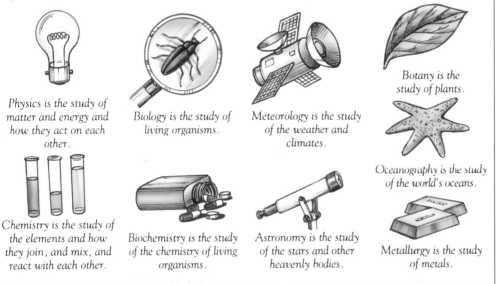

Physics is the study of matter and energy and how they act on each other.

Biology is the study of living organisms.

Meteorology is the study of the weather and climates.

Botany is the study of plants.

Oceanography is the study of the world's oceans.

Chemistry is the study of the elements and how they join, and mix, and react with each other.

Biochemistry is the study of the chemistry of living organisms.

Astronomy is the study of the stars and other heavenly bodies.

Metallurgy is the study of metals.

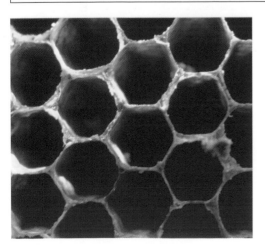

There are many different ways of looking at the natural world. An engineer might be interested in the strength and structure of a honeycomb. A biochemist might want to look at the composition of the material from which the honeycomb is made. A naturalist might study whether bees learn to make these hexagonal chambers or hatch already possessing the skill.

HOW ARE EXPERIMENTS DESIGNED?

IN THE WORLD around us, nothing happens in isolation. One event affects another. The activity of one living thing changes the lives of other organisms. As the natural world is very complicated, it can be difficult to see clearly how and why things are happening. One of the most important factors in designing an experiment is to try to isolate the particular event or substance being studied, so that the results of the experiment are not influenced by other things. For example, to see if a plant needs sunlight to live, you can put it in the dark and watch what happens. But it is important to make sure that the plant still has the same soil, amount of water and temperature as before, so that you can be sure that any changes in the plant are a result of the lack of sunlight.

water but no sunlight   sunlight but no water   sunlight and water

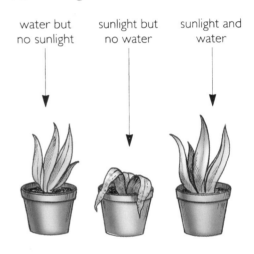

Many experiments use something called a control. For example, to test a new drug, a hundred people may be given it and their health monitored very carefully. A hundred similar people may be given no drug or a harmless substance and their health monitored just as accurately. They are the control. It is the difference in results between the two groups of people that is important. The control group is designed to show what would have happened to the first group if it had received no drugs. Only then can scientists tell if the drug has had an effect.

WHAT IS A HYPOTHESIS?

ANYONE can make a guess, but scientists set about finding out if their ideas are true in an organized way. A hypothesis is a theory – an idea – about why something happens or what makes something work. A scientist will then try to think of a way of testing whether this idea is correct. Often this will mean designing a special experiment.

HOW HAVE COMPUTERS HELPED SCIENTISTS?

SCIENTIFIC STUDY relies on collecting and interpreting information (data). Sometimes thousands of different observations or measurements are made. Computers can help to collect and organize the data. For example, an astronomer might want to study the movement of a planet. A computer, attached to a radio telescope, can measure the position of the planet every five minutes for weeks – a task that would be very tedious for a scientist. Having collected the data, the computer can also process it and use it to predict future patterns of movement. Likewise, computers can perform very complex calculations at incredible speed, working out in less than a second something that a century ago might have taken a lifetime to calculate. Other computer programs can draw three-dimensional plans of objects as tiny as an atom or as large as a cathedral. These models can be turned on screen so that all sides can be viewed. Finally, scientists can search for information on the Internet, instead of visiting libraries that may be in other countries.

Without computers, space exploration would be impossible. Computers monitor all the astronauts' equipment and keep the ground crew informed of any problems before the astronauts are aware of them.

HOW IS SCIENTIFIC KNOWLEDGE PASSED ON?

IT IS INCREDIBLE to us now that five hundred years ago it was possible for a person to have a good understanding of every branch of science then known. Today there is so much information available that no one person can be informed about every area of science, and even specialists have difficulty in keeping up with new developments. There is a long established tradition that scientists who have made a new discovery publish a "paper" or article on the subject in scientific journals. People working in the same field can then read this to keep up to date with their subject. Some discoveries are so important or amazing that they reach the general public, through radio, television, books and newspapers.

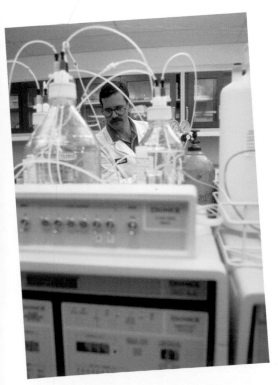

DO ALL SCIENTISTS WORK IN LABORATORIES?

SOME SCIENTISTS do wear white coats and work with test tubes, but many do most of their work in the world outside. A geologist, for example, may have to clamber a cliff face to obtain samples of rock.

Science is rarely easy, and scientists sometimes face dangerous situations where good preparation and equipment are vital. That is as true of a chemist dealing with dangerous chemicals in the laboratory as it is of a geologist looking for rock samples.

fast facts

HOW ARE IMPORTANT SCIENTIFIC DISCOVERIES MADE?

Scientific discoveries, like all great human achievements, are made by a combination of very hard work and luck. Although one person is often credited with an importartant discovery, it is likely that hundreds of other people also did work that made the discovery possible.

WHAT WERE THE FOUR ELEMENTS?

The ancient Greeks believed that everything was made from different proportions of four "elements": earth, water, air and fire.

WHAT WAS AN ALCHEMIST?

It is from the word *alchemy* that the modern word chemistry comes. Alchemists were early chemists, who discovered that metals could be extracted from minerals by heating them. The knowledge that one thing could apparently be changed info another led them to search for a way of changing "base" metals, such as copper lead and iron, into gold. We know now that this is not possible, but while working on this problem, alchemists made other useful discoveries.

WHAT DOES THE WORD "LABORATORY" MEAN?

This word comes from the Latin word laborare, meaning "to work". So a laboratory is a place where scientific work is done.

WHAT IS SOCIAL SCIENCE?

Social Science is the study of human behaviour and societies.

WHAT IS MATTER?

Matter is the stuff that the universe is made of. The planets, this page, your body and the air that you breathe are all made of matter. Matter itself is made of very small particles called atoms, much too small to be seen with the naked eye or even with many microscopes. The kinds of atom that matter contains and the way in which they are joined together are what determine the kind of matter it is.

ARE ATOMS THE SMALLEST PARTICLES OF MATTER?

THE WORD "atom" comes from an ancient Greek word for a tiny piece of matter too small to be split up. Today we know that even atoms are made up of smaller parts, called subatomic particles. Protons and neutrons are the particles that make up the nucleus of an atom, while electrons can be thought of as circling around the nucleus like orbiting planets. However, these are not the only subatomic particles. Scientists have found hundreds more and are still discovering others by using a machine called a particle accelerator. Quarks, for example, form part of neutrons and protons.

WHAT IS THE STRUCTURE OF AN ATOM?

Each atom has a nucleus containing protons, and all except the hydrogen nucleus have neutrons as well. Neutrons have no electrical charge, but protons have a positive charge. Moving at high speed around the nucleus are little particles of energy called electrons, which have a negative charge. The number of protons and electrons in an atom is always the same. As opposite charges attract each other, the attraction between the protons and the electrons keeps the electrons around the nucleus, just as the force of gravity keeps the Moon circling around the Earth.

fast facts

WHAT IS AN ISOTOPE?

An element always has the same number of protons and electrons, but it may have different forms with different numbers of neutrons. These different forms are called isotopes. Chemically, the isotopes have the same properties, but physically they may differ.

HOW ARE NEW ATOMS NAMED?

Newly discovered atoms are often named in honour of a place or a famous scientist. For example, the element called curium is named after the chemists Marie and Pierre Curie. Marie Curie herself called an element that she discovered polonium, in honour of her native Poland.

WHICH IS THE MOST COMMON ELEMENT?

Hydrogen and helium are the most common elements by far in the universe, but the most common element in the Earth's crust is oxygen.

WHO WAS DIMITRI MENDELEYEV?

Dimitri Mendeleyev was a Russian scientist who, in 1869, suggested the method of setting out elements in a periodic table that we still use today. Mendeleyev was a far-sighted man. He even left gaps in his table for elements that he felt sure would be discovered in the future.

WHO DISCOVERED ATOMS?

The idea of atoms was first put forward by a Greek philosopher called Democritus about 400BC, but it was not until the beginning of the nineteenth century that an English chemist called John Dalton suggested that different atoms made different elements.

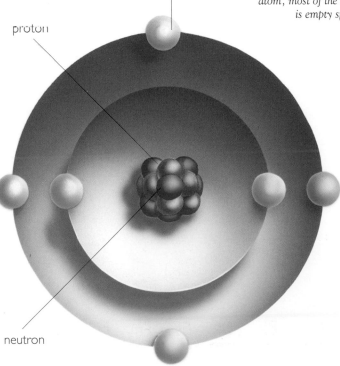

electron

proton

Although there may be many subatomic particles within an atom, most of the atom is empty space.

The electrons that move round the nucleus of an atom travel in different orbits, called shells. The number of electrons in each shell is limited. For example, there cannot be more than two electrons in the first shell, eight in the second shell, 18 in the third, and 32 in the fourth.

neutron

HOW MANY DIFFERENT ATOMS ARE THERE?

AN ELEMENT is a substance that is made up of only one kind of atom. The periodic table below shows all the elements currently known. However, there are more than 109 different atoms because some elements have more than one isotope.

The way that the periodic table is designed gives useful information about each element, depending on its position in the table. The elements are organized so that each has one more proton in the nucleus than the one before. The rows of the table are called periods. The elements in each period all have the same number of shells of electrons. The columns of the table are called groups. Each group has the same number of electrons in its outer shell. Elements in the first column have one, in the second two, and so on.

WHAT IS AN ATOMIC NUMBER?

THE ATOMIC NUMBER of an element is the number of protons it contains. For example, hydrogen has one proton, so its atomic number is one. Tin has an atomic number of 50 because it has 50 protons in its nucleus.

WHAT IS A MASS SPECTROMETER?

A MASS SPECTROMETER is a machine that can measure the mass of atoms and so identify them. In the table below, the relative atomic mass for radioactive elements is shown in parentheses: (242).

atomic number
chemical symbol
name
relative atomic mass (RAM)

1 H Hydrogen 1.0																		2 He Helium 4.0
3 Li Lithium 6.9	4 Be Beryllium 9.0											5 B Boron 10.8	6 C Carbon 12.0	7 N Nitrogen 14.0	8 O Oxygen 16.0	9 F Fluorine 19.0	10 Ne Neon 20.2
11 Na Sodium 23.0	12 Mg Magnesium 24.3											13 Al Aluminium 27.0	14 Si Silicon 28.1	15 P Phosphorous 31.0	16 S Sulphur 32.1	17 Cl Chlorine 35.5	18 Ar Argon 39.9
19 K Potassium 39.1	20 Ca Calcium 40.1	21 Sc Scandium 45.0	22 Ti Titanium 47.9	23 V Vanadium 50.9	24 Cr Chromium 52.0	25 Mn Manganese 54.9	26 Fe Iron 55.9	27 Co Cobalt 58.9	28 Ni Nickel 58.7	29 Cu Copper 63.5	30 Zn Zinc 65.4	31 Ga Gallium 69.7	32 Ge Germanium 72.6	33 As Arsenic 74.9	34 Se Selenium 79.0	35 Br Bromine 79.9	36 Kr Krypton 83.8
37 Rb Rubidium 85.5	38 Sr Strontium 87.6	39 Y Yttrium 88.9	40 Zr Zirconium (91.2)	41 Nb Niobium 92.9	42 Mo Molybdenum 95.9	43 Tc Technetium (97.9)	44 Ru Ruthenium 101.1	45 Rh Rhodium 102.9	46 Pd Palladium 106.4	47 Ag Silver 107.9	48 Cd Cadmium 112.4	49 In Indium 114.8	50 Sn Tin 118.7	51 Sb Antimony 121.8	52 Te Tellurium 127.6	53 I Iodine 126.9	54 Xe Xenon 131.3
55 Cs Caesium 132.9	56 Ba Barium 137.3		72 Hf Hafnium 178.5	73 Ta Tantalum 181.0	74 W Tungsten 183.9	75 Re Rhenium 186.2	76 Os Osmium 190.2	77 Ir Iridium 192.2	78 Pt Platinum 195.1	79 Au Gold 197.0	80 Hg Mercury 200.6	81 Tl Thallium 204.4	82 Pb Lead 207.2	83 Bi Bismuth 209.0	84 Po Polonium (210)	85 At Astatine (210)	86 Rn Radon (222)
87 Fr Francium (223)	88 Ra Radium (226)		104 Db Dubnium (260)	105 Jl Joliotum (262)	106 Rf Rutherfordium (263)	107 Bh Bohrium (262)	108 Hn Hahnium (265)	109 Mt Meitnerium (266)									

Key
- Alkali metals
- Transition metals
- Non-metals & semi-metals
- Lanthanides
- Alkaline-earth metals
- Poor metals
- Noble gases
- Actinides

57 La Lanthanum 138.9	58 Ce Cerium 140.1	59 Pr Praseodymium 140.9	60 Nd Neodymium 144.2	61 Pm Promethium (145)	62 Sm Samarium 150.4	63 Eu Europium 152.0	64 Gd Gadolinium 157.3	65 Tb Terbium 158.9	66 Dy Dysprosium 162.5	67 Ho Holmium 164.9	68 Er Erbium 167.3	69 Tm Thulium 168.9	70 Yb Ytterbium 173.0	71 Lu Lutetium 175.0
89 Ac Actinium (227)	90 Th Thorium (232.0)	91 Pa Protactinium (231)	92 U Uranium (238.1)	93 Np Neptunium (237)	94 Pu Plutonium (242)	95 Am Americium (243)	96 Cm Curium (247)	97 Bk Berkelium (245)	98 Cf Californium (251)	99 Es Einsteinium (254)	100 Fm Fermium (253)	101 Md Mendelevium (256)	102 No Nobelium (254)	103 Lr Lawrencium (257)

WHAT IS RADIOACTIVITY?

Most elements do not change unless a force is applied to them that causes them to join with another element. They are said to be stable. But some elements are not stable. Their nuclei are constantly breaking down, or decaying, as they shed particles in an attempt to become stable. This is radioactivity, and the particles that are given off are known as radiation. Three types of particles are known to be emitted: alpha, beta and gamma rays.

α
β
γ

Radioactive radiation is named after three letters of the Greek alphabet: alpha, beta and gamma.

WHAT IS A NUCLEAR REACTION?

THERE ARE TWO KINDS of nuclear reaction, both of which give off huge amounts of energy. Nuclear fusion happens when two nuclei collide and combine to form one larger nucleus. This gives off enormous power. Nuclear fission happens when neutrons bombard the nucleus of an atom, causing the nucleus to split apart.

HOW DOES CARBON DATING WORK?

THE ISOTOPE called carbon-14 has a half-life of 5730 years. All living things on our planet contain this form of carbon, but they stop taking it in when they die. Scientists can examine ancient substances to see how much the carbon in it has decayed. They can then give a fairly accurate date for when the substance was alive. This is particularly useful for archaeologists and historians, who can date objects they find, helping to build up a picture of the past.

WHAT IS MEANT BY A HALF-LIFE?

THE HALF-LIFE of a radioactive substance is a measure of the rate at which the nuclei of its atoms are breaking up or decaying. It is the time it takes for half the atoms in a sample to decay. Thorium, for example, has a half-life of 24 days, while radium-221 has a half-life of only 30 seconds. Uranium has a half-life of 4.5 thousand million years. Of course, as each isotope of an element has a certain number of protons and neutrons in its nucleus, it changes as it decays, forming other elements. For example, plutonium-242 decays to become uranium-238, which in turn breaks down to become thorium-234.

Archaeologists use many clues to discover what happened in the past. Carbon dating is a useful tool to add to their skills.

WHEN WERE NUCLEAR WEAPONS FIRST USED?

NUCLEAR WEAPONS were first used in the Second World War. Two bombs were dropped on the Japanese cities of Nagasaki and Hiroshima, killing hundreds of thousands of people.

The mushroom shape of the cloud produced by a nuclear explosion is now a familiar image. With the development of nuclear weapons, human beings for the first time possessed the power to destroy the living world within seconds. Relationships between nations and the development of strategies for peace have never been so important.

This peace memorial park in Japan honours those who died when two nuclear bombs were dropped on the country in 1945.

HOW IS NUCLEAR POWER USED?

NUCLEAR FUSION releases so much energy that it is hard to control. At the moment, only nuclear fission is used to give nuclear power. In power stations with pressurized water reactors, a radioactive substance, such as uranium, is bombarded with neutrons so that its atoms split and release energy. This energy heats water. The resulting steam turns a turbine to create electricity. Nuclear power has also been used to power submarines. One problem with nuclear power is that the waste material left behind is still radioactive and must be disposed of safely.

WHAT DOES A GEIGER COUNTER MEASURE?

A Geiger counter measures the radiation being given off by a substance. It has both a dial, giving a reading, and a loudspeaker that transmits a regular clicking sound if radiation is detected. The faster the clicking, the more radiation there is.

WHO DISCOVERED RADIOACTIVITY?

Antoine Becquerel (1852–1908) discovered "rays" coming from uranium. These were investigated by Marie and Pierre Curie, who later shared the Nobel Prize with Becquerel. Marie Curie may have died of cancer caused by radiation.

WHAT IS RADIOTHERAPY?

It is because radiation has an effect on the human body that it can be used for medical purposes. Radiotherapy involves directing radiation at harmful cells in the body, such as cancer cells, to kill them.

HOW ARE RADIOACTIVE MATERIALS HANDLED?

Exposure to radioactive radiation can be fatal to living organisms. For this reason, radioactive materials are carried in lead-lined containers and wherever possible robots rather than humans are used to deal with them. When people do need to handle such substances, they wear protective clothing and a meter that records the amount of exposure to radiation they are receiving.

WHO INVENTED THE GEIGER COUNTER?

Although the idea for the machine had already been suggested by other scientists, the Geiger counter was perfected by a German physicist called Hans Geiger (1882–1945).

This symbol on a container or building warns that there is radioactive material inside.

WHAT ARE MOLECULES?

In nature, it is rare to find one atom on its own. Atoms are usually grouped together in larger structures called molecules. A molecule is the smallest particle of a substance that can exist by itself. The atoms in a molecule are chemically bonded together. They may be atoms of the same element or they may be of different elements. A molecule of carbon dioxide, for example, has two atoms of oxygen and one of carbon.

HOW DO SOLIDS, LIQUIDS AND GASES DIFFER?

MANY SUBSTANCES can exist in three different states of matter: as solids, liquids and gases. In each state, the substance has the same chemical make-up – the elements in its molecules have not changed, but the way in which they are connected to each other has. Scientists think of all matter as being constantly in motion. The atoms and molecules of which it is made have energy, called kinetic energy.

In solids, the energy is not strong enough for the particles to break free of the attraction they have for each other. It is as though they are vibrating but not moving from their positions.

The molecules in a liquid have more energy and can move away from neigh-bouring molecules, so that a liquid will flow to cover as wide an area as it can.

The molecules of a gas have most kinetic energy. They will move apart from each other until they fill the space in which they are contained.

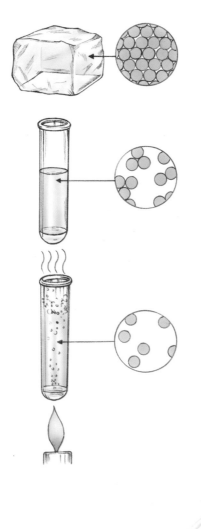

WHAT HAPPENS WHEN MOLECULES ARE HEATED?

WHEN MOLECULES are heated, they gain heat energy in addition to the kinetic energy they already have. If the molecules in a solid gain enough energy, they can break free of each other and become liquid. This is called melting. If they gain even more heat energy, the liquid becomes a gas.

Water freezes, or becomes solid, at temperatures of 0°C (32°F) or below. If the temperature outside drops to this level, the water on the surface of ponds and lakes will freeze, although the water below may hold enough heat to remain liquid.

When solid water (ice) is heated, it melts to become liquid. Generally speaking, we think of water as being liquid. That is because it is liquid at a "room temperature" of 20°C (68°F), or, in other words, under normal conditions. Copper, however, is a solid under such conditions, because it needs a temperature of 1083°C (1981°F) to melt into a liquid.

When water is heated and boils, it turns into a gas. We can see this when a kettle boils. In fact, it is not the billowing steam that is the gas – that is the water turning back into tiny droplets of liquid as it comes into contact with cool air. The real steam is invisible. It can be "seen" in the gap between the spout of the kettle and the visible vapour.

IS HEATING THE ONLY WAY TO CAUSE CHANGES OF STATE?

As well as heating or cooling, changing the pressure acting on a substance can also cause it to change state. If the pressure on the molecules in a substance is increased, it becomes harder for them to move apart from each other, so the temperature at which they become a liquid is increased. Similarly, at low pressure, changes happen at lower temperatures. It is impossible to make a good cup of tea or coffee at the top of Everest, for example, because water boils at a temperature almost 30°C (50°F) less than at sea level.

On top of a mountain, where the atmospheric pressure is less than at sea level, everything feels cold – not just the coffee!

WHAT IS MASS?

THE MASS of a substance is the amount of matter it contains. This is different from its weight, which is a measurement of the pull of gravity on this mass. For example, an astronaut would have the same mass on Earth as on the Moon, but his weight would be much less in the Moon's gravity than in the Earth's.

WHAT IS DENSITY?

THE AMOUNT of space that a substance takes up is called its volume. It is measured in cubic units. For example, a cube measuring one metre on each side has a volume of one cubic metre or 1m³. But a cubic metre of lead has a much greater mass than a cubic metre of wood. That is because the lead has a much higher density than the wood. Its particles are more tightly packed together. The density of an object is calculated by dividing its mass by its volume and is expressed as kilograms per cubic metre (kg/m³) or pounds per cubic foot (lb/ft³).

When water freezes, it expands. The water still has the same amount of matter in it when it is frozen – its mass is the same – but its volume has increased. This means that its density has decreased. Liquid water is denser than ice. That is why icebergs float in water.

HOW BIG IS A MOLECULE?

Although it is larger than an atom, because it is made up of more than one atom, a molecule is still much too small to see with the naked eye.

WHAT IS SUBLIMATION?

A few substances pass from a solid state to a gas without becoming a liquid in between. This is known as sublimation.

WHAT IS IN A MOLECULE OF WATER?

A molecule of water contains two atoms of hydrogen and one atom of oxygen.

WHAT IS A CHEMICAL FORMULA?

A chemical formula is a short way of writing down the "recipe" for a molecule. It uses the chemical symbols from the periodic table for each atom, plus numbers to show how many atoms there are. The chemical formula for water is well known: H_2O. That is a short way of saying that there are two hydrogen atoms and one oxygen atom in a molecule of water.

HOW MANY DIFFERENT MOLECULES ARE THERE?

At present we know of more than a hundred different atoms, but these atoms can combine in millions of ways to form different molecules. So there are literally millions of different kinds of molecules.

Scientists often make models of molecules. Each coloured ball represents an atom. The picture below shows a molecule of water, which is quite simple, but for more complex molecules, hundreds of balls may need to be used.

hydrogen atoms   oxygen atom

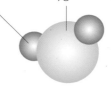

HOW DO ATOMS AND MOLECULES MIX AND JOIN?

Elements do not usually exist on their own. In the natural world, they are found in combination with other elements. By under-standing how elements combine, scientists have been able to make new combinations, creating molecules that are not found in nature. These combinations are not made simply by mixing two or more substances together. Brown sugar and salt can be stirred together, for example, but this does not create a new substance. Each little particle is either a grain of sugar or a grain of salt – they have remained separate. Mixtures can usually be separated again, but when elements are chemically joined together, they are said to be bonded and have created a new substance.

HOW DOES BONDING WORK?

BONDING is caused by a chemical reaction. Most chemical reactions need some form of energy to start them. Usually, this energy is supplied in the form of heat. Many compounds are made by heating two or more substances together until their molecules are moving so fast that they react with each other.

When we cook food, chemical reactions take place as heat energy is supplied to the ingredients. New compounds are formed, so that the cooked dish usually has a different appearance, texture and taste from the mixed raw ingredients.

WHAT IS A COMPOUND?

A COMPOUND is a substance that is created when two or more elements are bonded by a chemical reaction. It is difficult to split a compound back into its original elements. Compounds do not necessarily take on the characteristics of the elements that form them. For example, sodium is a metal and chlorine is a gas. Together they form a compound called sodium chloride, which is not like either of them. In fact, sodium chloride is the chemical name for the salt that we put on our food.

WHAT IS MEANT BY VALENCY?

IT IS USEFUL to think of an atom as having electrons circling in layers around its nucleus. These layers are known as "shells". Each layer can only have a certain number of elec-trons before a new shell must be started. Atoms that have as many electrons as possible in the outer shell (or some other particular numbers) are said to be stable. They do not easily form bonds with other atoms. Atoms that are not stable try to become so by sharing electrons with, or borrowing elec-trons from, or giving electrons to, another atom. The number of elec-trons that an atom needs to give or gain to achieve a stable outer shell is called its valency.

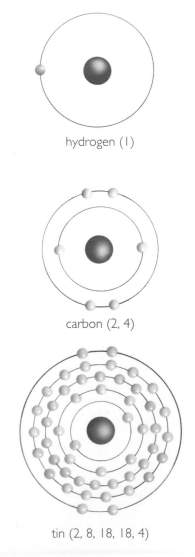

hydrogen (1)

carbon (2, 4)

tin (2, 8, 18, 18, 4)

The way in which the electrons of an atom are aranged around the nucleus can be written as numbers after its name.

WHAT IS A COVALENT BOND?

COVALENT BONDS usually take place between non-metals. Many substances made in this way are gases or liquids at room temperature. A covalent bond is one in which two atoms share one or more electrons in order to complete their outer shell of electrons. Water is an example of a covalent bond. A water molecule has two hydrogen atoms and one oxygen atom. The hydrogen atoms have one electron, while the oxygen atom has six electrons in its outer shell. By sharing the hydrogen electrons, the oxygen atom has eight electrons in its outer shell, creating a stable molecule.

When water freezes in the form of snow, it forms crystals with a regular, six-sided shape. The way in which hydrogen bonds with oxygen is responsible for these forms.

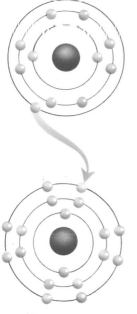

sodium (2, 8, 1)

chlorine (2, 8, 7)

When sodium and chlorine bond to make sodium chloride, the sodium atom gives the single atom from its outer shell to the chlorine atom, which then has eight electrons in its outer shell. This is an ionic bond.

Quartz crystals are made of silicon and oxygen. When an electric current is passed through them, they vibrate at a regular rate. This has meant that they can be used in clocks and watches to give very accurate timing.

WHAT IS AN IONIC BOND?

IONIC BONDS happen when one atom gains one or more electrons from another atom. The electrons in an atom have a negative charge and are equal in number to the positively charged protons in the nucleus. When an atom gains or loses electrons, the balance of charges is broken, so the atom becomes either positively or negatively charged. It is called an ion. An atom that has gained electrons has a negative charge and is called an anion. One that has lost electrons has a positive charge and is called a cation. As opposite charges attract each other, the two atoms that have gained and lost electrons are pulled together into a bond.

HOW DO METALS AND NON-METALS DIFFER?

The chlorophyll in the leaves of this plant contains magnesium.

Lead is added to glass to make it soft enough to cut into intricate patterns.

There are over 80 different metals. They tend to conduct heat and electricity well, and many of them can be shaped by pulling, beating, or melting and pouring into a mould. Metals with similar properties are often grouped together, although a metal may sometimes appear in more than one group, as these pages show. Unlike most non-metals, metals are shiny when cut. Metals have played an enormous part in the history of human activity, which is why some periods, such as the Iron Age and the Bronze Age, are known by the names of metals. Some people say that our present period should be called the Silicon Age. But silicon is what is known as a semi-metal, having some but not all of the properties of metals.

WHAT IS REACTIVITY?

THE ABILITY of an element to take part in a chemical reaction is called reactivity. Metals vary in their reactivity. Some alkali metals, such as sodium and potassium, are so reactive that they have to be stored in oil. They would react strongly with the oxygen in air or water. The least reactive metal is gold.

Tin cans are made of steel, not tin, but they do have a coating of tin to stop food inside corroding the steel. Drinks cans are often made of aluminium.

The stainless steel used in this sink is an alloy of iron, chromium and nickel. The nickel stops the iron from corroding.

Another way to prevent steel from corroding is to galvanize it. That means giving it a coating of zinc.

Copper wires conduct electricity. They are usually wrapped in a non-conducting plastic covering for safety.

Three-quarters of all known elements are metals, so it is not surprising that metals are found in most everyday objects. Even the human body contains large amounts of calcium and trace amounts of iron and other metals.

The paint used on white electrical goods may contain compounds of titanium.

WHAT ARE THE NOBLE METALS?

NOBLE METALS are those that can be found in their pure state, not mixed with other substances. As might be expected, they are not very reactive, which is why they do not readily form compounds in their natural state. This also means that they do not corrode easily, making them traditionally suitable to be formed into coins or jewellery. Noble metals include gold, silver, platinum and copper.

WHAT ARE ALKALI METALS?

AN ALKALI METAL is one that reacts vigorously with water to make an alkaline solution. Lithium, sodium, potassium, rubidium, caesium and francium are all alkali metals. They appear in the first column, or group, of the periodic table. All alkali metals are soft enough to cut with an ordinary knife and are a whitish silvery colour.

Streetlights that give off a yellowish orange light have sodium vapour inside.

Gold is sometimes found in its pure state as nuggets in streams that pass over gold-bearing rocks. The great gold rushes of America and Australia saw many prospectors panning for gold.

WHY DO METALS CORRODE?

SOME METALS corrode badly on contact with air and water. This means that the surface of the metal reacts with oxygen to form an oxide. The metal loses its shine as a layer of oxide covers it. This is sometimes known as tarnishing. When a bowl covered with silver is cleaned, for example, what is really happening is that the layer of tarnish is being rubbed away. Over a long period of time, all the silver may be rubbed off. Iron corrodes in air and water to produce rust. Non-reactive metals are less likely to corrode than reactive ones.

The Golden Gate Bridge in San Francisco needs to be painted regularly to stop it from corroding.

WHAT IS MEANT BY A TRANSITION METAL?

Transition metals are those in groups three to 12 of the periodic table, including iron, chromium, nickel, copper, gold and silver. Transition metals have a high melting point and are not too reactive. They are easy to shape and have thousands of uses in industry.

WHAT IS BRONZE?

Bronze is an alloy of tin and copper. It was probably the first alloy made by humans, thousands of years ago.

WHAT IS A DUCTILE METAL?

A ductile metal can be drawn out into a wire. Copper, for example, can form very fine wire that conducts electricity efficiently.

WHAT DOES "MALLEABLE" MEAN?

The word "malleable" comes from a Latin word, *malleus*, meaning a hammer. Malleable metals can be beaten into very thin sheets. Gold, for example, may be beaten into gold leaf – a very, very thin layer that can be used to decorate picture frames and other ornaments.

WHAT IS SPECIAL ABOUT MERCURY?

Mercury is the only metal that is not solid at room temperature.

WHAT KIND OF METAL IS CALCIUM?

CALCIUM is one of a group of metals called the alkaline-earth metals. They form alkaline solutions with water and are found in many natural substances. Calcium is an important constituent of bones, making them hard and stable. Magnesium is found in chlorophyll, the green part of plants that can make energy from sunlight by photosynthesis. Alkaline-earth metals form the second group of the periodic table.

Aluminium has a low density, so it is very light. That makes it ideal, mixed with other metals, for use in building aircraft, where weight must be controlled.

WHY IS ALUMINIUM KNOWN AS A POOR METAL?

POOR METALS have a low melting point and are quite soft, but they are still very useful. The seven metals that come to the right of the transition metals in the periodic table are known as poor metals. They are aluminium, gallium, indium, thallium, tin, lead and bismuth. Lead has a very high density, so radiation cannot easily pass through it. That is why radioactive materials are often carried in lead-lined containers and the operators of x-ray machines wear lead aprons. Poor metals may be combined with other metals to form useful alloys.

WHAT IS AN ACID?

The word "acid" comes from a Latin word meaning sour. Acids contain hydrogen and, when dissolved in water, produce positively charged hydrogen ions. Our tongues are able to detect acidic flavours, such as those of vinegar or citrus fruits, but these are very weak in comparison to some acids used in industry, such as sulphuric acid, which burns badly if it comes into contact with skin.

The juice of citrus fruits, such as lemons, limes and oranges, contains a weak acid called citric acid.

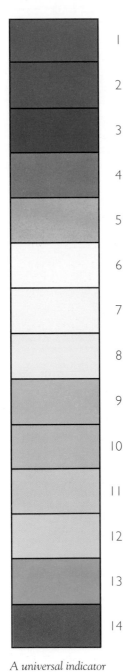

A universal indicator can be matched to pH numbers to measure a substance's acidity or alkalinity.

ARE BASES AND ALKALIS THE SAME THING?

A BASE is the opposite of an acid. Most soap and many household cleaners are bases. An alkali is a base that can be dissolved in water.

WHAT DOES A pH VALUE MEASURE?

THE ABBREVIATION pH stands for "power of hydrogen". It describes how concentrated the hydrogen ions in a substance are. A pH value below seven shows that the substance is acid. Above seven, it is an alkali.

WHAT IS AN INDICATOR?

AN INDICATOR is a substance that changes colour when it comes into contact with something acid or alkali. Several materials occuring in nature will do this, including litmus, which comes from lichen, and a substance in red cabbage. By using a range of different dyes, scientists make something called a universal indicator, which is able to show how acidic or alkali a substance is.

WHICH INTERNATIONAL SYMBOLS WARN ABOUT CHEMICALS INSIDE CONTAINERS?

INTERNATIONAL SYMBOLS warn people that the contents of containers are dangerous. The symbol on the left means "harmful chemical inside", while the other means "corrosive chemical inside".

HOW ARE ACIDS AND ALKALIS USED IN INDUSTRY?

MANY PRODUCTS and processes require the use of acids and alkalis. Here are just some of them.

Car batteries contain acid. Acids are also used to make fertilizer, paint, detergents, plastics, dyes and some artificial fabrics.

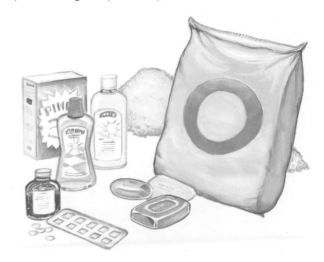

Alkalis are used in the manufacture of soap, floor cleaners, indigestion tablets and cement.

HOW DO ACID AND ALKALI SOILS DIFFER?

IT IS POSSIBLE to measure the acidity or alkalinity of soil. Acid soils are usually found in peaty or forest areas, while alkali soils often occur where the underlying rocks are chalk or limestone. Most plants prefer a soil that is neither too acid nor too alkali, but some are only happy in a particular soil. Heathers and rhododendrons, for example, prefer an acid soil.

Some plants are indicators themselves. Hydrangeas have pink blooms in alkaline soils and blue ones in acid soils.

Rainwater is not neutral. It is slightly acidic because carbon dioxide from the air is dissolved in it. This reacts with limestone, made of alkaline calcium carbonate. Minerals dissolved in the water gradually build up into the strange rock formations known as stalagmites (rising from the floor of caves) and stalactites (hanging from the ceiling).

HOW DO WASP AND BEE STINGS DIFFER?

ALTHOUGH both feel painful, wasp stings are alkali and bee stings are acid. That means that it is best to treat them with acid and alkali substances respectively.

Both stinging ants and stinging nettles produce an acid called methanoic acid (formic acid). Ants use it to immobilize their prey, while nettles use it to protect themselves from being eaten.

WHERE DOES ENERGY COME FROM?

Energy is what makes things happen. Nothing can live, move and grow, or give off light, heat or sound, without energy. There are many different kinds of energy, but nearly all the energy on our planet comes, directly or indirectly, from the Sun.

WHAT ARE THE DIFFERENT KINDS OF ENERGY?

CHEMICAL ENERGY is released when chemical reactions take place. It is stored in many different kinds of substances, such as foods and fuels. Kinetic energy is the energy of movement. An object that is being acted on by a force is said to have potential energy.

Chemical energy is stored in the food we eat. After we have eaten it, it is stored in our fat and muscles. When we move, some of the store of chemical energy in our bodies is converted into kinetic energy.

A rolling ball, a moving bicycle and a running person all have kinetic energy.

Electrical energy can be converted into light energy, sound energy or heat energy.

HOW DOES A POWER STATION WORK?

COAL, OIL OR GAS may be used to fuel a power station. All of these are fossil fuels, formed millions of years ago when the bodies of plants and animals were crushed under enormous pressure.

When the fuel is burned, a chemical reaction takes place that converts its chemical energy into heat energy.

The heat energy is used to heat water until it becomes a gas: steam.

The steam is used to turn a turbine, converting the heat energy into kinetic energy.

A generator converts the kinetic energy into electrical energy.

The electrical energy is carried along wires to homes and factories, where it is converted into heat, light or sound energy by electrical appliances.

A ball being held in the air is being acted on by the force of gravity. If it is dropped, its potential energy will become kinetic energy.

HOW DO HUMAN BEINGS GET THEIR ENERGY?

OUR ENERGY comes from the Sun – but not directly. Plants convert sunlight into chemical energy. We then eat the plants or other animals that have fed on them, so the chemical energy is stored in our bodies. For this energy to be released, chemical reactions need to take place in our bodies. These reactions require oxygen, which we take in from the air we breathe. That is why we get breathless when we are running and turning a lot of chemical energy into kinetic energy.

HOW CAN ENERGY BE STORED?

ENERGY from the Sun is stored in the leaves of plants, but it is also possible to store electrical energy in batteries. Inside a dry-cell battery there is a chemical paste called an electrolyte (which contains charged particles), a positive terminal (or electrode) and a negative terminal. When the battery is put into an electrical circuit, chemical reactions cause electrons to flow out through the negative terminal, through the circuit, and back through the positive terminal. When all the chemical reactions have taken place, the battery is "dead" and has to be replaced or, in the case of some batteries, recharged.

This is a single cell. Larger batteries contain several single cells. Car batteries are not dry cells but contain dilute sulphuric acid and electrodes made of lead and lead oxide.

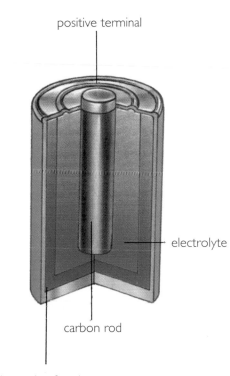

positive terminal

electrolyte

carbon rod

zinc casing forming
the negative terminal

WHAT IS A JOULE?

A JOULE (J) is a small unit of energy. More commonly, we measure energy in kilojoules (kJ), which are units of a thousand joules each. A medium orange probably contains about 250kJ of chemical energy. The same weight of chocolates might contain 1700kJ of energy.

WHAT IS GEOTHERMAL ENERGY?

THE EARTH itself is a store of energy, as the rocks inside it are extremely hot. Water in underground streams and lakes can be heated by running over hot or molten rock. It may then come to the surface in hot springs or geysers. In some parts of the world the hot water or steam is used to turn turbines to produce electricity. This is called geothermal energy.

Steam may come out of the ground naturally in geysers, or water can be pumped underground and heated by hot rocks.

fast facts

WHAT IS PERPETUAL MOTION?

Today we are concerned about conserving energy, ensuring that it is used efficiently so that we do not run out of non-renewable sources of energy too quickly. Once inventors dreamed of a perpetual motion machine, which would carry on working without more energy being supplied to it. In fact, this is impossible. No matter how efficient a machine is, some energy is lost as heat. Eventually, this uses up all the energy available to the machine unless more is supplied.

HOW CAN ROTTING PRODUCE ENERGY?

When plants or animals decay, they give off gases. One of these is a gas called methane, which can be used for heating water and homes.

CAN ENERGY BE DESTROYED?

One form of energy can change into another form but, like matter, it cannot be destroyed or created.

WHAT DOES A WATT MEASURE?

A watt (W) is a unit of power, which means the amount of energy used in a certain time. One watt is the same as one joule of energy used in one second. So a 100-watt light bulb is one that uses 100 joules in one second.

WHAT IS A CALORIE?

A calorie is a unit of energy that is sometimes used instead of the joule. One kilocalorie (Kcal) is equal to approximately 4.2 kilojoules (kJ).

WHAT IS A FORCE?

There are forces acting on us – and everything on our planet – all the time. The push and pull of forces is what keeps things where they are or starts them into motion. Forces enable something to stay the same size and shape or to change size and shape. They can slow down a moving object or speed it up, or change the direction of its motion. Whenever energy is being used, forces are at work.

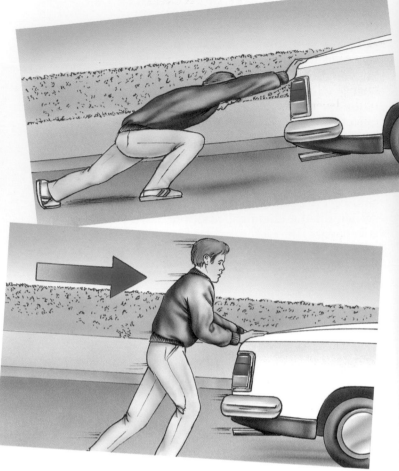

ARE THERE DIFFERENT KINDS OF FORCE?

THERE ARE many different kinds of force. They are affecting everyday objects around us all the time. Here are just some of the many forces that we experience.

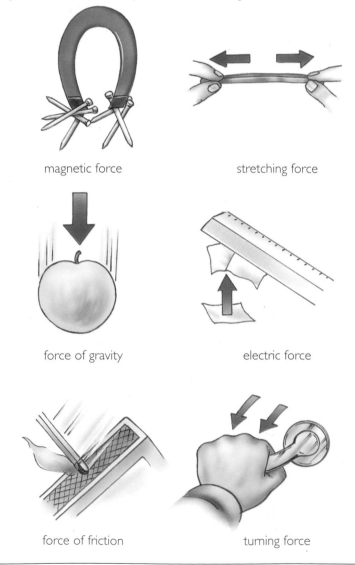

magnetic force

stretching force

force of gravity

electric force

force of friction

turning force

WHAT IS INERTIA?

WHEN A FORCE is applied to an object, it may change its position, movement or shape, but objects have a resistance to change that scientists call inertia. An object will always find it easier to carry on doing the same thing, unless a strong force acts on it. For example, if a car has broken down, a stronger force is needed to push it into motion than is required to keep it moving once it is on its way.

IS FRICTION A USEFUL FORCE?

FRICTION is a force that slows the motion of two surfaces when they move across each other. An engine has many moving parts. If they rub against each other, creating friction, the efficiency of the engine is affected. The friction creates heat and the engine needs more energy to work. The parts also wear down as they come into contact. To reduce the friction in an engine, a lubricant, such as oil, is put between the moving parts.

The grooves on a tyre help to push water on the surface of the road out of the way. This means that there is more friction between the tyre and the road, preventing the car from skidding.

There are also times when friction is useful. For example, if there were no friction between our feet and the ground, we would fall over. This can happen when a floor is polished or there is ice on the ground. There is less friction between our feet and these surfaces, so we easily slip.

HOW CAN THE DIRECTION OF FORCES BE CHANGED?

A DEVICE that can change the direction of a force is called a machine. It may be very simple, such as a lever. This can change a force pushing *down* on one end of the lever into a force pushing *up* on an object at the other end of the lever. A bicycle is able to move along because the crankshaft changes the force of your feet pushing *down* into the *turning* force of the wheels going round.

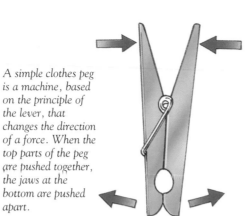

A simple clothes peg is a machine, based on the principle of the lever, that changes the direction of a force. When the top parts of the peg are pushed together, the jaws at the bottom are pushed apart.

WHAT HAPPENS WHEN MORE THAN ONE FORCE ACTS ON AN OBJECT?

MOST OBJECTS have more than one force acting on them at any one time. If an object is not moving, it is said to be in equilibrium, meaning that all the forces acting on it cancel each other out.

If both dogs are pulling with equal force, the shirt will not move. It will be in equilibrium. Of course, if the forces on it are too strong, the fabric itself will tear apart.

Often, the forces acting on an object are not balanced but combine together to have a certain effect, called the resultant. If the direction and size of all the forces acting on an object are known, the resultant can be calculated.

There are many forces operating on this balloon. The force of gravity is pulling it downwards towards the ground. The hot air is creating an upward force called lift. The pushing force of the wind is blowing the balloon along. The friction force of the air on the balloon is slowing it down. If the size and direction of all the forces are known, the direction and speed of the balloon can be worked out.

WHAT IS A CENTRIFUGAL FORCE?

FORCES act in a straight line unless something changes their direction. A carriage travelling around a fairground ride would go straight on if the track did not take it round in a circle, forcing it to change direction all the time. The forward-acting force keeps the carriage on the tracks, even when it is upside down. This is known as a centrifugal force.

IS GRAVITY A FORCE?

Gravity is a force of attraction between two bodies. It is present between any two objects, but it is only with very large items, such as planets and stars, that we notice it most of the time. The force of gravity of the Sun is so great that it keeps the planets of the Solar System in orbit around it.

WHAT IS A FORCE FIELD?

A force field is the area in which a force can be felt, such as the area around a planet within which the force of gravity operates.

HOW IS FORCE MEASURED?

Force is measured in newtons (N). One newton is the force needed to cause a mass of one kilogram to accelerate one metre per second per second ($1m/s^2$).

WHAT IS HOOKE'S LAW?

Hooke's Law, named after the Englishman Robert Hooke, says that the amount a body is stretched out of shape is in proportion to the force acting on it. That means that a spring can be used to measure forces, as the greater the force, the more the spring is stretched.

WHAT IS A CONTACT FORCE?

Some forces do not work unless one thing is touching another. These are known as contact forces. Other forces, such as gravity, work even if an object is not being touched.

WHAT IS A VECTOR QUANTITY?

A vector quantity is one that has both size (magnitude) and direction, as a force has. A quantity that has magnitude but not direction, such as temperature, is known as a scalar quantity.

WHAT IS A MAGNETIC FIELD?

A magnetic field is the area around a magnet in which its magnetic force operates. A magnetic object that is placed within the field will be attracted or repelled by the magnet. When iron filings (tiny slivers of iron) are placed near a magnet, they line up to show its magnetic field. In fact, each tiny piece of iron has become a small magnet. The mini-magnets show how strongly each part of the large magnet attracts them.

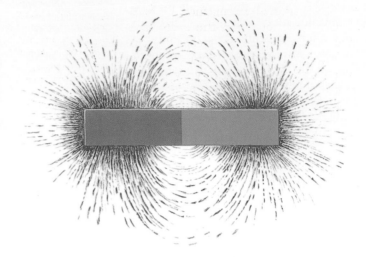

HOW IS AN ELECTROMAGNET MADE?

WHEN AN ELECTRIC CURRENT runs through a wire, it creates a magnetic field. If the wire is wound round and round an iron core, the coil and core become strongly magnetized whenever the current is turned on. The coil of wire is called a solenoid.

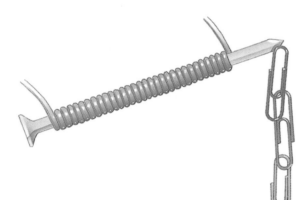

When the wires are connected to a power source so that current runs through them, the iron nail becomes a magnet and can attract iron and steel objects.

HOW DOES A COMPASS WORK?

THE EARTH has a core of molten iron and is itself a huge magnet. Its magnetic field acts as though there were a bar magnet running along the axis of the Earth. A compass contains a magnetized needle, which can turn freely. No matter which direction the compass is facing, the needle will turn to point towards the North Pole. The compass can then be rotated so that its north point lines up with the needle and the other directions can be read.

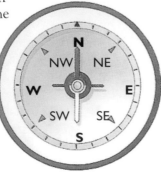

The abbreviations round a compass stand for North, North-East, East, South-East, South, South-West, West and North-East, reading clockwise from the top.

WHAT ARE THE POLES OF A MAGNET?

LIKE THE EARTH itself, each magnet has a north and a south pole. If it can turn freely, the north pole of a magnet will turn towards the North Pole of the Earth. The south pole of a magnet will be attracted towards the South Pole of the Earth. Confusingly, the Earth's North Pole actually has a south magnetic pole, which is why the north pole of a magnet is attracted to it. For the rule is that like poles repel each other (push each other away), while unlike poles attract.

The north and south poles of the two magnets attract each other.

The two north poles repel each other.

Two south poles would also repel each other.

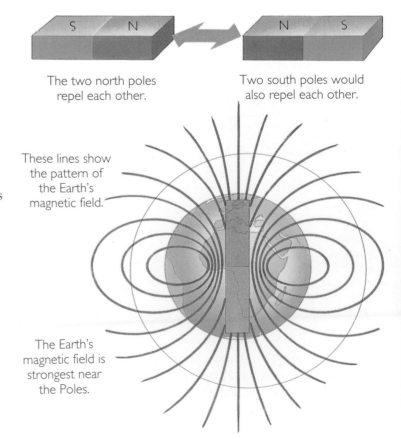

These lines show the pattern of the Earth's magnetic field.

The Earth's magnetic field is strongest near the Poles.

WHAT ADVANTAGES DO ELECTROMAGNETS HAVE OVER ORDINARY MAGNETS?

THE FACT that an electromagnet ceases to become a magnet when the current is turned off can be used to great effect in large and small machines. For example, a powerful magnet can lift very heavy weights of iron and steel in a factory, but that would be no good if the magnet could not be persuaded to release them. With an electromagnet, the current can be stopped and the load released.

An electromagnet can save people who live up several flights of stairs from having to walk down to the front door when the bell rings. They can simply find out who is calling by means of an intercom and then press a switch to let the caller in. The switch turns on a current that activates an electromagnet. The magnet attracts the door latch, pulling it back and allowing the visitor to enter. Then a spring allows the latch to slip back into place.

HOW DOES MAGNETISM CREATE A MAGNIFICENT LIGHT SHOW?

THE EARTH'S North and South Poles attract charged particles from the Sun. Within the atmosphere, these collide with molecules of gas to cause spectacular light shows, called the *aurora borealis* (northern dawn), which can be seen in the Arctic Circle.

When the weather conditions are right, the aurora borealis, also known as the northern lights, can sometimes be seen outside the Arctic Circle in the northern hemisphere.

Maglev trains are very quiet for the passengers, as there is no sound of wheels rattling on tracks.

WHERE ARE TRAVELLERS MAGNETICALLY LEVITATED?

IN JAPAN, "maglev" trains run just above, not on, their tracks. Both the bottom of the train and the track itself are magnetic. The magnets repel each other, so the train hovers just above the track, enabling it to run with less friction and so reach higher speeds.

WHO DISCOVERED ELECTROMAGNETISM?

Electromagnetism was discovered by a Danish physicist called Hans Christian Oersted. In 1820, he noticed that an electric current could cause a compass needle to deflect. Previously, only magnets had been seen to do this.

HOW CAN MAGNETS HELP WITH RECYCLING?

Before cans used for food and drink are melted down to be recycled, they need to be separated into those made of steel and those made of aluminium. As steel is magnetic but aluminium is not, a huge magnet is held over the pile of cans and the steel ones are picked up by it, leaving the aluminium ones behind.

WHERE DOES THE WORD "MAGNET" COME FROM?

Magnets are so called because the ancient Greeks found magnetic rocks in an area called Magnesia, in what is now Turkey.

WHAT ARE FERROMAGNETIC METALS?

Ferromagnetic metals are those that can be magnetized: iron and steel.

WHAT WAS A LODESTONE?

A lodestone was an early compass, used by sailors to navigate their ships. It was a piece of magnetite, a rock containing iron, that was naturally magnetic.

CAN MAGNETS WORK THROUGH NON-MAGNETIC MATERIALS?

Depending on its strength and the thickness of the material between it and a magnetic material, a magnet can still work. For example, it can be attracted to a refrigerator door through a piece of paper.

WHY IS ELECTRICITY SO USEFUL?

Electricity is a very flexible form of energy. It can easily be converted to heat, light or sound energy. It can be carried long distances through wires and cables. It is clean and safe if used in the right way. In fact, electricity is now so much a part of our lives that it is difficult to imagine being without it.

WHAT IS ELECTRICITY?

ELECTRICITY is the movement of electrically charged particles. Atoms contain positively charged protons and negatively charged electrons. Usually, these balance each other, so that the atom is electrically neutral, but electrons sometimes move from one atom to another, leaving the first positively charged and the second negatively charged. Just as unlike poles of magnets attract each other, so atoms with different charges attract each other. When electrons move through a substance, they create a flow of electricity called a current.

Once the brightest things to be seen at night were the Moon and stars. Electricity has enabled cities to be lit as brightly by night as by day.

WHAT IS STATIC ELECTRICITY?

STATIC ELECTRICITY is what sometimes makes a nylon jumper crackle and spark in dry weather. Or you may get a small electric shock from a metal surface after walking across a carpet made of artificial fibres. Rubbing something made of amber or plastic can cause it to pick up electrons from your clothes or hair, giving them a positive charge. If you then touch something with a slightly negative charge, a small spark may fly across just before you touch it, or, if it is light, the oppositely charged object may be attracted to you.

A balloon rubbed on your jumper picks up electrons from it. Your jumper is then slightly positively charged and the balloon is slightly negatively charged. As opposite charges attract, the balloon will cling to you.

HOW DOES A LIGHTNING CONDUCTOR WORK?

A LIGHTNING CONDUCTOR is a metal rod that is placed so that it points upwards above the highest point of a tall building. If lightning does strike the building, it is the lightning conductor, not the building itself, that the spark hits. The electrical charge then runs harmlessly down the lightning conductor to Earth.

We cannot see electricity, but we can see its effects. Lightning happens when the electrical charge of a cloud discharges itself to the Earth or to another cloud that has an opposite charge.

WHAT IS AN ELECTRIC CIRCUIT?

A CIRCUIT is a path along which an electric current can flow. Each part of the circuit must be connected to the next, and each must be able to conduct electricity. In a series circuit, there is only one path for the current to follow, and it passes through each component of the circuit in turn. If one component fails, the current will no longer be able to flow. Christmas tree lights are usually connected to each other in series. When one bulb blows, the circuit is broken and all the lights go out.

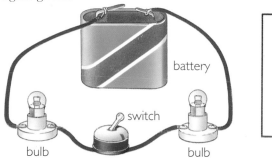

When the switch is turned on, the circuit is completed and the bulbs light. It does not matter what the order of the components is.

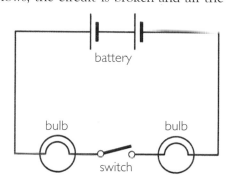

The same series circuit can be shown as an electrical diagram. Special symbols are used to represent the bulbs, the switch and the battery.

Instead of being connected in a series circuit, the same components could be connected in a parallel circuit. In this kind of circuit, there is more than one pathway for the electrical current to flow along.

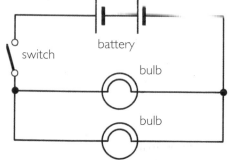

With this parallel arrangement of the bulbs, when the circuit is switched on, one bulb will still light if the other blows.

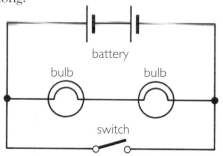

The order of components in a parallel circuit is very important. This circuit will still work even when the switch is turned off, making the switch useless.

WHAT IS A CONDUCTOR?

MATERIALS that allow electric currents to pass through them are called conductors. One of the best conductors that is fairly cheap to obtain is copper, which is why many electric cables and wires are made of this metal.

Tools such as screwdrivers, which may be used on electrical appliances, have plastic handles to provide insulation for the electrician in case the current is accidentally turned on.

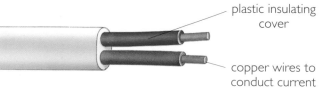

plastic insulating cover

copper wires to conduct current

WHAT IS AN INSULATOR?

AN INSULATOR is the opposite of a conductor. It is a material that will not allow electrical current to run through it because its electrons are not free to move. Plastic is a very good insulator. That is why it is used to cover copper wire. The wire can then safely conduct electricity along its length without allowing it to come into contact with other conductors.

WHAT DOES A VOLTMETER MEASURE?

A voltmeter measures voltage. An electrical current flows from an area with a high electrical potential to an area of low electrical potential, such as from one terminal of a battery to the other. The difference in electrical potential between the two terminals is measured in volts (V). A single cell has a voltage of 1.5V, which you will see written on the side of a battery of this size.

WHAT IS AN AMPERE?

An ampere, or amp (A), is a unit of measurement of electrical current. It is named after André-Marie Ampère, a French scientist working at the beginning of the nineteenth century. One amp is equivalent to a current of about six million million million (6,000,000,000,000,000,000) electrons per second.

WHERE DOES THE WORD "ELECTRICITY" COME FROM?

Our word "electricity" comes from the Greek word *elektron*, meaning amber. Thousands of years ago, the ancient Greeks realized that if amber is rubbed, small pieces of cloth will be attracted to it. We know now that this effect is caused by static electricity.

WHY DO BIRDS SITTING ON WIRES NOT GET AN ELECTRIC SHOCK?

An electric current can be very dangerous to a living body if it passes through it to the Earth. That is why you sometimes hear of people surviving electric shocks because they were wearing rubber soles that insulated them from the ground. Birds on wires are not in contact with the ground, so the circuit is not completed and they are safe.

HOW CAN ELECTRICITY BE USED TO SEPARATE COMPOUNDS?

Some compounds can be separated into individual elements by passing an electric current through them when they are in a liquid state. This process is called electrolysis. For this to happen, the compound must be able to conduct electricity, and its elements must be held together by ionic bonds. Many industrial processes use electrolysis, especially those concerned with purifying metals or applying thin layers of metal to other objects.

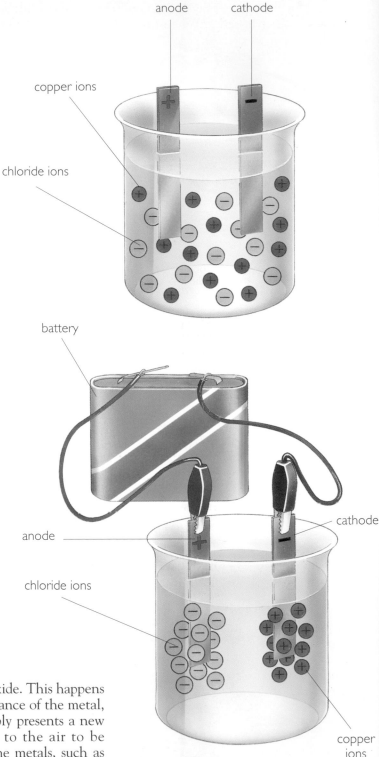

WHAT IS AN ELECTROLYTE?

AN ELECTROLYTE is a liquid that can conduct an electric current. A metal may become an electrolyte if it is molten (melted) or dissolved in another liquid. Water can also conduct an electric current. That is why it is very dangerous to touch an electric socket with wet hands.

WHAT ARE CATHODES AND ANODES?

CATHODES AND ANODES are electrodes. These are carbon or metal rods that are connected to an electric current. When they are placed in an electrolyte, current can pass through the liquid from one electrode to the other, so completing the circuit. The cathode has a negative electrical charge and the anode has a positive electrical charge. Ions in the electrolyte are being held together because they have opposite electrical charges, which attract each other. These bonds are broken because the ions with positive charges are more strongly attracted to the negative charge of the cathode than they are to the negative charge of the ions with which they are bonded. In the same way, negatively charged ions are attracted to the anode.

WHAT IS ANODIZING?

WHEN A METAL reacts with oxygen, it forms a compound called an oxide. This happens on the surface of metals such as silver. As the oxide dulls the appearance of the metal, it is often rubbed off ornaments and jewellery, but in fact this simply presents a new surface of pure metal to the air to be oxidized. However, some metals, such as aluminium, are deliberately coated, by means of electrolysis, with a layer of their oxide. This process is known as anodization. It protects the metal underneath from oxidizing further.

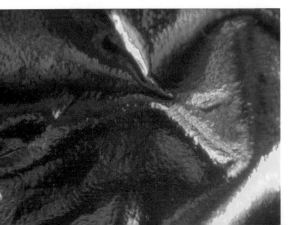

Anodized aluminium foil can be coloured by dyeing the layer of oxide.

This diagram shows copper chloride being separated into copper and chlorine by means of electrolysis. The copper ions have a positive charge, so they are attracted to the negative charge of the cathode and form a coating on this electrode. Chloride ions have a negative charge, so they are attracted to the positive charge of the anode. Here they give up their extra electrons and so become chlorine gas.

WHAT IS ELECTROREFINING?

ELECTROREFINING, as the word suggests, is a way of purifying metals by using electrolysis. Copper can be purified by making the impure copper the anode in an electrolyte of copper sulphate. The cathode is made of pure copper. When an electric current is passed through the copper sulphate, positively charged copper ions from the anode are attracted to the cathode of pure metal. The impurities, which may be tiny amounts of other metals, such as mercury, gold and silver, fall to the bottom of the electrolyte.

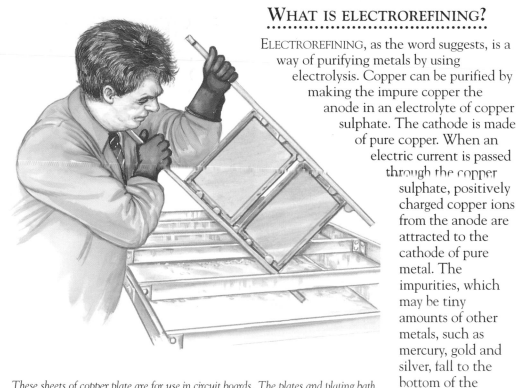

These sheets of copper plate are for use in circuit boards. The plates and plating bath have to be carefully arranged so that the copper is distributed evenly over the surface.

HOW DID HUMPHRY DAVY DISCOVER NEW ELEMENTS?

HUMPHRY DAVY (1778–1829) was an English chemist who conducted some early experiments using electrolysis. This process offered a way of isolating metals from the compounds in which they are naturally found. As a result, Davy discovered potassium, sodium and calcium because he was able to separate the metals into their pure form.

WHAT IS ELECTROPLATING?

ELECTROPLATING uses electrolysis to deposit a thin layer of metal on another substance. The item to be plated is used as one electrode. Copper, silver, tin and chromium are often applied to surfaces in this way.

WHAT HAPPENS TO WATER WHEN A CURRENT IS PASSED THROUGH IT?

When water is used as an electrolyte, it separates into hydrogen and oxygen – the two elements that, as the compound H_2O, form water.

WHICH METALS ARE EXTRACTED FROM THEIR ORES BY ELECTROLYSIS?

Electrolysis is used for the extraction of very reactive metals. Aluminium, for example, is extracted in this way from bauxite that has been dissolved in molten cryolite, a substance containing aluminium and sodium.

CAN ELECTROLYSIS BE REVERSED?

When electrolysis is being used to plate an object with a layer of metal, it is sometimes possible to remove the plating by reversing the electrodes. In other words, the cathode becomes the anode and the anode the cathode.

WHICH KINDS OF OBJECT ARE ELECTROPLATED?

OBJECTS may be electroplated for protection or to enhance their appearance. Very often, the object itself is made from a much cheaper material than the plating.

Almost any solid object can be electroplated. Some parents have their baby's first shoes electroplated as a keepsake.

Plating may protect the material underneath. Tin plate on steel cans stops the steel from corroding. Chromium plating was once common on cars to prevent bumpers and headlights from rusting.

BWM 960

Items made from cheaper metals can be electroplated with silver to look like solid silver articles.

WHO DISCOVERED GRAVITY?

The fact that objects dropped from a height fall to the ground, that the Moon is near enough to be seen from Earth, and that we do not float into the air when we are standing still has, of course, been known for thousands of years. What was not known was the reason for these phenomena. It was a British scientist, Isaac Newton, who, in 1666, put forward the idea that the same force – gravity – might be responsible for all these events. Gravity is a force of attraction caused by the huge mass of the Earth.

HOW DOES GRAVITY AFFECT THE TIDES?

THE MOON, too, has gravity. Its gravitational pull is much less than the Earth's, as its mass is smaller, but it still has an effect on Earth. On the side of the Earth nearest the Moon, the oceans are pulled out by the Moon's gravity, causing a high tide. Exactly the same thing happens on the opposite side of the Earth, but this time because the Moon is exerting less pull on the waters of the oceans. As the Earth rotates on its axis, each part of the Earth is turned towards the Moon once in every twenty-four hours. That means that the seas have two high tides every twenty-four hours – once when they are facing the Moon and once when they are on the opposite side of the Earth from the Moon.

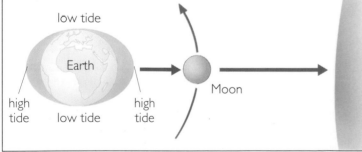

WHY DO ASTRONAUTS FLOAT IN SPACE?

OUTSIDE THE EARTH'S gravitational field, astronauts experience "weightlessness". Their mass has not changed, but with no gravity to act upon this mass, they have no weight. When working outside a spacecraft, astronauts are tethered to prevent them from floating away into space. Inside the spacecraft, liquids have to be sucked through straws. Liquid would not be held in an ordinary cup by gravity, as it is on Earth, but would spray all over the interior. One of the reasons that astronauts are spending longer and longer periods in space is so that scientists can study the effects of weightlessness on their bodies, so that future space flights can last for months or even years.

IS GRAVITY THE SAME ALL OVER THE UNIVERSE?

THE FORCE of gravity depends on the mass of the object exerting the gravitational pull. Generally, large planets have a greater gravitational force than smaller ones. As the Moon's mass is smaller than that of the Earth, it exerts a gravitational pull only a sixth as strong as the gravity on Earth. That is why astronauts appear to bounce along on the Moon's surface – the Moon is pulling them down much less strongly than on Earth. But the principle of gravity holds true throughout the universe.

This chart shows the force of gravity on each of the planets of our Solar System, compared to the gravity on Earth.

Mercury	Venus	Earth	Mars	Jupiter	Saturn	Uranus	Neptune	Pluto
0.38	0.9	1	0.38	2.64	0.925	0.79	1.12	0.05

WHAT IS A CENTRE OF GRAVITY?

THE CENTRE OF GRAVITY or centre of mass of an object is the point from which all its weight seems to act. The lower an object's centre of gravity, the more stable it is. That is why decanters for holding water or wine often have wide, heavy bases, giving them a low centre of gravity, to make them difficult to knock over. When an object is tilted, it is still stable while its centre of gravity is over its base. If the object is tilted further, so that its centre of gravity is no longer over its base, it becomes unstable and will fall over.

base | centre of gravity

base | centre of gravity is still over base

This toy has been designed so that when a young child knocks it over, it will almost always bounce back up. In other words, it is extremely stable. Similar principles are used to build boats that are very difficult to capsize and will right themselves if they do turn over.

IN WHICH SPORTS IS A LOW CENTRE OF GRAVITY IMPORTANT?

ANY SPORT that requires a participant or piece of equipment to be stable uses the principle of the centre of gravity.

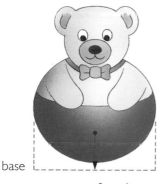

Boxers aim not to be knocked down! They try to keep a wide-legged stance to give themselves a low centre of gravity and maximum stability.

A racing car has wide wheels and a low body, giving it a low centre of gravity. This makes it stable at high speeds and when cornering.

DOES GRAVITY PULL HEAVY OBJECTS MORE STRONGLY THAN LIGHT ONES?

AS OBJECTS are dropped and pulled towards Earth by its gravitational force, they accelerate, travelling faster and faster the further they fall. That is why a person falling one metre might sustain only bruises but a person falling one kilometre would be unlikely to survive. The body would be hitting the ground at a much higher speed. However, an Italian scientist called Galileo Galilei, working some years before Newton, showed that the weight of a body does not affect the speed with which it falls.

HOW DO ROCKETS ESCAPE FROM THE EARTH'S GRAVITY?

The further away from the centre of the Earth that an object travels, the less the Earth's gravity pulls on it. In fact, you weigh very slightly less at the top of a mountain than at the bottom. At a certain distance, a rocket can escape the Earth's gravitational pull. A rocket uses up a great deal of fuel in the first part of its journey from Earth, as its booster rockets fire to push it beyond the planet's gravity.

WHY DO TIGHTROPE WALKERS OFTEN CARRY A POLE?

By carrying a pole, tightrope walkers are able to lower their centre of gravity and so increase their stability as they balance on the narrow rope.

HOW IS EARTH'S GRAVITY USEFUL IN COMMUNICATIONS?

It is not only the Moon that the Earth's gravity keeps in orbit around our planet. Satellites made by human beings are also circling the Earth. Radio signals can be bounced off them so that telephone calls, television programmes and other communications can be sent rapidly around the world.

DOES THE SUN HAVE GRAVITY?

The Sun is a massive body and so its gravity is very high. If you could jump to a height of one metre or one yard on Earth, you could not even jump three centimetres or one inch on the Sun. Of course, it would not be possible to stand on the surface of the Sun in any case!

A pingpong ball and a ball of lead of the same size and shape, dropped from the same height at the same moment, will reach the Earth together.

WHAT MAKES UP THE AIR WE BREATHE?

The air around us is a mixture of gases. Its content varies depending on where and when it is measured, but on average the air is made up of just over one-fifth oxygen and just under four-fifths nitrogen. There are also very small quantities of other gases, such as argon and carbon dioxide, some pollutants and water vapour, and tiny solid particles, such as soot and pollen.

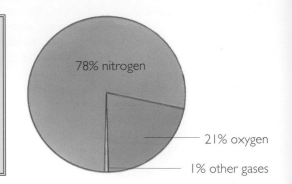

78% nitrogen

21% oxygen

1% other gases

exosphere

thermosphere

ionosphere

mesosphere

stratosphere

troposphere

The Earth's atmosphere has layers of cooler and warmer air. On this diagram, warm air is shown in pale blue, becoming darker as it gets colder.

WHAT IS ATMOSPHERIC PRESSURE?

THE AIR around the Earth is pulled towards it by the planet's gravity. This causes it to press down on the Earth with a force known as atmospheric pressure. This is measured in units called millibars (mb). At sea level, the average atmospheric pressure is around 1000mb. It is changes in atmospheric pressure, caused by the air being heated by the Sun, that make the air flow from place to place, causing the winds and weather that we experience on Earth. Most weather events happen in the lowest layer of the Earth's atmosphere – the troposphere.

Cyclists aiming for high speeds crouch low over their machines to reduce the air resistance that would slow them down.

WHY IS THE SKY BLUE?

AS THE SUN'S LIGHT passes through the atmosphere, its rays are scattered by the tiny particles of pollen, soot and dust to be found there. As blue light is scattered most, the sky appears blue. At sunset and sunrise, sunlight has further to travel to reach us. Only red light can be seen because the blue light has been absorbed by the atmosphere.

WHAT IS AIR RESISTANCE?

ALTHOUGH we cannot see the air, it is still made of atoms and molecules, just like everything else. When an object passes through the air, these molecules push against it, causing a force of friction called air resistance.

HOW DOES A PARACHUTE WORK?

A PARACHUTE offers an enormous surface area on which air resistance can operate. The friction slows the descent of the parachutist, so that he or she can land safely. Without a parachute, a human body would accelerate towards the Earth, hitting it with fatal force.

WHAT IS A PNEUMATIC MACHINE?

A PNEUMATIC MACHINE is one that is driven by compressed air. If no other forces are acting on them, the molecules in gases, such as air, spread out to fill the space that is available to them. If the space is sealed and then reduced, the air is compressed – the molecules are pushed closer together. This means that the pressure that the compressed air exerts on the inside of its container is greater than the atmospheric pressure pushing down on the outside of the container. A pneumatic drill, also known as an air-hammer or jack-hammer, uses compressed air to push its bit forcefully against the ground being broken up. The compressed air is supplied to the drill through a hose by a machine called a compressor.

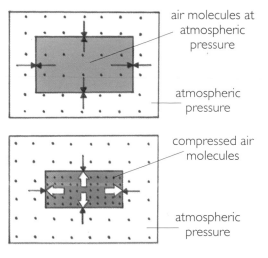

air molecules at atmospheric pressure

atmospheric pressure

compressed air molecules

atmospheric pressure

When air is compressed, the same number of molecules are squeezed into a smaller space. The pressure they exert is greater than the atmospheric pressure outside. This pressure can be used in pneumatic machines to drive a piston.

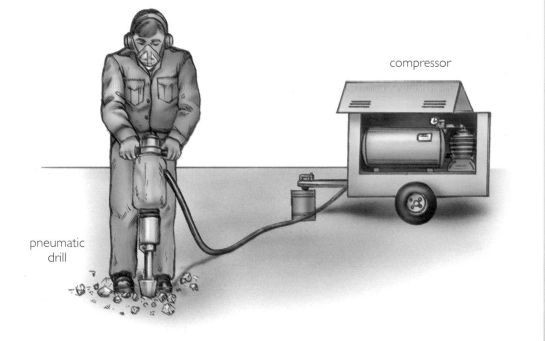

compressor

pneumatic drill

HOW DEEP IS THE EARTH'S ATMOSPHERE?

OUR PLANET'S ATMOSPHERE is not very deep compared with the diameter of the Earth. While you would have to travel 6370km (3956 miles) to reach the centre of the Earth, the edge of the Earth's atmosphere is only about 500km (310 miles) away.

WHY IS WATER VITAL TO LIFE ON EARTH?

All living things contain a large proportion of water. For example, around two-thirds of the human body is made up of water. Although most people could survive quite a long time without food, they would die within a few days if they had no water. More of the surface of the Earth is covered by water than by land – a fact that has an enormous effect on the climate of all parts of the Earth. Although it is a simple compound of oxygen and hydrogen, water plays a very complex role on our planet.

WHAT IS A SOLUTION?

IN CHEMICAL TERMS, a solution is not the answer to a problem but a mixture of a solid substance dissolved in a liquid. The solid is called a solute and the liquid is called a solvent. Some solids dissolve very easily and are said to be soluble. Something that will not dissolve in liquid is insoluble.

WHAT IS SURFACE TENSION?

WATER MOLECULES are attracted to each other strongly, which is why they stay as a liquid until heated to a temperature where the bonds between them are broken and they rise into the air as vapour. At the surface of still water, there are no water molecules above pushing or pulling against the surface molecules, so the surface molecules are even more strongly drawn together than usual. This causes them to act as though they form a skin over the surface. It is this effect that is called surface tension.

Insects that are as light as this pond skater can literally walk on water. Their feet make little indentations where they press down on the "skin".

Some drinks are supplied in concentrated form, as syrups of sugar and flavouring. When water is added, the syrup is diluted. A solution has been made.

Milk contains a large proportion of water, but it is not a solution. It is a suspension: a mixture of tiny particles of fat and other substances floating in water.

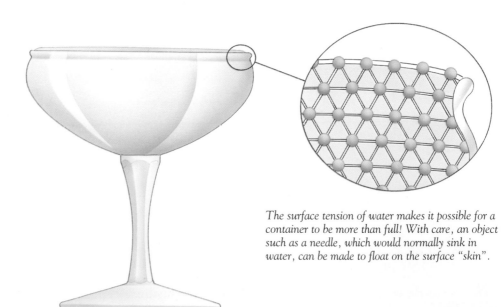

The surface tension of water makes it possible for a container to be more than full! With care, an object such as a needle, which would normally sink in water, can be made to float on the surface "skin".

CAN GASES BE DISSOLVED IN WATER?

GASES, as well as solids, can be soluble. For example, fizzy drinks have carbon dioxide gas dissolved in them. Inside the can or bottle, the carbon dioxide is at higher pressure than the outside atmosphere. When the bottle is opened, there is often a loud pop or fizz as the pressure is equalized and the carbon dioxide starts to escape into the air. If left for a few hours, the drink will lose most of its dissolved gas and taste "flat".

Fish breathe oxygen from the water with their gills. If pollution decreases the amount of oxygen dissolved in the water, fish cannot survive.

WHAT IS DISTILLED WATER?

BECAUSE WATER is an excellent solvent, we very rarely find it in a pure form. Even water from the tap has tiny amounts of a number of chemicals dissolved in it. If pure water is needed, it can be obtained by distillation.

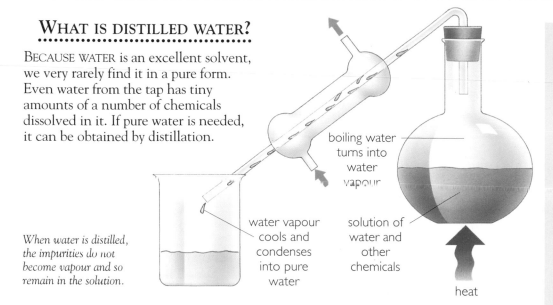

boiling water turns into water vapour

water vapour cools and condenses into pure water

solution of water and other chemicals

heat

When water is distilled, the impurities do not become vapour and so remain in the solution.

WHY IS EVAPORATION USEFUL?

EVAPORATION is another way of separating water from chemicals dissolved in it. It works in the same way as distillation, except that evaporation is usually used when it is the substances in the water that are needed, not the water itself. The water is usually allowed to drift away as steam. In other words, distillation is used to obtain the solvent, while evaporation is used to obtain the solute.

The sea is salty because there are many minerals dissolved in it. Some people prefer to use sea salt to flavour their food. This is obtained simply by boiling sea water, so that it evaporates. The water escapes as steam, while the salt is left behind as crystals.

HOW CAN DRYING GOODS PRESERVE THEM?

LIKE all other living things, bacteria need water to survive and reproduce. If foods, such as pulses and cereals, are dried, most bacteria cannot attack them, so they are very slow to decay.

Pasta is made of a mixture of flour and eggs. It is shaped when damp and then dried. In this form, it will keep for months. When it is boiled in water, pasta takes in water molecules and becomes soft. Pulses are dried peas and beans. Before they can be eaten, they are soaked in water to replace the liquid they lost in drying.

WHAT IS HARD WATER?

WATER is said to be "hard" when it has certain minerals dissolved in it. The most noticeable effect of hard water is that soap does not lather well in it, instead forming a kind of scum. There are two kinds of water hardness, depending on which chemicals are dissolved in it. Temporary hardness can be removed by boiling the water. The chemicals become a solid, which is the scale that sometimes furs up kettles and shower heads. Permanent hardness can be removed by using a water softener, which exchanges the calcium and magnesium ions that cause the hardness with sodium ions.

Oils and fats do not mix with water, so washing greasy clothes or hair in water alone will not clean them. Soap contains ions that are attracted to water at one end and to grease at the other. This end of each ion attaches itself to the grease, while the other end, attracted to the water, pulls the grease away from the fabric or hair. Hard water is a problem because the ions react with the chemicals in the water to form scum.

fast facts

WHY DO WATER PIPES SOMETIMES BURST IN COLD WEATHER?

Water expands when it freezes. If it is trapped in a pipe with no room for expansion, water may burst even a strong pipe as it freezes. Good insulation around pipes can keep the water inside above freezing point and prevent problems in all but the very coldest weather.

HOW DOES ANTIFREEZE WORK?

As liquids are cooled, they become solid, but this happens at a different temperature for each liquid. Water freezes at 0°C (32°F). By mixing water with a liquid, called antifreeze, that freezes at a much lower temperature, motorists can ensure that the water in their cars does not freeze in winter weather.

WHAT IS SATURATION?

Solutes can be added to a solvent only until its saturation point is reached. This is the point at which the liquid cannot dissolve any more of the solid.

WHAT IS DESALINATION?

In some parts of the world, there is little rain or fresh water. One answer is to remove the salt from sea water to make drinking water. This process is called desalination.

WHAT TRAVELS FASTEST IN THE UNIVERSE?

Nothing that has a physical existence travels faster than light. In a vacuum it travels at 300,000km (186,000 miles) per second. We tend to think that we are seeing things as they are, but that is not quite true. We are seeing them as they were at the moment that the light left them to travel to us. Of course, for most purposes, as light travels so quickly, this makes no difference at all. It is only when we are looking at the stars, which are unimaginably huge distances away, that we really are seeing the distant past. Light from our Sun takes about eight minutes to reach the Earth, but it takes less than a tenth of a second to travel across the Atlantic.

DOES LIGHT ALWAYS TRAVEL IN A STRAIGHT LINE?

BEAMS OF LIGHT do travel in straight lines, but those lines can be deflected. Light travels at different speeds in different substances. When the light passes from one substance to another, its beam bends. This is called refraction.

WHAT IS ELECTROMAGNETIC ENERGY?

LIGHT is not the only kind of energy to travel at the speed of light! In fact, every kind of energy in what is called the electromagnetic spectrum travels at that speed. Electromagnetic energy travels in waves. Only a small part of the electromagnetic spectrum is visible to us – the part that makes up the colours of the rainbow – but all of it has proved to be useful to us.

HOW ARE ELECTROMAGNETIC WAVES MEASURED?

THE DISTANCE from the peak of one wave to the peak of the next is called its wavelength. The height of a wave, from its rest position to a peak or trough, is its amplitude. The number of waves per second is known as the frequency and measured in hertz (Hz).

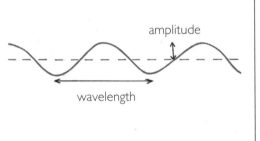

radio waves | microwaves | infra-red radiation | visible light | ultraviolet rays | x-rays | gamma rays

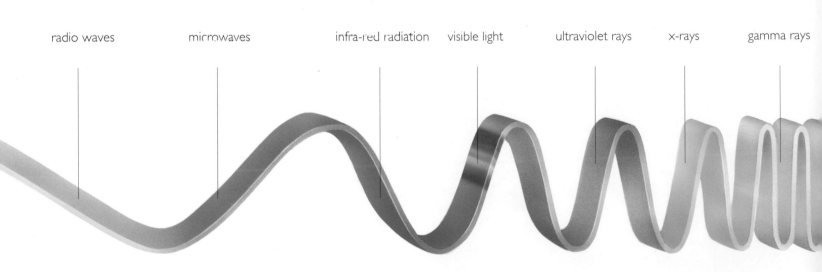

The longest wavelengths of electromagnetic energy are radio waves. They are used for communications and entertainment – radio and television.

Microwaves are best known for their use in microwave ovens.

Infra-red rays cannot be seen, but they can be felt as warmth. Infra-red cameras allow photographs to be taken in the dark. They create images showing areas of heat and cold.

Visible light appears colourless to us, but it is made up of different colours, each one of which has its own wavelength.

Ultraviolet (UV) rays are what cause some people's skin to tan. We now realize that large amounts of these can be harmful, but small amounts help our bodies to produce vitamin D.

X-rays can pass through the soft parts of the bodies of animals but are absorbed by their skeletons, which can be shown on x-ray film. X-rays are harmful in large quantities but useful in small ones.

Gamma rays are given off by radioactive materials. They can harm living cells.

HOW CAN SHADOWS MEASURE TIME?

AS THE EARTH turns each day, shadows cast by the Sun move and change length. This fact has been used for thousands of years to measure the time of day. A sundial has a time scale and a central pole called a gnomon. The shadow cast by the gnomon falls on the scale and the time can be read.

WHICH MATERIALS REFLECT LIGHT?

MOST THINGS do not create their own light. We can see them because they reflect light coming from another source, such as the Sun or a light bulb. A very smooth surface reflects more light than a rough one. Surfaces that are extremely smooth, such as mirrors, are the best reflectors.

A car wing mirror is slightly curved so that the image is smaller and more of the view along the side of the car can be seen.

Enormous buildings with glass sides seem almost to disappear as they reflect the images of everything around them.

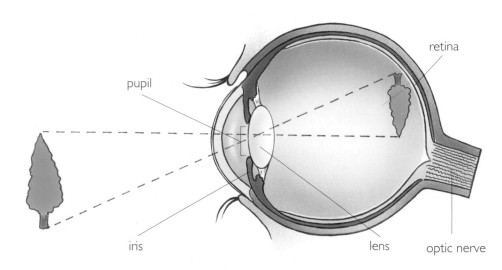

Builders and designers can use reflections to great effect. Here the water acts as a mirror, making the arches of the bridge appear circular, not semi-circular.

HOW DOES THE HUMAN EYE WORK?

THE HUMAN EYE is a ball containing a kind of jelly that keeps it round, just as the air in a balloon keeps that round. At the front is a lens, through which light can enter the eye. The lens can change shape to focus light from different distances. Like a slide projector, the lens throws an image onto the back of the eye, which is called the retina. In fact, the image is upside down, but your brain, which makes sense of everything you see, sorts out the image so that you "see" it the right way up.

retina

pupil

iris

lens

optic nerve

HOW DO SPECTACLES IMPROVE VISION?

Sometimes the lens in the human eye causes the image to fall behind or in front of the retina. This results in a blurred image. Vision can be corrected by placing another lens in front of the eye. This adjusts the image so that it falls directly on the retina and can be seen clearly. The corrective lens may be worn in spectacles or on the surface of the eye itself, as a contact lens.

WHAT ARE LASERS?

The word *laser* stands for Light Amplification by the Stimulated Emission of Radiation. Laser light has very focused beams that give it power and precision. Lasers are used for delicate medical and industrial cutting operations, to read barcodes and to make holograms.

WHAT IS GEOTROPISM?

Many seeds germinate in the dark, underground. Yet when shoots first appear, they at once start to grow towards the light. This behaviour is known as geotropism.

WHAT IS FLUORESCENCE?

Some substances absorb non-visible electromagnetic energy, such as UV rays, and then release it as bright, visible light. They are said to be fluorescent. Modern washing powders contain fluorescents to make washed clothes look whiter and brighter.

WHAT IS THE BLIND SPOT?

THE BACK of the eye is very sensitive, but at one point the optic nerve leads to the brain. If the image falls on this point, called the blind spot, it cannot be seen. The blind spot is particularly important for drivers, as there is a point behind them on either side where their vision can be misleading as they check for vehicles behind before overtaking.

WHAT ARE THE COLOURS OF THE SPECTRUM?

Although light appears to be white or colourless, in fact it is made up of all the colours of the spectrum. Each colour has a different wavelength. The colours can be seen if a beam of light is split by a prism. The prism refracts each of the wavelengths differently and so splits them into a visible band of colours. Although the colours merge together so that it is hard to see them separately, there are seven of them: red, orange, yellow, green, blue, indigo and violet.

In nature, the colours of the spectrum can sometimes be seen as a rainbow. Drops of rain in the air have acted as prisms to split the light into its seven colours. One way to remember the order of the colours is to memorize the sentence, "Richard Of York Gave Battle In Vain."

WHAT HAPPENS WHEN COLOURED LIGHTS ARE MIXED?

WE ARE USED to thinking of red, yellow and blue as the three primary colours. Paints of these colours can be mixed to create the other colours of the spectrum. But coloured lights work in a different way. The primary colours of light are red, green and blue. When lights are mixed in pairs, they create the secondary colours of magenta, cyan and yellow. When all three colours are mixed together in equal amounts, white light is the result.

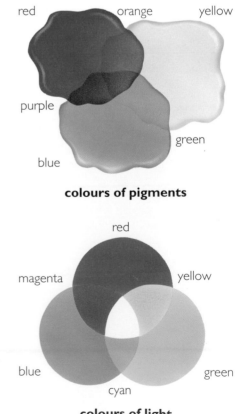

colours of pigments

colours of light

HOW CAN COLOURS FOOL THE EYE?

OPTICAL ILLUSIONS are often said to fool the eye, but it is the brain, which interprets the information that our eyes take in, that is really fooled. Our brains are working hard all the time to make sense of the world we see. They have so much information to process, coming in from all our senses, that they take short cuts, working on patterns they have met before. Sometimes those patterns do not make sense of a new situation.

Even in black and white, our brains can be confused. This picture can be seen as two faces or as a vase but not as both at once. The information being given to the brain is the same in either case.

The red squares in the middle of the coloured squares are the same size each time, but some colours appear more prominently to our brains, so some squares seem to be bigger than others.

WHY WERE THE COLOURS OF THE OLYMPIC RINGS CHOSEN?

THERE ARE five Olympic rings, to represent the five continents of the world. The colours – blue, black, red, yellow, green – were chosen because every national flag in the world includes at least one of these colours.

HOW DO COLOURS WORK AS CODES?

AS WE TAKE IN the huge amounts of information around us, different colours take on various meanings. They work as a kind of code. For example, everyone knows without thinking about it that red means "stop" and green means "go" at a traffic light. Seeing the colour is much quicker than reading or hearing the word. Similarly, certain colours become associated with certain products. When you go out to buy a can of drink, you probably do not have to *read* the label. You simply look for a certain combination of colours on the can.

HOW CAN MIXED COLOURS BE SEPARATED?

WHEN COLOURS are mixed together to form a coloured ink, it seems impossible to separate them, but chromatography is a method that may work. If a drop of ink is placed in the middle of a piece of filter paper and then some water is dropped on top of it, some of the dyes in the ink will travel across the paper more easily than others, resulting in rings of different colours spreading out from the centre. This method is also used by scientists to test whether chemicals are pure.

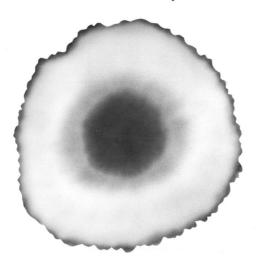

WHAT IS A COLOUR WHEEL?

GARDEN AND INTERIOR DESIGNERS sometimes make use of a colour wheel. This helps them to choose colours that are in harmony with each other when that is appropriate. When a more striking effect is required, colours that contrast can be chosen. One half of the wheel has colours that give a warm feeling, while the other half has cooler hues.

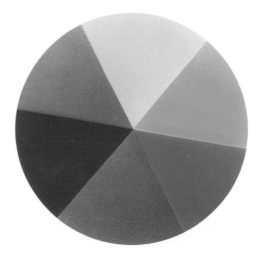

Colours opposite each other on the colour wheel generally contrast, while colours next to each other harmonize.

fast facts

WHAT IS COLOUR BLINDNESS?

Some people cannot distinguish easily between red and green. This type of "colour blindness" is more common in boys than in girls. About one out of every fifteen boys is affected but only one out of a thousand girls.

WHAT IS POINTILLISM?

Pointillism is a painting technique, used most famously by the Impressionist painter Georges Seurat, which uses tiny dots of pure colour to build up images. Viewed from a distance, these seem to blend together to produce a wide range of colours and tones.

WHAT IS SEPIA?

Sepia is a reddish-brown pigment (colour) made from the black, inky fluid secreted by cuttlefish. It was used for drawings and watercolour painting before artificial pigments were created. Giving a photograph a sepia tint is still a way of making it look instantly older.

HOW CAN PIGMENTS REVEAL FORGERIES?

Pigments for painting once came only from natural sources, such as the earth, plants and rocks. Many modern pigments are made by chemical processes. By analyzing the paint on a canvas, scientists can tell whether it could have been painted at the date claimed for it. Forgers rarely take the trouble to use original pigments.

HOW DO WE SEE COLOURS?

On the retina of the human eye are about seven million cells, shaped like cones, that help us to see colour. There are three different kinds of cone. Each can respond to one of the primary colours: red, green and blue.

CAN SOUNDS BE HEARD IN SPACE?

Like light, sound travels in waves, but while light can travel through a vacuum, sound cannot. Sound energy moves through vibration. Part of the instrument making the noise vibrates (moves backwards and forwards very quickly). This in turn pushes against the air, causing the air molecules to collide, transferring the sound energy from molecule to molecule away from its source, until it reaches our ears. Sound does not only travel through air molecules. It can also cause the molecules of other gases, liquids and even solids to vibrate. But space is silent. There are no molecules for the sound waves to vibrate.

WHAT IS SONAR?

SONAR uses ultrasonic sounds to find out where and how far away something is. This is called echo-location. The sounds are transmitted and bounced back by the object. The time that passes between the transmission and the reception of the reflected sound tells how far away the object is. Sonar is used particularly at sea to establish the depth of water beneath a boat.

Dolphins use ultrasound for echo-location to find food and avoid predators. They also communicate with each other using ultrasonic frequencies.

HOW IS SOUND MEASURED?

SOUNDS travel as waves. It is the shape of the wave that determines the kind of sound that is produced. The pitch of a sound (whether it is high or low) depends on the frequency of the sound waves. The frequency is how many waves, or vibrations, the sound makes in one second. This is measured in hertz (Hz). One vibration per second is one hertz. How loud the sound is depends on the magnitude (or height) of its waves. The more energy the waves carry, the louder the sound. Loudness is measured in decibels (dB).

As sounds push air molecules together, air pressure rises. Between vibrations, air pressure falls. It is this change in air pressure that can be shown as waves on a screen when sounds are made near a microphone.

WHAT IS MUSICAL NOTATION?

MUSICAL NOTATION is a way of writing down musical sounds so that a singer or instrumentalist can reproduce them as the composer intends. As well as showing the pitch and length of the sounds, the notation gives information about how the notes should be played.

This is a treble clef. It shows the pitch of the notes on this stave (five lines).

This is a key signature. It shows whether certain notes should be flattened or sharpened throughout the music.

A quaver is half a beat long.

The bar line divides the music into bars.

This is a time signature. It shows that there are three beats of music in each bar (small section).

A crotchet is one beat long.

pp

This is short for the Italian word *pianissimo*. It shows that the music should be played very quietly.

A minim is two beats long.

The higher on the stave a note is, the higher its pitch. The first two notes are an octave apart. The upper note has twice the frequency of the lower note.

WHAT IS A SONIC BOOM?

SOME AIRCRAFT can travel faster than the speed of sound. They travel ahead of the sounds they make. This produces a build-up of sound energy behind them that becomes a shock wave, heard as a sonic boom.

Aircraft travelling faster than the speed of sound are said to be moving at supersonic speeds. The speed of sound is described as Mach 1. Concorde, which can travel at twice the speed of sound, reaches Mach 2.

WHAT ARE HARMONICS?

MOST SOUNDS are not pure sounds of a single wavelength and frequency. Other frequencies are mixed in with the sound, creating the particular texture and tone of an individual voice or instrument. These frequencies are called harmonics.

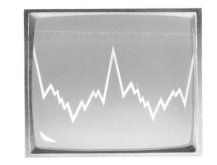

Complex sounds produce distinctive sound waves when viewed on a screen. These are so individual that a person's voice can be recognized from the wave patterns it makes. Voice-recognition systems use this fact to ensure that only certain people have access to buildings or computer files.

WHAT ARE THE INSTRUMENTS OF AN ORCHESTRA?

AN ORCHESTRA has instruments that produce sounds in different ways, but all cause air to vibrate to carry the sound to listening ears. String instruments have vibrating strings that are bowed or plucked. Wind instruments cause a column of air to vibrate when the player blows into them. Instruments that create sounds by being struck or shaken are percussion instruments. Brass instruments resonate when air is blown into them.

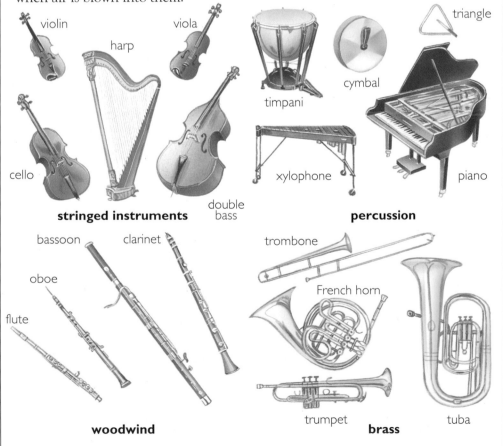

violin
viola
harp
triangle
cymbal
timpani
cello
xylophone
piano
double bass
stringed instruments
percussion
bassoon
clarinet
trombone
oboe
French horn
flute
trumpet
tuba
woodwind
brass

CAN SOMETHING BE HOT AND COLD AT THE SAME TIME?

When we describe an object as hot, we are really comparing it with something else. The word does not mean anything by itself. We can say that we feel hot after exercise, that a cup of coffee is hot, and that the surface of the Sun is hot, but we mean something quite different each time.
An object can be hot compared with an ice cube but cold compared with boiling water. In fact, both the ice cube and the boiling water contain heat energy, but their temperatures are quite different. Temperature is a measure of how hot something is compared with an agreed scale. A small object with a temperature of 100°C may not have as much heat energy as a very large object with a temperature of 0°C.

WHAT IS CONVECTION?

HEAT ENERGY is always on the move. It flows from a hotter object towards a cooler one until both are the same temperature. In liquids and gases, heat energy usually moves by convection. This means that the molecules nearest to the heat source begin to move more rapidly and spread apart, so that this area of the fluid is less dense. As the less dense part of the liquid or gas rises, denser parts sink to take its place.

The upwardly moving currents of warmed liquid or gas are known as convection currents. In the air, convection currents are called thermals. Birds (and even gliders containing passengers) are able to rise with them.

HOW DOES CONDUCTION WORK?

IN SOLIDS, heated particles also begin to vibrate in their positions, but while the substance remains solid, they cannot move upwards. Instead, one moving particle bumps into the next and so transfers some energy. This continues until the heat energy is transferred throughout the solid. If enough heat energy is transferred to the solid, the particles move so rapidly that they break free from each other and the substance melts to become a liquid.

Solids through which heat passes easily are said to be good conductors. Metals, such as copper, conduct heat quickly and evenly, which is one reason why cooking pans are often made from them.

WHAT KIND OF HEAT ENERGY IS RADIATION?

RADIATION is a means of transferring heat that does not cause particles to vibrate. Instead, it travels in waves, called infra-red rays. Infra-red radiation has a longer wavelength than light but travels at the same speed. Unlike other methods of heat transfer, radiation can work in a vacuum.

The Sun's heat travels through space by radiation. Ice reflects radiation, which is one reason why the temperature at the Poles is always low.

HOW DOES A THERMOSTAT WORK?

THERMOSTATS are devices that switch an appliance on and off when certain temperatures are reached. They work on the principle that some materials conduct heat better than others. A strip made of two metals, such as copper and iron, is connected to an electrical circuit. As the strip is warmed, the molecules in the upper metal vibrate more strongly than those in the lower one. The upper metal expands and bends, pulling the lower metal up and breaking the circuit. No more heat is transferred until the metal cools and drops back into position, completing the circuit again.

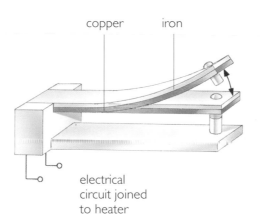

copper   iron

electrical circuit joined to heater

A scale on the glass tube shows the temperature in degrees Centigrade or Fahrenheit.

As it warms, the liquid inside the glass tube rises.

A narrow part near the base of the column of liquid stops the liquid from flowing back into the bulb before the temperature can be read. That is why thermometers are shaken before use to return all the liquid to its lowest point.

HOW IS HEAT ENERGY MEASURED?

HEAT ENERGY, like other forms of energy, is measured in joules (J). Temperature is measured in degrees Fahrenheit (°F), Celsius (°C) or Kelvin (K). In Fahrenheit, water freezes at 32° and boils at 212°. The Celsius scale is based on the boiling and freezing points of water, so these are 100°C and 0°C respectively. Kelvin units are the same as Celsius degrees but they start from the lowest temperature possible. On this scale, water freezes at 273K.

HOW DOES A THERMOMETER WORK?

AS SUBSTANCES get hotter, their molecules move around more rapidly and they may take up more space. A thermometer contains a liquid that expands as it gains heat energy. This causes the level of the liquid to rise in a narrow tube. A scale beside the tube allows the temperature to be read.

fast facts

WHAT IS THE NORMAL TEMPERATURE OF THE HUMAN BODY?

The normal temperature of the human body is around 37°C (98.6°F). When a thermometer shows a higher figure, we say that someone "has a temperature", but in fact they have one all the time!

WHY DO LIGHT-COLOURED CLOTHES KEEP US COOLER?

Light-coloured clothes reflect heat radiation, while dark-coloured ones absorb it. That is why houses in hot countries are often painted white, so that they remain cooler inside.

WHICH IS THE HOTTEST PLANET?

Venus has the highest surface temperature of any planet in our Solar System. Its average temperature is 465°C (839°F).

WHAT IS LATENT HEAT?

Heat flows from a warmer to a cooler substance, but materials cannot continue to absorb heat indefinitely. At some point the heat energy no longer increases the temperature of the material but changes its state from solid to liquid or from liquid to gas. The heat energy held in the liquid or gas is called latent heat. If the substance cools and turns back into a solid or liquid, the latent heat is given off into the surroundings.

HOW DO FIREFIGHTERS PROTECT THEMSELVES FROM HEAT?

FIREFIGHTERS need to wear clothing that is both fire retardant (slow to catch on fire) and offers good insulation (does not conduct heat easily). Fireproof clothing often has a shiny surface, because this helps to reflect the radiated heat away from the body.

ARE HUMAN BEINGS THE ONLY ANIMALS TO USE TOOLS?

The simplest tools often act as extensions of parts of the body. For example, if your arms are too short to reach a ball that has fallen into a pond, you may use a stick to lengthen your reach. The stick is a tool. Many non-human animals use simple tools: chimpanzees use sticks to scoop ants from their mounds; thrushes drop snails' shells onto a flat stone or "anvil" to crush them; some vultures drop stones onto other birds' eggs to break the shells. Tools, used by humans or other animals, help to make work easier to do.

Lifting your body to the top of the slide would be difficult if you had to go straight upwards. The steps are a kind of slope, making it easier to reach the top.

It would be hard work for one child to lift another into the air over and over again. A see-saw makes it easy because it is a kind of lever.

This cart and bricks would be much too heavy for a small child to lift and carry. Wheels make it possible for a small force to move them long distances.

A bicycle has gears that change the amount of force needed to turn the pedals.

IN SCIENTIFIC TERMS, WHAT IS WORK?

TO A SCIENTIST, work is done when a force causes something to move. The unit of measurement used for work is the joule. A joule of work is done when a force of one newton moves something one metre (3.3 feet). The force needed to lift a small apple is about one newton.

WHAT ARE SIMPLE MACHINES?

LEVERS, wedges, slopes, screws, wheels, gears and pulleys are all known as simple machines. They make work easier by enabling a small force to move a large load. Machines may magnify (increase) a force or a movement.

HOW CAN A SLOPE MAKE WORK EASIER?

A SLOPE, or inclined plane, makes work easier because the force needed to move a load is spread out over a longer distance. The amount of work needed to move an object from one point to another does not change, but as the distance is lengthened, less force is needed.

Steps are a form of inclined plane. The shallower the steps, the further you have to travel, and the easier the climb is.

HOW CAN THE PRINCIPLE OF THE SCREW BE USED?

A SCREW is really an inclined plane wrapped around a cone or cylinder. It works on the opposite principle to a staircase. This time, by lengthening the distance travelled in the circular motion of the screw, the forward force (as the screw moves into the wood or metal) is magnified.

fast facts

WHEN WAS THE WHEEL INVENTED?

The wheel was probably invented around 3300BC by the Mesopotamians. However, free-rolling logs, the forerunners of wheels, were probably used in many parts of the world long before that.

HOW IS WORK CALCULATED?

Work done (J) = force (N) x distance moved in the direction of the force (m).

WHAT IS ARCHIMEDES' SCREW?

Archimedes' screw is a device that uses the principle of the screw to lift water from a lower level to a higher one. The screw is inside a tube. With each turn, water trapped between the thread of the screw and the side of the tube is raised up the tube.

WHAT IS A GEAR?

A gear is a toothed wheel. Its teeth can fit into the teeth of another gear, so that when one turns, the other turns also. By using combinations of gears, engineers can change the magnitude or direction of a force. This technique is often used to slow or speed up machines. For example, a large gear, turning slowly, will make a smaller gear turn more quickly.

HOW DO LEVERS WORK?

THERE are three different kinds of lever, depending on where the force applied and the load are in relation to each other. A lever is a rod that can turn on a pivot, or fulcrum.

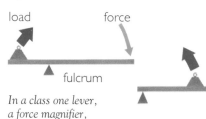

load   force

fulcrum

In a class one lever, a force magnifier, the fulcrum is between the force and the load. A crowbar is an example of such a lever.

In a class two lever, also a force magnifier, the load is between the effort and the fulcrum. Nutcrackers are class two levers.

A class three lever is a distance magnifier. It has the force between the fulcrum and the load. Tweezers are class three levers.

The further from the fulcrum the force is applied, the larger the load that can be moved, which is why a crowbar has a long handle.

WHY IS THE WHEEL SO USEFUL?

STRICTLY SPEAKING, a wheel on its own is not very useful, but a wheel on an axle is the basis of a huge number of machines. A wheel can be used to magnify a force. A steering wheel, for example, has a force applied to the outer edge, which moves a much longer distance than the centre (axle). The axle moves a much shorter distance and therefore exerts a greater force. When a force is applied to the axle, a wheel can be used to magnify distance, which is what happens in wheeled vehicles. A force applied to the axle moves a much greater distance at the outer edge of the wheels. Finally, a wheel can be used to change the direction of a force. Wheels convert the circular motion of the axle into the forward motion of the vehicle.

HOW CAN WHEELS HELP LIFT HEAVY LOADS?

PULLEYS are wheels with grooves through which a rope can run. It is much easier to pull something down than to lift it up, as you can use your body weight to help. A pulley enables a downward force to be converted into an upward force. Lifts often use this principle by employing a counterweight. The dropping *down* of the lift causes the counterweight to *rise*. Then the dropping of the counterweight helps the lift to go up again.

WHAT IS AN ELECTRONIC CIRCUIT?

An electronic circuit is made up of a number of components linked together to form a circuit through which electricity flows. Components are devices that have different jobs within the circuit. They may be fixed in position on a circuit board. Electronic components can be made so tiny that thousands of them will fit into a chip a fraction of the size of a postage stamp.

On a circuit board, individual components are held in position by soldering. The wiring that connects them runs along the underside of the board.

WHAT ARE THE MOST COMMONLY USED ELECTRONIC COMPONENTS?

ELECTRONIC COMPONENTS affect the way that current flows around a circuit. Four of the most commonly used are capacitors, diodes, resistors and transistors.

Capacitors are tiny storage devices. They can store electrical energy and release it when it is needed.

Diodes are components that allow electrical current to flow through them in only one direction. Some of them can give off light when a current passes through them.

Resistors can control the amount of current flowing through a circuit. An LDR (Light-Dependent Resistor) will increase resistance (decrease the current) in a circuit as available light increases. A thermistor is a variable resistor that is sensitive to temperature.

WHAT IS A SILICON CHIP?

A SILICON CHIP is also known as an integrated circuit. It is a complete circuit, perhaps containing thousands of electronic components, that is printed on a thin wafer of an element called silicon. The chip is protected by a covering called a capsule, which is the part we normally see. Little metal feet allow the chip to be connected to other chips and components.

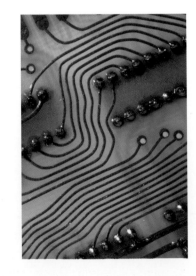

HOW ARE INTEGRATED CIRCUITS CONNECTED?

SILICON CHIPS are too small to be connected by ordinary wire, however fine it is. Instead, minute "tracks" of a conducting material such as copper are printed on the circuit board to link the silicon chips.

WHY DO ELECTRONIC CIRCUITS USE BINARY CODE?

ALTHOUGH APPLIANCES containing electronic circuits can perform very complicated tasks and even appear to think for themselves, they are operated entirely by electrical current. This cannot "think" but it can be turned on or off, increased or decreased, or caused to change direction by electronic components. The activity in any one part of a circuit depends on whether electrical current is detected or not. This can be represented by a 1 if a current is detected or a 0 if it is not. Binary code uses only the digits 0 and 1, so it enables an electronic device to perform calculations.

HOW DOES AN ELECTRONIC CALCULATOR WORK?

AN ELECTRONIC CALCULATOR has many integrated circuits inside, capable of making complicated calculations. The key pad sends signals through the circuits. The display shows the digits as they are keyed in and gives the answer when the calculation is finished. Keys marked with an M cause circuits to memorize certain numbers so that they can be reintroduced later in the calculation. As there is a key for entering the decimal point, the calculator can deal with both very small and very large numbers.

WHAT IS A LOGIC GATE?

LOGIC GATES are combinations of resistors that make it possible for an electronic circuit to carry out calculations. Different kinds of gates affect the output of electrical current, depending on the input. Most logic gates have two input points and one output point.

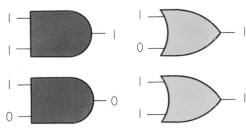

An AND gate gives an electrical signal only if it receives a signal at both input points.

An OR gate gives an electrical signal if either or both input points receive a signal.

A NOT gate gives an electrical signal if the input point does NOT receive a signal. If the inpoint point does receive a signal, there is no output. The effect of this is always to reverse the signal.

WHAT IS A LIQUID CRYSTAL DISPLAY?

MANY ELECTRONIC DEVICES nowadays have liquid crystal displays. Watches, music centres, calculators and even cars give information by means of liquid crystals. These are crystals, held inside cells, that become opaque or change colour when they are heated. The circuits behind the display pass a voltage across the crystals, so that some of them change while the others remain the same. In this way, numbers, letters and symbols can be displayed.

The cells are often straight lines arranged as a figure eight. Individual cells can be coloured to form a variety of numbers, letters and symbols.

WHERE IS SILICON VALLEY?

Silicon Valley is an area south of San Francisco, California, in the United States, where there are many companies concerned with electronics and computers.

WHAT IS THE BIGGEST ADVANTAGE OF THE SILICON CHIP?

By far the biggest advantage of the silicon chip is its size. Even very small devices can now be "smart", containing thousands of electronic circuits to enable them to perform complicated tasks or do several jobs at once. However, scientists are working on even smaller chips, which would enable almost all everyday objects, such as your clothing, to contain electronic components.

WHAT IS AN LED?

An LED is a Light-Emitting Diode. It does not use a bulb, so rarely fails and may be used, for example, in the light that shows whether an electrical device is switched on.

WHAT IS THE DIFFERENCE BETWEEN DIGITAL AND ANALOGUE SIGNALS?

Analogue signals, like sound waves, flow in a continuous wave. Digital signals contain the same information but are broken up into pulses, which can be expressed in binary code and are therefore in a form that electronic circuits can use.

WHAT IS A SEMICONDUCTOR?

Semiconductors are materials that conduct electricity more or less well, depending on certain outside conditions. In silicon chips, they are made by adding other chemicals to very thin layers of silicon.

HOW CAN TIME BE MEASURED?

Our experience of time is that it flows forwards. It cannot be stopped or reversed but goes on in a continuous stream. We can only measure time in relation to other things that have a regular pattern: the rising of the Sun, the swinging of a pendulum or the vibration of a crystal.

WHAT IS A DAY?

A DAY is the time that it takes for the Earth to turn once around its axis, or one day and one night. It is probably the earliest measurement of time used, although early people had no idea that the Earth was turning. They assumed that the Sun was moving, because it appeared to rise above the horizon each morning and disappear behind the opposite horizon at night.

The Earth orbits the Sun once every 365.24 days. This is one year.

The Moon circles the Earth once every 27.3 days.

The Earth takes 24 hours to turn on its axis. This is one day.

WHAT IS THE DIFFERENCE BETWEEN A LUNAR AND A CALENDAR MONTH?

AFTER THE DAY, the next measurement of time that early people used was probably the month. They noticed that the Moon changed shape on a regular cycle, with 28 days passing from one full Moon to the next. In fact, the true figure is about 29.5 days. This is a lunar month. The phases of the Moon do not divide exactly into the 365 or 366 days in a year, so over time the months that we use today, known as calendar months, came to have slightly different lengths. April, June, September and November have 30 days each. All the other months have 31 days, except February, which has 28 days, or 29 in a leap year.

WHY DO WE HAVE LEAP YEARS?

THE YEAR is not an exact number of days but about 365 and one quarter days. By adding an extra day into the calendar every four years, we ensure that the year does not gradually become out of step with the seasons.

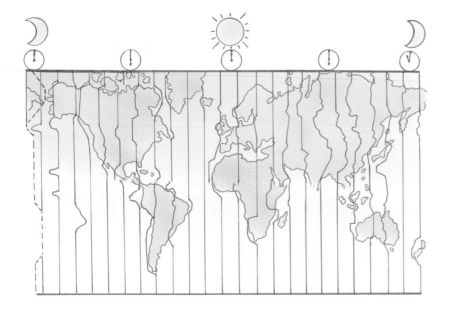

WHAT ARE TIME ZONES?

AS THE EARTH SPINS, different parts of it face the Sun. Therefore, it cannot be the same time all over the world at the same moment. When it is the middle of the night in one country, it is dawn in another part of the world. To keep expressions of time consistent in every part of the world, the Earth is divided into 24 time zones, each one exactly an hour apart.

WHAT IS GREENWICH MEAN TIME?

GREENWICH MEAN TIME is the local time at the Greenwich Observatory in London, England. The line of 0° longitude, along which the Sun passes overhead exactly at noon, runs through the Observatory. Greenwich Mean Time (GMT, also known as Universal Time, or UT) is used as a standard time all over the world.

WHAT WERE THE FIRST CLOCKS LIKE?

IT WAS probably the Babylonians who first divided the day into 24 hours, with 60 minutes in each hour. These are numbers that can easily be divided by 2, 3 and 4. The very first clocks, like the first calendars, were based on the Sun, using the movements of its shadow to read the time from a marked area of Earth or stone. Later methods of time measurement were based on actions that happened at a fixed rate, such as the pull of gravity on grains of sand.

Prehistoric standing stones may have been used as clocks or calendars.

Water clocks measured either the water that had dripped from a container, or the water left inside, to tell the time.

Hourglasses were used from the early middle ages. Sand drained from one bulb to the other in a few minutes or as much as two hours.

Candle clocks were used in the ninth century but were not very accurate as a draught could cause the candle to burn more quickly.

DOES THE WHOLE WORLD USE THE GREGORIAN CALENDAR?

FOR INTERNATIONAL COMMUNICATIONS, the whole world does use the Gregorian calendar, but other religious and traditional calendars are still in use around the world. The Jewish calendar has a year that varies between 353 and 385 days. The Muslim calendar has 354 or 355 days in a year.

fast facts

WHAT DID CHRISTIAAN HUYGENS INVENT?

Christiaan Huygens, a Dutch physicist, invented the first pendulum clock in the middle of the seventeenth century.

WHY WAS 46BC KNOWN AS "THE YEAR OF CONFUSION"?

Julius Caesar was the first person to try to take account of the fact that the year is slightly longer than 365 days. He instituted the Julian calendar in 46BC, but because the lack of leap years in previous years had made the year and seasons out of step, he decreed that the first year of the new calendar should have 445 days. The difficulties this caused resulted in the nickname "the year of confusion".

WHAT HAPPENED ON 5 OCTOBER 1582?

On 4 October 1582, Pope Gregory XIII introduced the Gregorian calendar, which was the most accurate yet and is still in use today. Like Julius Caesar before him, he needed to make an adjustment, so he declared that 4 October would be followed by 15 October. Therefore, strictly speaking, nothing at all happened on 5 October 1582.

WHY ARE THE 1900s KNOWN AS THE TWENTIETH CENTURY?

Our calendar is measured from an early estimate of the date of the birth of Christ. The next hundred years after this are called the first century. That means that the next century, with years beginning with the digit 1, is the second century, and so on.

WHAT ARE DECIMAL NUMBERS?

> *Decimal numbers use 10 digits, which are combined to make numbers of any size. The position of the digit determines what it means in any number. For example, the 2 in the number 200 is ten times the size of the 2 in the number 20. Each position of a number gives a value ten times higher than the position to its right. So 9867 means 7 units, plus 6 x 10, plus 8 x 10 x 10, plus 9 x 10 x 10 x 10. As decimal numbers are based on the number 10, we say that this is a base-10 number system.*

HOW ARE ROMAN NUMERALS USED?

THE ROMANS had a number system with a base of 10, as we do, but they used different numerals to write it down. For the numbers one to nine, instead of using nine different numerals, they used only three different letters, combining them to make the numbers. This made it very difficult for them to do even simple calculations, so their advances in mathematics and related fields were not as great as might have been expected from such a far-reaching civilization.

I	1	XX	20
II	2	L	50
III	3	C	100
IV	4	M	1000
V	5		
VI	6		
VII	7		
VIII	8		
IX	9		
X	10		

Roman numerals are still used for certain purposes. They appear on watch and clock faces (usually with IIII instead of IV for 4) and when numbers have a certain importance, such as in the title of a monarch.

WHAT IS THE BINARY SYSTEM?

THE BINARY SYSTEM is another way of counting. Instead of being a base-10 system, it is a base-2 system, using only two digits: 0 and 1. Again, the position of a digit gives it a particular value. 1010101 means 1 unit, plus 0 x 2, plus 1 x 2 x 2, plus 0 x 2 x 2 x 2, plus 1 x 2 x 2 x 2 x 2, plus 0 x 2 x 2 x 2 x 2 x 2, plus 1 x 2 x 2 x 2 x 2 x 2 x 2. 1010101 is the same as 85 in decimal numbers.

WHAT IS AN ABACUS?

AN ABACUS is a frame of beads used in China and neighbouring countries for making calculations. A skilled abacus user can produce answers to some calculations almost as quickly as someone using an electronic calculator.

64	32	16	8	4	2	1	
						1	= 1
					1	0	= 2
				1	0	1	= 5
			1	0	1	0	= 10
		1	0	0	0	1	= 17
1	0	1	0	1	0	1	= 85

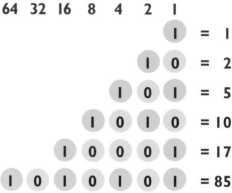

An abacus usually has wires or bamboo rods with five beads at the bottom and two beads at the top.

WHAT IS GEOMETRY?

GEOMETRY is the branch of mathematics that is concerned with points, lines, surfaces and solids, and their relation to each other. Shapes, both flat and three-dimensional, are an important part of geometry. When we describe something as geometric, we mean that it has a regular, often angular pattern of lines or shapes.

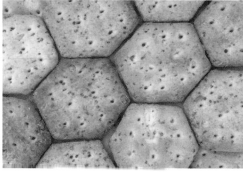

One branch of geometry is concerned with tesselation, which means covering a surface by repeated use of a single shape. This has many applications in construction and industry. These hexagonal biscuits, for example, can be cut from dough with no wastage at all.

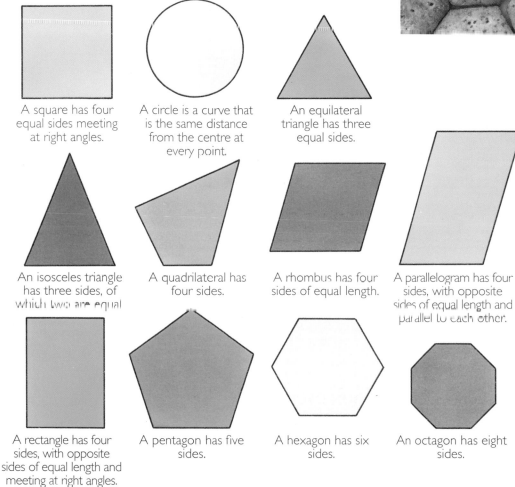

A square has four equal sides meeting at right angles.

A circle is a curve that is the same distance from the centre at every point.

An equilateral triangle has three equal sides.

An isosceles triangle has three sides, of which two are equal.

A quadrilateral has four sides.

A rhombus has four sides of equal length.

A parallelogram has four sides, with opposite sides of equal length and parallel to each other.

A rectangle has four sides, with opposite sides of equal length and meeting at right angles.

A pentagon has five sides.

A hexagon has six sides.

An octagon has eight sides.

WHAT ARE MATHEMATICAL FORMULAE?

MATHEMATICAL FORMULAE are useful rules expressed using symbols or letters. The formulae below show the volume of various three-dimensional shapes. $\pi = 3.142$

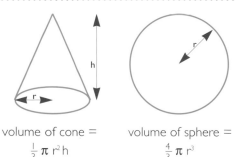

volume of cone = $\frac{1}{3}\pi r^2 h$

volume of sphere = $\frac{4}{3}\pi r^3$

volume of pyramid = $\frac{1}{3}h \times$ base area

WHO WAS PYTHAGORAS?

PYTHAGORAS was a Greek living in the sixth century BC. He was a mathematician and scientist who is now best remembered for Pythagoras' Theorem, a formula for calculating the length of one side of a right-angled triangle if the other sides are known. However, this theorem was, in fact, already known hundreds of years earlier by Egyptian and Babylonian mathematicians.

$a^2 + b^2 = c^2$ or
$(a \times a) + (b \times b) = (c \times c)$

fast facts

WHAT IS ALGEBRA?

Algebra is a branch of mathematics in which letters or symbols are used in place of numbers. At its simplest level, this means that if we know that there are 40 boys in a group of 100 children, we can say that g stands for the girls in the group and

$$40 + g = 100 \quad \text{or}$$
$$g = 100 - 40 \quad \text{so}$$
$$g = 60$$

WHAT IS THE LARGEST POSSIBLE NUMBER?

There is no such thing as the largest possible number. No matter how big a number you think of, someone else can simply add one to it to make a bigger number.

WHAT IS A PLANE FIGURE?

A plane figure is a flat shape, with only two dimensions, like the geometric shapes above.

WHAT IS A PRIME NUMBER?

Prime numbers are those that can only be divided by themselves and 1. For example, 23 is a prime number, as it can only be divided by 23 and 1. However, 24 can be divided by 1, 2, 3, 4, 6, 8, 12 and 24.

WHAT IS A POLYHEDRON?

A polyhedron is a three-dimensional figure with flat (plane) faces, such as a pyramid.

WHAT IS ALCOHOL?

Alcohol is an organic compound. That means that it is one of the substances studied in a whole branch of chemistry called organic chemistry. Organic chemistry concerns carbon compounds, many of which are made by living (organic) things. Alcohol is a compound of carbon, oxygen and hydrogen. There are many kinds of alcohol, with different properties and uses in industry. Ethanol and glycerol are both useful forms of alcohol.

HOW DOES FERMENTATION PRODUCE ALCOHOL?

FERMENTATION is a natural process that uses a kind of fungus called yeast. When given the right conditions of warmth and moisture, yeast will digest sugars in fruit or other plant materials and give off carbon dioxide gas and alcohol. Fermentation is used on a huge scale to make alcoholic drinks and ethanol for use in industry.

HOW WAS ALCOHOL DISCOVERED?

IT IS LIKELY that the effects of alcohol were discovered before the chemical! Grapes may have a natural yeast on their skins that will cause the fruits or juice squeezed from them to ferment in warm conditions without the addition of further yeast. Early peoples may have discovered that fermented grape juice had an unusual flavour and effect on the body.

WHAT IS THE CARBON CYCLE?

CARBON is an essential element in all living things. It is constantly being recycled on Earth in the carbon cycle shown below.

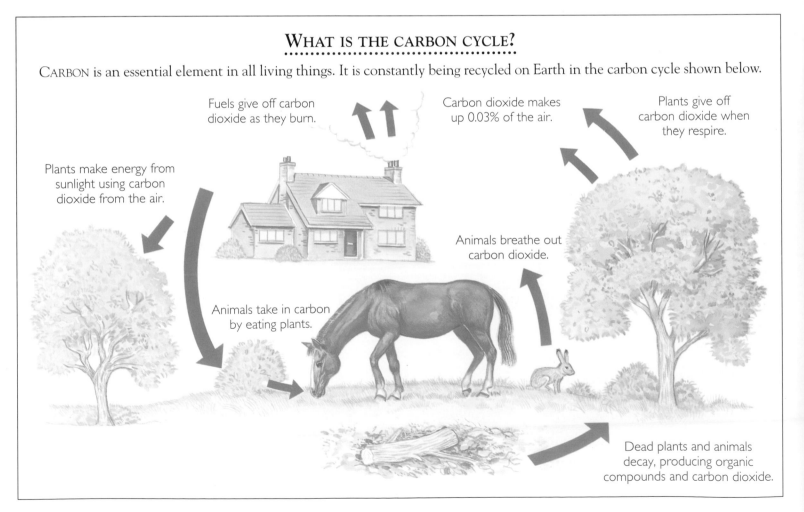

Fuels give off carbon dioxide as they burn.

Carbon dioxide makes up 0.03% of the air.

Plants give off carbon dioxide when they respire.

Plants make energy from sunlight using carbon dioxide from the air.

Animals breathe out carbon dioxide.

Animals take in carbon by eating plants.

Dead plants and animals decay, producing organic compounds and carbon dioxide.

WHAT ARE CARBOXYLIC ACIDS?

CARBOXYLIC ACIDS contain carbon, oxygen and hydrogen. Many naturally occurring acids are carboxylic acids, such as the acid that causes nettles to "sting" and the acid in vinegar. This is called ethanoic acid. It is created when alcohol reacts with oxygen (oxidizes).

Some carboxylic acids are found in fats and oils from animals and plants. They are called fatty acids. When they react with alcohol, they create compounds called esters, which give flowers their scent. Some expensive perfumes are still made by distilling the scent from flowers and preserving it in alcohol.

WHAT IS A HOMOLOGOUS SERIES?

A HOMOLOGOUS SERIES is a group of compounds that are made of the same elements and share some of the same properties and features but have different numbers of atoms in their molecules. Alkanes, alkenes and alcohols all form homologous series.

Cosmetics contain many organic compounds. Solvents dissolve other ingredients to produce a liquid consistency. Pigments give the cosmetics a wide range of colours. Oils give a smooth texture that is resistant to moisture.

Aniline is one of the many organic compounds that can be extracted from coal tar. It forms an important part of aniline dyes, which give very bright colours for textiles.

Plastics, made from organic compounds such as ethene, can be incredibly strong. The bodies of racing cars are made from plastic reinforced by fibres.

WHAT IS AN ALKANE?

An alkane is a compound of carbon and hydrogen (a hydrocarbon) in which the atoms are held together by single covalent bonds. Methane, propane and butane, gases used as fuels are examples of alkanes.

WHAT IS AN ALKENE?

An alkene is also a hydrocarbon but its atoms are held together by double covalent bonds. Alkenes are very reactive and can be used in industry to make many products, such as plastics, dyes and paints.

WHAT CAN WE TELL FROM THE NAMES OF ORGANIC CHEMICALS?

The names of some organic compounds tell us how many carbon atoms there are in their molecules. Compounds whose names begin with "meth" have one carbon atom. Molecules with two carbon atoms have names beginning with "eth", while three carbon atoms in a molecule are indicated by a name beginning with "prop".

WHY IS CARBON ABLE TO FORM SO MANY COMPOUNDS?

Carbon is extraordinary in that it can form over two million different organic compounds. This is because carbon atoms are able to bond with each other and with other atoms in single, double and triple covalent bonds, forming molecules in the shape of strings or rings.

WHAT IS A CHLOROFLUOROCARBON?

A chlorofluorocarbon, as its name suggests, is a compound of chlorine, fluorine and carbon. Chlorofluorocarbons were widely used in aerosols, but it was feared that they helped to destroy the ozone layer, so they are now avoided where possible.

WHY DO WE NEED ACCURATE MEASUREMENT?

For many purposes, an approximate idea of a length or weight or distance is fine. We may say that something is five-minutes' walk away, for example. That does not tell us how far it is – that would depend on how quickly a person walked – but it does give a rough idea that it is neither hundreds of kilometres nor just a few centimetres distant. However, if you need to know whether a new car would fit in your garage, you need a more accurate measurement, at least within a few centimetres. An Olympic highjumper, in fierce competition, will certainly need to measure to the nearest centimetre. And so it goes on, until scientists measuring the size of atoms need units of measurement much too small to be seen with the naked eye. The important thing is that units of measurement must be standard (agreed by everyone who uses them).

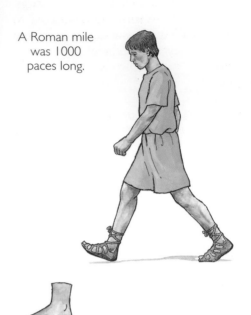

A Roman mile was 1000 paces long.

A foot was as long as ... a foot!

At one time, the timing of international athletics races was measured by an official with a stopwatch. Now winning margins of as little as one hundredth of a second are recorded by electronic timers.

WHAT WAS THE EARLIEST SYSTEM OF MEASUREMENT?

IT IS LIKELY that the first systems of measurement were based on the human body. As every person had a body, they could use themselves as reference! Of course, since people vary greatly in size, this was not a very accurate system.

From elbow to fingertips was one cubit.

The width of the hand was four fingers.

WHAT ARE SI UNITS?

SI UNITS are internationally agreed units for scientific measurements. SI stands for a French phrase: Système Internationale d'Unités (International System of Units). The base units are those used for the basic measurements that can be made, while derived units are those that need to be worked out using one or more base units. For example, a newton is the force needed to accelerate a mass of one kilogram by one metre per second.

BASE UNITS

Quantity	Unit	Abbreviation
distance	metre	m
mass	kilogram	k
time	second	s
electrical current	ampere	A
temperature	kelvin	K
amount of substance	mole	mol
luminous intensity	candela	cd

DERIVED UNITS

Quantity	Unit	Abbreviation
frequency	hertz	Hz
energy	joule	J
force	newton	N
power	watt	W
pressure	pascal	Pa
electrical charge	coulomb	C
electromotive force	volt	V
electrical resistance	ohm	Ω
electrical conductance	siemens	S
electrical capacitance	farad	F
magnetic flux	weber	Wb
inductance	henry	H
luminous flux	lumen	lm
illumination	lux	lx

HOW ARE LATITUDE AND LONGITUDE MEASURED?

IN ORDER to be able to pinpoint where we are on the Earth, we cover it with a grid of imaginary lines. Those running from North to South are called lines of longitude, while those running from East to West are called lines of latitude. These lines are measured in degrees. The line of longitude running through Greenwich, England is taken as 0° and lines on either side of it are so many degrees East or West. The line of latitude that is counted as 0° runs around the equator. Lines either side of it are said to be so many degrees North or South. Each degree is divided into sixty minutes (60').

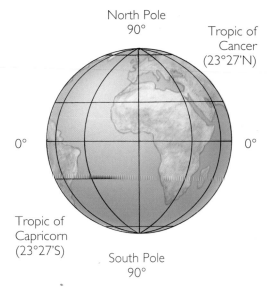

North Pole
90°

Tropic of
Cancer
(23°27'N)

0°   0°

Tropic of
Capricorn
(23°27'S)

South Pole
90°

HOW CAN STANDARD UNITS BE USED FOR VERY SMALL AND VERY LARGE MEASUREMENTS?

METRIC UNITS can be multiplied or divided by 10 as often as is needed to create units of a useful size for measuring the object under consideration. For example, a unit of 1000 metres, which is the same as 10 x 10 metres, and can be written as 10^2 metres, is called a kilometre. The prefix "kilo", meaning one thousand, can be applied to other units. A kilogram (kg) is equal to one thousand grams. Similarly, there is a prefix meaning one thousandth (10^{-3}): milli-. So one milligram is the same as a thousandth of a gram. On the right is a list of other prefixes and their meanings.

Prefix	Symbol or abbreviation	Factor
deca-	da	10
hecto-	h	10^2
kilo-	k	10^3
mega	M	10^6
giga-	G	10^9
tera-	T	10^{11}
peta-	P	10^{15}
exa-	E	10^{18}
deci-	d	10^{-1}
centi-	c	10^{-2}
milli-	m	10^{-3}
micro-	µ	10^{-6}
nano-	n	10^{-9}
pico-	p	10^{-12}
femto-	f	10^{-15}
atto-	a	10^{-18}

HOW ARE ANGLES MEASURED?

ANGLES are measured in degrees, using a protractor. There are 360° in a circle, and 90° in a right angle. A triangle has a total of 180° in its three inner angles, so that if the size of two angles is known, it is always possible to work out the third. Since pairs of inner and outer angles must add up to 360°, it is also possible to work out the inner angles if two of the outer angles are known.

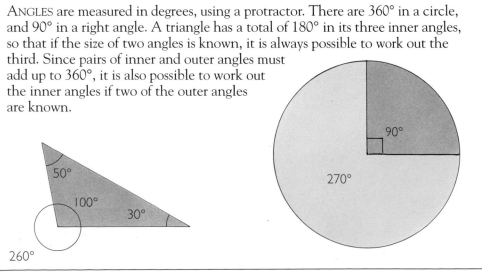

50°

100°

30°

260°

90°

270°

HOW LONG IS A METRE?

When the metre was first defined in 1791 by the French Academy of Sciences, it was expressed as the distance from the North Pole to the equator along a line passing through Paris, France, divided by 10,000,000,000.

HOW CAN CELSIUS BE CONVERTED INTO FAHRENHEIT TEMPERATURES?

To convert Celsius into Fahrenheit, multiply the degrees Celsius by 9, divide the answer by 5, and add 32. To convert Fahrenheit into Celsius, subtract 32 from the degrees Fahrenheit, multiply by 5, and divide by 9.

HOW ARE THE VAST DISTANCES OF SPACE MEASURED?

The distances in space are so huge that dealing with them in metres would result in numbers stretching right across this page. Instead, astronomers usually talk about a star being a certain number of light years away. Since light is the fastest thing in the universe, the distance it can travel in a year is enormous. In fact one light year is almost 100,000,000,000,000 kilometres.

WHAT IS THE PRIME MERIDIAN?

This is another way of referring to the line of longitude running through Greenwich, England.

WHAT IS TRIGONOMETRY?

Trigonometry is the measurement and calculation of angles, and their relationship to the lines that join them, especially in triangles.

WHAT IS A ROBOT?

A robot is a machine that can carry out a complicated series of actions automatically. Electronic circuits make it able to move, which may be controlled by radio signals from a distance. When we think of robots, we may think of machines shaped approximately like human beings, but robots can be any shape or size.

HOW ARE ROBOTS USED FOR DANGEROUS JOBS?

THERE ARE MANY SITUATIONS in which human beings can operate safely only by wearing bulky protective clothing and working for short periods at a time. Sometimes even that is not enough to protect them. If it is suspected that a booby-trapped bomb has been left in an abandoned vehicle, for example, a controlled explosion may be the only way of deactivating it. No matter how much protection a bomb disposal expert has, the explosion could be fatal if he or she is nearby. The answer is to use a robot carrying an explosive charge. The robot can be sent into the danger zone while experts remain at a safe distance. Although no one wants to destroy an expensive machine, the alternative is much worse.

In recent years, minefields have often caused dreadful injuries to civilians long after a war has ended. Clearing them is extremely dangerous. This is another area in which robotics can save lives.

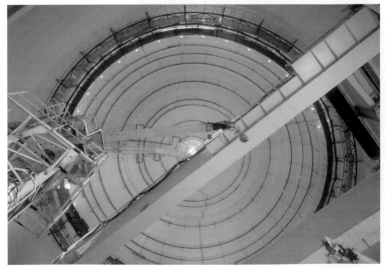

This is the interior of a nuclear reactor containment dome. Within radioactive environments, robots can perform tasks that would be dangerous for human beings.

HOW ARE ROBOTS USED IN INDUSTRY?

AS WELL AS BEING USEFUL in dealing with chemicals that would be dangerous to humans, robots have their uses in manufacturing industry. On production lines, the same action is done over and over again as part-made products pass along a conveyor belt. This is very tedious for human workers. Specialist robots, which can perform only one action, are ideal for this work, but humans are still needed to control them and to act if something goes wrong, as most robots are not designed to respond to unusual situations.

These robots are welding cars on a production line. They can work quickly and accurately twenty-four hours a day if necessary.

WILL ROBOTS EVER BE ABLE TO THINK FOR THEMSELVES?

IN MANY WAYS, robots already do think for themselves, in the sense that they may have the ability to assess all the information available in a particular situation and make a decision based on what they "know". Some robots can also "learn", so that if an action is unsuccessful, they do not repeat it. But any robot is only as good as the electronic circuits that cause it to move and the engineering that has enabled it to respond physically to electronic signals. As computer technology becomes more sophisticated, so will robots. It is likely that they will play an important role in all our lives in the twenty-first century.

fast facts

HOW CAN COMPUTERS BEAT CHESS EXPERTS?

Computers are able to perform calculations at lightning speed. Before making a chess move, they can review all available moves and choose the best one. But chess experts can sometimes beat a computer by understanding the basis on which it makes decisions.

WHERE DOES THE WORD "ROBOT" COME FROM?

The word "robot" was first used in a Czech play in 1920. It comes from the Czech word for work or labour.

WHAT IS AN ANDROID?

An android is a robot shaped like a human being.

ARE HUMAN-SHAPED ROBOTS USEFUL?

In most cases, a robot does not need to be shaped like a human, but sometimes this can be useful. People who have lost limbs can now be fitted with a robotic arm, leg, hand or foot that is made to look as much like a living body part as possible.

CAN ROBOTS FEEL?

Robots cannot feel emotions but they can be built to have senses. Television cameras and light sensitive cells can "see" for the robot, while touch-sensitive pads enable it to grip a very delicate object without crushing it.

WHAT IS ANIMATRONICS?

A METHOD of animating models by using specially developed robotic techniques is called animatronics. It is specially useful for museum displays and cinema work, where animatronic models of such creatures as dinosaurs, monsters or aliens can "act" alongside human actors.

Animatronic dinosaurs have realistic "skin" covering the engineering and electronics inside.

HOW HAVE ROBOTS BEEN USED IN SPACE TRAVEL?

ROBOTS have already been sent to distant planets, such as Mars. They are able to land on surfaces that might be hostile to human beings, to take soil and atmospheric samples, analyze them and send the results back to Earth. Missions "manned" by robots are much cheaper than those including humans, and robots do not necessarily have to be brought home again!

A robotic arm on the space shuttle enables astronauts to carry out repairs on satellites and space stations.

WHAT IS VIRTUAL REALITY?

VIRTUAL REALITY is a series of effects produced by a computer that enables someone wearing special equipment to feel as if they are really within an artificially created world. The person experiencing the effect wears a helmet through which sounds and pictures are relayed, but this is not like watching a movie. The computer technology makes it possible to turn round and "see" what is behind you. You can also move through the created world, exploring and having adventures. Wearing electronically controlled gloves and other clothing even makes it possible for you to "feel" objects in the virtual world.

In virtual reality, you can experience worlds as strange as the imagination of the programmer can create. But virtual reality is not just amazing entertainment. It can be used for training, especially where real experience could be dangerous or very expensive. Pilots, firefighters, divers and astronauts are just some of the people who can benefit from virtual reality training.

WHAT IS THE DIFFERENCE BETWEEN SPEED AND VELOCITY?

Speed is a measure of how quickly something is moving. Usually when we are talking about speed, we mean average speed. This is the time that it takes to travel from one point to another divided by the distance travelled. So speed is expressed in units such as kilometres per hour (km/h) or metres per second (m/s). Velocity, however, is a vector quantity. It measures the direction of movement as well as the speed.

The velocity of a flying bird can change even if its speed remains constant, as it can change direction.

WHAT IS RELATIVE VELOCITY?

RELATIVE VELOCITY is the velocity that one object has when viewed from another moving object. It is something that we are frequently aware of throughout the day, although we are not thinking in scientific terms. For example, if you are sitting still and a dog walks past, it seems to be moving quite quickly. If you later go for a run and pass the dog, still moving at the same velocity, it will seem to be travelling much more slowly.

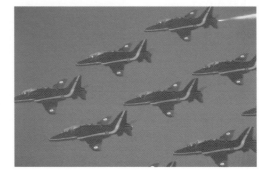

The aeroplanes are moving in formation, at the same speed and in the same direction. Viewed from the ground, they are clearly moving very quickly, but their velocity in relation to each other (relative velocity) is zero.

WHAT IS ACCELERATION?

ACCELERATION is a change in the velocity of an object. We often think of it as "speeding up", but there is also negative acceleration, known as deceleration. Acceleration is measured in metres per second per second (m/s^2). A change of direction is also an acceleration, as the velocity is changed.

A sprinter accelerates from zero velocity by pushing against the blocks. This propels her forward, but she will still be accelerating for several metres before she reaches her fastest velocity. Her momentum carries her forward even after she has passed the finish line, but as she stops using energy to push her feet against the ground, she gradually slows and stops.

fast facts

HOW FAST CAN THE FASTEST HUMAN RUN?

The fastest male sprinter in the world reaches speeds of over 43km/h (almost 27mph) over very short distances.

WILL WOMEN EVER BE ABLE TO RUN AS FAST AS MEN?

Since records have been kept, the difference between male and female speed in athletics has been narrowing. Because men are usually taller and more muscular, it is likely that some men will always be faster than the fastest women at shorter distances. But at longer distances – longer even than the marathon – the difference between the genders is much less marked and may one day be negligible.

HOW ARE FAST-MOVING VEHICLES SLOWED DOWN?

Most vehicles are slowed by braking, which means applying a force to the wheels to slow their turning motion. However, some aeroplanes and cars that move at very high speeds use parachutes to slow their forward motion. Air resistance acting on the parachute counters the forward motion of the vehicle, causing it to slow.

CAN ANYTHING KEEP MOVING FOR EVER?

Nothing can keep moving for ever, as friction or lack of energy input will gradually slow it down. The turning of the planets and other astronomical movements will continue for millions and millions of years, but even those will be affected when the star around which they orbit ages and dies.

WHAT IS TERMINAL VELOCITY?

WHEN SOMETHING IS DROPPED and is pulled by gravity towards the Earth, it accelerates as it falls until it reaches a velocity from which it can accelerate no further. This is called its terminal velocity. Terminal velocity happens when the force of the air resistance against the falling object increases to the point where it equals the force of gravity pulling the object. The terminal velocity of an object depends on how much air resistance it experiences. This is not affected by its weight but by its surface area and the streamlining of its shape.

A body experiences more friction passing through water than through air. That is why swimmers in a race try to dive as far as possible through the air before they enter the water. To reduce air resistance and increase their speed through the air as much as possible, they maintain a streamlined shape, with legs and arms held tightly in line with the body.

HOW FAST ARE YOUR REACTIONS?

INVOLUNTARY REACTIONS, which happen without conscious thought, such as blinking an eye when an object approaches it, happen in fractions of a second. You can make a comparison of the speed of your *conscious* reactions and those of a friend by asking him or her to hold a ruler upright from the bottom. Put your fingers around the ruler without touching it. As your friend shouts "Go!" and drops the ruler, close your fingers as quickly as you can. Use the ruler's scale to compare measurements with friends.

WHAT ARE NEWTON'S LAWS OF MOTION?

IN THE SEVENTEENTH CENTURY, Sir Isaac Newton developed three laws of motion that can be illustrated by a boy standing in a boat.

Newton's First Law of Motion states that an object will stay still or continue to move at the same velocity unless it is acted on by a force. Several forces are, in fact, acting on the boy and the boat, but they are balanced, so neither moves.

Newton's Second Law says that when a force acts upon an object, it will cause it to move, change direction, speed up or slow down. A gust of wind blowing against the boy and boat pushes them towards the bank.

Newton's Third Law states that every action produces an equal and opposite reaction. As the boy pushes himself forward, the boat pushes itself backward! The same thing happens when a gun is fired. When the bullet moves forward, the gun recoils.

WHAT IS MOMENTUM?

ALL MOVING OBJECTS have momentum. It is their tendency to keep moving unless a force acts upon them. Momentum is calculated by multiplying the mass of an object by its velocity. The greater its mass, the greater its momentum. That means that a train travelling at 25km/h (15mph) along a straight track has a greater momentum than a bird flying at the same speed above it. A much greater force will be needed to stop the train than to stop the bird.

WHAT IS THE IDEAL TEMPERATURE FOR LIFE?

Living things have evolved and adapted over millions of years to live successfully in very different temperatures. Penguins at the South Pole may live quite happily in temperatures of –50°C (–58°F), while some bacteria live near deep-sea vents that are gushing out water at close to boiling point.

HOW DOES A REFRIGERATOR WORK?

A REFRIGERATOR is basically a box that is very cold inside. The heat inside the box is made to move outside, where it flows out into the air. This is achieved by means of a pipe that contains a fluid called a refrigerant. The refrigerant flows around the pipe, becoming a vapour and then condensing back into a liquid. As it becomes a vapour, the refrigerant takes heat from inside the refrigerator. When it becomes a liquid again, it gives off the heat outside at the back of the refrigerator. This cycle of evaporation and condensation is caused by changes in pressure as the fluid is pumped from a high pressure part of the pipe (the condenser) into a lower pressure area (the evaporator).

CAN THE SEA FREEZE?

THE MINERALS dissolved in sea water, which make it taste salty, lower the temperature at which the water will freeze. But at the temperatures found at the far north and south of the globe, the sea is frozen all the time. Further from the Poles, it may also freeze in winter. In fact, the North Pole is permanently frozen sea – there is no land beneath the ice.

The condenser is where the refrigerant turns back into a liquid.

Strongly built ships called icebreakers are needed to keep some shipping lanes open during the winter when the sea freezes over. Ships with less strong hulls can be crushed by the ice.

WHERE DO ICEBERGS COME FROM?

ICEBERGS are huge chunks of ice that break off from the frozen seas at the North and South Poles as the weather becomes warmer. They can be enormous and are all the more dangerous for shipping because nine-tenths of the iceberg is invisible under water. The famous *RMS Titanic* was sunk by an iceberg in 1912.

A pump compresses the vapour, so that it is at higher pressure in the condenser than in the evaporator.

HOW WAS ICE-CREAM MADE IN THE DAYS BEFORE ELECTRICITY?

TWO THINGS have to happen to the mixture of dairy products and flavourings that make up ice-cream: they must be frozen and they must be stirred, to prevent large ice crystals from forming. Before electrical freezing machines were available, the ice-cream mixture was put into a churn, around which a mixture of salt and ice was packed. Heat from the ice-cream mixture gradually passed into the colder ice, until the cream itself was frozen. Meanwhile, the mixture was stirred by means of a paddle connected to a handle outside the tub. This became harder work as the icecream froze!

Iced desserts were probably first made by the Chinese as long ago as 3000BC.

WHY DO SOME FOODS FREEZE SUCCESSFULLY WHILE OTHERS DO NOT?

PLANTS AND ANIMALS are made up of cells, each of which is surrounded by a cell wall. Some foods contain a great deal of water. As the water freezes, it expands, breaking the cell walls. When the food is defrosted, its texture has been changed and what remains may well be just a mushy mass. It is not dangerous to eat this food, but it may not look or taste very pleasant.

Melons, which have a very high water content, do not freeze successfully. Other fruits may still be edible after freezing but have a different texture.

WHY IS THERE FROST MORE OFTEN ON A CLEAR NIGHT THAN ON A CLOUDY ONE?

FROST IS FORMED overnight when the air temperature drops below 0°C (32°F) and the dew freezes. Clouds in the sky act as insulation, preventing the heat from the Sun that has built up in the land, sea and air during the day from escaping. This means that the temperature is less likely to drop below freezing. When the sky is clear, the day's heat is able to escape easily, and a frost is likely.

A sharp frost can result in even the smallest branches having a sparkling covering of ice.

fast facts

WHAT IS ABSOLUTE ZERO?

Absolute zero is a theoretical temperature at which particles could no longer move and so there could be no heat. It is calculated as −273.15°C (−459.69°F).

WHAT IS DRY ICE?

Dry ice is frozen carbon dioxide. When it begins to melt, it turns into a gas without becoming a liquid first. The melting dry ice looks like rolling mist and is often used in theatrical shows to give a mysterious effect.

WHAT IS A GLACIER?

When layers of snow build up in a mountainous region, their weight may cause the crystals to freeze together into a massive sheet of ice that is too thick to melt during the summer. This is called a glacier. Often, glaciers move very, very slowly downhill, carving out new valleys as they do so.

WHAT IS BLACK ICE?

If roads are already wet when the temperature drops, the water may freeze into a layer of ice. The layer may be so thin that the road is visible underneath and the ice can hardly be seen. This black ice poses a serious problem for drivers, as they may be quite unaware of the danger before they begin to skid.

WHAT IS PERMAFROST?

In the Arctic and Antarctic Circles, there are seasons, but even in summer it is very cold. However, in the Arctic Circle, the top few centimetres of soil may defrost, and the land becomes tundra: an area where sparse vegetation can grow and flower. Beneath this defrosted layer, there is soil that is always frozen and in which nothing can grow. This is called permafrost.

WHAT IS MEANT BY A BALANCED DIET?

Human beings need a certain amount of food each day to supply them with energy. Almost all foods can supply some energy, but our bodies have other requirements as well. In order to make sure that we are taking in everything we need, we should eat a wide variety of foods, with the correct amounts of carbohydrates, fat and protein. A diet that fulfils these requirements is called a balanced diet.

Nutritionists recommend that we should eat something from each of these food groups every day. Carbohydrates give us energy. Protein is needed to build and repair cells and to keep our bones, muscles, blood and skin healthy. Fruits and vegetables contain energy and a wide range of essential vitamins and minerals. Dairy foods contain protein and calcium for healthy bones and teeth.

carbohydrates

protein

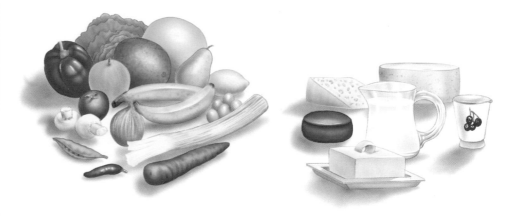
fruits and vegetables   dairy foods

WHERE DOES DIGESTION BEGIN?

DIGESTION begins as soon as we put food in our mouths. Saliva starts to digest the carbohydrates in the food as we chew it. Chewing breaks the food up into small pieces that can pass easily down the oesophagus and into the stomach, where powerful acids begin to digest proteins and kill harmful bacteria. The stomach is not still. Its muscular walls churn the food into a thick, soupy consistency.

Saliva begins to flow when we see or even think about food. Making food look appetizing is a first step towards good digestion.

WHAT ARE VITAMINS?

VITAMINS are chemicals that we need to stay healthy. They are referred to by the letters A, B, C and so on. Some of them are stored in the body but others, such as vitamin C, need to be eaten every day.

WHY WERE SAILORS ONCE GIVEN LIME JUICE TO DRINK?

IN THE DAYS of sailing ships, sailors could be at sea for months on end. Fresh fruits and vegetables, containing vitamin C, could not be kept fresh for long voyages. As a result of a lack of vitamin C, also known as ascorbic acid, sailors developed a condition called scurvy. This distressing condition caused bleeding gums, weakness and dizziness. In the eighteenth century it was discovered that limes could cure these symptoms.

Although ships began to carry limes in the eighteenth century, it was not until the twentieth century that it was understood that citrus fruits contain vitamin C, and that this vitamin is effective against scurvy.

HOW DOES HUMAN DIGESTION WORK?

THE FOOD that we eat travels slowly through our bodies, a journey of up to ten metres (nearly eleven yards), taking about two days. As it passes through the various stages of our digestive system, chemicals called enzymes act on the food to make different parts of it useful to the body. Anything that cannot be used is passed out when we go to the toilet.

HOW DOES FOOD MOVE THROUGH THE DIGESTIVE SYSTEM?

IT IS NOT GRAVITY that causes food to move through the long tube that is our digestive tract. In fact, even if you stood on your head, food would still move through your oesophagus and intestines. Muscles in the walls of these organs squeeze and release rhythmically to move the partly digested food along.

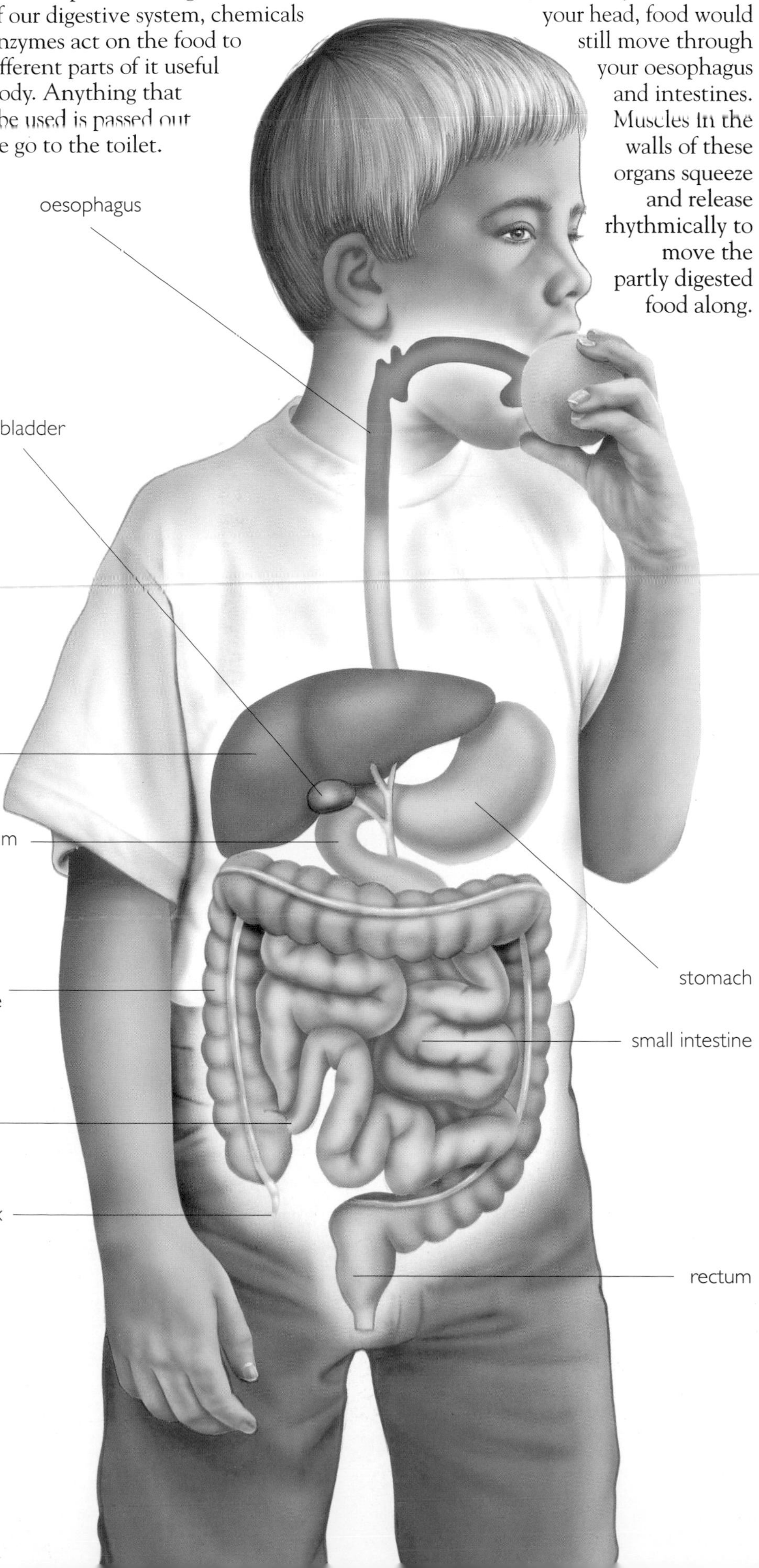

oesophagus

gall bladder

liver

duodenum

large intestine

ileum

appendix

stomach

small intestine

rectum

fast facts

WHY ARE SOME PEOPLE FATTER THAN OTHERS?

If we take in more energy from our food than we use, it is stored as fat. However, people naturally have different body shapes, and two people of very different builds may both be entirely healthy.

WHY IS DIETARY FIBRE IMPORTANT?

Dietary fibre is found in the tough parts of seeds, fruits and vegetables that are not broken down and digested. It is useful because it sweeps through the digestive system like a broom, preventing blockages.

WHICH MINERALS DO HUMANS NEED?

As well as vitamins, we need tiny amounts of minerals in our food. These include iron, for making red blood cells, and calcium for healthy bones and teeth.

WHY SHOULD BANANAS NOT BE STORED WITH OTHER FRUIT?

Ripe bananas give off a gas that causes other fruit to ripen rapidly and then rot.

WHY DO NEWBORN BABIES ONLY DRINK MILK?

The best food for a newborn baby is its mother's milk, which contains just the right amounts of the nutrients needed, all in a form that is easily digestible. Babies' digestive systems are not sufficiently developed to deal with other foods until they are about four months old.

WHAT IS AN RDA?

RDA stands for Recommended Daily Allowance. It is used to describe the quantity of vitamins and minerals that should be eaten each day to maintain good health.

WHY IS IRON AN IMPORTANT METAL?

Iron is the most widely used of all metals. It is cheap and very strong, so it can be used to make the supports for huge buildings and bridges. The Industrial Revolution would not have been possible without iron to make the machinery used in new factories. Today most iron is made into steel, a metal that can be used for a wider variety of purposes than any other metal on Earth.

WHAT IS SMELTING?

SMELTING is what is known as a reduction reaction. It is a method of extracting iron from iron ore. Iron ore, or haematite, is a rock that contains iron and oxygen. The process of smelting takes place in a blast furnace, where iron ore, limestone and coke (a form of carbon) are heated together while hot air is blasted into the furnace. The carbon in the coke reacts with the oxygen in the air to form carbon monoxide. This is turn takes oxygen from the iron ore, leaving behind iron mixed with a little carbon.

WHERE IS THE BIGGEST IRON MOLECULE IN THE WORLD?

SO IMPORTANT was the metal-working industry of Belgium that a building in Brussels called the Atomium was made in the shape of a molecule of iron – magnified two billion times!

The blast furnace gets its name from the hot air that is blasted into it. The air reacts with the carbon to form carbon monoxide, which reacts with the oxygen in the ore, leaving the iron behind.

The temperature inside the furnace reaches 2000°C (3450°F).

Iron ore, coke and limesto are fed into the blast furnace.

A waste material called slag is produced as the limestone reacts with impurities in the ore.

WHAT IS STEEL?

STEEL IS AN ALLOY of iron and carbon. Iron extracted from iron ore contains about 4% carbon and some other impurities. The carbon makes it hard but weakens it. Removing some of the carbon and other impurities in an oxygen furnace produces steel.

Molten iron and scrap steel are placed in an oxygen furnace called a converter.

A jet of oxygen is blasted into the converter. The oxygen reacts with most of the carbon to form carbon monoxide.

The furnace tips to pour the molten steel into a ladle.

WHAT IS MADE FROM STEEL?

A HUGE RANGE of items can be made from steel, from tiny paperclips to huge girders forming the frames for skyscrapers. One useful property of steel is that it can be recycled and used over and over again.

Alloys of steel, in which steel is combined with other metals, can be very useful. Railway tracks are often made of an alloy of steel and manganese.

Cutlery can be made from stainless steel. Unlike other metals, it will not rust or react with acids in foods.

Most screws, nails, nuts and bolts are made of steel. The thread of a screw can be given a sharp edge that is strong enough to drive through wood and other materials.

The huge cranes that make modern construction possible are made of steel. They are capable of carrying enormous weights, including the steel girders that form the skeleton of many new buildings.

Inside the dome of the Capitol, in Washington DC, there are massive cast-iron girders supporting the stone cladding.

fast facts

WHO WAS HENRY BESSEMER?

Henry Bessemer was a British scientist who, in 1856, invented a cheap method of extracting most of the carbon from iron ore in a blast furnace. The methods used today are still based on his process.

WHAT IS CAST IRON?

Cast iron is iron that has been poured into a mould while still in a molten state.

WHAT IS STAINLESS STEEL?

Stainless steel contains small amounts of nickel and chromium to make a metal that does not corrode.

WHEN WAS THE IRON AGE?

Although people probably learned how to work iron over 6000 years ago, the period known as the Iron Age relates to the centuries after 1000BC, when the technique of smelting spread throughout Europe.

HOW IS WIRE MADE?

To make wire, rolled steel is pulled through a very small hole in a process called drawing.

WHAT IS MEANT BY FORGING?

Forging is a method of shaping hot steel by pressing it between blocks and rollers.

HOW MUCH CARBON IS LEFT IN STEEL?

Low-carbon steel is more malleable than high-carbon steel, but the latter can be shaped to have a sharp cutting edge, used for the blades of knives and industrial guillotines. All steel contains less than 1.7% carbon.

HOW ARE GREAT INVENTIONS MADE?

An invention is a new method, material or machine that applies theoretical principles to a practical use. That does not mean that the inventor necessarily understands why his invention works! Inventions may be the result of hard work, or luck, or both. Very often, it is the name of the person who popularized the new idea that we remember, not the person who first thought of it.

WHAT DID BENJAMIN FRANKLIN RISK HIS LIFE TO DISCOVER?

IN THE EIGHTEENTH CENTURY, wealthy and influential men often interested themselves in more than one branch of learning. The American Benjamin Franklin was a statesman, printer, author and scientist. He left school at twelve, being the fifteenth child of seventeen, but soon made up for his lack of formal education. As well as his political work, he conducted many experiments concerning electricity. In 1752, he flew a kite in a thunderstorm, attaching a metal key to the damp string. An electrical charge ran down the string and Franklin was able to feel it jump to his finger when he approached the key. From this he concluded that lightning was an electrical spark and in 1753 launched his invention of the lightning conductor.

Inventions such as the Spinning Jenny heralded the arrival of the Industrial Revolution, which brought enormous changes to methods of production and the speed of scientific discovery. Modern industry could not have developed as it has without such beginnings.

WHAT WAS THE SPINNING JENNY?

THE SPINNING JENNY was one of the inventions that revolutionized textile production in the eighteenth century. For thousands of years, spinners were able to produce only one thread at a time, using devices such as spinning wheels. Then in 1764, James Hargreaves, an English weaver, invented a machine that could be operated by one person but spin several threads at the same time.

WHY IS GALILEO REMEMBERED?

GALILEO GALILEI (1564–1642) was an Italian scientist who worked on many mechanical problems but is perhaps best known for his astronomical observations. These supported the ideas developed by Nicholas Copernicus (1473–1543), a Polish scientist. He claimed that rather than the Sun orbiting the Earth, the Earth orbits the Sun. This idea went against the teachings of the Church, so Copernicus did not tell many people about it. Indeed, when Galileo spoke out in its support, he was put on trial and forced to withdraw his claim. Even today, scientific discoveries are not always popular when they go against long-held beliefs.

Aristotle (384–322BC) was a Greek thinker who put forward a theory of the universe in which the stars moved in circles around the Earth. These ideas were held for at least another 1800 years, until the work of Copernicus and Galileo began to show people a different view.

HOW DOES SIR EDMOND HALLEY'S NAME LIVE ON?

SIR EDMOND HALLEY'S name is remembered because he was the first person to predict that the comet he saw in 1682 followed a path that would bring it within sight of the Earth again in 1758. Unfortunately, he was no longer alive at that date to see his prediction come true, but his achievement was recognized and his name attached to the comet ever afterwards. In fact, the comet can be seen from Earth every 75–79 years. Its appearance was first recorded by Chinese astronomers in 240BC. The comet, still an unexpected visitor, also appeared in 1066 and was embroidered onto the Bayeux Tapestry, which records the Norman invasion of England.

A comet is a huge, dirty snowball, perhaps with a nucleus of small pieces of rock. Glowing gas or dust reflecting the Sun's light makes up the comet's "tail"

Hundreds of years ago, news about new products travelled very slowly. Today, advertising is aimed at individual markets and ensures that as many people as possible are aware of what is available.

HOW LONG DOES IT TAKE FOR NEW INVENTIONS TO BECOME WIDELY AVAILABLE?

AT ONE TIME tens or even hundreds of years might have passed between a scientist's discovery of a potentially useful fact or method and its use by a wide range of other people. Nowadays, the process is much quicker. This is partly because research is often very expensive and there is pressure to find a commercial use for an invention to help to pay for new research. Modern methods of mass production and global advertising also mean that new products can become popular very quickly.

WHAT DID JOSEPH PRIESTLEY DISCOVER?

IN 1774, the English chemist Joseph Priestley announced that he had discovered an element within the air. Previously it had been thought that air itself was an element. However, Priestley's achievement is an example of something that happens quite frequently in science. Although Priestley undoubtedly did discover the presence of oxygen, he was not the first to do so. A Swedish chemist called Carl Scheele had discovered it some months before, and it was not until some months later that a French chemist, Antoine Lavoisier, used Priestley's work to explain what oxygen is and its importance in respiration and combustion. He also gave oxygen its name. The sharing of scientific knowledge moves our understanding of the world forward. No one person can put together all the pieces of the jigsaw puzzle.

Joseph Priestley is less well known for the fact that he discovered soda water! This is the basis of most fizzy drinks.

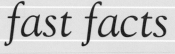

fast facts

WHAT IS THE BIG BANG THEORY?

The Big Bang theory of the beginning of the universe is based on the discovery made in 1929 by Edwin Hubble that the galaxies of the universe are moving apart. The idea is that this movement is still the result of an enormous explosion (the Big Bang) that began the universe billions of years ago.

WHAT DID GREGOR MENDEL DISCOVER?

Mendel (1822–84) showed how an individual's dominant and recessive characteristics are inherited from its parents. This explained why, for example, two white flowers could produce a pink flower.

WHAT IS ARCHIMEDES SAID TO HAVE DISCOVERED IN HIS BATH?

It is said that Archimedes (287–212BC) jumped out of his bath one day and ran naked through the streets, shouting "Eureka!" ("I've found it!") Whether this story is true or not, Archimedes did find that an object displaces its own weight of water when floating or submerged.

WHEN WERE SPECTACLES FIRST USED?

The first recorded wearing of spectacles to improve sight was in Italy in 1289. No one knows who made this very useful invention, but Ibn-al-Haytham, an Arab physicist, was investigating the properties of lenses as early as AD1000.

WHEN WAS GUNPOWDER FIRST USED?

By 1230, the Chinese were using gunpowder in warfare, making bombs to blow up the walls of towns being attacked.

GLOSSARY

Axis   The imaginary line around which a wheel or planet rotates.

Alloy   A mixture of metals, or of metals and non-metals.

Barcode   A pattern of lines, which represent numbers and can be read by a light pen or scanner using lasers.

Bit   The end piece of a drill that turns or vibrates at high speed to bore into rock, wood or metal.

Characteristic   A distinctive or typical feature of a material or person.

Component   A part of a larger machine or system, such as an electrical or electronic circuit.

Constituent   A part of something, such as one of the elements in a compound.

Deflection   A bend, turn or deviation in a light beam or the path of a moving object.

Dominant   When describing a characteristic shown by a living thing, an inherited feature that is shown although it has only been inherited from one parent. The gene inherited from the other parent that affects this part of the organism is carried, but not shown.

Efficiency   When used of a machine, the amount of useful work done compared with the amount of energy or heat supplied to the machine.

Experiment   A procedure designed to test whether an idea (hypothesis) about why or how something happens is true.

Extraction   Removing a metal or other substance from the mixture of elements in which it is found in nature.

Guillotine   A powerful cutting machine, using a sharp blade, named after a Doctor Guillotin, who recommended using a beheading machine for executions during the French Revolution.

Hologram   A three-dimensional image created using beams of laser light.

Indentation   A cut, notch or hollow in a flat surface or angle.

Lubricant   A substance, usually oil or grease, that is used to reduce friction between moving parts.

Nucleus (nuclei)   The central part of a cell, which controls what it does, or the central part of an atom, containing protons and neutrons.

Ozone   A gas with molecules made of three oxygen atoms, found in a layer of the Earth's atmosphere.

Philosopher   A person who uses reason and argument to discover what is real and true.

Pressure   A force being exerted on an object or material. Atmospheric pressure, for example, is the force exerted by the Earth's atmosphere on the planet and everything on it.

Prism   A shaped material, through which light can pass. A prism usually has a triangular cross-section.

Recessive   A term describing a characteristic that is inherited from one parent but not shown. However, it can be passed on to offspring.

Refraction   The change in direction of a beam of light passing from one material to another, such as from air to water.

Saturation   The condition of a solution when it can dissolve no more of a solute.

Soldering   Joining together metal parts by causing another molten metal to solidify between them.

Supersonic   Moving faster than the speed of sound.

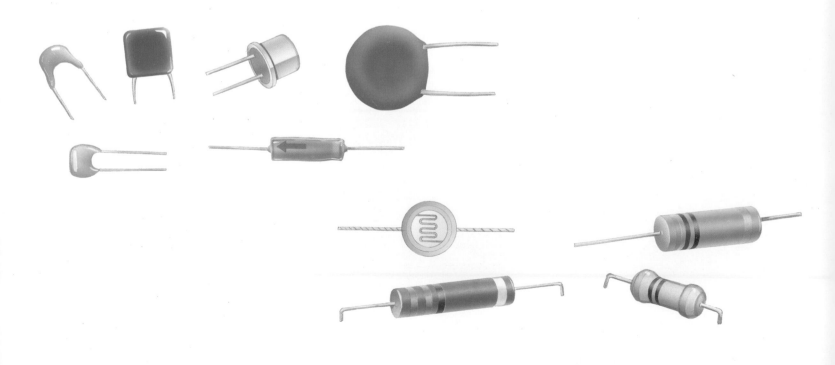

How
things
work

WHAT ARE THE SYSTEMS OF THE HUMAN BODY?

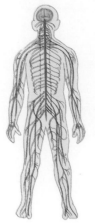

The central nervous system includes the brain and the nerves that carry messages to and from it.

Our bodies are very complicated. It is impossible to think about all the processes that are going on inside them at the same time, so doctors often consider the body as being made up of several different systems, each one with different organs and mechanisms working together to perform particular functions.

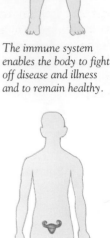

The immune system enables the body to fight off disease and illness and to remain healthy.

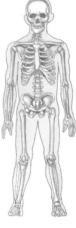

The skeletal system is the framework that supports and protects the soft parts of the body.

The muscular system enables the body to move. Muscles contract to cause movement.

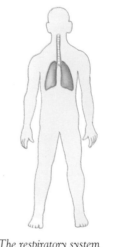

The circulatory system is concerned with the way in which blood flows around the body.

The respiratory system works to supply the body with the oxygen it needs from the air we breathe.

The digestive system enables us to absorb nutrients from what we eat and drink.

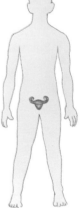

The reproductive system differs in males and females, allowing new humans to be born.

HOW DOES THE BRAIN WORK?

THERE IS MUCH that we do not yet know about how the brain works, but we do know that the brain communicates with the rest of the body through a thick cord of nerves running down the middle of the spine and branching off to reach the limbs and internal organs. The nerves are pathways for messages *to* the brain, to inform it about what is happening elsewhere in the body, and *from* the brain to tell the rest of the body how to act. These messages, and the processes happening within the brain, are made up of tiny electrical impulses. By far the largest part of the brain is the cerebrum, which is divided into two halves, called hemispheres. The rest of the brain is made up of the cerebellum, the pons and the medulla, which join together at the top of the spinal cord.

One very important function of the brain is memory, without which we would all be like tiny babies. Repetition seems to help the brain to memorize things. These dancers have probably repeated their actions over and over again.

HOW MUCH FOOD DO WE NEED?

FOOD IS THE FUEL that our bodies need for movement. But we also need some fuel simply to maintain all the parts of our bodies. Individual cells are being renewed all the time. And even if we do not move the *outside* of our bodies at all, there are many parts *inside* that are constantly in motion. How much food we need depends on our size, age, gender and level of activity.

Food energy is measured in kilojoules (kJ) or kilocalories (kcal). Until puberty, boys and girls need the same amount of food energy, but after that boys tend to need more. Of course, every person has different requirements, and a more active person will always require more food than an inactive one.

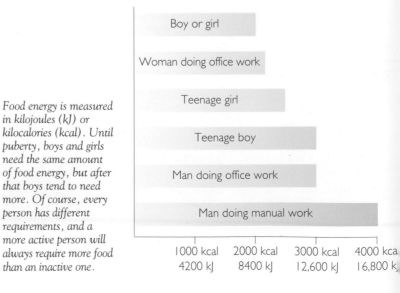

Boy or girl

Woman doing office work

Teenage girl

Teenage boy

Man doing office work

Man doing manual work

1000 kcal	2000 kcal	3000 kcal	4000 kcal
4200 kJ	8400 kJ	12,600 kJ	16,800 k

HOW MANY MUSCLES DO WE HAVE?

THERE ARE more than 600 muscles in the human body. Over 100 of these are in our faces, which is why we can have so many different expressions. Although we can perform a great variety of movements, each muscle can only do one thing: contract. That is why muscles often work in pairs, so that one muscle can move a part of the body in one direction, while its partner can move it back again. Perhaps the most important muscle in the human body is the heart, which is contracting and relaxing all the time to pump blood around the body.

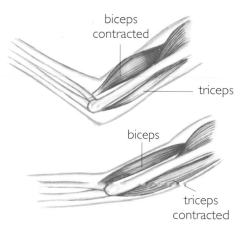

Two muscles work together in our upper arms. When the biceps muscle contracts, the forearm is lifted. When the triceps muscle contracts, the forearm is lowered again.

Once almost everyone did manual work of some kind. It was essential for survival. Human bodies were not designed for the sedentary lives many of us now lead. That is why exercise is important for good health.

HAVE HUMAN BODIES CHANGED THROUGH THE CENTURIES?

OVER MILLIONS OF YEARS, evolution is changing the way humans look. Over a shorter period, improved nutrition and medical discoveries have meant that people in some parts of the world today are generally bigger and stronger than their ancestors. But we are also losing some abilities that no longer seem useful. The smallest toe, for example, can no longer be moved independently by most people. As recently as Roman times, some people may have been able to "prick up their ears", moving them slightly towards sounds as some animals can.

WHAT IS THE DIFFERENCE BETWEEN VEINS AND ARTERIES?

VEINS ARE BLOOD VESSELS that carry blood to the heart, while arteries carry it from the heart. The heart acts as a pump, pushing blood to every part of the body. Adults have between five and six litres (between nine and ten pints) of blood. As well as containing red cells to carry oxygen to the body's organs, blood also plays an important part in fighting infection. White blood cells attack and digest harmful bacteria, while platelets in the blood form clots so that wounds can heal and no further infection can enter the body.

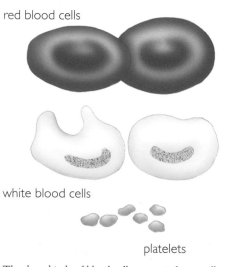

red blood cells

white blood cells

platelets

The three kinds of blood cell are carried in a yellowish liquid called plasma. Plasma is 90% water.

fast facts

WHICH IS THE LARGEST HUMAN CELL?

The largest human cell is the female egg cell. It is just visible as a tiny dot to the naked eye.

WHICH IS THE SMALLEST HUMAN CELL?

Strangely, the smallest human cell is the male sperm cell, which can fertilize an egg to create an embryo.

WHAT ARE HORMONES?

Hormones are substances made in glands that travel through the bloodstream to trigger various actions in different parts of the body. We create over 50 different hormones, such as insulin.

DO BABIES HAVE FEWER BONES THAN ADULTS?

In fact, babies have *more* bones than adults. Some bones in babies, such as in their skulls, hands and feet, are in separate parts when they are born and only fuse together later, as the baby grows.

HOW MANY TEETH DO HUMANS HAVE?

Humans usually have two sets of teeth. As babies, they grow 20 first teeth, often called milk teeth. Later, these fall out and a second set of 32 adult teeth grows, although the last four of these, called wisdom teeth, may not appear until a person is 18 or older, and sometimes do not grow at all.

WHY IS SMOKING BAD FOR HEALTH?

Your lungs have over 350 million tiny air sacs, called alveoli, in which oxygen is taken from the air and passed into your blood. Smoking coats these sacs with sticky tar, so that they cannot do their job.

WHICH IS THE MOST WIDELY SPOKEN LANGUAGE?

Languages are living things, changing all the time to meet the needs of their speakers and writers. It is only in the last few hundred years that attempts have been made to standardize the way in which languages are used, so that people using the same language can understand each other as well as possible. In the world today, Mandarin Chinese is the most widely used language, with over a billion speakers. English is next, with around half a billion speakers.

Chinese characters can be very complicated, with up to 26 strokes in each. The Japanese have adapted over two thousand characters to write their language, but they also have two alphabets, one for Japanese words and one for foreign words!

Perhaps the nearest thing we have to a universal language is road signs!

DO ALL LANGUAGES HAVE ALPHABETS?

ALPHABETS consist of letters that represent sounds. By writing different combinations of letters, all the sounds in a language can be represented. The first alphabet was probably developed by the Phoenicians before 1500BC. Even if they use the same letter forms, not all languages have the same number of letters in their alphabets. English, for example, uses 26 letters to write all its sounds, but Italian uses just 21, with j, k, w, x and y seen only in foreign words. However, the most widely spoken language of all, Chinese, does not use an alphabet. Instead, it has over 50,000 characters, each representing a word or part of a word.

ARE ALL LANGUAGES RELATED?

NOT ALL LANGUAGES are related, but they do seem to form related groups. Most languages that were originally European, some of which are now spoken all over the world, are thought to have developed from an ancient and unknown language that linguists know as "Proto Indo-European".

IS THERE A UNIVERSAL LANGUAGE?

MANY PEOPLE have dreamed of a world in which everyone speaks the same language. Some international jobs use one language to avoid dangerous misunderstandings. However, even gestures can be misunderstood, as a shake of the head can mean "yes" in some countries and "no" in others!

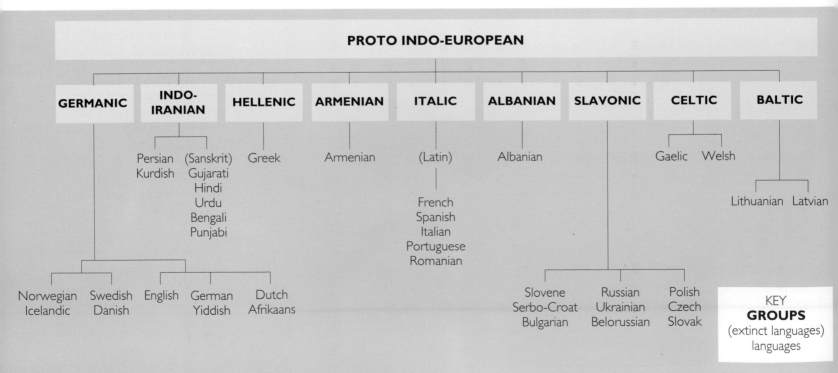

PROTO INDO-EUROPEAN

GERMANIC	INDO-IRANIAN	HELLENIC	ARMENIAN	ITALIC	ALBANIAN	SLAVONIC	CELTIC	BALTIC

Persian Kurdish — (Sanskrit) Gujarati Hindi Urdu Bengali Punjabi — Greek — Armenian — (Latin) — Albanian — Gaelic Welsh

French Spanish Italian Portuguese Romanian

Lithuanian Latvian

Norwegian Icelandic — Swedish Danish — English — German Yiddish — Dutch Afrikaans

Slovene Serbo-Croat Bulgarian — Russian Ukrainian Belorussian — Polish Czech Slovak

KEY
GROUPS
(extinct languages)
languages

HOW AND WHY ARE NEW WORDS INVENTED?

LANGUAGES grow and change because they need to. New words are invented when new ideas or articles require a name. Usually, new words are based on earlier ones. When the television was invented, the word chosen to describe it was a combination of an ancient Greek word, meaning "far" and a Latin word to do with "seeing". Sometimes a writer takes delight in inventing words. Lewis Carroll wrote a poem about a creature he called the "Jabberwock", for example.

Sometimes a "new" word is simply borrowed from another language. "Chocolate" came into the English language as a version of the word that the Aztecs used to describe a drink made from the cocoa bean. This drink was unknown in Europe until the Spaniards discovered the Aztecs in South America. Once it was known, it had to be named! Borrowing the local name for it was an easy solution.

WHAT IS THE ROSETTA STONE?

THIS STONE was found near Rosetta, in Egypt. On it was an inscription, given three times in three different languages. One of the versions was in Greek, which scholars could read. Another version was in ancient Egyptian hieroglyphs, a kind of picture-writing that no one in modern times had been able to decipher. Given the Greek "key", it became possible to read the hieroglyphs on the stone, and later, thousands of other hieroglyphs carved on monuments and buildings.

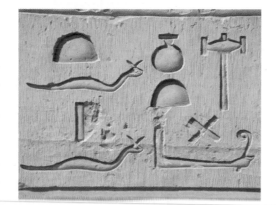

Until Egyptian hieroglyphs were deciphered, it was not known that most of them represent sounds and syllables, not whole words.

WHEN WAS BRAILLE DEVELOPED?

BRAILLE is a system of writing that uses raised dots, punched into paper or plastic. It enables people with little or no vision to read with their fingers. The system was invented in the first half of the nineteenth century by Louis Braille (1809–52), a Frenchman who had himself been blind since the age of three.

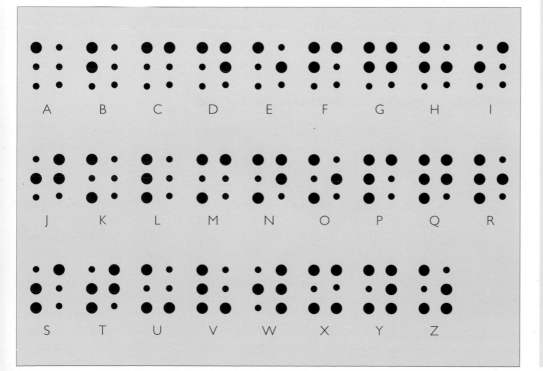

fast facts

WHAT IS A DIALECT?

A language may have speakers who use different accents, vocabularies and ways of putting words together. Varying forms of the same language are called dialects, especially when they are found in particular regions.

WHICH ARE THE RAREST LANGUAGES?

Usually, when the last person to speak a language dies, the language dies too, even if it has been recorded. Each year, a few languages or dialects disappear for ever. This is specially true at the moment of some native American languages.

CAN ANYONE SPEAK ANY LANGUAGE?

Babies are born with the ability to make the sounds of any language, but as they learn one language, they gradually lose this ability.

WHAT IS ESPERANTO?

Esperanto is a language invented in 1887 by a Polish doctor called Zamenhof. He hoped that it would become a worldwide language.

HOW SOON DO CHILDREN RECOGNIZE THEIR NATIVE LANGUAGE?

Researchers have found that children as young as three months can tell the difference between the language they hear most frequently and other languages or even dialects.

HOW CAN WE TELL HOW ANCIENT LANGUAGES WERE PRONOUNCED?

We cannot be sure how languages of long ago sounded. However, by studying how languages change over time and looking at poetry in the dead languages, it may be possible to make a good guess about how they sounded.

HOW HAVE MODERN COMMUNICATIONS CHANGED OUR LIVES?

Modern communications have affected our lives in numerous ways. Being able to pass information down telephone wires or via satellites means that some people can work from anywhere in the world and still keep in constant touch with their offices. A surgeon in Arizona, via a satellite link, can assist a colleague in Beijing with a complicated operation. News can travel halfway around the world as quickly as it can reach the next town. Perhaps the biggest effect of communications has been to make us all feel that the world is a smaller place, and that we need to be concerned about its future and the futures of people thousands of miles away.

Communication satellites usually circle the Earth in what is called a geostationary orbit. This means that the satellite is always above the same point on the Earth's surface.

HOW MUCH HAS THE SPEED OF COMMUNICATION INCREASED?

ONLY A FEW HUNDRED YEARS ago, the fastest way that a piece of news could travel was to be carried by a person on horseback. Messages sent overseas could only travel as fast as the fastest sailing ship and were at the mercy of the wind and weather. The development of steam loco-motives and steamships made it possible for information to move around the world more quickly, but it still had to travel physically from one place to another, as a letter. The breakthrough came with the invention of the electric telegraph and messages in Morse Code. The message was sent down a wire in bursts of electric current. Today, images of written docu-ments, sound recordings or television pictures can be flashed around the globe in less than a second by means of satellites and radio communications.

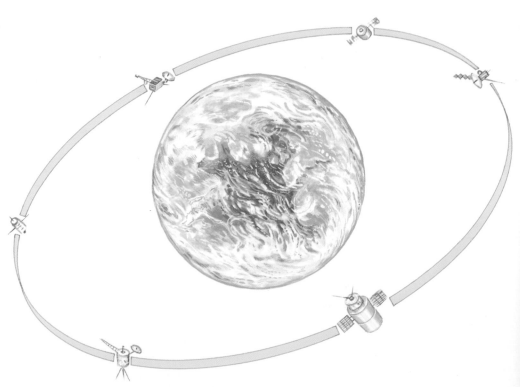

Satellites have different shapes and sizes, depending on the job they have to do. They are launched into orbit around the Earth by rockets. As a result, they are very expensive to put into position. Astronauts are sometimes sent to repair damaged satellites.

HOW DO COMMUNICATION SATELLITES WORK?

THE LAYER of the Earth's atmosphere called the ionosphere can reflect some radio waves back to Earth. This is used for sending messages over fairly short distances, but for messages to travel further across the Earth, the radio signals can be bounced off a satellite, orbiting almost 36,000km (22,000 miles) above the Earth's surface. Several satellites, in different orbits, are required to give coverage over the whole globe, and different satellites are used to reflect signals for different media, such as telephone messages and television pictures.

WHAT IS SEMAPHORE?

SEMAPHORE is a means of signalling using pairs of flags. Different flag positions stand for different letters and numbers. Semaphore signals are useful when the signaller is within sight of the receiver of the message but too far away to call out. It was widely used between ships sailing near each other in the days before ship-to-ship radio.

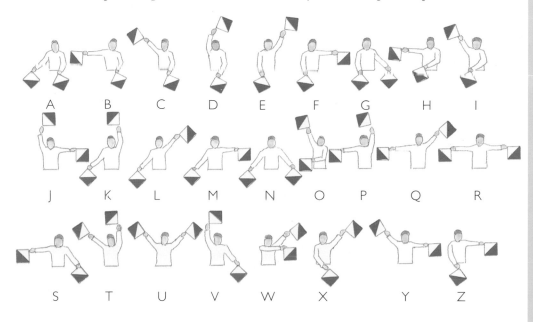

HOW DOES A TELEPHONE WORK?

A TELEPHONE works by sending and receiving electrical signals that represent sounds, including the human voice. When the required number is dialled, a signal passes to the called telephone, causing it to ring, buzz, flash a light, or even vibrate to attract the attention of the person using it. When the telephone is picked up or switched on, a connection is made, and a conversation can take place.

The receiver of the telephone converts the electric current back into sounds by using an electromagnet to make a diaphragm vibrate.

The mouthpiece contains a microphone. Sound vibrations are converted into an electric current which varies as the sounds do.

Telephone messages can travel as electrical signals along wires or through the air as radio waves. As signals take time to travel, you may notice a very slight delay in the response of the person being called if they are thousands of miles away.

Messages reach the right telephone by means of a dialled number. Pressing the keys of the telephone causes different electrical pulses or varying tones to pass to electronic equipment at the telephone exchange. This "reads" the pulses or tones and routes the call to the correct area and telephone.

WHAT IS E-MAIL?

E-mail is short for "electronic mail". It is a way of sending messages between computers along telephone wires or using radio signals.

HOW WILL COMMUNICATIONS IMPROVE IN THE FUTURE?

In the future it is likely that each one of us will be able to carry a full communications system with us, as telephones, computers and even television screens become smaller and smaller.

WHAT IS AN OPTICAL FIBRE?

An optical fibre is made of fine strands of glass, along which pulses of light can travel. Optical fibres are used to carry signals, such as telephone messages. Each optical fibre can carry thousands of telephone messages at the same time.

WHEN WAS THE TELEPHONE INVENTED?

The invention of the telephone is often attributed to Alexander Graham Bell (1847–1922), a Scottish-American inventor who patented a practical telephone in 1876. As is often the case, other inventors had already proposed similar machines.

HOW DOES A FAX MACHINE WORK?

"Fax" is a short way of saying "facsimile", meaning an exact copy of a document. A fax machine scans each tiny section of a document and sends signals by telephone wires or radio waves to another fax machine, communicating whether the section is light or dark. The receiving machine converts these signals back into light and dark sections on light-sensitive paper, or prints them onto plain paper.

WHY DO SHIPS FLOAT?

Ships float, even if they are made of iron, because their overall density is less than that of the water that supports them. The water displaced (pushed aside) by the hull of the ship pushes back upwards with a force called upthrust or buoyancy. If this is equal to or greater than the force of gravity pulling the ship's mass downwards, the vessel will float. In fact, ships need a certain amount of weight to give them stability in the water, so many of them have hulls weighted with concrete or another kind of ballast. Without it, the ship would bob around on the water like a cork.

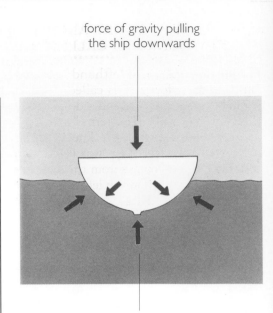

force of gravity pulling the ship downwards

upward force of the displaced water

ARE SHIPS STILL IMPORTANT NOW THAT AIR, ROAD AND RAIL TRAVEL ARE SO MUCH FASTER?

SHIPS are of vital importance to the world's economy. They carry over 90% of the freight that travels around the globe. Although air travel is a quicker way of crossing the oceans, it is very expensive, and weight is always a problem. Ships may be slower, but they can carry enormous loads. Nowadays many loads are carried in large steel containers, which can be stacked on the ship and then lifted by crane directly onto the back of a truck in the port, doing away with the need to pack and unpack cargo at each change of carrier.

Containers protect the goods inside. They can be stored in stacks on the dockside until transferred to a ship, truck or train.

HOW DOES A SUBMARINE SUBMERGE AND SURFACE?

SUBMARINES, unlike most ships, are not always required to float! In order to make a submarine sink beneath the surface, its density must be increased to be greater than that of the water. This is done by taking in water, which fills ballast tanks within the outer hull of the submarine. The amount of water entering can be controlled, so that the vessel sinks slowly. To bring a submarine back to the surface, pumps force the water out of ballast tanks. The submarine's density becomes less than that of the water it is displacing, so it rises.

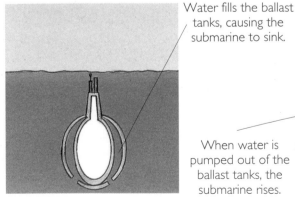

Water fills the ballast tanks, causing the submarine to sink.

When water is pumped out of the ballast tanks, the submarine rises.

WHAT IS A PERISCOPE?

A PERISCOPE is a metal tube that can be extended above the submarine while it is underwater. The tube contains lenses and mirrors, which enable an image of the scene above the surface to be seen below in the submarine. The periscope can swivel, so that a 360° view is obtained.

The operator turns the periscope by means of the handles on the side. These fold up when it is not in use, as space is always at a premium in a submarine.

WHY ARE PORT AND STARBOARD SO CALLED?

TRADITIONALLY, the lefthand side of a ship, looking forward, is called the port side, while the righthand side is called the starboard side. The term "starboard" comes from "steerboard". The large oar used to steer early ships was usually on the right. "Port" comes from the fact that ships had to tie up on the left side in port so that their steering oar would not be crushed against the dock.

At night, ships show a green light on their starboard side and a red light on their port side.

In a race, it is often the efficiency with which a boat tacks, compared with its competitors, that makes it a winner.

HOW DOES A YACHT TACK?

SAILORS cannot change the direction of the wind, but they are not powerless to change the direction of their sailing boats. By steering a zigzag course, called tacking, they are able to sail in the direction they require. This can be a time-consuming process. It is important that the navigator keeps an accurate check on the boat's position, so that it does not travel too far off course while tacking.

third tack

wind direction

second tack

first tack

WHAT WERE THE FIRST BOATS LIKE?

IT IS LIKELY that the first boats were made of hollowed-out tree trunks. Perhaps early humans saw fallen hollow logs floating along a river and realized that they could carry goods and people. Tree trunks were hollowed using stone axes and fire. A dugout pine canoe, found in the Netherlands, is thought to be at least 8000 years old.

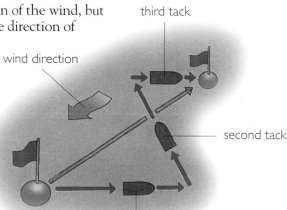

WHAT HAPPENED TO THE MARIE CELESTE?

The *Marie Celeste* was a sailing ship, found floating at sea in 1872. The sailors who found the ship claimed that everything was in its place, with an untouched dinner on the captain's table. Many suggestions have been made as to the fate of the ten crew, but the likeliest explanation is that the sailors who discovered the ship exaggerated in the stories they told, ignoring signs of pirate attack or illness.

WHAT WAS A TRIREME?

A trireme was an ancient Greek warship, powered by three rows of rowers, positioned above each other on both sides of the ship. The oars of the upper rows needed to be longer than the lower ones to reach the water.

WHAT IS A PLIMSOLL LINE?

A Plimsoll Line, named after the man who proposed it in 1876, is a line or series of lines on the side of a ship, marking the highest safe water level in various conditions. It ensures that merchant vessels are not overloaded.

WHY ARE SHIPS OFTEN REFERRED TO AS "SHE"?

One reason for ships being thought of as female may date from the days when, during a voyage that might take months or even years, male sailors came to think of the ship as home, supplying all they had of comfort and security. In this way, the ship was like the mothers and wives that the men had left in their homes on shore.

WHICH WAS THE FIRST CAR?

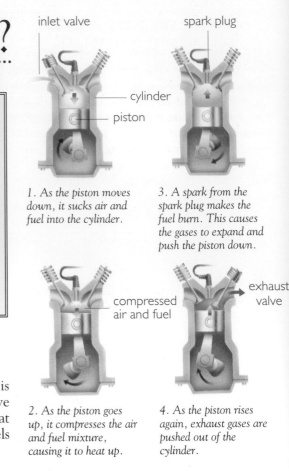

inlet valve   spark plug

cylinder

piston

compressed air and fuel

exhaust valve

The very first vehicle able to run on the open road was powered by steam. It was a three-wheeled tractor, built in 1769 by a Frenchman, Nicolas Cugnot (1725–1804). However, it was not until the development of the internal combustion engine in the second half of the nineteenth century that motor transport began to be successful. Both Gottlieb Daimler (1834–1900) and Karl Benz (1844–1929) were working on such engines in the 1880s in Germany. It is said that neither knew about the other's work, although they lived less than 100km apart.

1. As the piston moves down, it sucks air and fuel into the cylinder.

2. As the piston goes up, it compresses the air and fuel mixture, causing it to heat up.

3. A spark from the spark plug makes the fuel burn. This causes the gases to expand and push the piston down.

4. As the piston rises again, exhaust gases are pushed out of the cylinder.

HOW DOES THE INTERNAL COMBUSTION ENGINE WORK?

INTERNAL COMBUSTION ENGINES are usually fuelled by petrol or diesel. This fuel is burnt (combusted) within metal cylinders. The burning fuel causes a piston to move up and down inside each cylinder, and it is this upward and downward movement that is translated into a turning movement by the crankshaft, causing the axles and wheels to turn and the car to move.

WHAT ARE THE MAIN SYSTEMS OF A CAR?

LIKE THE HUMAN BODY, a car can be thought of as having systems with different functions, all working together to make the vehicle operate effectively. The most important systems are shown in the illustration below.

Electrical system
As well as moving the wheels, the engine also powers an alternator, or dynamo, which generates electrical current. This current is stored in the battery. This supplies energy for the car's lights, windscreen wipers, radio and such features as electric windows.

Suspension system
The suspension is a system of springs and shock absorbers that prevents every jolt caused by an uneven road surface being felt by the driver and passengers inside the car.

Transmission system
The transmission system consists of the crankshaft, gears and the differential. This is a system of gears on the axles that allows the wheels to travel at different speeds when going round corners, when the outer wheel travels further than the inner one.

Braking system
Each wheel has a brake unit, connected to the brake pedal by a tube full of brake fluid. Pushing the pedal forces the fluid down the tube, causing a brake shoe to press against a metal disk or drum on the inside of the wheel. Friction causes the wheels to slow and stop.

WHAT IS A CUSTOM CAR?

A CUSTOM CAR is one that has been altered from the manufacturer's original specifications to suit the wishes of its owner. This may involve painting it with extraordinary designs, making the engine more powerful, or even "stretching" it by cutting the entire car in half and inserting additional body parts. Some cars have been made very long indeed by this method. The one below has 26 wheels and contains a swimming pool!

This car was designed by Jay Ohrberg of California, USA. It is over 30m (100ft) long.

WHEN WERE SPEED LIMITS INTRODUCED?

Speed limits are almost as old as cars themselves. Early motor vehicles were thought to travel at a dangerous speed, so the first cars in Britain, for example, were required to have a man with a red flag walking in front of them, and had to observe a speed limit of less than 5 miles per hour!

WHAT WAS SPECIAL ABOUT THE MODEL T FORD?

The Model T Ford was the first car to be built on a moving production line. This made the manufacturing process much cheaper and put motor cars within reach of many more people. Henry Ford (1863–1947) began the mass-production of motor cars that continues today.

WHAT IS FOUR-WHEEL DRIVE?

In most modern cars, the engine drives the front wheels of the car. In rear-wheel drive cars, it turns the back axle. In four-wheel drive cars, both axles are driven by the engine, enabling the car to travel powerfully over rough ground.

HOW DO RACING CAR DRIVERS ACHIEVE HIGH SPEEDS?

FORMULA 1 drivers cannot win races by themselves. Large teams of mechanics and technicians are needed to enable the car to perform well. The driver spends more time testing the car than he does racing, and no aspect of the vehicle is ignored. Even while the car is waiting at the start of a race, special electric heaters are warming the tyres so that they give their best performance. Every second counts in motor racing, so mechanics practise until they can change all four tyres of the car in under three seconds! Controlling the car at high speed puts enormous physical and mental strain on the driver. There is no power steering in Formula 1 cars, so the driver needs great strength and split-second reactions.

Non-professional drivers enjoy competing at many levels of motor racing. Here the actor Paul Newman is preparing to practise for the Daytona 24-hour race.

WHAT IS THE DIFFERENCE BETWEEN A VETERAN CAR AND A VINTAGE CAR?

A VETERAN CAR was made between 1896 and 1903, while a vintage car was built after 1904 and before 1930.

This vintage car is an Austin 7 "Chummy" Tourer, built in 1923.

HOW WILL MOTOR CARS CHANGE IN THE FUTURE?

TWO AREAS of car design have been researched very thoroughly in the past few years. One of these concerns fuel consumption and exhaust gases, as the realization grows that the world's fossil fuels are polluting the atmosphere. The other is safety. It is likely that future cars will be able to prevent some accidents by assessing the distance to an obstacle and taking evasive action without prompting from the driver.

Streamlining helps to save fuel by reducing air resistance. Modern cars tend to have rounded angles and door handles that are flush with the bodywork, as this Chrysler Showcar does.

WHICH WAS THE WORLD'S FIRST PUBLIC RAILWAY?

The first public railway in the world to run a regular service was opened on 27 September 1825. It ran between Stockton and Darlington in the north of England. A steam train called The Locomotion pulled 34 wagons, some of which carried coal, while others were adapted to carry passengers. Both the locomotive and its track were built to the design of George Stephenson (1781–1848). Stephenson's background was in mining engineering. Coal mines had long used tracks to move wagons of coal, and it was with steam engines for these wagons that Stephenson first experimented.

WHAT DO THE NUMBERS BEFORE STEAM TRAIN NAMES MEAN?

STEAM LOCOMOTIVES are described by the arrangement of their leading, driving and trailing wheels. In fact, only the driving wheels are connected to the cylinders that provide the engine's power. So a 2-8-2 has two leading wheels, eight driving wheels and two trailing wheels.

Steam trains are still running scheduled services in some parts of the world. This is a 2-6-2 engine in Sumatra.

WHO INVENTED THE LOCOMOTIVE?

A LOCOMOTIVE is an engine that can travel under its own power, not pulled by horses, for example. But we usually think of it as running on tracks, or tramways, as they were first called. In 1804, Richard Trevithick (1771–1833), an English inventor, designed a train to pull coal wagons in a Welsh colliery. Trevithick was convinced that steam engines had a great future and later travelled to Peru and Costa Rica, where he introduced steam engines into the silver mines.

ROCKET

In 1829, Stephenson built an engine called The Rocket, which won a competition of steam trains called the Rainhill Trials by running at 48km/h (30mph).

fast facts

WHAT WAS THE ORIENT EXPRESS?

Some special trains have gained a romantic image over the years. The Orient Express was a luxurious train running between Paris, France, and Istanbul, Turkey, from 1883. Today, the train still travels over part of this route.

WHAT IS THE LONGEST JOURNEY THAT CAN BE MADE BY TRAIN?

Without changing trains at any point, the longest journey that can be made is 9297km (5777 miles) between Moscow and Vladivostok on the Russian Trans-Siberian line.

WHEN DID RAILWAYS FIRST CROSS THE UNITED STATES?

Railways spread across the world very quickly. In the 1850s, settlers suffered hardship crossing the American continent in wagons. By 1869, the journey could be made by train in relative comfort.

WHAT IS A MONORAIL?

A monorail, as the word suggests, is a railway with only one rail, on which an electric train can run.

WHERE WAS THE FIRST UNDERGROUND RAILWAY BUILT?

THE WORLD'S FIRST city underground railway line was opened in 1863 in London. It was called the Metropolitan.

HOW ARE UNDERGROUND RAILWAYS BUILT UNDER EXISTING CITIES?

BENEATH CITIES are the foundations of large buildings and many pipes carrying water, electricity, gas and telephone cables. Builders have either to tunnel very deeply or to use a technique called "cut-and-cover", which means that they run the railway under existing roads, so that they simply have to dig a huge trench along the road, build the railway, and cover it up again.

WHAT IS THE GAUGE OF A RAILWAY?

THE GAUGE of a railway is the distance between its rails. At one time, the standard gauge in several countries was 1.48m (4ft 10.25in), which was thought to have been the width of Roman chariot tracks. Today, many different gauges are used.

WHAT IS A COWCATCHER?

A COWCATCHER is a V-shaped metal part on the front of a train, designed to push obstacles – including cows! – off the line before the wheels hit them. The American Denver and Rio Grande steam engine below has an example.

HOW DO TRAINS CHANGE TRACKS?

THE INTERSECTIONS that allow a train to move over onto another track are called switches or points. Short pieces of rail are able to move across to bridge the gap between the two tracks, so that the train's wheels cross over as smoothly as possible.

The TGV (Train à Grande Vitesse) of France (left) and the Bullet Train of Japan (below) are two of the fastest trains in the world, aiming to run at 300km/h (186mph) in regular service.

Underground railways help to ease surface congestion in cities around the world. The underground railway in Paris, France, is called the Metro, which is short for Metropolitan, the first underground railway.

HOW DO PLANES FLY?

Aeroplanes fly when two of the four forces acting upon them are greater than the other two. The force of thrust, created by the aeroplane's propellers or jet engines, moves the plane forward. The force of lift is caused by air flowing over the wings. This keeps the plane in the air. The two forces working against thrust and lift are gravity, which pulls the plane towards the Earth, and drag, caused by air resistance, which slows the plane's forward motion.

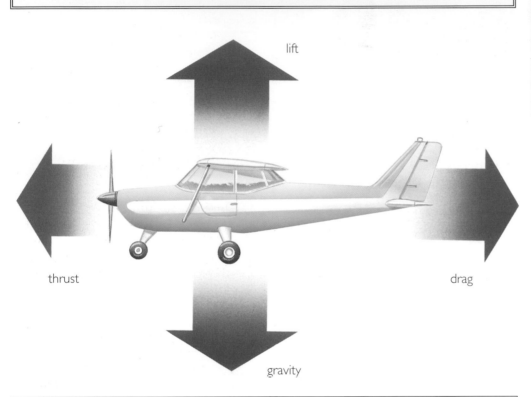

lift

thrust

drag

gravity

Although they cannot fly in very rough weather, helicopters are extremely useful for rescues at sea, as they can hover over the site of a wreck.

WHY IS A HELICOPTER SO MANOEUVRABLE?

HELICOPTERS have rotor blades above them that are aerofoils. When they turn rapidly, they create lift. The blades are tilted slightly, so that they also provide thrust. The helicopter's tail rotor blades stop the helicopter from spinning and enable it to turn. With this combination of rotors, a helicopter can move in any direction or simply hover. Without long wings, helicopters can manoeuvre in tight places, such as alongside cliff faces, so they are particularly useful for rescue and emergency work.

HOW DO AN AEROPLANE'S WINGS CREATE LIFT?

THE SHAPE of all parts of a plane is important, as the more streamlined it is, the less air resistance will cause drag to slow the plane. But the form of the wings is particularly important. The wings of most planes are shaped so that the upper surface is more curved than the lower surface. As the diagram shows, this affects the way in which air moves over them. The air travelling over the upper surface of the wing has further to travel and therefore moves faster than that passing under the wing. This creates an area of lower pressure above the wing, which sucks the wing upwards, creating the force of lift.

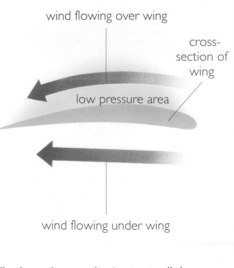

wind flowing over wing

cross-section of wing

low pressure area

wind flowing under wing

The shape of an aeroplane's wing is called an aerofoil.

HOW CAN GLIDERS FLY WITHOUT ENGINES?

GLIDERS are so light that the lift created by their wings can overcome the opposing pull of gravity. However, without engines, gliders cannot take off. There are two widely used methods of launching gliders into the air. They can be catapulted upwards from the ground, or they can be towed up by an aeroplane. The cable between the plane and the glider is then released, and the glider can fly solo. A glider flight is an extraordinary experience, as it is almost silent except for the sound of the wind.

HOW DO AIR TRAFFIC CONTROLLERS COMMUNICATE WITH PILOTS?

AIR TRAFFIC CONTROLLERS have screens on which they can see the planes in their sector. It is their job to see that planes are kept safely apart and guided appropriately during take-off and landing. When aeroplanes are near enough, the air traffic controllers can speak to them directly, but they cannot be expected to speak all the languages of international pilots. For this reason, to make communications as safe and clear as possible, all instructions and discussions take place in English all over the world.

Air traffic controllers use an aircraft's registration mark when calling it by radio. As one letter can sound rather like another, words are used instead, each one standing for the letter that begins it.

A Alpha
B Bravo
C Charlie
D Delta
E Echo
F Foxtrot
G Golf
H Hotel
I India
J Juliet
K Kilo
L Lima
M Mike
N November
O Oscar
P Papa
Q Quebec
R Romeo
S Sierra
T Tango
U Uniform
V Victor
W Whisky
X X-Ray
Y Yankee
Z Zulu

WHAT IS AN AIRSHIP?

AN AIRSHIP is a cigar-shaped balloon, filled with a gas. Nowadays, this is usually helium, as it cannot catch fire, unlike the hydrogen used in earlier airships. Beneath the balloon, a cabin (often called a gondola) and engines are suspended. In the 1930s, the Germans developed airships called Zeppelins, although the tragic crash of the Hindenburg in the USA in 1937 really spelled the end of the age of the airship.

Today's airships are usually built for publicity purposes rather than as passenger carriers.

This is a 1939 Piper J-3 Cub, flying over Clear Lake, California, USA.

WHICH PLANES CAN LAND ON WATER?

SEAPLANES and flying boats have floats instead of wheels, so that they can land on water. In the 1930s, flying boats were often larger and more luxurious than ordinary aircraft, as they could be made larger without the expense of creating longer runways at airports around the world. Instead, they took off and landed at sea, taxiing in and out of existing harbours.

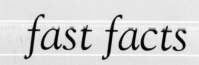
fast facts

WHICH PLANE CAN AVOID RADAR DETECTION?

Small planes may be able to avoid radar detection by flying very low, but the Northrop B2 Stealth bomber is made of special materials that can absorb radar, while its "flying wing" shape also helps it to avoid detection.

WHEN WAS THE FIRST AEROPLANE FLIGHT?

On 17 December 1903, Orville Wright took off in a plane called the Flyer and travelled 37m (121ft) – only just over half the length of a modern Boeing 747. Orville Wright had designed and built the plane with his brother Wilbur.

WHAT DOES A FLIGHT RECORDER RECORD?

A flight recorder is an electronic recording device contained in a waterproof and fireproof box. It records the plane's speed, height and direction, as well as the conversations of the crew with each other and with ground control. If the plane crashes, the flight recorder can give vital information that will help to save lives in the future.

HOW DO PLANES REFUEL WITHOUT LANDING?

Sometimes planes need to refuel in mid-air. Perhaps they are crossing an ocean or enemy territory. In this case, by very skilful manoeuvring, it is possible for another plane to transfer fuel through a flexible pipe. This is a difficult and potentially dangerous operation.

WHY DOES A ROCKET HAVE STAGES?

A rocket needs enormous power to escape from the Earth's gravity. The velocity required to achieve this is called the escape velocity, which is about 49,000km/h (29,000mph). The rocket's power comes from burning liquid hydrogen and oxygen. Each stage of a rocket is a fuel tank, which is jettisoned when its fuel is used up. After all, carrying an empty fuel tank will only use up more fuel. Only the top stage of the rocket, called the payload, makes the whole journey and brings the crew back to Earth.

A crew of up to eight people has to train for several months to become familiar with the controls in the shuttle's cockpit.

HOW CAN THE SPACE SHUTTLE BE USED OVER AND OVER AGAIN?

AT LIFT-OFF, the space shuttle has two rocket boosters. These are jettisoned when the shuttle reaches a height of 43km (27 miles). The shuttle usually remains in orbit around the Earth for about seven days, although it can continue for 30 days. When it returns to Earth, the shuttle lands on a runway, in a similar way to an ordinary aircraft. The rocket boosters are reattached to it, so that it is ready for another mission.

HOW DO ASTRONAUTS MOVE OUTSIDE THE SHUTTLE?

ASTRONAUTS outside the shuttle are encumbered by a heavy spacesuit, but this is not really a problem in weightless conditions. Controlled movement is more difficult, however. Astronauts wear a unit called a manned manoeuvring unit (MMU) on their backs. This is fuelled by nitrogen and is rechargeable in the shuttle. Several small thrusters allow the astronaut to move in all directions.

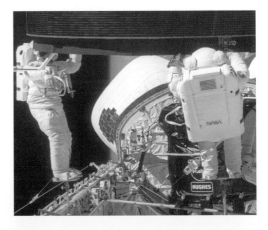

WHAT IS THE SPACE SHUTTLE USED FOR?

THE SPACE SHUTTLE has many uses and, because it is reusable, has made it possible to pursue some space activities that would otherwise have been too expensive. It is used to launch satellites and to make repairs to existing satellites. The shuttle can also be used as a laboratory, in which to carry out experiments that are only possible in zero gravity.

CAN ANY HUMAN STRUCTURE BE SEEN FROM SPACE?

THE GREAT WALL, which stretches for over 3640km (2150 miles) across China, is the only human structure that can be seen from space.

HOW DOES A SPACESUIT WORK?

A SPACESUIT is all that stands between an astronaut on a space walk and the emptiness of space. It must supply all his or her needs. There is no breathable atmosphere in space, so a spacesuit supplies oxygen to the astronaut.

Within the helmet, headphones and a microphone enable the astronaut to communicate with crew members and mission control.

A specially treated dark visor protects the astronaut's eyes from the glare of the Sun, while lights can illuminate dark areas.

A camera may be fixed to the astronaut's shoulder, so that other crew members and the ground crew can watch what is being done.

All the joins in the spacesuit must be absolutely airtight. Inside, the spacesuit is pressurized, like a deep-sea diver's suit.

The temperature, pressure and oxygen levels inside the suit are monitored by a control pack on the astronaut's front or back.

Under the outer suit, a body suit contains pipes through which cool liquid flows to protect the astronaut from the heat of the Sun.

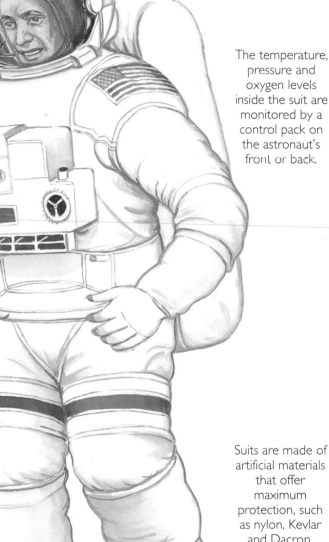

The visor and outer layer of the spacesuit must be tough enough not to be torn or cracked by tiny meteorites that may bounce off the astronaut.

Suits are made of artificial materials that offer maximum protection, such as nylon, Kevlar and Dacron.

The astronaut is completely sealed within his or her suit, so urine is collected inside for disposal later!

On Earth, a spacesuit can be as difficult to walk in as a suit of armour, but in the weightlessness of space, the pull of gravity is not a consideration.

fast facts

HOW DO ASTRONAUTS SLEEP IN ZERO GRAVITY?

In order to prevent themselves floating around as they sleep, astronauts have to strap themselves down. Of course, it is important that everything else in the cabin is also firmly fixed.

WHO WAS THE FIRST PERSON IN SPACE?

The Russian cosmonaut Yuri Alekseyevich Gagarin was the first person to travel into space on 12 April 1961 in *Vostok 1*.

WHAT WAS THE SPACE RACE?

In the 1960s and 70s, both the USA and the USSR were investing considerable resources in space exploration at a time when tension between the two countries was high. Their endeavours to outdo each other in outer space were known as the space race. Today, Russian cosmonauts and American astronauts work together on international projects.

WHAT HAPPENS TO SPACE PROBES WHEN THEIR TASK IS DONE?

Most space probes are sent out with a particular job in mind, such as taking photographs or testing the atmosphere of a certain planet. But when this is done, those that have not landed on a planet's surface simply travel on through space. The American probe *Pioneer 10*, for example, sent to Jupiter on 2 March 1972, was still sending back signals from outside our Solar System 25 years later.

WHO WAS THE FIRST MAN ON THE MOON?

Neil Armstrong became the first man to step onto the Moon on 20 July 1969.

WHO WERE THE FIRST GREAT ROAD-BUILDERS?

From the earliest times, humans and animals have created trackways along well-used routes, but it was the Romans who were the first to set about road-building in a systematic manner. The Roman Empire stretched from North Africa to Scotland. In order to govern successfully, the occupying forces needed to be able to reach trouble spots quickly. Roman roads were built so that armies could march rapidly for hundreds of miles.

Medieval bridges often used arches for support and had shops built along them to catch the passing trade of travellers who had no option but to cross the bridge.

An arch bridge uses the strength of an arch for support, although the roadway itself is usually straight.

A top level of paving stones gave a smooth surface for carts and marching armies.

Roman roads were made in layers. First the route was cleared of large stones and boulders. Then the bed of the road was levelled with sand.

The Romans tried to build straight roads as far as possible. Straight roads were easier to march along and reduced the risk of ambush, as the view was clear in both directions.

Rubble and crushed stone were rammed down on top of the sand.

Drainage ditches beside the road kept it dry.

A bascule bridge has two sections that can be opened so that shipping can pass through.

Suspension bridges have towers from which steel cables stretch to support the bridge beneath.

WHAT ARE THE DIFFERENT KINDS OF BRIDGES?

THE EARLIEST BRIDGES were probably tree trunks across streams or flat slabs of rock. Gradually, people learned to span wider rivers and ravines by supporting the bridge in the middle. Since then, engineers have devised ways of spanning very wide distances.

Beam bridges usually have fairly short spans. Today they are often supported by concrete piers.

WHEN WAS THE HEYDAY OF CANAL-BUILDING?

FOR THOUSANDS OF YEARS, people have transported heavy goods along waterways. The first canals were probably built to join existing navigable rivers. In the fifteenth century, the Aztec city of Tenochtitlan had a sophisticated series of canals, providing transport for goods and people. Venice, in Italy, although a smaller city, was also built on a system of canals rather than roads. However, the golden age of canal-building probably came with the Industrial Revolution, when there was an enormous need for cheap and easy ways to carry the goods made in factories to the nearest port. Canal boats, powered at first by a horse on the towpath and later by coal-fired steam engines, could carry enormous loads much more conveniently than horsedrawn carts on bumpy roads.

In England, barges and narrowboats were often brightly painted with patterns and scenes from life on the canals.

HOW DO CANALS CLIMB HILLS?

WATER, left to its own devices, always flows from its highest point to its lowest, until the two points are on the same level. If a canal sloped as it climbed a hill, its water would simply flow to the bottom. One solution is to bore a tunnel through the hill, so that the canal can continue on a level course, but sometimes this is too costly or geologically impossible. Building locks can solve this problem.

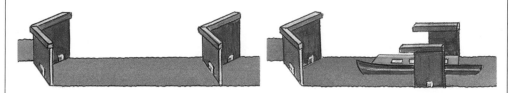

A lock consists of two gates across the canal, with mechanisms for opening them on the towpath.

To climb to a higher level of the canal, a boat enters the first lock gate, which is closed behind it.

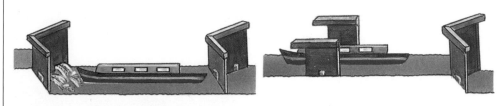

Paddles in the second lock gate are opened so that water can flow in, gradually raising the level of water in the lock.

When the water ahead is level with that in the lock, the gates are opened and the boat can move on.

WHICH IS THE WORLD'S LONGEST ROAD SYSTEM?

The longest road in the world that can be travelled in a motor vehicle is the Pan-American Highway. This runs from north-west Alaska, USA, to Santiago in Chile. It then turns to the east to reach Buenos Aires, Argentina, before coming to an end in Brasilia, Brazil.

WHICH COUNTRY HAS THE MOST ROADS?

The USA has about 6,284,500km (3,905,000 miles) of roads – more than any other country in the world.

WHEN WERE PARKING METERS INTRODUCED?

The first parking meter appeared in Oklahoma City, USA, in 1935.

WHEN WERE TRAFFIC LIGHTS FIRST USED?

The first traffic lights were used in Detroit, USA, in 1919.

WHEN WAS THE FIRST METAL BRIDGE BUILT?

The first metal bridge was built of iron in Shropshire, England, in 1779.

ARE ROAD SIGNS INTERNATIONAL?

ALTHOUGH ROAD SIGNS do differ across the world, many rely on pictures and symbols rather than words. These are often faster for the motorist to recognize, and avoid some language problems for international travellers.

Whatever language a traveller understands, this sign is very clear.

HOW IS PAPER MADE?

Paper is made from plant fibres. These are very tiny cellulose tubes that make up the stem or leaves of a plant. The fibres are mixed with water and then poured onto a mesh, so that the water can drain through, leaving the fibres behind. The mat of fibres is rolled and dried until it becomes a strong sheet of paper. Although traditionally paper was made by hand, today it is usually made in one large machine, which takes in the water and fibres at one end and produces reels of paper at the other end.

HOW ARE DIFFERENT PAPERS DESCRIBED?

THERE is no such thing as good or bad paper, just paper that is good or bad for a particular job. Blotting paper needs to be able to absorb ink, for example, while paper for printing must let the ink sit on the surface, so that the printing is crisp and clear. Most paper is described firstly by weight. Paper for a children's picture book might weigh 150 grams per square metre. It is said to be 150gsm paper.

The mixture of water and fibres is called stock. It enters the machine through a pipe.

The stock flows into a breast or flow box. This pours the liquid evenly onto a mesh called the wire. Water drains out through the wire and is collected below.

Heated rollers called drying cylinders help to dry the paper.

A couch roll transfers the wet mat of fibres to a felt blanket, which supports it until it becomes drier.

Press rolls squeeze more water out of the mat of paper.

Calender rolls smooth the surface of the paper.

WHAT DOES A DANDY ROLL DO?

A DANDY ROLL has raised patterns on it. As it presses onto the wet paper at the end of the wire, it leaves impressions called watermarks. If you hold a piece of paper up to the light, you may see a pattern or wording left by a dandy roll.

Coatings may be applied to the paper by a size press.

The paper is wound onto a huge reel.

fast facts

HOW CAN YOU MEASURE A PAPER'S OPACITY?

Nowadays a computer can test how opaque paper is (how difficult it is to see through it). A simpler test is to draw a letter in thick black ink on a piece of paper and then place sheets of the paper to be tested on top of it until the letter can no longer be seen. The fewer sheets needed, the more opaque the paper.

HOW IS PAPER RECYCLED?

It is easy to recycle paper. Old paper is soaked in water and put into a giant liquidizer, to blend it into stock. This is poured into the paper-making machine in the usual way.

WHAT IS PAPIER MÂCHÉ?

Papier mâché is French for "torn paper." Paper is torn or cut into small pieces. These are then pasted in layers over a mould. When the glue and the paper are dry, the mould can be removed and the article decorated. Bowls, boxes and even furniture can be made like this.

WHAT IS THE GRAIN OF A PIECE OF PAPER?

If you try to tear an article out of a newspaper, you will find that it tears in quite a straight line in one direction but not in the other. That is because the movement of the wire causes the fibres to settle in one direction, giving the paper a grain. When paper is printed, it is important that the direction of the grain is known, or the pages will buckle.

WHO INVENTED THE FIRST PAPERMAKING MACHINE?

Louis Robert, a Frenchman, invented a papermaking machine in 1799. Four years later, the Fourdrinier brothers in London developed the idea. Papermaking machines are still called Fourdrinier machines today.

WHAT KIND OF PLANT FIBRE IS USED TO MAKE PAPER?

NOWADAYS most paper is made from specially grown trees. These trees are usually softwoods, grown in the cooler parts of the world where little else can thrive. Fir, pine, spruce, larch and cedar trees are all used. The trees do not have to be very tall or straight, as they do for timber. Almost all parts of the tree, except the bark, can be ground up into fibres for papermaking.

Felled trees are heavy. Where possible, the trunks are floated down a river to the sawmill, where they are ground up into fibres.

HOW IS STRONG CARDBOARD MADE?

CARDBOARD is really just very thick paper. The machine that makes it is slightly different because the card is not wound onto a reel at the end, but cut up into sheets. For making strong, light boxes, corrugated cardboard is often used. This has paper pressed into a ridged shape sandwiched between two outer sheets.

WHERE WAS PAPER FIRST MADE?

PAPER WAS FIRST MADE 2000 years ago in China. It was made from pulped rags and old fishing nets, drained on a sieve made of bamboo! Paper may not immediately seem to be an ideal building material, but it is light and cheap, and allows a certain amount of light to pass through it. It is ideal for use with bamboo, which is also very light. Paper has been used in China and Japan for centuries to make screens and internal sliding walls in houses. Although these are not soundproof, they are very attractive and easily replaced if damaged.

CAN PAPER ONLY BE MADE FROM WOOD FIBRES?

PAPER can be made from almost any kind of plant fibre. In some parts of the world, banana stalks and sugar-cane stems made fine, strong paper. On the whole, the longer the fibres, the stronger the paper.

Paper money is folded, pushed into wallets and pockets, and passed from hand to hand. It needs to be very strong. A special paper is made that may contain cotton fibres (which come from cotton plants) or linen fibres (from flax plants).

WHEN WAS PRINTING INVENTED?

Printing – producing identical copies of a picture or piece of writing by pressing an inked block onto a surface – was introduced by the Chinese over a thousand years ago. However, the breakthrough of movable type, which meant that a new block could be made up from existing pieces of type, without having to carve it from scratch, was developed in 1438 by Johannes Gutenberg, in Germany. This was still a fairly slow, manual method, although much faster than the alternative of writing documents out by hand. It was not until the invention of steam and, later, electrical machinery to power the presses that documents could be printed rapidly on a large scale.

HOW MANY COLOURS ARE USED IN COLOUR PRINTING?

HOWEVER COLOURFUL a page in a book may be, it is probably made up of only four colours. Tiny dots of yellow, blue, red and black inks are used to print the page. The dots are so small that they cannot usually be seen with the naked eye. Instead, they "mix" visually to form all the colours on the final page.

WHAT IS REGISTRATION?

THE PAGE to be printed passes between inked rollers or plates four times, each time with a different coloured ink being used. In order to make sure that the final image is clear and sharp, the four printings must line up exactly on top of each other. This is known as registration. Registration marks, at the corners of a page, help the printer to position the images accurately. You may have seen a strip of coloured shapes on the edge of a printed food packet. These also enable the printer to see at a glance if the four printings have been properly positioned.

Registration marks normally fall outside the main printed area. When the pages are trimmed to their final size, the marks are cut off.

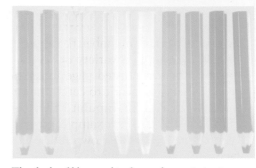

A photograph is scanned to separate the image into a piece of film for each of the four "process" colours.

The shade of blue used in four-colour printing is called cyan.

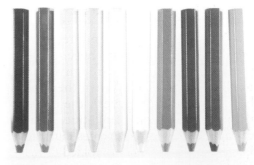

The red ink is a pinkish colour called magenta. Brighter reds are created when magenta is added to yellow.

Black ink gives a deeper black than mixing the three other colours and gives crisper black type.

When the four colour separations are printed one on top of the other, a full-colour picture is produced.

HOW ARE DIFFERENT TONES OF COLOUR PRINTED?

SOME PRINTED IMAGES use one solid colour. These words are printed in solid black ink, for example. The dots are so close together that no background colour shows through. Using increasingly widely spaced dots creates the impression of paler tones of grey.

| 100% cyan | 50% cyan | 30% cyan | 10% cyan |

The tone of a colour being printed is described by the percentage of paper that is covered with ink.

WHAT IS A TYPEFACE?

A TYPEFACE is an alphabet that has been specially designed for printing. It can usually be used in a variety of sizes and styles. The typeface chosen has a huge effect on how a printed page looks. Some typefaces are designed to be easy to read. Others are meant to catch the eye in headings and titles. Today, computers make it easy to manipulate type, s t r e t c h i n g i t or squashing it, for example, to create special effects. It is also easy to adapt typefaces or create your own. Each set of letters, numbers and symbols in a typeface is called a font.

WHY CAN THE NUMBER OF PAGES IN A BOOK USUALLY BE DIVIDED EXACTLY BY 16?

PAGES IN A BOOK are not printed one by one. They are printed on huge sheets of paper that then pass through another machine to be folded. When the book is bound (put into its cover), the edges of the pages are cut on a guillotine. A piece of paper folded in half creates four pages. Larger sheets of paper are folded to make 16, 32 or even 64 pages.

HOW IS A HARDBACK BOOK COVER MADE?

GLUEING, sewing or stapling pages together and placing them within a cover is called binding. Several pieces of card and paper are required to bind a hardback book. It is also possible to add bookmark ribbons and little pieces of fabric called headbands at the top and bottom of the spine (back) of the book.

Pieces of card are glued to a printed cover paper, the edges of which are folded over.

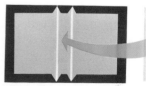

The book block is placed in the cover (or case).

Endpapers – the first and last pages of the book block or separate pieces of paper – are glued down to hold the book block in place.

WHAT IS A TEXTILE?

> *The word "textile" may be used to describe any woven material, or, more broadly, any cloth. Most fabrics are made from threads. These may be looped or passed under and over each other to create a firm cloth, or they may simply be matted together to form a kind of felt. There are thousands of different kinds of textile, each with its own properties and uses.*

WHERE DO FIBRES FOR TEXTILES COME FROM?

AT ONE TIME, fibres for textiles came from either plants or animals. The former included cotton from the cotton plant and linen from flax, but also coarser fibres for rope, sacking and matting, such as hemp, jute, sisal and even coconut fibres. Animal-based fibres have been spun from the coats of sheep, goats, camels, llamas and, by real enthusiasts, dogs! Nowadays, there are also artificial fibres, spun from mixtures of chemicals. By mixing different fibres together, it is possible to make fabrics for every purpose.

Spun threads are twisted together for strength, forming yarn of different thicknesses.

WHAT IS SPINNING?

THREADS from plants and animals are usually not more than a few centimetres long. To make a long, strong thread for weaving or knitting, they must be spun. A carding machine combs the fibres so that they are all lying in the same direction and form a loose rope. This rope is then gently drawn out into a thinner thread and twisted into yarn.

These loose ropes of cotton fibres are called slivers. They will gradually be pulled into a thinner rope, called roving, before being twisted into thread. Years ago, this process was done by hand, using a spinning wheel.

Dyed thread may be wound onto small reels for sewing at home, or huge reels for use on powerful industrial weaving, knitting or sewing machines.

HOW ARE THREADS AND TEXTILES COLOURED?

SUBSTANCES called dyes are used to colour threads and textiles. In the past, natural dyes were used, made mainly from plants. Onion skins, for example, give a soft, reddish colour. Most natural dyes fade gradually when washed or exposed to light, which can be very attractive. Many people like the faded colour of denim jeans, for example, dyed with a natural plant-based dye called indigo. Modern chemical dyes do not fade so easily. They give strong, bright colours. Either skeins of thread or finished fabrics may be dyed by passing them through a dye bath, then fixing the dye with other chemicals and drying the result.

WHAT IS THE DIFFERENCE BETWEEN KNITTING AND WEAVING?

BOTH KNITTING AND WEAVING are methods of making threads into cloth, but knitting involves looping one long thread together, while weaving usually involves passing threads lying in one direction over and under threads lying at right angles to them.

In handweaving, the loom holds the lengthways threads (warp), while the weaver passes a shuttle, carrying the crossways thread (weft) between them. The finished fabric cannot be wider than the weaver's outstretched arms.

Threads in woven fabrics can be crisscrossed in hundreds of different ways to add texture to the cloth.

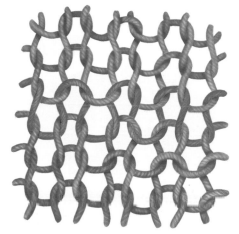

It is not only woollen jumpers that are knitted. The fabric that T-shirts are made from is knitted cotton.

HOW ARE FABRICS PATTERNED?

THERE ARE TWO main ways of patterning fabrics. By using coloured threads in the knitting or weaving, patterns can be made in the fabric itself. This is a very easy way to create stripes and checks, and it is quite cheap to use lots of colours, so the resulting fabric can be very bright. Another method of patterning fabric is to print it, using special dyes. This may be done by big rollers or by squeezing dye through patterned screens. Since only one colour can be printed at a time, each additional colour adds to the cost.

When threads of different colours pass under and over each other, it is as if the colours mix. Here black and cream threads combine to make a grey colour.

WHAT IS SILK MADE FROM?

NATURAL SILK is spun as a thread by silk-worms. They use it to form a cocoon. Unlike other natural threads, the silk-worm's thread is very long – up to one kilometre (0.62 miles). Traditionally made in Asia, silk was such a sought-after textile that the route from Europe to the East became known as the Great Silk Road.

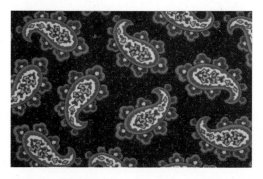

The curved shapes on this printed fabric are described as paisley, after a town in Scotland, although this was originally an Indian design.

HOW LONG DOES IT TAKE TO SHEAR A SHEEP?

IN 1957, a New Zealander sheared a sheep in just 47 seconds!

Expert shearers can remove the fleece from hundreds of sheep in a day.

WHO WAS THE FIRST PHOTOGRAPHER?

The first person to take a photograph was a Frenchman, Joseph Nicéphore Niepce, in 1822. However, as is often the case with new inventions, many other scientists had been experimenting with light, lenses and light-sensitive chemicals. Working with Niepce was a man called Louis Daguerre, who later improved on Niepce's process. Some early photographs were called daguerreotypes.

HOW DOES A CAMERA WORK?

A CAMERA is a lightproof box containing light-sensitive film. To take a picture, the photographer presses a button to open a shutter and let light pass through the aperture, a hole in the front of the camera. The camera's lens focuses the light so that it forms a sharp image on the photographic film, just as the lenses in our eyes focus the light onto our retinas. Then the shutter closes again so that no more light reaches the film. The whole process usually takes just a fraction of a second.

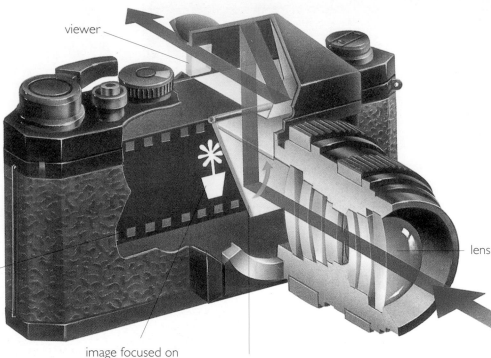

viewer

lens

sprocket holes guide the film through the camera

image focused on light-sensitive film

mirror

When the camera is not in use, a lens cap stops dirt and grit from getting onto the lens.

HOW IS FILM DEVELOPED?

AFTER AN IMAGE has been recorded on light-sensitive film in a camera, the film is moved along, so that the next photograph will be taken on a fresh piece of film. No more light must hit the exposed film until it is developed, or the picture would be spoiled. When all the photographs on a roll of film have been taken, the film is wound into its case, which is lightproof. The development process then takes place in a darkroom, or in a specially made machine.

The film is taken out of its case and immersed in a chemical solution that develops the image.

After rinsing, the film is bathed in more chemicals to fix the image onto the film.

A final rinse and the film is dried. The image is negative: dark areas look light and vice versa.

HOW ARE FILMS PRINTED?

PRINTING converts the negative image of the film into a positive image on paper. Light is shone through the film onto light-sensitive paper. Passing the light through lenses makes the image larger. The print is then developed and fixed just as the film was.

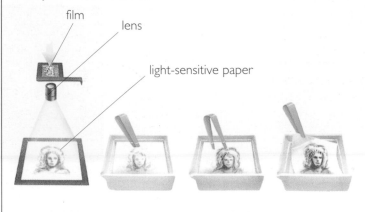

film

lens

light-sensitive paper

HOW CAN PHOTOGRAPHS BE MADE TO MOVE?

MOVING PICTURES, or movies, do not really have moving images at all. They are simply a series of still photographs, shown rapidly one after the other. Our brains are not able to distinguish the individual images at that speed, so we see what appears to be a moving picture.

HOW CAN LENSES CHANGE OUR VIEW?

THE WAY in which we see the world has been greatly influenced by photography. We are used to seeing printed images that we could never see with our naked eyes, either because they happen too fast, or because a special camera lens has allowed an extraordinary view to be taken.

Macrophotography is a way of photographing very small objects by using special macro lenses. Used for both still and moving pictures, macrophotography has transformed our knowledge of the way that tiny living things, such as insects, behave.

These Chicago skyscrapers do not really lean so alarmingly, but by using a special lens, the photographer has been able to emphasize the way in which the massive buildings tower over the church in the foreground of the picture.

Once only wealthy people could have pictures of themselves, painted by an artist. Now most people have family photographs. Before photography, we could only see mirror images of ourselves in a looking glass. Now we can see ourselves as others see us.

fast facts

WHERE DOES THE WORD "CINEMA" COME FROM?

"Cinema" (or "kinema" as it was originally) comes from a Greek word meaning "movement".

WHY DO CARRIAGE WHEELS APPEAR TO GO BACKWARDS IN MOVIES?

As the carriage moves forward, the spokes of its wheels go round, but a movie is just a series of still pictures. Because we cannot distinguish between the different spokes, it can appear that the same spoke is seen in a slightly earlier position each time, when in fact it is simply another spoke that has moved forward that is being seen.

HOW DOES COLOUR FILM WORK?

Colour film has three layers, each sensitive to blue, green or red light. When colour film is processed, the layers are coloured with yellow, magenta and cyan dyes to produce the full-colour image.

WHAT IS A POLAROID CAMERA?

A Polaroid camera uses special film that can develop itself. When the picture has been taken, chemicals are released onto the film, and the final image appears within a minute.

WHICH WAS THE FIRST MOVIE TO HAVE ITS OWN SOUND TRACK?

Full-length movies were silent until 1927, when *The Jazz Singer* was released by Warner Brothers.

WHERE IS BOLLYWOOD?

Just as the movie industry of the United States is based in Hollywood, California, the thriving movie industry of India is centred on Bombay, nicknamed "Bollywood".

WHEN WERE RADIO WAVES FIRST USED TO SEND A MESSAGE?

Although several scientists, including Heinrich Hertz, experimented with sending and receiving radio waves, the first person to patent a useful system for using them to send signals through the air was an Italian engineer called Gugliemo Marconi (1874–1937) in 1896. He created enormous publicity for his work by claiming to have sent the first radio signal across the Atlantic in 1901. Today there is disagreement about whether such a signal was received, but Marconi was right that sending radio messages between Europe and the Americas was possible, and his work encouraged the enthusiasm for and development of radio communications that continues to this day. As Marconi's messages did not pass through wires, the system was known as wireless telegraphy.

A	• – –	S	• • •
B	– • • •	T	–
C	– • – •	U	• • –
D	– • •	V	• • • –
E	•	W	• – –
F	• • – •	X	– • • –
G	– – •	Y	– • – –
H	• • • •	Z	– – • •
I	• •		
J	• – – –	1	• – – – –
K	– • –	2	• • – – –
L	• – • •	3	• • • – –
M	– –	4	• • • • –
N	– •	5	• • • • •
O	– – –	6	– • • • •
P	• – – •	7	– – • • •
Q	– – • –	8	– – – • •
R	• – •	9	– – – – •

WHY WAS MORSE CODE INVENTED?

MORSE CODE was ideal for sending messages by telegraph because it used only two kinds of signal: a long one, called a dash, and a short one, called a dot. By sending long and short bursts of radio waves along a wire, a transmitter could send a clear message. Samuel Morse (1791–1872) was an American engineer who invented a practical magnetic telegraph. His invention was more or less ignored on both sides of the Atlantic, until, in 1843, the United States government allotted 30,000 dollars for a telegraph line between Washington and Baltimore. Morse invented Morse Code for use on his telegraph, which became very successful.

WHY HAVE RADIO MESSAGES BEEN BEAMED INTO SPACE?

NO ONE KNOWS if we are alone in the universe. In order to try to make contact with other intelligent life forms in our galaxy, some laboratories regularly send radio signals out into space. In fact, distant constellations do emit radio waves, but so far they do not seem to have been transmitted intentionally by living creatures. Scientists watch for a regular pattern of signals that might indicate a living transmitter.

WHAT ARE TELECOMMUNICATIONS?

TELECOMMUNICATIONS include sending and receiving messages by radio, television, telephone and fax. They began when the telegraph used electrical pulses, sent down a wire, to send information. Radio waves, electricity, or light can carry telecommunications. As well as a method of carrying the message, telecommunications also require a transmitter, to send the signals, and a receiver.

Modern telecommunications make it possible for people all over the world to make contact with each other, however remote their locations.

HOW DOES A TELEVISION SHOW PICTURES?

TELEVISION TECHNOLOGY uses electric signals through cables or ultra-high frequency (UHF) radio waves to transmit pictures and sound to a television set, which acts as a receiver. The signals come into the television through a cable or an aerial. The picture signals are divided into three – one each for red, green and blue. In the television, there is an electron gun for each colour, which fires electron beams (also known as cathode rays) onto the screen. The screen is covered with chemicals called phosphors. The electron beams scan rapidly across the screen, causing tiny dots of phosphors to glow red, green and blue. Viewed with normal vision, from a distance, the dots blur into a full-colour picture.

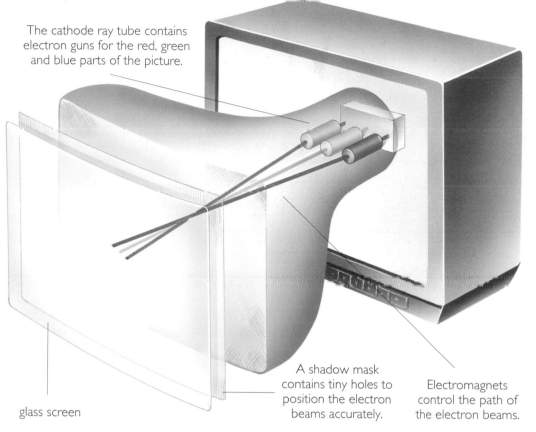

The cathode ray tube contains electron guns for the red, green and blue parts of the picture.

glass screen

A shadow mask contains tiny holes to position the electron beams accurately.

Electromagnets control the path of the electron beams.

HOW CAN RADIOS HELP NATURALISTS?

BY PUTTING COLLARS with radio transmitters onto wild animals, naturalists have been able to track their movements, night and day, adding enormously to our knowledge of animal behaviour. The collars do not interfere with the animals' normal lives. As well as learning about animal migrations and hunting patterns, naturalists are also able to discover more about the life span of animals in the wild, which may differ enormously from that of those kept in zoos and wildlife parks.

Polar bears can be fiercely protective of their young, and the conditions of the Arctic in winter make it difficult for naturalists to follow their movements. A harmless tranquillizer is used to send the animal to sleep while a transmitting collar is fitted.

HOW DOES A VIDEO RECORDER WORK?

A VIDEO RECORDER stores television sound and pictures on a magnetic tape. It receives the electric signal that comes through a cable or aerial into the machine, then records it on tape in much the same way as a tape recorder does, although the video recorder makes diagonal tracks so that more information can be held on the tape. A record–replay head in the video recorder enables the information on tape to be sent to a television set.

fast facts

CAN SENDERS OF MORSE CODE BE ANONYMOUS?

Of course, the receiver of a message in Morse Code may be thousands of miles away from its sender, so he or she may not be sure who is pressing the Morse key. But when sending Morse manually, everyone has his or her own style and rhythm. An experienced Morse receiver can often recognize the sender by the way the message is sent, just as we may recognize the sender of a letter by his or her handwriting.

HOW DO RADIO WAVES ACT AS BABYSITTERS?

Many parents with small children use baby alarms. These transmit radio signals of the sounds a child makes to a receiving radio in another room or even a nearby home. They can help to reassure a parent that a child is still sleeping while they are out of hearing range.

WHAT IS CLOSED-CIRCUIT TELEVISION?

Closed-circuit television, which is most commonly used for security purposes, is a system in which the television pictures travel directly from the camera taking them to a screen. This does not mean that they cannot be stored. The pictures can be captured on videotape in the normal way.

Videotape has many uses in sport. For example, it may be used for an "action replay", to check what really happened in a fast-moving sport. Athletes are also able to study videotape in order to see where they are making errors and so improve their technique.

WHAT WAS THE EARLIEST SOUND RECORDING?

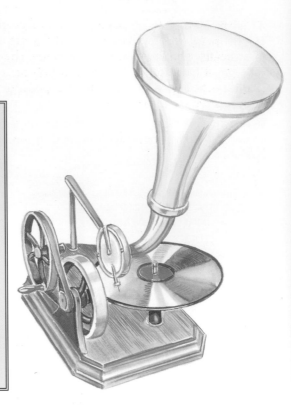

In 1877, the American inventor Thomas Edison (1847–1931) experimented with a machine called a "phonograph", which converted sound vibrations into grooves on a cylinder covered with tinfoil. A sharp needle, called a stylus, was attached to a diaphragm at the narrow end of a large horn. When sound waves travelled into the horn, they made the diaphragm vibrate, causing the needle to move up and down, and cutting a groove of varying depth in the tinfoil. If this process was reversed, so that the needle was made to run over the grooves, it caused the diaphragm to vibrate. Vibrations passed through the horn, pushing air in front of them, to reach the listener's ear as sound. Later, wax-coated cylinders were used instead of tinfoil, to give a better result.

HOW DOES A CASSETTE TAPE RECORD AND PLAY?

DISCS were the main method of recording and playing music for the first half of the twentieth century, but sound recording on steel tape was used in the 1930s by radio stations. In 1935, two German companies developed a strong plastic tape, which had a layer of iron oxide on the surface. This invention eventually made it possible for smaller, domestic tape recorders to come into use. In 1963, Philips introduced something they called a "compact cassette", which contained a thin tape within a plastic case. This was much lighter and more convenient for home use.

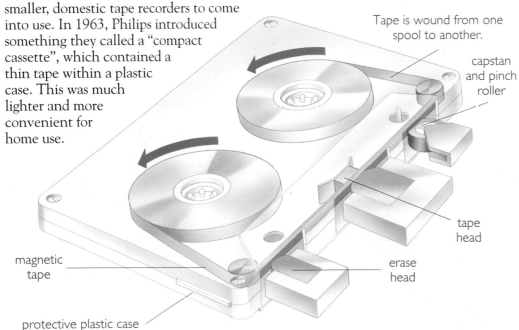

Tape is wound from one spool to another.

capstan and pinch roller

tape head

erase head

magnetic tape

protective plastic case

On blank magnetic tape, the magnetized particles are all facing in the same direction. Electrical signals created by recorded sounds cause the magnetized particles to move into patterns that match the sound signal. When the tape is played, the head "reads" the magnetized particles and creates electrical signals to match them, which are relayed to a loudspeaker to be played. In order to wipe the recording from the tape, all that needs to happen is for the tape to be passed through a strong magnetic field, which lines up the magnetized particles once more.

WHO INVENTED THE GRAMOPHONE?

In 1888, the German-American inventor Emile Berliner (1851–1929) invented a system of sound recording that could be mass produced. He devised a flat disc, called a gramophone record. On the disc, a groove ran in a spiral from the outer edge of the disc to the centre. Side-to-side, rather than up-and-down movements of the stylus recorded and played the sound vibrations. Once one disc had been made, it could be used as a mould to make a metal die, which could then stamp out exact copies of the disc in large numbers.

In the second half of the twentieth century, magnetic tape has been an important storage medium for sound and computerized information. Today compact discs and other recording methods are taking over.

HOW DOES A COMPACT DISC WORK?

A COMPACT DISC (CD) has a plastic surface on which sounds are stored in binary code as very small holes, called pits, and flat areas, called lands. These can be "read" by a laser beam. The laser beam scans across the surface of the disc. When the light falls on a pit, it is scattered, but when it falls on a land, it is reflected back to a light-sensitive detector. This in turn causes a pulse of current to pass to a loudspeaker, which converts it back into sound.

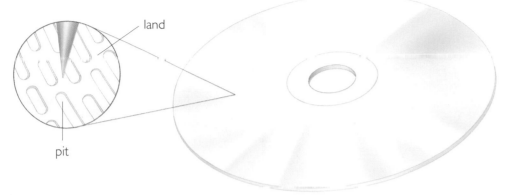

land

pit

As the laser scans the disc, a motor spins the CD round. CDs can be used to store words and pictures as well as sounds. The photographs in this book were stored on compact discs before being used.

HOW DO MICROPHONES WORK?

INSIDE A MICROPHONE is a metal disc, called a diaphragm. When a sound wave hits the sensitive diaphragm, it makes it vibrate at the same frequency. This causes a wire coil, beneath the diaphragm, to move up and down. As the coil comes near to a magnet below, it creates a pulse of electric current in the wire. The pattern of these pulses matches the pattern of the sound wave. The pulses can be sent along a wire to a loudspeaker, to be turned back into sound, or they can be recorded on a tape or compact disc.

diaphragm

magnet

coil of wire

Microphones and loudspeakers make it possible for huge numbers of people to hear speakers or performers at public events. For actors and singers, very small microphones can now be attached to their faces, near their cheekbones, so that the audience cannot see them at all.

fast facts

WHY DID SINGERS ONCE PERFORM IN CAVES?

We do not hear our own voices as others hear them, because the sounds pass through flesh and bone to reach our ears. Today singers can hear recordings of their voices, but before sound recording, the only way they could judge their own singing was to perform in a cave and listen to the echo!

HOW CAN RECORDINGS HELP HISTORIANS?

Written records give historians lots of useful information, but do not tell the whole story. Recordings of the voices of ordinary people, recalling their own views and memories, give vivid pictures of the past. Imagine how interesting it would be to hear people from five hundred years ago speaking. In four hundred years time, that will be possible!

WHAT IS SAMPLING?

Sampling involves recording different sounds and then using digital technology to manipulate them, changing pitch, volume, tone and tempo to create special effects.

Face microphones are very useful in musical theatre, where actors have to sing and dance at the same time.

HOW DOES A LOUDSPEAKER PRODUCE SOUND?

A LOUDSPEAKER works like a reversed microphone. Electric current flows into a coil of wire, turning it into an electromagnet. This attracts the coil to another magnet inside the loudspeaker, causing the coil to vibrate. This vibrates a diaphragm at the same frequency as the original sound, pushing air in front of it to carry the sound to the ears of the listeners. Many loudspeakers can be connected together, so that sound is heard all around a large outdoor or indoor space.

DID EARLY BUILDERS HAVE PLANS TO FOLLOW?

For thousands of years, people have been building homes, temples and monuments, but until only a few centuries ago, they had no proper plans to follow before building began. They based their work on tried and tested methods, estimating how strongly walls had to be built to support the floors above and the roof. Of course, many buildings collapsed or subsided, but others are still standing to this day, a tribute to the skill of builders in times past.

HOW WERE THE PYRAMIDS BUILT?

THE EGYPTIANS were building massive pyramids almost 5000 years ago. We are still not sure how they achieved this without the mechanical lifting and cutting equipment that we have today, but the answer must be that they used huge numbers of slaves to shape and haul the enormous stones with which they built. Recently, scientists have calculated that as many as 10,000 slaves were probably needed to work on these structures.

WHAT ARE THE EARLIEST BUILDINGS KNOWN?

THE EARLIEST HUMAN HOMES that we know of are caves. We know that they were inhabited because paintings have been found on the walls, but these homes were not built – they were made by nature, not human beings. The earliest mud and wooden shelters and huts have not survived intact, but from about 2700BC people began to build some of the huge stone structures that have survived to this day. Apart from the Egyptian pyramids, one of the earliest was the circle of stones known as Stonehenge, in England. It is not known exactly what this was for, but it probably had religious significance. Throughout history, religion has spurred builders to create many of the largest and most impressive buildings ever seen.

DO ALL HUMAN SOCIETIES BUILD HOMES?

WHEN PREHISTORIC PEOPLES began to farm, they built settlements. However, some peoples preferred to continue to move about in search of food, following a nomadic lifestyle. Nomads do not need settled homes, but they do need shelter from the weather, so many of them carry tents made of skins or woven fabric. Tents are light to carry and can be put up very quickly.

Some Native Americans made shelters from skins and sticks. A hole in the top let out smoke.

HOW HAVE BUILDING STYLES DEVELOPED THROUGH HISTORY?

ALTHOUGH many traditional building styles are still in use, the appearance of buildings and the way in which they are built changes as outside influences are brought to bear on their architects and builders. Naturally, buildings are based on shapes that give the strongest structures: rectangles, cylinders, triangles and domes. In the search for new forms, architects have often looked back to the past. In the fourteenth century in Italy, for example, designers rediscovered the architecture of ancient Rome and neo-classical ("new" classical) buildings in the subsequent centuries were built all over the world, especially where a building was meant to embody power, learning and dignity. New buildings today still combine recent ideas with traditional motifs.

Doric column   Ionic column   Corinthian column

Classical styles of architecture were divided into orders, of which the Doric, Ionic and Corinthian were three that may still frequently be seen on large houses, churches and public buildings.

fast facts

WHICH ARE THE BEST BUILDING MATERIALS?

On the whole, building materials are not better than one another. Some are simply more suitable in some situations and for some purposes than others. Traditionally, people have built with the materials nearest to hand, using wood in forest areas, mud in dry areas, and bricks where there was clay to make them. The towering structures built today require modern building materials, such as reinforced steel, concrete and glass.

HOW IS CONCRETE REINFORCED?

Used since the 1850s, reinforced concrete has metal bars or wires embedded in it for extra strength.

WHAT WAS A ZIGGURAT?

Ruins of ziggurats can still be seen. They were ancient Mesopotamian stepped towers, with temples on top.

WHAT DO AN ARCHITECT'S PLANS SHOW?

AN ARCHITECT'S plans give all the information needed to build the structure shown. The plans show the materials to be used, how they fit together, and all the measurements necessary to complete the building. Plans usually show several elevations (different views) of the structure, including a floor plan and a plan of each side of the building. Nowadays, computers are increasingly used to draw up plans. They can provide lists of the materials and equipment needed as the plans are drawn, and work out costings.

IS CONCRETE A NEW BUILDING MATERIAL?

CONCRETE is a mixture of sand, water and cement, a powder made of lime and clay. Far from being a new material, concrete was used by the Romans in the first century AD to build the dome of the Pantheon in Rome.

HOW ARE SKYSCRAPERS BUILT?

SKYSCRAPERS have a frame, usually made of steel or concrete, to support the floors and walls, which are attached to the frame. The frame is rather like the skeleton inside a human body. It is not designed to be completely rigid, but to sway a little in high winds, thus reducing the force of the wind upon the structure.

WHAT ARE CERAMICS?

Ceramics are objects made of materials that are permanently hardened by being heated. Usually, the word is used to mean articles made of various forms of clay. Sticky clay is dug from the Earth and needs to have impurities, such as stones, removed before it can be used. The clay may be naturally red, yellow, grey or almost white, but can be coloured before shaping or covered with a coloured glaze.

WHAT CAN BE MADE FROM CLAY?

CLAY CAN BE USED to make a huge variety of ceramic articles, from tiny electronic components to bricks and baths. It is a good insulator and, when covered with a glaze, is completely waterproof. Unlike many metals, glazed clay is unreactive, so that acidic foods will not stain it, and exposure to water and the air will not tarnish or corrode it.

HOW ARE CLAY ARTICLES SHAPED?

CLAY CAN BE SHAPED when it is wet by squeezing it between the fingers, "throwing" it on a potter's wheel, or pushing it into a mould. Before using any of these methods, the potter must make sure that there are no air bubbles in the clay. If there are, the air will expand when the clay is baked, and the article may explode, breaking other items in the kiln as well. However ceramic articles are produced, they are made a little larger than the finished product needs to be, as they shrink slightly when baked.

A potter's wheel consists of a turntable, powered by a treadle or motor. The clay is placed (or "thrown") into the middle of the wheel and shaped with wet hands or tools as it turns. A skilled potter can make a perfectly symmetrical pot in this way.

Mass-produced items are usually produced by moulding. A machine called a jolley pushes a piece of clay into a mug-shaped mould. Then a profiling tool presses round inside to push the clay against the sides of the mould and leave the inside of the mug empty. The handle is added later.

WHY ARE CERAMICS BAKED?

CERAMICS are baked to make them hard and waterproof. Until they are baked (fired), ceramics can be mixed with water again to form clay. Firing is done in a large oven called a kiln. In large ceramics factories, the kilns are heated all the time. They are like long tunnels, through which ceramics move slowly on trolleys in a never-ending process. The first firing that a clay article receives is called a biscuit firing. It makes the article hard and brittle, but it is still porous. Water can be absorbed by it.

Pots for plants grown outside need to be chosen carefully if the gardener lives in an area that has frosts in the winter. If the pots are too porous, they will absorb a lot of water. If this freezes, it will expand and crack the pot.

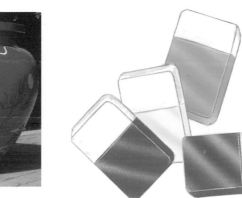

This Chinese bowl has intricate patterns painted onto it in coloured glazes. In English, some kinds of pottery are often called "china". This is because fine pottery was first imported from China.

Glazes often change colour in the kiln, so test pieces of clay, dipped in glaze, are fired to make sure that the colour will come out as required.

HOW IS POTTERY DECORATED?

THERE ARE MANY WAYS of decorating pots. They can be dipped in a glaze, made of tiny particles of glass in a liquid, and fired for a second time. The glassy covering melts onto the pottery, making it completely waterproof. Pottery can also be decorated after glazing, with transfers, hand-painted designs, or by screen-printing. It may then be fired for a third time to fix the decoration.

WHAT IS SLIP?

SLIP IS A MIXTURE of clay and water, forming a thick liquid. It can be used as a kind of glue to stick a handle onto a cup when both are "leather hard" (hard enough to handle but still soft enough to cut with a knife). Slip can also be poured into plaster moulds to form intricate shapes. The plaster absorbs water from the slip, causing it to dry on the outside first. If the rest of the slip is poured away, hollow vessels and ornaments can be made.

WHY ARE THERE UNGLAZED PARTS ON THE UNDERSIDE OF A CERAMIC OBJECT?

IN THE HEAT of the kiln, glaze would fuse with the shelf that the object stands on, so glaze is carefully wiped from the base of the object before it is fired.

WHAT IS GLASS MADE OF?

Glass is an extraordinarily useful material. The substances from which it is made are easy to find and very cheap. Glass is mainly melted, cooled sand, but other ingredients are added, such as sodium carbonate (soda ash) and limestone. Although it appears solid to us, glass is in fact a liquid, flowing incredibly slowly. When windows that are hundreds of years old are measured, they are found to be slightly thicker at the bottom than at the top, as the glass very gradually flows downwards.

Coloured glass is made by adding metallic oxides, such as iron, copper, manganese and chromium.

HOW IS PLATE GLASS MADE?

PLATE GLASS is thick, good quality glass made in huge sheets for shop windows. Its very smooth surface is made by floating the molten glass onto a bath of molten tin. Tin melts at a lower temperature than glass, so the glass begins to set on the tin and is then passed over rollers as it finishes cooling. The larger the bath of molten tin, the larger the glass that can be made.

HOW IS GLASS CUT?

HARDENED METAL BLADES can cut glass but are easily blunted. More often, glass is cut with the hardest natural substance known – a diamond. If a furrow is made in glass with a diamond, it will usually break cleanly when pressure is applied to it.

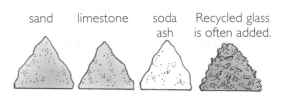

sand   limestone   soda ash   Recycled glass is often added.

Heating the ingredients in a furnace makes molten glass.

The molten glass floats on top of a bath of molten tin.

The cooled glass can be cut into smaller sheets.

HOW IS GLASS BLOWN?

GLASSBLOWERS dip a long tube into molten glass, then blow air into it as it cools, causing the glass to form a bubble. While it is still very warm, this bubble can be shaped, cut with shears, or added to other glass shapes. A slightly different method is used when glassware is made by machine. Then, lumps of hot glass are placed in a mould and air is blown in to force the glass to the sides of the mould. With both methods, the glass can be engraved, or sandblasted to give it a rough texture, after it has cooled.

Sweden is famous for its handblown glass. Here the glassblower is positioning molten glass to be shaped.

The more air that is blown into the glass, the thinner it becomes. Very delicate objects can be made.

HOW ARE STAINED GLASS WINDOWS MADE?

SINCE MEDIEVAL TIMES, glorious decorative windows have been made by joining small pieces of coloured and painted glass together with lead strips. The lead is soft and easy to bend but strong enough to hold the glass.

Stained glass has been popular for centuries. In the days when most people could not read, the stained glass in Christian churches told biblical stories in a way that the congregation could understand. It also meant that no one could look out of the window during lengthy sermons!

HOW ARE MIRRORS MADE?

MIRRORS are made by coating the back of a sheet of glass with an alloy of mercury and another metal. This means that light does not pass through the glass, but is bounced back to give a reflection.

As mirrors show us ourselves, they have often been thought of as slightly mysterious, as in the story of Snow White.

HOW WERE WINDOWS MADE BEFORE GLASS WAS WIDELY AVAILABLE?

WINDOWS have three main purposes: to let light into a building, to allow ventilation, and to allow the occupants to see out. Although glass has been made for thousands of years, it is only comparatively recently that techniques have been developed for making large sheets of glass for windows. Before that, although small sheets of glass were available, they were expensive. Small windows were sometimes covered with thin panels of horn. Although this could not be seen through, it did let in a certain amount of light and kept out cold winds.

This castle has very small windows so that there are few entrances for enemy arrows and bullets. A narrow slit was all that was necessary for the castle's inhabitants to fire on attackers outside. In any case, large windows would have been terribly draughty.

Buildings dating from the sixteenth century or earlier usually have very small windows, in which little panes of glass can be fitted into wooden frames. Strips of lead may be used to hold them in place.

Nowadays we are used to seeing entire buildings covered with glass, but vehicles need windows too. This boat allows tourists an uninterrupted view of Paris, as it travels down the River Seine in France.

fast facts

WHAT IS GLASS FIBRE?

Glass fibre is a material made of glass that is spun info very, very fine fibres. It is used to add strength to some plastics and for insulation Both heat and sound are unable to pass through it easily.

HOW IS OVENPROOF GLASS MADE?

Glass in which food is cooked needs to be very tough and resistant to rapid changes in temperature. A chemical called boron oxide is added to the glass to give it these properties.

WHAT IS REINFORCED GLASS?

Everyone knows that most glass shatters quite easily, but when glass is used to make a roof, for example, breakage could be extrmely dangcrous. For this reason, in places where increased security is needed, glass is reinforced by having a mesh of wire embedded in it. Even if the glass breaks, the wire will remain in place and prevent the glass from shattering into large, sharp pieces.

WHEN WAS GLASS FIRST MADE?

Ancient civilizations, such as the Egyptian and Roman Empires, certainly used glass, and glass objects were being made in Mesopotamia 4500 years ago.

HOW IS GLASS RECYCLED?

It is very easy to recycle glass. It is simply broken up and melted, before being shaped again in the normal way.

HOW IS GLASS ENGRAVED?

Expert engravers decorate glass using various methods depening on the number of objects and the intricacy of the design, it is possible to use hydrochloric acid. The basic technique involves covering the glass inside and out with an acid resistant wax or a varnish. The design is then inscribed through the wax with a sharp point either free hand or with the use of a template. The object is then immersed in acid which eats into the glass leaving deep lines where the resistant coating has been removed.

WHY DO WE COOK FOOD?

There are several reasons why food is cooked. Most obvious is the fact that cooking makes food hot! In cold weather, hot food is especially warming and comforting. Cooking also alters the flavour and texture of food. Heat causes chemical reactions to take place, altering the way that the food tastes and feels in our mouths. Because of these chemical reactions, cooking may also make food easier to digest. Finally, cooking can make food safer to eat by killing bacteria within it.

Preservatives extend the life of foods, so that bacteria do not cause them to deteriorate within days or even hours.

HOW DOES YEAST WORK?

YEAST is a single-celled living organism that digests starches and gives off carbon dioxide gas in the process. Bread can be made light and airy by mixing yeast into the flour and water that make up bread dough. The dough is then left to rise in a warm place. The warmth encourages the yeast to give off tiny bubbles of carbon dioxide, which are trapped within the elastic dough. When the dough is put into the oven, some water evaporates from the flour mixture, and the dough becomes firmer, with the tiny bubbles trapped within it.

In a bakery, huge machines mix and knead the dough. Different kinds of flour are used to make different breads, while flavourings, fats and other ingredients may also be added.

Flavourings and flavour enhancers can intensify natural flavours or provide a cheaper way to flavour food.

WHAT MAKES A CAKE RISE?

IN ORDER for a cake to rise and become light and spongy, air has to be trapped inside the mixture, just as it does in bread. Instead of yeast, most cakes contain a raising agent, such as bicarbonate of soda. When it is heated with flour and liquid, chemical reactions take place to produce little bubbles of carbon dioxide, which are then trapped in the mixture as it becomes firm. Another way of incorporating air into cakes is to whisk eggs before adding them to the mixture. The air is trapped in the egg mixture, which becomes firm as it cooks. This method is used in cakes that do not contain fat.

Colourings make foods and drinks more enticing. They may replace the colour lost when food is cooked.

Emulsifiers enable fats to be suspended in tiny globules in liquids.

Uncooked cake mixture is a very thick liquid. As it cooks, bubbles form in it, and it expands. This expansion causes the mixture to move upwards (rise) as the baking tin prevents it from expanding in any other direction. As the cake cooks, it becomes solid, taking on the shape of the container in which it is cooked.

WHY ARE CHEMICALS ADDED TO FOOD?

WHEN WE READ the lists of ingredients on food packaging, they sometimes sound more like a chemistry lesson than a recipe! Nowadays, food safety regulations and the demand of consumers for products with a reliable taste and texture mean that many different additives are found in some foods.

HOW CAN FOODS BE PRESERVED WITHOUT FREEZING?

BACTERIA that cause food to go bad need certain conditions in which to grow. If they are deprived of those conditions, they may die or be unable to reproduce themselves. One thing that bacteria need is water, so drying foods can help to preserve them. Bacteria cannot reproduce at temperatures below 6°C (39°F) or above 37°C (98°F), so making them hot or cold can prevent them from being active. Canning preserves food by sealing it into a can and then heating it to a high temperature, killing off the bacteria inside. As no more bacteria can enter the can, the food is safe for a long time, until the can is opened. High concentrations of salt or sugar prevent bacteria from being able to use available water, as can acids, so foods such as pickles and preserves are cooked and stored in brine (a mixture of salt and water), vinegar or sugar.

WHAT ARE THE BASIC FOOD FLAVOURS?

MOST OF US can recognize hundreds of different flavours if tested blindfold, but food technologists see these as mixtures of four basic flavours: sweetness, sourness, bitterness and saltiness. Flavour receptors on different parts of the tongue are best at sensing these flavours. You can test this for yourself with a little sugar for sweetness, salt for saltiness, vinegar for sourness and squeezed lemon peel for bitterness, but hold your nose as you test so that aromas do not affect your judgment.

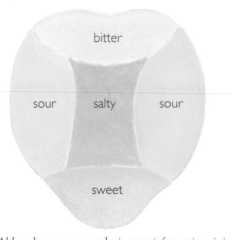

Although our tongues take in taste information, it is our brains that process it.

HOW DOES PACKAGING HELP TO PRESERVE FOOD?

THE MAIN WAY in which packaging helps to preserve food is by preventing bacteria from contaminating its contents, but modern packaging is very sophisticated. Some foods are vacuum packed, so that plastic wrappings exclude any air from the product. Other kinds of packaging are designed to trap gases such as oxygen, nitrogen and carbon dioxide. Mixtures of these help to preserve different foods and to give them a pleasant appearance. Meats, for example, can be kept pink and fresh-looking. Sometimes you will see that meat looks browner where it touches the packaging. This is because the gases cannot reach it at this point. As these are gases that we breathe in every day, they are perfectly safe.

fast facts

DOES FREEZING PREVENT FOODS FROM GOING BAD?

Freezing does not kill the bacteria that cause food to spoil, but it does slow them down so that they are unable to multiply. That means that when a food is defrosted, it will continue to deteriorate at the same rate it would have done if it had not been frozen.

WHAT IS EXTRUSION?

Extrusion is a means of shaping foods by squeezing a mixture through a nozzle and then cooking it quickly so that it retains the shape. Breakfast cereals shaped like hoops or stars are made like this, as is spaghetti and other pasta shapes.

WHAT IS IRRADIATION?

Irradiation is a way of killing the bacteria in food by bombarding it with gamma rays.

WHAT DID LOUIS PASTEUR INVENT?

This French chemist invented a way of making milk safe by heating it. It is not boiled, which would change the flavour, but kept at a high temperature for several minutes. This process is now known as pasteurization.

WHY DO FOODS SOMETIMES SEEM TASTELESS IF YOU HAVE A COLD?

Although we do taste food with the sensitive areas of our tongues, we also use our sense of smell a great deal. Some "flavours" are really aromas. When we have a cold, our sense of smell can be affected, which in turn affects the way our food tastes.

Today's food packaging is often brightly coloured to encourage consumers to buy. But packages also have important nutritional information and a date by which the food should be eaten, while it is still fresh.

WHAT ARE FOSSIL FUELS?

Fossil fuels, which include coal, oil and natural gas, were formed millions of years ago when prehistoric plants and animals died, and their decaying bodies, pressed under layers of rock and earth, became fossilized. Life as we know it would not be possible without fossil fuels. Not only are they burned to supply heat and energy to homes and industry, but by forming the fuel for power stations, they also supply most of the electricity we use. In addition, fossil fuels can be processed to produce many other useful materials, including plastics, dyes and bitumen.

On land, oil is brought up to the surface by a pump called a nodding donkey. It gets its name from the upward and downward motion of its "head"

HOW IS OIL MINED?

THE ROCKS in which deposits of crude (unrefined) oil are found may be hundreds of metres beneath the soil or the sea bed. In either case, a shaft must be drilled down to the deposits. On land, the drill can be set up on a steel structure called a derrick. At sea, a drilling platform is needed. This may have legs that stand on the sea bed or, in very deep water, the drilling platform may float on the surface. Floating platforms must still be anchored firmly to the sea bed so that they can withstand high winds and tempestuous seas.

Helicopters are an oil rig's lifeline, bringing workers, food and supplies.

Some gas from the oil is burnt off on the rig.

Oil rigs need teams of skilled divers to check the drilling platform below the surface and make any necessary repairs.

A pipeline carries crude oil to shore, where it will be refined.

HOW IS OIL REFINED?

CRUDE OIL is refined in a process known as fractional distillation. The oil is heated to about 350°C (660°F) and its vapour is piped into a round column, about 50m (165ft) high. Inside the column, there are perforated trays at different levels. The vapour cools as it rises up the column. Different substances within the crude oil condense at different temperatures (and therefore different levels). They are called fractions.

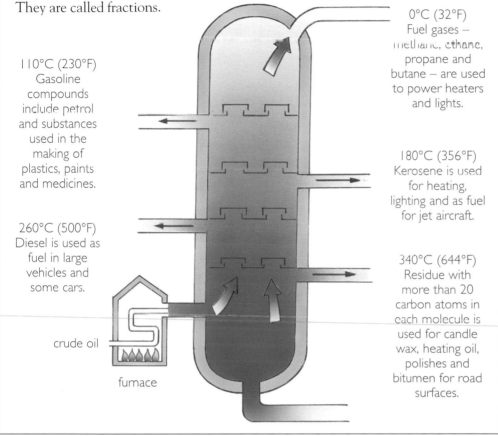

110°C (230°F) Gasoline compounds include petrol and substances used in the making of plastics, paints and medicines.

260°C (500°F) Diesel is used as fuel in large vehicles and some cars.

crude oil

furnace

0°C (32°F) Fuel gases – methane, ethane, propane and butane – are used to power heaters and lights.

180°C (356°F) Kerosene is used for heating, lighting and as fuel for jet aircraft.

340°C (644°F) Residue with more than 20 carbon atoms in each molecule is used for candle wax, heating oil, polishes and bitumen for road surfaces.

WHAT IS CRACKING?

CATALYTIC CRACKING is another method of refining crude oil. By applying pressure and heat to some of the heavier fractions obtained by distillation, lighter, more useful fractions are produced.

In an oil refinery, crude oil is separated into usable compounds. By mixing these with other substances and treating them in various ways, literally thousands of useful materials can be made.

WHAT IS PEAT?

PEAT IS partly carbonized vegetable matter, which has decomposed in water. If placed under enormous pressure for millions of years, peat would become coal. Although it does not give off as much heat as coal or oil does when burned, peat is still a useful fuel in some parts of the world, where it is dug from peatbogs. Peat has also been much prized by gardeners for improving the condition of soil.

Peat has been a traditional Irish fuel for centuries. Nowadays, conservationists are concerned that too much digging of peatbogs is destroying the environment that they provide, so alternative fuels and soil conditioners are recommended.

fast facts

HOW IS OIL FOUND?

Geologists know what kinds of rocks are likely to contain or cover oil deposits. When they find a likely area, on land or at sea, test drilling is carried out to find out if there is oil beneath the surface.

WHAT ARE THE DIFFERENT KINDS OF COAL?

Coal is found in three forms. Lignite, or brown coal, provides the least heat, as it contains less carbon and more water than the other two kinds, which are bituminous coal and anthracite.

HOW ARE OIL RIG FIRES EXTINGUISHED?

If the gas gushing from an oil well is ignited, the fire burns far too fiercely to be put out with water or normal fire extinguishers. Instead, firefighters use a special crane to position an explosive device in the flames. It seems strange to fight a fire with an explosion, but when the explosion occurs, it takes the surrounding oxygen, temporarily depriving the fire and putting it out.

WHY WERE CANARIES TAKEN INTO MINES?

Traditionally, in British mines, a canary in a cage was taken down to the coal face with the miners. The small birds were very sensitive to the dangerous gases that might build up in the shafts. If the canary died suddenly, miners knew that they must run for their lives. Now, the practice seems cruel, but it did save many human lives.

WHAT WAS A DAVY LAMP?

In deep mines, lamps were needed, but naked flames might cause an explosion. In 1815, Humphry Davy invented a safety lamp with a wire mesh around the flame, so that gases would not be ignited.

WHICH MINERALS ARE OBTAINED BY MINING?

Strictly speaking, all "minerals" are obtained by mining, as that is one meaning of the word, although it is sometimes used to refer to other inorganic substances. Mining usually involves digging in the Earth's crust, although a few minerals, such as gold, sometimes come to the surface naturally and are found in rivers or on the seashore. Metals, precious and semi-precious stones, and minerals such as sulphur and salt are all obtained by mining.

Rocks found beneath the Earth's surface have many uses in industry. Others, such as malachite, are used for decoration.

WHERE ARE THE WORLD'S MOST IMPORTANT MINING AREAS?

FOR MINING to be economical, minerals need to be found in high concentrations. Sometimes they occur in seams. These are layers of minerals or mineral ores occurring between other rocks. In different parts of the world, rocks dating from various periods of the Earth's history are nearest the surface. This gives mineralogists their first clue as to the minerals that may be found within them.

IS WATER USEFUL IN MINING?

IN DEEP MINES, water can pose a great danger, undermining layers of rock and causing collapses and flooding, but other types of mining use water to great advantage. Sulphur, for example, can be mined in an unusual process using water. Three pipes of different sizes, one inside another, are drilled into the sulphur reserves. Then extremely hot water, under pressure, is pumped down the outer pipe. This melts the sulphur. Compressed air is then pumped down the central pipe, causing the melted sulphur to move up the middle pipe to the surface. This system was developed by an American engineer, Herman Frasch (1851–1914).

KEY
- ▢ precious metals, such as gold, platinum and silver
- ◇ precious stones, such as diamonds
- ○ base metals, such as copper, lead, mercury, tin and zinc
- ■ light metals, such as aluminium, lithium and titanium
- ▽ rare metals, such as uranium
- ⊘ iron, chromium, cobalt, manganese and nickel
- ▲ industrial minerals, such as asbestos, china clay, mica and talc
- △ chemicals, such as borax, nitrates, phosphate, potash, salt and sulphur

CAN MINERALS BE OBTAINED FROM PLACES OTHER THAN THE EARTH'S CRUST?

FOR PRACTICAL PURPOSES, the Earth's crust is the only source of minerals. There are, of course, huge amounts of minerals in the Earth's core and in space, but at the moment it is not possible for us to reach and use them.

Despite modern safety regulations, mining is still a dangerous occupation. However, opencast mines are less hazardous than deep-shaft mines, where miners have to work hundreds of metres below the surface.

WHAT IS OPENCAST MINING?

OPENCAST MINES are used when the deposit lies near the surface. Overlying earth and rock can be moved by machine or washed away with water. Although opencast mining is cheaper than digging deep mines, some people feel that the environmental costs of it are high, as large areas of land are laid bare and wildlife destroyed. Nowadays great attention is often paid to landscaping the area after an opencast mine has been abandoned. Many are made into parks or wildlife refuges. Planting the areas also helps to stabilize heaps of spoil.

COULD THE EARTH'S MINERALS BE USED UP?

ALTHOUGH there are enormous reserves of iron and aluminium in the Earth's crust, other metals, such as tin, lead, silver, zinc, mercury and platinum are not so plentiful. Some further sources of such metals are known, but at present it would prove too expensive to reach them. As with other non-renewable resources, it is important that we recycle metals or use other materials where possible.

HOW DO UNDERGROUND MINES OPERATE?

DEEP DEPOSITS are reached by driving a shaft vertically into the ground. Miners descend the shaft in a lift. An air shaft takes fresh air down into the mine, where poisonous gases may accumulate. Trucks carry the mined material to a freight lift, which brings them to the surface. Trucks may also be used to take miners to the nearest deposits. Drift mines are dug where the deposit lies in an outcrop of rock near the surface. The seam can be mined directly from the surface, which is often on the slope of a hill.

WHAT IS A CARAT?

A carat is a unit of weight for precious stones, equivalent to 200 milligrams (0.007oz). It is also used as a measure of purity of gold. Pure gold is 24 carats.

WHICH IS THE LARGEST DIAMOND EVER FOUND?

A diamond called the *Cullinan* was found in 1905 at the Premier Diamond Mine, in South Africa. It weighed 3106 carats and was cut into 106 polished diamonds.

HOW DEEP IS THE DEEPEST MINE?

A gold mine at Carltonville, in South Africa, has reached a depth of 3581m (11,749ft).

WHICH ARE THE MOST COMMON MINERALS IN THE EARTH'S CRUST?

Aluminium, in the form of the ore bauxite, is the most common mineral in the Earth's crust, followed by iron and magnesium.

WHAT ARE 'CONFLICT DIAMONDS'?

Conflict diamonds are stones that originate from regions controlled by forces of factions who use the income from selling diamonds for violent ends.

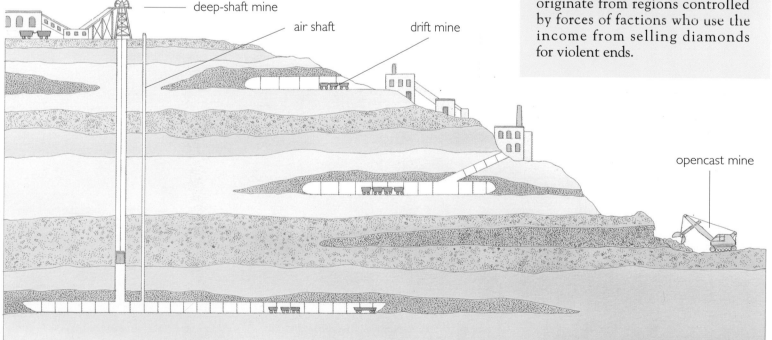

deep-shaft mine

air shaft   drift mine

opencast mine

HOW ARE MODERN MAPS MADE?

A map is similar to an aerial view of the Earth. The landscape is shown as though you are looking down on it, so that the relation of one place to another is clear. But maps are much more than simply bird's-eye views. A great deal of information about the names of places and what they are like can be given in words, numbers and symbols. Although maps are more than aerial snapshots, surveying by plane or satellite has helped mapmakers considerably. Surveying on the ground is time-consuming and may be difficult in remote places. Computer-controlled aerial surveying can give very accurate results and show overall changes in such features as vegetation and coastlines much more clearly than traditional methods.

An aerial view can show roads, rivers, buildings and vegetation, but it cannot tell you the name of a street or the height of a hill. This information has to be added to maps by the mapmakers themselves, known as cartographers.

WHAT IS A PROJECTION?

GLOBES can represent the Earth in miniature, with features shown in a true relationship to each other, but they are not practical to put in your pocket for an afternoon walk. Paper maps are much easier to use, but an adjustment needs to be made in order to show a curved land surface on a flat map. The adjustment chosen is called a projection. Several different projections can be used, depending on the purpose of the map.

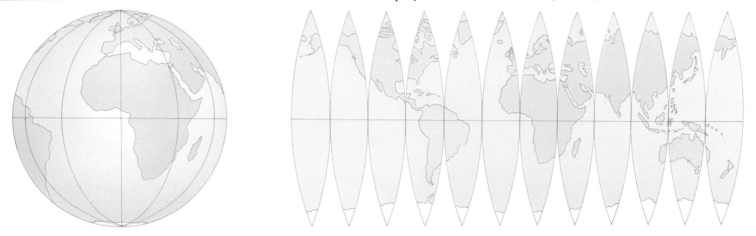

In order to flatten out the Earth's surface, it can be thought of as being divided into segments, like peeling an orange. But that leaves gaps at the top and bottom that make the map impossible to use.

WHO WAS GERARDUS MERCATOR?

GERHARD KREMER (1512–94) was called Gerardus Mercator, meaning merchant, because he made maps for merchants travelling from country to country. In 1569, he made a world map using a projection that has come to be known as Mercator's projection. It is a map that seems familiar to us, but in fact it makes countries at the far north and south of the globe appear much larger than they really are.

This map is based on Mercator's projection, but it does not look very much like the map that he produced in 1569. For one thing, Mercator had no idea of the existence of Australia or New Zealand.

This map of the world is based on Peters' projection. In the 1970s, Arno Peters devised a projection that gave each land mass its true area, but to do so he had to distort the shapes of the oceans and continents.

SCALE : 1:10,000

WHAT IS A KEY?

A MAP must be as easy to read as possible, which means that symbols and colours can often give more information than words. A key explains what the symbols and colours mean, as the one on the right does for the map above.

KEY

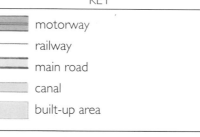

- motorway
- railway
- main road
- canal
- built-up area

WHAT IS THE SCALE OF A MAP?

MAPS ARE MADE for many purposes. The details that an airline pilot needs to see, for example, are very different from those needed by a person following a local foot-path. In addition to the actual content of the map, it needs to be drawn to an appropriate scale. That means that a distance on the map will need to be multiplied by a certain figure to find the distance on the ground itself. On a scale of 1:10,000, for example, one millimetre on the map will be equivalent to 10,000 millimetres (or 10 metres) in real life. The scale of the map above is shown on the map itself.

Many leisure maps for walkers and cyclists are drawn at a scale of 1:50,000.

fast facts

WHAT IS AN ASTRAL MAP?

An astral map is a map of the stars ans other heavenly bodies. Astral maps are usually made from the viewpoint of Earth, but still present difficulties as they do not represent a definite surface as maps of the Earth do. The stars are millions and millions of kilometres apart but are shown on maps as though they were merely distant in two dimensions, not three.

WHAT USE ARE OUT-OF-DATE MAPS?

Out-of date maps are not much use for finding your way today, but they are extremely interesting to histo-rians, who can tell a great deal about the knowledge and interests of the pepple who made them. Medieval maps of the world, for example, show how much of the Earth was known to European map-makers at that time. Huge areas of Africa and Asia are left blank, while the Americas and Australasia are not present at all.

WHAT IS A THEODOLITE?

A theodolite is an instrument used by surveyors and mapmakers. It measures horizontal and vertical angles, enabling surveyors to chart the distance between features of the landscape and their relative posi-tions above sea-level.

WHAT IS ORIENTEERING?

Orienteering is a sport that combines map-reading and running. Competitors follow a cross-country course, reaching checkpoints as quickly as possible by using a map. At each checkpoint, there is a rubber stamp, which runners use to show that they have completed all parts of the course.

WHAT ARE THE EARLIEST SURVIVING MAPS?

The oldest maps in existence are ancient Babylonian clay tablets from the 6th century BC, they show the world as a small, flat landmass entirely encircled by a ribbon of water. They are almost entirely without mathematical principles to determine where things are - not like to the maps of today.

HOW IS FITNESS MEASURED?

Fitness is the physical condition of an individual. When considered in terms of sports and other physical activity, it is often thought of as having four aspects: endurance, strength, flexibility and speed. Sports differ in the degree to which each of these factors is important. For example, weightlifting requires enormous strength, while a sprinter needs the greatest possible speed. The four aspects of fitness are measured in different ways, but one general way of measuring fitness is to see how the heart responds to physical activity. During exertion, the rate at which the heart beats increases, as it pumps more oxygenated blood around the body. How quickly the heart rate returns to normal after exercise is one way to assess how fit someone is and how exercise is improving their fitness.

Modern exercise bicycles have computers that can give instant readings of the time and distance pedalled and monitor the exerciser's heart rate.

HOW CAN TRAINING IMPROVE PERFORMANCE?

TRAINING improves performance by building up endurance, strength, flexibility and speed. This is done by improving the techniques used in a particular sport, strengthening the muscles used, improving athletes' understanding of how their bodies are performing and giving them confidence to try even harder. There are lots of training methods, and variety can help to prevent boredom setting in.

Decathlon

100m, 400m and 1500m races

long jump

shot put

high jump

110m hurdles

discus

pole vault

javelin

Modern pentathlon

fencing

freestyle swimming

pistol shooting

cross-country running

riding

Triathlon

swimming 3.8km

cycling 180km

running 42.2km

Many people use weight training to increase their strength. Lifting light weights and repeating the exercise a specified number of times builds muscle strength without creating bulk.

WHAT ARE MULTI-DISCIPLINARY SPORTING EVENTS?

SOME ATHLETES do not specialize in just one sport but maintain a very high standard at several. For them, multi-disciplinary sports, in which points are awarded for performance in a variety of events, are ideal. Some of the most popular are shown above.

HOW ARE RACES ON A CIRCULAR TRACK MADE FAIR?

WHEN ATHLETES are running a circuit, those on the inside tracks have to run less far than those on the outside. In order to ensure that everyone runs the same distance, the start is staggered, so that those on the inside appear to start much further back than those on the outside. It is not until the final straight that it is really possible to see who is winning. Longer races often start from a simple curved line. Athletes break out of their lanes quite quickly and each runs as close to the inside of the track as possible.

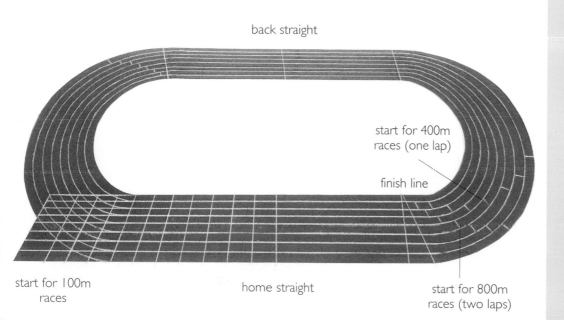

back straight

start for 400m races (one lap)

finish line

start for 100m races

home straight

start for 800m races (two laps)

WHEN WERE THE MODERN OLYMPIC GAMES INTRODUCED?

THE ANCIENT GREEKS held sporting contests over 2000 years ago. In 1896, a Frenchman called Baron Pierre de Coubertin prompted the revival of the Olympic Games. The first modern Olympics were held in Athens, Greece, in honour of their origin. Since then they have been held every four years, except in wartime, in cities all over the globe.

The Olympic flame is a symbol of the Olympic spirit of striving to do one's best. Before each Olympic Games, a series of runners carries the flame from Greece to the site of the Games, where it is used to light the main flame at the opening ceremony.

WHAT ARE THE PARALYMPICS?

IN 1960, in Rome, Italy, the first Paralympics were held. These are Olympic Games for athletes with disabilities. They are now held after each Olympic Games, often on the same site, and give disabled athletes from all over the world an opportunity to compete against each other.

Athletes at the Paralympics train just as hard as their Olympic colleagues. Wheelchairs are specially built for various sports, including track and field events.

fast facts

WHEN WAS THE FIRST MARATHON RUN?

The marathon, a race of 42.195km (26.2 miles), is named after a famous journey by a Greek called Pheidippides, who ran almost that distance to report a Greek victory at the Battle of Marathon in 490BC.

WHAT DOES A SPORTS PHYSIOTHERAPIST DO?

Hard training and harder competition causes many athletes to sustain injuries. A sports physiotherapist uses techniques such as massage, remedial exercises and heat treatment to help the injury to heal properly and quickly.

WHY DO MALE SWIMMERS SHAVE THEIR BODIES?

Competitive swimmers want to move through the water as quickly as possible. Hair may increase the friction between their bodies and the water, so they shave it off. Some even shave their heads!

WHY IS IT IMPORTANT TO WARM UP BEFORE EXERCISE?

Stretching muscles and raising the heart rate before exercise is called warming up. It is important because it helps to prevent injury to muscles and allows the body to enter a higher level of activity gently.

IS SQUASH THE FASTEST BALL GAME?

During a squash match, the rubber ball may travel at over 230km/h (143mph). But in the fast-moving game of pelota (or jai alai), ball speeds of over 300km/h (186mph) have been recorded.

HOW DO GOLF COURSES AND GOLF LINKS DIFFER?

Strictly speaking, links are near to the seashore.

WHAT IS A PLASTIC?

> *Plastics are polymers, which means that they are made of lots of small molecules joined together to form larger molecules in the form of long chains. Polymers can be manufactured from crude oil, natural gas, or coal. They include artificial fibres and many kinds of plastic. Plastics are extremely useful because they are extraordinarily versatile. They are easy to shape and colour. They can be made into rigid objects or thin, pliable sheets. Some plastics are heatproof, while others melt at low temperatures.*

WHAT CAN BE MADE FROM PLASTIC?

ALMOST ANYTHING can be made from plastic! Plastic packaging keeps food fresh and protects it from bacteria. A plastic coating, called Teflon, can prevent food from sticking to cooking pans. Plastic can be elastic, like the skin of a balloon, or very rigid and reinforced with other fibres, as in a protective helmet. Plastic can also be a good insulator. A plastic sleeve on electrical wiring protects the wires from corrosion and the user from electric shocks. Polystyrene packaging can help to keep take-away food warm. Plastic can be dyed in bright colours or completely transparent, to make spectacles and contact lenses. Without plastics, there would be less music in our lives, with no cassette tapes, compact discs or even old-fashioned records.

HOW IS PLASTIC SHAPED?

PLASTIC may be shaped in various ways. It can be extruded (pushed through a nozzle when liquid) to form sheets, tubes and fibres. Molten plastic can be poured into moulds. Vacuum forming is a way of making complicated plastic shapes. A sheet of warm plastic is placed over a mould, then the air is sucked from under it so that the sheet is pulled firmly against the sides of the mould. When the plastic is cooled, it retains the mould's shape. Disposable cups are often made in this way.

WHAT IS THE DIFFERENCE BETWEEN THERMOPLASTICS AND THERMOSETS?

SOME PLASTICS, such as polythene, can be melted and reshaped over and over again. These plastics are recyclable and are called thermoplastics. Other plastics are more resistant to heat and cannot be melted and reshaped. They are known as thermosets. Plastic kitchen worksurfaces and the hard plastic casings around some electrical goods are made from thermosets.

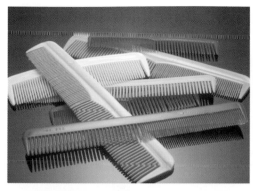

Many inexpensive plastic products are made from fairly flexible thermoplastics, such as polythene. This can be formed in thin sheets or moulded.

The plastic casing of this glue gun is made from thermoset plastic. It needs to be rigid and to resist the heat generated inside it.

ARE THERE ANY NATURAL POLYMERS?

STARCH, rubber, wool, silk and hair are all natural polymers. Their molecular structure, under the right conditions, makes them strong and flexible.

The sap of rubber trees is a white, milky substance called latex. It is collected by cutting the bark and allowing the latex to run into a cup underneath. When heated and treated, the latex solidifies into rubber.

HOW HAVE PLASTICS CHANGED OUR LIVES?

PLASTIC MATERIALS can be shaped very efficiently by machines, so plastic objects are cheaply made in great numbers. Some people think that this has contributed to the "disposable society", where we are inclined to throw something away when it is worn or broken, instead of trying to mend it, as would have happened in the past. They warn, too, that most plastics do not easily decay, so our thrown-away food cartons and shopping bags will remain to pollute the planet for years to come. However, plastics have also brought great benefits, playing a part in so many aspects of our lives that it is difficult now to imagine the world without them.

Once tennis equipment was made entirely of natural materials: wood, cat gut, rubber and wool. Now synthetic polymers may be used to make the racket frame, strings and tennis balls.

It was a natural polymer, rubber, that was used to make the first truly waterproof clothing, when Scottish chemist Charles Macintosh (1766–1843) sandwiched a layer of rubber between two pieces of cloth. Today, many different waterproof materials are made from polymers, using plastic coatings and artificial fibres.

WHO BUILT THE FIRST COMPUTER?

In the early 1830s, an English inventor called Charles Babbage (1792–1871) designed the first programmable computer and began to build it. In fact, he never finished, as the machine was extremely complicated! This computer was entirely mechanical. Over a hundred years had to pass before the electronic components that are used today were invented.

monitor

central processing unit (CPU)

keyboard

mouse

WHAT ARE THE MAIN PARTS OF A COMPUTER?

THE CENTRAL PROCESSING UNIT (CPU) is the "brain" of a computer, where its calculations take place. It is contained within a larger processing unit. In order to give instructions to the computer, input devices, such as a keyboard, stylus, mouse, or joystick, are needed. The monitor enables the user to see data on a screen. Many other machines, called peripherals, can also be connected to the computer. They include printers, scanners and modems.

HOW IS INFORMATION STORED IN A COMPUTER?

INSIDE A COMPUTER is a "hard disk", which is able to store information (data) even when the machine is turned off. But there are also two other kinds of storage in a computer. ROM (read-only memory) stores the instructions that tell the computer how to start working when it is first switched on. RAM (random-access memory) stores data that is in use. To make sure that data is permanently stored, it must be "saved" on the hard disk before the computer is switched off.

WHAT IS THE DIFFERENCE BETWEEN HARDWARE AND SOFTWARE?

THE HARDWARE of a computer consists of all the parts described above: the machine itself and any other machinery that is attached to it. But a computer by itself is simply a collection of components. In order to do anything at all, it must be programmed (given a set of instructions). Programs are what is known as software. They are written in a code that a computer can "understand" and act upon. The codes in which programs are written are sometimes called languages.

floppy disk   compact disc   cassette   optical disk

An enormous amount of data can be stored in a computer's memory, but as a back-up and so that data can be shared between machines, several different portable storage devices are used.

HOW DOES A MOUSE WORK?

A MOUSE is a device for giving the computer information (an input device). When the mouse is pushed around on a mat, a pointer on the computer's screen is moved, indicating how data needs to be changed, moved or processed. Tiny beams of light inside the mouse shine through slotted wheels. The ball of the the mouse moves as it is pushed across the mat, and the beams of light are interrupted in a way that tells the computer the direction that the mouse is moving.

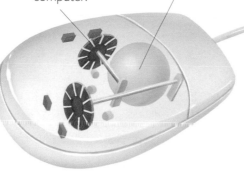

Slotted wheels send information on the mouse's position to the computer.

mouse ball

WHAT IS INSIDE THE PROCESSING UNIT OF A COMPUTER?

INSIDE the processing unit of a computer are collections of integrated circuits (microchips) and other components, usually positioned on circuit boards. There are also slots for floppy disks and CDs to be inserted, a "hard disk" on which data is stored, and perhaps devices such as fans to keep the components cool. Portable computers also have space for a battery, which can be recharged.

Many computers have what are known as expansion slots. Special circuit boards can be inserted into these to increase the computer's power or allow it to perform a particular function.

WHAT IS A PIXEL?

A PIXEL is a tiny dot of colour, which, together with millions of other dots, makes up a picture on a computer or television screen. It is short for "picture element".

fast facts

WHAT DOES CAD STAND FOR?

CAD stands for "computer aided design". There are very few areas of manufacturing and production that do not now call on computers to help with designing new products and improving existing ones.

WHAT DOES THE WORD "COMPUTER" MEAN?

A computer is simply something that can "compute", or calculate. Although today computers can be used for much more than simple calculations, all their functions are based on mathematics.

WHAT IS PROCESSING?

Processing is anything that the computer does to data. It could include sorting it, changing the way it looks, performing calculations on it, or any number of other activities.

WHAT IS A MODEM?

A modem is a device that links a computer to a telephone line or other communication system. It enables information to be shared between computers directly or via the Internet, which is a huge "net" of computer connections stretching across the world.

HOW DO COMPUTERS TODAY DIFFER FROM THE FIRST ELECTRONIC ONES?

Early computers took up whole rooms, which were filled with machinery and spools of whirring magnetic tape. Today, a personal computer (PC) can sit on top of a desk, yet offers many times more power than those huge machines. Today's computers are much faster and have huge memories compared with their ancestors. They are also able to handle pictures and even video footage in a way that was impossible even a few years ago.

HOW DOES AN ELECTRIC MOTOR WORK?

An electric motor uses a current and a magnetic field to create motion. A specially shaped coil of wire, called an armature, is positioned between the poles of a permanent magnet. When an electric current is fed into the wire, the coil becomes a magnet too and forces of attraction and repulsion between it and the permanent magnet cause the armature to move around its axis. A device called a commutator then reverses the current, so that the armature's magnetic poles are reversed and it turns through 180 degrees. If the current is continually reversed, the armature is always turning on its axis. It is this motion that can be used to drive a huge number of machines, such as washing machines, hairdriers and food processors.

armature

commutator

Carbon brushes transfer current to the commutator.

permanent magnet

source of electrical current

WHAT IS THE LEFT-HAND RULE?

FLEMING'S LEFT-HAND RULE enables you to use your hand to work out the direction of motion of a current-carrying wire in a magnetic field. Hold your hand as in the picture, with the first finger pointing in the direction of the magnetic field and your second finger in the direction of the electric current. Your thumb will now point in the direction of motion of the wire.

WHAT IS THE RIGHT-HAND RULE?

FLEMING'S RIGHT-HAND RULE enables you to tell in which direction a current flows in a wire that is moved in a magnetic field. Hold your hand as shown and point your thumb in the direction of motion and your first finger in the direction of the magnetic field. Your second finger will then point in the direction in which current flows in the wire.

HOW DOES AN ELECTRIC LIGHT WORK?

INSIDE many electric light bulbs is a wire called a filament, made of tungsten. When current is passed through the wire, it glows white hot, giving off light and some heat. As the oxygen has been removed from the bulb, combustion cannot take place, so the wire does not burn out immediately.

sealed glass bulb

filament

metal contacts through which current can flow

WILL ELECTRICALLY POWERED VEHICLES EVER BE POSSIBLE?

ELECTRICALLY POWERED VEHICLES have been in use for many years! Powering motor cars with electricity does present certain problems, as batteries are heavy and a car's energy requirement is high. This means that the distance an electric car can travel before it is recharged may be too low for many uses. In hot countries, engineers have experimented quite successfully with supplementing a car's battery power with solar power, using solar panels on the roof of the car.

Where vehicles can obtain electrical energy from a fixed wire or track, there is no problem about electrical supply. Electrically powered trains, such as the French train shown above, are the fastest in the world.

We are used to thinking of small domestic electric light bulbs, but in some situations a great deal more light is needed. Some lighthouses have their own generators, which must be kept working all the time if the light is not to fail.

Specially designed electrically powered wheelchairs and vehicles enable disabled people to move about at the same speed as pedestrians.

WHAT IS A GENERATOR?

A GENERATOR is a machine that produces electrical current by moving a wire in a magnetic field. Energy is needed to move the wire. This may come from steam, wind, moving water, or, in the case of the small generator called a dynamo that may be found on some bicycles, from the movement of human legs! Dynamos produce just enough electrical energy to power the lights of a bicycle, but this energy is not stored. If the cyclist stops pedalling, the lights dim and go out.

WHO BUILT THE FIRST ELECTRIC MOTOR?

The first electric motor was based on the work of Michael Faraday (1791–1867), an English physicist. Not only was he the first to show how current and a magnetic field could produce motion, but he also discovered the principle of the generator.

WHAT IS ALTERNATING CURRENT?

Alternating current is electrical current that continually changes direction. This happens many times in a second.

WHAT IS DIRECT CURRENT?

Direct current is electrical current that flows in only one direction.

HOW DOES A FUSE WORK?

A fuse is a short piece of wire, often sealed in a plastic and metal casing, that forms the weakest link in a circuit. If the current in the circuit becomes too high, the fuse wire will melt, breaking the circuit.

WHAT IS A SOLENOID?

A solenoid is another name for a coil of wire in which an electromagnetic field is created when a current passes through it.

The windmills of a wind farm can power generators to produce electricity for hundreds of homes.

WHAT IS ARABLE FARMING?

Arable farming is the growing and harvesting of crops, particularly where the ground is ploughed between harvests, as the term comes from the Latin word for ploughing. Arable farming is of enormous importance to the world's population, since most of us rely on grains or vegetables for our staple foods.

WHICH ARE THE WORLD'S MOST WIDELY GROWN CROPS?

Wheat is the most widely grown crop, as its various hybrids can grow in a variety of soils and climates. Apart from some grains kept for seed, harvested wheat is ground into flour to make bread, pasta and baked goods.

Rice is the main food for over half the world's population, largely in Asia and South America. Up to three crops of rice per year can be harvested from the same well-watered land. Rice needs a growing-season temperature of over 21°C (70°F).

Maize, or corn, originated from the Americas but is now grown in all warm parts of the world. It is used for human food, as a vegetable, and in the form of maize flour and breakfast cereals. It is also milled and fed to animals.

WHICH CROPS ARE NOT GROWN FOR FOOD?

NOT ALL CROPS are grown for human or animal food. Cotton, flax and jute are grown to be made into fabric. Esparto grass may be cultivated for the manufacture of rope and paper. Tobacco is grown for smoking, while bamboo canes have hundreds of varied uses.

Other non-food crops, such as lavender, are grown for the perfume and cosmetics industries.

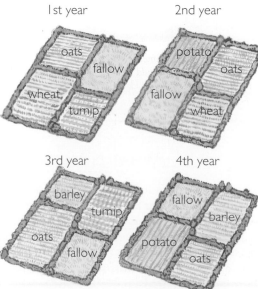

A typical four-year rotation is shown here. During fallow years, grass or clover was grown. The latter was particularly good for restoring nitrogen to the soil.

WHAT WAS THE AGRICULTURAL REVOLUTION?

IN EUROPE in the Middle Ages, large fields were often divided into strips, with individuals farming their strip as intensively as possible. Since little was understood about the nutrients that plants need and the use of fertilizers, the soil in these strips soon became exhausted, with poorer and poorer yields resulting. The Agricultural Revolution was a change in farming practice that took place gradually during the eighteenth century. The technique of resting ground for a year (leaving it fallow) and rotating crops, so that the same crop was not grown year after year on the same plot, was tested and found to improve harvests. A two-year rotation, and later three- and four-year rotations came to be widely practised.

WHICH ARE THE MOST COMMONLY FARMED ANIMALS?

LIVESTOCK is farmed chiefly to supply foods such as meat, eggs and milk, but also for leather, fur and wool. Animal by-products may also include glue, gelatin and fertilizer. The most commonly farmed animals in the world today are shown below.

Cattle are found all over the world, reared for meat, milk and as draught animals. Cows remain in milk for up to 10 months after the birth of a calf. Different breeds of cattle are suited to almost all climates.

Bred for meat, eggs and feathers, poultry may be chickens, turkeys, ducks or geese. Recently, ostriches have also been farmed. Poultry are often reared indoors for all of their comparatively short lives.

Sheep are kept for meat, milk and wool. They can survive on poorer pasture than cattle. Huge numbers of sheep are raised in Australia and New Zealand, where vast areas of land are given over to them.

There are very few parts of the pig that cannot be used as meat, leather, bristles or fat. Traditionally allowed to roam in woodland, they are now kept in purpose-built huts and intensively farmed.

HOW CAN FISH BE FARMED?

FISHING in the open seas is expensive, dangerous and increasingly difficult as some fish stocks diminish. Fish farming involves using lakes, rivers and netted-off coastal areas to raise fish that can be harvested more easily. Freshwater fish and shellfish have been most successfully farmed in this way. Many deep-sea fish require conditions that are impossible to recreate in managed waters.

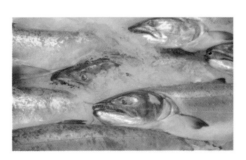

The oceans are so immense that it seems impossible that they could be over-fished, but modern fishing boats are like huge floating factories. They can be at sea for weeks, processing and freezing on board the fish that they literally scoop from the sea. The latest ultrasonic aids help in finding shoals of fish.

HOW HAS MACHINERY CHANGED FARMING?

MACHINERY has made it possible for the work of a dozen farm workers to be done twice as quickly by one worker. There are fewer people working on the land in developed countries than ever before. Machinery exacts a price from the environment as well, as hedges and ditches are removed to allow larger machines to work the enormous fields. Crops have been bred for the machine age, too. They need to ripen together, not over a period of time, so that machinery can harvest them in one operation.

There are still many parts of the world where traditional farming methods are used, but the use of machinery is increasing year by year.

fast facts

WHAT IS FACTORY FARMING?

Factory farming is an intensive farming method in which animals are kept in buildings until they are slaughtered. They have little space to move and so need less food energy to bring them to the desired size. While some consumers are glad of the cheaper food that is available from this method, others feel that the quality of life of the animals is unacceptably low.

WHAT IS IRRIGATION?

Irrigation involves bringing water to cultivated land, by means of ditches, reservoirs, pipes or sprayers.

WHAT IS HYDROPONICS?

Hydroponics is a way of growing food crops in gravel or polythene. All the nutrients they need are dissolved in water, which is pumped directly to their roots.

WHICH CROP TAKES LONGEST TO GROW?

Trees, grown for timber and paper-making, may need to grow for 50 or 60 years before they are harvested.

WHAT IS PASTORALISM?

Pastoralism is another term for livestock farming, although strictly speaking it does not include factory farming.

WHO WAS HIPPOCRATES?

Hippocrates is often described as "the father of modern medicine". He was a Greek doctor, living in the fourth and fifth centuries BC, who taught that a doctor's first duty is to his or her patient and that the aim must at all times be to try to do good rather than harm. When they qualify, many modern doctors take the Hippocratic Oath, promising to follow these principles throughout their careers.

The anaesthetist usually sits at the patient's head, monitoring breathing and heart rate.

Nurses pass instruments to the surgeons. They also make sure that no instruments are left inside the patient by mistake!

Those in the operating theatre wear sterile clothing and cover their noses, mouths and hair to prevent bacteria infecting the open wound.

Sterile drapes cover the patient except for the area where the operation is taking place.

WHAT WAS THE EARLIEST OPERATION?

ARCHAEOLOGISTS have found skulls, dating from at least 10,000 years ago, that have holes drilled into them. Because bone has begun to grow around the holes, they were clearly made while the person was still alive. It is believed that this technique, called trepanning, was the first operation. It was probably done to relieve headaches or to let out evil spirits that were thought to be trapped inside the patient's head.

WHEN WAS ANAESTHESIA FIRST USED?

ANAESTHESIA prevents pain signals from being received by the brain, so that the pain is not felt by the patient. Hundreds of years ago there were few ways to relieve a patient's pain during surgery. Alcohol might be used, but it was not very effective. It was not until the nineteenth century that anaesthetic drugs began to be widely used. The first operation to be performed using a general anaesthetic was by an American surgeon, Crawford Long, in 1842.

fast facts

WHAT IS ACUPUNCTURE?

Acupuncture is an ancient Chinese technique for improving or maintaining health by pushing needles into certain points in the body.

WHAT IS ENDOSCOPY?

Endoscopy is a way of looking inside the body without major surgery. An instrument called an endoscope is inserted into the body through a small hole. Inside it, optical fibres enable the doctor to see internal organs through an eyepiece or on a screen. Endoscopy also enables some operations to be performed using a technique called keyhole surgery, in which only a small incision needs to be made, as the endoscope enables the surgeon to manipulate instruments inside the patient.

HOW DID JOSEPH LISTER HELP TO SAVE LIVES?

Joseph Lister (1827–1912) was an English chemist who introduced the first widely-used antiseptic. By spraying the operating theatre with carbolic acid, he was able to kill harmful bacteria and reduce the infection of wounds dramatically.

WHEN WAS THE FIRST HEART TRANSPLANT?

In 1967, the South African surgeon Christiaan Barnard performed the first transplantation of a heart from a person who had recently died into the body of a man with terminal heart disease. The recipient lived for 18 days. Since then, many patients have lived for years following successful surgery, and the transplantation of other organs, such as kidneys and lungs, is routinely undertaken.

In past centuries, many children did not survive to adulthood. Today, many of the illnesses from which they died can be treated quite easily.

HOW ARE NEW DRUGS DEVELOPED?

RESEARCH CHEMISTS examine different chemicals to find out how they react with other chemicals and with living cells. When a mixture of chemicals is thought to have potential in the treatment of certain conditions, various combinations of the chemicals will be tested to see whether they might be dangerous to living things. Tests on individual cells and on animals are made before human beings are given the new drug. Many people think that drug-testing on animals is wrong, but others feel that this is the best way to make sure that drugs are safe. Trials of the drug, in which some patients are given a placebo (a drug with no active ingredients), are carried out to assess the drug's effectiveness. It is usually only after many years of testing and monitoring that the drug is released for use by doctors.

HOW DO VACCINATIONS WORK?

IN 1796, an English doctor called Edward Jenner (1749–1823) gave the first vaccination. He realized that milkmaids who caught cowpox did not catch the very dangerous disease of smallpox. By injecting the cowpox virus into a child, he was able to vaccinate him against the more serious disease. As the body fights the virus, antibodies are formed in the blood that prevent further infections or infection by some similar viruses. Today, huge vaccination programmes ensure that most children are protected against a range of diseases.

WHAT CAUSES ILLNESS?

UNDERSTANDING the cause of an illness can often help a doctor to bring a patient back to good health or to suggest ways to prevent the illness from recurring or affecting other people. Illness may be caused by an accident, which physically affects part of the body, or it may be brought about by tiny organisms such as bacteria and viruses. Antibiotics are used to treat bacterial infections, while antiviral drugs attack viruses. In both cases, some disease-causing organisms are resistant to drug therapy. Occasionally, the cells of the body seem to act in destructive ways for no obvious reason. This is what happens in some forms of cancer. However, researchers are finding new ways to combat disease all the time.

Drugs in powder form may be pressed into tablets or contained in capsules that dissolve in the stomach. To help pharmacists and patients to distinguish between drugs, they are shaped and coloured in different ways.

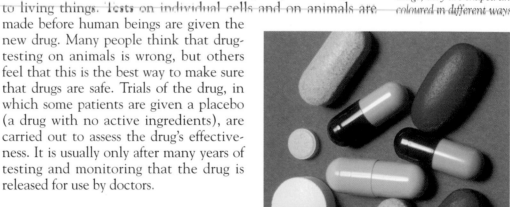

Vaccinations are given with hypodermic needles. These are manufactured in sterile conditions and packaged so that bacteria cannot contaminate them.

GLOSSARY

Aerial   A wire or rod that is used to transmit or receive radio waves.

Ballast   Heavy material placed in the hull of a boat or ship to increase its stability.

Book block   The pages of a book, sewn or glued together, before the cover is put onto them.

By-product   A secondary product, resulting from a process mainly designed to extract or manufacture another product.

Cockpit   The place in the fuselage of a plane in which the pilot sits.

Diaphragm   A thin disc or sheet used to separate two areas. The diaphragm is usually designed to vibrate or move up and down when the pressure on one side of it is higher than on the other.

Die   An engraved stamp used for decorating coins and other objects, or a hollow mould for shaping metal or plastic items.

Fuselage   The body of an aeroplane.

Gender   Whether a plant or animal is male or female.

Incision   A cut, such as that made by a surgeon to open the skin for an operation.

Leaf (of a book)   The two sides of a page.

Mica   Any one of several minerals made of aluminium silicate or other silicates with a layered structure.

Organ   Part of the body of an animal or plant that performs a particular function. The lungs, for example, are organs of respiration. The stomach is an organ of digestion.

Piston   A disc or cylinder of metal, wood or plastic that fits closely within a tube and is able to move up and down within it. Pistons create motion in steam and petrol engines.

Receptor   In a living body, a receptor is an organ that is able to sense aspects of the outside world, such as light, heat, aromas and flavours.

Repulsion   The act of repelling: pushing something back or away.

Reservoir   A tank or lake in which large amounts of liquid, especially water, can be stored.

Scanner   A device that can gather information about an image by passing a beam of light across it. Scanners are used to separate colour pictures into four films for printing, and to store an image digitally so that it can be processed and output by a computer.

Spoil   Earth, rocks and minerals brought to the surface during mining but not needed for further processing. Spoil may often be seen piled in heaps near mines and quarries.

Surveying   Determining the nature of a piece of land by measuring distances and angles. Surveys are needed before a new building is constructed and for making maps or finding new deposits of minerals.

Talc   A form of magnesium silicate used, in powdered form, as a lubricant between moving parts or to stop two surfaces from sticking together.

Tempo   The speed of a piece of music, and sometimes its characteristic rhythm as well.

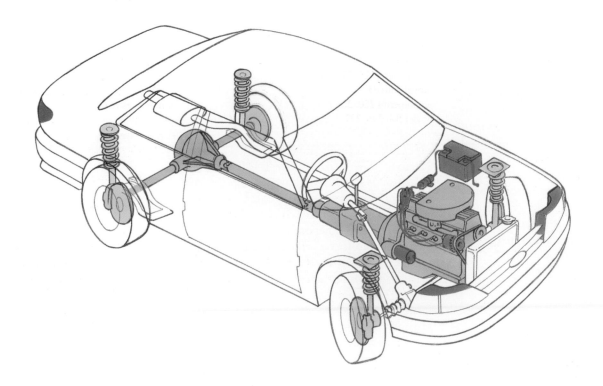

INDEX

MY BIG BOOK OF
QUESTIONS
AND
ANSWERS

ARMADILLO

This paperback edition printed in 2008

© 1997, 2002 Bookmart Limited
Revised and updated in 2007

ISBN: 978-1-84322-607-9

3 5 7 9 10 8 6 4 2

Published by Armadillo Books,
an imprint of Bookmart Limited,
Registered Number 2372865
Trading as Bookmart Limited, Blaby Road
Wigston, Leicester, LE18 4SE, England

Material for this publication has been taken from
1000 Questions and Answers and *1001 Questions and Answers*,
published by Bookmart Limited

Produced for Bookmart Limited by Omnipress Limited, UK

Printed in Thailand